To

9-14-19

LAW

Historical and Theological Foundations of Law is a remarkable book. John Eidsmoe canvasses all of recorded history to analyze the legal systems of the world's great civilizations. In doing so, he raises important questions that are often ignored by modern legal scholars and policymakers: What are the sources of liberty and the rule of law? Is there a higher law? Is law naturally evolving from the primitive and crude to the sophisticated and effective?

The book is both accessible and thought-provoking. And it opens the door for further discussion and research on the issues and legal cultures it addresses. We recommend *Historical and Theological Foundations of Law* to anyone with an interest in knowing more about the roots of law and justice.

Jeffrey A. Brauch, Dean
Doug Cook, Associate Dean
Eric DeGroff, Professor
Regent University School of Law

John Eidsmoe sets forth the Christian vision of law, centered on man's relation to God, encompassing all the great cultures of the world from ancient to the early modern eras. For citizens and lawyers, leaders and students, this book relates the great Christian story underlying the history of law: how man's awareness of God's desire for justice and liberty under law has made itself felt in age after age. Our law students—early readers of the book, drawn from twenty different countries—have been inspired by it to carry on this universal story in their own legal ministries.

Eric Enlow, Dean
Handong International Law School
Pohang, South Korea

It has been said, *"If the foundations are destroyed, what can the righteous do?"* (Ps. 11:3). In the United States, the foundations have not been destroyed, but they are being ignored. Every nation's legal and political system rests upon certain philosophical tenets concerning the nature of man, the source of rights, and purpose of civil government. Professor Eidsmoe addresses the question of what is the philosophy of government of America's constitutional republic by exploring the different views of government and cultures known to our Founders when they created a new nation. This comprehensive discussion of the historical and theological foundations of law—from the ancient to the modern—supplies the documentation for any intellectually honest person to consider why our Founders chose the theory of government expressed in the Declaration of Independence.

Robert J. Barth,
Associate Dean
Oak Brook College of Law

John Eidsmoe's book, *Historical and Theological Foundations of Law* is magisterial in its sweep of history, scholarly in the thoughtfulness of its reflection, and remedial in its correction of what is modernly a much-neglected question: why obey the law? This work does not break new ground so much as survey the ground upon which all civilization has been attempted. Eidsmoe illustrates that the Darwinian notion of an ever-improving species is belied by any number of examples where what is ancient is sturdier, more captivating, or more consistent with human nature. If the pyramids outclass their Las Vegas counterparts, why would we think law follows an opposite path? Because our founders "built better than they knew," America is cocooned from some of the international incoherence spinning in a secular frame that oppresses the yearning for the transcendent. But no wall of separation is high enough to protect us against the ill consequence of an arrogant complacency that denies either moral or physical realities.

Unless law is well-founded, and for that to happen schools must teach what Dr. Eidsmoe has assembled here, we likely will not have to wait for a tsunami to repay our environmental degradation. Not everyone, of course, believes in climate change; just as not everyone grasps the insight of the Divine. There is a truth, however, and law no more than science can long retain its coherency or its usefulness if the ultimate meaning and source of authority or meaning is ignored. This timely book is an essential recollection of the vast knowledge of the past needed to have any hope of navigating into the future.

Douglas W. Kmiec, U.S. Ambassador (ret.)
Caruso Family Chair in Constitutional Law & Human Rights,
Pepperdine University

As an admirer of the work of Professor John Eidsmoe for many years, I am very pleased to learn that he has completed his three-volume treatise on the *Historical and Theological Foundations of Law*. For many years I have assigned the students in my "Origins of the Constitution of the Unites States of America" to read a very enlightening article he wrote about the theological foundations of the U.S. Constitution. He draws the connection between the development of core ideas of theology and the core ideas about government, particularly self-government, in a very persuasive manner.

I have reviewed the Table of Contents for *Historical and Theological Foundations of Law* and they outline a very thorough and fascinating set of materials. The scope and breadth are exceptional and the clear genealogy of ideas about freedom and responsibility, from ideas about man's relationship with God to man's relationship to other men is impressive.

I have read the overview of his three-volume treatise and it describes a work that should be in every law library and every library of religion, political science, and history. I commend Colonel Eidsmoe on this publication and strongly encourage serious students of legal history to get and use this comprehensive resource.

Lynn Wardle,
Professor of Law, J. Reuben Clark School of Law
Brigham Young University

There has been a lot of confusion over the role that faith has played in the development of our legal systems. John Eidsmoe's book does a great deal to address that problem. This comprehensive survey of the foundations of law contributes significantly to the discussion of the source of our legal order.

Myron Steeves,
Dean and Professor, Trinity Law School

It's been noted that he who is not aware of his own ignorance will only be misled by his knowledge. One memorable cartoon depicts a professor confiding to his academic colleague, "Thirty percent of what I say is pure nonsense... but nobody knows which 30%!" America's nonsense quotient has been rising sharply in recent years—especially in relation to the subject of law. Thus, it is timely that Professor John Eidsmoe is releasing his *Historical and Theological Foundations of Law* three-volume set at this time. A fellow Alabaman, U.S. District Judge Brevard Hand (1924–2008) once wrote of "... pebbles on the beach of history from which scholars and judges might attempt to support the conclusions that they are wont to reach." Knowledgeable readers who are wont to see a return to America's Godly heritage will no doubt find that Dr. Eidsmoe's pebbles make for refreshing reading indeed.

Retired Judge Darrell White
American Judicial Alliance
Baton Rouge, LA

THEOLOGY

John Eidsmoe effectively demolishes the evolution-compatible theory that modern law is a product (still continuing in motion) of the crude and ignorant protective devices of the ancient primitives extending to the relative societal consensus represented variously in civilized societies today. Finding the "cornerstone" in Hebrew law, he traces its alternating influences on nations and movements up to the advent of American common law in the constitution of the United States. The reader will discover in this massive volume a wealth of valuable historical information gleaned from the author's thorough-going research and will recognize and affirm from this convincing well-documented testimony that the common source of all just law is divine.

Dr. Francis W. Monseth, Dean
Association Free Lutheran Theological Seminary
Plymouth, MN

John Eidsmoe's *Historical and Theological Foundations of Law* will, I believe, become a cultural landmark in centuries to come, because it will long serve as a lighthouse, beaming desperately needed historical and legal and governmental good sense, based on unchanging principles of divine truth. It shines out light in a time of educational darkness and political storms and confusion. It is a rare and happy day when a scholar of massive erudition and genuine humility is able to bring into his vision a multitude of facts and underlying principles from broad fields of culture, and think them through together, giving his readers a bright and harmonious synthesis of truth from thousands of years, thereby making sense of competing national histories and world religions.

To my mind, Charles Norris Cochrane in the 1940s provided a remarkable synthesis of religion, culture, and law in his *Christianity and Classical Cultur*e, as has Niall Ferguson (2011) in his *Civilization*. John Eidsmoe is certainly in their league, and I have felt that the synthesis he offers is not forced, but naturally flows out of the massively documented content (which somehow never overwhelms the reader). None could properly accuse Colonel Eidsmoe of "Eurocentrism," for one of the qualities of his book is the lucid discussions on the development of Law in China, Polynesia, South America, and—what particularly piqued my interest—law systems among the North American Indian confederations: the Cheyenne and the Iroquois. Throughout this large volume is an intelligent and fair-minded discussion of this underlying question: does the evidence support the evolutionary scenario of development of law (and the religion behind it) from primitive, polytheistic sources, or does it rather indicate a Creator God, who imprinted his moral standards into the human conscience across space and time? One quote will summarize the debated point: "... If the people of the ancient world possessed such sophisticated knowledge of building construction, writing, medical skills, and so many other forms of knowledge, is it not possible, is it not likely, that they possessed sophisticated systems of law as well? In fact, would not a sophisticated system of law and government be a prerequisite for the other achievements? If so, then modern Darwinian theories that law evolved from the simple to the complex, definitely need to be re-examined" (p. 11).

I cordially recommend this amazing volume; I fully expect it to be known as a classic a century hence, and I shall be mentioning it with appreciation to my classes.

Douglas F. Kelly,
Professor of Systematic Theology
Reformed Theological Seminary, Charlotte, NC

Eidsmoe's massive work chronicles the development of law from widely disparate cultures (e.g., Egyptian, Chinese, Mesopotamian, Indian, Polynesian, Mayan, Cheyenne and Iroquois) through the common law basis of the United States Constitution. Throughout Eidsmoe courageously argues that there are universal features within particular legal codes and systems that point to a non-natural source for human law, a source oftentimes apprehended more clearly at the origins of these civilizations and subsequently occluded as governmental power centralizes. This book should be of significant interest to those who take the reality of God seriously, who believe that human beings are created in the image of this real God, and who venture to claim that truth about God's relationship to culture must be unitary, that is, that theological claims about God's primary intentionality for human beings must be ultimately consonant with the moral and legal understandings present among the divergent cultural traditions of humankind.

Dr. Dennis Bielfeldt,
Vice President of Academic Affairs
Institute of Lutheran Theology

Christian academia spawns multiple disciplines and produces a variety of dissertations. I have read from these varieties for decades; yet, none has been more intriguing, or more comprehensive than *Historical and Theological Foundations of Law* by Colonel John A. Eidsmoe. Originally presented to the faculty of Emmanuel College of Christian Studies as a doctoral dissertation, this monumental, multi-volume work of almost incalculable proportions, spans ancient civilizations, examining their laws and religions, before ultimately reaching the rational conclusion that the source of all law is Almighty God! Authored by one of our nation's foremost authorities on the Constitution of the United States, this compendium of historical and theological truth comes in an easy-to-read style that simply begs not to be laid aside.

Gene L. Jeffries, Th.D.,
President, Emmanuel College of Christian Studies

There have been studies in the past to show the influence of the Christian faith on the founders of the American constitution and the representative form of government. My former student Colonel Eidsmoe has been a strong contributor to this study.

In this comprehensive study he researches history to show a common strain that has demonstrated itself in many primitive and modern cultures. Mesopotamia, Egypt, Persia, India, China, Hawaii, Malaysia, Inca, Aztec and several modern civilizations.

Col. Eidsmoe comes to this task with training and experience in law and religion. This study is destined to become a classic in the history of law and religion.

Rev. Omar Gjerness, Professor (Ret.)
Lutheran Brethren Seminary

Professor Eidsmoe has written a "Summa Legem" which in its vastness and erudition reveals the author's grasp of the historical, theological, and juridical foundations of civilization. As a competent lawyer, theologian, and historian, he has employed these disciplines successfully in his effort to demonstrate the truth of his thesis, namely, that law and government cannot be understood or preserved without an understanding of and commitment to the religious/moral underpinnings of the culture. The reader will be intrigued by the wealth of anecdotal detail in Colonel Eidsmoe's description of the religion, law, and government of ancient civilizations from the Sumerian culture of ca. 4000 BC to the Incas and Aztecs of ca. AD 1000 as well as of the classical civilizations of the Hebrews, Greeks, and Romans. The author gives in-depth insights into the more immediate antecedents of our American culture in the religion and laws of the Celtic, Viking, Anglo-Saxon, and Norman invaders and colonizers of the British Isles. Pastor Eidsmoe concludes by delineating the profound effect which Christianity has had on the legal and governmental culture which was transferred to American shores by colonists and immigrants and took root to produce the Laws and Constitutional form of government of the United States. This scholarly work has my highest recommendation.

Press on in the Lord!
Med vennlig hilsen,

Rev. Dr. Duane R. Lindberg,
Presiding Pastor Emeritus, The American Association of Lutheran Churches

---

HISTORY/HERITAGE

John Eidsmoe has masterfully synthesized a broad array of primary sources into a comprehensive survey of legal philosophy. Eidsmoe is equally at home in the fields of law, theology, and history. What's more, he energetically guides his readers on a journey from the ancient Near East to the founding of the American Republic, gracefully distilling complex ideas into short, accessible sentences. Study questions conclude each section, making the text readily adaptable to the classroom. By including frequent block quotations from history's greatest legal thinkers, *Historical and Theological Foundations of Law* achieves an encyclopedic chronicle of human endeavors to maintain ordered societies. Eidsmoe's narrative also links salient facts into an interpretative essay, culminating in a reflection upon natural law and the divine Lawgiver who established it.

Ryan C. MacPherson, Ph.D.
Chair, Dept. of History, Bethany Lutheran College, Mankato, Minnesota
Founding President, The Hausvater Project

John Eidsmoe's tremendous work, *Historical and Theological Foundations of Law*, is an amazing overview of world history. After reading his examination of the development of the law throughout the centuries, one cannot help but come to the conclusion that what we have experienced in America is truly rare. Americans have been the beneficiaries of the most individual freedom, opportunity, and prosperity than of all previous cultures. This phenomenal book not only pulls aside the curtain to help us understand the origins of law, but inspires us to want to preserve it for future generations.

William J. Federer,
Author/Producer, The American Minute

Professor John Eidsmoe presents an irrefutable case for the excellence of the Biblically based common law tradition that birthed America's constitutional liberty. Eidsmoe clearly explains what is the only unchanging source for a just and prosperous society. Every American who values freedom should read these volumes.

Marshall Foster
World History Institute
worldhistoryinstitute.com

John Eidsmoe is a great intellectual of our time. He understands so well the Christian roots of America, including some of the nuances to avoid lest we fall into exaggeration. He has a grasp of the big picture of history and the ability to communicate that, so we can see God's hand in civilization—including the foundation of America's law. What a great trilogy from a great scholar.

Jerry Newcombe, D.Min.
Spokesman for Truth in Action Ministries (formerly Coral Ridge)
Author, *The Book that Made America*

In the *Historical and Theological Foundations of Law,* John Eidsmoe does a thorough and masterful job of presenting the origins and development of law, and in particular of the laws of liberty. He clearly shows that true law originates with God, and that law is right and true when it emanates from Him. Understanding God as the source of law leads to voluntary obedience, since such obedience to truth brings great blessing to men and nations.

Stephen McDowell,
President, Providence Foundation Biblical Worldview University

---

MILITARY

My friend Colonel John Eidsmoe has defended our country throughout his distinguished military service. Now he defends our country as an attorney, with meticulous research and lucid explanation of the long history of America's Godly Heritage, including the foundations of American law and civil government, from ancient times to the founding of our nation. Everyone who is concerned about the source and nature of the Higher Law in America should read this excellent book. The U. S. Supreme Court has declared four times that America, as a matter of law and fact is a "Christian Nation." Colonel Eidsmoe provides a readable account of this crucial history, suitable for lawyers, judges, legislators, and laymen.

Ronald D. Ray, Colonel, USMC (Ret.)
Former Deputy Assistant Secretary of Defense
Counselor and Co-Founder of First Principles, Inc.

CULTURE

John Eidsmoe has written arguably the most comprehensive—likely, at least, the most wide-ranging—genealogy of legal systems ever published in English. In tracing the influence of Christianity and the Bible on Western legal systems, Eidsmoe has left us deeply in his debt. This is a massive, towering work, a *magnum opus* to which few could attain, and it will furnish legal students intellectual grist for many, many years to come."

P. Andrew Sandlin,
President, Center for Cultural Leadership

John Eidsmoe has presented the world with a book that it has long needed. His three-volume *Historical and Theological Foundations of Law* offers a richly comprehensive account of the historical development and supra-historical foundation of the law. Though his focus is Judeo-Christian and Greco-Roman, Eidsmoe offers fascinating glimpses into how the law has manifested itself in non-Western cultures; he also challenges his readers to preserve the future by looking backward to the past. Most vitally, he equips his reader to understand that the law is neither a man-made artifact nor something that varies wildly from culture to culture and age to age.

Louis Markos,
Professor in English and Scholar-in-Residence, Houston Baptist University; author of *From Achilles to Christ: Why Christians Should Read the Pagan Classics, Apologetics for the 21st Century*, and *Restoring Beauty: The Good, the True, and the Beautiful in the Writings of C. S. Lewis.*

As a former law student of Professor Eidsmoe and now a government and legal studies professor myself, I have read many of his books and am currently using one of his books as a text in my introductory American government class. In this, his most current work, John Eidsmoe has crafted a premier text on the subject of law and theology from a distinctly historical perspective. I can think of no better treatment of the subject for use in the classroom to inform the reader of the historical sources of our law and theology than this multi-volume work. It is destined to be a classic for the ages.

Bryan H. Sanders, J.D.
Chair, Department of Social Sciences. Professor of Government and Legal Studies
Evangel University, Springfield, MO

Written from a Protestant evangelical viewpoint, John Eidsmoe's three-volume work provides material difficult to find in similar works on the subject: ancient and primitive law and the legal traditions of non-western societies provide the background for his deep appreciation of American common law developments. Those in the legal field and students wanting to delve into the intricacies of legal history as it interacts with theology will surely want to add it to their bookshelves.

John Warwick Montgomery
Distinguished Research Professor of Philosophy and Christian Thought, Patrick Henry College. Professor Emeritus, University of Bedfordshire, England. Ph.D. (Chicago), D.Théol. (Strasbourg, France), LL.D. (Cardiff, Wales, U.K.). Member of the California, D.C., Virginia, Washington State, and U. S. Supreme Court bars; Barrister-at-Law, England and Wales; Avocat à la Cour, Paris.

"Law is a back stage pass to theology," as one man put it. John Eidsmoe has, with meticulous research articulated in plain language, granted us VIP seats in the theater of theology playing in the legal culture. He connects the contextual dots, thereby allowing us to see how the WHAT's of legal history are linked to the WHEN's, WHERE's, and WHY's animating that history. And, in doing so, he provides much needed clarity and context in the sea of relativist confusion. This project underscores with Paul, that "we know that the law is good, if one uses it lawfully" (1 Tim. 1:8, ESV).

Jeffery J. Ventrella, Esq.
Senior Vice President, Strategic Training
Alliance Defense Fund

Fascinating, interesting, knowledgeable, and wise are just a few words that describe Professor Eidsmoe. As his former law student and now lawyer, I can say firsthand that he has an extraordinary ability to communicate and educate, and *Historical and Theological Foundations of Law* is the proof. Two of my sons had the privilege of cite-checking two chapters of this book and found the information intriguing. They could not seem to get the work done for reading the rest of the book! This book is well written and so full of well-researched facts that it is a must have for every homeschooling family. As a homeschooling mother, *Historical and Theological Foundations of Law* is an invaluable tool.

Stacy Harris
Attorney, home-schooling mother, and author of
Happy Healthy Family Tracking the Outdoors In

Colonel Eidsmoe's comprehensive historical survey of the foundations of law from a Biblical perspective will be an outstanding resource for Christian students and scholars.

Roger Schultz, Ph.D.
Dean, College of Arts and Sciences
Liberty University

Congratulations to Professor John Eidsmoe on the completion of his magnum opus! *Historical and Theological Foundations of Law* is a landmark accomplishment, not just for the study of the history of law in general but also for the demonstration of the vital impact of the Judeo-Christian worldview on the development of western culture. Scholars, lawyers, pastors, and theologians will benefit greatly from Eidsmoe's tour de force.

Peter A. Lillback,
President, Westminster Theological Seminary
President, The Providence Forum

Historical *and* Theological Foundations *of* Law

HISTORICAL *and* THEOLOGICAL FOUNDATIONS *of* LAW

VOLUME I
Ancient Wisdom

JOHN EIDSMOE

NORDSKOG PUBLISHING INC.
VENTURA, CALIFORNIA

Historical and Theological Foundations of Law
VOLUME I: ANCIENT WISDOM

First Edition, printed November 2012
ISBN: 978–1–936577–17–0

Expanded Second Edition, printed August 2016
ISBN: 978–1–9903774–6–7

Library of Congress Control Number: 2016913222

Second Edition Editing and Production by Desta Garrett, Managing Editor

Second Edition Index by Desta Garrett and Michelle Shelfer

Copyediting by Michelle Shelfer

Cover Design by Luis Lovelace

COVER ART*:* An Egyptian clay engraving of *Maat*, goddess of justice. The Egyptian word *ma'at* meant "straight," or "true," and thus "just." The "feather of justice," erect on the headdress, was her emblem, and her image was worn on a gold collar by the Egyptian Chief Justice.

Printed in the United States of America.

Published by:

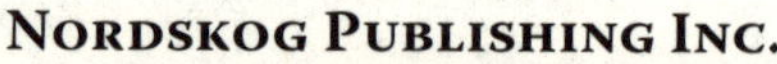

2716 Sailor Ave
Ventura, CA 93001 USA
1-805-642-2070 • 1-805-276-5129

www.NordskogPublishing.com

In Dedication

I lovingly dedicate this book

To my parents,
Russell and Beulah Eidsmoe,

to my brother
Robert,

to my wife
Marlene,

to my children and their spouses,
David (Donna), Kirsten (Chris), and Justin,

and to my grandchildren,
Elizabeth, Erik, and Amelia.

Author's Preface to the Second Edition

Greetings!

Please embark with me on a journey through time and space, to explore the foundations of law from their very beginnings.

We will begin, in **Book I, The Foundation**, by exploring the ancient legal systems of Egypt, Mesopotamia, Persia, India, China, Polynesia, the Inca, the Maya, the Aztec, the Cheyenne, and the Iroquois Confederacy. We will study the facts about their legal systems, but we will consider much more: How did these systems arise? How did they develop, or degenerate? What common characteristics did they possess? And what was their source, or sources, or Source?

Then, in **Book II, The Cornerstone**, we will focus upon the legal system that has influenced the world more than any other—the laws and institutions of the ancient Hebrews. What is the secret of the Hebrews' genius, and why are the Laws of Moses so often overlooked by scholars today?

In **Book III, The Structure**, we will turn to the Greek and Roman legal systems, with their many strengths and equally many weaknesses. What was the source of their strength? And what were their fatal flaws? Out of Roman law we will see the rise of the Canon Law of the Church, and we will also survey the Sharia law of Islam.

Book IV, The Centerpiece, chronicles the birth of the Common Law of the West, with its Celtic, Anglo-Saxon, Viking, Jewish, and Norman roots. What is the Common Law? If it is so common, why is it so seldom defined? How does it relate to Canon Law or Civil Law? And is it Christian, or Roman, or a fusion of both?

Book V, The Pinnacle, views the Common Law as resurrected by the Lutheran Reformation of Germany and Scandinavia and the Calvinist Reformation of Switzerland, France, the Netherlands, Scotland, and England. Following in the footsteps of the Reformers, we will see how legal philosophers like Selden, Milton, Althusius, Grotius, Pufendorf, Vattel, Locke, Coke, Montesquieu, and Blackstone crystalized the Common Law and articulated its timeless principles in a more modern form.

And finally, **Book VI, The Beacon**, dramatizes the Common Law's journey across the Atlantic to the American colonies, how it gave form and life to their colonial governments and provided the background for the Declaration of Independence and the Constitution.

I hope this book provides information and answers, but just as important are the questions it raises about the nature, purpose, and *source* of law. Jurists have articulated it, philosophers have theorized about it, theologians have explored the moral principles that underlie it. Statesmen have enacted it, judges have interpreted it, sheriffs have enforced it, soldiers have defended it, kings have implemented it. And then, after the fact, people like me have written about it, to try to explain what it is, and what it should be.

With a scope as wide as this, I certainly have not exhausted the subject. Not even close! Already, just before this book goes to print, I have come across materials that I wish I had included, and in coming years I'm sure I'll discover much more. Some years from now, perhaps, I will revise this work into a third edition. But it will never be truly complete.

History consists of objective reality, but because of our human fallibility, our understanding of history is often incomplete and imperfect. Especially in ancient history, the original sources often conflict, and the more recent interpretations of ancient history conflict even more. Faced with these conflicts, I have tried to select the interpretation and explanation that seems most likely to be true. If you, the reader, believe I have interpreted something wrongly, or if you have information that I have overlooked, I would be pleased to hear from you; you may contact me at eidsmoeja@juno.com. Unfortunately, I may not be able to answer all communications. I will also try to be available for speaking engagements on topics related to this book.

If you, the reader, are as blessed and edified by reading this book as I have been by writing it, my purpose in writing will have been fully accomplished.

Soli Deo gloria!

Volume I Table of Contents

Contents of Volume II

Contents of Volume III

A Persian horse archer in *The Battle of Gaugamela*

Foreword

I have known John Eidsmoe for many years. We have taught together and had many discussions over several decades, as well as serving together on the Board of Directors for the Plymouth Rock Foundation. John is articulate, balanced, and a thorough investigator when it comes to historic gems hidden in the soil of the past. Like a good investigator, he puts the pieces together to form a picture worth observing and considering. What makes John's work so compelling, however, is that he knows and admires the "book of books"—the Bible. His commitment to Biblical truth guides his work in uncovering what is valuable, bringing forth lessons often missed by those who have no compass when it comes to the past.

The work you are about to study has taken John years to compile, and will take you years to digest. However, the time could not be more ripe both for John to release this work and you and others to digest it. The American Republic, like the Titanic of one hundred years ago, faces the iceberg of debt, ignorance, loss of self-government, and injustice. Blinded to these faults through its pride, it sails on at full speed toward disaster.

John Eidsmoe has given to us further proof through his exhaustive research, however, that our nation is unique and exceptional, especially in our history. It is unlike the ancient law systems for a very clear and good reason. They were based on nature by the mind of man with no guiding light. Without the light of the Bible, Americans were and are no smarter than any of these systems—in fact, as evidence shows, the brilliance of many of these systems is apparent. But intellectual prowess alone will not rescue us any more than the most experienced Captain Smith of the Titanic who took her on her maiden voyage in 1912.

Eidsmoe's work demonstrates proof that truly our nation has a Judeo-Christian heritage. Though much evidence is now in print of the influence of Christianity upon our founding through the work of many, John Eidsmoe provides tremendous evidence of the roots of that influence—the Hebrew institutions and laws of the Old Testament. Just as the Bible demonstrates that Israel was unique among the ancient nations in the Old Testament era, we now have further evidence that confirms the position of Scripture all along. Israel was the most prosperous, literate, free, and just nation among the ancient empires. So too has America been the most prosperous, literate, free, and just nation among the modern empires. This was not by chance—but rather by design, for the United States of America has sailed in the wake of the ancient Hebrews—following the path set forth in Holy Scripture.

The comparison of ancient Israel to America was a frequent illustration among the colonial clergy prior to the writing of the Declaration of Independence and our Articles of Confederation and Constitution. It was also Sam Adams' (father of the American Revolution) favorite illustration as well. You now have the evidence of what these scholarly pastors knew all along. I heartily endorse this work. Though it will take time to digest it, the result will be, if applied, just the right fruit we need to restore the prosperity, literacy, freedom, and justice we once knew as a nation."

Paul Jehle,
Executive Director, Plymouth Rock Foundation
www.plymrock.org

Introduction

Philadelphia, May 25, 1787: Delegates from twelve states gathered at Independence Hall, as authorized by the Continental Congress, to revise the Articles of Confederation. They drafted a new Constitution that has enabled Americans to enjoy freedom, order, justice, and prosperity for more than two centuries, and that has served as a model for many other constitutions throughout the world.

Thomas Jefferson was in France and did not attend the Convention. But when he saw a list of delegates, he wrote to John Adams, "It is really an assembly of demigods."[1] Later he added, "A more able assembly never sat in America."[2] Nor, we may add, has a more able body ever sat since that time.

But the Convention delegates did not write on a blank slate. Their way of putting ideas together was new; the Constitution they drafted, consisting of levels of government, branches of government, checks and balances among those levels and branches, and reserved individual rights, was unique and arguably the finest the world has ever seen. But the ideas that underlie those constitutional provisions were far from new. Those Founding Fathers, with their varied backgrounds and their knowledge of history, drew upon the wisdom of the past: the English common law with its Celtic, Anglo-Saxon, Viking, and Norman antecedents; the classical systems of Greece and Rome, with their many successes and at least as many failures; the laws of ancient systems throughout the world, not least of which were the Christian tradition and the laws of the ancient Hebrews.

They also knew from history and from observation that, in the course of human events, government tends to grow and centralize, and politics and law involve a constant and universal conflict between those who would increase and centralize government power and those who would keep government power limited and localized. Jefferson put it so well: "The natural progress of things is for liberty to yield and government to gain ground."[3]

---

1. Thomas Jefferson to John Adams, August 30, 1787, reprinted in *The Works of Thomas Jefferson,* ed. H. A. Washington (Townsend, 1884) 2:260.

2. Thomas Jefferson to M. Dumas, September 10, 1787 in *Works,* 2:264.

3. Thomas Jefferson, letter to Colonel Edward Carrington, May 27, 1788; Albert Ellery Bergh, ed., *The Writings of Thomas Jefferson,* 20 vols. (Washington, DC: The Thomas Jefferson Memorial Association, 1907) VII:37. "Yeild" is Jefferson's original spelling.

But the Founding Fathers were determined that America would be the exception, that the dangerous servant government would be securely bound by the chains of the Constitution, so it would not become a fearful master.

In the struggle between liberty and power, both sides commonly invoke a Supreme Being. One side believes God, or the gods, or the Tao or Ground of Being, possesses all power and delegates a portion of that power to the king, who in turn delegates power to lower officials, who rule over the people. The other side agrees that God possesses all power, but He delegates a portion of that power to the people, who in turn delegate power to localized officials, who in turn establish the national government, and that national government governs only by the consent of the governed. This struggle has been waged for thousands of years and continues today.

For law is as old as civilization itself. And as Edward Gibbon observed, "The laws of a nation form the most instructive part of its history."[4]

Ever since people began living together in groups, they needed rulers to lead them, standards to govern them, and laws to protect them from others.

But whence come our laws? And how have they developed? Are the laws of a large and complex society different from those of a small and primitive tribe? Are our laws today different from those of our ancestors thousands of years ago? Are the laws of primitive tribes today similar to those of our primitive ancestors? As we examine the laws of complex and primitive societies today, and compare them with those of ancient societies, what common patterns can we see?

Sir Henry Maine believed that the patriarchal family was the earliest basis of social organization, and that law developed from judgment to custom to legislation.[5] That is, law begins as judgments deciding individual cases; then these judgments form patterns or customs to which tribespeople and their leaders generally conform. Finally these judgments and customs are enacted into rules or laws that bind all who are within the jurisdiction. In the process the patriarchal family unit expands to include more distant kin, and eventually the social unit becomes based more on

4. Edward Gibbon, *History of the Decline and Fall of the Roman Empire* (Oxford University Press, 1776), IV: 524ff.

5. Sir Henry Maine, *Ancient Law* (Dorset Press, 1861, 1986), 101ff.

territory rather than blood relationships. Out of this eventually arises the modern political state.

Others see it differently. Some believe law originates in commercial exchange. Hunters exchange their quarry for the vegetables grown by others, and both exchange their products with those who make clothing, pottery, and other goods. Out of these exchanges the laws of commerce develop.

Still others believe law has its origins in the blood feud.[6] When Alf of Clan A kills Bill of Clan B, Clan B seeks vengeance by killing Alf, or failing that, they kill someone else of Clan A. But Clan A comes to the defense of Alf, perhaps because they believe he was justified in killing Bill or perhaps just because he is their kinsman, and several are killed on each side. The thirst for revenge leads to a feud that claims many lives over generations. Eventually both clans, and others as well, conclude that this is an unacceptable state of affairs, so they agree on laws and procedures for judging and punishing murderers.

These divergent theories have several points in common. They agree that law has evolved as man has evolved, from basic primitivism to advanced civilization, from the simple to the complex, from rudimentary customs to modern legislation.

In other words, modern theories of legal origins conform to Darwinian theories of the origin and development of man.

They assume that early man evolved from an apelike creature to modern Homo sapiens, and that his intelligence gradually increased during the evolutionary process.

They assume that as man's intelligence evolved, so his level of culture, technology, philosophy, and theology evolved as well.[7]

---

6. William Seagle, *The History of Law* (New York: Tudor, 1946), 36.

7. Herbert F. Hahn noted that the documentary hypothesis of many higher critics, which contends that the first five books of the Bible were not written by Moses but by several later writers, "did not grow merely from an objective reading of the sources. In a larger sense, it was a reflection of the intellectual temper of the times. The genetic conception of Old Testament history fitted in with the evolutionary principle of interpretation prevailing in contemporary science and philosophy.... From the evolutionary point of view, which assumed that development invariably took place from lower to higher forms, it was inconceivable that the nomadic ancestors of the Israelites could have held the lofty, monotheistic conceptions ascribed to Abraham.... [A]fter Herbert Spencer had popularized the notion that biological evolution had an analogue in the cultural history of mankind, the ideas of unilinear evolution and parallel development dominated anthropological research." Hahn, *The Old Testament in Modern Research* (Philadelphia: Fortress Press, 1954, 1966), 9–10, 12, 46–47.

They assume that societies that have primitive technology and culture will have primitive laws and governments.

They assume that the legal systems of our primitive ancestors must have been similar to the legal systems of primitive societies today.

But does the evidence support these assumptions? Does the evidence show a gradual development from primitivism to advanced civilization? All across the world, strong and startling evidence reveals advanced civilizations with remarkable technologies, thousands of years ago.

Consider the following:

- The pyramids of Egypt are among the greatest wonders of the ancient world. The Great Pyramid, sometimes called the Cheops Pyramid, is usually dated around 2700 BC,[8] though some date it even earlier. The millions of stones that comprise this pyramid are enormous—tens of thousands weighing 15 tons or more, millions more weighing an average of two and one-half tons—and were not only transported to this site, but also carefully cut to fit perfectly together, and somehow put into place. They are held together by a mortar stronger than any commonly used

8. In the 1600s AD the Reverend James Ussher, Archbishop of Armagh and Primate of Ireland, compiled a detailed scholarly work titled *The Annals of the World Deduced from the Origin of Time and Continued to the Beginning of the Emperor Vespasian's Reign and the Total Destruction and Abolition of the Temple and Commonwealth of the Jews.* The *Annals* were published in 1658, two years after Archbishop Ussher's death. The *Annals* are detailed, well-organized, and contain numerous references to other scholarly works of history, many of which are lost today. Archbishop Ussher accepted as literal truth the Biblical narrations that Adam lived 130 years and then begat Seth (Genesis 5:3), that Seth lived 105 years and then begat Enos (Genesis 5:6), and so on down to the birth of Jesus Christ. Based upon these chronologies and other sources, Archbishop Ussher concluded that the world was created in the year 4004 BC, and that the worldwide Deluge occurred in 2348 BC, at which time the world's population was reduced to eight persons, Noah and his wife, his three sons and their wives. The Ussher Chronology conflicts with the records of ancient Egypt and other societies that date their civilizations to 3000 BC and before. This writer will not attempt to resolve that conflict, but will only make the following observations: (1) The ancient records of the Egyptians, the Babylonians, and other civilizations are not always reliable, nor are modern scholars agreed as to their meaning. As only one of many examples, the 43-year reign of King Hammurabi of Babylon is dated by Durant and other historians in the 2100s BC, and perhaps more commonly by others in the 1700s BC. (2) It is possible to read the Biblical chronologies literally without accepting the Ussher Chronology. The Hebrew word translated "begat" can mean "became the parent of" or "became the ancestor of." Some conservative scholars who believe the Bible is literally true, have concluded that there are gaps in the Biblical chronologies. Throughout this book we will at times use the dates given in the records of various ancient societies and the dates given by ancient and modern historians for various persons and events. By doing so we neither endorse those dates nor reject the Ussher Chronology. We will simply make sure the reader is aware that these dating conflicts exist and leave their resolution to others.

today, so strong that if one tries to separate a stone from the pyramid, the stone will break rather than the mortar.

- The Great Pyramid remains today the heaviest building in the world. It is over 450 feet tall, covers 13.1 acres or several city blocks, and its measurements are far more precise than almost any modern building—the northern face is aligned almost perfectly to true north, and the other faces similarly to east, south, and west, with an average variation of only three minutes of arc, or 0.015 percent. The lengths of the shortest and longest sides differ by only eight inches, and the pavement around the Great Pyramid is level to within less than an inch.

Do we see an evolution of smaller, cruder pyramids, culminating in the Great Pyramid? Almost the exact opposite: The largest, best-constructed, and best preserved pyramids are the earliest ones, those built before 2000 BC. The later pyramids, including those which were possibly constructed with Hebrew slave labor around 1500 BC, are inferior in size, quality, and preservation. From the beginning of recorded Egyptian history there is little if any evolution in the art of pyramid-building; it emerges almost from the beginning as a high technology and then declines as we move into the later centuries and dynasties.

Ancient Egypt was remarkable in other ways. The Sphinx may predate the pyramids in its antiquity. Egyptian doctors had a well-developed theory and practice of medicine centuries before Hippocrates and the Greeks, and Egyptians were a literate people at least as early as 2000 BC.

How did the Egyptians develop this kind of technology? Many have speculated, but no one knows with certainty.[9]

---

9. One of the best and most balanced discussions of the pyramids is found in Peter James and Nick Thorpe, *Ancient Mysteries* (New York: Ballentine, 1999), 201–28. James and Thorpe believe there was a brief evolution in pyramid-building but thereafter the art declined. Graham Hancock's *Fingerprints of the Gods* (New York: Three Rivers Press,1995) makes more extreme claims, arguing that the pyramids were the work of a much more ancient civilization around 10,500 BC, and that the Sphinx shows evidence of water damage near the head despite the fact that there has been no flood of that consequence in Egypt for thousands of years (273–410). Hancock provides much useful information and documentation, but some of his conclusions seem fantastic and some of his documentation could be improved. *Mysterious Places: The World's Unexplained Symbolic Sites, Ancient Cities, and Lost Lands,* ed. Jennifer Westwood (New York: Galahad Books, 1987), 62–67, gives balanced coverage of the Pyramids and contains excellent photography, as does *100 Great Archeological Discoveries,* ed. Paul G. Bahn (New York: Barnes and Noble, 1995), 28–41. Some writers have speculated that the pyramids of Egypt, like Stonehenge and the pyramids of Central America, were used by aliens for interplanetary travel and communication, or a vestige of the lost civilization of Atlantis. One need not engage in such fanciful theories to recognize that the ancient Egyptians possessed some remarkable technological knowledge.

• In Zimbabwe in southern Africa lie the remains of another remarkable civilization. Now referred to as Great Zimbabwe, the ruins include an enclosure surrounded by a wall 830 feet in circumference and ranging from 16 to 35 feet high. The wall was built of carefully cut brick-like granite stones. Inside the enclosure are various smaller walls, rooms, and passages, and a 30-foot-tall conical tower.

Who built Great Zimbabwe? Various theories have been advanced. From their discovery by Portugese explorers in 1532 through the 1800s and early 1900s, various explorers concluded that the ruins were the palace of the Queen of Sheba who had visited King Solomon in Jerusalem in the 10th century BC. Others thought this could be the site of the long-sought King Solomon's mines. Still others attributed the structure to Sabaeans between 2000 and 1000 BC, or to Phoenicians around 1100 BC. The more common opinion today is that they were built by the Bantu people some time after AD 1000.

And why were they built? As a religious shrine? As a palace or fortress? As an enclosure for cattle? As a holding place for black slaves being transported to Arabia? As a trading center? Artifacts found at the site are mostly African but do include a Persian bowl from the 13th or 14th century, Chinese dishes, and engraved and painted Near Eastern glass.

Most amazing of all, no mortar or other adhesive was used in the construction of Great Zimbabwe. The structure is held together by the force of gravity and precise craftsmanship alone—and much of it remains standing today! Whether Great Zimbabwe is eight hundred years old, a thousand years old, or several thousand, this is truly an amazing feat of technology.[10]

How many structures that we are building today will be standing a thousand years from now?

• Ur of the Chaldees, the early home of Abraham (Genesis 11:31) in Mesopotamia (now part of Iraq), was an early center of civilization. By 3500 BC, Ur featured elaborate temples with intricate art of gold and mother-of-pearl, and by at least 2100 BC, the Sumerian people were building huge towers called ziggurats. These are not as well-preserved as the pyramids of Egypt; stone was not plentiful in Mesopotamia, so the

---

10. Basil Davidson, *The Lost Cities of Africa* (New York: Little, Brown and Company, 1959, 1987), 193–311; *Mysterious Places,* op. cit., 162–67.

builders used mostly clay bricks. But even these ruins reflect a highly advanced culture.[11]

• Starting perhaps as early as 3000 BC and until its destruction by earthquake around 1500 BC, the Minoan civilization on the island of Crete in the Mediterranean was one of the most remarkable of the ancient world. The palace of King Minos was four stories high, covered over five acres, and contained 1,500 rooms.

The Minoan capitol of Knossos featured an elaborate plumbing and drainage system with lavatories, sinks, and manholes, underground pipes of various sizes with perfectly tapered socket joints, elaborate bathtubs with hot and cold water, and flush toilets. Excavations have revealed two-story condominiums that would be comfortable even by the standards of today.[12]

• Moving northward to the British Isles, Stonehenge has haunted the human imagination for thousands of years. Composed of sarsen megaliths (large stones) weighing up to 26 tons or 52,000 pounds as well as many bluestone megaliths, Stonehenge is a marvel of ancient technology. These sarsens were quarried some twenty miles away and transported to the site of Stonehenge; the bluestones may have been transported as far as 200 miles.

Who built Stonehenge? Speculation has ranged from aliens to stone-levitating wizards to a prehistoric race of giants. A common belief is that Celtic Druids built Stonehenge. But the general belief today is that while the Druids may have used Stonehenge, it was built before the Celtic peoples arrived in the British Isles. Today the prevailing theory is that Stonehenge was built in increments. The earthen bank and ditch were constructed around 3000 BC; wooden structures were erected from 2900 to 2500 BC; and the sarsen and bluestone megaliths were transported and erected between 2500 and 1600 BC.

Not only were the megaliths cut and shaped by expert craftsmen and transported a considerable distance; they were erected at such places and angles that they accurately reflect the movements of the heavens and the solstices and equinoxes—even allowing for settling of the earth!

---

11. *100 Great Archeological Discoveries,* op. cit., 142–45.

12. *100 Great Archeological Discoveries,* op. cit. 96–97; *Ancient Inventions,* op. cit., 361–64, 442–63; *The History of Plumbing—Crete,* www.historywiz.com/minoanplumbingandheating.html (accessed 28 April, 2016).

And what was Stonehenge? A "Neolithic computer" to predict lunar eclipses? An altar for animal (or human) sacrifice? A crematorium? A temple for sun-worship? All these and many other theories have been seriously advanced, and the truth may always be shrouded in mystery.

This much is clear: the builders of Stonehenge, whoever they were, were far from primitive.[13]

• On the other side of the world, in the Andes Mountains of Peru, stand the remains of a civilization that once rivaled anything in Europe, Africa, or Asia. The capital of the Inca Empire, Cuzco, contained public buildings of superior construction and stonemasonry, and the Temple of the Sun at Moche is 340 feet square, 75 feet tall, and contains an estimated 130 million adobe bricks. The Empire was linked together by a complex system of roads, paved and unpaved.

Near Cuzco is an immense fortress known as Sacsahuaman, 1800 feet long with stone walls 60 feet tall, made of perfectly cut stones, some weighing over 100 tons (200,000 pounds), held together with no mortar but gravity alone.

Even more breathtaking is the city of Machu Picchu, located on a mountain 8,000 feet above sea level. To construct Machu Picchu the stonemasons worked with hard granite blocks weighing up to 50 tons (100,000 pounds) and shaped them so tightly that a knife blade cannot fit between them. The city contains palaces, temples, baths, storage rooms, 150 homes, terraced mountainsides for agriculture, and a large Intihuatana (Hitching Post of the Sun) Stone that precisely indicates the autumn and spring equinoxes. Despite being abandoned for nearly half-a-millennium, the stone structures of Machu Picchu stand in excellent condition today, minus only their thatched roofs.

Inca surgeons even performed operations called "trephining" which involved cutting away part of the skull, either to ease pressure on the brain or to let out evil spirits. Yet despite this and many other evidences of incredible technology, the Inca knew neither writing nor the wheel!

While the Incas enjoyed an advanced civilization beginning shortly after the time of Christ, they began to expand into an empire only around AD 1300. But other civilizations preceded the Incas, and some believe many of these impressive structures were the work of earlier people.[14]

---

13. David Souden, *Stonehenge: Mysteries of the Stones and Landscape* (London: Collins & Brown, 1997); *Mysterious Places*, 26–31; *Ancient Mysteries*, 184–200.

14. *World Book Encyclopedia* (Chicago: World Book, 1985), "Inca," "Machu Picchu;" J. Alden

• When the Spanish conquistadors arrived in Mexico in AD 1519, they confronted a civilization in many ways far in advance of their own. The Aztec capital of Mexico City was larger than any city in Spain and better fortified than any city in Europe except possibly the Alhambra in Granada. Their temples and pyramids rivaled those of Egypt though not as large, and the city featured shopping malls and zoological gardens. The Aztecs employed a better mathematical system and more accurate calendar than any known in Europe, and a better system of communications.

And yet, the Aztecs were relative newcomers. Preceding them were the Toltecs, the Mixtecs, and perhaps others whose names have been lost. Teotihuacan, the spectacular abandoned city near Mexico City (Tenochtitlan), flourished from around the time of Christ to about AD 700–800. Its Pyramid of the Sun, about 750 feet square and 200 feet high, is the largest ancient structure in the Western Hemisphere.

• Equally impressive was the Maya civilization in Mexico's Yucatan Peninsula and Central America, which began around 1800 BC, entered its classical period around AD 250, began to decline around AD 900, and collapsed around AD 1100. And the Maya were preceded by an older civilization, the Olmecs.[15]

The technology of the ancients is revealed not only in their amazing construction projects but in more intricate aspects as well. Peter James and Nick Thorpe, in their book *Ancient Inventions,* presents convincing evidence of ancient medical procedures such as eye operations, brain surgery, false teeth, false limbs, anesthetics, and acupuncture; ships and canal-building; primitive computers, clocks, magnets, and magnifying glasses; impressive military technology; watermills, windmills, fish and oyster farms, pesticides; and many others.[16]

The ancient world valued learning and compiled impressive libraries. Some of the finest libraries of the ancient world were in the Assyrian capital Nineveh, Persia, Greece, Rome, and China, as well as in those kept in the Western Hemisphere by the Maya, the Aztecs, and the Toltecs. Most

---

Mason, *The Ancient Civilizations of Peru* (London: Penguin Books, 1957, 1988); *100 Great Archeological Discoveries,* 230–31; *Mysterious Places,* 142–49; http://sacredsites.com/americas/peru/machu_picchu.html (accessed 28 April, 2016).

15. Michael D. Coe, *The Aztecs: From the Olmecs to the Aztecs* (London: Thames and Hudson, 1962, 1995); Michael D. Coe, *The Maya* (London: Thames and Hudson, 1966, 1988); *World Book Encyclopedia* "Aztecs," "Maya," "Mexico;" *Mysterious Places,* 156–59; *100 Great Archeological Discoveries,* 206–07, 214–19, 228–29, 232–33.

16. *Ancient Inventions,* op. cit.

impressive of all was the library of Alexandria in Egypt, which housed over 700,000 volumes (some say more than 1,000,000) and was a working library where scientists and scholars conducted extensive research projects. Who knows today what ancient wisdom, perhaps preserved from civilizations extinct for thousands of years, might have been stored on those shelves?

We may never know the answer. The library of Alexandria was raided by vandals and later by Muslims, and when the Ottoman Turks conquered the Byzantine Empire in AD 1453, they brought the remnants of the library to Constantinople. Who knows what valuable works were lost over the years?

In the early 1500s a Turkish admiral named Piri Reis spent years researching in the library of Constantinople. In 1513 he produced a map known today as the Piri Reis Map which, many believe, depicts the southern tip of South America and, with astounding accuracy, the coastline of Antarctica—even though the coast of Antarctica has been under an ice cap for thousands of years! Charles H. Hapgood, in *Maps of the Ancient Sea Kings,* discusses the Piri Reis Map in detail, and compares it to the Oronteus Finaeus Map of AD 1531 and the Mercator Map which appears in Mercator's Atlas of AD 1569—even though Antarctica was unknown to the modern world until its discovery by Captain James Cook in 1772 and its coastline under the ice cap could not be determined until the early 1900s.[17]

So, what does all of this have to do with the history and development of law? If people of the ancient world possessed such sophisticated knowledge of building construction, writing, medical skills, and so many other forms of knowledge, is it not possible, is it not *likely,* that they possessed sophisticated systems of law as well? In fact, would not a sophisticated

17. Charles H. Hapgood, *Maps of the Ancient Sea Kings* (Kempton, IL: Adventures Unlimited Press, 1966, 1996), 4–111; cf. *World Book Encyclopedia,* op. cit., "Antarctica." Donald E. Chittick, in *The Puzzle of Ancient Man* (Newberg, OR: Creation Compass, 1997), 41–43, accepts Hapgood's thesis and connects it to Genesis 10:25: "And unto Eber were born two sons: the name of one was Peleg; for in his days was the earth divided; and his brother's name was Joktan." Chittick suggests that the word used for *divided* in Genesis 10:25, "pelag," can also mean "surveyed." He suggests that the days of Peleg, the great-great-grandson of Noah, saw voyages of discovery to survey and map the new post-Flood world (32–35). Graham Hancock likewise accepts Hapgood's thesis (*Fingerprints of the Gods,* 3–25). However, James and Thorpe believe it is "highly questionable" that these maps actually depict Antarctica, though they do not totally reject the possibility *(Ancient Mysteries,* 61–77). Still others question Chittick's thesis that "pelag" in Genesis 10:25 can mean "surveyed."

system of law and government be a prerequisite for the other achievements?

If so, then modern Darwinian theories, that law evolved from the simple to the complex, definitely need to be re-examined.

Those of our age have conflicting views about ancient people. On the one hand we picture them as primeval savages, whose ability to think and build a civilization was only slightly above that of apes. On the other hand we speak of the "wisdom of the ancient sages" as though they possessed knowledge and even technology that have somehow been lost through the passage of time.

Rawlinson suggests that both are not only possible but probable:

> Man can and does often, perhaps most usually, pass from the savage into the civilized condition. We have numerous instances of this transition, which we can follow step by step, and put (as it were) under a metaphysical microscope. We see the Greek pass from the simple semi-savage state described by Homer to the condition of high civilization placed before us by Thucydides and Xenophon....
>
> But, while this is the more ordinary process, or at any rate one which most catches the eye when it roves at large over the historic field, there are not wanting indications that the process is occasionally reversed. Herodotus tells of the Gelonia (Herod. iv. 108.), a Greek people, who, having been expelled from the cities on the northern coast of the Euxine, had retired into the anterior, and there lived in wooden huts, and spoke a language "half Greek, half Scythian." By the time of Mela this people had become completely barbarous, and used the skins of those slain by them in battle as coverings for themselves and their horses (Pomp/ Mel. ii.1.). A gradual degradation of the Greco-Bactrian people is apparent in the series of their coins, which is extant.... We trace a certain degeneration in the Jews of the post-Babylonian period, if we compare them with their compatriots from the accession of David to the captivity of Zedekiah. The modern Copts are very degraded descendants of the ancient Egyptians, and the Romans of Wallachia have fallen away very considerably from the level of the Dacian colonists of Trajan....
>
> Civilization, as evident from these and various other instances, is liable to decay, to wane, to deteriorate, to proceed

> from bad to worse, and in course of time to sink to so low a level that the question occurs, Is it civilization any longer?...
>
> Thus, on the whole, there would seem to be grounds for believing, broadly, that savagery and civilization, the two opposite poles of our social condition, are states between which men oscillate freely, passing from either to the other with almost equal ease, according to the external circumstances wherewith they are surrounded.[18]

This book will explore the world's legal systems, ancient, classical, medieval, and beyond, and ask the piercing questions: Where did they come from? On what foundation are they based? How did man develop them? Or were they given to man by another source, or Source? How have they developed—or have they developed? Is increasing complexity a sign of progress?

In Book One, The Foundation, we will tour ancient civilizations and examine their laws and governments, ranging from Egypt and Mesopotamia to India and China and then, by way of Hawaii, to the Incas, Maya, Aztecs, Cheyenne, and Iroquois of America. Book Two, The Cornerstone, will focus upon the laws of the ancient Hebrews. Book Three, The Structure, will explore the classical world of Greece and Rome and the development of Christian jurisprudence in the late classical period and early Middle Ages. Book Four, The Centerpiece, will trace the development of the common law through its Celtic, Germanic, Roman, Anglo-Saxon, and Norman periods. And Book Five, The Pinnacle, will examine the relevance of the Reformers, the philosophers, and the colonial experiences. And Book Six, The Beacon, will narrate the sending of the common law across the Atlantic to the North American colonies.[19]

---

18. George Rawlinson, *The Origin of Nations* (1889); quoted by Katherine Dang, *Universal History, Vol. I: Ancient History: Law Without Liberty* (Oakland, CA: Dang, 2000), I: 139–41.

19. Frequently, as we explore ancient legal systems, we find that the sources give conflicting information. In such circumstances this writer has endeavored to use the information that is most likely to be correct, recognizing that in some instances readers may disagree with me. The reader should also bear in mind that civilizations and legal systems change with time. For example, the legal theory and structure of China might not be the same during the reign of the Xia Dynasty around 2000 BC, as under the Zhou Dynasty around 700 BC, or the Han Dynasty around AD 200, or the Tang Dynasty around AD 900. And new discoveries frequently change the way we assess the age of civilizations. Several decades ago conventional wisdom taught that the Maya of Central America rose a few centuries before Christ, but more recent discoveries indicate that the Maya civilization arose as early as 1800 BC and had a written language by the time Rome was founded around 750 BC.

So, as we search for the sources of the Founding Fathers' ideas, let's begin our tour of ancient civilizations and ancient laws.

Questions for Reflection, Discussion, and More Reflection

1. Why is it important to know the sources of the concepts contained in the U. S. Constitution?
2. Does it detract from the significance of the Constitution to know that its basic concepts did not originate with its Framers?
3. If the concepts contained in the Constitution originated with earlier, even ancient sources, then what if anything makes the Constitution unique?
4. According to Thomas Jefferson, what trend in the "natural progress of things" poses a perpetual threat to liberty?
5. How did the Framers guard against that trend when they designed the U. S. Constitution?
6. How does one's belief about the existence and nature of God affect one's view of law and government?
7. Describe some of the more common secular explanations of the beginning of law? What do these explanations have in common?
8. What evidence supports the theory that law evolves from the primitive and simple to the sophisticated and complex? What evidence refutes this theory?
9. Could an ancient (or modern) society have a complex and sophisticated legal system but a simple and primitive technology and culture? What about the reverse?
10. Can you think of other ancient civilizations that possessed remarkable technology and culture? What does this tell us about law and government?

Book I

The Foundation:
Ancient Legal Systems

Ruins in Karnak, Egypt. Francis Frith (ca. 1856–1860).

The Foundation: *Ancient Legal Systems*

History is Philosophy teaching by example.
—Thucydides

Since many societies of the ancient world enjoyed high levels of technology, it would be reasonable to think they might have been highly advanced in literature, art, theater, philosophy, and other aspects of culture. And we should not be surprised to find that many of them had sophisticated laws and legal systems as well.

We will find that the jurisprudence of almost every ancient society tried to answer the basic legal questions we ask and try to answer today:

- What is the source of law?
- Why should people obey the law, and when, if ever, should they disobey?
- What is the true nature of man, and how does the answer to this question affect law and government?
- Are the standards of law fixed and absolute, or do they change with time?
- What is justice?
- What is liberty, and how is liberty to be balanced against the need for social order?
- Does the individual possess natural rights, and if so, what are they, and what is their source?
- How does one balance the rights and needs and desires of the individual against those of the group, or the state?
- What is true equality, and how (if at all) should government seek to create equality?

- What form of government is most likely to secure order, liberty, equality, and justice?
- What is the best way to ensure an orderly and peaceful transition of power from one ruler to the next, and thereby perpetuate a stable society?
- How does a government balance the interests of the upper, middle, and lower classes?
- To what extent should government be centralized or decentralized?
- Should the law protect and preserve the family as the basic unit of society, and if so, how?
- How does a ruler secure the loyalty of the military without giving the military too much power?
- What is the proper relationship of law and government to religion?
- How can a society maintain virtue and moral vigor in its populace?
- What is the best way to ensure that the best-qualified people become leaders in law and government?
- What is the best way for a nation to govern conquered nations?
- As a nation becomes prosperous and civilized, how can its people retain their physical and mental toughness so they do not become easy prey for rising barbarians?
- And last but far from least, how does a nation deal with the ever-recurrent problem of human evil? By denying its existence? Through education? By giving the government and its police force absolute power? If so, don't those in power have the same evil tendencies as others? Or is battling evil solely the responsibility of the church?

We will find that in diverse times and in many places, various societies have answered these questions in different ways. But we will also find that in many respects, their answers are similar.

As we seek answers to these questions, we will find that the answers often turn upon one underlying question: was man originally polytheistic or monotheistic? Did ancient societies begin with polytheism and evolve toward monotheism, or did they begin with an original monotheism and degenerate into polytheism?

Many academicians, imbued with the Darwinist worldview, assume that man evolved from a lower form of life and that, in his early stages, he was incapable of sophisticated monotheistic thought. Gradually he began to wonder about things that did not seem to occur naturally, so he began to think that objects like rocks, rivers, mountains, trees, and animals had certain supernatural powers. As his intellectual powers developed through the evolutionary process, he began to worship these powers and to seek their favor or avert their wrath by shamanism, rituals, charms, vows, and sacrifices. Eventually he came to believe that one god took special care of him, and that god became his patron divinity with whom he entered into covenants and to whom he offered sacrifices. The next step was a recognition that his personal god (often the sun god or sky god) was greater than all of the other gods, and from there he came to believe that his god was the only god, or that all of the gods are simply different manifestations of the same god. And some would go a step further and say that as science provided answers to man's questions about the world around him, he began to limit the role of God and ultimately would abandon belief in God in favor of secularism and atheism.

But others question this theory. Augustine said of God, "Thou hast made us and drawn us to Thyself, and our hearts are restless until they rest in Thee."[1] According to this view God created man and placed in man's heart a knowledge of and longing for God. But after the Fall man increasingly fell into the snare of sin, rebelled against God, and degenerated into polytheism, animism, pantheism, and ultimately materialism.

The conclusion one draws on this question may affect one's view of the origin and direction of law. If man is (or has been) evolving from less intelligent forms of life, it is reasonable to assume that his theology must be more profound and sophisticated today than it was thousands of years ago. Likewise, if *Law* is simply the product of man's mind, then it follows that as man becomes more intelligent and capable of rational and philosophical thought, his concept of law will become increasingly wise and sophisticated.

On the other hand, if man is a created being, it is reasonable to assume that his Creator placed within him a knowledge of right and wrong that forms the basis for *Law,* and that as man rebelled against his Creator,

1. Augustine, *Confessions* Book I Ch. 1.

his knowledge of right and wrong, and therefore his knowledge of true *Law,* diminished.

So, is human history the story of man's rise from the slime to the stars, or the story of man's fall from Eden, with no hope of anything except further degeneration, apart from the Creator's intervention?

The evolutionary hypothesis pervades the thinking of many jurists, historians, archeologists, paleontologists, and even many theologians today. But if we accept this view, what basis do we have for determining that some law and legal systems are just and some are unjust? If law is a formulation of man's mind, why is any one person's "law" any better than that of any other person? If there are many gods, why are the laws of Themis better or worse than the laws of Marduk? Can there be a just legal order apart from a monotheistic Creator God?

The twentieth-century theologian H. Richard Niebuhr argued that the defining mark of monotheism is not God's *oneness* but rather His *goodness.*[2] Even if there is only one god, but a god who is amoral and indifferent to issues of right and wrong, the existence of that god cannot form the basis for a just social order. Only a God Who is just and righteous can be the basis for a just system of law.

As we look at these various societies, we will see evidence that many of them, perhaps all of them, began with monotheism. George Rawlinson, professor of ancient history at Oxford, has written that a

> historical survey has shown us that in the early times, everywhere, or almost everywhere, belief in the unity of God existed —barbarous nations possessed it as well as civilized ones— it underlay polytheism that attempted to crush it—retained a hold on language and thought—had from time to time its special assertors, who never professed to have discovered it.[3]

The Church Father Justin Martyr (ca. AD 100–165) argued that the ancient Greeks were monotheists; he quoted the 6th century BC poet Orpheus as saying, "Look to the one and universal king—One, self-begotten, and the only One, of whom all things and we ourselves are sprung.... And, other than the great King there is none."[4] Gordon Holmes Fraser noted

2. H. Richard Niebuhr, *Radical Monotheism and Western Culture* (Harper & Row 1960).

3. George Rawlinson, quoted by Wayne Jackson, *Biblical Studies in the Light of Archeology* (Apologetics Press 1982), 5–6.

4. Justin Martyr, quoted in *The Apostolic Fathers with Justin Martyr and Irenaeus,* ed. A.

that "Anthropologists, working with primitive tribes in a number of world areas and unaware of each other's findings, were reporting with a striking coincidence the concept of a Supreme Being among supposedly primitive peoples."[5] He noted Dr. Wilhelm Schmidt's observation that primitive cattle-herding people steadfastly believe in and worship a supreme sky-god, and that

> In proportion as we withdraw from the most primitive peoples and approach the semi-civilized ones, these three elements, magic, ghost-worship and nature worship, take deeper root and finally overrun the ancient veneration of the Supreme Being to such a degree as to render it no longer visible.[6]

Dr. Schmidt further noted that in these primitive cultures the "Supreme Being Himself is, in the fullness of His attributes and functions, an ideal personification of the highest essential and moral character, and well calculated to inspire the peoples that acknowledge and honor Him with the high value of active life and solemn moral virtue."[7]

Writing in the *Encyclopedia of Religion and Ethics,* George Foucart noted the common belief of primitive cultures in one high god who

> occupies the same place in the semi-civilized religions of Pre-Columbian America as we find in all groups of so-called non-civilized religions without exception. We may safely presume that the concept of sky-god belongs to the most ancient period in the history of religious feeling, and that it is at least as ancient as primitive naturism and animistic fetishism. Whether it is even pre-animist in its fundamental aspect is a question which must be reserved in the meantime.
>
> The nature, role, and characteristics of this universal sky-god may be concealed under the most diverse forms, but he is always more or less recognizable to the historian of religions

---

Cleveland Coxe (Eerdmans: 1972), 279.

5. Gordon Holmes Fraser, "The Gentile Names of God," *A Symposium on Creation* (Baker Book House, 1975), 11–38; www.creationism.org/english/symposium/symp5no1.htm (accessed 28 April, 2016).

6. Fr. Dr. Wilhelm Schmidt, *Primitive Revelation* trans. Joseph J. Baierl (R. Herder 1939), 123 (quoted by Fraser).

7. Schmidt, 125 (quoted by Fraser op. cit). He notes that one herding nomadic tribe, the Samoyeds of Lapland and Siberia, distinctly spoke of God in terms of "Heaven."

> and always identical in essential definition. America shows him in the mythology of the Toltecs, the Mayas and the Incas as well as in Brazil, in the Andes, among the Caribs, in Tierra del Fuego, and at the extreme north among the Eskimos.
>
> The sky-god has reigned everywhere; his kingdom still covers the whole of the uncivilized world. No historical or proto-historical motive can be assigned as a cause, and neither the migrations of races nor the diffusion of myths and folk-lore affords the slightest justification of the fact. The universality of the sky-god and the uniformity of his essential characteristics are the logical consequences of the constant uniformity of the primitive system of cosmogony.[8]

Fraser developed a detailed and convincing argument that the terms for "God" in ancient languages are often morphemes (words that cannot be broken down into smaller words), demonstrating that those who spoke those languages must have been monotheistic.[9]

Old Testament scholar Friedrich Delitzsch noted that in ancient societies the number of gods tends to increase with time. This, he concluded, indicates an origin in monotheism rather than polytheism.[10] Stephen Langdon of Oxford came to the same conclusion:

> In my opinion the history of the oldest civilization of man is a rapid decline from monotheism to extreme polytheism and widespread belief in evil spirits. It is in a very true sense the history of the fall of man.[11]

Likewise Shuckford, after examining the religious systems of many ancient civilizations, concluded that "…at first, there was a general agreement about religion in the world; and if we look into the particulars of the heathen religion, even after they were much corrupted, we may evidently find several practices, as well as principles, sufficient to convince us, that

8. George Foucart, "Sky Gods, Universality and Antiquity," in *Encyclopedia of Religion and Ethics,* 13 vols., ed. James Hastings (New York: Scribner's, 1908–1927), 11: 580; (quoted by Fraser, op. cit.)

9. Fraser, op. cit.

10. Friedrich Delitzsch, *Babel and Bible* (Williams & Norgate 1903), 144ff. P. Le Page Renouf makes similar observations in *Lectures on the Origin and Growth of Religion as Illustrated by the Religion of Ancient Egypt* (Williams & Norgate, 1897).

11. Stephen H. Langdon, *Semitic Mythology, Mythology of All Races* (Archeological Institute of America 1931), V: xviii.

the ancient religion in all parts of the world was originally the same."[12] These similarities included sacrifices, a priestly caste, and ritual cleansings.

Rawlinson suggested that originally man believed in one God with many attributes, but with time people came to ascribe the different attributes of God to many different gods:

> The deity, once divided, there was no limit to the number of His attributes of various kinds and of different grades; and in Egypt everything that partook of the divine essence became a god. Emblems were added to the catalogue; and though not really deities, they called forth feelings of respect which the ignorant could not distinguish from actual worship.[13]

Don Richardson, in his fascinating book *Eternity in Their Hearts,* examined the ancient Greeks, the Incas of Peru, the Santal people of India, the Mbaka of Africa, the ancient Chinese and Koreans, those of Burma, of Hawaii, and many others. He contended that when missionaries came to preach Christianity to these people, the people frequently responded that they had known this God in the distant past but had lost contact with Him. Richardson believed this has serious implications for missionary evangelism: missionary approaches might be very different if the people being evangelized had once known God, even imperfectly or by a different name, than if they had never known Him at all.[14]

If man was originally monotheistic, his concepts of law, and the Source of that law, might be very different from what they would be if we cling to the assumption that man was originally polytheistic. We will explore the evidence and those assumptions further as we look at the world of ancient man. And we will look for clues and evidence as to whether ancient civilizations in different parts of the world held common concepts of morality, a common Law of Nature, that may indicate a common bond, a common origin, or a common Source.

We will not be surprised to find that people's beliefs about religion influence and even drive their beliefs about law and government.

12. Samuel Shuckford, *The Sacred and Profane History of the World Connected* (1727; 1824; reprinted by Tolle Lege Press, 2009), I: 285.

13. George Rawlinson, *The History of Herodotus: A New English Version* (D. Appleton & Co. 1859), II: 249.

14. Don Richardson, *Eternity in Their Hearts* (Regal, 1981, 1984).

Ultimately, law constitutes the determination of social values, giving them the sanction of government, and imposing them by governmental force. Law, then, cannot be divorced from moral values, and moral values have their origin in religious belief, broadly defined. That which Ed Bishop and Charles Pellegrino describe as their "first law" may be an overstatement but is worth thinking about:

> All philosophy ultimately dovetails with religion—which is ultimately reducible to history. All history is ultimately reducible to biology. Biology is ultimately reducible to chemistry. Chemistry is ultimately reducible to physics. Physics is ultimately reducible to mathematics. And mathematics is ultimately reducible to philosophy.[15]

Do morality, law, and government fit somewhere in this circle?

As we consider that question, we're now ready to begin our tour, going back to the beginnings of recorded history and surveying law in the ancient world.

Tomb of Cyrus the Great. 1898.

---

15. Ed Bishop's and Charles Pellegrino's "First Law," in Charles Pellegrino, *Return to Sodom and Gomorrah* (Avon Books, 1994), 4. Readers who question how mathematics can be reducible to philosophy and ultimately religion are encouraged to read James Nickel, *Mathematics: Is God Silent?* (Ross House Books, 2001).

CHAPTER 1

EGYPT:
LAW AND JUSTICE—
Human and Divine

Egypt has never been a major world empire. The Assyrians, the Persians, the Greeks, and the Romans each in turn dominated Egypt. And yet each of these empires has crumbled into dust. But like the pyramids and the sphinx, Egypt remains to this day. How has Egypt maintained itself as a distinct culture and civilization through these thousands of years? Let's look at this land on the Nile and try to find the secret to Egypt's stability.

George Rawlinson observed that in Egypt

> ...there is no indication of any early period of savagery or barbarism. All the authorities agree that, however far we go back, we find in Egypt no rude or uncivilized time out of which civilization is developed. Menes, the first king, changes the course of the Nile, makes a great reservoir, and builds the temple of Phtah at Memphis. (Herodotus, ii: 99) Athothis, or Tosorthmus, his son and successor, is the builder of the Memphite palace, and a physician, who wrote books on anatomy.... The Pyramid period falls very early in Egyptian history, but "the scenes depicted in the tombs of this epoch show that the Egyptians had already the same habits and arts as in after-times, and the hieroglyphics in the Great Pyramid prove that writing had been long in use. We see no primitive mode of life in Egypt, no barbarous customs; not even the habit, so slowly abandoned by all people, of wearing arms when not on military service, nor any archaic art.... In the tombs of the Pyramid period are represented the same flowing and fishing scenes as occur later; the rearing of cattle, and wild animals of the desert, the scribe using the same kind of reed for writing on the papyrus an inventory of the estate, which was to be presented to the owner; the same boats,

> though rigged with a double mast instead of the single one of late times; the same mode of preparing for the entertainment of guests; the same introduction of music and dancing; the same trades as glass-blowers, cabinet-makers, and others, as well as similar agricultural scenes, implements, and granaries.[1]

John Maxcy Zane, in his *The Story of Law* in which he endeavors to present the history of law as an evolutionary process, candidly acknowledged that he omitted coverage of the Egyptians because they did not fit his desired pattern of evolutionary development.[2]

The first Egyptian king of great reputation, so far as history records, was Menes, who began his reign around 3100 BC and reigned 60 (Eusebius) or 62 (Africanus) years.[3] Menes established Egypt's first ruling dynasty, and he also was Egypt's first notable lawgiver. But he claimed his laws were given to him by the god Thoth, so we must first examine the religion of Egypt to see how Egyptian religion influenced Egyptian law.

Herodotus said of the Egyptians, "They are religious to excess, far beyond any other race of men."[4] A common belief is that ancient Egyptian religion was polytheistic, and their gods often represented forces of nature. Greatest of all the gods was Ra (also sometimes called Horus), the sun god, who fertilizes Mother Earth with heat and light. The moon, stars, and constellations were also gods, and there were gods on the earth as well. Most notable of the earth gods was the god of the Nile, as Egyptian subsistence and commerce depended so much on the great river.[5] Animals, too, were considered divine and some were worshipped, such as snakes, dogs, hawks, ibises, and cats. Various Egyptian rulers differed as to which god should receive supreme worship and obedience.

But many scholars reject this theory. Sir Flinders Petrie, the archeologist who is commonly called the "father of modern Egyptology," wrote in 1908,

---

1. George Rawlinson, *The Origin of Nations* (1889), reprinted in Dang, I: 143. Rawlinson quoted from Sir. G. Wilkinson.

2. John Maxcy Zane, *The Story of Law,* 2nd ed. (Indianapolis: Liberty Fund, 1927, 1998), xix, 47.

3. Alan Gardiner, *The Egyptians* (Oxford: Oxford University Press, 1961; London: Folio Society, 2000), 418.

4. Herodotus, *The Histories of Herodotus,* trans. George Rawlinson (The Everyman Library 1992), II: 136.

5. Durant, I: 197–205; cf. Gardiner, 206–239.

> Were the conception of a god only an evolution from such spirit worship, we should find the worship of many gods preceding the worship of one god.... What we actually find is the contrary to this, monotheism is the first stage traceable in theology....
>
> Wherever we can trace back polytheism to its earliest stages, we find that it results from combinations of monotheism. In Egypt even Osiris, Isis, and Horus, so familiar as a triad, are found at first as separate units in different places: Isis as a virgin goddess, and Horus as a self-existent God.[6]

Likewise, Le Page Renouf declared in 1880,

> The sublimer portions are not the comparatively late results of a process of development or elimination from the grosser. The sublimer portions are demonstrably ancient, and the last stage of the Egyptian religion, that known to the Greek and Latin writers, was by far the grossest and most corrupt.[7]

Another Egyptologist, Sir Wallis Budge, noted that the number of gods increased as Egyptian history progressed. This, he suggests, indicates a beginning with monotheism, not polytheism. He further observes that the Egyptian *Book of the Dead* contains hymns addressed to the chief god of the Egyptian pantheon, Ra or Amen-Ra, that reflect monotheism:

> A Hymn to Amen-Ra...president of all the gods...Ra, whose word is truth, the Governor of the world, the mighty one of valour, the chief who made the world as he made himself.... Adoration be to thee, O Maker of the Gods, who hast stretched out the heavens and founded the earth!... Lord of eternity, maker of the everlastingness...creator of light.... Hail to thee, O thou maker of all these things, thou only one. In his mightiness he taketh many forms.[8]

Shuckford wrote,

---

6. Sir Flinders Petrie, *The Religion of Ancient Egypt* (London: Constable, 1908), 3–4.

7. Le Page Renouf, *Lectures on the Origin and Growth of Religion as Illustrated by the Religion of Ancient Egypt* (London: Williams and Norgate, 1897), 90.

8. Sir Wallis Budge, *The Book of the Dead*, www.gutenberg.org/files/7145/7145-h/7145-h.htm (accessed 28 April, 2016); also quoted in "Monotheism: The Original Religion of Man," Zenith Harris Merrill.

> The heathen writers give us some hints, that the Egyptians were at first worshippers of the true God. Plutarch testifies, that, in Upper Egypt, the inhabitants of that country paid no part of the taxes which were raised for the idolatrous worship, asserting, that they owned no mortal being to be a god, but professed to worship their god Cneph only, whom they affirmed to be without beginning and without end. Philo-Biblius informs us, that in the mythologic times they represented this deity, called Cneph, by the figure of a serpent, with the head of a hawk in the middle of a circle. But then he further tells us, from the ancient records, that the God thus represented was the Creator of all things, a Being incorruptible and eternal, without beginning and without parts; with several other attributes belonging to the Supreme God. Agreeable to this, Porphyry calls this Egyptian Cneph *ton demiourgon*, i.e., the Maker, or Creator, of the Universe. If we search the Egyptian antiquities, we may find in their remains as noble and true notions of the Deity as are to be met with in the antiquities of any other people. These were certainly their first principles, and as long as they adhered to these, so long they preserved the knowledge of the true religion; but afterwards, when they came to add to these speculations of their own, then by degrees they corrupted and lost it.[9]

Still another scholar, Rudolphe Anthes, has written, "It may appear striking to find both the concepts of the universal, eternal god and the trinity of this god as early as 3000 BC.... As for the trinity, the earliest evidence is the carving on the ivory comb of King Zet, 'the Serpent,' of about 2900 BC."[10]

At least one ancient pharaoh believed himself the servant of the one true God. The name he used for this one true God was Aton, which comes from the same root as a Hebrew word for God, Adonai.[11] Amenhotep IV, also known as Ikhnaton, reigned from 1380–1362 BC, shortly after the time of Moses, the plagues, and the Hebrews' exodus from Egypt. Ikhnaton's hymns seem to address a loftier God than those of the Egyptian pantheon:

---

9. Samuel Shuckford, *The Sacred and Profane History of the World Connected* (1824) (Reprinted by Tolle Lege Press, 2009), 1: 284–85.

10. Rudolph Anthes, "Mythology in Ancient Egypt," *Mythologies in the Ancient World,* ed. Samuel Noah Kramer (Anchor 1961), 34.

11. My thanks to British author and historian William Cooper for bringing the *Aton/Adonai* connection to my attention.

Thy dawning is beautiful in the horizon of the sky,
O living Aton, Beginning of life.

When thou risest in the eastern horizon,
Thou fillest every land with thy beauty.[12]

Ikhnaton warred against the priests and their corruptions and ordered that the names of all gods but Aton be erased and chiseled from all public inscriptions, closed the old temples, declared all polytheistic creeds illegal, forbade images of the gods because the one true God Aton had no form, and seems to have practiced monogamy as well as monotheism.

But whether he sought to introduce a new monotheistic religion, or a return to the monotheism of the ancients, he apparently pushed too hard and too fast. He incurred the enmity of the priesthood, as well as his generals who blamed military defeats on Ikhnaton's abandonment of the gods. He died in 1362 BC facing a general revolt and collapse, "broken with the realization of his failure as a ruler, and the unworthiness of his race."[13]

Besides their belief in a god or gods, another key feature of Egyptian religion was belief in life after death, or more specifically, the transmigration of souls. Clare writes,

> The belief in the transmigration of the soul was closely connected with the reverence for animals. Bunsen says the Egyptians viewed the human soul and the animal soul as the same, and for this reason the animal was considered sacred to man.... The Egyptian doctrine, according to Herodotus, was that every human soul must pass through all animals, fishes, insects, and birds, thus completing the whole circuit of animated existence, after which it would again enter the human body, from which it came.... Herodotus further says that the complete circuit of transmigration is performed by the soul in three thousand years.... This explains the extraordinary care taken in ornamenting the tombs, as the permanent resting-places for the dead during a long period. Diodorus says that the Egyptians ornamented their tombs as the enduring residences of mankind. The doctrine of transmigration also accounts for the custom of embalming the

12. Durant, I: 206. Ikhnaton reigned about a century after the Israelites' exodus from Egypt. Is it possible that God's plagues upon the Egyptians and His deliverance of the Israelites, caught the attention of Ikhnaton, even if his predecessors had ignored them?

13. Durant, I: 210–12.

> dead, in order to preserve the body from decay, and to render it fit to receive the soul on its return.[14]

To please the gods and gain their favor, Egypt maintained an elaborate caste of priests. Since Egypt had a well-developed system of writing well before 2000 BC, the priests wrote their doctrines and rituals in forty-two sacred books. Unfortunately, only one of these, the *Necromicon* or *Book of the Dead,* has been discovered.

In every nome (region) of Egypt was a sacred lake that the body of a deceased person must cross before he or she could be buried in the city of the dead. This lake symbolized the spiritual lake that the soul must cross. Thalheimer describes the human judgment and divine judgment a person must undergo after death:

> At death all became equal; the king or the highest pontiff equally with the lowest swineherder must be acquitted by the judges before his body was permitted to pass the sacred lake and be buried with his fathers. Every nome had its sacred lake, across which all funeral processions passed on their way to the city of the dead. On the side nearest the abodes of the living, have been found the remains of multitudes who failed to pass the ordeal, and whose bodies were ignominiously returned to their friends, to be disposed of in the speediest manner.
>
> Beside the earthly tribunal of forty-two judges, who decided the fate of the body, it was believed that the soul must pass before the divine judgment-seat before he could enter the abodes of the blessed. *The Book of the Dead*—the only one yet discovered of the forty-two sacred books of the Egyptians—contains a description of the trial of the departed soul. It is represented on its long journey as occupied with prayers and confessions. Forty-two gods occupy the judgment-seat. Osiris presides; and before him are the scales, in one of which the statue of perfect Justice is placed; in the other, the heart of the deceased. The soul of the dead stands watching the balance, while Horus examines the plummet indicating which way the beam preponderates; and Thoth, the Justifier records the sentence. If this is favorable, the soul receives a mark or seal, "Justified."[15]

---

14. Israel Smith Clare, *Sixty Centuries of Progress,* Vol. I, reprinted in Dang, I: 317–18.

15. Mary E. Thalheimer, *A Manual of Ancient History* (Cincinnati: Wilson, Hinkle & Co., 1872), 63–64.

Thalheimer adds, "The rewards and punishments of a future life were powerful incitements to right dealing in the present."[16] However, Durant says that for the most part,

> Egyptian religion had little to say about morality; the priests were busier selling charms, mumbling incantations, and performing magic rites than inculcating ethical precepts. Even the *Book of the Dead* teaches the faithful that charms blessed by the clergy will overcome all the obstacles that the deceased soul may encounter on its way to salvation; and the emphasis is rather on reciting the prayers than on living the good life.[17]

However, Hutchinson believed the Egyptians emphasized both right ceremonies and right living:

> It was very important, in the opinion of the Egyptians, that the gods at each place, and of each kind, should be worshipped with the exactly right ceremonies. If the ceremonies were not rightly performed the god might be angry and bring all kinds of calamities upon you. It seemed far more important that these rites should be properly performed than that those who performed them should lead very good lives. They had their laws and their customs which regulated their conduct, but they do not seem to have feared that the gods would visit them with punishment in this life for any wrong-doing. They did, however, consider that any acts of injustice, such as robbery or dishonesty, would affect the state of their soul after death. That would be the business of Osiris, the ruler of the dead, to look after.[18]

This picture of the judgment before Osiris is difficult to reconcile with the concept of transmigration of souls. Possibly the judgment before Osiris was necessary before the transmigration could begin. Possibly different Egyptians believed differently at different times of history. Or possibly, as Thalheimer suggests, the priests kept the "sacred mysteries" to themselves and taught the common people "only those convenient doctrines which would render them submissive to kingly and priestly authority."[19]

---

16. Ibid, 63.

17. Durant, I: 204.

18. Horace G. Hutchinson, *The Greatest Story in the World* (New York: DeWitt and Davenport, 1923,1928); reprinted in Dang, I: 318

19. Thalheimer, 62.

A society that believed so strongly in the gods, that believed so strongly in life after death, that had such a strong and well-organized priesthood, very naturally would see divine influence in law and government. As Israel Smith Clare wrote,

> The government of Egypt was a theocratic monarchy, the king being the earthly representative of the Deity. His body was considered sacred, and he was worshiped as a god. His title of Phrah, or Pharaoh, signifying the Sun, ranked him as the emblem of Helios, or Phrah, or Ra, the Sun-god. His right and duty was to preside over the sacrifices and to pour out libations to the gods. He was thus the head of the national religion, as well as the civil and political head of the state.[20]

The pharaoh was the representative of the Sun-god, and he was a lesser deity himself. The very term *pharaoh* may stem from *Phrah,* a variant of Ra, the Sun-god. As such, he not only spoke the law, he *was* the law. The pharaoh was the sole and supreme ruler, but the exercise of his power was carefully circumscribed by law. The *Cambridge Ancient History* observes that "The whole structure of the Egyptian constitution was founded on the general acceptance that its rulers were divine.... In virtue of his supposedly divine nature, the king ruled as an absolute monarch with complete authority over both secular and religious affairs."[21]

Early Egyptian documents refer to a code of laws, but this code has not been found, and some scholars question whether it actually existed prior to the 700s BC.[22] But long before that time, a body of law existed, whether it consisted of unwritten custom, precedents, and decrees, something like the common law, or a written code that has been lost to historians.

The Egyptian concept of law was represented by the goddess Ma'at; she stood by the god Osiris (or in some accounts Horus) at the judgment of the dead. Judges were priests of Ma'at and often wore a figurine of the goddess around their necks. Her name became an abstract term for the concept of law and justice, and *ma'at* is essential to an understanding of Egyptian jurisprudence. VerSteeg says *ma'at* represented the natural order and balance of life, with religious, ethical, and moral connotations.

20. Israel Smith Clare, reprinted in Dang, I: 320.

21. *Cambridge Ancient History I,* 2: 35–37.

22. Rus VerSteeg, *Law in Ancient Egypt* (Carolina Academic Press, 2002), 9–10, 17; Wigmore, I: 13–14.

It required conformity with the principles of the universe which were established by the gods at the time of creation. This order is maintained through truth, justice, balance, and tradition.[23] Wilson says *ma'at* can be

> variously translated as "truth," "justice," "righteousness," "order," and so on. Each of those translations may be apt in a certain context, but no one English word is always applicable. Ma'at was a quality which belonged to good rule or administration, but it cannot be translated as "rule," "government," "administration," or "law." *Ma'at* was the proper quality of such applied functions. Basically, *ma'at* had some of the same flexibility as our English terms "right," "just," "true," and "in order." It was the cosmic force of harmony, order, stability, and security, coming down from the first creation as the organizing quality of created phenomena and reaffirmed at the accession of each god-king of Egypt. In the temple scenes the pharaoh exhibited *ma'at* to the other gods every day, as the physical evidence that he was carrying out his divine function of rule on their behalf. Thus there was something of the unchanging, eternal, and cosmic about *ma'at.* If we render it "order," it was the order of created things, physical and spiritual, established at the beginning and valid for all time. If we render it "justice," it was not simply justice in terms of legal administration; it was the just and proper relationship of cosmic phenomena, including the relationship of the rulers and the ruled. If we render it "truth," we must remember that, to the ancient, things were true not because they were susceptible of testing and verification but because they were recognized as being in their true and proper places in the order created and maintained by the gods. *Ma'at,* then, was a created and inherited rightness, which tradition built up into a concept of orderly stability, in order to confirm and consolidate the status quo, particularly the continuing rule of the pharaoh. The opposites of *ma'at* were words which we translate as "lying," "falsehood," and "deceit." That which was not consonant with the established and accepted order could be denied as being false. *Ma'at* comes closest to the moral connotation of our word "good."[24]

23. VerSteeg, 21; cf. Wigmore, I: 13.

24. John A. Wilson, *Culture of Ancient Egypt* (1948), quoted by VerSteeg, 22.

The duty of a judge, and of a pharaoh as chief judge, was to judge in accordance with truth, righteousness, and the eternal laws established by the gods at creation, thereby fostering the condition the Egyptians called *ma'at.*

To create and preserve *ma'at,* the Egyptians established a complex legal structure. The pharaoh was the supreme judge of all matters, but he delegated most of his judicial functions to an assistant or Visier, sometimes called the "prophet of Ma'at." In the Old Kingdom (2700–2200 BC) the land was divided into six judicial districts called "Great Houses" with "Great Courts." Each of these Great Courts had a chief justice with various associate justices. Under these were forty-two nomes or districts, twenty-two in the northern kingdom and twenty in the southern kingdom, each of which had an administrator who served as a judge, and such additional personnel (generally priests and elders) as were necessary to establish tribunals to administer justice.[25]

In the Middle (2200–1552 BC) and New (1552–1069 BC) Kingdoms, the judicial structure retained the same basic form but became more fixed and permanent. At all levels, judging was usually one of several functions performed by an administrator. The concept of three functions of government—legislative, executive, and judicial—was present in the ancient world, but the idea of dividing those three functions into separate branches of government did not become prevalent until much later.[26]

The Egyptian judicial system made extensive use of written legal proceedings. Lawyers proliferated, but they functioned more as scribes drafting legal documents than as advocates in the courtroom. Litigants commonly argued their own cases in the courtroom, and oratory was a prized art. We gain much insight into Egyptian court procedure from a story written during the age of the Middle Kingdom or possibly earlier, titled "The Tale of the Eloquent Peasant." The highly articulate peasant Khunanup eventually prevails in his lawsuit to recover his livestock, but only after lengthy delays, brought on by the judges because they immensely enjoyed listening to the peasant as he argued his case! The judges pretend to ignore him, making him come back and argue again and again. In his nine speeches Khunanup offers sage advice to judges of his day and ours as well, such as "be patient

25. VerSteeg, 38–41.

26. Ibid., 41–43. However, Wigmore believed the office of prime minister and the office of chief justice were originally distinct but were merged toward the end of the Old Kingdom (2700–2200 BC), I: 12.

that you may learn justice," and manage your caseload efficiently and diligently because "pass over a case, and it will become two." The themes of the story are that justice should be available to the poor on an equal basis with the rich, justice is a natural force, but also that justice is a natural force that judges somehow can and should control.[27]

Early Egyptian law was based on the edicts of the divine pharaoh, applied and interpreted by the judges. Where the pharaoh had not spoken or where his decrees were ambiguous, custom and case precedents were very important, although judges occasionally overruled or distinguished precedents.

A plaintiff began his lawsuit by filing a written petition with the Visier, or with a lower court judge, who examined it to determine whether it was legally sufficient. If the petition was deficient, it was dismissed and returned to the plaintiff.[28] If it sufficiently stated a case, the court notified the defendant of the lawsuit and gave the defendant the opportunity to file a written answer. Sometimes the plaintiff was allowed to rebut the defendant's answer, followed by a further answer by the defendant.

The judge then held a hearing, at which both parties stated their cases and presented witnesses, documents, and other evidence to support their positions. Testimony was under oath, and there were strict penalties for perjury. Since the parties were not represented by attorneys, the judges commonly took an active role in questioning witnesses. The judge then pronounced his judgment, after which the parties faced each other and promised to abide by the judgment.[29]

An Egyptian court record from about 2500 BC is, according to Wigmore, the oldest court record in the world yet discovered. It reads:

> The party Sebekotep alleges that one Usser, now deceased, father of the other party Thau, made the said Sebekotep to be guardian of his, the said Usser's wife and children, and to that

---

27. VerSteeg, *Egypt*, 15–17, 28–36. One wonders whether future historians and archeologists will try to understand our legal system by reading the novels of Earl Stanley Gardner and John Grisham.

28. VerSteeg, 69–70. This "gatekeeper" feature of Egyptian legal proceedings has much to commend it today. In many American appellate courts, the judges or justices pass judgment on the legal sufficiency of a pleading. If they determine that it is legally insufficient, often because of some minor technical detail, the appeal is dismissed, and often the litigant cannot correct the deficiency and refile because, by this time, the deadline for filing has expired. The party is therefore not allowed to seek justice because of the technical, procedural error of his attorney.

29. Ibid., 63–95.

> end delivered all his property to the said Sebekotep, to be applied to the use of the said Usser's family, whether or not the property increased or decreased. But the party Thau denies that his father ever made any such conveyance.
>
> If the said Sebekotep produces credible witnesses who will make oath that the said Usser did in their presence deliver the property on the terms set forth in the said Sebekotep's written pleading, then the property is to remain in his possession. But if he does not produce such witnesses, then none of the said Usser's property shall remain in Sebekotep's possession, but shall be delivered to the said Thau, son of Usser.[30]

Judgments could be appealed to higher courts, which usually involved several appellate judges. The pharaoh himself was the court of last resort, though he usually delegated that function to the Visier. One appeal that has been preserved through history is *Mes v. Khay* around 1300 BC. The lower court had resolved this land dispute in favor of Khay, but Appellant Mes claimed Appellee Khay had procured the lower court judgment by means of fraudulent entries in the land register and forged documents of title. Court records summarize the argument

> *MES*: . . . I am the son of Hui, the son of Urnero, the daughter of Neshi. A division of the property was made for Urnero and her brothers and sister in the Great Court in the time of Horemheb. They sent the clerical Iniy, who was an officer of the Great Court, to the district of Neshi: and a division was made for me and my brothers and sisters; and they made my mother, the dweller in the town, Urnero, administrator for her brothers and sisters.
>
> Then my father Hui died.
>
> And Nubnofret my mother came to till the portion of Neshi my [grand]father, but she was not allowed to till it. Then she laid a plaint against the administrator Khay, and they caused them to appear before the Court in Heliopolis in the year 14. . . of King Ramses II. . . .
>
> The administrator Khay laid a plaint in the Great Court in the year 18, and they sent for the clerical Amenemiopoet, who was an officer of the Great Court, together with him, having

30. Wigmore, I: 32–34.

> a false register in his hand, whereby I ceased to be a child of Neshi....
>
> *KHAY*: I am the son of the administrator Userhat, the son of Thani...the son of Prehotep.... I laid a plaint before the Judge in Heliopolis, and he caused me to plead together with Nubnofret before the Judge in the Great Court. I brought my testimonies...in my hand since Amosis I, and Nubnofret brought her testimonies in like manner. Then they were unrolled before the Judge in the Great Court.... Then the judge said to Nubnofret: "Who is thy heir among the heirs who are upon the two registers that are in our hand?" And Nubnofret said: "There is no heir in them." "Then thou art in the wrong," said the Judge to her.

The record then summarizes the testimony of the witnesses, including a goatherd, a honey-maker, an administrator, and a priest. Unfortunately, the portion of the record that has survived does not include the appellate court's ruling, so we are forever in the dark as to the outcome.[31]

Because Egypt was an agricultural society, property was a foremost concern of early Egyptian law. The deeds, titles, and conveyances clearly reflect private ownership of property, though some believe all property titles originally come from the pharaoh. In one early case, *Kenna v. Peikharu,* Peikharu had originally owned a house but allowed it to fall into disrepair, and Kenna rebuilt it. The court ruled that the house rightfully belonged to Kenna, suggesting that labor can beget an ownership interest in property.[32]

Egyptian property law recognized bailments, life estates, leases, easements, and other concepts associated with modern property law. Property was subject to taxation, but property of priests and judges was tax-exempt.[33]

Family law was another feature of the Egyptian legal system. Monogamy was the norm, but some royalty and nobility practiced polygamy or had a harem in addition to the one wife. A husband was responsible to support his wife throughout the marriage, and property acquired during the marriage was considered to be owned jointly by both parties, two-thirds by the husband and one-third by the wife. Divorce seems to have been fairly common, and at least in the later period (500 BC), either the

31. Wigmore, I: 34–39.

32. VerSteeg, *Egypt,* 109. VerSteeg suggests that this presages John Locke's theory that labor can create a property right by several thousand years.

33. Ibid., 109–23.

husband or the wife could sue for divorce. The husband was usually required to either return his wife's dowry or pay alimony, though these were excused if the wife was guilty of adultery or otherwise at fault. In one case a wife was found to be at fault where she had sold the joint property without her husband's consent and abandoned her husband while he was ill.[34]

A last will and testament dated around 1805 BC reads,

> I, Uah, devise to my wife Sheftu, the woman of Gesab called Teta, daughter of Sat Sepdu, all properties given to me by my brother Ankh-ren. She shall give it to whomsoever she may see fit of her issue born to me.
>
> I devise to her the Eastern slaves, 4 persons, that my brother Ankh-ren gave me. She shall give them to whomsoever she may see fit of her children.
>
> As to my tomb, let me be buried in it with my wife alone.
>
> Moreover, as to the house built for me by my brother Ankh-ren, my wife shall dwell therein and shall not be evicted by any person.
>
> The deputy Sebu shall act as guardian of my son. Done in the presence of these witnesses:
>
> Kemen, Decorator of Columns,
> Apu, Doorkeeper of the Temple,
> Senb, son of Senb, Doorkeeper of the Temple.[35]

Criminal laws were enforced strictly but not brutally in the Early and Middle Kingdoms. Restitution was a common punishment, and in cases of theft, multiple restitution was employed as a deterrent.[36] Other punishments could include forfeiture of property, forced labor, divestment of civic status, deprivation of burial (which could affect one's status in the afterlife), and, for murder and other serious cases, death (usually by decapitation). In the Middle Kingdom, beatings became a common form of punishment, and the standard means of execution became impalement. In the New Kingdom, punishments became much more severe: amputation of ears, nose, hands, or tongue, death by burning, or casting to the crocodiles. Incarceration seems not to have been a common punishment;

34. Ibid., 132–34.

35. Wigmore, I: 22.

36. Multiple rather than simple restitution might be necessary as a deterrent for an obvious reason: the potential thief has little incentive to be honest if the worst thing that can happen to him is that, if he is caught and convicted, he might have to return what he stole.

jails existed, but they were used primarily to house prisoners awaiting trial or sentence. Egyptian law also prescribed strict penalties for judges and other public officials who misused their offices: the punishment for judicial misbehavior in the New Kingdom was 100 blows, removal from office, and forced common labor.[37]

Durant describes Egyptian law and government as it worked in practice:

> With... scribes as a clerical bureaucracy the Pharaoh and the provincial nobles maintained law and order in the state. Ancient slabs show such clerks taking the census and examining income-tax returns. Through Nilometers that measured the rise of the river, the scribe-officials forecast the size of the harvest and estimated the government's future revenue; they allotted appropriations in advance to governmental departments, supervised industry and trade, and in some measure achieved, almost at the outset of history, a planned economy regulated by the state.
>
> Civil and criminal legislation were highly developed, and already in the Fifth Dynasty the law of private property and bequest was intricate and precise. As in our own days, there was absolute equality before the law—whenever the contesting parties had equal resources and influence.... Judges required cases to be pled and answered, reargued and rebutted, not in oratory but in writing—which compares favorably with our windy litigation. [Other historians believe that Egyptian court proceedings used both written pleadings and oral argument.] Perjury was punished with death. There were regular courts, rising from local judgment-seats in the nomes to supreme courts in Memphis, Thebes, or Heliopolis. Torture was used occasionally as a midwife to truth; beating with a rod was a frequent punishment, mutilation by cutting off nose or ears, hand or tongue, was sometimes resorted to, or exile to the mines, or death by strangling, impaling, beheading, or burning at the stake; the extreme penalty was to be embalmed alive, to be eaten slowly by an inescapable coating of corrosive natron. Criminals of high rank were saved the shame of public execution by being permitted to kill themselves, as in samurai Japan. We find no signs of any system of police; even the standing army—always small because of Egypt's protected isolation between deserts and seas—was

37. VerSteeg, *Egypt*, 152–77.

> seldom used for internal discipline. Security of life and property, and the continuity of law and government, rested almost entirely on the prestige of the Pharaoh, maintained by the schools and the church. No other nation except China has ever dared to depend so largely upon psychological discipline.
>
> It was a well-organized government, with a better record of duration than any other in history.[38]

And the evidence indicates that at least some of Egypt's rulers strove to rule justly. *Ma'at*, comprising an order maintained through truth and justice, is a worthy ideal for any jurist. "The Tale of the Eloquent Peasant" reflects the Egyptian concern for equal justice under the natural order of *ma'at*. The Pharaoh Thutmose III, when he appointed Rekhmire to be the Grand Visier around 1500 BC, gave him advice that modern judges would do well to heed:

> Take heed to thyself for the hall of the chief judge; be watchful over all that is done therein. Behold, it is a support of the whole land; behold, as for the chief judge, behold, he is not sweet, behold, bitter is he, when he speaks.... Behold, he is not one setting his face toward the officials and councilors, neither one making brethren of all the people.... Mayest thou see to it for thyself, to do everything after that which is in accordance with law; to do everything according to the right thereof...lo, it is the safety of an official to do things according to the law, by doing that which is spoken by the petitioner....
>
> It is an abomination of the god to show partiality. This is the teaching: thou shalt act alike to all, shalt regard him who is known to thee like him who is unknown to thee, and him who is near...like him who is far.... An official who does this, then shall he flourish greatly in the place.
>
> Do not avoid a petitioner, nor yet nod thy head when he speaks. As for him who draws near, who will approach to thee, do not...the things which he saith in speaking. Thou shalt punish him when thou has let him hear that on account of which thou punishest him.
>
> Be not enraged toward a man unjustly, but be thou enraged concerning that about which one should be enraged.

38. Durant, I: 161–62.

> Show forth the fear of thee; let one be afraid of thee, for a prince is a prince of whom one is afraid. Lo, the true dread of a prince is to do justice.
>
> Thou shalt do thy office, as thou doest justice. Lo, one shall desire to do justice.... Lo, one shall say of the chief scribe of the chief judge: "A scribe of justice," shall one say of him.[39]

And on the Visier Rekhmire's tombstone are inscribed his words:

> I judged both [the insignificant] and the influential; I rescued the weak man from the strong man; I deflected the fury of the evil man and subdued the greedy man in his hour.... I succoured the widow who has no husband; I established the son and heir on the seat of his father. I gave [bread to the hungry], water to the thirsty, and meat, oil and clothes to him who had nothing.... I was not at all deaf to the indigent. Indeed, I never took a bribe from anyone....[40]

Because of its location in the northeast corner of Africa, with Arabia to the east and with Greece and Rome across the Mediterranean, Egypt was less isolated than much of the rest of Africa and more influenced by other parts of the world. But Egypt also interacted with other parts of Africa. To the south of Egypt was the substantial Empire of Cush, at various times ruled by the Numidian kings and the Meroite kings, which reached the zenith of its power around 1700–1500 BC, then fell under Egyptian domination for several centuries, and reasserted its independence around 1000 BC. Then, in the 800s BC, the Cushites invaded Egypt, and their kings formed that twenty-fifth pharaonic dynasty that ruled Egypt until the Assyrian conquest in the 700s BC. The Cushites resembled the Egyptians in their religion and culture, although their pantheon included gods from southern African cultures, but unlike the Egyptian pharaohs the Cushite kings were elected from the royal family, and they followed a customary law that was interpreted by the priests.

The Numidian Empire, at times associated with Cush but centered west of Egypt in what is now Algeria, flourished in the 200s BC. During the Punic Wars, the Numidian kings sometimes allied themselves with Carthage and sometimes with Rome, and after the Punic Wars a Numidian king, Jugurtha, fought against Rome but was ultimately defeated.

39. Wigmore, I: 16–17.

40. VerSteeg, *Egypt,* 23. Cf. 1 Samuel 12:1–5.

Throughout its history, Cush served as a link between Egypt and the more southern portions of Africa.

Southeast of Cush was Ethiopia, a civilization that arose at least as early as 800 BC and probably earlier. At times, Egypt and Ethiopia were ruled by the same kings. The early inhabitants spoke a Semitic language, and some believe the Kingdom of Sheba, where the Queen of Sheba came from to visit King Solomon in Jerusalem (I Kings 10:1–10; cf. Matthew 12:42, Luke 11:31), was actually Ethiopia, although others place it in Yemen and elsewhere. Many Ethiopians believe King Solomon and the Queen of Sheba (Makeda in the Ethiopian account) had a child, Menelik I, who became Ethiopia's first emperor. Haile Selassie (AD 1892–1975) and other modern Ethiopian emperors have claimed to be descended from Menelik I.

Other ancient empires existed in Africa. The Kingdom of Ghana, an authoritarian theocratic kingdom that arose in the early Middle Ages, considered its kings to be so divine that they could not communicate directly with their subjects. Muslim historians related that the Ghanian kings could field an army of 200,000, but between 1054 and 1076 the kingdom gradually fell to Islamic jihad. The Kingdom of Mali, whose famous city of Timbuktu was a center for the slave trade and also for Islamic scholarship, was conquered by the Songhai, whose ruler was called the King of Kings. Greater Zimbabwe is remembered for its impressive stone structures that survive today; but like most of the African empires, its law and government is shrouded in mystery because of the lack of written records.[41]

Consider the influence upon Egypt of a Hebrew youth sold into slavery in Egypt and cast into prison on a false charge of seducing the wife of his owner, Pharaoh's officer, Potiphar. And yet Joseph rose to prominence and became Egypt's prime minister. He carefully planned Egypt's economy and saved the Egyptian people and many others from starvation and ruin during a seven-year famine (Genesis 37–50). Did he learn these principles of government and economics from the Egyptians? Or did he teach those principles to them? Where, or from Whom, would he have learned them?

---

41. See generally, Kenneth P. Vickery, *The African Experience: From "Lucy" to Mandela,* (The Teaching Company, 2006); http://archive.archaeology.org/9807/abstracts/africa.html (accessed 28 April, 2016); Basil Davidson, *The Lost Cities of Africa* (Little, Brown & Co. 1987). For different points of view, see Isak Dinesen, *Out of Africa* (Modern Library, 1992), and Mary Lefkowitz, *Not Out of Africa: How Afrocentrism Became an Excuse to Teach Myth as History* (Basic Books, 1996).

And consider further the influence of Egypt upon another man. Born a Hebrew slave and condemned to die by Pharaoh's decree, Moses was rescued from the waters by Pharaoh's daughter. Raised and educated in the royal palace, Moses cast his lot with his fellow Hebrews, and after being strengthened and honed during a wilderness sojourn, he returned to lead his people out of Egyptian bondage into freedom (Exodus 1–15). What did Moses learn from the Egyptians? And what did they learn from him?

What was the secret of Egypt's success and stability? One might point to the Egyptians' strong respect for tradition, the awe in which they held their gods and rulers, the stability and efficiency of the Egyptian bureaucracy, and the orderliness of succession of Egyptian rulers. Absolute rules of succession—that the eldest son always succeeds his father as the ruler—reduced the instability that other nations like Persia experienced when royal relatives battled for power. But it also led to stagnation when the succeeding son was a mediocre ruler.

Writing in 1935, Durant summarized Egypt's legacy:

> Today there is a place called Egypt, but the Egyptian people are not masters there; long since they have been broken by conquest, and merged in language and marriage with their Arab conquerors; their cities know only the authority of Moslems and Englishmen, and the feet of weary pilgrims who travel thousands of miles to find that the Pyramids are merely heaps of stone.... On all sides gigantic ruins, monuments, and tombs, memorials of a savage and titanic energy; on all sides poverty and desolation, and the exhaustion of an ancient blood. And on all sides the hostile, engulfing sands, blown about forever by hot winds, and grimly resolved to cover everything in the end.
>
> Nevertheless the sands have destroyed only the body of ancient Egypt; its spirit survives in the lore and memory of our race. The improvement of agriculture, metallurgy, industry, and engineering; the apparent invention of glass and linen, of paper and ink, of the calendar and the clock, of geometry and the alphabet; the refinement of dress and ornament, of furniture and dwellings, of society and life; the remarkable development of orderly and peaceful government, of census and post, of primary and secondary education, even of technical training for office and administration; the advancement of writing and literature, of science and medicine; the first clear formulation

> known to us of individual and public conscience, the first cry for social justice, the first widespread monogamy, the first monotheism, the first essays in moral philosophy; the elevation of architecture, sculpture, and the minor arts to a degree of excellence and power never (so far as we know) reached before, and seldom equaled since: these contributions were not lost, even when their finest exemplars were buried under the desert, or overthrown by some convulsion of the globe. Through the Phoenicians, the Syrians and the Jews, through the Cretans, the Greeks and the Romans, the civilization of Egypt passed down to become part of the cultural heritage of mankind. The effect or remembrance of what Egypt accomplished at the very dawn of history has influence in every nation and every age.... We shall do well to equal it.[42]

And even the sands of time have not covered these marvels of Egyptian engineering that have no equal even today. "All the world fears Time," says an Arab proverb, "but Time fears the Pyramids."[43]

42. Durant, I: 216–17.

43. Ibid., I: 150.

1 Egypt: *Law and Justice—Human and Divine*

Questions for Reflection, Discussion, and More Reflection

1. To what do you attribute Egypt's stability over the millennia?
2. Does the evidence indicate an original monotheism or polytheism in Egypt? Why and how is this important for an understanding of Egyptian history, government, and law?
3. Which is more likely to be tolerant of other religions—monotheism or polytheism? Why?
4. Why was Egyptian religion so occupied with death and the afterlife? How and why did Egyptian justice mirror their concept of the last judgment?
5. What was the Egyptian legal concept of *ma'at*? Does it provide a basis for natural law theory?
6. Describe the Egyptian court structure. How did it parallel the Egyptian concept of judgment after death?
7. How would you explain the fact that a pagan society like that of Egypt would place so much emphasis on ethics and integrity in law? What is the source of that emphasis?
8. Note the feature of the "gatekeeper" in Egyptian courts who examined written pleadings for legal sufficiency before they were filed and served. Could our court system benefit from a similar "gatekeeper"?
9. Did the Egyptian rule for succession to the office of pharoah promote stability or mediocrity—or both?
10. How did Egypt influence Greece and Rome? And consider the Israelites, Joseph in Genesis, and Moses in Exodus: did they learn from their sojourns in Egypt, or did the Egyptians learn from them?

Ziggurat of Warka, Mesopotamia (ca. 1898–1946).

CHAPTER 2

MESOPOTAMIA: *Where West Met East*

Ask anyone to name the world's #1 hotspot, and they'll probably point to the Middle East. The wars of the West with Iraq, Iraq's war with Iran, the Arab/Israeli conflict, and other conflicts of our time focus the world's attention on this region.

And so it has been throughout history: Assyria v. Babylonia, Babylonia v. Egypt, the rise of Islam, the Crusades, the Ottoman Turks, the British, the Jews, the Arabs, and a host of others. And often this conflict has focused on a region between the Tigris and Euphrates rivers called Mesopotamia.

Mesopotamia is often called the cradle of civilization, though others give that title to Egypt, India, China, and various other nations of the ancient world. Located between the Tigris and Euphrates Rivers in northern Iraq, northeastern Syria, and southeastern Turkey, Mesopotamia was a crossroads between eastern, western, and southern nations. From the Mesopotamian city known as Ur of the Chaldees (in present-day Iraq), Abraham came forth at the call of his God to the promised land of Palestine (Genesis 11:26–12:5).[1]

The earliest known culture in Mesopotamia was that of the Sumerians, who had a thriving civilization between 3000 and 2000 BC. Gradually they were conquered and absorbed by the Babylonians, who reigned

1. The credibility of the Biblical account is attested by the recent discovery of cuneiform tablets in the Mesopotamian town of Ebla. Dated approximately 1800 BC, the Ebla Tablets make reference to Abraham (though one may not say for certain that this was the Abraham of the Bible as Abram was a common name at the time), Sodom and Gomorrah, and other Biblical places and names. Other archeological work has uncovered the ruins of the cities of Ur, Shechem, Hebron and Haran, all of which figure prominently in the Genesis account. Werner Keller, *The Bible as History* (New York: Bantam, 1965, 1980), 83; Jeffery L. Sheler, *Is the Bible True? How Modern Debates and Discoveries Affirm the Essence of the Scriptures* (San Francisco: Harper and Zondervan, 1999), 72–76.

supreme in the region until the rise of the Assyrian Empire around 1300 BC. Assyria was the dominant power in the Middle East until shortly before 600 BC, when the Chaldeans or Neo-Babylonians from the South arose and restored Babylon's greatness under Nabopolassar and his son Nebuchadnezzar (Daniel 1–4). But Babylon's resurrection was short-lived; in 539 BC Cyrus the Great of Persia conquered Babylon. The Persian Empire dominated the Middle East for two centuries until, grown decadent, it fell to Alexander the Great of Greece in 331 BC.[2]

A clear separation between the Sumerian and Babylonian empire is nearly impossible; the former flows into the latter. But the Babylonians were a Semitic people, while the Sumerians probably were not.[3] The Sumerians drained the swamps, excavated canals, and created impressive works of metal, wood, bone, stone, and clay. They developed a system of writing using a symbolic alphabet known as cuneiform; the writing was commonly preserved on clay tablets. Durant says of them,

> The remains show them as a short and stocky people, with high, straight, non-Semitic nose, slightly receding forehead and downward-sloping eyes. Many wore beards, some were clean-shaven, most of them shaved the upper lip. They clothed themselves in fleece and finely woven wool; the women draped the garment from the left shoulder, the men bound it at the waist and left the upper half of the body bare.... The head was usually covered with a cap, and the feet were shod with sandals; but well-to-do women had shoes of soft leather, heel-less, and laced like our own. Bracelets, necklaces, anklets, finger-rings, and ear-rings made the women of Sumeria, as recently in America, show-windows of their husbands' prosperity.[4]

---

2. Sumeria is not the same as Samaria. The Sumerian Empire flourished before 2000 BC over a large area including Mesopotamia. Samaria was the region of Palestine between Galilee and Judea in the time of Christ and a few centuries before; the Samaritans were of mixed Jewish and Babylonian ancestry. Likewise, Assyria should not be confused with the Syria of Bible times or the Syria of today. The Assyrian Empire dominated the Middle East from about 1500 BC until about 612 BC when its capital, Nineveh, fell to the Babylonians. Syria during this time was a small nation northeast of Israel.

3. Durant simply says, "Despite much research we cannot tell of what race the Sumerians were, nor by what route they entered Sumeria. Perhaps they came from Central Asia, or the Caucasus, or Armenia, and moved through northern Mesopotamia down the Euphrates and the Tigris... perhaps, even, they were of remote Mongolian origin, for there is much in their language that resembles the Mongol speech. We do not know." Will Durant, *The Story of Civilization* (New York: Simon & Schuster, 1954, 1963), I: 118–19.

4. Durant, I: 119.

Babylonian civilization was largely a continuation of Sumerian culture. The Babylonians were noted for their astronomy and astrology (which were one and the same according to their worldview), their mathematics, and their architecture, although their buildings are not well preserved because they used mostly clay bricks due to a shortage of stone. And they were voluminous writers. Hundreds of thousands of clay cuneiform tablets have been discovered that give us good insight into their thinking and their way of life.

Religion was central to Sumerian culture and life. The Sumerians are commonly thought to have been polytheists, believing in a host of gods and goddesses who directed all aspects of earthly affairs. But others have argued that the earliest Sumerians were monotheists, and that instead of polytheism evolving into monotheism, monotheism degenerated into polytheism. In 1931 Stephen Langdon of Oxford wrote concerning Sumeria, "In my opinion the history of the oldest civilization of man is a rapid decline from monotheism to extreme polytheism and widespread belief in evil spirits."[5] Five years later he wrote,

> The history of Sumerian religion, which was the most powerful cultural influence in the ancient world, could be traced by means of pictographic inscriptions almost to the earliest religious concepts of man. The evidence points unmistakably to an original monotheism, the inscriptions and literary remains of the oldest Semitic peoples also indicate a primitive monotheism, and the totemistic origin of Hebrew and other Semitic religions is now entirely discredited.[6]

And Friedrich Delitzsch wrote in 1903 of a fragmentary tablet in which the various gods of the Babylonian pantheon are designated as one with and one in the supreme god, Marduk.[7] Sir Flinders Petrie wrote that "Babylonian cities each had their supreme god, and the combinations of these and their transformations in order to form them into groups when their

5. Stephen H. Langdon, *Semitic Mythology, Mythology of All Races*, Vol. V (Archaeological Institute of America,1931), xviii.

6. Stephen H. Langdon, *The Scotsman,* November 18, 1936.

7. Friedrich Delitszch, *Babel and Bible* (London: Williams and Norgate, 1903) 1441; (Chicago: The Open Court Publishing Co., 1903), 65.

homes were politically united show how essentially they were solitary deities at first."[8]

In any event, the Sumerians eventually embraced polytheism. Some of their gods, like the sun god Shamash, were believed to rule over a vast domain. Others were patrons of specific areas of life, like the gods and goddesses of love, fertility, springtime, harvest, thunder, warfare, the ocean, and others. Still others were local deities worshipped in a particular town, or by a particular family, or by workers in a particular occupation.[9]

The Sumerians and their successors were also animists, believing that all of nature, including animals, trees, rocks, rivers, mountains, and oceans, possessed spirits. Knowing how to communicate with these spirits, supplicate them, gain their favor, and invoke their aid, became the central role of Sumerian and later Babylonian religion. The *shaman,* a priest who supposedly had great skill in dealing with spirits, was a respected and powerful figure in Sumerian and Babylonian society.

Sacrifice was an important way of gaining the favor of the gods or averting their anger. By sacrifice one either gave the god something the god supposedly wanted, or one showed his or her devotion to the god by giving up something of value—like grain, or an animal, or a firstborn child.[10]

Astrology, and astronomy, which to the Babylonians was the same as astrology, was considered the highest order of science. The movements of the stars controlled events here on earth, so by charting the movements of the stars, planets, comets, and meteors, one could foretell the future.

8. Sir William M. Flinders Petrie, *The Religion of Ancient Egypt* (Constable 1908), 4.

9. Durant, I: 127–30; *International Standard Bible Encyclopedia* (Grand Rapids: Eerdmans, 1929, 1939) "Babylonia and Assyria, Religion of" Alexander Hislop presented persuasive evidence that pagan religion throughout much of the world originated in Sumeria, that the Biblical figure of Nimrod (Genesis 10:9–11, 11:1–9) was an early Sumerian king who, together with his legendary wife Semirami, were later deified and worshipped as the king and queen of the Babylonian pantheon of gods, the name Nimrod eventually metamorphosizing into Marduk. This same mythology, with many local variations, became the mythology of much of the rest of the world; Nimrod and Semirami become Marduk and Sarpanitum (or Bellona) for the Babylonians, Zeus and Hera for the Greeks, Jupiter and Juno for the Romans, Wotan and Frigg for the Germans, and Odin and Frigg for the Norse. Alexander Hislop, *The Two Babylons* (Neptune, NJ: Loizeaux Brothers, 1916, 1959), 1–90, 302–04, 312.

10. Some see the sacrifices of the Old Testament as another form of trying to please a particular god. Others see the pagan sacrifices as corrupted forms or counterfeits of the true sacrifice commanded by God in the Old Testament. Those Old Testament sacrifices, in turn, are types that find their fulfillment in the ultimate sacrifice of Jesus Christ on the Cross. In either event, an important difference exists: The pagan sacrifices were a means of manipulating the gods and gaining their favor; the Biblical sacrifices were an atonement for sin and a substitutionary satisfaction of God's perfect justice.

The Babylonians, and probably the Sumerians before them, constructed many ziggurats, large towers that were probably used for stargazing and probably also contained temples for rituals of worship and sacrifice. The Tower of Babel described in Genesis 11:1–9 may have been the original ziggurat.[11] Not surprisingly, then, when we read in the Book of Daniel of Daniel's captivity in Babylon and of King Nebuchadnezzar's desire for an interpretation of his dream, "Then the king commanded to call the magicians, and the astrologers, and the sorcerers, and the Chaldeans, for to shew the king his dreams" (Daniel 2:2; cf. 4:7, 5:7). These were his royal cabinet, the wise men of the kingdom, the intelligentsia of the day.

This understanding of Babylonian pagan religion, and pagan religion in general, is essential to an understanding of law and government in pagan societies. Pagan societies commonly consider the state as divine, and frequently the ruler as well. The king in a pagan society is commonly thought to be a god, or descended from the gods, or ascended to the level of a god, or in some way to have divine ancestry. Undoubtedly many sincerely believed in the king's divinity. Very possibly, others doubted but saw the utility of the myth in gaining public respect and obedience.

Jews, Christians, and Muslims regard this concept as absurd and blasphemous. God, in their view, is One, and He is all-powerful, all-knowing, and all-present. He is also perfectly truthful, perfectly righteous, and perfectly just. The difference between God and man is infinite, and the idea that a man could become God, or even partially God, is incomprehensible and blasphemous.[12] And Moses commanded his people to have nothing to do with pagan and occult practices:

> *When thou art come into the land which the Lord thy God giveth thee, thou shalt not learn to do after the abominations of those nations.*

11. H.C. Leupold, *Exposition of Genesis* (Grand Rapids: Baker Book House, 1942, 1977) I: 386–93. Josephus (AD 37–circa 100) wrote that the Tower of Babel was the work of Nimrod, who tried to establish himself as a tyrannical ruler over the whole world. Flavius Josephus, *The Antiquities of the Jews;* reprinted in *Josephus: Complete Works* (Grand Rapids: Kregel, 1963, 1972), 30. The Bible calls Nimrod "a mighty hunter before the Lord" (Genesis 10:9), though the Hebrew term for hunter can also mean killer or conqueror. The Genesis account further says of Nimrod that "the beginning of his kingdom was Babel, and Erech, and Accad, and Calneh, in the land of Shinar," (Genesis 10:10), but the Bible does not directly connect Nimrod with the Tower of Babel of Genesis 11. It is of course possible that Josephus used other historical sources in addition to the Bible.

12. The exception, of course, in Christian thought, is the incarnation of Jesus Christ, in Whom man did not become God, but God became man. (John 1:14)

> *There shall not be found among you any one that maketh his son or his daughter to pass through the fire, or that useth divination, or an observer of times, or an enchanter, or a witch,*
>
> *Or a charmer, or a consulter with familiar spirits, or a wizard, or a necromancer.*
>
> *For all that do these things are an abomination unto the LORD: and because of these abominations the LORD thy God doth drive them out from before thee.*
>
> *Thou shalt be perfect with the LORD thy God.*
>
> *For these nations, which thou shalt possess, hearkened unto observers of times, and unto diviners: but as for thee, the LORD thy God hath not suffered thee so to do.*
>
> *The LORD thy God will arise up unto thee a Prophet from the midst of thee, of thy brethren, like unto me; unto him ye shall hearken.* (Deuteronomy 18:9–15; cf. Malachi 3:5)

But in the pagan view, gods are plural; and while they are superhuman, they are not all-powerful, all-knowing, or all-present. Nor are they always truthful, righteous, or just; they have their own intrigues, deceits, struggles, and problems, which are on a much more colossal plain than those of humans but are finite nevertheless.

In the Biblical view, then, God and man are an infinity apart; and man can know God only because God has chosen to reveal Himself to man. But in the pagan view, gods and men are merely part of a continuum, with animals and plants beneath them and heroes[13] and spirits between them. To the pagan mind, then, the idea that a ruler, with all his splendor and power, might be divine or at least superhuman, is not that unreasonable. Certainly many of the ceremonies and regalia of pagan kings were intended to inculcate and reinforce that kind of respect and worship.

From the beginning, the people of Mesopotamia believed their law came from a higher source than man. Sumerian myth taught that the god Enki became intoxicated and began lavishing gifts upon Innin, the goddess of Erech. Those gifts included justice, truth, and falsehood.[14]

---

13. In Greek mythology a hero was a mortal such as Hercules who by great deeds was transformed into immortality.

14. Russ VerSteeg, *Early Mesopotamian Law* (Durham, NC: Carolina Academic Press, 2000), 44.

Early Sumerian society consisted of semi-independent city-states, each ruled by a *patesi* or priest-king, "indicating by the very word that government was bound up with religion."[15] Gradually these city-states were centralized under one empire, in a feudal system in which local kings became vassals to the higher king. As Durant says,

> To this system of royal and feudal administration was added a body of law, already rich with precedents when Ur-engur and Dungi codified the statutes of Ur; this was the fountainhead of Hammurabi's famous code.... Courts of justice sat in the temples, and the judges were for the most part priests; professional judges presided over a superior court. The best element in this code was a plan for avoiding litigation: every case was first submitted to a public arbitrator whose duty it was to bring about an amicable settlement without recourse to law. It is a poor civilization from which we may not learn something to improve our own.[16]

It seems generally agreed that two ancient peoples, the Sumerians and the Accadians, amalgamated to become the Babylonians. Babylonian thought and jurisprudence generally continued that of Sumeria, but with some changes which are apparent in the law code of early Babylon's most famous king.

Best-known of the early Babylonian rulers was Hammurabi. Historians generally agree that he reigned about forty years but disagree as to when that reign took place. Durant dates Hammurabi's reign from 2123–2081 BC[17]; VerSteeg dates his reign from 1792–1750 BC[18] Whichever date is accepted, Hammurabi is recognized as a great Babylonian king, conqueror, and lawgiver.

The Code of Hammurabi, probably promulgated in the last years of his reign,[19] consists of about 282 provisions arranged by subject.[20] The most complete copy was found by French archeologists in 1902 in Susa,

15. Durant, I: 126.

16. Durant, I: 127.

17. Durant, I: 219.

18. VerSteeg, 30.

19. VerSteeg, 30.

20. VerSteeg, 31. The exact number of provisions varies from 275–300 depending on which version is used; several versions of the Code of Hammurabi have been found, but none is complete.

having apparently been carried to Susa from Babylon. It is engraved on a 7-foot-tall cone-shaped black diorite cylinder. Durant says, "Like that of Moses, this legislation was a gift from Heaven, for one side of the cylinder shows the King receiving the laws from Shamash, the Sun-god himself."[21] The sun-god would naturally be the god of justice, because his light shines everywhere, he sees all, and he therefore has the greatest capacity to discover truth.[22] The Preamble reads in part,

> When the lofty Anu, King of the Anunaki and Bel, Lord of Heaven and Earth, he who determines the destiny of the land, committed the rule of all mankind to Marduk;...when they pronounced the lofty name of Babylon; when they made it famous among the quarters of the world and in its midst established an everlasting kingdom whose foundations were firm as heaven and earth—at that time Anu and Bel called me, Hammurabi, the exalted prince, the worshiper of the gods, to cause justice to prevail in the land, to destroy the wicked and the evil, to *prevent the strong from oppressing the weak,... to enlighten the land and to further the welfare of the people.*[23]

VerSteeg perceives an orderly arrangement to the Code of Hammurabi:

The first five provisions deal with procedure, and include the death penalty for perjury in capital cases such as murder or witchcraft.[24] This was a recognition that a judge cannot do justice unless he is able to ascertain the truth, and perjury is a crime not only against the judicial system but also against the person who is falsely accused.

Provisions 6–25 relate to property and include laws dealing with contracts, slaves, children, purchase and sale of goods, and theft. Note that Babylonian law did not make a clear distinction between civil and criminal law.

Provisions 26–41 deal with military matters and particularly protect the rights of veterans. Under these laws, if a soldier is away at battle, even if he is gone for years as a prisoner of war and presumed dead, when he

21. Durant, I: 219.

22. VerSteeg, 44–45.

23. Code of Hammurabi, quoted by Durant, I: 219.

24. Some are surprised to learn that witchcraft, or "black magic," was a capital offense even in many pagan societies. They recognized its destructive effects, even if they did not recognize its unholy source.

returns he may reclaim his property and may even reclaim his wife if she has remarried. Other laws provide punishments for military officers who abuse their authority.

Provisions 42–65 protect land and agriculture and concern landlord-tenant matters, farmers, debts, irrigation, and liability for crop failures.

Provisions 66–99 involve miscellaneous matters including debtor-creditor issues, interest rates, businesses, and partnerships.

Provisions 100–112 cover the rights and responsibilities of merchants and agents, and special considerations for female innkeepers.

Provisions 113–126 deal with debt and address issues like self-help for repayment, holding a member of a debtor's family as "debt-hostage," and responsibility for loss or damage of goods.

Provisions 127–195 address family matters. They include marriage and divorce laws (127–153), prohibitions on incest (154–158), property transfers, dowries, and gifts between brides, grooms, and their families (159–164), inheritance and gifts (165–175), slave owners and marriages to slaves (176–177), priestesses and their inheritances (178–184), adoptions (185–193), a requirement that if a child dies in the care of a wetnurse, the wetnurse must obtain the father's permission before caring for someone else's child (194), and punishment for a child who strikes his father (cutting off the child's hand) (195).

Provisions 194–214 involve personal injury matters. Normally these laws follow the principle of *lex talionis,* or law of like punishment, which means "let the punishment fit the crime." If a defendant negligently caused the loss of someone's hand, the defendant would lose his hand. As applied, however, this principle often involved restitution, whereby the defendant would pay the victim the value of his hand. These punishments varied according to the class of offender and the victim. If the victim was an aristocrat, the punishment was more severe. Likewise, if the offender was an aristocrat, his punishment was more severe. The aristocrats enjoyed more protection, but they were also held to a higher standard.

Provisions 215–277 cover wages and liability. The fees to be charged by doctors, veterinarians, barbers, boatmen, and many other professionals were strictly regulated.

Finally, Provisions 278–282 address the sale and purchase of slaves. One provision allowed a purchaser to revoke the agreement if the slave was stricken with epilepsy within one month of the purchase.[25]

25. VerSteeg, 32–41.

Despite all its detail, many believe the Code of Hammurabi was not intended to be an exhaustive compendium of statutes like the Justinian Code (6th century AD). They suggest the Code is simply a compilation of court precedents or a set of amendments to existing law.[26]

In addition to the Code, there was in Babylonia a large body of unwritten law, consisting of basic principles of equity to be applied in specific cases. Jean Bottero offers insight into Babylonian jurisprudence:

> The Babylonians used especially two words that we can associate more or less with the word "justice": *kittu* and *mesaru,* which they often combined: *kittu mesaru,* and always in this order, as if the second complimented and enclosed the first. *Kittu* by its basic meaning *(kanu: to establish firmly)* evokes something firm, immobile, and is best understood as that which derives its solidity from its conformity to the law (abstracting from the law's presentation, written or unwritten). We translate it best by *honesty* or by *justice* in the narrow sense, depending on the context. *Mesaru,* derived from *eseru (to go straight, in the right way; to be in order)* contains a more dynamic element; one can understand it, depending on the context, as a state or as an activity. As a state it reflects the *good order* of each thing in its place and according to its ways, in other words, its nature and its role (its "destiny" one would have said in Mesopotamia). As a type of activity or of conduct it renders or attributes to each being and to each man that which comes to him by nature or by his place in society: again his "destiny"—*justice* in short.[27]

Kittu, then, might be identified with principles of natural law that have permanent validity. *Mesaru* might be the specific decree by which a judge attempts to apply *kittu* to the facts and persons of a particular case. When *kittu* and *mesaru* are combined, justice has been achieved and human affairs are in balance with the law of nature.

Professor Wigmore of Northwestern University School of Law presented some examples of Babylonian legal documents. The following deed for the sale of a storehouse reads as though a modern-day lawyer had drafted it:

26. VerSteeg, 13–17.

27. Jean Bottero, *Mesopotamia: Writing, Reasoning, and the Gods* (Chicago: U. of Chicago Press, 1982), 182; quoted by VerSteeg, 43–44 (italics original).

> A 12-reed storehouse, a finished house having a built-in threshold, a covered house with a door having a firm bolt, of the bright storehouse of Ezida; on the upper north side adjoining the storehouse of Bel-epush, son of Apla, son of Mubanni; on the lower south side adjoining the storehouse of Etillu, son of Marduk-abishu; on the upper west side along the Tarrabshu road; on the lower eastern side adjoining the storehouse of Nabu-iddina, son of Arkat-Damqu. Total 12 reeds is the measurement of that storehouse.
>
> With Bel-uballit, son of Amelai, the riqqu of Marduk, Marduk-kudurri-usur, son of Irani-Marduk, the Tu oficer of the house of Marduk, according to 3 minas, 10 shekels of silver and 5 kors of dates, the full price of his storehouse, Bel-uballit, son of Apla, the riqqu officer of Marduk, received from Marduk-kudurri-usur, son of Irani-Marduk, the Tu officer of the house of Marduk. The buyer has a fee simple, there shall be no recourse. They shall not return and complain to one another.[28]

A stone marker fixing the boundary of a cornfield around 1100 BC sets forth a clear legal description:

> This stone is named Perpetual Fixer of Landmark. One acre of corn-land, rated at 5 bins of seed, lying along the Baddar Canal and Khanbi estate, bounded by Khanbi estate on the north, by Imbiati estate on the south, by Khanbi estate on the west, and by the canal bank on the east, bought from Amel Enlil by Marduk-nasir and surveyed by Shapiku, for the price of 1 chariot value 100 shekels of silver, 1 western ass value 30 shekels silver, 2 saddles value 50 shekels silver, 1 ox value 30 shekels silver,... If any agent or official of the said Khanbi estate shall lay claim to or take this land or shall wrongfully reclaim it or transfer it to any other party, or shall dispute this grant from the king, or shall send any fool or blind man or ignorant person to remove or destroy or hide this landmark, may the great gods curse him with incurable evil. May Shamash judge of heaven smite his countenance. May his

28. John Henry Wigmore, *A Panorama of the World's Legal Systems* (St. Paul: West Publishing Co., 1928), I: 63–65. In the early 1900s Wigmore was Dean of Northwestern Law School and was considered America's leading authority on rules of evidence.

> posterity perish among the people. This stone is named Perpetual Fixer of Landmark.[29]

Ancient Babylonians entered into business agreements much like people of today. Some worked out, some didn't. The following document dated around 600 BC is an agreement to dissolve a partnership, either because it didn't work out or because the purposes of the partnership had been completed:

> As to the business-capital used in partnership between Nabu-kin-aplu and his son Nabu-bil-shunu, and Shula son of Zir-ukin, and Mushizib-bil...official, from the 8th year of Nabu-kudur-usur, king of Babylon: An accounting has been had by the parties on oath in the presence of the judges, and it was agreed that 50 shekels gold are to be received by [the first-named two parties] Nabu-bil-shunu and his father Nabu-kinaplu. No recourse or claim will be made. The partnership-venture is dissolved, and each party will go his own way. In the name of...the gods, each party has made oath, and the accounting is finished. The original instrument executed by the parties have been cancelled.[30]

The Babylonian legal system was fully functional well before 2000 BC, with professional judges, professional clerks and notaries, and standard forms for legal writs and other legal process. According to Babylonian legal theory the gods gave divine guidance to the king, thus enabling him to judge cases rightly. The king delegated his authority to lower judicial officers who acted in his name, and the losing party could appeal to a higher court and, in some cases, ultimately to the king.[31]

The following incomplete cuneiform inscription records the proceedings of a lawsuit between two priestesses which was tried in a Babylonian court around 2000 BC. The plaintiff claimed the defendant had signed a contract to purchase land and failed to pay:

> ...1 rod of improved house-lot, which Ilusha-negal, priestess, daughter of Ea-ellazu, had bought from Belizunu, priestess of Zamama, daughter of...in the year when King Abi-eshuh....

29. Wigmore, I: 67.

30. Wigmore, I: 71.

31. Wigmore, I: 73–77; see also VerSteeg, 53–62.

being 1 rod of house-lot adjacent on one side to the house of Ili-ikisha son of Idin-shamash, and on the other side to the house of Ili-ikisha son of Itti-marduk-balatu, and on the front to the house of Ili-ikisha son of Idin-shamash, and on the rear to the house of Nabi-ilishu.

[Defendant Pleads.] "From the priestess Ilusha-negal daughter of Ea-ellazu, for 15 silver shekels, my wife Belizunu [a different person from the above-named B.], priestess of Marduk, and daughter of... did indeed buy the lot in the year when King Ammi-ditana... and I received the deeds duly executed by seal. And I have as witness Ili-ikisha above-named, possessor by inheritance of the two lots adjacent, who affixed his seal. But now the priestess Ilishu-negal, daughter of Ea-ellazu, is claiming this 1 rod of house-lot, although the executed deed bears her seal."

[Plaintiff Pleads.] After he had thus pleaded, the priestess Ilusha-negal, daughter of Ea-ellazu, answered thus in person: "When the 1 rod of improved house-lot, adjacent to 1 rods of house-lot, which I had bought from Belizunu, priestess of Zamama, was sold to me by Belizunu, [the other B.], priestess of Marduk, wife of defendant Addi-liblut, for 15 silver shekels, she did not pay me the 15 silver shekels." Thus the plaintiff replied.

[Evidence.] Then the judges called upon [the plaintiff] Ilusha-negal to produce either witnesses that the [defendant] priestess Belizunu had not paid the money, or an instrument of debt for the unpaid price, but she did not produce them, for none came. Then [the defendant] Addi-liblut produced the executed deed for the 1 rod of house-lot, and the judges read it, and called for the testimony of the witnesses signing the executed deed, and they in the presence of the judges stated that the 15 shekels, the price for the 1 rod of house-lot, had been received by [the plaintiff] Ilusha-negal, and that she had acknowledged receipt.

[Judgment.] After the judges had examined the facts, they imposed a fine on [the plaintiff] the priestess Ilusha-negal, daughter of Ea-ellazu, because she had denied her authentic seal; and directed that she sign the following release of claim....[32]

32. Wigmore, 77–79.

Babylonian law, as reflected in the Code of Hammurabi and earlier codes of previous kings, protected property rights, including the right to enter into and enforce a contract, and the right to bequeath and inherit property. The strict penalties for perjury show a strong commitment to finding the truth. But Martha Roth has observed that

> an overwhelming number of law provisions protect the downtrodden and powerless in Babylonian society who are largely dependent on the whims and good-will of the empowered: the falsely accused, the soldier away on a tour of duty, the depositor, the unwary victim of poorly trained physicians, boat builders, and construction workers, the small-time renter of oxen and agricultural tools, and especially women and children whose property rights (in marriage, adoption, and inheritance) are most easily usurped by the adult free males.[33]

For better or worse, Durant notes an interesting feature of Babylonian law: "We find no evidence of lawyers in Babylonia, except for priests who might serve as notaries, and the scribe who would write for pay anything from a will to a madrigal. The plaintiff preferred his own plea, without the luxury of terminology."[34]

And Durant makes another interesting observation:

> There was nothing in the Code [of Hammurabi] about the rights of the individual against the state; that was to be a European innovation. But articles 22–24 provided, if not political, at least economic, protection. "If a man practice brigandage and be captured, that man shall be put to death. If the brigand be not captured, the man who has been robbed shall, in the presence of the god, make an itemized statement of his loss, and the city and governor within whose province and jurisdiction the robbery was committed shall compensate him for whatever was lost. If it be a life (that was lost), the city and governor shall pay one *mina* ($300) to the heirs." What modern city is so well governed that it would dare to offer such reimbursements to the

33. Martha Roth, *The Law Collection of King Hammurabi: Toward an Understanding of Codification and Text.* (Strasbourg Codification Conference, 1997), 11–12; quoted by VerSteeg, 41. See generally VerSteeg, 19–41

34. Durant, I: 232.

> victims of its negligence? Has the law progressed since Hammurabi, or only increased and multiplied?[35]

Mesopotamian law changed over time, but the changes were not necessarily for the better:

- Early Sumerian law provided for the death penalty in very few types of cases, and even in those cases the death penalty was seldom imposed.[36] Later Babylonian law made much greater use of capital punishment.
- Early Sumerian and Babylonian law recognized the rights of women to own property, enter into contracts, marry and divorce, inherit property, and participate in civic affairs. Later Babylonian law curtailed these rights.[37]
- In early Sumeria (2900–2350 BC) there were very few slaves, and even those were mostly prisoners of war. As time went on, slavery proliferated.[38]
- And early Sumeria may have been more democratic than those who came after them. H.W.F. Saggs suggests that early Sumerians governed themselves by means of a "general assembly of all citizens—probably including women as well as men—who came together to decide upon action when some emergency threatened."[39] Others believe this general assembly decided court cases as well as other matters.[40] As time progressed, the general assembly was limited to men, and then largely superceded by professional judges and courts.[41]

---

35. Durant, I: 232.

36. VerSteeg, 20.

37. Durant, I: 130.

38. Durant, I: 19–20.

39. H.W.F. Saggs, *The Greatness That Was Babylon* (1962), quoted by VerSteeg, 51.

40. Samuel Greengus, "Legal and Social Institutions of Ancient Mesopotamia," in *Civilizations of the Ancient Near East* ((Jack M. Sasson ed., 1995), I: 469, 475; cited by VerSteeg 52; A. Leo Oppenheim, *Ancient Mesopotamia: Portrait of a Dead Civilization* (1977), 112; cited by VerSteeg, 52; G.R. Driver and John C. Miles, *The Babylonian Laws* (1952), I: 242, 493; quoted by VerSteeg, 52.

41. VerSteeg, 52–57.

With the passage of time, the laws of Mesopotamia became more numerous and complex, the judicial system became more institutionalized, and the government became more centralized—a trend we will see repeated over and over throughout history.

But is that really progress?

The Assyrian Interval

The Book of Jonah begins with these words,

> *Now the word of the LORD came unto Jonah the son of Amittai, saying,*
>
> *Arise, go to Nineveh, that great city, and cry against it; for their wickedness is come up before me.*
>
> *But Jonah rose up to flee unto Tarshish from the presence of the LORD, and went down to Joppa; and he found a ship going to Tarshish: so he paid the fare thereof, and went down into it, to go with them unto Tarshish from the presence of the LORD.* (Jonah 1:1–3)

As we learn more about the Assyrian Empire, we will understand why Jonah was not exactly enthusiastic about the Lord's calling to preach judgment to Assyria's capital city, Nineveh.

Assyria was one of the most militaristic societies in all history. By 800 BC they had built the most powerful empire the Middle East had ever seen and possibly the most powerful empire in the world up to that time. Originally located north of Babylonia in an area that included the upper Tigris and Euphrates Rivers and part of Asia Minor, Assyria eventually conquered Babylonia, Armenia, Media, Palestine, Syria, Phoenicia, Sumeria, Elam, and Egypt. The *Cambridge Ancient History* says the Assyrians "were expansion-minded throughout their history.... The first Assyrian ruler who adopted both the title *sarrum* (king) and the more ambitious and programmatic 'king of the universe' was Shamshi-Adad I, who actually assembled an empire of impressive proportions under his sceptre."[42]

Conquest, of course, requires an army. The Assyrian army was large and well-disciplined, and Assyrian military strategists developed superb tactics using cavalry, chariots, infantry, and sappers in flexible formations,

42. *Cambridge Ancient History* (London: Cambridge University Press, 1928, 1969), Vol. I, Part 2, 736.

striving for rapid movement of attack. The infantry wore armor and carried large shields, and fought with lances, cutlasses, maces, clubs, slings, battle-axes, and bows and arrows. They innovated the use of cavalry and developed the art of siege, using a metal-tipped battering ram. Their treatment of conquered foes may seem brutal:

> Soldiers were rewarded for every severed head they brought in from the field, so that the aftermath of a victory generally witnessed the wholesale decapitation of fallen foes. Most often the prisoners, who would have consumed much food in a long campaign, and would have constituted a danger and nuisance in the rear, were dispatched after the battle; they knelt with their backs to the captors, who beat their heads in with clubs, or cut them off with cutlasses. Scribes stood by to count the number of prisoners taken and killed by each soldier, and apportioned the booty accordingly; the king, if time permitted, presided at the slaughter. The nobles among the defeated were given more special treatment: their ears, noses, hands and feet were sliced off, or they were thrown from high towers, or they and their children were beheaded, or flayed alive, or roasted over a slow fire.[43]

Durant says of the Assyrian King Ashurbanipal after his victory over Elam:

> The severed head of the Elamite king was brought to Ashurbanipal as he feasted with his queen in the palace garden; he had the head raised on a pole in the midst of his guests, and the royal revel went on; later the head was fixed over the gate of Nineveh, and slowly rotted away. The Elamite general, Dananu, was flayed alive, and then was bled like a lamb; his brother had his throat cut, and his body was divided into pieces, which were distributed over the country as souvenirs.[44]

One now begins to understand why Jonah was less than enthusiastic about this preaching assignment in Nineveh! Instead, Jonah went to Joppa, a Phoenician port on the Mediterranean, and booked passage on a ship to Tarshish. Tarshish was a city on the west coast of the Iberian peninsula (now Spain and Portugal)—as far in the known world from Nineveh as Jonah could possibly travel!

---

43. Durant, I: 271.

44. Durant, I: 269.

But military conquest does not tell the whole story of Assyria. As Durant says,

> It never occurred to Ashurbanipal that he and his men were brutal; these clean-cut penalties were surgical necessities in his attempt to remove rebellions and establish discipline among the heterogeneous and turbulent peoples, from Ethiopia to Armenia, and from Syria to Media, whom his predecessors had subjected to Assyrian rule; it was his obligation to maintain this legacy intact. He boasted of the peace that he had established in his empire, and of the good order that prevailed in its cities; and the boast was not without truth. That he was not merely a conqueror intoxicated with blood he proved by his munificence as a builder and as a patron of letters and the arts. Like some Roman ruler calling to the Greeks, he sent to all his dominions for sculptors and architects to design and adorn new temples and palaces; he commissioned innumerable scribes to secure and copy for him all the classics of Sumerian and Babylonian literature, and gathered these copies in his library at Nineveh, where modern scholarship found them almost intact after twenty-five centuries of time had flowed over them.[45]

Assyria's policy toward subjugated nations varied. Sometimes the Assyrian rulers allowed the conquered people to keep their own gods, rulers, and laws, provided they paid tribute and pledged loyalty to Nineveh.[46] But at other times they deported conquered people to other parts of the empire, hoping they would intermingle with other nations, lose their identity, and be less likely to rebel. 2 Kings 15–18 describes the Assyrian conquest of the ten northern tribes of Israel, the Assyrian deportation of these Israelites to other parts of the Empire, and their replacement in Israel and Samaria by people of other nations.[47] 2 Chronicles 32 and Isaiah 36 describe an unsuccessful Assyrian attempt to subjugate the southern kingdom of Judah; the Bible attributes Judah's victory to divine intervention.

45. Durant, I: 269.

46. *Cambridge,* I: 2: 715–16.

47. What eventually happened to these "ten lost tribes" remains a mystery. Many believe they intermarried with other nations and lost their identity as Israelites. Others believe they may have migrated to Europe, or to the Americas, or to other parts of the world. Solving this mystery may be impossible (although DNA may provide new evidence from old bones) and is at any rate beyond the scope of this book. See, *Quest for the Lost Tribes* DVD (dvdempire.com/690709/quest-for-the-lost-tribes-movie.htm) (accessed 6/6/2016).

The Assyrians, too, believed in divine intervention, but their gods were a pagan pantheon similar to those of Babylon and Sumeria. The moon-god was especially important and perhaps provides the key to understanding Assyria's expansionism:

> The idea of a universal empire as that created by the Akkadian rulers and aimed at by subsequent generations of Assyrian rulers had its origin in the cult of the moon, which, throughout Assyrian history, played an important role in the pantheon. The moon was the prototype of a universal god in contrast to the various national deities. It is visible everywhere; it was worshipped and had sanctuaries wherever Semites settled or travelled.... Since it was assumed that each of the national deities bestowed upon the king of his choice the region which was the centre of his worship, the moon-god evidently could convey the entire Semitic world upon the king he selected.[48]

But the moon-god was a subordinate being who ushered the Assyrian king into the presence of the chief deity, Ashur. As the Assyrians subjugated Babylon, the Babylonian Marduk became a servant of Ashur. The *Cambridge Ancient History* attributes further significance to this god:

> Their national god Ashur embodied for them more or less their homeland and their capital city.... The fact...that the supreme court building was at the foot of the Ashur temenos also suggests that it actually represented a religious court over which the king presided as Ashur's earthly representative.[49]

Besides representing the heavenly sphere, Ashur was the Assyrian god of justice. The Assyrians were a Semitic people whose language and laws were similar to those of the Babylonians, but the punishments imposed upon offenders were more severe.[50] Durant says Assyrian justice

> ...was distinguished by a martial ruthlessness. Punishment ranged from public exhibition to forced labor, twenty to a hundred lashes, the slitting of nose and ears, castration, pulling out the tongue, gouging out the eyes, impalement, and beheading.

48. *Cambridge,* I: 2: 736.

49. *Cambridge* I: 2: 764. "Temenos" is a sacred enclosure containing a temple or dedicated to a god.

50. *World Book Encyclopedia,* (Chicago: World Book, 1947, 1985), "Assyria" I: 785.

The laws of Sargon II prescribe such additional delicacies as the drinking of poison, and the burning of the offender's son or daughter alive on the altar of the god; but there is no evidence of these laws being carried out in the last millennium before Christ. Adultery, rape, and some forms of theft were considered capital crimes. Trial by ordeal was occasionally employed; the accused, sometimes bound in fetters, was flung into the river, and his guilt was left to the arbitrament of the water. In general Assyrian law was less secular and more primitive than the Babylonian Code of Hammurabi, which apparently preceded it in time.[51]

The Neo-Babylonian Empire

In the 600s BC, the power of Assyria began to wane, and the Babylonians in the south began to reassert themselves. In 625 BC, a Chaldean or Neo-Babylonian army officer named Nabopolassar took control of the City of Babylon and proclaimed himself king. Warfare ensued between Assyria and Babylon; and in 612 BC, Nineveh fell to Nabopolassar and his son Nebuchadnezzar. An ally and subject of Assyria, Pharaoh Neco of Egypt led his armies to Assyria's defense. As the Egyptian armies marched northward toward Nineveh they passed through Judea. King Josiah and his army met them in battle, but the Judeans were overwhelmed and Josiah was killed in the battle (2 Chronicles 35:20–27). Pharaoh Neco continued his march and met Nebuchadnezzar and the Babylonian forces at Carchemish. In the Battle of Carchemish (606 BC), one of the most decisive battles of all history, Crown Prince Nebuchadnezzar soundly defeated Pharaoh Neco, and Babylonian preeminence in the Middle East became an established fact.

Nebuchadnezzar proceeded southward toward Egypt, but while passing through Judea he became enamored by the City of Jerusalem—all of which is the background behind Daniel 1:1–6:

In the third year of the reign of Jehoiakim king of Judah came Nebuchadnezzar king of Babylon unto Jerusalem, and beseiged it.

And the Lord gave Jehoiakim king of Judah into his hand, with part of the vessels of the house of God: which he carried into

51. Durant, I: 272. Durant adds that abortion was a capital crime in Assyria: "a woman who secured miscarriage, even a woman who died of attempting it, was to be impaled on a stake." I: 275.

the land of Shinar to the house of his god; and he brought the vessels into the treasure house of his god.

And the king spake unto Ashpenaz the master of his eunuchs, that he should bring certain of the children of Israel, and of the king's seed, and of the princes;

Children in whom was no blemish, but well favored, and skilful in all wisdom, and cunning in knowledge, and understanding science, and such as had ability in them to stand in the king's palace, and whom they might teach the learning and the tongue of the Chaldeans.

And the king appointed them a daily provision of the king's meat, and of the wine which he drank: so nourishing them three years, that at the end thereof they might stand before the king.

Now among these were of the children of Judah, Daniel, Hananiah, Mishael, and Azariah.

As understood by the Jews and later by Christians, this happened as part of a divine plan for the chastening and eventual restoration of Judea.[52] But Nebuchadnezzar had a different plan in mind. This deportation of Jewish youths to Babylon around 605 BC, followed by more massive deportations of Jews to Babylon in 597 and 586 BC, furthered the Babylonian policy of moving peoples around to break down their national identity and amalgamate them into a giant Babylonian melting pot. But the Neo-Babylonian Empire, sometimes called the Chaldean Empire, lasted only about seventy years. Nebuchadnezzar died around 562 BC,[53] and no ruler of similar strength followed him. Meanwhile, to the east, the Medes and the Persians were gaining strength and beginning their conquests.

---

52. These events were prophesied by Isaiah over a century earlier, around 720 BC (Isaiah 39).

53. Nebuchadnezzar initially followed the pagan gods of Babylonia, but Daniel 2–4, especially Chapter 4, indicate that later in life he may have become a believer in the God of the Bible. An inscription found in Babylon is attributed to Nebuchadnezzar; Durant believes Nebuchadnezzar was addressing Marduk, but the language sounds more like the words he addressed to the God of the Bible in Daniel Chapter 4. The inscription is reproduced below; the reader may judge:

> Without thee, Lord, what could there be
> For the king thou lovest, and dost call his name?
> Thou shalt bless his title as thou wilt,
> And unto him vouchsafe a path direct.
> I, the prince obeying thee,
> Am what thy hands have made.
> 'Tis thou who art my creator,
> Entrusting me with the rule of hosts of men.
> According to thy mercy, Lord,…
> Turn into loving-kindness thy dread power,

In 539 BC, Cyrus the Great, having united the Medes and Persians into the Persian Empire, laid siege to Babylon. Belshazzar, the Crown Prince of Babylon, apparently believed his capital city could survive a siege; the walls were forty feet thick, the Euphrates flowed through the city to supply water and was protected by a watergate, and the city boasted grain supplies that could feed the populace for thirty years. But Cyrus overcame the city's defenses, and Babylon became a province of the Persian Empire.[54]

What caused the decline and fall of Babylon? Durant says, "The army fell into disorder; business men forgot love of country in the sublime internationalism of finance; the people, busy with trade and pleasure, unlearned the arts of war."[55] And Durant's homily could be the epitaph of many nations including our own:

> A nation is born stoic, and dies epicurean. At its cradle (to repeat a thoughtful adage) religion stands, and philosophy accompanies it to the grave. In the beginning of all cultures a strong religious faith conceals and softens the nature of things, and gives men courage to bear pain and hardship painfully; at every step the gods are with them, and will not let them perish, until they do. Even then a firm faith will explain that it was the sins of the people that turned their gods to an avenging wrath; evil does not destroy faith, but strengthens it. If victory comes, if war is forgotten in security and peace, then wealth grows; the life of the body gives way, in the dominant classes, to the life of the senses and the mind; toil and suffering are replaced by pleasure and ease; science weakens faith even while thought and comfort weaken virility and fortitude. At last men begin to doubt the gods; they mourn the tragedy of knowledge, and

---

And make to spring up in my heart
A reverence for thy divinity.
Give as thou thinkest best.
Durant, I: 241.

54. The fall of Babylon is narrated in Daniel Chapter 5. By this account Belshazzar committed the ultimate sacrilege, holding a drunken feast during which he brought out the sacred vessels of Jerusalem (Isaiah 39; Daniel 1) and used them to toast the gods of Babylon. The handwriting on the wall appeared, and Babylon fell to Persia that night. Exactly how Cyrus overcame Babylon's defenses is uncertain. Durant suggests that city officials, disgusted with Belshazzar, opened the gates and welcomed Cyrus (I: 263). Another theory is that Cyrus's General Gobryas, working upstream, diverted the channel of the Euphrates, and with the watergate unguarded because of the great festival, the Persian armies entered through the dry riverbed. J. M. Cook, *The Persians* (London: Folio Society, 1983, 2000), 44–45.

55. Durant, I: 263.

seek refuge in every passing delight. Achilles is at the beginning, Epicurus at the end. After David comes Job, and after Job, Ecclesiastes.[56]

Questions for Reflection, Discussion, and More Reflection

1. Who were the Sumerians, the Babylonians, the Assyrians, and the Neo-Babylonians (Chaldeans)? How were they different from one another?
2. What evidence exists that the earliest Mesopotamians were monotheists? What evidence exists that they were polytheists? Which do you think is more likely? How is this question relevant to the study of the history and nature of law?
3. What is the underlying reason for human sacrifice? How is this a legal concept?
4. Why were the ancient Mesopotamians so interested in the stars? What premises underlie the discipline of astrology?
5. How did the Babylonian religion lend itself to emperor-worship? Why does emperor-worship or state-worship seem so strange to us today?
6. Why is the discovery of the Code of Hammurabi so important to history and archeology? To whom does the Code ascribe its origin? Even if one does not believe in the Babylonian gods, is it still possible to ascribe a divine origin to the laws of Babylonia?
7. Why would even pagan law codes criminalize witchcraft? Is there something about witchcraft that offends the Law of Nature?
8. What does the term *lex talionis* mean, and why is this such a central feature of criminal law codes throughout history?
9. What did the Babylonians mean by the terms *kittu* and *mesaru?* How are these concepts relevant to an understanding of Babylonian law? How do they compare to the Egyptian *ma'at?*

Questions continued on next page....

56. Durant, I: 259.

Questions *continued*

10. Are you surprised to learn that the ancient Babylonians had a complex multi-tiered court system, and contracts and other written legal documents much like those of today? Why, do you suppose, is modern man so surprised to learn of great wisdom and achievements among the ancients? Why do we think we are the wisest generation in history? Is it only because we are the most recent?

Baghdad, Iraq (once Mesopotamia), Haidar Khana Mosque, 1932.

Chapter 3

Persia:
Where West Became East

"Persian" means more than carpets and cats. It is more than the "law of the Medes and the Persians, which altereth not."[1] Persia was a major empire in ancient times; as the Parthian Empire, it was the main rival of the Roman Empire; during the Middle Ages, it was the stronghold of Shi'ite Islam; and as Iran, it is a major player in world affairs today.

In 539 BC, Cyrus and the Persians were the "new kid on the block" in the Mediterranean regions. But the Persian or Elamite people already had a long and impressive history.

Unlike the Semitic nations of the Middle East, including the Babylonians, Assyrians, Chaldeans, and Jews, the Persians were a Japhetic people. They probably descended from the Indo-Europeans, who sometime before 2000 BC began a mass migration from their home on the steppes of Central Asia near the Caucasus Mountains and the Caspian Sea. Originally they were nomadic herdsmen, but they established an early capital at Ecbanata in the mountains of Iran. They brought to the Middle East their Indo-European or Aryan language, an advanced and excellent commercial code, and some unique views of theology, law, and government. During the 500s BC, when Cyrus the Great united the Persians with a related people called the Medes, the Persian Empire became the most powerful the world had seen up to that time.

Early Persian religion is shrouded in mystery. Some authorities believe the early Persians (Elamites) practiced paganism but eventually became monotheistic.[2] Others believe Persia was essentially monotheistic from the beginning. Shuckford wrote in 1743,

1. Daniel 6:8,15.

2. Edwin M. Yamauchi, *Persia and the Bible* (Grand Rapids: Baker Book House, 1990, 2000), 410–11.

> The Persians...for some time adhered to the pure and true worship of God. They are remarkable beyond other nations, for having had amongst them a true account of the creation of the world; and they adhered very strictly to it, and founded all their religion upon it.... Dr. Hyde remarks, that he could not find any reason to think, but that they were for some time very strict professors of it, tho' by degrees they corrupted it, by introducing novelties and fancies of their own into both their faith and practice.[3]

And Rawlinson wrote in 1884,

> At a time which is difficult to date, but which those best skilled in Iranian antiquities (Haug) are inclined to place before the birth of Moses, there grew up, in the region whereof we are speaking, a form of religion marked by very special and unusual features, very unlike the religions of Egypt and Assyria, a thing quite *sui generis,* one very worthy of the attention of those who are interested in the past history of the human race, and more especially of such as wish to study the history of religions.[4]

The conclusion one draws about early Persian religion may depend primarily upon one's basic worldview. If one believes man has evolved from a simple creature to a complex and intelligent Homo sapiens, one is likely to believe his religious beliefs developed from primitive animism to monotheism. But if one believes God orginally created man as an intelligent being and revealed true religion to him, one is more likely to believe early man was monotheistic, and his beliefs gradually degenerated into polytheism and animism.

Regardless of the origin of Persian religion, a religious leader came to Persia, saw the corrupted state of Persian religion, and led the Persians to a purified form of monotheism. This man was known to the Persians as Zarathustra and to the Greeks as Zoroaster. His followers were known as Zoroastrians, and Zoroastrianism remains a potent force in Iran and parts of India today. His followers gathered his sayings and prayers into a collection of books called the *Avesta.*

---

3. Samuel Shuckford, *The Sacred and Prophane History of the World Connected* (1824; Reprinted Tolle Lege Press, 2009), I: 278.

4. George Rawlinson, *The Religions of the Ancient World,* (John B. Alden Publishers, 1885), 65.

The time of Zarathustra's appearance is uncertain. Ancient, medieval, and modern scholars have suggested dozens of possible dates for his life, ranging from 6347 BC (Greek tradition) to 558 BC (Arabic tradition), with many scholars dating him between 2000 and 1000 BC.[5] Zarathustra found his people steeped in idolatry and taught the worship of the true supreme God, Ahuramazda ("Wise Lord"), which may have been a new god to the Persians or possibly an older god under a new name. Yamauchi says, "Whether Zoroaster also preached a monotheism, a henotheism—that is, the exaltation of one god over other gods—or a dualism is also disputed.... It is certain that he preached an ethical dualism, teaching that each man must choose between righteousness and the Lie."[6]

While there is some uncertainty about how much of modern Zoroastrian doctrine comes from Zarathustra's teachings and how much from later Zoroastrian teachers, he apparently taught that the true God Ahuramazda is engaged in a struggle with Angramanyu (sometimes Ahramanyus or Ahriman, meaning "Spirit of Evil"). Zarathustra called upon people to join this struggle against evil by engaging in "good thoughts, good works, good deeds."[7] Ahuramazda has revealed his divine law *(daena)* to man through Zarathustra, and

> According as man obeys or disobeys this Divine law his future lot will be decided; by it he will be judged at his death.... Moral good, righteousness, sanctity *(asha)* is according to the Divine will and decrees; Man by his free will conforms to, or transgresses, these.... It is well to emphasize this basis of Avestic moral theology, because it at once marks off the Avesta system from the fatalistic systems of India with their *karma* and innate pessimism.... A characteristic note of Iranian religious philosophy is its essential optimism; if there is human sin, there is also repentance and expiation.[8]

Man's chief duty, in Zoroastrian thought, is the worship of Ahuramazda. Professor Grant Hardy notes that although the evil god Angramanyu is a powerful deity comparable to Ahuramazda, he is not to be worshipped,

5. Yamauchi, 412–14.

6. Yamauchi, 417–18.

7. W. S. LaSor, *Evangelical Dictionary of Theology* (Grand Rapids: Baker Book House, 1984), "Zoroastrianism," 1202.

8. *The Catholic Encyclopedia* (New York: Gilmary Society, 1907, 1913), "Avesta," II: 155.

and he will be defeated in the end. As Hardy says, Zoroastrianism is doctrinally dualistic but devotionally monotheistic.[9] Human and animal sacrifice are forbidden; instead, one worships through the offering of *haoma* (fermented juice of a sacred plant); the care of the Sacred Fire (because fire is either a god or a symbol or sacrament of a god); ritual hymns and prayers, goodness in thought, word, and deed; and truthfulness, purity, and generosity to the poor.[10]

Zoroastrianism teaches that there is a war between good and evil involving gods and spirits, humans, animals, and even plants on each side, and that the conflict will continue until the end of time. At that time the last great Prophet, Saoshyant (Savior) will appear and do battle with Angramanyu and his forces of evil. At the victory of Saoshyant and the forces of good, the Resurrection of the Dead shall occur, followed by a Great Judgment in which the earth shall be burned in a great conflagration followed by a great flood to extinguish the fire. This great flood will purify all creatures of all stains of sin, and even hell will be cleansed and added to the new heavens and new earth.[11]

Another aspect of Persian religious life is the cult of the magi, or *magoi* as the term appears in the Greek Septuagint. Like Zoroastrianism, the Magi are shrouded in mystery. They appear to have been an ancient priestly caste that existed in Babylonia, Persia, and other parts of the ancient Middle East. They play a role in the Book of Daniel (2:2,27; 4:7,9), where the term is translated "magicians," where they are numbered among the "wise men" of the kingdom and are trusted advisors to the king, and where Daniel is described as *"master of the magicians* (*magoi*)*"* (4:9).

Some believe the early magi were polytheists and clashed with Zarathustra and his followers. Others believe Zarathustra himself was a magus or even the master of the magi. Still others suggest that the magi eventually came to accept Zarathustra's teachings and worship the one true

9. Grant Hardy, *Great Minds of the Eastern Intellectual Tradition* Lecture 11 (The Teaching Company, 2011).

10. *The Catholic Encyclopedia,* II: 155–56.

11. *The Catholic Encyclopedia,* II: 156. One can see certain similarities between Zoroastrianism and Christianity. Father Ernest Hull, a Jesuit priest, described Zoroastrianism as "the highest religious result to which human reason unaided by revelation, can attain." II: 156. However, one Christian concept that seems to be missing from Zoroastrianism is that of salvation by grace and substitutionary atonement.

God.[12] It is possible, even probable, that all magi did not think exactly alike during all periods of their lengthy history.

The magi have also been closely identified with stargazing or astrology.[13] In a pagan worldview, events in the heavens and events on earth are bound together by a cosmic unity, and by watching and interpreting the movements of the stars and planets, one can predict events on earth. If the magi became worshippers of the one true God, they could have concluded that this God revealed his will to men through the movements of the stars and other signs in the heavens.

While the magi were not kings, they were, in Tertullian's words, "well-nigh kings."[14] Kings regularly consulted them for their advice on matters of state, and they played a major role in the selection of a new king, again consulting the stars as they made their prognostications.

With good reason, many Christians have identified the magi with the *"wise men [magoi] from the east"* who came to Judea to worship Jesus Christ (Matthew 2:1–12).[15] Through the influence of Zarathustra they may well have been worshippers of one God. As part of their official function, they were deeply interested in the birth of new kings, and in keeping with their traditional practices as magi, they were accustomed to consulting the heavens for signs concerning such matters. And Daniel, living in Babylon and Persia and serving in high governmental positions in both kingdoms (Daniel 2:48–49, 6:1–3, 28), was *"master of the magi"* (Daniel 4:9). Surely the Magi of Christ's time were familiar with Daniel's writings, particularly his prophecy concerning the coming of *"Messiah the Prince"* (Daniel 9:24–27). They may well have identified Daniel's *"Messiah the Prince"* with Zarathustra's prophecy of the savior-king Saoshyant and were therefore especially interested in signs of His coming.

Ethelbert Stauffer, in his classic work *Christ and the Caesars,* has two fascinating chapters titled "Myth and Epiphany" and "Art Thou He That Should Come?"[16] Mythology, he says, expresses man's deepest longings; epiphany is God's fulfillment of those desires. Beset by turmoil in national and international affairs, ancient man constantly looked for a coming king

12. Yamauchi, 468–69.

13. Yamauchi, 472–74.

14. *Catholic Encyclopedia,* "Magi" IX: 528.

15. *Catholic Encyclopedia,* "Magi," IX: 527–30; Yamauchi, 481–91.

16. Ethelbert Stauffer, *Christ and the Caesars* (Philadelphia: Westminster Press, 1952, 1955), 15–41.

who would set all things right, establish peace and justice, and usher in a golden age. Throughout the ages, countless kings and emperors have claimed to be this coming savior-king. All have failed and died. Jesus Christ, God's Epiphany, fulfilled this ancient mythological longing, though in a way few expected or even understood.

The emperors of Persia were influenced by the magi and the Zoroastrians. Cyrus the Great, who ruled from 560–530 BC and by his conquests transformed Persia from a nation into an empire, seems to have accepted the Zoroastrian faith, though he granted his subject nations the right to follow their own religions.[17] His successor, Cambyses (530–522 BC), seems to have rejected his father's beliefs; but upon his death the magi placed Smerdis on the throne. Smerdis was assassinated a year later, and his successor, Darius I (522–486 BC) was a zealous Zoroastrian.[18] The remaining kings were probably influenced by Zoroastrianism, though the old Aryan paganism and the Cult of Mithras may have influenced some of them as well.

The Persians practiced tolerance on religious matters, reflecting a general Persian policy concerning subjugated peoples. Unlike the Babylonians and Assyrians who often suppressed local religions and customs to break down the identity of conquered nations and make them less likely to revolt, the Persian policy was to demand an oath of loyalty from conquered nations, after which the conquered nation was allowed to keep its own laws, system of government, rulers, customs, language, religion, and culture. As Durant says of Cyrus,

> Cyrus was one of those natural rulers at whose coronation, as Emerson said, all men rejoice. Royal in spirit and action, capable of wise administration as well as of dramatic conquest, generous to the defeated and loved by those who had been his enemies—no wonder the Greeks made him the subject of innumerable romances, and—to their minds—the greatest hero

17. J. M. Cook, The Persians (Folio Society, 1999), 63–64; See also, Pierre Bryant, *From Cyrus to Alexander: A History of the Persian Empire* (Eissnbeauns, 2002).

18. Yamauchi, 424–46. Darius I was not the same person as Darius the Mede who, according to Daniel 5:31, received the rule of Babylonia after its conquest by Cyrus the Great. Darius the Mede was Cyrus's father-in-law, whom Cyrus placed over Babylon after the conquest. Some have speculated that Darius the Mede was Zoroastrian. They note that unlike the Babylonian King Nebuchadnezzar who used a fiery furnace for executions (Daniel 3), Darius the Mede used a den of lions (Daniel 6). A possible reason could be that Zoroastrians regarded fire as divine or at least sacred, and using fire for executions (or even cremations) would be a sacrilege.

> before Alexander. It is a disappointment to us that we cannot draw a reliable picture of him from either Herodotus or Xenophon....
>
> So far as we can visualize him through the haze of legend, he was the most amiable of conquerors, and founded his empire upon generosity. His enemies knew that he was lenient, and they did not fight him with that desperate courage which men show when their only choice is to kill or die.... The first principle of his policy was that the various peoples of his empire should be left free in their religious worship and beliefs, for he fully understood the first principle of statesmanship—that religion is stronger than the state. Instead of sacking cities and wrecking temples he showed a courteous respect for the deities of the conquered, and contributed to maintain their shrines; even the Babylonians, who had resisted him so long, warmed towards him when they found him preserving their sanctuaries and honoring their pantheon. Wherever he went in his unprecedented career he offered pious sacrifice to the local divinities. Like Napoleon he accepted indifferently all religions, and—with much better grace—humored all the gods.[19]

The Jews were particular beneficiaries of Persian benevolence. Shortly after Nebuchadnezzar captured Jerusalem around 605 BC, he deported many of the Jewish people to Babylon and tried to reeducate them in Babylonian culture to break down their Jewish identity.[20] After Babylon fell to the Persians in 539 BC, Cyrus issued a decree that the Jews could return to Judea. Many did return, though others remained in Babylon. Cyrus gave orders for the rebuilding of the Temple in Jerusalem (2 Chronicles 36:23; Ezra 1:2, 5:13, 6:3), restored the sacred vessels of the Jews which Nebuchadnezzar had taken to Babylon and Belshazzar had profaned on that fateful night of Babylon's demise (Isaiah 39:1–8; Daniel 1:1–2; 5:1–4; Ezra 1:7), and provided funds to bring cedar trees from Lebanon (Ezra 3:7). Isaiah called Cyrus God's shepherd (44:28) and the Lord's anointed (45:1). Cyrus, whatever his relation to God may have been, was faithfully following the Persian policy toward subjugated nations.

The Persian policy is commendable in many ways. It makes conquest easier; it makes opponents more willing to surrender; it provides

19. Durant, I: 352–53.

20. Daniel 1.

continuity; and it saves the necessity of setting up a whole new government for the conquered nation. But this policy may reap negative results later. As Durant observed,

> It is in the nature of an empire to disintegrate soon, for the energy that created it disappears from those who inherit it, at the very time that its subject peoples are gathering strength to fight for their lost liberty. Nor is it natural that nations diverse in language, religion, morals, and traditions should long remain united; there is nothing organic in such a union, and compulsion must repeatedly be applied to maintain the artificial bond. In its two hundred years of empire Persia did nothing to lessen this heterogeneity, these centrifugal forces; she was content to rule a mob of nations, and never thought of making them into a state. Year by year the union became more difficult to preserve. As the vigor of the emperors relaxed; the boldness and ambition of the satraps grew.... The frequency of revolt and war exhausted the vitality of little Persia; the braver stocks were slaughtered in battle after battle, until none but the cautious survived; and when these were conscripted to face Alexander they proved to be cowards almost to a man.[21]

A second aspect of Persian political theory, in the early years, was decentralization of power. We see this again in Daniel 6 where Darius the Mede set 120 princes or satraps over the kingdom of Babylonia. As a check, he appointed three presidents to govern over the 120 satraps; Daniel was the first of these three presidents. This, too, is in accordance with Persian policy. These satraps were responsible for collecting taxes in their provinces or satrapies. To check against the possibility that they would extort too much money from their subjects, the kings fixed the amount of tax revenue so the satraps could not overcharge. He also had secretaries and other officers who would report directly to the king about any misconduct by the satraps. The satraps were also responsible for provisioning the military forces and for administering justice; but many of the ordinary duties of civil government were left to the local rulers.[22]

Third, at least in the early days, the Persians were less likely than their Semitic and Asiatic neighbors to practice emperor-worship and state-worship. The Indo-Europeans in general were less inclined to deify the

21. Durant, II: 382.

22. Cook, 114–34.

king and the state. Zarathustra taught that the one true God Ahuramazda was above all other gods and the source of law and justice. It was much more difficult to identify a king with the almighty Ahuramazda than to merely deify him as one of many smaller gods. As the *Cambridge Ancient History* observes,

> In Asia deities either were, or were tending to become, cosmic forces, while their worshippers, unlike the Greeks, remained devoutly religious. Hence a Darius was as incapable, almost, of being approximated to Ahuramazda as a Solomon to Yahweh.[23]

Gradually, though, Persia followed the universal path: political power became centralized, and the power of the Persian kings increased. Some of the later Persian emperors may have come to believe they were gods, or if not, they found it convenient that others should believe them so. By the time Alexander invaded Persia in 325 BC, the Persian kings had been elevated to the status of gods, although lesser gods, and the style of their rule had become almost as despotic as that of any Oriental monarch.

But this was not true in the early days. In those days the Persian kings were thought to speak for God, but they were not thought to be God.

That vital distinction—that the king spoke for God but was not God himself—laid the basis for a very important concept of Persian law: that law was supreme, and no one, not even the king, was above the law. Durant puts it well:

> ...it was a proud boast of Persia that its laws never changed, and that a royal promise or decree was irrevocable. In his edicts and judgments the king was supposed to be inspired by the god Ahura-Mazda himself; therefore the law of the realm was the Divine Will, and any infraction of it was an offense against the deity.[24]

The example that comes readily to mind is that of Darius the Mede, whom Cyrus placed over the Babylonians after the conquest in 539 BC. As noted earlier, Daniel tells us that Darius placed 120 satraps over the realm of Babylon, and over the 120 satraps three presidents of whom Daniel was the first (6:1–2). Darius preferred Daniel over the other presidents and proposed to place Daniel in charge of them, perhaps as a prime minister

23. *Cambridge Ancient History,* VI: 15.

24. Durant, I: 361.

(6:3). The other presidents and satraps, apparently jealous of Daniel, tried to find some incident in Daniel's administration that they could use to discredit him, but there was none, so they determined that the only way to get rid of Daniel was to maneuver him into a situation in which he would have to choose between obeying Darius or obeying his God (6:4–5).

They devised an ingenious plan. They prepared a decree for Darius to sign, requiring that for the next thirty days *"whosoever shall ask a petition of any God or man for thirty days, save of thee, O king, he shall be cast into the den of lions."* (6:7b) They advised Darius that *"all the presidents of the kingdom, the governors, and the princes, the counsellors, and the captains, have consulted together"* (6:7a) to prepare this decree (an obvious lie; Daniel was the first of the presidents, and he wasn't consulted). They urged Darius to sign the decree, and he did so (6:8–9). Why would Darius sign such a foolish decree? Possibly he was persuaded that, as a newcomer to Babylon, he needed to consolidate his power and gain the favor of his people by putting them into the habit of coming to him with their petitions and requests.

As they well knew he would, Daniel chose to obey God rather than Darius. Knowing the decree was signed, Daniel went to his house and with the windows open, prayed facing Jerusalem three times a day, as had been his continuous practice over a lifetime (6:10). When the other presidents and satraps accused Daniel before the king, Darius realized that he had been tricked, and he *"was sore displeased with himself, and set his heart on Daniel to deliver him: and he laboured till the going down of the sun to deliver him"* (6:14). Undoubtedly Darius consulted earnestly with his best judges and legal advisors, trying to find a legal way to revoke the decree or at least make an exception to it. But repeatedly Daniel's accusers reminded him, *"Know, O king, that the law of the Medes and Persians is, That no decree nor statute which the king establisheth may be changed"* (6:15b; cf. 6:8, 6:12).

If a Babylonian king like Nebuchadnezzar had been tricked into signing such a decree, he could just as quickly revoke it. But Darius could not, because a basic Persian principle was that the king was under the law. Once Ahuramazda had spoken the law through the king, the king himself was bound by the law, since he was not God but only the spokesman for God. (Fortunately, by its very terms this decree was effective for only thirty days.) Under Persian law Darius had no legal alternative but to commit Daniel to the den of lions and trust that God—Daniel's God—would deliver him, which He did (6:16–28).

John Adams declared that, "The very definition of a republic is 'an empire of laws, and not of men.'"[25] Americans commonly interpret that phrase to mean that no one, not even the President, is above the law. That bedrock principle of American constitutionalism has a forerunner in the laws of the Medes and the Persians.

Nevertheless, occasionally Persian jurists had to bend this lofty principle in the face of political reality. The Greek historian Herodotus records that the Persian emperor Cambyses (530–522 BC) fell in love with his sister and summoned a council of judges to inquire whether Persian law allowed him to marry her. They did not want to compromise their principles, but they also did not want to share the fate Sir Thomas More would face two thousand years later in a similar confrontation with King Henry VIII. So according to Herodotus,

> By them [the judges] justice is administered in Persia, and they are the interpreters of the old laws, all disputes being referred to their decision. When Cambyses, therefore, put his question to these judges, they gave him an answer which was at once true and safe. "They did not find any law," they said, "allowing a brother to take his sister to wife, but they found a law, that the king of the Persians might do whatever he pleased." And so they neither warped the law through fear of Cambyses, nor ruined themselves by over stiffly maintaining the law, but they brought another quite distinct law to the king's help, which allowed him to have his wish.[26]

The uncertain dating of Zarathustra makes it difficult to determine the extent to which he influenced the earliest Persian legal codes, the laws of the Vendidad, which were only a fragment of a vast system of jurisprudence. Of the twenty-one Nasks, or Holy Books, of the Zoroastrians, one-third comprised law, one-third science, and one-third religion. The one-third that comprised law included court and magisterial law, accusations, injuries to person and property, theft, misappropriation of and cruelty to animals, soldiers and military organizations, church law, family

25. John Adams, *Letters to George Wythe* (1776).

26. Herodotus, *The Histories* (431 BC; trans. George Rawlinson, The Everyman Library 1910, 1991), III: 31, 232.

law and law of pedigree and descent, medical practice, business transactions, property, debt and interest, purity, health, sanitation, agriculture, colonization, and finally, the heavenly kingdom and the divine government of the universe.[27] Farrukh-Mart Vahram, an early compiler of the Zoroastrian Holy Books, believed that the purpose of law is to further the word and knowledge of Ahura-Mazda and defeat falsehood. Ahura-Mazda, he believed, had embedded in humanity the basic principle of "Law-abidingness," which included obeying secular rulers but ultimately meant obeying the law of Ahura-Mazda. Law must therefore be subservient to religion if it is to have an eternal moral basis.[28]

Bulsara says of early Persian history, "The Iranians were a free people, and although their Sovereign had great prerogatives he could not misuse them with impunity."[29] The king was responsible to a two-house legislature which included the Grand Senate composed of nobles, prelates, grand marshalls, and imperial ministers and secretaries, and a Popular Assembly which represented the people. The king could not take office without confirmation by the Grand Senate and Popular Assembly, and those bodies could try him and depose him for misconduct or malfeasance. Bulsara says the Popular Assembly may have had more power than the Grand Senate, noting that in one instance the Grand Senate had opposed the accession of Bahram V to the throne, but he still became king when the Popular Assembly voted in his favor. Bulsara adds that if a complaint was presented against the king, the king had to immediately leave the throne, remove his crown and place it on the empty throne, hand the complaint to the Supreme Spiritual Lord, and ask him to hold an inquiry and pronounce an impartial judgment. If the judgment went against the king, he had to immediately make amends to the injured party before he could reclaim the crown and resume the throne.[30]

In the early days of Persia, Bulsara says, the king was accessible to the people, and even the humblest peasant was entitled to come into the presence of the king to plead his cause. But in all civilizations the trend seems to be toward centralization of executive power, and by the days of King

---

27. S.J. Bulsara, *The Laws of the Ancient Persians* (Bombay, 1937) http://www.parstimes.com/law/ancient_persia_laws.html (accessed 28 April, 2016).

28. Farrukh-Mart Vahram, quoted by Bulsara.

29. Bulsara.

30. Bulsara.

Ahasuerus (486–465 BC), according to the Book of Esther, it was a capital offense to enter the king's presence without permission (Esther 4:10–17).

The Persian legal system included the sacred law of the temple and also secular law, both of which were referred to as *kabussum,* or legal paths or guide routes.[31] But the *Cambridge History* adds that

> it is not possible to draw a dividing line between divine and secular law, nor would it be possible even to make out an opposition between the two established forms of law. On the contrary, everything points to the fact that for the Elamites all law, even secular law, was rooted in the numinous [spiritual]. To such a view of things the ruler-legislator appears completely united with the deity. This is illustrated by a late Elamite inscription, which says: "The law which the God In-Shushinak and King Shutruk-Nahhunte (II) have graciously given...." In Elam divine and secular law always form one whole.[32]

Another old Elamite term that helps us understand the role of the gods in law and justice is *kiten. Kiten* is a special protection the gods give, something like a magic charm or a shield from evil or bad fortune, but even more, that vital cosmic substance without which life is impossible or at least unthinkable. So long as one lived obediently to the law of the gods, one enjoyed kiten. But when one disobeys the gods, their kiten is removed from the individual, and he or she is unprotected from a host of evils. The *Cambridge Ancient History* observes that "anyone losing the *kiten,* the magical protection of the deity, will be 'outlawed'—and not infrequently the text adds laconically: 'he dies!' On one occasion, too, it says: 'He will be delivered up to the god In-Shushinak'—meaning that he will be executed."[33]

The strengths of the Persian legal system included the best commercial code of any society up to that time. Persian law recognized and protected the family as a holy institution, though polygamy and concubinage were allowed. Early in Persian history, women enjoyed a high status; they owned and managed property, they moved freely in society, they could enter into contracts, testify in court, sue and be sued, and inherit from

31. *Cambridge History,* II: 1: 272–74.

32. *Cambridge History,* 275. Il-Shushinak may be the old Elamite form for Ahuramazda; however, this is uncertain.

33. *Cambridge History,* 276.

their parents' estates.[34] Later, after the reign of Darius I (522–486 BC) their status declined. Interestingly, lower class women and concubines had greater freedom than upper class women, because they had to work.[35] Durant adds that "Even in the later reigns women were powerful at the court, rivaling the eunuchs in the persistence of their plotting and the kings in the refinements of their cruelty."[36]

These legal principles were enforced by a well-organized judicial administration. The king acted as a supreme court, but he normally delegated that function to an assistant. Below them was a High Court of Justice composed of seven judges, and lower courts existed in the various regions of the Empire. The priests formulated the laws, and most though not all of the judges were priests. Judges were required to be learned in the law, and they had the authority to find people in contempt of court if necessary to preserve order or enforce their decrees.[37]

The Greek historian Herodotus, writing around 430 BC, noted that "the royal judges are certain picked men among the Persians, who hold their office for life, or until they are found guilty of some misconduct"[38]—a system very similar to the federal judiciary under Article III of the United States Constitution.

Unlike the practice of many ancient legal systems, lawyers abounded in ancient Persia and regularly represented clients in court. Lawyers could not charge excessive fees, but the contingent fee was common in civil lawsuits, with the fee commonly ranging from 22% to 30% of the property's value, and a lesser percentage in smaller cases.[39] An individual charged with a crime could be released on bail except in the most serious cases, and a statute of limitations existed to prevent unreasonable delays in bringing cases to trial. A system of alternative dispute resolution existed to settle cases out of court. Litigants commonly represented themselves in court, but "speakers of the law" were available to explain the law to litigants and help them present their cases. Witnesses testified under oath, and bribery in a legal matter was a capital offense. "Cambyses improved the integrity of the courts by causing an unjust judge to be flayed alive,

34. Durant, I: 375; *Cambridge Ancient History* II: 1286–88.

35. Durant, I: 376.

36. Durant, I: 376.

37. Bulsara, op. cit.

38. Herodotus, *The Histories* (ca. 430 BC) III: 31, 232.

39. Bulsara, op. cit.

and using his skin to upholster the judicial bench—to which he then appointed the dead judge's son."[40]

Criminal punishments included flogging and fines for lesser crimes, and branding, maiming, mutilation, blinding, imprisonment, or death for more serious crimes. Capital crimes included treason, rape, sodomy, murder, "self-pollution," burning or burying the dead (both contrary to Zoroastrian teaching; burying the dead could pollute the land, and burning was a sacrilege because of the fire-god), intruding upon the king's privacy, approaching one of the king's concubines, or sitting upon the king's throne.[41]

The Persians left us an excellent example of a well-organized empire, practicing decentralized government, well-administered laws, the belief that law comes from God, and the vital concept that no one including the king is above the law.

But the Persian system had a fatal flaw—an inadequate procedure for succession, that is, transferring power from one king to the next. Not being gods, the Persian kings died, and before they died, they customarily chose which son was to succeed them in power. But the disappointed sons and their supporters often refused to accept the father's verdict, and the result was intrigue, betrayal, and violence seldom equaled in any kingdom. As Durant says,

> Only the records of Rome after Tiberius could rival in bloodiness the royal annals of Persia. The murderer of Xerxes was murdered by Artaxerxes I, who, after a long reign, was succeeded by Xerxes II, who was murdered a few weeks later by his half-brother Sogdianus, who was murdered six months later by Darius II, who suppressed the revolt of Terituchmes by having him slain, his wife cut into pieces, and his mother, brothers, and sisters buried alive. Darius II was followed by his son Artaxerxes II, who at the battle of Cunaxa, had to fight to the death his own brother, the younger Cyrus, when the youth tried to seize the royal power. Artaxerxes II enjoyed a long reign, killed his son Darius for conspiracy, and died of a broken heart on finding that another son, Ochus, was planning to assassinate him. Ochus ruled for twenty years, and was poisoned by his general Bagoas. This iron-livered Warwick placed Arses, son

40. Durant, I: 361.

41. Durant, I: 361.

> of Ochus, on the throne, assassinated Arses' brothers to make Arses secure, then assassinated Arses and his infant children, and gave the sceptre to Codomannus, a safely effeminate friend. Codomannus reigned for eight years under the name of Darius III, and died in battle against Alexander at Arbela, in the final ruin of his country. Not even the democracies of our time have known such indiscriminate leadership.[42]

A nation can rise to greatness in a short time, but it can maintain that greatness over the long term only if it manages to preserve the moral virtue, discipline, and toughness of its people. In this respect, also, Persia failed. The teachings of Zarathustra undoubtedly prolonged the virtue and lengthened the life of the Empire, but even these failed in the end. Corrupt and duplicitous leaders, a weak and demoralized army, and a soft and cowardly populace all combined to make the Empire a sitting duck for a fresh and vigorous conqueror.

That conqueror came in the person of Alexander the Great, whose vastly outnumbered armies, superbly disciplined and brilliantly led, cut through their Persian opponents like a knife through soft butter. Persia, the greatest empire in world history up to that time, suddenly became a Greek province.

But in a subjugated state, Persia survived, and after the death of Alexander and the dissolution of his empire, Persia reasserted itself as the Parthian Empire and became a rival to the Romans and Byzantines in the West, and the Mongols and the Chinese in the East.

And sometime around 4 BC, perhaps influenced by the teachings of Zarathustra and the writings of the master of the magi known to us as Daniel the Prophet (Daniel 4:9; 9:24–27), Persian Magi saw a Star in the East and came to worship the newborn King (Matthew 2:1–12).

---

42. Durant, I: 381–82.

3 Persia: *Where West Became East*

Questions for Reflection, Discussion, and More Reflection

1. How is the ethnic background of Persia different from that of most nations of the Middle East? Is that difference relevant to an understanding of Persian religion and law?
2. How was Persian religion different from that of other Middle Eastern societies? To what do you attribute this difference? How was Persian religion similar to, and different from, Judaism and Christianity?
3. What are the distinctives of Persian law? Specifically, how did Persian religion influence these distinctives?
4. What is meant by the term "dualism"? Are Judaism and Christianity dualistic religions? How does Zoroastrianism differ from Judaism and Christianity?
5. How did the Persian policy of treating conquered peoples differ from that of Babylonia and Assyria? What are the advantages and disadvantages of each? How did the Jews believe the policies of Assyria, Babylonia, and Persia, each in its own time, served God's plan concerning the disciplining and delivery of His people?
6. Do the favorable references to Cyrus the Great in 2 Chronicles 36:23, Ezra 1:2, 3:7, 5:13, 6:3, Isaiah 44:28 and 45:1, mean that Cyrus was a believer in the God of Israel, or only that God used him for certain purposes?
7. How does the phrase repeated in verses 8, 12, and 15 of Daniel 6, "the law of the Medes and Persians, which altereth not," reflect a unique feature of Persian law?
8. What does Daniel 6:1–3 tell us about Persian governmental organization?
9. What were the special strengths of Persian law and government? What were its weaknesses? What was its greatest weakness, and how was that weakness demonstrated in later Persian history?
10. What lessons can we learn from the religion, law, government, and history of Persia?

Fortified Northwestern Railway bridge over the Indus River at Attock (modern day Pakistan). William Henry Jackson (1843–1942). Photograph taken in 1895.

CHAPTER 4

INDIA:
A Study in Contrasts and Blended Cultures

There is a struggle between the Oriental and the Occidental in every nation; some who would be forever contemplating the sun, and some who are hastening toward the sunset. The former class says to the latter, When you have reached the sunset, you will be no nearer to the sun. To which the latter replies, But we so prolong the day.[1]

We now move eastward in our survey of ancient law, not only geographically but philosophically as well. Writers often speak of the divergence of eastern and western thought, but seldom articulate how, at bottom, eastern and western thought differ.

The fundamental difference goes back to that basic philosophical problem of the one and the many. In its political and legal manifestations, Western thought values the individual, his rights and his freedoms, above those of the group. Eastern thought values the group, society, social control, and the state above the individual. In Western thought, the individual has rights that the state is (or should be) powerless to take away. Eastern thought historically has subordinated the rights of the individual to the needs of the group and the interests of society.

Similarly, Western religious thought, exemplified by Judaism and Christianity, views God as personal; that is, God has the attributes of personhood; He thinks; He feels; He acts, both now and throughout all time. Eastern religious thought, exemplified by religions such as Buddhism,

1. Henry David Thoreau (1817–1862), U.S. philosopher, author, naturalist. "A Week on the Concord and Merrimack River" (1849), in *The Writings of Henry David Thoreau,* (Houghton Mifflin (1906), I: 147.

Hinduism, Taoism, Shinto, and others, views God as an impersonal force, a cosmic unity without distinct personality.

Joseph Campbell said the "geographical divide between the Oriental [Eastern] and Occidental [Western] ranges of myth and ritual is the tableland of Iran. Eastward are the two Spiritual provinces of India and the Far East; westward, Europe and the Levant."[2] He described the difference:

> Throughout the Orient the idea prevails that the ultimate ground of being transcends thought, imaging, and definition. It cannot be qualified. Hence, to argue that God, Man, or Nature is good, just, merciful, or benign, is to fall short of the question. One could as appropriately—or inappropriately—have argued, evil, unjust, merciless, or malignant. All such anthropomorphic predications screen or mask the actual enigma, which is absolutely beyond rational consideration; and yet, according to this view, precisely that enigma is the ultimate ground of being of each and every one of us—and of all things.
>
> The supreme aim of Oriental mythology, consequently, is not to establish as substantial any of its divinities or associated rites, but to render by means of these an experience that goes beyond: of identity with that Being of beings which is both immanent and transcendent; yet neither is nor is not. Prayers and chants, images, temples, gods, sages, definitions, and cosmologies are but ferries to a shore of experience beyond the categories of thought, to be abandoned on arrival; for, as the Indian Kena Upanishad states: "To know is not to know, not to know is to know"; and the Chinese Tao Te Ching: "Those who know are still."[3]

To further illustrate the difference, Campbell said:

> In the Western ranges of mythological thought and imagery… the ground of being is normally personified as a Creator, of whom Man is the creature, and the two are not the same; so that here the function of myth and ritual cannot be to catalyze an experience of ineffable identity. Man alone, turned inward, according to this view can experience only his own creaturely soul, which may or may not be properly related to its Creator.

2. Joseph Campbell, *The Masks of God: Occidental Mythology* (Secer & Warburg, 1965), 2.

3. Campbell, 2.

> The high function of Occidental myth and ritual, consequently, is to establish a means of relationship—of God to Man and Man to God. Such means are furnished, furthermore, by institutions, the rules of which cannot be learned through any scrutiny of nature, whether inward or with-out. Supernaturally revealed, these have come from God himself, as the myth of each institution tells; and they are administered by his clergy, in the spirit of the myth.
>
> However, certain exclusively Occidental complications result from the fact that, where two such contradictory final terms as God and Man stand against each other, the individual cannot attach his allegiance wholly to both. On the one hand, as in the Book of Job, he may renounce his human judgment in the face of what he takes to be the majesty of God: "Behold, I am of small account; what shall I answer thee?" Or, on the other hand, as in the manner of the Greeks, he may stand by his human values and judge, according to these, the character of his gods. The first type of piety we term religious and recognize in all traditions of the Levant: Zoro-astrianism, Judaism, Christianity, and Islam. The other we term, in the broadest sense, humanistic, and recognize in the native mythologies of Europe: the Greek, Roman, Celtic, and Germanic....
>
> Much of the complexity and vitality of the Occidental heritage must be attributed to the conflicting claims—both of which are accepted—on the one hand, of the advocates of what is offered as the Word of God, and, on the other, of the rational individual. Nothing quite of the kind has ever seriously troubled the mentality of the Orient east of Iran, where the old hieratic Bronze Age cosmology of the ever-circling eons—static yet turning ever, in a round of mathematical impersonality, from everlasting to everlasting—endures to this day as the last word on the universe and the place of man within it.[4]

According to Campbell, in the West—and of course this is an overgeneralization—the dominant theme is the split between the Creator and the created; the individual is not identical with God, but rather exists in a state of relationship to God. In Oriental thought, the dominant theme is the unity of all things divine and human and the transcendent and immanent nature of all being.

4. Campbell, 4–5.

But was this always the way of things? Not necessarily. As we will see in this chapter and the next, evidence exists that in the early days the Orient was monotheistic.

We now visit an eastern country, India, and we naturally expect India's laws and government to be based on concepts of Eastern thought. Generally this is true. But Westerners and Western thought have penetrated India several times throughout history: the Indo-Europeans around 2000 BC, the Greeks under Alexander around 330 BC, Muslims in the 7th century AD, and the British in the 19th century. Each of these in turn has exercised a unique influence upon India, its thought, religion, laws, and institutions. India is truly a crossroads between East and West.

And India is a land of great variety, from the frozen Himalayas in the north to the lowland jungles of the south, from the Indo-Europeans to the darker Dravidians, from the Brahmins to the untouchables, from Hindu to Buddhist to Muslim to Sikh to Hebrew[5] to Christian[6] and to many others, India is a land of multiple cultures, multiple ethnic backgrounds, multiple languages, and multiple religions. All of these have impacted India's history, law, and government.

Since the 1800s, the prevailing view of India's history has been that the earliest recorded inhabitants were the Dravidians, a dark-skinned people possibly related to the Aborigines of Australia. This civilization centered around the Indus River and is known as the Harappan culture. It was essentially a city culture that carried on commerce with lands as far away as Sumeria and Mesopotamia. Archeology has revealed that all of these Harappan cities were "built on almost identical plans, of well laid-out streets, elaborate drainage systems, public baths, differentiated residential areas, flat-roofed brick houses, and fortified administrative-

---

5. Recent DNA testing supports the claim of the *Bene Israel* ("Sons of Israel"), an ethnic group living in Mumbai, Pune, Thane, and Ahmedabad, that their ancestors came from Palestine to India over 2,000 years ago. http://www.indiadivine.org/audarya/hinduism-forum/188694-indias-jews-original-jews.html (accessed 28 April, 2016); *Jews of India,* http://www.the-south-asian.com/March2001/Jews_of_India-Intro.htm (accessed 28 April, 2016).

6. According to Church tradition, Thomas the Apostle traveled to India to evangelize for Christianity. The Thomasene Christians, or St. Thomas Christians, of the Kerala State on the southwest coast of India, number around 300,000 today and claim an unbroken descent from those early converts of the Apostle Thomas. In AD 325 their bishop attended the Council of Nicea. Many medieval travelers reported contact with the St. Thomas Christians, and in the 1200s, when Marco Polo wrote of his travels to the Far East, he reported having seen the old tomb of Thomas in India, and the Cathedral of St. Thomas was built over that tomb. William Steuart McBirnie, *The Search for the Twelve Apostles* (Tyndale House 1973, 1978), 142–73.

cum-religious centers enclosing meeting halls and granaries."[7] Archeologists have also found realistic engravings of animals and human figures, with short inscriptions that as of this time are undecipherable.[8] Interestingly, the oldest of these are of higher quality than the later ones.[9]

The conventional view, advanced in the 1800s by Max Muller and others, is that sometime around 2000–1500 BC, the Harappan civilization was conquered by invading forces from the north and west. These invaders were part of a larger movement of the Indo-Europeans, or Aryans, or Indo-Aryans, who for unknown reasons left the steppes of Central Asia and migrated in different directions. Out of this migration came the Celts and Germans of northern Europe, the Greeks and Romans of southern Europe, the Persians or Parsee of modern Iran, and others.[10] As they conquered the Harappan cities, they did not exterminate them but rather subjugated them and kept them under control by imposing a rigid caste system, with themselves as the upper or Brahmin caste. The Vedas, their ancient writings that became the foundation for Hinduism, represent the original religion of this Aryan or Indo-European people.

In recent years the Aryan invasion theory has come under attack. With one exception, excavation of the Harappan cities does not indicate destruction or invasion. The inhabitants of the Harappan cities appear to have been of more than one race. What little we know of the religious beliefs of the Harappans indicates that they were similar to those of the Indo-Europeans. The Rig Veda refers to the greatest and holiest river not as the Indus or the Ganges but rather the Saraswati, a river that dried up around 1900 BC. And it is hard to explain why the Vedas are devoid of any references to places outside India if they are truly the work of Indo-Europeans from Central Asia.[11]

---

7. Richard F. Nyrop, ed., *India: A Country Study* (Washington, D.C.: Dept of the Army, 1985), www.shsu.edu (accessed 28 April, 2016).

8. Nyrop.

9. Durant, I: 395.

10. The mummified remains of an Indo-European man, woman, and child have been discovered in the plains of China, the man and woman both about six feet tall, with light-colored hair, and wearing Celtic clothing of the type produced in Western Europe around 2000–1500 BC. Stephen L. Goldman, "Science in the Twentieth Century: A Social-Intellectual Survey," Part III (The Teaching Company, 2004), "Mysterious Mummies of China," *NOVA*, http://www.pbs.org/wgbh/nova/chinamum (accessed 28 April, 2016).

11. Goldman *op. cit.;* see also David Frawley, "The Myth of the Aryan Invasion of India," http://www.scribd.com/doc/400594/The-Myth-of-the-Aryan-Invasion-of-India; Dr. Dinesh Agrawal, "Demise of the Aryan Invasion Theory," www.hindunet.org/hindu_history/ancient/aryan/aryan

This does not mean the Aryan migration did not take place, or that Indo-Europeans did not migrate to India. It may mean they came earlier than Muller and others supposed. It may mean they were the original inhabitants of the Harappan cities, or, more likely in my opinion, that they intermingled with the Dravidians rather than subjugating them. And it may mean that the Vedas and the Hindu religion were developed by the Aryans (and perhaps the Dravidians as well) after the migration rather than before.

A series of writings called the Vedas, or books of knowledge, are the prototype of Hinduism, and they are definitely among the oldest religious documents in the world, whether one dates them as late as 1500 BC, as early as 12,000 BC, or anywhere in between. Some believe they existed in oral tradition long before they were committed to writing. Some scholars believe the Vedas represent the original religion of the Aryans which they carried with them when they left the steppes of Central Asia; others believe the Vedic religion developed after the Aryans arrived in India. Possibly the Vedas represent an amalgamation of the Aryan and Dravidian religious beliefs and practices. Hindus regard the Vedas as revelations of the Divine nature and its relation to us. The *Rig Veda* is considered the oldest and contains hymns and rituals as well as information about astronomy, astrology, and medical science. The *Sama Veda*, *Yajur Veda*, and *Atharva Veda* are thought to have developed from the *Rig Veda*.

Each of the Vedas has three parts: the *Samhitas,* which contain prayers and hymns; the *Brahmanas,* which include ritual and theology; and the *Upanishads,* which are philosophical works, probably dating from 600–400 BC, that teach the inner spiritual meaning of the Veda and explain the sciences of yoga, meditation, transmigration of souls, and realization of one's oneness with God.

Other sacred writings include the *Puranas,* which contain stories about Hindu gods and goddesses, and epic stories called the *Ramayana*

_agrawal.html (accessed 6/7/2016). The debate appears to have some political and ideological overtones. Frawley and Agrawal argue that the Aryan invasion theory prevents India from developing its own identity and causes India to see itself as a divided people. They also suggest that the Aryan invasion theory was used to justify British domination of India in the 1800s and early 1900s. Did Hinduism as taught in the Vedas really reflect the original religion of the Indo-Europeans? It does not reflect the religious beliefs of Indo-Europeans in northern Europe, in Greece or Rome, or in Persia, though a few parallels may exist, such as the dualistic conflict between light and darkness. And the caste system supposedly established by these Aryan conquerors bears little resemblance to the social and governmental systems established by Indo-Europeans in other countries they came to dominate.

and the *Mahabharata*. The *Mahabharata* includes a philosophical work called the *Bhagavad Gita,* in which the god Krishna and the warrior Arjuna carry on a discourse about the meaning and nature of existence.

Westerners often do not realize the depth of Indian interest in philosophy. In America neighboring communities compete with each other in high school football games; in India, both historically and to the present, neighboring communities challenge each other to philosophical debates.

There are many varieties of Hinduism, and the religion has changed over time. Hinduism is generally considered to be polytheistic, worshipping or at least acknowledging millions of gods. But unlike the polytheistic religions of the west, the gods and goddesses of Hinduism are less personal beings and more identified as forces of nature. Robert Brow writes,

> The earliest literature of India, the Sanskrit *Vedas,* picture the nomadic Aryan tribes who fought their way eastwards across the Indus and Ganges plains.
>
> The head of the tribe offered animal sacrifice with the same simplicity as Abraham. When they settled in India the Aryans developed a regular priesthood, and the *Vedas* are hymns which the priests chanted as the sacrificial smoke ascended to God. The hymns address God under various names such as "The Sun," "The Heavenly One," and "The Storm," but the interesting thing is that, whatever name they gave to God, they worshipped him as the supreme Ruler of the universe. This practice is called Henotheism. God has several names, just as Christians today have several names for God, but the names do not indicate different gods. They are different facets of one God. Henotheism changes into Polytheism when the names of God are so personified that the various gods are separated, and they begin to disagree and fight among themselves. The later Vedic literature has certainly become polytheistic by, say, 1000 BC, but the earliest Aryans must have been Monotheists.[12]

Brow is not alone in this conclusion. Recreating the early Brahmin priests as Enlightenment figures similar to himself, Voltaire saw the early Vedic writers as ethical monotheists.[13] Coleman, in his book *Hindu Mythology,* says,

12. Robert Brow, *Religion: Origins and Ideas,* (Tyndale Press, 1966), 3.

13. Voltaire, cited by Jyoti Mohan, "*La civilization la plus antique:* Voltaire's Images of India," *Journal of World History* XVI:2 June 2005, 1–11, http://www.muse.jhu.edu/article/190240 (accessed 28 April, 2016).

> The early writers exhaust language in endeavours to express the lofty character and attributes, and the superlative power and dignity of this great unity—the highest conception of which man is capable. He is spoken of as "The Almighty, Infinite, Eternal, Incomprehensible, Self-existent Being—He who sees everything, though never seen—He who is not to be compassed by description—He from whom the universe proceeds—who rules supreme—the Light of all lights—whose power is too infinite to be imagined—the One Being—the True and Unknown brahm.[14]

And in the *Bhagavad Gita* or "Sacred Song," composed between two and three thousand years ago, we read:

> I am the Creator of all things, and all things proceed from me. I am the beginning, the middle, and the end of all things; I am time; I am all-grasping death; and resurrection.[15]

The skeptic Voltaire wrote concerning the Brahmins of India,

> They continued to acknowledge one supreme God, in the midst of the multitude of subordinate deities, which popular supersitition adopted in all countries of the world. Strabo expressly says that, in the main, the Brahmins acknowledge only one God.... They held one God, the creator, preserver and avenger, and believed the fall and degeneracy of man; and this opinion is everywhere to be met with among the people of antiquity.[16]

In 1857 the Norwegian missionary Lars Skrefsrud and the Danish layman Hans Børreson visited the Santal region of India north of Calcutta. As Skrefsrud proclaimed the Gospel, he heard the Santal sages saying to one another, "What this stranger is saying must mean that Thakar Jiu has not forgotten us after all this time!" Fluent in the Santal tongue, Skrefsrud recognized that the phrase *Thakar Jiu* means "Genuine God." The Santals

14. Coleman, *Hindu Mythology,* quoted by J.H. Titcomb, "Prehistoric Monotheism," *Journal of the Transactions of The Victoria Institute,* 1872–73, http://www.creationism.org/victoria/VictoriaInst1872_pg141.htm (accessed 28 April, 2016).

15. James George Roche Forlong, *Faiths of Man: A Cyclopaedia of Religions* (London: Bernard Quaritch 1906), I:39, Thomas Maurice, *Indian Antiquities* (Univ. of Virginia, 1793–1800), 288.

16. Francois-Marie Arouet, aka Voltaire, "Dialogue Entre un Brachmane et un Jesuite" ("Dialogue Between a Brahman and a Jesuit") 1756; in *Melanges* (Paris 1961); *The Works of M. de Voltaire,* trans T. Smollett, et al. (Newsberry, 1763).

then told Skrefsrud how Thakar Jiu had created the world, how He had caused a flood but preserved two people by hiding them in a cave on Mt. Harata (note the similarity to Ararat), and numerous other parallels to the Biblical account. Skrefsrud concluded that the Santal people at one time knew the true God and continued to remember Him imperfectly.[17]

And many Hindus thinkers, both historically and at present, have regarded the various gods and goddesses as simply different forms or manifestations of one universal spirit, or that the one Self-existent God created the lesser gods out of himself, just as he created the earth and all that is therein out of himself, so that all things including the lesser gods are really part of this one ultimate God. In this way ancient Indian thought combines monotheism, henotheism, monism, pantheism, and polytheism. As Creuzer observed,

> The very vastness of Hindoo mythology obliges it to be inconsistent. It is an effort to represent a Being who can only be grasped by infinite thought. Were it consistent, its failure would be still more signal, the many being but fractions of the one, and this one an infinite spirit. It therefore takes refuge in poetry, and struggles to utter, by luxuriant similitudes, what language cannot with accuracy express.[18]

Dr. Hundersmarck of Fordham University says,

> With the *Upanishads,* we see a turn away from the hymnology of god and goddess to an earnest search for one universal reality that sustains the flux of being. This Upanishadic shift is analogous to pre-Socratic thought in the Greek world seeking to find a universal principle in contradistinction to Homeric polytheism....
>
> The *Upanishads* advise the inward journey into the self, rather than the outward movement into the world. While the Vedic tradition rejoiced in the vitality of the universe, the Upanishadic tradition make a deliberate turn to the human subject, and with this turn offers an intense preoccupation with human consciousness and all that flows from acts of self-reflection. In such acts, the enlightened person realizes that the deepest human longing is for meaning and purpose, an end to human

17. Don Richardson, *Eternity in Their Hearts* (Regal 1981, 1984), 41–48.

18. Creuzer, quoted by Titcomb, *op. cit.*

> restlessness, a final peace. In a world where all that is good appears to be destroyed by age and death, the seeker longs for the infinite in the finite, the absolute in the relative. Throughout the Upanishadic texts, the fulfillment of this longing is called *Brahman.*[19]

Brahman, in Hindu thought, represents the one universal world spirit. This world spirit is made up of many gods, three of the most important of which are Brahma, the creator of the universe; Vishnu, the preserver of the universe; and Shiva, the destroyer of the universe. Brahman is absolute truth, pure consciousness, the source of all being, and the essence of every good. And yet Shiva the destroyer is also part of Brahman, as is Kali the feared goddess of destruction. This is the essence of eastern monism, the unity of all things, in contrast to western dualism that sees good and evil as diametrically opposite forces.

Brahman is also the essence of man, called the *Atman*, a Hindu concept roughly comparable to the Christian concept of the human soul. Understanding that one's Atman is part of Brahman is somewhat like thinking, in Western terminology, that one's soul is part of God and one with God. Not only does each person have an Atman, but animals likewise have an Atman, and all are part of Brahman; therefore animals, humans, and the ultimate Brahman are all part of one essential unity.

The Atman, or inner self, is eternal, and goes through many incarnations. What state one occupies in this life, and in lives to come, is determined by the law of *karma*. *Karma* simply means that one's next existence will be determined by one's actions in this and previous existences. In other words, we reap what we sow. Whatever one's status in this life, one has certain duties and obligations to perform, and these are called *dharma*. How one fulfills one's *dharma* in this life may cause one to be reincarnated in a higher caste or status than in this life, or a lower status, or even that of an animal. This process continues through almost endless reincarnations until one has perfectly fulfilled one's *dharma*, worked off all the accumulated *karma* of previous lives, and enters an eternal state called *moksha* or *Nirvana*. Westerners often assume Nirvana is the equivalent of the Christian heaven, but it is very different. When one enters Nirvana, one becomes part of Brahman, the universal world spirit, and all

19. Lawrence F. Hundersmarck, "Upanishads," *Great Thinkers of the Eastern World*, Ian McGreal, ed. (New York: HarperCollins, 1995), 155–56.

individual existence and consciousness ceases, like the water of a stream that enters the ocean and becomes part of one great whole.[20]

Max Muller, one of the chief architects of the Aryan invasion theory, wrote of Indian thought:

> Greece and India are, indeed, the two opposite poles in the historical development of the Aryan man. To the Greek, existence is full of life and reality; to the Hindu it is a dream, an illusion. The Greek is at home where he is born; all his energies belong to his country: he stands and falls with his party, and is ready to sacrifice even his life to the glory and independence of Hellas. The Hindu enters this world as a stranger; all his thoughts are directed to another world; he takes no part even where he is driven to act; and when he sacrifices his life, it is but to be delivered from it.[21]

India's caste system is directly related to the Hindu religion. The four castes are thought to have been established around 1500 BC by the Aryans to keep the subjugated peoples under their control. But they also reflect one's status in this present life, based upon the individual's accumulated *karma* and the laws and duties of *dharma*. The four castes consist of (1) the Brahmins[22] or priests, who wield both ecclesiastical and governmental power; (2) the kshatriyas, the princes and warriors; (3) the vaisyas, the merchants and landowners; and (4) the sudras, the farmers, laborers and servants.[23] Below all of these castes were the "untouchables," or social outcasts, who could perform only such work as was forbidden for the four

20. Hundersmarck, 155–60; see also *World Book Encyclopedia,* "Hinduism," IX: 224–25. We should also note at this point that around 500 BC another great world religion, Buddhism, arose in India. Buddhism is variously described as an outgrowth of Hinduism and as a reaction against Hinduism, and perhaps it is both. Buddhism had great influence in China, Japan, Korea, and Southeast Asia. But except for a brief period during the reign of the Buddhist King Asoka (circa 270–232 BC), Buddhism has been a minority religion in India and its influence on India's legal system has been negligible. We will examine Buddhism in greater detail in the chapter on China.

21. F. Max Muller, *A History of Ancient Sanskrit Literature So Far As It Illustrates the Primitive Religion of the Brahmans,* revised and edited by Dr. Surendra Nath Sastri, 1968 (Dang, 677–78).

22. The term *brahmin* always means a member of the highest caste. The term *brahman* usually means "world spirit" or one who has achieved unity with the world spirit, but it is sometimes used interchangeably with *brahmin* for a member of the highest caste.

23. *World Book Encyclopedia,* "Hinduism," IX: 225. A similar though not identical class system existed in medieval Europe: (1) "Those who pray," the clergy; (2) "Those who fight," the knights and nobility; and (3) "Those who work," the merchants and peasants.

castes. Officially at least, the 1950 India Constitution eliminated the "untouchable" class and gave its members full citizenship.

Ancient India's form of government reflects its diverse heritage. The Indo-Europeans brought with them the decentralized system of government that characterized Indo-European societies elsewhere, and the local city-states retained a great deal of local autonomy. Each comparatively independent village was governed by an assembly of family heads; villages were grouped together into a tribe which was governed by a raja who was limited by a tribal council. The tribes formed a state; each state was ruled by a king, but the king was subject to a council of warriors.[24]

The family was the basic unit of Hindu society; families rather than individuals owned property. Families were basically patriarchal, but women had greater freedom and status in the earlier Vedic period (2000–1000 BC) than in later India. As Durant says,

> She had more to say in the choice of her mate than the forms of marriage might suggest. She appeared freely at feasts and dances, and joined with men in religious sacrifice. She could study, and might...engage in philosophic disputation. If she was left a widow there were no restrictions upon her remarriage. In the Heroic Age [1000–500 BC] woman seems to have lost something of this liberty. She was discouraged from mental pursuits...the remarriage of widows became uncommon; *purdah*—the seclusion of women—began; and the practice of *suttee* [burning the widow on the funeral pyre of her husband], almost unknown in Vedic times, increased. The ideal woman was now...that faithful Sita who follows and obeys her husband humbly, through every test of fidelity and courage, until her death.[25]

As India moved from the Vedic to the Heroic Age, government became more centralized; and a well-organized bureaucracy regulated prices, weights and measures, customs, frontiers, passports, communications, excises, mines, agriculture, cattle, commerce, warehouses, navigation, forests, gambling and prostitution (both of which were legal but government-controlled), and intoxicating drinks; and the government owned and regulated many industries. The government owned all land and leased

---

24. Durant, I: 398. Durant also suggests that the kshatriyas were originally the highest caste but were gradually eclipsed by the Brahmins.

25. Durant, I: 401–02.

it to individuals or families, and kept a monopoly on mines, salt, timber, fine fabrics, horses, and elephants. Indian monism was not conducive to personal liberty and individual rights, but the government seems to have been benevolent most of the time.[26]

The general view is that ancient India, like the Orient in general, was a stranger to republican or democratic government. Durant says Vedic India was ruled by an Aryan oligarchy, and even in the Heroic Age, the government "made no pretense to democracy" and was "based frankly on military power."[27] It was well-organized and efficient, but the "one defect of this government was autocracy, and therefore continual dependence upon force and spies,... always fearing revolt and assassination."[28]

But this view is not unanimous. Greek writers from the time of Alexander's conquest of India (330–320 BC) suggest that, at least in northwestern India, Alexander came upon independent city-states with democratic forms of government.[29]

India's earliest known written legal code is known as the Laws of Manu, a compendium of 2,685 legal maxims that forms the basis of Indian law. The origins of the Laws of Manu are shrouded in mystery, as is Manu himself, and the Hindu view of time and history as cyclical rather than linear makes it even more difficult to trace. Buhler dates the Laws of Manu around 1500 BC;[30] others date them much later and some much earlier, dating back to the early part of the Vedic era and possibly even before the Aryans came to India. Muhlberger describes Manu as a moral philosopher and legislator who lived between 200 BC and AD 200.[31] Durant says Manu was "the mythical ancestor of the Manava tribe (or school) of Brahmans near Delhi; he was represented as the son of a god and as receiving his laws from Brahma himself."[32] A Hindu legend claims the name Manu belongs to "fourteen mythological progenitors of mankind and rulers of the earth, each of whom holds sway for the period called a

26. Durant, I: 443–44.

27. Durant, I: 443

28. Durant, I: 445.

29. Steve Muhlberger, "Democracy in Ancient India," www.faculty.nipissingu.ca/muhlberger/HISTDEM/INDIADEM.HTM (accessed 28 April, 2016).

30. G. Buhler, *India History Sourcebook:* "The Laws of Manu, ca. 1500 BCE," http://www.fordham.edu/halsall/india/manu-full.html (accessed 28 April, 2016).

31. Muhlberger, 2.

32. Durant, I: 484.

Manwantara (manu-antara), the age of a Manu, i.e., a period of no less than 4,320,000 years. The first of these Manus was Swayam-bhuva, who sprang from Swayambhu, the Self-existent.... The law-book commonly known as Manu is ascribed to this Manu, and so also is a sutra work on ritual bearing the same name."[33]

The people of ancient India clearly believed the Laws of Manu were of divine origin. The Laws themselves begin with sages seeking divine truth:

> I.
>
> 1. The great sages approached Manu, who was seated with a collected mind, and, having duly worshipped him, spoke as follows:
>
> 2. "Deign, divine one, to declare to us precisely and in due order the sacred laws of each of the (four chief) castes (varna) and of the intermediate ones.
>
> 3. "For thou, O Lord, alone knowest the purport, (i.e.) the rites, and the knowledge of the soul, (taught) in this whole ordinance of the Self-existent (Svayambhu), which is unknowable and infathomable."
>
> 4. He, whose power is measureless, being thus asked by the high-minded great sages, duly honored them, and answered, "Listen!"[34]

Manu then revealed to the sages a creation account that in some respects parallels Genesis 1:

> 5. This (universe) existed in the shape of Darkness, unperceived, destitute of distinctive marks, unattainable by reasoning, unknowable, wholly immersed, as it were, in deep sleep.
>
> 6. Then the divine Self-existent (Svayambhu, himself), indiscernible, (but) making (all) this, the great elements and the rest, discernible, appeared with irresistible power, dispelling the darkness.

33. *Encyclopedia,* http://www.http://www.mythfolklore.net/india/encyclopedia/manu.htm (accessed 28 April, 2016).

34. "The Laws of Manu, ca. 1500 BCE," trans. G. Buhler, *Indian History Sourcebook,* http://www.fordham.edu/halsall/india/manu-full.html (accessed 28 April, 2016) (parenthetical phrases supplied by translator).

> 7. He who can be perceived by the internal organ (alone), who is subtle, indiscernible, and eternal, who contains all created beings and is inconceivable, shone forth of his own (will).
>
> 8. He, desiring to produce beings of many kinds from his own body, first with a thought created the waters, and placed his seed in them.
>
> 9. That (seed) became a golden egg, in brilliancy equal to the sun; in that (egg) he himself was born as Brahman, the progenitor of the whole world.[35]

Like the Judeo-Christian God in the Genesis account, the God who is later known to the Hebrews as Yahweh ("I Am Who I Am"), the Self-existent Svayambhu brought all things into being by his own will. But unlike the transcendent God of Genesis who stands above His creation, the Self-existent Svayambhu is part of the cosmos, and he creates the cosmos out of himself:

> 14. From himself (atmanah) he also drew forth the mind, which is both real and unreal, likewise from the mind egoism, which possesses the function of self-consciousness (and is) lordly....
>
> 22. He, the Lord, also created the class of the gods, who are endowed with life, and whose nature is action; and the subtle class of the Sadhyas, and the eternal sacrifice....
>
> 26. Moreover, in order to distinguish actions, he separated merit from demerit, and he caused the creatures to be affected by the pairs (of opposites), such as pain and pleasure....
>
> 32. Dividing his own body, the Lord became half male and half female; with that (female) he produced Virag.[36]

Like India itself, Manu's account of creation blended aspects of western and eastern thought. The western concept of an omnipotent and omniscient creator is present, but the Self-existent Svayambhu is an impersonal force, lacking the aspects of personality that characterize the God of the Bible. And the Self-existent Svayambhu has created opposites, like male and female and merit and demerit, but in keeping with eastern monism

35. *Id.*

36. *Id.*

he has created them out of himself, so they are all part of him. The God of the Bible is in no way the Author of sin (1 John 1); sin and evil are part of Satan's rebellion against God. And we may also see here a mixture of polytheism and monotheism: there are many gods, but they are created by the one Self-existent Svayambhu.

Having explained the origin of the cosmos through the will of the Self-existent Svayambhu, Manu in Chapter II instructed the sages to

> 1. Learn that sacred law which is followed by men learned (in the Veda) and assented to in their hearts by the virtuous, who are ever exempt from hatred and inordinate affection.[37]

Manu then set forth an order of authority, much as American jurists would say the Constitution is the supreme law of the land, followed by federal law, state constitutions and laws, etc.:

> 6. The whole Veda is the (first) source of the sacred law, next the tradition and the virtuous conduct of those who know the (Veda further), also the customs of holy men, and (finally) self-satisfaction.[38]

Manu proceeded to give wise maxims ("2. To act solely from a desire for rewards is not laudable, yet an exemption from that desire is not [to be found] in this [world]."), practical suggestions ("33. The names of women should be easy to pronounce, not imply anything dreadful, possess a plain meaning, be pleasing and auspicious, end in long vowels, and contain a word of benediction."), reinforcements of the superiority of the Brahmin caste ("135. Know that a Brahmana of ten years and a Kshatriya of a hundred years stand to each other in the relation of father and son; but between those two the Brahmana is the father."), exhortations to humility and openness to correction ("162. A Brahmana should always fear homage as if it were poison; and constantly desire [to suffer] scorn as [he would long for] nectar.") and study ("165. An Aryan must study the whole Veda together with the Rahasyas, performing at the same time various kinds of austerities and the vows prescribed by the rules [of the Veda].")

Chapters III and IV set forth caste distinctions, duties, privileges, and penalties:

---

37. *Id.* The maxims of each chapter are numbered beginning with one.

38. *Id.*

III.

1. The vow (of studying) the three Vedas under a teacher must be kept for thirty-six years, or for half that time, or for a quarter, until the (student) has perfectly learned them....

17. A Brahmana who takes a Sudra wife to his bed, will (after death) sink into hell; if he begets a child by her, he will lose the rank of a Brahmana....

20. Now listen to (the) brief (description of) the following eight marriage-rites used by the four castes (varna) which partly secure benefits and partly produce evil both in this life and after death....

57. Where the female relations lie in grief, the family soon wholly perishes; but that family where they are not unhappy ever prospers....

62. If the wife is radiant with beauty, the whole house is bright; but if she is destitute of beauty, all will appear dismal....

286. Thus all the ordinances relating to the five (daily great) sacrifices have been declared to you; hear now the law for the manner of living fit for Brahmanas.

IV.

1. Having dwelt with a teacher during the fourth part of (a man's) life, a Brahmana shall live during the second quarter (of his existence) in his house, after he has wedded a wife.

2. A Brahmana must seek a means of subsistence which either causes no, or at least little pain (to others), and live (by that) except in times of distress....

12. He who desires happiness must strive after a perfectly contented disposition and control himself; for happiness has contentment for its root, the root of unhappiness is the contrary (disposition)....

> 44. A Brahmana who desires energy must not look at (a woman) who applies collyrium to her eyes, has anointed or uncovered herself or brings forth (a child).[39]

Chapters V and VI consist of dietary restrictions, ritual purification laws, and rules concerning sacrifice. In Chapter VII Manu moved to governmental subjects and declares that a king is not only created by "the Lord"; he is in fact a lesser god himself:

VII.

> 1. I will declare the duties of kings, (and) show how a king should conduct himself, how he was created, and how (he can obtain) highest success.
>
> 2. A Kshatriya, who has received according to the rule the sacrament prescribed by the Veda, must duly protect this whole (world).
>
> 3. For, when these creatures, being without a king, through fear dispersed in all directions, the Lord created a king for the protection of this whole (creation).
>
> 4. Taking (for that purpose) eternal particles of Indra, of the Wind, of Yama, of the Sun, of Fire, of Varuna, of the Moon, and of the Lord of wealth (Kubera).
>
> 5. Because a king has been formed of particles of those lords of the gods, he therefore surpasses all created beings in lustre;
>
> 6. And, like the sun, he burns eyes and hearts; nor can anybody on earth even gaze on him.
>
> 7. Through his (supernatural) power he is Fire and Wind, he Sun and Moon, he the Lord of justice (Yama), he Kubera, he Veruna, he great Indra and of the Lord of wealth (Kubera).
>
> 8. Even an infant king must not be despised, (from an idea) that he is a (mere) mortal; for he is a great deity in human form....

39. *Id.*

> 12. The (man) who in his exceeding folly hates him, will doubtlessly perish, for the king quickly makes up his mind to destroy such (a man).[40]

Manu declared that punishment is a divine ordinance, necessary for the protection of law-abiding citizens and to enable people to pursue their *dharma* without interference from criminals:

> 14. For the (king's) sake the Lord formerly created his own son, Punishment, the protector of all creatures, (an incarnation of) the law, formed in Brahman's glory.
>
> 15. Through fear of him all created beings, both the immovable and the movable, allow themselves to be enjoyed and swerve not from their duties.
>
> 16. Having fully considered the time and the place (of the offence), the strength and the knowledge (of the offender), let him justly inflict that (punishment) on men who act unjustly.
>
> 17. Punishment is (in reality) the king (and) the male, that the manager of affairs, that the ruler, and that is called the surety for the four orders' obedience to the law.
>
> 18. Punishment alone governs all created beings, punishment alone protects them, punishment watches over them while they sleep; the wise declare punishment (to be identical with) the law.
>
> 19. If (punishment) is properly inflicted after (due) consideration, it makes all people happy; but inflicted without consideration, it destroys everything.
>
> 20. If the king did not, without tiring, inflict punishment on those worthy to be punished, the stronger would roast the weaker, like fish on a spit....
>
> 25. But where Punishment with a black hue and red eyes stalks about, destroying sinners, there the subjects are not disturbed, provided that he who inflicts it discerns well....

---

40. *Id.*

> 28. Punishment (possesses) a very bright lustre, and is hard to be administered by men with unimproved minds; it strikes down the king who swerves from his duty, together with his relatives....
>
> 31. By him who is pure (and) faithful to his promise, who acts according to the Institutes (of the sacred law), who has good assistants and is wise, punishment can be (justly) inflicted.
>
> 32. Let him act with justice in his own domain, with rigour chastise his enemies, behave without duplicity toward his friends, and be lenient towards Brahmanas.
>
> 33. The fame of a king who behaves thus, even though he subsist by gleaning, is spread in the world, like a drop of oil on water.[41]

Manu exhorted kings to develop good character, to live according to the Vedic laws, and to always be respectful and even worshipful toward Brahmanas. In Chapter VIII he set forth principles for the adjudication of legal disputes:

> 1. A king, desirous of investigating law cases, must enter his court of justice, preserving a dignified demeanor, together with Brahmanas and with experienced councillors....
>
> 8. Depending on the eternal law, let him decide the suits of men who mostly contend on the titles just mentioned.
>
> 9. But if the king does not personally investigate the suits, then let him appoint a learned Brahmana [priest] to try them....
>
> 11. Where three Brahmanas versed in the Vedas and the learned (judge) appointed by the king sit down, they call that the court of (four-faced) Brahman....
>
> 14. Where justice is destroyed by injustice, or truth by falsehood, while the judges look on, there they shall also be destroyed.
>
> 15. Justice, being violated, destroys; justice, being preserved, preserves: therefore justice must not be violated, lest violated justice destroy us;

41. *Id.*

> 19. But where he who is worthy of condemnation is condemned, the king is free from guilt, and the judges are saved (from sin); the guilt falls on the perpetrator (of the crime alone).[42]

Manu moved on to the resolution of property disputes and gave the king a special admonition to care for the property of orphans and women and unclaimed property:

> 27. The king shall protect the inherited (and other) property of a minor, until he has returned (from the teacher's house) or until he has passed his minority.
>
> 28. In like manner care must be taken of barren women, of those who have no sons, of those whose family is extinct, of wives and widows faithful to their lords, and of women afflicted with diseases.
>
> 29. A righteous king must punish like thieves those relatives who appropriate the property of such females during their lifetime.
>
> 30. Property, the owner of which has disappeared, the king shall cause to be kept as a deposit during three years; within the period of three years the owner may claim it, after (that term) the king may take it.
>
> 31. He who says, "This belongs to me," must be examined according to the rule; if he accurately described the shape, and the number (of the articles found) and so forth, (he is) the owner, (and) ought (to receive) that property.
>
> 32. But if he does not really know the time and place (where it was) lost, its colour, shape, and size, he is worthy of a fine equal (in value) to the (object claimed).
>
> 33. Now the king, remembering the duty of good men, may take one-sixth part of property lost and afterwards found, or one-tenth, or at least one-twelfth.
>
> 34. Property lost and afterwards found (by the king's servants) shall remain in the keeping of (special) officials; those whom

42. *Id.*

> the king may convict of stealing it, he shall cause to be slain by an elephant.[43]

Manu then presented rules of evidence somewhat similar to those followed by our courts today:

> 57. Him also who says "I have witnesses," and, being ordered to produce them, produces them not, the judge must on these (same) grounds declare to be non-suited. [have his case dismissed]....
>
> 63. Trustworthy men of all the (four) castes (varna) may be made witnesses in lawsuits, (men) who know (their) whole duty, and are free from covetousness; but let him reject those (of an) opposite character.
>
> 64. Those must not be made (witnesses) who have an interest in the suit, nor familiar (friends), companions, and enemies (of the parties), nor (men) formerly convicted (of perjury), nor (persons) suffering under (severe) illness, nor (those tainted [by mortal sin]).
>
> 65. The king cannot be made a witness, nor mechanics and actors, nor a: Srotriya, nor a student of the Veda, nor (an ascetic) who has given up (all) connexion (with the world),
>
> 66. Nor one wholly dependent, nor one of bad fame, nor a Dasyu, nor one who follows forbidden occupations, nor an aged (man), nor an infant, nor one (man alone), nor a man of the lowest castes, nor one deficient in organs of sense,
>
> 67. Nor one extremely grieved, nor one intoxicated, nor a madman, nor one tormented by hunger or thirst, nor one oppressed by fatigue, nor one tormented by desire, nor a wrathful man, nor a thief.[44]

Most of those whose testimony is forbidden are persons who are not likely to be credible: those who are biased because of a personal interest in the suit or because of their friendship or enmity with the parties, those who have been untruthful in past, those whose perception of reality may be

43. Execution by elephant was conducted in several ways, including having an elephant step on the condemned person's head. Wigmore, I: 254.

44. *Id.*

altered by illness, those of bad reputation, those who are so old as to be incompetent, or who are suffering from grief, guilt of sin, intoxication, insanity or anger, and ascetics who are preoccupied with otherworldly matters. Likewise the king may invoke "executive privilege" because he should not be distracted from his duties by litigation. But when competent witnesses are lacking, the court may invoke the "best evidence" rule and accept testimony from less qualified witnesses:

> 70. On failure (of qualified witnesses, evidence) may be given (in such cases) by a woman, by an infant, by an aged man, by a pupil, by a relative, by a slave, or by a hired servant.[45]

Women may testify in cases involving other women (68) or in cases in which "qualified" witnesses are unavailable, but Manu took a lower view of such testimony:

> 77. One man who is free from covetousness may be (accepted as) witness; but not even many pure women, because the understanding of females is apt to waver, nor even many other men, who are tainted with sin.[46]

Manu stressed that those who perjure themselves incur bad *karma* with eternal consequences:

> 81. "A witness who speaks the truth in his evidence, gains (after death) the most excellent regions (of bliss) and here (below) unsurpassable fame; such testimony is revered by Brahman (himself).
>
> 82. "He who gives false evidence is firmly bound by Varuna's fetters, helpless during one hundred existences; let (men therefore) give true evidence....
>
> 123. But a just king shall fine and banish (men of) the three (lower) castes (varna) who have given false evidence, but a Brahmana he shall (only) banish.[47]

Manu then set forth practical rules for commercial disputes, rules that indicate men by this time had experienced these various commercial

45. *Id.*

46. *Id.*

47. *Id.*

problems and had considered practical principles for resolving them. For example:

> 157. Whatever rate men fix, who are expert in sea-voyages and able to calculate (the profit) according to the place, the time, and the objects (carried), that (has legal force) in such cases with respect to the payment to be made.)....
>
> 163. A contract made by a person intoxicated, or insane, or grievously disordered (by disease and so forth), or wholly dependent, by an infant or very aged man, or by an unauthorized (party) is invalid....
>
> 222. If anybody in this (world), after buying or selling anything, repent (of his bargain), he may return or take (back) the chattel within ten days.
>
> 223. But after (the lapse of) ten days he may neither give nor cause it to be given (back); both he who takes it (back) and he who gives it (back, except by consent) shall be fined by the king six hundred (panas).[48]

After establishing remedies for both "buyer's remorse" and "seller's remorse," Manu moved to criminal law, setting forth the categories of crimes commanding the king to punish violent crime without clemency:

> 345. He who commits violence must be considered as the worst offender, (more wicked) than a defamer, than a thief, and than he who injures (another) with a staff.
>
> 346. But that king who pardons the perpetrator of violence quickly perishes and incurs hatred.
>
> 347. Neither for friendship's sake, nor for the sake of great lucre, must a king let go perpetrators of violence, who cause terror to all creatures.[49]

Nevertheless, Manu did recognize self-defense as a justification for violence:

48. *Id.*

49. *Id.*

> 350. One may slay without hesitation an assassin who approaches (with murderous intent), whether (he be one's) teacher, a child or an aged man, or a Brahmana deeply versed in the Vedas.
>
> 351. By killing an assassin the slayer incurs no guilt, whether (he does it) publicly or secretly; in that case fury recoils upon fury.

Adultery was forbidden, partly because it threatened to break down caste distinctions:

> 352. Men who commit adultery with the wives of others, the king shall cause to be marked by punishments which cause terror, and afterwards banish.
>
> 353. For by (adultery) is caused a mixture of the castes (varna) among men; thence (follows) sin, which cuts up even the roots and causes the destruction of everything.[50]

The Laws of Manu enjoined moral virtue and clearly were intended to establish justice, but they cannot be called egalitarian. Manu carefully preserves the privileged status of the upper castes, especially the Brahmana, and women are placed in a protected but subordinate position. The German philosopher Friedrich Nieztsche, who thought he saw in the Vedic writings the earliest expression of the core beliefs of his own Aryan race, wrote,

> I know of no book in which so many tender and kind remarks are addressed to woman as in the law-book of Manu, these old greybeards and saints have a way of being polite to women which has perhaps never been surpassed.[51]

But while the Laws of Manu command that women be treated kindly and with respect, they definitely place women in a subordinate status. As noted earlier, women normally may not testify in court because the "understanding of females is apt to waver" (VIII:77), but one of the most

---

50. *Id.*

51. Friedrich Nietzsche, *The Antichrist* trans. R. J. Hollingdale (Harmondsworth, 1968); quoted by Dr. V.V. Bedekar, "Law and Justice in Ancient India," Institute for Oriental Study, http://www.orientalthane.com/speeches/speech_6.htm (accessed 28 April, 2016).

severe criminal punishments in the Laws of Manu is reserved for a woman caught in adultery:

> 371. If a wife, proud of the greatness of her relatives or (her own) excellence, violates the duty which she owes to her lord, the king shall cause her to be devoured by dogs in a place frequented by many.
>
> 372. Let him cause the male offender to be burnt on a red-hot iron bed; they shall put logs under it, (until) the sinner is burned (to death).[52]

Chapter XI addressed penances for those who have committed certain crimes or sins, many of which clearly reflect underlying Hindu theology. Believing that cattle are likely to be reincarnations of departed ancestors who are working off bad *karma* in this bovine existence, the Laws of Manu commanded kindness toward cattle and strict punishment for those who mistreat cattle:

> 113. (When a cow) is sick, or is threatened by danger from thieves, tigers, and the like, or falls, or sticks in a morass, he must relieve her by all possible means:
>
> 114. In heat, in rain, or in cold, or when the wind blows violently, he must not seek to shelter himself, without (first) sheltering the cows according to his ability.
>
> 115. Let him not say (a word), if a cow eats (anything) in his own or another's house or field or on the threshing-floor, or if a calf drinks (milk).
>
> 116. The slayer of a cow who serves cows in this manner, removes after three months the guilt which he incurred by killing a cow.[53]

And compare the punishment for killing certain other animals, compared to that for killing a eunuch or an adulterous woman:

> 131. He who has slain a Sudra [person of the laboring caste], shall perform that whole penance during six months, or he may also give ten white cows and one bull to a Brahmana.

---

52. "The Laws of Manu," *op. cit.*

53. *Id.*

> 132. Having killed a cat, an ichneumon, a blue jay, a frog, a dog, an iguana, an owl, or a crow, he shall perform the penance for the murder of a Sudra;
>
> 133. Or he may drink milk during three days, or walk one hundred yoganas, or bathe in a river, or mutter the hymn addressed to the Waters.
>
> 134. For killing a snake, a Brahmana shall give a spade of black iron, for a eunuch a load of straw and a masha of lead;
>
> 135. For a boar a pot of clarified butter, for a partridge a drona of sesamum-grains, for a parrot a calf two years old, for a crane (a calf) three years old.
>
> 136. If he has killed a Hamsa, a Balaka, a heron, a peacock, a monkey, a falcon, or a Bhasa, he shall give a cow to a Brahmana.
>
> 137. For killing a horse, he shall give a garment, for (killing) an elephant, five black bulls, for (killing) a goat, or a sheep, a draught-ox, for killing a donkey, (a calf) one year old;
>
> 138. But for killing carnivorous wild beasts, he shall give a milch-cow, for (killing) wild beasts that are not carnivorous, a heifer, for killing a camel, one krishnala.
>
> 139. For killing adulterous women of the four castes, he must give, in order to purify himself, respectively, a leathern bag, a bow, a goat, or a sheep.[54]

The Hindu belief in the transmigration of souls is further recognized in that, while sin and crime incur punishment by civil government, the bad *karma* incurred by such acts is primarily worked off in future incarnations and intermediate hells, as described in Chapter XII:

> 54. Those who committed mortal sins (mahapataka), having passed during large numbers of years through dreadful hells, obtain, after the expiration of (that term of punishment), the following births.

54. *Id.*

> 55. The slayer of a Brahmana enters the womb of a dog, a pig, an ass, a camel, a cow, a goat, a sheep, a deer, a bird, a Kandala, and a Pukkasa.
>
> 56. A Brahmana who drinks (the spirituous liquor called) Sura shall enter (the bodies) of small and large insects, of moths, of birds, feeding on ordure, and of destructive beasts.
>
> 57. A Brahmana who steals (the gold of a Brahmana shall pass) a thousand times (through the bodies) of spiders, snakes and lizards, of aquatic animals and of destructive Pisakas.
>
> 58. The violator of a Guru's bed (enters) a hundred times (the forms) of grasses, shrubs, and creepers, likewise of carnivorous (animals) and of (beasts) with fangs and of those doing cruel deeds.
>
> 59. Men who delight in doing hurt (become) carnivorous (animals); those who eat forbidden food, worms; thieves, creatures consuming their own kind; those who have intercourse with women of the lowest castes, Pretas.[55]

The Laws of Manu closed with a recognition that, exhaustive and complete as these 2,685 verses have been, they cannot possibly address every situation. Matters that have not been specifically addressed in the Laws of Manu are to be resolved by the priestly caste, much as in our constitutional system questions that are not specifically addressed by the Constitution or by statute are resolved by judges:

> 108. If it be asked how it should be with respect to (points of) the law which have not been (specially) mentioned, (the answer is), "that which Brahmanas (who are) Sishtas propound, shall doubtlessly have legal (force)."[56]

One more ancient ruler and lawgiver deserves mention, King Ashoka who ruled from approximately 270–232 BC. The Buddhist religion arose in India around 500 BC, partly as an outgrowth of Hinduism and partly as a reaction against Hinduism. But while Buddhism became very influential in China, Hinduism remained the dominant religion in India. However King Ashoka had undergone a religious conversion and had become

55. *Id.*

56. *Id.*

a devout Buddhist. His edicts reflect his Buddhist compassion, and his reforms were a reaction against the harshness of the Hindu system. In numerous edicts in which Ashoka referred to himself as "Beloved of the Gods," he called for religious tolerance, individual morality, sometimes clemency for criminals, and more appellate rights for those sentenced to death. For example, one of his edicts states,

> This edict has been written for the following purpose: that the judicial officers of the city may strive to do their duty and that the people under them might not suffer unjust imprisonment or harsh treatment. To achieve this, I will send out Mahamatras every five years who are not harsh or cruel, but who are merciful and who can ascertain if the judicial officers have understood my purpose and are acting according to my instructions.[57]

Another edict reads,

> The people of the unconquered territories beyond the borders might think: "What is the king's intentions towards us?" My only intention is that they live without fear of me, that they may trust me and that I may give them happiness, not sorrow. Furthermore, they should understand that the king will forgive those who can be forgiven, and that he wishes to encourage them to practice Dhamma so that they may attain happiness in this world and the next... you should perform your duties and assure them (the people beyond the borders) that: "The king is like a father. He feels towards us as he feels towards himself. We are to him like his own children."[58]

And still another:

> Beloved-of-the-Gods, King Piyadasi, speaks thus: These and other principal officers are occupied with the distribution of gifts, mine as well as those of the queens. In my women's quarters, they organize various charitable activities here and in the provinces. I have also ordered my sons and the sons of other queens to distribute gifts so that noble deeds of Dhamma and the practice of Dhamma may be promoted. And noble deeds of

57. Ven. S. Dhammika, "The Edicts of King Ashoka," http://www.cs.colostate.edu/~malaiya/ashoka.html (accessed 28 April, 2016).

58. *Id.*

> Dhamma and the practice of Dhamma consist of having kindness, generosity, truthfulness, purity, gentleness and goodness increase among the people.[59]

Durant agrees that Ashoka was a compassionate reformer but adds, "His outstanding fault was egotism; it is difficult to be at once modest and a reformer."[60] Ashoka incurred the enmity of the Brahmin caste and that of others who felt threatened by his reforms. Durant compares him to the Emperor Marcus Aurelius of Rome and his removal from the throne to that of the Egyptian Pharaoh Ikhnaton by the priests of Thebes.[61] In the short run it may appear that Ashoka failed as a reformer in India, but his reign helped to spread Buddhism to the East and served as a model for Buddhist rulers in other countries.

Professor Muhlberger of Nipissing University argues that, while ancient India was not purely democratic, many of its cities did contain some seeds of republicanism. He cites ancient Greek visitors to India, such as Megasthenes and Diadorus Siculus, who claimed that in their time (circa 300 BC) many of the cities of Northern India were at least semi-independent and democratic.[62] In most instances these city-states seem more like oligarchies than democracies, but at least there was a ruling class that could check the power of the king, and Mulberger claims that in some of these cities the enfranchised ruling class was quite broad-based, and that the castes were not as rigid as they became in later years.[63] And Justice Rama Jois of the High Court of Karnataka believes ancient India contained the seeds of modern public law, with its emphasis on the needs of society over those of the individual and the responsibility of government to work for the public good. He claims that ancient Indian law separated the legislative and executive powers of government. Because of the high respect accorded to *dharma*, the king had little power to legislate; rather, he simply implemented the laws that had been adopted according to *dharma*.[64] But *dharma* was not declared by a legislative body; it was

59. *Id.*

60. Durant, I: 449.

61. *Id.*

62. Steve Muhlberger, "Democracy in Ancient India," http://www.nipissingu.ca/muhlberger/HISTDEM/INDIADEM.HTM (28 April, 2016).

63. *Id.*

64. Justice Rama Jois, *Seeds of Modern Public Law in Ancient Indian Jurisprudence* (Lucknow: Eastern Book Company, 1990), 30–31.

the divine pronouncement of the Self-existent Svayambhu as revealed by lesser gods to the Brahmana.

CONCLUSIONS

We may draw the following conclusions from our study of ancient India:

(1) The Hindus believed their laws came from the Self-existent Svayambhu.

(2) The Hindus believed their kings were lesser gods and that the administration of the laws was entrusted to these divine kings and the priestly Brahamas.

(3) The Hindu legal system closely mingled the priestly and governmental, spiritual, and legal duties (*dharma*) of man.

(4) The Hindu legal system established and preserved the caste system with all its privileges and duties as necessary for the good ordering of society.

(5) Many of the crimes and punishments in the Laws of Manu reflect the Hindu thought upon which they are based.

(6) The Hindus had an orderly system of criminal justice, commercial regulation, dispute resolution, trial procedure, rules of evidence, and other means of ensuring justice.

(7) The Hindu system relies heavily upon the need for severe punishment because of the evil nature of man.

(8) Over the centuries the castes became more rigid, the rights of women became more restricted, punishments (except during the Ashoka interval) became harsher, government became more centralized and its powers more nearly absolute. This is not necessarily progress.

(9) The legal, moral, and social duties the Indians called Brahma and *dharma* constitute a higher, eternal, god-given law similar to that higher law concept that the Babylons called *kittu*, the Persians called *kiten*, the Egyptians called *ma'at*, the Chinese called the *Tao*, and many classical, medieval, and modern thinkers call natural law.

Writing in 1861, Sir Henry Sumner Maine first published his classic work, *Ancient Law.* He observed that law can help a society progress, or it can hinder that progress, and that "Brahminical India has not passed beyond a stage which occurs in the history of all the families of mankind, the stage at which a rule of law is not yet discriminated from a rule of religion. The members of such a society consider that the transgression of a religious ordinance should be punished by civil penalties, and that the violation of a civil duty exposes the delinquent to divine correction."[65]

Certainly the belief that law is divinely ordained can limit progress, especially if that law is distorted or misunderstood. But recognition of a divine sanction upon law can also be a barrier against tyranny, because it can impel rulers to take their duties seriously, recognize the divinely-ordained limits on their authority, and respect the God-given rights of their people. The belief that law is divinely ordained can also give law and government a stability that makes enduring progress possible.

Perhaps 35 centuries have passed since the time of Manu and 23 centuries since the time of Ashoka. In Ashoka's day the Greek invasions were a fresh memory. Since then India has been invaded by Persians, Muslims, British colonialists, and others who have placed their stamp on this second largest nation of the world. To Alexander, India was one more nation to conquer; to the Persians, they were a rival to the East; to the Muslims, they were infidels; to the British colonialists, they were a backward people in need of civilization; to the missionaries they were lost sinners in need of salvation.

But in Hindu thought, all of this reflects the cyclical nature of time, and much of the Indian mind remains unchanged through the centuries. And throughout all time, undisturbed by this parade of invaders, the sages of India continued their contemplations. Can the Western mind even begin to comprehend what they were thinking?

65. Henry Sumner Maine, *Ancient Law* (New York: Dorset Press, 1861, 1986), 19.

4 India: *A Study in Contrasts and Blended Cultures*

Questions for Reflection, Discussion, and More Reflection

1. In what ways do the history, institutions, and culture of India reflect a meeting or blending of Eastern and Western cultures?
2. What is the Indo-Aryan invasion theory? Why is the theory being challenged today? Does the evidence tend to prove or disprove the theory? How is the theory relevant to an understanding of Indian law and culture?
3. What are the Vedas? Summarize their basic teachings and explain how they set the stage for Indian law and government.
4. What is "henotheism," and how does it differ from monotheism and polytheism? Which of these terms best describes Indian religion, both historically and presently?
5. Explain the following concepts of Hindu thought: Brahma, *dharma, karma, atman,* Nirvana. Based upon these concepts, what is the Hindu view of man and of history? How does this view affect the nature and purpose of law?
6. According to Manu, what is the ultimate source of law? How is Manu's conception of Svayambhu similar to the Moses's concept of Yahweh? How are they different?
7. How is the Hindu belief in reincarnation manifested in the Laws of Manu?
8. How do you think India's caste system developed, and how does it fit with Hindu beliefs? How is it different from the class systems of other nations?
9. Do you think the Laws of Manu reflect an ancient Law of Nature that the people of ancient India possessed in common with other nations? What evidence do you see for and against this hypothesis?
10. What does the experience of Lars Skrefsrud in the Santal region of India suggest concerning Indian history and the original Indian beliefs?

Dragon Throne of Chinese Emperors in Beijing, China. 1928.

CHAPTER 5

CHINA:
The Multi-form Mandate of Heaven

On the exterior west wall of the United States Supreme Court Building, just below the roof, is a panel of large sculpted figures, each portraying a prominent lawgiver. The largest and centermost figure is Moses, seated and holding two stone tablets. Standing on Moses' left is the Greek lawgiver Solon and on his right the Chinese philosopher Confucius.

Each of these men made a major contribution toward our understanding of law.

We continue our eastward journey, this time stopping in China, the most populous nation in the world and a cradle of Oriental civilization. Westerners often do not realize that in the days when the Roman Empire was said to rule the world, to the east the Chinese had an empire approximately equal to that of Rome in size, culture, and military power, separated from Rome by the Persian Empire and India.

China has a rich cultural tradition, and colonialists who looked condescendingly on the Chinese as hopelessly backward, might have been surprised to know that at least until the twentieth century, the Chinese looked upon the people of Europe and America as "barbarians."

Durant wrote, "Chinese society was built not on science but on a strange and unique mixture of religion, morals, and philosophy. History has known no people more superstitious, and none more skeptical; no people more devoted to piety, and none more rationalistic and secular; no nation so free from clerical domination, and none but the Hindus so blessed and cursed with gods."[1]

The religion of the earliest Chinese is shrouded in mystery, and many have therefore assumed that the earliest Chinese religion was polytheistic. Durant describes early Chinese religion as "an animistic fear and worship

1. Durant, I: 783.

of spirits lurking anywhere, a poetic reverence for the impressive forms and reproductive powers of the earth, and an awed adoration of a heaven whose energizing sunlight and fertilizing rains were part of the mystic rapport between terrestrial life and the secret forces of the sky."[2] But presaging later Chinese thinking, "heaven and earth were bound together as two halves of a great cosmic unity, and were related very much as man and woman, lord and vassal, *yang* and *yin*. The order of the heavens and the moral behavior of mankind were kindred processes, parts of a universal and necessary rhythm called the *Tao*—the heavenly way; morality, like the law of the stars, was the cooperation of the part with the whole."[3]

Dr. Herbert A. Giles, Professor of Chinese at the University of Cambridge, describes the ancient Chinese explanation of origins:

> Before the beginning of all things, there was Nothing. In the lapse of ages Nothing coalesced into Unity, the Great Monad. After more ages, the Great Monad separated into Duality, the Male and Female Principles in nature; and then, by a process of biogenesis, the visible universe was produced.[4]

Dr. Giles described ancient Chinese religion as "primitive monotheism"[5] and said the two main Chinese terms for "God" are "T'ien," which refers to the sky, and "Shang Ti" which means Supreme Ruler. Shang Ti is a more personal name for God, while T'ien is more generic.[6] Dr. Giles emphasized that the two terms both referred to the same God, as evidenced by the fact that the Emperor Yung Lo (AD 1403–1425) had a dream in which an angel appeared to him with a message from Shang Ti, after which the emperor remarked, "Is not this a command from T'ien?" T'ien might be roughly comparable to the generic Hebrew word for God, Elohim, while Shang Ti might be comparable to the personal Hebrew name for God, Yahweh or Jehovah.[7] Nelson, Broadberry, and Chock demonstrate convincingly that

---

2. Durant, I: 783.

3. Durant, I: 783.

4. Herbert A. Giles, "Religions of Ancient China: the Ancient Faith" (London: Constable & Co., 1906), http://www.gutenberg.org/files/2330/2330-h/2330-h.htm (accessed 28 April, 2016).

5. *Id.*

6. *Id.* See also, C.H. Kang and Ethel R. Nelson, *The Discovery of Genesis: How the Truths of Genesis Were Found Hidden in the Chinese Language* (St. Louis: Concordia, 1979) .

7. Giles, op. cit.

the characters of the written Chinese language reveal an original monotheism and many parallels to the Bible.[8]

As we have seen with other societies such as India, belief in one supreme God did not necessarily constitute a belief that this supreme God was the only God. This one supreme God may have created lesser gods, either out of and as part of himself (as in India) or separate from himself (as in Persia). Judaism and Christianity both teach that God created lesser spiritual beings, but the Bible calls them angels rather than gods.

Whether China was polytheistic from the beginning or degenerated from monotheism into polytheism, the unique blend of Chinese religion and Chinese philosophy has given China a remarkable stability from its earliest history down even through its current Marxist regime. The first recorded dynasty to rule China was the Xia Dynasty, which governed from at least 2000 BC to about 1500 BC. During this time the Chinese worked with bronze and wrote with a pictorial alphabet, and practiced a cult of ancestor-worship that lent stability to society. The Shang Dynasty followed, ruling from about 1500 BC to 1045 BC. Writing proliferated during this time, particularly in the form of "oracle bones," animal bones upon which messages were inscribed as questions to the ancestors. Diviners read and interpreted the cracks in the bones as the ancestors' answers to these questions.

The Zhou people, who lived on the western periphery of Shang China, believed the Shang rulers had become corrupt and oppressive. So over the course of several generations they plotted an overthrow, which finally succeeded around 1045 BC. The kings of the new Zhou Dynasty felt compelled to justify their rebellion, so they developed the doctrine of the "Mandate of Heaven." "Heaven" in this sense may be more like an Eastern cosmic force than a Judeo-Christian concept of God or heaven. The doctrine held that Heaven, which is the guiding power in the universe, had given the right to rule to the Shang kings. But when the Shang Dynasty became cruel and oppressive, the Mandate of Heaven was lifted from them and placed instead on the Zhou rulers. Professor Kenneth Hammond believes this represented more than a change of dynasties; it also represents a change from the primacy of ancestor worship to the worship of Heaven instead.[9]

---

8. Dr. Ethel R. Nelson, Richard E. Broadberry, and Dr. Ginger Tong Chock, *God's Promise to the Chinese* (Read Books Publisher, 1997).

9. Kenneth J. Hammond, "From Yao to Mao: 5000 Years of Chinese History," (Chantilly, VA:

In the 8th century BC, the Zhou Dynasty began to fragment into many smaller states. Times of crisis often bring major developments in theology, philosophy, and literature, and Taoism (sometimes called Daoism) and Confucianism apparently developed out of this crisis, as did many other schools of thought, and this period of Chinese history is sometimes called the time of the Hundred Schools. One of these was Moism, based on the teachings of Mozi that men should treat one another as they would want to be treated (cf. Matthew 7:12). Mozi also taught defensive warfare as a means of discouraging aggression among the various states.

In the 4th century BC, Shang Yang, the prime minister of one of these states (Qin), promulgated a school of thought called Legalism. Much like the English philosopher John Locke (1632–1704), the Legalists taught that human nature is essentially a "blank slate," and people therefore need strict rules, with rewards and punishments, to develop good habits and live in an orderly way. Enforcing these rules was the role of government. In the 3rd century BC, the Qin rulers began to consolidate other states under their rule. By 221 BC their conquest of China was complete, and the Qin ruler assumed the title Qinshihuangdi, meaning First Emperor.

The Qin Dynasty established a unified administrative system, with uniform regulation of such matters as weights and measures, coinage, and cart axle width. But Qinshihuangdi also sought to regulate the thoughts of his subjects, and executed "unorthodox" scholars and burned their books. This, coupled with high taxes and labor levies, caused great resentment. After Qinshihuangi died in 210 BC, his son could not maintain control, and the Qin Dynasty collapsed around 207 BC.

After three years of civil war, the Han Dynasty took control and ruled China, despite periods of unrest, until AD 220. During this era China enjoyed great political, economic, and military strength and constituted an empire that rivaled that of Rome to the west. Probably during the earlier part of this period a military leader named Sun Tsu compiled his classic treatise on military strategy and tactics, *The Art of War*, a work that is still studied in American military schools today. Sun Tsu taught that the wisest general gains his objective without having to fight. No rational commander joins a battle he knows he cannot win. So the wise general uses timing, mobility, positioning, training, and superior numbers and

The Teaching Company, 2004), Part I, Lectures 2 and 3, Course Guidebook, I: 7–12. Note that because the Chinese language has many dialects and uses a pictorial alphabet, transliteration of Chinese names into English results in many variant spellings.

arms, and deploys his troops in such a show of strength that his opponent knows he cannot win and therefore comes to the bargaining table. The ramifications of Sun Tsu's teachings[10] extend far beyond the battlefield to diplomacy, business, and other areas of life.

Another major development during the Han Dynasty was the introduction of Buddhism, the ramifications of which will be discussed later.

After the stagnation and collapse of the Han Dynasty around AD 220, China entered an era of instability, with divided kingdoms and various seizures of power. Buddhism had many adherents among the Turkic migrant peoples of northern China, while Confucianism still held sway in the south. The Sui Dynasty reunified China in the late 500s, and the Tang Dynasty came to power in AD 618 and gave China both power and stability into the 9th century. Their rulers were mostly Buddhist, but some also had Taoist leanings; the Eastern subjective view of truth meant that these various Oriental religions were not mutually exclusive. Not trusting the local Confucian intelligentia, the Tang rulers tended to employ foreigners as military commanders and bureaucrats. The days of the Tang Dynasty were a golden age for the Chinese economy and commerce, and saw the flowering of theology, philosophy, literature, and art as well.[11]

Toward the end of the 8th century, Confucianism revived and Buddhism waned, and with it waned the Tang Dynasty. The Tang Dynasty collapsed around AD 900 and after half a century of turmoil, the Zhao brothers, Kuangyin and Kuangyi, seized and consolidated power, and established a stable bureaucracy which held China together long after the Zhao brothers' dynasty was history. They ensured that the bureaucracy attracted the most qualified civil servants by a system of civil service examinations. These exams were open to all classes of applicants except women and the sons of merchants. They consisted of three days in isolation writing essays, and they tested writing ability, knowledge of Confucian philosophy, and other subjects. Those who passed these exams became China's new elite or literati, and these Confucian-oriented civil service exams continued in various forms until the British abolished them after the Boxer Rebellion of 1905.

The reign of the Zhao brothers gave way to the Liao Dynasty, the Song Dynasty, the Mongol rulership of Genghis and Kublai Khan, the Ming

10. This writer personally studied the writings of Sun Tsu at the Air Command and Staff College, Maxwell Air Force Base, Alabama.

11. Hammond, I: 13–41.

Dynasty, the Manchurian conquest, European colonialism, the Nationalists led by Sun Yat Sen and Chiang Kai Shek, and the communist conquest of 1949. But a detailed study of these developments is beyond the scope of our study of ancient law.

Taoism

Several major religions have influenced the development of Chinese law and government. We will look first at Taoism. Its founder, Lao-tzu (also known as Lao tze, Laozi, Laotze),[12] is usually thought to have lived around 604–531 BC, though some scholars date him several centuries later. *Tao,* sometimes expressed "Dao" or "Do," literally means "the Way, " and Taoism's central tenet is that there is a natural order of things, the Tao.

The Tao is difficult to define. For the Taoist believer the Tao may occupy a place comparable to that of God, but unlike the western God, the Tao is an impersonal force. Taoists emphasize that the Tao that can be expressed is not the eternal Tao, so Taoist religion of necessity contains an element of mysticism, as all knowledge is partial and provisional. The Tao encompasses natural law, but it is more than that. It is a cosmic unity, a cosmic flow of energy, the first cause of the universe, a force that flows through all of life. If one lives in accordance with the Tao, one will enjoy Heaven's blessing and earthly success; to go against the Tao is like swimming against the current of a mighty river; one has to swim harder to succeed, and one probably will not succeed at all. The contemporary cliche, "Go with the flow," expresses Taoism well.

The yang and yin symbol is common to Taoism, though not unique to it. The white and black shapes are opposites, as male and female, hard and soft, light and dark, good and evil, but they complement each other and fit together in a circle, as together they are one and they flow out of the same source. And in the center of the dark mass is a small white dot, and a dark dot in the white mass, because all light has an element of darkness and all darkness has an element of light. And these endlessly flow in and out of each other, through the endless cycles of time.

12. *Tze* or *zi,* difficult to transliterate into a Western alphabet, simply mean "master teacher." We will see this title with many Chinese names.

Taoism teaches that man's goal should be non-interference with the Tao, or more properly, go with the Tao rather than against it. Going with the Tao can include doing what seems natural, preferring nature to civilization, going with gut instincts rather than systematic thought, being spontaneous and creative, probing into one's deepest consciousness, adjusting one's breathing patterns to the rhythms of the universe, ruling in accordance with the Mandate of Heaven, meditation, alchemy, dietary practices, learning to yield rather than resist, seeking the simple life. Like Rousseau two millennia later, Lao-tzu believed that man in the natural state was good but was corrupted by civilization. Many of the "soft" martial arts, like aikido, judo, ju jitsu, ninjitsu, tai chi, and some styles of kung fu, frequently incorporate Taoist philosophy and practice.[13]

Taoism incorporates older Chinese concepts, such as the yang and yin, the opposite principles of male and female, light and darkness, good and evil, all ultimately flowing from the same ultimate source, the Tao. Some say Taoism originally did not recognize a Supreme Being, but a host of gods and goddesses became incorporated into Taoist thought after Lao-tzu's death. Others insist these were always part of Taoism, and that the Tao itself is the Supreme Being, but Taoists would agree that the Tao is not a personal God like the Judeo-Christian God of the Bible.

Applying Taoism to law and government, one would see first a higher law, perhaps a form of natural law, to which human law and human government must conform. One would see, second, a skepticism about vigorous government action, even those programs designed to improve the lot of the people. Lao-tzu is quoted as saying,

> In the kingdom the multiplication of prohibitions increases the poverty of the people. The more implements to add to their profit the people have, the greater disorder is there in the state and clan; the more acts of crafty dexterity men possess, the more do strange contrivances appear; the more display there is of legislation, the more thieves and robbers there are. Therefore a sage has said: "I will do nothing, and the people will be

13. Two excellent books that discuss the martial arts and their philosophical/theological underpinnings are Major Forrest E. Morgan, *Living the Martial Way* (New York: Barricade Books, 1992), and Bob Orlando, *Martial Arts America: A Western Approach to Eastern Arts* (Berkeley, CA: North Atlantic Books, 1997). See also Keith D. Yates, "The Demystification of Ki," *Inside Karate*, March 1985, 6–7. For those who are interested in a Christian approach to the martial arts, the author recommends the publications of the Gospel Martial Arts Union (gmau.org) and Black Belts of the Faith, International (blackbeltsoffaith.com) (accessed 28 April, 2016).

> transformed of themselves; I will be fond of keeping still, and the people will of themselves be correct. I will take no trouble about it, and the people will of themselves become rich; I will manifest no ambition, and the people will of themselves attain to the primitive simplicity....
>
> In a little state with a small population I would so order it that though there would be individuals in it with the abilities of ten or a hundred men, there should be no employment for them; I would make the people, while looking upon death as a grievous thing, yet not remove elsewhere [to avoid it]."[14]

Elsewhere Lao-tzu stated,

> Those who are skilled do not dispute; the disputatious are not skilled.... When we renounce learning we have no troubles.... The sage constantly keeps men without knowledge and without desire, and where there are those who have knowledge, keeps them from presuming to act.... The ancients who showed their skill in practicing the Tao did so not to enlighten the people, but to make them simple and ignorant.... The difficulty in governing the people arises from their having too much knowledge. He who tries to govern a state by his wisdom is a scourge to it, while he who does not do so is a blessing.[15]

Taoist political theory is well summarized by the observation of Lao-tzu that a good ruler is feared by his people, a better ruler is loved by his people, but "the best of all rulers is but a shadowy presence," barely noticed by his people.[16] Thomas Jefferson would be pleased, having declared that "That government governs best which governs least"; likewise Henry David Thoreau, who said "That government governs best which governs not at all." And Ronald Reagan once quoted a Taoist proverb that governing a nation is like cooking a small fish; one shouldn't overdo it.[17]

---

14. Durant I: 654

15. Durant, I: 653.

16. *Tao Te Ching* (also called the Daodejing) Chapter XVII, verses 39–41; cf. Grant Hardy, *Great Minds of the Eastern Intellectual Tradition* (Teaching Company, 2011), Lecture, 7.

17. Hardy, Lecture 7. One might also note Texas Gov. Rick Perry's declaration in his 13 August 2011 announcement of his candidacy for President, that "I'll promise you this: I'll work every day to make Washington, D.C. as inconsequential in your life as I can." www.wsj.com/articles/SB100 01424053111904253204576510303805465220l (accessed 28 April, 2016).

Confucianism

Around the same time another Chinese thinker arose, known to the world as Confucius.[18] Living around 551–479 BC, Confucius served as prime minister of the Chinese state of Lu, but resigned around 495 BC to protest the king's evil ways. Some say Confucianism is a philosophy rather than a religion, but to the extent that Confucianism addresses basic questions like the nature of ultimate reality, the nature of man, and the purpose of existence, the distinction between philosophy and theology is difficult to draw.

Confucius's primary focus was the role of man in society: what virtues should be inculcated in people so that they will benefit society? In particular, Confucius contemplated the character and role of the "superior man." Drawing upon ancient Chinese concepts of yang and yin, Confucius taught that the way of the superior man was a golden mean, a life of balance between extremes. The superior man should be taught cardinal virtues such as loyalty to the state, duty to parents, and veneration of ancestors. Duty to parents and veneration of ancestors provides continuity with the past and a respect for habit and tradition; loyalty to the state means not just blind obedience but active and dedicated service.

Confucius was concerned that people should learn to live together peaceably. To do so, they need to understand their respective roles in society, beginning with their roles in the family as a microcosm of the wider society. He stressed what he called the Five Great Relationships: ruler and subject, father and son, husband and wife, elder and younger brother, and friend and friend. Each relationship, and each role in that relationship, involves both reciprocity and hierarchy, with superiors and subordinates, and mutual obligations and responsibilities.

The superior man should develop certain virtues that will facilitate these Five Great Relationships; the four most important virtues are sincerity, benevolence, filial piety, and propriety. Confucius stressed the importance of ritual (called *li)* in developing these virtues and understanding the Great Relationships.

To the westerner, Confucianism might seem very restrictive. But the restrictions were largely by social custom. By weaving together a fabric of social control consisting of respect for family, worship of ancestors, loyalty to government, and adherence to custom, Confucius hoped to

18. "Confucius" is actually a Western Latinized version of Kong Fu Zi.

foster a closely knit society in which government control could be kept to a minimum. And in practice Confucianism was tempered by Taoism. In many ways, the Taoist heritage of individual freedom, laissez-faire government, social primitivism, and mystical self-transformation is the antithesis of Confucian moral duties, community standards, and governmental responsibilities. But they did manage to co-exist, partially because neither believed truth to be absolute. Confucianism had greater appeal among the wealthier and better-educated classes, while Taoism held sway among the common people.

It is sometimes said that Confucius did not believe in any gods or spiritual reality, and that supernaturalism was added to the system by later Confucian thinkers. But Professor Giles disagrees. He acknowledges that Confucius depersonalized God by always referring to Him as T'ien rather than Shang Ti. But he sacrificed to the spirits and is quoted as saying that "he who offends against God has none to whom he can pray."[19] He believed in a higher moral law which took precedence even over duty to parents and government.[20] Confucius' rather ambivalent attitude toward religion might be summarized in his utterance, "respect the spirits, but keep them at a distance."[21] The later Confucian philosopher Mencius (372–289 BC) tied this higher moral law into the "Mandate of Heaven" and formulated a right to revolution when a regime, through disregarding the higher moral law, had the Mantle of Heaven lifted from itself and placed upon another regime.[22] And Confucius gave a warning from history:

> Before the sovereigns of the Shang [Dynasty] had lost [the hearts of] the people, they were the mates of God. Take warning from the house of Shang. The great decree is not easily preserved.[23]

Between these twin poles, Confucianism and Taoism, Chinese thought and political theory moved for hundreds of years. Confucian regimentation and Taoist laissez faire balanced one another, and the Tao and the bureaucracy held each other in check. By no means could ancient China be thought democratic or even republican; the Chinese had known

19. Giles, op cit., 22.

20. Giles, op. cit.; cf. Durant, I: 671.

21. Giles, op cit., 21.

22. Durant, I: 673, 682–86.

23. Durant, I: 671.

monarchy throughout their history and accepted it as the natural order. The philosopher Mo Ti (Mozi) tried to preach a personal God and a doctrine of universal love and peace. He incurred the opposition of Yang Chu who argued that there is no God, that life is full of suffering, and that the purpose of life is pleasure. Mencius (or Men Ke) argued against both positions, saying,

> The words of Yang Chu and Mo Ti fill the world.... Now Yang's principle is, "Each for himself"—which does not acknowledge the claims of the sovereign. Mo's principle is "To love all equally"—which does not acknowledge the peculiar affection due to a father. To acknowledge neither king nor father is to be in the state of a beast. If their principles are not stopped, and the principles of Confucius set forth, their perverse speaking will delude the people, and stop up the path of benevolence and righteousness.[24]

Mencius remonstrated against wickedness in high places and threatened revolution as the remedy:

> The King Hsuan asked about the high ministers.... Mencius answered: "If the princes have great faults, they ought to remonstrate with him; and if he do not listen to them after they have done so again and again, they ought to dethrone him."[25]

As Professor Hardy says, "Confucianism is associated with hierarchy, order, social responsibility, conformity, moralism, activism, service, and seriousness. Daoism prefers individualism, freedom, noncomformity, nature, retirement, tranquility, mysticism, and wit. Both are wary of competition, confrontation, and coercion; both are attractive and have much to teach us about how to live the best life."[26]

Over the centuries, Confucian regimentation and Taoist laissez faire, Confucian activism and Taoist passivity, Confucian passion for civilized culture and Taoist return to nature, balanced one another, while the Confucian higher moral order and Mandate of Heaven formed some common ground with Lao-tzu's Tao. But in the first century AD another religion challenged both.

---

24. Durant, I: 681–82.

25. Durant, I: 685–86.

26. Hardy, Lecture 7; Course Guidebook, 22.

Buddhism

Buddhism wasn't really a new religion. It began around 500 BC and was imported to China from the "west"—India. But over the next five centuries Buddhism took hold in China as it never had in India, and the Chinese in turn gave Buddhism a distinctively Oriental character.

Around 500 BC a young prince in northern India named Siddhartha Gautama was anguished over the pain and sadness in the world and sought an answer to the problem of human suffering. He began with the basic principles of Hinduism: a pantheon of gods and goddesses, all manifestations of one ultimate reality, belief in the *atman* or human soul, and belief in the transmigration of souls (reincarnation). Good and bad *karma* determine one's future existences, and by working off one's bad *karma*, fulfilling one's *dharma* (duty), and perfecting one's *atman*, one could be liberated from the cycle of reincarnation and enter the eternal state of Nirvana. But he found all of this unsatisfying, so he wandered across India searching for the answer. Death was not the answer, because that would only lead to rebirth and new anguish. He tried study, fasting, asceticism, and everything he could think of to find the answer.

Then one day, while meditating under a Bodhi tree, the young prince received a sudden enlightenment, after which he became known as the Buddha, or enlightened one. The solution to the problem of suffering, he concluded, is found in the Four Noble Truths: (1) Suffering is part of the normal life of people; (2) Suffering is caused by our attachment to material things; (3) The way to be free of suffering is to be free from these attachments to material things; and (4) People can free themselves from these attachments through meditation and renunciation.[27]

The best way to meditate is to follow the Eightfold Path: (1) Right View; (2) Right Intention; (3) Right Speech; (4) Right Conduct; (5) Right Livelihood; (6) Right Effort; (7) Right Mindfulness; and (8) Right Concentration.[28]

Like Christianity with its many denominations, Buddhism has divided into various schools. Theravada Buddhism stresses that people must work

27. Hammond, I: 30. These Four Noble Truths are sometimes stated in different ways. Dr. Scott Shaw states them this way: (1) All beings are bound by *karma* (the law of cause and effect) and, thereby, are subject to suffering. (2) The cause of suffering is desire. (3) The chain of suffering can be broken by obtaining enlightenment. (4) Enlightenment is obtained by following the path of *dharma*. Scott Shaw, *The Warrior Is Silent: Martial Arts and the Spiritual Path* (Rochester, VT: Inner Traditions, 1998), 11.

28. Shaw, 11.

out their own salvation without help from the gods, by means of an ascetic existence. Mahayana Buddhism taught that Siddhartha Gautama had become a divine being, and that many other enlightened Buddhas have come and will come. Bodhisattva Buddhism taught that every person could potentially become a god by awakening the Buddha within. And Zen Buddhism turned inward, stressing the inner life of contemplation.[29]

Buddhism began making inroads into China during the 1st century AD, especially in northern and western China, and was a major force by AD 500. During the Tang Dynasty several rulers, such as the Empress Wu Zetian (AD 690–705) and the Emperor Xuanzong (AD 713–756) were devout Buddhists. Buddhism and Taoism shared many common beliefs, such as the subjective view of truth, the cyclical concept of time, a monistic view of reality, pantheism, a pantheon of impersonal gods, and the inner life of contemplation, and their followers formed an uneasy synthesis.

But Buddhists and Confucians clashed bitterly. The Buddhist life of contemplation contrasted with the Confucian ideal of the man of excellence, and the Confucian who venerated his ancestors and believed he would be blessed after death as his descendants venerated him, despaired at the thought that his descendants might forsake the old ways and become celibate Buddhist monks. As Durant says,

> For a thousand years the Taoist faith had millions of adherents, converted many emperors, and fought long battles of intrigue to wrest from the Confucians the divine right to tax and spend. In the end it was broken down not by the logic of Confucius, but by the coming of a new religion even better suited than itself to inspire and console the common man. For the Buddhism that began its migration from India to China in the first century after Christ was not the hard and gloomy doctrine that the Enlightened One had preached five hundred years before; it was no ascetic creed, but a bright and happy faith in helping deities and a flowering paradise.... When, after the fall of the Han [Dynasty, circa AD 220], China found herself torn with political chaos, and life seemed lost in a welter of insecurity and war, the harassed nation turned to Buddhism as the Roman world was at the same time turning to Christianity. Taoism opened its arms to take in the new faith, and in time became inextricably

29. Major Forrest Morgan, *Living the Martial Way* (New York: Barricade Books, 1992), 240–45; cf. Hammond, I: 30–31.

> mingled with it in the Chinese soul. Emperors persecuted Buddhism, philosophers complained of its superstitions, statesmen were concerned over the fact that some of the best blood of China was being sterilized in monasteries; but in the end the government found again that religion is stronger than the state; the emperors made treaties of peace with the new gods; the Buddhist priests were allowed to collect alms and raise temples, and the bureaucracy of officials and scholars was perforce content to keep Confucianism as its own aristocratic creed. The new religion took possession of many old shrines, placed its monks and fanes along with those of the Taoists on the holy mountain Tai-shan, aroused the people to man pious pilgrimages, contributed powerfully to painting, sculpture, architecture, literature, and the development of printing, and brought a civilizing measure of gentleness into the Chinese soul. Then, it, too, like Taoism, fell into decay; its clergy became corrupt, its doctrine was permeated more and more by sinister deities and popular superstitions, and its political power, never strong, was practically destroyed by the renaissance of Confucianism under Chu Hsi. [AD 1130–1200][30]

In the third century AD Buddhism gradually gave way to neo-Confucianism. Nevertheless, Durant says, Buddhism has "sunk into the national soul, and is still part of the complex but informal religion of the simpler Chinese. For religions in China are not mutually exclusive as in Europe or America, nor have they ever precipitated the country into religious wars. Normally they tolerate one another not only in the state but in the same breast; and the average Chinese is at once an animist, a Taoist, a Buddhist and a Confucianist. He is a modest philosopher and knows that nothing is certain; perhaps, after all, the theologian may be right, and there may be a paradise; the best policy would be to humor all these creeds, and pay many diverse priests to say prayers over one's grave."[31]

Together, Taoism, Confucianism, and Buddhism form the basic values of the Chinese nation, influenced in turn by other Oriental cultures: the Japanese, the Koreans, the Manchurians, the Tibetans, and the Mongols. How, then, does this mixture affect Chinese law and government? Georges Padoux says of Chinese jurisprudence,

30. Durant, I: 786–87.

31. Durant, I: 787.

Since the dawn of its history, China has believed in the existence of a natural order of things, or law of Nature, including all parts of the universe and adjusting them harmoniously with one another. This order of Nature was not made; it exists and is its own reason for existence. Humanity is a part of it, and must conform to it. And as the elements in this order of Nature are interdependent, whatever affects one element reacts on the others also....

The consequences of this theory in the field of law and government and of justice may be readily perceived; here are the most important:

This natural law does not yield precedence to positive law, i.e., laws representing human experience and wisdom. Positive law ought to confine itself to translating the natural law into written formulas. If this translation is correct, the written law is good and binding; if the translation is incorrect, i.e., if the prince or the governor in formulating his decrees has misinterpreted the law of nature, the written law is not binding. A Chinese will regard as binding a rule promulgated even by doubtful constitutional authority if he deems it conformable to "the edicts from on High"; and he will deem himself free to disregard it if he finds it in disaccord with the natural law....

[T]he Confucian philosophers never formulated or defined the natural law even in its broad lines; but... in general the Chinese look to Moderation, Humanity, Equity, as the governing idea for social relations. The conception of strict logical law, independent of the purpose in hand and the personality of the parties to a dispute, remains an alien notion. The Chinese does not conceive of an absolute right or wrong in law.

It follows that in general, he seeks a middle road, the golden mean, a compromise which will "save the face," an adjustment by settlement between the differing contentions. The magistrate, for the Chinese, is a friendly arbitrator, rather than a dominating authority bound to declare the law and to secure its respect....

And finally, since positive law is the expression of natural law, its violation, even of rules purely civil (as we should say), will involve at the same time a penal sanction, for it will be a breach of the preexisting order of nature,—a transgression liable to cause dangerous disturbance in the community.[32]

32. *Philosophy of Life,* trans. from Georges Padoux (Peking: China Booksellers Ltd., 1926); quoted by Wigmore, I: 143–45.

Because the Oriental concept of truth is more subjective than that of the West, the law of nature and the concept of justice will turn to some extent on the personalities involved, rather than on purely abstract legal principles. Therefore, Dean Wigmore says, the western concept of a "government of laws and not of men" gives way to a more subjective and personal view of law. He quotes Confucius as saying,

> Let there be Men, and Government will flourish. But without the right men, government decays. Therefore the success of government lies in getting proper men. If you lead the people correctly, who will dare not to be correct? Hence the institutions of a ruler are rooted in his own character and conduct.[33]

A primary goal of the Chinese legal system was to resolve disputes by compromise or mediation rather than declaring one party right and the other wrong. Dean Wigmore says, "The 'struggle for rights,' which the great German jurist, von Ihering, inculcated as the basis of civic law and order, is alien to Chinese thought. An unyielding insistence on principle, and a rigid demand for one's due, are almost as reprehensible as a vulgar physical struggle. Moral force, and the 'rule of reason,' should control, rather than strict technical rights. Compromise is the highest virtue; intolerance and obstinacy, a mark of defective character. Nothing is so important that it cannot be compromised for human welfare or comfort or dignity. Hence the significance (so misunderstood by the Occidental) of 'saving the face,' i.e., of obtaining a respectable compromise in a dispute."[34]

The earliest known legal code of China is the Chow Li, or Regulations of Chow, dating from the Chow Dynasty around 1100 BC. A legal code properly consists of Lu, which is the unchanging legal text, and Li, the annual edicts and judicial interpretations which interpret and apply the Lu.[35] Lu seems to reflect the law of nature, while Li is the positive law that seeks to implement the law of nature. When Lu and Li are in harmony, the Mandate of Heaven rests upon the nation and its rulers. Chinese law codes generally made no distinction between civil and criminal law; even civil violations carry civil penalties because they breach public order.

Another important concept of Chinese thought is *chi*, sometimes written ch'i, ki, or qi, a "life force" or "energy field" that may be comparable

33. Confucius; quoted by Wigmore, I: 145.

34. Wigmore, I: 150.

35. Wigmore, I: 158–62.

to the Dao in Taoism. *Chi* plays an important role in Oriental philosophy, medicine, feng shui, martial arts, and other fields. It pervades all things and may also be developed within each person.[36]

An Arab traveler around AD 850 wrote that the Chinese "administer justice with great strictness in all their tribunals."[37] An incident of criminal justice is recorded by a Portugese merchant named Perera around AD 1560. Perera and his party had been mistaken for pirates and arrested; they resisted and several Chinese deaths ensued. Perera and his party were understandably apprehensive as they faced the justice of a foreign court, but the Chinese judges found them innocent and punished the Chinese officials who had wrongfully arrested them. Perera wrote,

> Now I will speake of the maner which the Chineans doe observe in doing of justice, that it may be known how farre these Gentiles do herein exceed many Christians, that be more bounden then they to deale justly and in trueth.... We poore strangers brought before them might say what we would, as all to be lyes and fallaces that they did write, ne did we stand before them with the usuall ceremonies of that Countrey; yet they did beare with us so patiently, that it caused us to wonder, knowing specially how litle any advocate or Judge is wont in our Countrey to beare with us. For wheresoever in any Town of Christendome should be accused unknowen men as we were, I know not what end the very innocents' cause would have. But we, in a heathen Countrey, having our great enemies two of the chiefest men in the whole Towne, wanting an interpreter, ignorant of that Countrey language, did in the end see our great adversaries cast into prison for our sake, and deprived of their Offices and honour for not doing justice,—yea not to escape death: for, as the rumour goeth, they shal be beheaded.[38]

The Chinese judicial system was a unique blend of Confucian professionalism, Taoist passivity, and Buddhist compassion. As Durant says, "If the

36. A good discussion of *chi* may be found in Bob Orlando, *Martial Arts America: A Western Approach to Eastern Arts* (Frog, Ltd., 1997), 123–48.

37. Wigmore, I: 154–55.

38. Wigmore, I: 155–56. Where possible, when quoting early documents, we will retain the original spelling, punctuation, capitalization, and grammar. Rules of spelling, punctuation, capitalization, and grammar have changed over the centuries, and in earlier times these rules were often unsettled. This writer believes retaining these documents in their original form helps us understand the spirit of the times.

ideal state is a combination of democracy and aristocracy, the Chinese have had it for more than a thousand years; if the best government is that which governs least, then the Chinese have had the best. Never has a government governed so many people, or governed them so little, or so long."[39]

Governmental authority flowed from the top down, rather than from the bottom up as in Western thought. In theory, the emperor ruled by divine right; "he was the 'Son of Heaven' and represented the Supreme Being on earth. By virtue of his godlike powers he ruled the seasons and commanded men to coordinate their lives with the divine order of the universe. His decrees were laws, and his judgments were the final court; he administered the state and was the head of its religion; he appointed all officials, examined the highest contestants for office, and chose his successor to the throne."[40] But in practice he was limited by custom and law, and a special officer called a Censor could rebuke him at any time for a breach of duty.[41] If he did not follow the higher law of nature, the "Mandate of Heaven" could be lifted from him and made to fall upon another. Not uncommonly, a strongman might consider himself the instrument of Heaven to remove the Mandate from one king and place it upon another, such as himself. Despite its seeming absolutism, Chinese thought did make room for resistance.

The emperor was surrounded by a Grand Council composed of four Great Ministers and by a group of advisers called the Inner Cabinet. The administration was divided into departments of civil office, revenue, ceremonies, war, punishments, and works.[42]

The empire was divided into provinces (*sheng*), the provinces into circuits (*tao*), the circuits into areas each ruled from a city (*fu*), these areas into towns (*hein*), and the towns into villages. The local village was ruled by a headman appointed by the central government and surrounded by a council of the heads of families. Trials were rare; people preferred to resolve their disputes by mediation if possible, and in many towns years could pass without a single case coming to court. A common saying was, "Win your lawsuit, lose your money." When they did take place, trials were simple, partly because lawyers were not allowed in court, although notaries could prepare and read statements in court. There were no juries, so

39. Durant, I: 795–96.

40. Durant, I: 797–98.

41. Durant, I: 798.

42. Durant, I: 798.

litigants were at the mercy of the judges; but the judges usually respected custom as reflecting the will of the people.[43]

And here is an irony: while individual rights were a foreign concept to China, government was limited and people did possess considerable freedom. As Durant says,

> the concept of the individual was weak, and lost him in the groups to which he belonged. He was, first of all, a member of a family and a passing unit in the stream of life between his ancestors and his posterity; by law and custom he was responsible for the acts of the others of his household, and they were responsible for his. Usually he belonged to some secret society, and, in the town, to a guild; these limited his rights to do as he pleased. A web of ancient custom bound him, and a powerful public opinion threatened him with ostracism if he seriously violated the morals or traditions of the group. It was precisely the strength of these popular organizations, rising naturally out of the needs and voluntary cooperation of the people, that made it possible for China to maintain itself in order and stability despite the weakness of law and the state.[44]

Since 1949, China has been ruled by a Marxist regime. Was the communist coup an accident of history, a well-planned operation of international Marxist strategists, or a natural result of thousands of years of Chinese thought and practice?

Certainly the impersonal nature of the deity in Chinese thought made Marxist atheism more palatable than in a Western society with a belief in a transcendent and personal God. And certainly traditional Chinese concepts of the state over the individual and the absence of a well-developed concept of individual rights made communist regimentation easier to achieve than in a society based on the belief that all men are "endowed by their Creator with certain unalienable rights."

But is China truly an atheistic nation today, or does the worship of Shang-Ti and T'ien still lurk beneath the surface?

And how will the next chapter of China's history read, after the Mandate of Heaven has been lifted from the present regime?

---

43. Durant, I: 796–97.

44. Durant, I: 796.

Questions for Reflection, Discussion, and More Reflection

1. What parallels can you cite between Chinese philosophical thinkers and those of the West? Despite these parallels, are there genuine differences between Eastern and Western modes of thought? If so, how would you characterize those differences?
2. What is the Tao in Chinese thought? Is the Tao comparable to the Western concept of God, or to the Law of Nature? What are some of the implications of Taoism for law and government?
3. Is the Oriental concept of *yang* and *yin* compatible with Western Christianity and Judaism? In what ways are they fundamentally different?
4. Is Confucianism a religion, a philosophy, or both? How does Confucianism impel its followers toward good citizenship? What did Confucius mean by the "Mandate of Heaven"? How does the Mandate of Heaven fit with the concepts of Li, Lu, Dao, and Chi? Do these concepts have a Western scientific explanation?
5. How does Buddhism address the problem of human suffering?
6. How and why have Taoism, Confucianism, and Buddhism conflicted with one another in matters of government and social policy?
7. How could China maintain a tight system of social control with a minimum of government intrusion?
8. How could China maintain a fair system of justice with neither juries nor lawyers?
9. How can a secular society practice emperor-worship? Are secularism and state-worship inconsistent, or does atheism naturally lead to state-worship?
10. Did the Chinese religious systems (Taoism, Confucianism, and Buddhism) facilitate the Communist takeover of China in the 1940s? Do these systems provide a way of freeing China from Communist domination?

but not necessarily that they in fact *did* so. Recent genetic testing points to Southeast Asia as the most likely place of origin.[2]

Separated by thousands of miles, the various Polynesian subgroups probably had little contact with each other. But they retained many similar beliefs and customs. Martha Beckwith, in her classic work *Hawaiian Mythology,* describes the Polynesians as a "nature-worshipping people."[3] But Daniel Kikawa, in his book *Perpetuated in Righteousness,* argues convincingly that the Hawaiian people originally were monotheistic, worshipping a triune god whom they called Io who had three personalities, Kane, Ku, and Lono, and that as time passed the Hawaiian people lost contact with Io and degenerated into polytheism.[4]

Beckwith explains further,

> Among Hawaiians the word for god (akua) is of indeterminate usage. Thus any object of nature may be a god; so may a dead body or a living person or a made image, if worshiped as a god. Every form of nature has its class god. . . .[5]

She continues:

> An animistic philosophy thus conditions the Hawaiian's whole conception of nature and of life. Much that seems to us wildest fancy in Hawaiian story is to him a sober statement of fact as he interprets it through the interrelations of gods with nature and with men. Another philosophic concept comes out in his way of accommodating himself as an individual to the physical universe in which he finds himself placed. He arrives at an organized conception of form through the pairing of opposites, one depending upon the other to complete the whole. So ideas of night and day, light and darkness, male and female, land and water, rising and setting (of the sun), small and large,

---

2. Thor Heyerdahl, *Kon Tiki: Across the Pacific by Raft* (Skokie, IL: Rand McNally, 1950); Howard Wolinsky, "Our History, Our Genes," *EMBO Reports;* http://www.nature.com/embor/ ournal/v9/n2/full/7401164.html (accessed 28 April, 2016).

3. Martha Beckwith, *Hawaiian Mythology* (Honolulu: U of Hawaii Press, 1940, 1976), 1.

. Daniel Kikawa, *Perpetuated in Righteousness: The Journey of the Hawaiian People from Eden ana i Hauola) to the Present Time,* 4th Ed. (Aloha Ke Akua Publishing, 1994); the title is taken the Hawaiian motto Ua Mau Ke Ea O Ka Aina I Ka Pono; translation: The Life of the Land etuated in Righteousness; cf. Don Richardson, *Eternity in Their Hearts* (Regal Books 1981, 124–28.

kwith, 2.

> little and big, hard and light (of force), upright and prostrate (of position), upward and downward, toward and away from (the speaker) appear paired in repeated reiteration as a stylistic element in composition of chants, and function also in everyday language, where one of a pair lies implicit whenever its opposite is used in reference to the speaker. It determines the order of emergence in the so-called chant of creation, where from lower forms of life emerge offspring on a higher scale and water forms of life are paired with land forms until the period of the gods (po) is passed and the birth of the great gods and of mankind ushers in the era of light (ao). It appears in the recitation by rote of genealogies in which husbands and wives are paired through literally hundreds of generations. It is notable that in similar genealogies such as the Hebrew, in which, as introduced by the missionaries, Hawaiians showed extraordinary interest, males alone are recorded.[6]

Beckwith says the Hawaiians originally recognized four primary gods. Ku was a great ancestral god who, with his wife Hina (note the Hawaiian pairing of opposites) had general control over the fruitfulness of the earth and of mankind.[7] Kane was also a god of procreation and was the ancestor of chiefs and commoners, who formed the three worlds—the heaven of the gods, the heavens above the earth, and earth itself.[8] Lono was the god of the waters and was associated with cloud signs and storms.[9] Kanaloa (also called Milu) was the god of the underworld and was associated with disease, poison, death, and evil.[10] Kane and Kanaloa are paired as opposites: "Kane draws the figure of a man in the earth, Kanaloa makes one also; Kane's lives, but Kanaloa's remains stone. Kanaloa is angry and curses man to die."[11] Beckwith refers to

> a tendency by Hawaiian antiquarians to equate Kanaloa with the Christian devil. His name is associated with various legends of strife against Kane in which Kanaloa and his spirits rebel and are sent down to the underworld. In the legend of Hawaii-loa

6. Beckwith, 3.
7. Beckwith, 3, 12–30.
8. Beckwith, 3, 42–66.
9. Beckwith, 3, 31–41.
10. Beckwith, 3, 60–66.
11. Beckwith, 60–61.

> belonging to the Kumu-honua epic account of the Kane tradition, Kanaloa is the leader of the first company of spirits placed on earth after earth was separated from heaven. These spirits are "spit out by the gods." They rebel, led by Kanaloa, because they are not allowed to drink awa, but are defeated and cast down to the underworld, where Kanaloa, otherwise known as Milu, becomes ruler of the dead.[12] [cf. Genesis 3; Isaiah 14:12–15; Revelation 12:1–9]

These four, and a host of lesser gods associated with each of them, make up the Polynesian pantheon.

Beckwith says the gods are represented as "chiefs dwelling in far lands or in the heavens and coming as visitors or immigrants to some special locality in the group sacred to their worship."[13] Some believe the gods were originally human, great chiefs who were deified after their deaths. However, Beckwith believes they were originally conceived as nature deities and later associated with human figures.[14] The Hawaiians in particular seemed to think of Tahiti, from whence their ancestors had come in the 700s and conquered the original Hawaiians, as the home of the gods. "The plot of many Hawaiian romances and hero tales turns upon such a claim to relationship with a chief in Tahiti through whom the child of the humbler parent lays claim to divine lineage."[15]

According to the conventional view, the Hawaiians lived in awe or fear of their gods, and human sacrifice was a regular means of appeasing them. But some believe the earlier Hawaiians still remembered the one supreme God Io and worshipped him until the Tahitian priest and navigator Paao arrived around AD 1300. As noted earlier, Kikawa believes that the ancient Hawaiians worshipped Io as a trinitarian god of three personalities, Kane, Ku, and Lono;[16] obviously the evil god Kanaloa would not be part of this trinity. Abraham Fornander claims that before Paao arrived, "the kapus were few and the ceremonials easy; human sacrifices

12. Beckwith, 60.

13. Beckwith, 3.

14. Beckwith, 4.

15. Beckwith, 6.

16. Kikawa, 54–55. The Let Us Reason website contains an attempted refutation of Kikawa's theory. www.letusreason.org/Current68.htm (accessed 28 April, 2016).

were not practiced; and government was more of a patriarchal than of a regal nature."[17]

Hawaiian society was a complex religious, governmental, and cultural system that reflected the Hawaiians' view of their place in nature, governed by *kapus* (from which we get our word "taboo") or divine edicts that keep society in order. Central to the *kapu* system was a strict caste society, reflecting each person's place in the divine order. This caste structure is very similar to that which the Aryan invaders may have imposed on Hindu India, and if the Tahitian invaders subjugated rather than eradicated the indigenous Hawaiian population, they may have imposed the caste system to keep their subjects in order.

The highest caste was the *alii,* chiefs who ruled specific territories. These chiefs were considered to be descendants of the gods, and the highest chiefs (*alii kapu*) were considered to be gods. They ruled with a divine power called *mana,* which seems to be a spiritual energy comparable to what the Orientals call *ki* or *chi.*

The next caste was the *kahuna,* priests and skilled craftsmen, who performed religious functions and also served as advisers to the chiefs.

Third was the largest caste, the *makaainana,* the commoners who comprised the working class.

Last was the *kauwa,* outcasts similar to the Hindu untouchables, who performed the most menial tasks and whose status was little better than slaves. They included prisoners captured in the frequent wars among the various Hawaiian chieftains, and they were often used for sacrifices to the gods.[18]

"Religion held ancient Hawaiian society together, affecting habits, lifestyles, work methods, social policy, and law."[19] The religious *kapu* covered all aspects of life from work to hunting and fishing to eating to sex, and was especially forward-looking on matters relating to the environment. The shadow of the chief must not be touched, because that would be stealing his *mana.* Hawaiians distinguished between *kapu akua,* the laws of the gods, and *kapu alii,* the laws of the chiefs. The laws of the

17. Abraham Fornander, *An Account of the Polynesian Race;* quoted at www.alternative-hawaii.com/hacul/history.htm (accessed 28 April, 2016).

18. *Id.*; see also wikipedia.org/wiki/Ancient_Hawaii (accessed 28 April, 2016).

19. Wikipedia, *Id.*

gods, *kapu akua*, were the most important; but since the chiefs were lesser gods, the *kapu alii* had divine sanction as well.[20]

The chiefs ruled with nearly absolute power, conducted trials themselves without the aid of juries, and could command death at will, even for an accidental violation of a *kapu*. But the *kapu akua* also provided for pardon, clemency, absolution, and mercy.[21] The law also provided for a place of refuge to which one accused of a crime could flee for sanctuary, similar to the *cities of refuge* of Old Testament Israel (Numbers 35, Joshua 20, Deuteronomy 19:2). In general, the ancient Polynesians seem to have been a gentle people, but at times they were capable of great cruelty. In this, of course, they were far from alone.

The first recorded European discovery of the Hawaiian Islands is that of English Captain James Cook in January 1778, but Hawaiian legends tell of earlier visits by white persons. Spanish or Dutch expeditions, and possibly a Japanese expedition as early as the 1500s, may have taken place.[22] Captain Cook himself noted that the Hawaiians possessed a few pieces of iron that appeared to have been left by previous Spanish visitors.[23] He commented extensively on the comeliness, friendliness, gentleness, and honesty of the Hawaiian people,[24] and the Hawaiians themselves seemed to think Captain Cook was the god Lono returned to them. However, Lieutenant James King later observed that "The satisfaction we derived from their gentleness and hospitality was, however, frequently interrupted by their propensity to stealing, which they have in common with all the other islanders of these seas."[25] Lt. King also noted the people's quick obedience to the orders of their Chiefs and commented, "The authority of the Chiefs over the inferior people appeared, from this incident, to be of the most despotic kind."[26]

20. *Id.*

21. *Id.*

22. *World Book Encyclopedia,* "Hawaii," op. cit. IX: 104.

23. James Cook, *Captain Cook's Voyages 1768–1779* (London: Folio Society, 1997), 401.

24. Cook, 392–404, 462–67.

25. Cook, 479. Captain Cook himself wrote the account of his voyage except for the last two chapters, which were written by Lt. King after Captain Cook was killed in a confrontation with Hawaiians on February 14, 1779. Perhaps this encounter sobered Lt. King's evaluation of the islanders.

26. Cook, 469.

Captain Cook's visit brought Hawaii's relative isolation to a close. A war broke out among the islands' various chiefs in 1782, and one chief, Kamehameha, with the aid of firearms obtained from European traders, succeeded uniting most of the islands under his control by 1795. He reigned as Kamehameha the Great until 1819 and engaged in extensive trade with Europe, Asia, and America.[27]

More changes were in store for Hawaii. The first Protestant missionaries arrived from New England in 1820, followed by Catholic and Mormon missionaries, and the timing of their arrival was providential. After Kamehameha the Great died in 1819, one of his wives, Queen Ka'ahumanu, declared herself co-ruler with Kamehameha's 19-year-old son Liholiho (by another wife, Queen Keopuolani). The two queens persuaded King Liholiho to abolish the old *kapu* legal system. This created widespread disorder, so when the missionaries arrived a year later, the islands were ripe for new moral direction. They listened carefully to the missionaries, noting many similarities to their own beliefs, and most of them accepted Christianity with enthusiasm. The missionaries translated the Bible into the Hawaiian tongue, served as advisors to the royal family, established schools and churches, produced Hawaiian newspapers and textbooks, and introduced Western medicine and other practices.[28]

By 1840 the Kingdom of Hawaii was ready for a Constitution and Declaration of Rights. The Declaration of Rights begins with a quotation from Acts 17:26:

> *"God hath made of one blood all nations of men to dwell on the earth,"* in unity and blessedness. God has also bestowed certain rights alike on all men and all chiefs, and all people of all lands.
>
> These are some of the rights which He has given alike to every man and every chief of correct deportment; life, limb, liberty from oppression; the earnings of his hands and the productions of his mind, not however to those who act in violation of laws.
>
> God has also established government, and rule for the purpose of peace; but in making laws for the nation it is by no

27. *World Book Encyclopedia,* "Hawaii," IX: 104–06.

28. "Maui History 101," http://hawaiian-roots.com/missionaries.htm (accessed 28 April, 2016).

> means proper to enact laws for the protection of the rulers only, without providing protection for their subjects. . . .[29]

The 1840 Constitution begins,

> It is our design to regulate our kingdom according to the above principles [found in the preceding Declaration of Rights] and thus seek the greatest prosperity both of all the chiefs and all the people of these Hawaiian Islands. But we are aware that we cannot ourselves alone accomplish such an object—God must be our aid, for it is His province alone to give perfect protection and prosperity.—Wherefore we first present our supplication to HIM, that he will guide us to right measures and sustain us in our work.
>
> It is therefore our fixed decree,
>
> I. That no law shall be enacted which is at variance with the word of the Lord Jehovah, or at variance with the general spirit of His word. All laws of the Islands shall be in consistency with the general spirit of God's law.
>
> II. All men of every religion shall be protected in worshipping Jehovah, and serving Him, according to their own understanding, but no man shall ever be punished for neglect of God unless he injures his neighbor, or brings evil on the kingdom. . . .[30]

The 1840 Constitution establishes the king as a constitutional monarch and sets forth his powers including his service as "chief judge of the Supreme Court, establishes a Premier who was appointed by the king, divides the kingdom into four provinces headed by four governors subject to the king and the premier, establishes a legislative branch similar to the English parliament in that it consists of a House of Nobles appointed by the king and a Representative Body elected by the people.[31]

---

29. "Kingdom of Hawaii Constitution of 1840," www.hawaii-nation.org/constitution-184.html (accessed 28 April, 2016).

30. *Id.* (emphasis original). The protection of every religion "in worshipping Jehovah" had not always been practiced. According to *World Book Encyclopedia,* "Hawaii," X: 196, the Catholic missionaries who arrived in 1827 faced stiff Protestant opposition; in 1831 they were expelled and many Catholics were imprisoned. In 1839 the French frigate *L'Artemise* blockaded Honolulu and its captain threatened to destroy the town if all of the imprisoned Catholics were not released and given religious freedom. The Kingdom of Hawaii relented, and the 1840 Constitution reflects that limited tolerance.

31. "Kingdom of Hawaii Constitution of 1840," *Id.*

A new Constitution of 1852 also recognized that "God hath created all men free and equal and endowed them with certain unalienable rights…," and that "All men are free to worship God according to the dictates of their own consciences; but this sacred privilege hereby secured, shall not be so construed as to justify acts of licentiousness or practices inconsistent with the peace or safety of this Kingdom."[32] This Constitution reaffirms the constitutional monarchy under the authority of God but reflects a Christian natural law philosophy.

In 1893, a bloodless revolution overthrew the monarchy and established the Republic of Hawaii, which became a territory of the United States in 1898, leading to statehood for Hawaii in 1959.[33]

Despite the changes, the laws of the State of Hawaii still recognize traditional Hawaiian customary law to some extent, particularly in the area of property law.[34]

And through their many changes, the Hawaiians have always recognized that their laws came from God, or the gods, whoever they may be.

Questions for Reflection, Discussion, and More Reflection

1. Discuss the various theories of the origin of the Polynesians. Which theory seems most likely to you? Was the Polynesian settlement of Hawaii an intentional colonization, or the accidental result of shipwreck?

Questions continued on next page….

32. "Kingdom of Hawaii Constitution of 1852," www.hawaii-nation.org/constitution-1852.html (accessed 28 April, 2016).

33. *World Book Encyclopedia,* "Hawaii," IX: 106. Many claim the revolution was really a coup led by wealthy American planters, but this is disputed by others. Some call for sovereignty for Hawaii, or part thereof, and special land privileges for those of Hawaiian ancestry; but others strongly disagree. See, "Kanaka Maoli (Hawaiian People) Subjected to Genocides at the Hands of U.S. and State," www.hawaii-nation.org/turningthetide-6-2.html (accessed 28 April, 2016); Kenneth R. Conklin, Ph.D., "Whose Land Is It? Hawaiian Spirituality, Kingdom Law, and Modern Law All Support Racial Equality," www.angelfire.com/hi2/hawaiiansovereignty/landequalityspiritlaw.html (accessed 28 April, 2016). [arguing that the spirit of equality of the ancient Hawaiian laws precludes sovereignty exclusively for those of Hawaiian ancestry].

34. See, for example, *Oni v. Meek,* 2 Haw. 87 (1858); *Public Access Shoreline Hawaii v. Hawaii County Planning Commission,* 79 Haw. 425, 903 P.2d 1246 (Haw. 1995), cert.den., 115 S.Ct. 1559 (1996); *Kalipi v. Hawaiian Trust Co.,* 66 Haw. 1, 656 P.2d 745 (1982); *Pai Ohana* 875 F.Supp. 680 (D. Haw. 1995), affirmed 76 F.3d 280 (1996); *Pele Defense Fund v. Paty,* 73 Haw. 578, 837 P.2d 1247 (1992), cert. den., 507 U.S. 918 (1993). See also, Damien P. Horigan, "Some Aspects of Law in Hawaii," *Journal of South Pacific Law,* Article 1, Vol. 5, 2001.

Questions *continued*

2. Does the evidence support Daniel Kikawa's theory that the Polynesians were originally monotheists, worshipping a triune God with whom they later lost contact?
3. If Kikawa is correct, how should that affect methods and approaches to Christian evangelism?
4. What does the term *kapu* mean, and how did the *kapu* system result in a caste society?
5. What was the distinction between *kapu akua* and *kapu alii?* Does this distinction have a counterpart in Western legal thought?
6. Explain the structure of Hawaiian government before European discovery. What parallels do you see between their judicial system and that of Old Testament Israel? What contrasts?
7. Why did the Hawaiian people embrace Christianity with such enthusiasm? Could this reflect dissatisfaction with their old religion and despotic rule of the chiefs?
8. The 1840 Constitution and Declaration of Rights has been called the most Christian in the world at that time. Do you agree? What were some of its distinctively Christian features?
9. Explain the process by which the Kingdom of Hawaii became a territory (and later a state) of the United States. Was this a popular revolution, or an American-orchestrated coup? Consider the long-range scheme of things: Did the American acquisition of Hawaii in 1898 prevent Japan from over-running Hawaii and the rest of the Pacific at the beginning of World War II?
10. Currently there is an indigenous movement to restore the old *kapu* law to Hawaii. Based upon the cases and authorities cited in a footnote at the close of this chapter, is this movement likely to succeed? Should it succeed?

CHAPTER 7

INCA:
Law—Short, Swift, and Severe

As we move to the western hemisphere, several observations are necessary.

First, time and space preclude us from covering every American Indian system of law and government. At least 500 Indian nations existed in North America alone, and many more in South America. We will focus upon five to provide a good cross-section: the Incas of South America, the Maya of Central America, the Aztecs of Mexico, the Cheyenne of the American west, and the Iroquois Confederacy of the American northeast.

Second, "Indian" is admittedly an imperfect term, given by Columbus who thought he'd reached islands off the coast of Asia. But consider the alternatives. Regardless of race, everyone who was born in America can claim the term "native American." "Aborigine" may be accurate, but it has negative connotations of primitiveness and is often associated with a particular group, the Bushmen of Australia. Accordingly, we will use the term "Indian" because, despite its inadequacies, no better term exists.

Third, at the time of their "discovery" by Europeans, these various Indian nations did not consider themselves "Americans." That term originated in the 1500s and may have come from an Italian writer named Amerigo Vespucci; he wrote about the land across the Atlantic; hence "Amerigo's land, although alternative explanations have been proposed. By 1492 the people of Europe were just beginning to think of themselves as Europeans; formerly they had considered themselves Franks, or Lombards, or Visigoths, Saxons, and the like. Only with the advent of the Crusades did they even begin to develop a pan-European identity. Likewise, there was little if any pan-American identity among Indians. They considered themselves Algonquin, or Cherokee, or Arapaho; and a

Chippewa would have felt no more cultural affinity with a Tlingit than he would feel with an Englishman or a Norseman.

Fourth, all American Indians are not necessarily related to one another, and uncertainty exists about their origin. The most common belief is that all American Indians descended from a common group of ancestors who migrated from Siberia to Alaska across the Bering Strait or possibly across a land bridge that then connected Siberia and Alaska. But others believe at least some American Indians descended from Polynesians who crossed the Pacific (perhaps involuntarily). Still others suggest that some Indians, possibly the Olmecs who preceded the Maya in the Yucatan, came from Africa or the Middle East. In the future, DNA testing may provide new answers to the question of Indian origins.

Fifth, except for the Maya, we cannot trace the legal and governmental history of American Indian institutions over 4,000 years as we can with ancient peoples of the Old World. Most did not have a system of writing except for pictographs. The Aztecs and Maya had written languages, but the Spanish conquerors considered their writings formulas for devil-worship and destroyed many of them. (In fairness we should note that when the Aztecs conquered Mexico they destroyed the writings of the Toltecs who preceded them, and throughout history this has been a common practice of conquerors.) So while this book purports to be a study of ancient law, some of the Indian laws and customs described in this chapter can be traced back only a few centuries.

Finally, as we shall see, the various Indian nations differed greatly in their systems of law and government, as in their dress, customs, and philosophical and religious beliefs. Most of them lived close to nature and deeply respected nature, sometimes to the point of pantheism (equating nature with God). Many believed in a host of nature gods and spirits. But like other people who live close to nature, many believed in a sky-god who is above all others, calling him Gitchie Manitou, Wakonda, the Great Spirit, and many other terms. Is this polytheism evolving into monotheism, or original monotheism degenerating into polytheism?

With these qualifying observations, let us journey first to the Andes Mountains of South America.

Of all the great buildings of ancient America, none are more breathtaking than those of ancient Peru. The Inca capitol Cuzco, is magnificent with its great walls and its gold-gilt Temple of the Sun, as is the great fortress Sacsayhuaman located just outside Cuzco. Of equal magnificence is Machu Picchu, the mountaintop fortress complex of temples, palaces, and observatories where, it is believed, the ruling class lived. These structures were built with stones of up to 200 tons (400,000 pounds) and up to 16 feet high, which had been quarried 35 miles away and fitted together so tightly that one cannot slip a penknife between them. Held together, they have stood through the centuries and are virtually earthquake-proof. Scholars disagree as to whether the Incas built these structures or whether they had been built by earlier cultures and occupied by the Incas after they conquered that area around AD 1200.[1]

The Inca Empire was knitted together by thousands of miles of roads, with runner/messengers placed at relay stations so they could carry messages up to 250 miles per day. These roads covered seashores, jungles, and mountains and were connected together over mountain gorges by a series of suspension bridges up to 330 feet in length. Made of rope from plant fibers, one such bridge was built around AD 1350 and was used for over 500 years until it was abandoned in 1890.

For all of their accomplishments, the Incas had no wheeled vehicles, no beasts of burden except llamas, no iron tools, no coinage, and no system of writing except for *quipu*, a device from which were suspended short knotted strings. The colors of the strings and the intervals between the strings and their knots conveyed a message, and a trained *quipucamayo* or memory expert could read the *quipu* and understand its message. After the Spanish conquest, the Incas lost the ability to read the *quipus*, and modern scholars have not yet been able to decipher them.[2]

In the long run of Peruvian history, the Inca Empire was a comparatively recent development. Much about this history is unclear because of the lack of a written language, but early civilizations seem to have settled in the coastal areas from around 1250–850 BC. Around 850 BC the Chavin

---

1. New evidence suggests that civilization in Peru is far older than was previously thought. Archeologists have uncovered a city known as Caral that is believed to date back to around 3,000 BC. Located in the mountains near the coast at an elevation of 11,500 feet, it appears to have been a planned community, with pyramid-shaped public buildings, an amphitheater complex, residential buildings, and a population up to 10,000—all predating the likely date of the construction of Egypt's earliest pyramids. www.crystalinks.com/incancd.html (accessed 28 April, 2016); http://www.labyrinthina.com/caral.htm (accessed 28 April, 2016).

2. William A. Fowler, "Origins of the Incas," http://autocww2.colorado.edu/~blackmon/E64ContentFiles/HistoryOfTheAmericas/IncaEmpire.html (accessed 28 April, 2016). A *quipu* has been found in a public building at the ancient Caral site described in footnote 1 above. The 1996 discovery of the "Ica stones" may indicate more advanced knowledge and communication, but their authenticity has yet to be established. Douglas Phillips, *Mysteries of the Ancient World* (Vision Forum CD album, 2009).

culture arose, known for its remarkable weaving, pottery, and agriculture which included a series of terraces on the mountainsides. Textiles and pottery were advanced in the Salinar culture from around 350 BC to AD 100, and around this time arose the Moche culture which built massive pyramids, and the coastal Nazca culture known for its petroglyphs and Nazca Lines in the coastal desert.

The first known true empire of the Andes was the Wari. Starting around AD 700, the Wari Empire conquered much of Peru and imposed their own culture and values upon the conquered peoples. But rivals arose, and the Wari Empire was overthrown around AD 1100. For several hundred years several rival states vied for power in Peru.[3]

One such rival group was the Incas, who lived by Lake Titicaca in southeastern Peru on the Chilean and Bolivian borders. Around 1200 the first Inca emperor, Manco Capac, led the Inca clans from Lake Titicaca to the valley of Cuzco, where they conquered the local tribes and began to establish the Inca Empire. The Incas then engaged in wars of conquest and expansion; and at its peak in the 1400s, the Empire covered about 350,000 square miles including about 2,500 miles of coastline and included about nine million people. The Empire centered in the Andes mountains but extended to the Amazon jungles and the Pacific coast.[4]

The Incas were an intensely religious people whose religious worldview dominated every aspect of their lives. Their supreme god was the creator, Viracocha, and Richardson believes they worshipped this God in ancient times, but their memory of Viracocha faded with time as they descended into polytheism and worshipped Inti, the sun god, and various nature gods.[5] They also believed certain objects were sacred; these were called *huacas* (revered objects) and could include temples, or streams or rocks, or small amulets.

---

3. "Peru at a Glance," http://texcolca1.tripod.com/body/peru.html (accessed 28 April, 2016).

4. Fowler, *op. cit.*

5. Don Richardson, *Eternity in Their Hearts* (Regal 1981, 1984), 33–41. Richardson cites recently restored beautiful hymns and psalms apparently composed by the Inca King Pachacuti who reigned from 1438 to 1471. The Incas did not have a system of writing, but a Catholic priest named Christobel de Molina collected and transcribed them in AD 1575. Their style is so different from that of the Spaniards that various modern scholars have concluded that they must be of Inca origin. The hymns note that Inti the sun god must not be the greatest of all gods, because the sun as a created being cannot be greater than the Creator. Also, the sun always follows a fixed path and cannot do anything original. Furthermore, any passing cloud can dim our view of the sun; if Inti were the supreme god, nothing could dim his sight. The hymn concludes that Viracocha, not Inti, must be the supreme god, and the Incas should worship Him.

The Incas believed strongly in life after death. In the afterlife, the good enjoyed a life of luxury, tranquility, and ease, while the wicked dwelt in the center of the earth and expiated their sins through ages of wearisome toil, under the rule of an evil spirit named Cupay.

They worshipped, or at least venerated, the spirits of their ancestors. They mummified the bodies of their ancestors and considered them *huacas*, especially the bodies of nobles and rulers, and they would even consult these bodies for advice. In certain religious rituals the mummified bodies of past rulers were brought into the public square with great ceremony, paraded through the city as the people prostrated themselves in veneration, and even seated at elaborate stately dinners.[6]

The Inca religion was highly formal and included extensive ceremony and a large and elaborate priesthood. The priests were thought to have power to heal the sick, since illness was thought to result from the ill will of a god, and some priests were thought to have prophetic powers. The rituals included live sacrifices, usually llamas or guinea pigs, but sometimes humans, usually women and children.

As we have seen in other societies, scholars disagree as to whether Inca religion was originally monotheistic and degenerated into polytheism, or whether it began with nature-worship and developed into worship of the sun-god Inti and the creator-god Viracocha. Prescott notes that the Incas believed in a worldwide deluge similar to that of Genesis 6–8, and that they held a special religious festival which resembled the Christian Eucharist:

> A fine bread or cake, kneaded of maize flour by the fair hands of the Virgins of the Sun, was also placed on the royal board, where the Inca [term for King], presiding over the feast, pledged his great nobles in generous goblets of the fermented liquor of the country, and the long revelry of the day was closed at night by music and dancing.... In the distribution of bread and wine at this high festival, the orthodox Spaniards, who first came into the country, saw a striking resemblance to the Christian

6. William H. Prescott, *History of the Conquest of Mexico and History of the Conquest of Peru* (New York: Modern Library), 745. Prescott, whose scholarship in this area is unsurpassed, wrote on Mexico and Peru as separate books in the 1840s; they are published today as a combined volume. In footnote 51 on page 749 Prescott quotes an earlier writer, Sarmiento, as saying that only princes were honored in this way, "whose souls, the silly people fondly believed, on account of their virtues, were in heaven, although in truth, they were all the time burning in the flames of hell!"

> communion; as in the practice of confession and penance, which, in a most irregular form, indeed, seems to have been used by the Peruvians, they discerned a coincidence with another of the sacraments of the Church. The good fathers were fond of tracing such coincidences, which they considered as the contrivances of Satan, who thus endeavored to delude his victims by counterfeiting the blessed rites of Christianity. Others, in a different vein, imagined that they saw in such analogies the evidence, that some of the primitive teachers of the Gospel, perhaps an apostle himself, had paid to these distant regions, and scattered over them the seeds of religious truth. But it seems hardly necessary to invoke the Prince of Darkness, or the intervention of the blessed saints, to account for coincidences which have existed in countries far removed from the light of Christianity, and in ages, in deed, when its light had not yet arisen on the world. It is much more reasonable to refer such casual points of resemblance to the general constitution of mankind, and the necessities of his moral nature.[7]

The "Virgins of the Sun" referred to above were young maidens, taken from their homes and educated in convents, and prepared for a life of service to Inti the sun-god. But since the king (called the Inca) was a direct descendant of the sun-god, the Virgins of the Sun also served as his concubines, and because at any given time the Virgins of the Sun numbered around 1,500, the Inca had a harem larger than that of Solomon,[8] as well as hundreds or thousands of children.

Despite this harem, the Inca had only one wife. Since the Inca was a direct descendant of the sun-god, his wife was chosen from among his sisters so the lineage from the sun-god would remain pure. As for the rest of the people, the nobility were allowed multiple wives, but among the common people monogamy was the rule.

Since the Inca was of divine lineage, his edicts necessarily had divine sanction. Prescott describes the Inca society as a people "who claimed a divine original for the founders of their empire, whose laws all rested on a divine sanction, and whose domestic institutions and foreign wars were alike directed to preserve and propagate their faith. Religion was the basis

7. Prescott, 786–87.

8. 1 Kings 11: 1–3.

of their polity, the very condition, as it were, of their social existence. The government of the Incas, in its essential principles, was a theocracy."[9]

The Inca himself was taken at an early age and instructed by *amautas* or "wise men," in religion, ceremony, polity, and military science. He was then educated with other youth of the nobility and forced to undergo rigorous ordeals to develop his own physical prowess. Once he became king, he was set apart from the people as befitted one who considered himself divine. He wore the richest wool in the finest tones, ornamented by gold and precious stones, a many-colored turban, and a crown of rare bird feathers. As Prescott says,

> The government of Peru was a despotism, mild in its character, but in its form a pure and unmitigated despotism. The sovereign was placed at an immeasurable distance above his subjects. Even the proudest of the Inca nobility…could not enter his presence without removing their shoes and carrying a light burden on their shoulders as a token of homage. As the representative of the Sun, he stood at the head of the priesthood, and presided at the most important of the religious festivals. He raised armies, and usually commanded them in person. He imposed taxes, made laws, and provided for their execution by the appointment of judges, whom he removed at pleasure. He was the source from which everything flowed,—all dignity, all power, all emolument. He was, in short, in the well-known phrase of the European despot, "himself the state."[10]

Under the Inca were the nobility, which consisted of two orders. The first were those of common descent, those who were distant relatives of the Inca and therefore had some divine lineage, or whose ancestors had been the original Incas who came in the early days from Lake Titicaca. They wore distinctive dress, held the most important governmental posts, were exempt from taxation, and had certain public lands which were appropriated for their use and income.

The second order of nobility was the Curacas, the leaders of conquered nations. The reader will recall that the Babylonians and Assyrians commonly eliminated the leaders of conquered nations and tried to forcibly assimilate those nations into the Babylonian or Assyrian melting pot, while

9. Prescott, 776.

10. Prescott, 743–44. The "European despot" refers to King Louis XIV of France, who allegedly said "L'etat c'est moi" (The state, this is me).

the Persians allowed conquered nations to keep their previous leaders and customs so long as they swore allegiance to Persia. The Inca policy was somewhere between these extremes. They tried to impose a common language, and they required conquered nations to worship Inti the sun-god. But so long as they worshipped Inti as supreme, they were allowed to continue worshipping their own gods, and the images of those gods were taken to Cuzco and added to the Incan pantheon of lesser gods.[11]

And usually they allowed the conquered leader to keep his post, or if it was necessary to remove him, he was succeeded by his rightful heir. But first, like Daniel in the days of King Nebuchadnezzar of Babylon,[12] the Curacas and their families were taken to Cuzco for a time, where they learned the Inca language, manners, usages, and general policies of the government, after which they were returned to their respective lands to rule after the Inca manner. Often they had to leave their eldest sons in Cuzco as a guaranty of their fidelity. If a subject nation seemed insubordinate, the Incas would move part of their population, up to 10,000 people, to a remote part of the Empire, and move an equal number of persons from that part of the Empire to replace them. As these differing nations lived side by side, they jealously checked each other and kept each other from rebellion.[13]

The Inca kept close tabs on his subjects through excellent communications. As Prescott says,

> Intelligence from the numerous provinces was transmitted on the wings of the wind to the Peruvian metropolis [Cuzco], the great focus to which all the lines of communication converged. Not an insurrectionary movement could occur, not an invasion on the remotest frontier, before tidings were conveyed to the capital, and the imperial armies were on their march across the magnificent roads of the country to suppress it. So admirable was the machinery contrived by the American despots for maintaining tranquility throughout their dominions! It may remind us of the similar institutions of ancient Rome, when, under the Caesars, she was mistress of half the world.[14]

---

11. Prescott, 770.

12. Daniel 1.

13. Prescott, 750, 772–73.

14. Prescott, 766–67.

Cuzco itself was divided into four quarters, as a microcosm of the empire, The empire itself was divided into four provinces, each ruled by a viceroy or governor with the assistance of councils for the various aspects of administration. Beneath them, the people were subdivided into sections of ten thousand, and further subdivided into groups of a thousand, five hundred, one hundred, fifty, and ten, remarkably like Moses' division of Israel at the direction of the Midianite Jethro (Exodus 18:5–27), and remarkably like that of Anglo-Saxon England. Each of these subgroups had a headman who was responsible for those in his subgroup, both to ensure their welfare and to bring them to justice if needed.[15] Professor William R. Fowler of Vanderbilt University has calculated that for every 10,000 people there were 1,331 government officials.[16]

The Empire also had a multi-tiered court system with magistrates in the smaller villages exercising jurisdiction over petty offenses and superior judges in the larger districts with jurisdiction over major offenses. All judges were appointed by the Inca and could be removed at his pleasure, and they decided cases without juries. Unlike the American system in which cases drag on for years, the Inca judges were required to resolve every case that came before them within five days.[17] A committee of visitors traveled the kingdom to investigate the conduct of the magistrates and reported up the chain of command. While there was no right of appeal from one judge to another, the Inca could on his own initiative reverse or modify the judgments of lower courts and rectify any perceived injustices.[18]

Prescott observes that

> The laws were few and exceedingly severe. They related almost wholly to criminal matters. Few other laws were needed by a people who had no money, little trade, and hardly any thing that could be called fixed property. The crimes of theft, adultery, and murder were all capital; though it was wisely provided that some extenuating circumstances might be allowed to mitigate the punishment. Blasphemy against the Sun, and malediction

15. Prescott, 752–53.

16. Fowler, *op. cit.*

17. Prescott, 753, 755. Prescott says the "Spaniards, familiar with the evils growing out of long-protracted suits, where the successful litigant is too often a ruined man, are loud in their encomiums of this swift-handed and economical justice." (755).

18. Prescott, 753–54.

> of the Inca,—offenses, indeed, of the same complexion,—were also punished with death. Removing landmarks, turning the water away from a neighbor's land into one's own, burning a house, were all severely punished. To burn a bridge was death. The Inca allowed no obstacle to those facilities of communication so essential to the maintenance of public order. A rebellious city or province was laid waste, and its inhabitants exterminated. Rebellion against the "Child of the Sun," was the greatest of all crimes.[19]

Land was divided into three categories: one for the Sun, one for the Inca, and one for the people. The land reserved for the Sun was worked to provide revenue for the temples and the priestly class. The land reserved for the Inca was worked to provide revenue for the Inca and his government. The remaining land was divided in equal shares per capita among the people, and this division was altered each year as the population changed. The people were required to till all three categories of land. First they worked the land of the Sun, and then they worked the land of the people, first tilling the land of those who were unable to till their own because of military service, infirmity, or other reasons, and then they could work their own land to support themselves. Finally, with great ceremony, they tilled the land of the Inca.[20]

This overview demonstrates that while the Inca Empire left little room for individual freedom, it was superbly well-organized and managed.

Like the missionaries who came to Hawaii in 1820, the Spanish conquistadors arrived in Peru at a providential or at least an opportune time. The Inca Empire had reached its peak around AD 1493, when Huayna Capac became the Inca. He died in AD 1525, along with his son and chosen heir. His remaining sons, Huascar and Atahualpa, engaged in a destructive civil war until 1532, when Atahualpa captured and executed Huascar. In that same year, Francisco Pizarro and his conquistadors landed on the coast of Peru and made their way inland to Cuzco. Weakened by civil war, the Incas at first worshipped Pizarro as the creator god Viracocha returned. These factors enabled the Spaniards to quickly conquer Cuzco and most of the Empire. The nobility held out for 36 years in the mountain fortress of Vilcabamba and finally fell in 1572.[21]

19. Prescott, 754.

20. Prescott, 757.

21. Fowler, *op. cit.*

We still have much to learn about the Incas. The Spaniards and their successors occupied most of the Inca territory, but the lofty fortresses were virtually inaccessible and lost in the mountain mists. The mountaintop city of Machu Picchu was rediscovered in 1911, and the last Inca stronghold Vilcabamba was rediscovered in 2002. Thousands of mummies, including ice mummies in the high Andes, are being discovered and analyzed. Archeology has uncovered advanced cities on the Pacific coast of South America and in the Nazca desert of Peru, and increasing evidence indicates that great civilizations once flourished in the Amazon jungle.[22] Who knows what secrets they will impart?

Questions for Reflection, Discussion, and More Reflection

1. What parallels do you see between Christianity and the religion of the Incas, and between the governmental structure of Old Testament Israel and that of the Incas? What, if any, conclusions would you draw from these parallels?
2. What do you see as the best features of Inca culture? What are the worst?
3. What evidence do you see that the Inca Empire was a centrally-planned society? What freedom, if any, existed among the Incas?
4. Describe the Inca criminal justice system. Do you think it possible for a court system to operate that quickly and do real justice? What is the proper balance between speed and efficiency verses thoroughness and fairness?
5. Does the lack of a writing system pose a formidable barrier to the effective administration of justice? What problems does it cause?
6. Why was the emperor's sister his only real wife? How did his divinity affect the validity of his decrees?
7. Why was the emperor kept in such extreme isolation from his subjects? Was this an effective way of maintaining control?

Questions continued on next page....

22. David Grann, *The Lost City of Z* (Vintage Books 2005), chronicles the expeditions of Colonel Percy Fawcett in which he searched for a lost civilization in the Brazilian jungle, and presents considerable evidence that such a civilization once existed.

Questions *continued*

8. Can the Inca government really have been as efficient and effective as historians suggest, when over 13% of all Incas served as government employees?
9. There are indications that the Inca Empire had already begun to collapse by AD 1532, when Pizarro and the Conquistadors arrived. What might have been the causes of that collapse?
10. At the time of this writing (AD 2011), much exploration and research concerning the Incas and neighboring tribes is underway. What new discoveries have taken place since that date, and what is the significance of those discoveries?

Inca ruins from Sacsayhuamán, near the town of Cusco, Peru. 2005.

Chapter 8

Maya: *Shining Cities, Built on Blood*

Long before the Incas became an empire, the dense jungles of the Yucatan peninsula of southeastern Mexico, as well as Honduras, Belize, and Guatemala, had already hidden from view an empire whose achievements rivaled that of the Incas. The Maya civilization developed a writing system about the time Rome was founded (circa 753 BC), established a hierarchical government of kings and nobles as Rome was rising to power, entered a golden age while Rome was entering its decline, continued to enjoy that golden age until around AD 900, when the cities in the southern lowlands suddenly and mysteriously collapsed. The magnificent temples at Copan and Tikal, the great palaces of Palenque and Xpuhil, the observatory at Chichen Itza, and hundreds of other sites, demonstrate a culture unequaled by anything in the Western Hemisphere at that time, and equaled by few anywhere in the world.

Like the Incas, the Maya were not the first to inhabit their part of the world. The Olmec culture began perhaps 1500 BC—a date that fresh archeological discoveries are regularly pushing backward—but little is known of its origins. Some believe it was an indigenous Indian culture, others that the Olmec migrated from or had contact with Asia, Africa, Egypt, or the Middle East. But the growing consensus is that the Olmec were the first advanced major civilization in the Western Hemisphere. By at least 900 BC the Olmec had developed a complex society governed by kings and priests, employed a syllabic system of writing and began building pyramids arranged around large plaza areas, a buried system of stone drain lines, a detailed calendar, and impressive statuary including colossal monolithic human heads ranging from five to eleven feet tall, the features of which are thought by some to appear African. At one time the Olmec were thought to be monotheistic, worshipping only the rain god, but further studies of Olmec art have revealed that the Olmec worshipped a pantheon of at least ten distinct gods, most of whom were the same gods worshipped in Central America generally.[1] Possibly the earliest Olmec worshipped one God, and polytheism was a later development. The extent to which the Maya learned from and borrowed from the Olmec culture is still uncertain.

Unlike the Incas, the Mayas developed an alphabetical system of writing and left detailed records of their history, customs, and beliefs. But after the decline and fall of the Maya Empire AD 900–1250, the surviving Maya lost the ability to read these inscriptions. And after the Spanish conquest of the 1500s, the Spanish missionaries considered the Maya writings to be formulas for devil-worship and destroyed many of them. Four major codices survived, and numerous smaller inscriptions, and many more have been discovered, but no one knew how to read them until the code was finally cracked in the 1900s. Reading these inscriptions tells us much about the Maya civilization, and we are learning more as archeology and translation continue.

The Maya had a mathematical system more advanced than anything known in Europe at that time, and they developed or inherited a calendar far more accurate than any calendar of the Old World. Their advanced mathematics also had a religious significance, as the Maya practiced astrology and numerology. Michael D. Coe, Professor of Anthropology and Curator of the Peabody Museum of Natural History at Yale University, says Maya mathematics and astronomy had reached a level comparable to that of the ancient Babylonians and surpassing in some respects that of the Egyptians. But he adds, "Science in the modern sense was not present. In its place we find, as with the Mesopotamian civilizations, a combination of fairly accurate astronomical data with what can only be called numerology, developed by Maya intellectuals for religious purposes."[2] The discovery of "new" inscriptions, coupled with our new-found ability to read Maya hieroglyphics and the Maya calendar, have unlocked the history of the Maya city-states. As Martin and Grube demonstrate in *Chronicle of the Maya Kings and Queens: Deciphering the Dynasties of*

1. See generally, "Olmec Civilization 1200 BC–AD 600," www.crystalinks.com/olmec.html (accessed 28 April, 2016); "The Olmec," www.mesoweb.com/olmec/ (accessed 28 April, 2016); "The Decipherment of the Olmec Writing System" Abstract of Paper presented at the 1997 Central States Anthropological Society Meeting, http://olmec98.net/olmecDecip.htm (accessed 28 April, 2016).

2. Michael D. Coe, *The Maya 4th Ed.* (New York: Thames and Hudson, 1966, 1987), 161.

the Ancient Maya, we are now able to trace the reigns of the various royal dynasties to the exact year and often the exact day.[3]

Like many Orientals, the Maya had a cyclical view of time. They believed the earth and the universe went through cycles of creation and destruction. Each of these cycles lasts around 5,200 years, and our current cycle began with creation in the year 3114 BC and ended [without the predicted destruction] on AD December 23, 2012.[4]

Coe says the Maya conceived of a flat, four-cornered earth, with a multi-tiered sky supported at the four corners by four gods called Bacabs. They pictured the earth as the back of a monstrous crocodile resting in a pool filled with water lillies and the sky as a double-headed serpent.[5] But Humbatz Men believes that is an overly literal interpretation, and the Maya worshipped forces of nature and understood complex concepts of astronomy. For example, the letter for "G" in the Maya alphabet actually represents the spiraling Milky Way.[6] According to Men, the Maya believed people are composed of several elements: the physical body, an ethereal material comparable to body heat, the mind, and the vital essence of energy.[7]

The Maya believed in many gods, which represented forces of nature and which often had differing aspects and differing names, and many of the gods had a goddess as a counterpart.[8] Some Maya codices (scripts) speak of a one-and-only god named Hunab Ku, who was incorporeal and omnipotent,[9] which could indicate an earlier monotheism. But Coe believes the Maya worshipped as a primary deity, Itzamna, who may have also been the sun-god Ah Kinchil, and whose wife was Ix Chel, the moon goddess. All other gods and goddesses are progeny of Ah Kinchil and Ix Chel. The sun god, during his nightly journey under the earth, becomes the fearsome Jaguar god of the underworld. Other important gods were

---

3. See generally, Simon Martin and Nikolai Grube, *Chronicle of the Maya Kings and Queens: Deciphering the Dynasties of the Ancient Maya* (London: Thames and Hudson, 2000).

4. Martin and Grube, 164. Others insist that this was an inaccurate or overly-literal reading of the Maya calendar and prophecies.

5. Martin and Grube, 164–65.

6. Humbatz Men, *Secrets of Mayan Science/Religion* (Santa Fe: Bear & Co., 1990), 34–39. Men's thesis is interesting, but he may be imposing upon the Maya the modern concepts of the New Age.

7. Men, 47. Same comment as in the footnote above.

8. Coe, *op. cit.,* 165.

9. Coe, 166.

the benevolent Chacs, the rain gods, and Kukulcan, the god of the ruling caste, who may be the Mayan counterpart of the Aztec Quetzalecoatl.[10]

The Maya believed in life after death, though apparently not in reincarnation.[11] After death one enters the underworld, known as Xibalba, the "Place of Fright."[12] But after a period of purgation, one would be resurrected and reborn as a star in the heavens, which also meant becoming a god.

A central feature of Mayan religious thought, like that of the Zapotec, Mixtec, Aztec, and other Central American societies, was the concept of a vital force that separated living from nonliving matter. This vital force seems similar to the Oriental concept of *ki* or the Hawaiian *mana.* The Maya called it *ik,* the Zapotecs *pi,* the Mixtecs *yni* or *ini,* and the Aztecs *tona.* As Robert Sharer describes Maya thought,

> All things, whether animate or inanimate, were imbued with an unseen power. In some cases—especially the "spirits" inhabiting rocks, trees and other objects (a concept we call animism)—the invisible power was amorphous. In other cases the unseen power was embodied in a "deity" perceived to take animal-like (zoomorphic) or humanlike (anthropomorphic) form.... In its normal state the world was seen as an ordered place. Order, the foundation of the Maya world, stemmed from the predictable movements of the "sky wanderers," the sun, moon, planets, and stars that marked the passage of time. Each of these celestial bodies was animate, a deity by our definition. Human destiny was linked with these celestial beings, and when cataclysmic events overwhelmed the Maya world, as they did from time to time, the sky wanderers and the calendar based books of prophecy would be consulted to find portents of change. Once found and recorded, such portents explained the disorder that had fallen upon the world and thus allowed the world order to be restored.[13]

10. Coe, 166.

11. This seems to be the majority view, but it is not unanimous. Martin and Grube, for example, think the Maya did believe in a form of reincarnation, sometimes with deceased persons being reincarnated in their grandchildren. Martin and Grube, *op. cit.,* 16.

12. Martin and Grube, 166–68. Xibalba, and the seven (or nine) Lords of Xibalba, figure prominently in the mythology of many Indians of the Southwest.

13. Robert Sharer, 1994: 514, www.angelfire.com/ca/humanorigins/religion.html (accessed 28 April, 2016).

In Maya thought, human society is a microcosm of the universe, and what happens on earth, what happens in our local society, affects the course of the heavens, and likewise the course of the heavens affects events on earth. As Sharer says, "The places where the Maya lived, from the smallest house to the largest city, were conceived of as symbolic representations of their universe."[14] The universe was engaged in a cosmic struggle between the forces of good and the forces of evil, and a primary mission of Maya society was to aid the forces of good, in particular the sun god, in his battle against the forces of evil. Schele and Miller put it well:

> For the Maya, the world was a complex and awesome place, alive with sacred power. This power was part of the landscape, of the fabric of space and time, of things both living and inanimate, and of the forces of nature—storms, wind, smoke, mist, rain, earth, sky, and water. Sacred beings moved between the three levels of the cosmos, the Overworld which is the heavens, the Middleworld where humans live, and the Underworld of Xibalba, the source of disease and death. The king acted as a transformer through whom in ritual acts, the unspeakable power of the supernatural passed into the lives of mortal men and their works. The person of the king was also sacred. His clothing reflected more than wealth and prestige: it was a symbolic array identifying rank, ritual context, and the sacred person he manifested.[15]

Reciprocity is another central feature of Maya thought. As David Carrasco, Professor of History and Religions at the University of Colorado, explains, "In the Maya world, as in many religious traditions, humans and gods have a relationship based on some form of mutual care and nurturance. The gods create humans, who are therefore in their debt. The ongoing existence of human life depends on the generous gifts of life, which the gods continue to dispense through children, germination, rain, sunshine, the supply of animals, and objects of power. But the gods are also dependent beings, at least in the Maya world. They depend on humans to care, nurture, acknowledge, and renew their powers."[16]

---

14. Sharer, 1994: 523–26.

15. Linda Schele and Mary Elen Miller, *The Blood of Kings: Dynasty and Ritual in Maya Art* (Fort Worth: Kimbell Art Museum, 1986), 300; quoted by David Carrasco, *Religions of Mesoamerica* (San Francisco: Harper Collins, 1990), 94.

16. Carrasco, 107.

One way of aiding the sun god and the forces of good was to engage in wars of subjugation against the surrounding nations. Restoring order on earth helped to restore order in the heavens. Another was to sacrifice to the sun god, and the sacrifice needed most was human blood. In theory at least, becoming a sacrifice to the sun-god was considered a high honor and privilege, and at first only nobles could be sacrificed. The victim sacrificed to the sun-god did not descend to the underworld but rather ascended directly to the heavens and became a star/god. Apparently this incentive did not produce enough willing victims, so as time went on, the Maya increasingly used prisoners of war for divine sacrifices, and wars therefore increased:

> Maya religion was probably the major ideological justification for the Maya political, military, and economic institutions. By building temples, for example, the rulers enhanced their own prestige and authority to rule, and created social unification. The use of war to obtain captives for sacrifice probably overlapped nicely with a ruler's desire to militarily "decapitate" neighboring polities to obtain economic tribute and eventually to expand their territory. Building pyramidical structures also probably reinforced and reminded the people of their place in the pyramidal hierarchy and structure of society....
>
> Both the Classic Maya and Zapotec systems linked politics, religion, economics, and social organization. Both systems required the effort of the masses to be harnessed in large community building projects related to religion and politics and justified wars against neighboring groups in cosmological terms that required human sacrifices to keep the universe in balance and food abundant.[17]

A blood sacrifice to the gods, however, did not always require the death of a victim. Bloodletting was a ceremonial act that gave reciprocity to the gods and accompanied a rite of passage for the bloodgiver. These rites of passage included birth, puberty, marriage, becoming a warrior or priest, death, and life after death. Just as caves could be passageways to and from Xibalba, so a sacrificial wound could be a passage through which gods could enter the world. Carrasco says, "The opening or passageway for this passage was the wound in the human body and blood. This opening was

17. www.angelfire.com/ca/humanorigins/religion.html (accessed 28 April, 2016).

especially crucial for lords seeking to become rulers. For it was through bloodletting that a real reciprocity was achieved. On the one hand the royal person was passing to a higher social and sacred status, that of the supreme ruler. On the other hand the gods were passing into the world of humans to be reborn. The Maya gave blood in order to receive a vision in which the gods and ancestors appeared in the world of the ceremonial center and in order to perceive the spiritual presence of their ancestors."[18]

Carrasco describes bloodletting as the "mortar of Maya life" because it integrated the levels of the cosmos and various social groups into a sense of wholeness. Bloodletting was practiced at the dedication of buildings and monuments, the birth of children, marriage ceremonies, public events, and rites of passage.[19] Male and female blood were each thought to have special significance, and blood from the genitals was thought especially potent. Those who gave blood often cut themselves in special patterns that somehow gave the sacrifice greater potency.[20] By giving blood, the Maya engaged in world-centering and world-renewing;[21] that is, he helped to stabilize the cosmos and give it new life.

In these bloodletting ceremonies, the king played the preeminent role. Schele and Freidel describe these royal bloodgiving ceremonies in intricate detail.[22] The kings were descended from sacred lineages, and their bodies contained divine fire and energy. Through special rituals their actions brought the divine into the terrestrial level of existence. The king was considered the "center of everything in heaven and earth."[23] His authority to rule came from cosmic beings, and his power was therefore immense. As Carrasco explains, this pattern of rulership was

> based on four basic assumptions lodged in the Maya worldview. First, it was believed that a powerful cosmic order permeated every level and dimension of the world from the heavens, through the clouds, through the things on the earth, and into

18. Carrasco, *op. cit.*, 110.

19. Carrasco, 110.

20. Carrasco, 110–13; cf. Linda Schele and David Freidel, *A Forest of Kings: The Untold Story of the Ancient Maya* (New York: Quill, 1990), 68–71, 89, 202, 233–35, 281, 286, 426–27, 447.

21. Carrasco, 105–06.

22. Schele and Freidel, generally; see esp. 233–35.

23. Carrasco, 103.

> the realms of the underworld. Second, it was believed that human society would be stable as long is it operated as a microcosm or approximate imitation of the cosmic order constructed by the gods. Third, it was the role of the sacred kings to align the social world of the humans with the supernatural world of the gods. Fourth, the king had to demonstrate through ritual his line of descent from the first ancestor who was the source of sacrality. The main technique for Maya kings to bring the social and supernatural world into alignment was ritual action.[24]

Coe says the "ancient Maya realm was no theocracy or primitive democracy, but a class society with strong political power in the heads of an hereditary class."[25] The top class was the nobles, or *almehen*, who held the top governmental and military positions and included wealthy landowners and priests. Beneath them were the commoners or free workers. Below them were the serfs who worked the lands of the nobles, and at the bottom were the slaves, largely captives taken in war and frequently sacrificial victims.[26]

Little is known about the political structure of the Maya Empire during the pre-classical era. It seems to have consisted of small city-states, each of which controlled the surrounding area and maintained suzerainty relationships with each other. Each of these was headed by a territorial ruler (called a *halach uinic)* who inherited his throne through his male bloodline. He appointed headmasters (*batabs*) over each of the smaller villages, who ruled with the assistance of a council of wealthy old men. The batab served as a manager, a judge, and a war leader.

More is known about the classical era (AD 300–900), but even then, the empire does not seem to have been unified under one head. The city-states still retained considerable independence and were loosely joined with others in a confederation. Each of these city-states had its own king, and occasionally a king seemed to rise above the others. One such ruler was Pacal the Great, who ruled the City of Palenque for sixty-eight years. From the precision of Maya records we learn that he was born AD March 23, 603, became king on AD July 26, 615, and reigned until his death AD August 28, 683.[27]

24. Carrasco, 104.

25. Coe, 159.

26. Coe, 159–60.

27. Martin and Grube, 162.

The Maya practiced primogeniture, that is, the eldest son normally was next in line for succession after his father the king died. The new king took office in an elaborate investiture ceremony replete with religious significance.

Until archeologists cracked the Maya code and learned to read their inscriptions, the Maya were generally thought to have been a peaceful nation. But the consensus has shifted, because the Maya chronicles reveal incessant warfare. As Coe says,

> The Maya were obsessed with war. The Annals of the Cakchiquels and the Popol Vuh speak of little but intertribal conflict among the highlanders, while the sixteen states of Yucatan were constantly battling with each other over boundaries and lineage honor. To this sanguinary record we must add the testimony of the Classic monuments and their inscriptions. From these and from the eye-witness descriptions of the conquistadores we can see how Maya warfare was waged. The holcan or "braves" were the footsoldiers; they wore cuirasses of quilted cotton or of tapir hide and carried thrusting spears with flint points, darts-with-atlatl, and in late Post-Classic times [AD 900–1100], the bow-and-arrow. Hostilities typically began with an unannounced guerrilla raid into the enemy camp to take captives, but more formal battle opened with the dreadful din of drums, whistles, shell trumpets, and war cries. On either side of the war leaders and the idols carried into the combat under the care of the priests were the two flanks of infantry, from which rained darts, arrows, and stones flung from slings. Once the enemy had penetrated into home territory however, irregular warfare was substituted, with ambuscades and all kinds of traps. Lesser captives ended up as slaves, but the nobles and war leaders either had their hearts torn out on the sacrificial stone, or else were beheaded, a form of sacrifice favored by the Classic Maya.[28]

The southern cities of the Maya Empire collapsed around AD 900 and, the rest of the empire declined and finally fell around AD 1250. Scholars disagree as to the cause. We do know that in the 900s the Toltecs from the north, perhaps pushed south by the Aztecs, began making incursions on Mayan territory, and occupied some of that territory themselves, expanded upon the building of some of the great cities like Chichen Itza,

28. Martin and Grube, 160.

and may have merged with the Maya civilization.[29] But this does not fully explain the collapse.

The destruction of the Maya Empire is variously attributed to foreign invasion, epidemic, famine, or economic collapse. A popular explanation is that the rural commoners revolted against the nobility who lived in the cities and exterminated them. But the commoners then found that they had no idea how to run the cities, being unable to read the Mayan codices, so they abandoned the cities and reverted to the primitive life of the jungle. After the Spanish conquest, some of the same missionaries who had destroyed the Maya codices, tried diligently to reconstruct Maya history, but found the surviving Mayans of little help since they could not read the Mayan script and had little understanding of classical Mayan science or theology. The friars took the legends of the commoners and compiled them into a work called the *Popul Vuh*,[30] but it is at best an incomplete record.

The fascination of the Maya lies in part in that which is hidden from view. Because of the lack of codices, and our inability to read what inscriptions we have until recently, scholars' attitudes toward the Maya have changed greatly over the past 30 years. They were once regarded as peaceful and egalitarian; further and deeper study indicates that they were regimented, stratified into classes, and chronically and intensely devoted to war. One point is very clear: their religious beliefs dictated their view of society, of kings, of government, of law, and of life itself.

Only about 40% of the currently-known Maya inscriptions have been deciphered, and more are being discovered each year. Those for whom every inch of ground is paved or plowed, have difficulty grasping the fact that much of the Maya homeland is still unexplored and covered with jungle so thick one needs a machete to move through it. The jungle hides its secrets so carefully that small abandoned villages cannot even be seen from a plane overhead.

What more lies hidden in those jungles, and what will it tell us about the Maya?

---

29. See, Peter G. Tsouras, *Warlords of the Ancient Americas: Central America* (London: Arms and Armour Press, 1996), 9–32.

30. *Popul Vuh: The Sacred Book of the Ancient Quiche Maya* (Norman: U. of Oklahoma Press, 1950, 1991).

Questions for Reflection, Discussion, and More Reflection

1. What parallels do you see between the civilization of ancient Egypt and that of the Maya? Are these parallels best explained by a common origin, by trans-Atlantic contact, or by another explanation?
2. Like the Incas, the most recent evidence indicates that the Maya civilization is much older than archeologists previously thought. Why is this significant?
3. What best explains the decline and fall of the Maya Empire?
4. Why do conquerors—Aztec over Toltec, Spaniard over Maya, Muslim over Egyptian, and others—tend to destroy the writings of their vanquished opponents? If the Spanish monks were correct in their belief that the Maya and Aztec writings contained formulas for devil-worship, were they justified in destroying them?
5. Explain the Maya worldview and its effect on the Maya view of law, government, and warfare.
6. How did the Maya obsession with bloodletting begin, and what was its significance?
7. Does it seem strange that even at the height of their civilization (AD 300–900), the Maya culture consisted of semi-independent city-states rather than a united empire? Does this suggest that confederation may be a better way to achieve lasting greatness than united empire? Or could the lack of unity have been a cause of the Maya downfall?
8. Maya city-states had territorial rulers, and beneath them over the smaller villages were headmasters who served as managers, judges, and war leaders, aided by a council of wealthy old men. Does this appear to have been government from the top down, or is there any evidence in Maya culture that political power rested with the people?

Questions continued on next page....

Questions *continued*

9. What was the role of the military orders, the Order of the Eagle and the Order of the Jaguar? Did they possess governmental authority? Do they have counterparts in armed forces today?
10. In your opinion, to what extent was the later Maya civilization influenced by the Toltecs, Olmecs, or other civilizations? Is this where they learned human sacrifice, or did that practice originate with the Maya themselves?

Tikal Maya Temple in Guatemala. Raymond Ostertag, 2006.

CHAPTER 9

AZTEC:
America's Roman Empire, or America's Third Reich?

Fascination with the Aztecs has not diminished since Cortez and his conquistadors first gazed upon the Aztec capital in 1519. As his foot-soldier Bernal Diaz described the scene,

> we saw so many cities and villages built in the water and other great towns on dry land and that straight and level causeway going towards Mexico [City], we were amazed and said that it was like the enchantments they tell of in the legend of Amadis, on account of the great towers and cues and buildings rising from the water, all built of masonry. And some of our soldiers even asked whether the things we saw were not a dream?
>
> ...the appearance of the palaces in which they lodged us! How spacious and well built they were, of beautiful stone work and cedar wood, and the wood of other sweet scented trees, with great rooms and courts, wonderful to behold, covered with awnings of cotton cloth.
>
> When we had looked well at all of this, we went to the orchard and garden, which was such a wonderful thing to see and walk in, that I was never tired of looking at the diversity of trees, and noting the scent which each one had, and the paths full of roses and flowers, and the many fruit trees and native roses, and the pond of fresh water. There was another thing to observe, that great canoes were able to pass into the garden from the lake through an opening that had been made so that there was no need for their occupants to land. And all was cemented and very splendid with many kinds of stone [monuments] with pictures on them, which gave much to think about. Then the birds of many kinds and breeds which came into the pond. I say again that I stood looking at it and thought that never in the

> world would there be discovered other lands such as these, for at that time there was no Peru, nor any thought of it. [Of all the wonders I then beheld] to-day all is overthrown and lost, nothing left standing.[1]

The Aztec Empire was a remarkable civilization, rivaling anything in Europe, Asia, or Africa at the time. Mexico City had an estimated 60,000 households, or a population of several hundred thousand (much larger than any city in Spain at that time), and a central marketplace in which 100,000 people could transact business. The capital featured aqueducts, watercourses, and a sanitation system far ahead of anything in Europe. Their mathematical system, knowledge of astronomy, and calendar were very advanced and possibly borrowed from the older Maya civilization. Like the Incas, they enjoyed an excellent network of roads; within 48 hours of Cortez's landing at Vera Cruz on the Gulf Coast, news of their landing and detailed sketches of Cortez had already reached Montezuma by an efficient system of relay runners.

The Aztecs are thought to have migrated to central Mexico around AD 1100, having previously lived in northern Mexico or possibly southwestern United States. By this time the Maya civilization had already declined, and central Mexico had witnessed the rise and fall of several great empires. The great Mexican city, Teotihuacan, had been built thousands of years earlier. The Aztecs displaced the Toltecs, who had come to central Mexico in the 7th or 8th century and had dominated the area until the coming of the Aztecs. The Toltecs apparently were skilled governors as well as fierce warriors, and Aztec rulers claimed descent from Toltec kings.[2] But the building of Teotihuacan started even before the Toltecs arrived. The building started around 300 BC, and the magnificent Pyramid of the Sun was built around 150 BC. At its height, around AD 150–450, Teotihuacan boasted a population of 150,000–200,000, and its rulers had included the Totonacs, the Zapotecs, the Mixtecs, the Maya, and the Nahua.

---

1. Bernal Diaz del Castillo, *The True History of the Conquest of New Spain by Bernal Diaz del Castillo, One of Its Conquerors* (London: Hakluyt Society, 1568, 1908), II: 87: 37–38. The Aztec capital was built upon a large inland lake which the Spaniards drained in the 1600s. Diaz's statement that "at that time there was no Peru" reflects the fact that the Spaniards did not encounter the Incas until AD 1532.

2. The Toltecs appear to have been a truly remarkable civilization, worthy of a book in their own right. David Allen Deal, in his *Discovery of Ancient America* (Irvine, CA: Kherem La Yah Press, 1984), 63–86, presents a unique theory of Toltec origins.

Teotihuacan appears to have been a planned metropolis, and it was planned around ancient Mesoamerican religion. Like the Inca capital and the later Aztec capital, the city was laid out in quarters, and its central axis was the Avenue of the Dead which linked the Ciudadela (Citadel) with the Pyramid of the Moon. The city also featured the Pyramid of the Sun, temples to the various gods, and palaces of the kings and lords, adorned with magnificent murals, almost all on religious themes. The pantheon of gods included the various phases of nature: Tlaloc the rain god, Chalchiuhtlicue the water goddess, the Spider Woman who wove together this creation, the sun god, the moon goddess, and others.

By the time the Aztecs migrated to central Mexico, Teotihuacan had long been abandoned. But the ruins still stood, as they do today. The Aztecs later came to believe the gods once gathered at Teotihuacan to sacrifice themselves to begin the creation of mankind and the present age.[3]

Aztec legend says they came from an island in a lake northwest of central Mexico, known as Aztlan, or Land of White Herons, and that they began their southward migration in AD 1111, led by their god Huitzilopochtli, whose image was borne on the shoulders of four priests as they marched southward. Coe says the Aztec myth of their tribal origin is similar to myths of other ancient people, and "Their function seems clear: to tell the world that the rule by a particular elite was given by history and supported by divine sanction."[4]

When they arrived in the Valley of Mexico, they at first accepted a subservient position, working the fields for the established and civilized inhabitants. But in the year 1323 the Toltec rulers of the city-state Colhuacans gave the Aztec chief a Colhuacan princess to be his bride, and the Aztecs sacrificed her in the belief that she would then become a war goddess. This and similar acts brought the Aztecs the hostility of nearly all of the civilized nations of the valley. As a result, the Aztecs' very survival required them to excel in warfare.

In the year 1367 the Aztecs began serving as mercenaries for the city-state of Atzcapotzalco and its powerful king, Tezozomoc. They conquered one after another city-state for Tezozomoc and shared in the spoils of conquest. But Tezozomoc died in 1426, and his son Maxtlatzin distrusted the Aztecs and tried to suppress them. The Aztec chieftain Itzcoatl

3. Michael D. Coe, *Mexico: From the Olmecs to the Aztecs* (London: Thames and Hudson, 1962, 1994), 91–100.

4. Coe, 159.

("Obsidian Snake") and his chief adviser Tlacaelel decided to fight. Together they defeated Atzapotzalco, and the Aztecs took control of the Valley of Mexico. Tlacaelel served as grand vizier to King Itzcoatl and two succeeding Aztec kings, dying around 1480. More than anyone else, he was the chief architect of the Aztec Empire and its form of government.[5]

But first he had to change the way the Aztecs thought of themselves. As Coe says,

> Tlacelel introduced a series of reforms that completely altered Mexican life. The basic reform related to the Aztec conception of themselves and their destiny; for this, it was necessary to rewrite history, and so Tlacelel did, by having all the books of conquered peoples burned since these would have failed to mention Aztec glories. Under his aegis, the Aztecs acquired a mystic-visionary view of themselves as the chosen people, the true heirs of the Toltec tradition, who would fight wars and gain captives so as to keep the fiery sun moving across the sky.[6]

The sun god, Huitzilopochtli, stood at the center of Aztec cosmology, theology, and ideology. Like the Maya and most other Central American nations, the Aztecs believed in a life force they called *tona,* similar to the Maya *ik* and the Oriental *chi.* Like the Maya, they believed this life force holds the universe together and gives it its life energy. Like the Maya, they believed that through this universal life force, events on earth affect events in the heavens, and vice versa. Like the Maya, they believed the sacrifice of human blood and human hearts was necessary to nourish the gods.

At this point, Aztec religion took a unique twist. The Maya believed human sacrifice was necessary to nourish the gods and keep the universe in balance. But the Aztecs believed the universe was out of balance, because the moon god and star gods had rebelled against the sun god, thus causing "star wars" in the heavens. As a result of this cosmic conflict, political affairs in the central American lands were in disarray. The sun god, Huitzilopochtli, had therefore commissioned the Aztecs as his divine legionnaires to subdue the surrounding nations, create order on earth, provide human sacrifices to nourish the sun god in his battle, and thus restore order and balance in the universe. As Jon White says of the Aztecs,

5. Coe, 159–60.

6. Coe, 160.

> To live was to fight. Indeed, they had early come to believe that heaven had appointed them its legionnaires on earth, and that to them had been given the divine duty and privilege of fighting on behalf of the gods against the cosmic forces of destruction.[7]

Alfonso Caso, Director of the National Museum in Mexico City, describes the role of the Aztecs in this cosmic struggle:

> Each day this divine combat [between the sun-god and the moon and star-gods] is begun anew, but in order for the sun to triumph, he must be strong and vigorous, for he has to fight against the unnumbered stars of the North and the South and frighten them all off with his arrows of light. For that reason man must give nourishment to the sun. Since the sun is a god, he disdains the coarse food of mortals and can only be [kept] alive by life itself, by the magic substance that is found in the blood of man, the chalchihuatl, "the precious liquid," the terrible nectar with which the gods are fed.
>
> The Aztecs, the people of Huitzilopochtli, were the chosen people of the sun. They were charged with the duty of supplying him with food. For that reason war was a form of worship and a necessary activity that led them to establish the Xachiyaoyotl, or "flowery war." Its purpose, unlike that of wars of conquest, was not to gain new territories nor to exact tribute from conquered prisoners, but rather to take prisoners for sacrifice to the sun. The Aztec was a man of the people chosen by the sun. He was a servant of the sun and consequently must be, above everything else, a warrior. He must prepare himself from birth for his most constant activity, the Sacred War. . . .[8]

Consequently, while human sacrifice was a regular practice in most central American nations, in Aztec society it grew into a holocaust. Diaz wrote that as he marched with Cortez and the Conquistadors through Mexico, "I remember that in the plaza where some of their oratories stood, there were piles of human skulls so regularly arranged that one could count them, and I estimated them at more than a hundred thousand. I repeat again that there were more than a hundred thousand of them. And in

7. Jon M. White, *Cortez and the Downfall of the Aztec Empire* (New York: St. Martin's Press, 1971), 114.

8. Alfonso Caso, *The Aztecs: People of the Sun* (Norman, OK: U. of Oklahoma Press, 1958, 1968), 13–14.

another part of the plaza there were so many piles of dead men's thigh bones that one could not count them; there was also a large number of skulls strung between beams of wood, and three priests who had charge of these bones and skulls were guarding them."[9] This sight was repeated in place after place.

In 1487, Montezuma's immediate predecessor, Ahuitzotl, dedicated a great temple to Huitzilopochtli and sacrificed around 20,000 human victims; the victims stood in four lines between three and four miles long, and the ceremony lasted four days and was conducted by eight teams of priests.[10] After each victim ascended the steps of the temple, the priests stretched him or her out on a stone slab, cut open the chest with an obsidian knife, and ripped out the beating heart to hold aloft before the sun god. The arms and legs were then cut off and eaten in a cannibalistic ceremony whereby the sacrificer acquired the victim's moral and spiritual qualities along with the physical flesh, and the remainder was rolled down the temple steps. As White says, "When we visit or study photographs of Aztec temples, we should picture to ourselves those tall staircases as they frequently appeared: covered from top to bottom with a tacky, crimson sheath of blood."[11]

The sacrificial victims included enemies captured in war, and also young men and women of other nations given to the Aztecs as tribute. But the sacrifices included Aztecs as well. The Aztecs believed, or at least tried to convince their victims, that being sacrificed was a great honor and a guarantee that the victim not have to pass through the underworld but would immediately be reborn as a star in the heavens.

Aztec society included two noble military orders similar to the orders of medieval knighthood in Europe and the Samurai in Japan. They were known as the Order of the Eagle and the Order of the Jaguar. The two orders frequently engaged in public athletic competitions; the losers (and sometimes the winners) would be sacrificed at the end of the games.[12]

On an even more macabre note, children were sacrificed to the rain god Tlaloc; the more they cried, the more likely were their tears to induce Tlaloc to send rain.

9. Diaz, I: 61: 222.

10. *Man, Myth & Magic: An Illustrated Encyclopedia of the Supernatural* (New York: Marshall Cavendish, 1970), II: 200.

11. White, 129.

12. Caso, 73–74.

The Aztecs shared the Mayas' cyclical view of time. The earth's history was a series of creation, destruction, and re-creation. The current age began when the four gods sacrificed themselves to facilitate the creation of man, and it will come to an end with destruction by fire. All of this gave the Aztecs a sense of fatalism, as though doom was at hand. And the Aztec doom was closely tied with what might seem the brightest star in the Aztec pantheon—Quetzalcoatl.

The Quetzalcoatl theme featured prominently in Aztec religion. Known as Kukulcan to the Maya and by other names throughout Central America, Quetzalcoatl was variously a man, a king, a god, a feathered serpent, or a combination of these. Originally he may have been a Toltec king who had been driven from his kingdom and who had promised to return to liberate his people from oppression. According to the Aztec prophets, the year of Quetzalcoatl's return would be the Year of the Rabbit, or AD 1519. Quetzalcoatl was a god who opposed human sacrifice (though the Aztecs sometimes gave him human sacrifices anyway), and he was associated with springtime and rebirth, goodness, science, learning, wind, light, and the morning star. The return of Quetzalcoatl brought hope to the hearts of subject nations and a sense of doom to their Aztec overlords, for Quetzalcoatl's return would bring about the downfall of the Aztec Empire.[13]

This religion was the source of the Aztecs' strength, and it was also their greatest weakness. The service of the sun-god impelled them to conquer and establish order. Without it they would never have become a great empire.

But the Aztecs' religion was also a major cause of their downfall. The Aztec prophets had seen visions of Quetzalcoatl's return and predicted the return would take place in the Year of the Rabbit, which in the Julian Calendar was AD 1519. Coincidentally or providentially, that was the precise year of Cortez' landing at Vera Cruz. Collis records the omens of doom:

> For a time the night sky was lit by a northern light; a volcanic disturbance caused the water in the Mexico lake to boil up and flood the city streets; the temple of the sun god went on fire; a spirit speaking in a woman's voice wailed at night: "My

13. For an intriguing alternative explanation of the Toltecs, Aztecs, and Quetzalcoatl, along with many other entities including Hebrews and Vikings, see David Allen Deal, *Discovery of Ancient America* (Kherem La Yah Press, 1984); Charles Michael Boland, *They All Discovered America* (Doubleday, 1961).

> children, my children, ruin is at hand." Magicians were called in to interpret these signs. They could not pretend that their meaning was good. Montezuma strangled them, for in magic it is some remedy to destroy the bearer of bad news.
>
> Sign followed sign, a comet, an earthquake. Montezuma felt his nerve giving away. A calamity was certainly approaching. His sister, Papantzin, after lying in a coma for four days, a condition that was taken for death, revived in her grave and on being carried back to the palace declared that she had seen strange beings entering the country and bringing it to ruin. This profoundly shocked him, but not more than what he himself saw shortly afterwards. He was sitting on his mat of state in the building called the Dark House of the Cord, the monastic university inside the precincts of the great temple of the Humming Bird, as the war aspect of the Smoking Mirror was called. "The sun had inclined already towards evening, but it was still day," says Sahagun, the Franciscan friar who a few years later took down the story from those, perhaps, who were present at the time. "Some people who earned their living by catching waterbirds, got a bird of ash grey colour like a crane and brought it to show Montezuma." As he looked at it he seemed to fall into a trance, and saw on the bird's head a magic mirror in which was reflected an ill-omened constellation. This alarmed him and when he looked more closely into the mirror he was horrified "to perceive reeds like men approaching, armed as for war and mounted on deer." It seemed to him that he saw the landing of Quetzalcoatl.[14]

The Aztec warriors fought against Cortez with stoic courage, but with a sense of foreboding as though the final outcome were foreordained. And the subjugated nations rallied around the banner of Cortez with a sense of exultation, for they regarded him as Quetzalcoatl returned, not a conqueror but their liberator from Aztec tyranny.

The Aztec sacrifices not only deprived them of their best young men as warriors; they also enraged the subject nations and inspired them to join Cortez and fight more fiercely to overthrow Aztec rule. And the Aztecs fought only during the daylight hours when the sun-god could watch over them. Cortez quickly learned this and used it to his advantage by surprise night attacks.

---

14. Maurice Collis, *Cortez and Montezuma* (London: Faber & Faber, 1954), 56–57.

Furthermore, Cortez and his men were horrified by the Aztec human sacrifice, cannibalism, and other pagan practices. They were men of war and inured to violence by decades of battles with Muslims and Moors; but human sacrifice was utterly alien to their traditions and beliefs. At least as much as the Muslim outrages of earlier centuries, the Aztecs' pagan practices imbued the conquistadors with crusader zeal to eradicate these demonic practices and establish the worship of the one true God.[15] As the French historian Jean Descola wrote,

> The Conquistadors believed in God fiercely and unreservedly. But they believed also—above all else!—in the Devil. Now, the New World was the empire of the Devil, a Devil with multiform face, always hideous. The somber Mexican divinities, Huitzilopochtli (the Sorcerer-Hummingbird) and Tezcatlipoca (the Smoking Mirror), the horrible Kinich Kakmo of the Mayas, the Peruvian Viracocha who symbolized boiling lava, the sinister totems of the Araucanians and the Diaguites.... Spaniards who in Estramaduran twilights had taken the flight of a bat for the passing of the Evil One were naturally terrified before these monsters of stone, with bared fangs and gleaming eyes, that seemed to come to fantastic life as night fell. How could they have watched an Aztec ceremony without nausea? The black-robed priests with matted hair, burrowing with their knives in the breasts of their victims, the human skulls piled up at the feet of the teocallis, the cannibal feasts around statues spattered with putrid blood, and the charnel-house stench which all the perfumes of Mexico were never able to hide....
>
> Such things froze the spirits of the Conquistadors, surpassing the nightmares of their childhoods. Satan himself was there, and his worship was celebrated among the dismembered corpses. His maleficent power was honored. He was no longer, as in Spain, a familiar accomplice that could be driven off by the flick of the finger, or the shameful specter slipping furtively through one's conscience but put to flight by a sprinkling of holy water. He was enthroned. Carved in granite, incrusted

15. See John Eidsmoe, *Columbus and Cortez: Conquerors for Christ* (Green Forest, AR: New Leaf Press, 1992), 147–298, in which this author discusses in detail the Spanish conquest of Mexico. Those who question whether Cortez and his conquistadors were motivated by Christian zeal should read the five-volume treatise by Bernal Diaz, a footsoldier who served under Cortez throughout the campaign: *The Conquest of New Spain by Bernal Diaz del Castillo, One of Its Conquerors* (London: Hakluyt Society, 1558, 1908), and Father Francisco Lopez de Gomara's *Cortez: The Life of the Conqueror by His Secretary* (Berkeley: U. of California Press, 1552, 1964).

with precious stones and encircled with golden serpents, he was the superb incarnation of Evil. He glorified sin. Nothing was lacking in this perfect representation of Hell, not even the pots in which certain tribes of the Colombian jungle cooked their enemies alive. This indeed was Satan himself, adorned with all his lugubrious attractions.

Why, therefore, should we be astonished at the reaction of the Spaniards? In the depths of the Indian sanctuaries they could see the Prince of Darkness standing in all his macabre splendor. Looking heavenward, they could distinguish the silvery figure of Saint James galloping across the clouds. The conflict between the true and the false, between good and evil, was manifest in this double apparition. The problem was simple and their duty was clear. The Indians were possessed of the Devil, who had to be exorcised, first, by destroying the material evidence of Devil worship. This is why the conquerors, activated by the same blind zeal as early Christians when they shattered the Roman statues, overturned the pre-Columbian idols and burned the ritual articles and the manuscripts that transmitted the sacred tradition—in short, showed a holy ardor to abolish the very memory of the heathen liturgy. This they counted as pious work and a salutary need.

But the Conquistadors did not limit themselves to casting down the idols. In order that the exorcism be fully effective, it was proper also to set up in their places the symbols of the True Faith. Just as holy medals were laid upon flesh that was eaten away with ulcers, the soldiers of Charles V planted crosses on the tops of the teocallis or at crossroads. On the stones that were still spattered with blood from the sacrificial tables, they raised altars to Our Lady of Guadalupe. Tolerance was not for them. Others would follow who would use gentler methods. No one doubts that these booted and armored Christians often lacked the Christian spirit and that charity was almost always missing from their pitiless fervor; but their Faith and their good faith were whole.[16]

16. Jean Descola, *The Conquistadors* trans. Malcolm Barnes (New York: Viking Press, 1957; selections reprinted by John Francis Bannon, *The Spanish Conquistadors: Men or Devils?* (New York: Rinehart & Winston, 1960), 37–38. A hauntingly beautiful collection of Aztec hymns from the 1500s is preserved in CD form titled *Guadalupe: Virgen de los Indios* (Iago/Talking Taco Music, Inc., 1998).

Despite their horror at the Aztecs' paganism, human sacrifice, and cannibalism, the Spaniards admired certain features of the Aztec system of government. It appears that, unlike the Incas, the Aztecs did not regard their rulers as gods during their lifetimes, though they may have deified their leaders after their deaths. Quetzalcoatl may have originally been a Toltec king, and Huitzilopochtli may have been an early Aztec chieftain. And the kings took a leading role in the religious rites of Aztec society, including the construction and dedication of the temples and the ever-present sacrifices.

Just as the Aztec wars were religious crusades to restore order to the land and correspondingly to the universe, so the Aztec system of law and government was an expression of the Aztec religious worldview and an attempt to create and preserve divine order.

Our knowledge of Aztec law is limited by several factors. First, at the time of the Spanish conquest the Aztecs were making a transition from pictorial writing to phonetic writing. Second, the Spanish destroyed many of the Aztec records, considering them to be demonic, just as the Aztecs had destroyed the records of the Toltecs who had preceded them. But some records survived, and some of the Spanish clerics saw the need to preserve the historical record of Aztec culture and custom. And portions of the legal code were preserved in Aztec hymns and passed down by the chanting of those hymns.[17]

Aztec law was not uniform throughout the Empire, because the Empire was actually a union of three powers known as the Triple Alliance, consisting of the Aztecs as the dominant partner in league with two smaller powers, Texcoco and Tacuba. This Triple Alliance controlled about thirty vassal states. The Alliance left the vassal states largely free to continue their own customs and laws, but they required that the vassals pay tribute in the form of goods, arms, soldiers, and victims for sacrifice.[18]

Like the Triple Alliance, the Aztec Empire was an absolute monarchy. The emperor, though, was chosen by the Aztec nobility, who elected four members of their class who in turn chose the emperor, four advisers, and a senior adviser. The emperor had to be of the noble class, over thirty years old, educated at the Calmecac school, brave, and just. (The Calmecac school was limited to children of the nobility between ages

17. Francisco Avalos, "An Overview of the Legal System of the Aztec Empire," *Law Library Journal* 86:2 (Spring 1994), 259–60.

18. Avalos, 260; see also Gomara, 44:95.

fifteen and twenty-two, where youths were educated by the priests and trained in religion and warfare, after which they took their places in the Aztec priesthood, government, or military.) Theoretically the new emperor could be any man of the noble class, but in practice the choices were limited to the heirs of one royal family.[19] Prescott says the emperor-to-be normally must have distinguished himself in war, though the last emperor (Montezuma II) rose in rank through the priesthood rather than through the military.[20]

Once chosen, and before he could be installed, the emperor-elect had to lead a victorious military campaign. When he returned with captives for his triumphal entry into Tenochtitlan, he was inaugurated in a dignified religious ceremony, complete with sacrifices of the captives. Once inaugurated, he held office for life, and his powers were absolute. Political power, in Aztec thought, flowed from the top down, not from the bottom up. His decrees had the full force of law, for all legislative and executive power was combined in the emperor. As Prescott says,

> The legislative power, both in Mexico and Tezcuco, resided wholly with the monarch. This feature of despotism, however, was, in some measure, counteracted by the constitution of the judicial tribunals,—of more importance, among a rude people, than the legislative since it is easier to make good laws for such a community, than to enforce them, and the best laws, badly administered, are but a mockery. Over each of the principal cities, with its dependent territories, was placed a supreme judge, appointed by the crown, with original and final jurisdiction in both civil and criminal cases. There was no appeal from his sentence to any other tribunal, nor even to the king. He held his office during life; and any one, who usurped his ensigns, was punished with death.[21]

Avalos, however, believes these supreme judges met together, at least on some occasions, as a supreme court. And while there was no right to appeal from the supreme judges to the emperor, the supreme judges themselves could send a case to the emperor for decision.[22]

---

19. Avalos, 260–61.

20. Prescott, 20.

21. Prescott, 22–23.

22. Avalos, 263–64.

Below these supreme judges, each province had a *teccalli* court consisting of three or four judges, and an appellate court likewise consisting of three or four judges. In civil cases the jurisdiction of the appellate court was concurrent with that of the supreme judge. In criminal cases, a decision of the provincial court could be appealed to the supreme judge. These provincial judges were appointed by the supreme judges. They held office for life terms and could be removed only for judicial misconduct. Certain lands were set aside for the judiciary, and the profits from those lands paid the judges' salaries. This was thought to give the judges independence and assure their impartiality in deciding cases.[23]

And then, in each neighborhood, was a *barrio* court, with a judge elected by the people of the neighborhood who handled minor cases similar to a modern justice of the peace. Neighborhoods also elected block watchers to help keep social order and report instances of misconduct to the *barrio* judge.[24]

Besides these courts, the Aztec Empire also had specialty courts, including commercial courts, fiscal affairs courts, artisans courts, a military affairs court, and a religious affairs court. The three commercial courts each had twelve judges; the military court had four military judges, and the religious affairs court had only one judge who was appointed by the Chief Priest.[25] The two lesser partners of the Triple Alliance, the Texcoco and the Tacuba, had their own judicial systems. Prescott says the Texcoco judicial system was highly refined, and the judges at all levels met together every eighty days as a parliament, over which the king presided in person.[26]

Avalos says of the judges,

> A career in the judiciary was highly esteemed among the Aztec people. It required immense preparation and previous experience, which was gained through a judicial apprenticeship system. The young apprentices would sit behind the judges hearing a case and learn by observing. These apprentices formed the pool from which judges were selected.
>
> All judges had to abide by professional ethical standards. A judge could not accept gifts. He was not to distinguish "entre

23. Avalos, 263, 265.

24. Avalos, 264; cf. Prescott, 23.

25. Avalos, 264.

26. Prescott, 23; cf. Jerome A. Offner, *Law and Politics in Aztec Texcoco* (London: Cambridge University Press, 1983).

> grandes, ni pequenos, ricos ni pobres" (between the noble nor the common, rich nor poor), when rendering a verdict or sentence. The judge was supposed to render honest verdicts based on impartial judicial wisdom. For the first minor offense, a judge received a reprimand; for the third minor offense, he lost the judgeship and his head was shaved, an act considered a great dishonor and humiliation among the Aztec people. A major breach of professional ethical standards meant death for the guilty judge. The Aztec bench was self-policing.[27]

As there was no legislature, law was based upon royal decree and historical custom. At the time the Spaniards arrived, the Aztecs were moving from pictorial writing to phonetic writing, and with that change came a movement to codify the Aztec laws. The Aztec word for justice was *tlamelahuacachinaliztli,* which literally means "straight line to a point," or to "straighten that which is twisted." This implied that the judge's duty was to use his wisdom to straighten out a problem, doing that which seemed just and reasonable without being bound by statute or precedent. Aztec judges did establish a system of case law which helped to make justice more predictable, but they seem to have been less bound by *stare decisis* (the practice of following previous case precedents) than are American judges today.[28]

Like many ancient judicial systems, the Aztecs apparently made no use of lawyers. A litigant usually represented himself, although a friend or relative could speak for him. Trials were public, and defendants had the right to confront their accusers. The process was inquisitorial, as the judges actively questioned the parties and their witnesses. Witnesses testified under oath, and admissible evidence included documents, testimony, circumstantial evidence, and confessions extracted by torture. To promote efficiency, no trial could last more than eighty days.[29]

Aztec justice was severe. Many crimes were capital, including treason, sedition, disrespect for parents, theft of an amount greater than twenty ears of corn, perjury, abortion, rape, serious defamation of character, highway robbery, destruction of crops, selling stolen property, weight and measure fraud, witchcraft, incest, official graft, pederasty, inciting a public disturbance, sedition, treason, use of the emperor's

---

27. Avalos, 265–66.

28. Avalos, 266

29. Avalos, 267.

insignia, and major judicial misconduct. Adultery was a capital offense, as was having knowledge of adultery and failing to report it. Homicide was a capital offense even if done in self-defense or with other justification, because one who killed another usurped the emperor's power over life and death. The form of execution depended on the nature of the crime; common forms included hanging, drowning, stoning, strangulation, impaling, beheading, beating, disembowelment, burning, quartering, opening the chest and removing the heart, and dropping a heavy stone on the condemned person's head. Clemency could be extended if the victim or his relatives forgave the criminal, in which case the condemned person became the victim's slave.[30]

Nobles and warriors were held to higher standards, and their crimes received more severe punishment than those of commoners. Guilt and punishment for some crimes could extend to family members up to the fourth degree of relationship. Children under the age of ten were considered incapable of committing criminal offenses. Lesser punishments included restitution, slavery, and incarceration. Avalos says,

> There were four types of prisons. Prisoners condemned to death went to the "cuauhcalli" prison to await their execution. "Teilpiloyan" prison was debtors' prison. Prisoners found guilty of minor crimes went to the "petlacalli" prison, where cells were so dark, harsh, and cruel... and food was so poor and inadequate, that a jail sentence usually meant the death of the prisoner. The fourth type of prison, reserved for minor crimes, was not a physical prison. Instead, the judge would draw lines or place sticks on the ground and tell the prisoner not to cross the parameters.[31]

Slavery was a fact of Aztec life, but slaves were not utterly destitute of rights. All persons in Aztec society were born free, but one could become a slave by being captured in war (in which case the slave likely would be sacrificed to the gods), by committing a crime, or by selling oneself or one's offspring into slavery. Slaves could marry, own property (including other slaves), substitute another person in their place, or buy their freedom.[32]

The family was a basic unit of Aztec society. Polygamy was common, but the first wife was always the leading wife. Persons could marry

30. Avalos, 269–71.

31. Avalos, 268.

32. Avalos, 268–69.

conditionally for a certain term of years, or unconditionally for life. Parents arranged marriages for their children, but the children had some say in the matter. A brother was obligated to marry his deceased brother's widow. Aztec law did not recognize divorce, but it did recognize legal separation, in which case the father took custody of their sons and the mother took custody of their daughters.[33]

The emperor owned ultimate title to all real property, and he gave limited title to his nobles and warriors as he saw fit. The *barrios* (neighborhoods) owned certain land and parceled it out among the commoners, but the commoners had no right to land ownership. The emperor took title to all newly conquered lands and parceled these out to his warriors and nobles. The conquered people usually continued to live on and work their lands, but they had to share the profits with their new landlords.[34]

All commerce had to be carried out in the marketplace, and goods could be exchanged only at designated places. The Empire had no formal coinage, but grains of cacao, squares of cotton cloth, pieces of tin, nuggets of gold, and precious feathers, served as mediums of exchange. Commerce employed credit and barter, and oral contracts were valid if witnessed by four persons.[35]

Fierce nationalists though they were, the Aztecs did recognize some form of international law. Before the Empire could engage in a war of conquest, a declaration of war was required, and fixed protocols had to be followed. The emperor sent envoys to the potential enemy and presented gifts to the enemy king along with certain charges or demands. The envoys gave the enemy twenty days to respond to those demands. If the enemy did not respond, the Aztecs repeated this protocol a second and third time, after which they would attack.[36] This is in keeping with international law today, that a declaration of war is required before just warfare can begin, so the opponent has notice of the causes of war and the opportunity to surrender or negotiate conditions for peace.

Let us return to our opening question: The Aztecs—America's Roman Empire, or America's Third Reich? The Aztec Empire was a curious mixture of triumph and tragedy, courage and cruelty, glory and gore, dignity and depravity, devotion and debauchery. They achieved order, but at the

33. Avalos, 271–72.

34. Avalos, 272–73.

35. Avalos, 274–75.

36. Avalos, 275–76.

expense of freedom. They were the sun god's legionnaires, and they became masters of their known world. But in so doing, they laid the seeds of their own destruction.

And what about Cortez—conqueror or liberator? A foreign devil, or Quetzalcoatl returned? Or was he sent by a Power even higher than Quetzalcoatl?

And the Aztec gods—are they dead? Or do they lurk in the shadows, waiting to return at the next cycle of rebirth?

Questions for Reflection, Discussion, and More Reflection

1. How did the Aztec religion or cosmology lead them to become a powerful empire in Central America?
2. Describe the Quetzalcoatl story. How did the Quetzalcoatl myth, coupled with the Aztecs' fatalism and cyclical view of time, lead to their downfall?
3. Describe the Aztec policy toward conquered vassal states. How does this policy compare to those of other empires we have studied—for example, the Babylonian and the Persian?
4. Why was human sacrifice such a central aspect of Aztec religion? Did this play a role in the decision of other Central American Indian nations to join with Cortez in bringing down the Aztec Empire?
5. Describe the Aztec system of government, as the foremost partner in the Triple Alliance. How was the emperor selected, what were his powers, and how did he relate to other officers of the Aztec government?
6. Explain the workings of the Aztec judicial system. Did an independent judiciary serve as a counterweight to executive and legislative power concentrated in the emperor?
7. Consider the Aztec method of judicial selection, the ethical standards required of judges. Do you see a parallel between the Aztec policy of appointing judges for life and making them

Questions continued on next page....

Questions *continued*

subject to removal only for judicial misconduct, and Article III § 1 of the U.S. Constitution? Is this a good policy?

8. What does the Aztec word for justice, *tlamelahuacachinaliztli*, literally mean? What does this word tell us about the Aztec view of the role of a judge?
9. The emperor had title to all real property and could dispose of it as he chose. Today, some legal theorists argue that the ultimate title to all real estate belongs to the state. Would you agree with this view?
10. Father Francisco Vitoria argued that the Spanish Conquest was justified because the Aztecs refused to allow their subjects to hear the Gospel, which all men have a God-given right to hear. Father Francisco Suarez argued that a Christian nation has a right to intervene militarily in the affairs of a non-Christian nation if that nation is engaged in practices that violate the Law of Nature, such as human sacrifice, cannibalism, and sodomy. Would you agree?

Aztec sacrificial stone. William Henry Jackson, 1880.

CHAPTER 10

CHEYENNE: *The Mystic Warriors of the Great Plains*

As we move from Central America northward, we find that the North American continent has been the home of at least 500 Indian nations. They have not left us the magnificent architectural and technological wonders of Central and South America, but that may be due to the fact that they built with earth and wood rather than stone and so their works have not survived. The cliff dwellings of the mysterious Anasazi at Mesa Verde, Colorado, and elsewhere, their stone structures at Hovenweep, Utah, the immense stone structures of the Chaco culture in New Mexico, and many other buildings that have stood for 1,000 years or more, are evidence that the North American Indians of the Southwest were capable of great architectural achievements.[1]

More recently archeologists have unearthed the secrets of the Hopewell Culture that flourished in the Ohio Valley and elsewhere in the Midwest around AD 500. Josephy tells us that "The mounds and other evidence suggest that Hopewellians had a highly developed social system that included a class structure, with rulers of hereditary rank and privileges; a strong religious system; specialists like artists, traders, and metalworkers; and organized direction over cooperative labor."[2] The Mississippian Culture that supplanted the Hopewell Culture around AD 700 and lasted until about AD 1150 developed large urban centers, built huge earthen mounds topped by temples and palaces, and established a trade network that included pottery, weaving, and copper from the Great Lakes, obsidian from the Yellowstone country of the Far West, mica and

1. See generally, David Grant Noble, *Ancient Ruins of the Southwest* (Flagstaff: Northland Publishing Company, 1991, 2000).

2. Alvin M. Josephy, Jr., *500 Nations: An Illustrated History of North American Indians* (New York: Gramercy Books, 1994), 37. This writer confirmed Josephy's observations during a visit to the Cohokia mounds in January, 2010.

crystal from the Appalachians, gold and silver from Canada, and conch shells from the Gulf of Mexico. One city of the Mississippian Culture, Cahokia in Illinois near St. Louis, Missouri, was an elite walled city of five square miles, contained more than a hundred large and small pyramids and earthen mounds, and boasted a population of at least 10,000, making it the largest city in the history of the territory that is now the United States until Philadelphia surpassed it in the 1800s. As Josephy says,

> At the top of the social system was Cahokia's absolute ruler, a revered chieftain known as the Great Sun, who dwelled with his relatives on the flattened top of Cahokia's biggest mound. Now called Monks Mound, it was ten stories high and had an earthen base far larger than that of any pyramid in Egypt or Mexico. From this forbidden holy estate, elevated toward the sky above the bustling urban center, Cahokia's hereditary monarch, the head of both state and religion, ruled like a god over all aspects of Mississippian life.[3]

We will focus on two North American Indian cultures, the Cheyenne of the West and the Iroquois of the Northeast. Due to the lack of written records, our information about these societies goes back hundreds rather than thousands of years—not that they had no legal systems before that, but we have no information about them. The legal systems we are going to explore cannot be considered "ancient" in the same sense as the Egyptian or the Mesopotamian, or even as ancient as the Maya. But they do show us well-developed systems of law and government that apparently arose prior to extensive contact with Old World civilizations.

The Cheyenne

The Cheyenne are usually regarded as Indians of the American West, but their early origins are uncertain. Like many other Indians, particularly those of the Southwest, the Cheyenne legend is that they originally lived underground and were led to the surface when one of their number perceived and followed a small source of light and discovered the world above them.[4] The common belief today is that their earliest known home was in Algonquin territory above the Great Lakes in Canada. The name "Cheyenne" means "people of a different speech" and was given to them

---

3. Josephy, 41.

4. "Cheyenne Lands," http://rebelcherokee.labdiva.com/cheyenne.html (accessed 28 April, 2016).

by the Sioux, probably because their language was similar to Algonquin; the Cheyenne called themselves "Tsististas," meaning "the beautiful people."[5] The first written record of them is a map drawn by the French missionary explorer Louis Joliet around 1673 which places them in the Great Lakes area in what is now Wisconsin. The French explorer Sieur de LaSalle recorded a visit by the Cheyenne in 1680 while he was building Fort Crevecoeur near present-day Chicago, Illinois.[6]

During the late 1600s they began to move westward, perhaps pushed by the Sioux and Ojibwa who were themselves moving westward, and throughout the 1700s the Cheyenne lived in eastern Dakota territory where the Sheyenne River bears their name although with a different spelling. A Cheyenne tradition says they were led westward by a great chief and prophet named Sweet Medicine, and that before he led them westward he journeyed alone to Bear Butte in western South Dakota northeast of the Black Hills. Bear Butte is a sacred site to at least 60 Indian nations,[7] and while Sweet Medicine was there, the Creator God Maheo instructed him on sacred matters, including the right way to organize and govern his people. Maheo also entrusted to Sweet Medicine four Sacred Arrows which, if properly kept and ritually purified, would ensure the well-being of the Cheyenne. Two of these were hunting arrows which, when pointed at animals, would render them helpless and easily killed; the other two were war arrows which, if carried into battle and pointed at the enemy, would blind and confuse them and ensure a Cheyenne victory.[8] He also visited Wind Cave in the Black Hills, one of the world's longest and most complex caves, also a sacred site to many Indian nations. According to Charmaine

---

5. Northern Cheyenne Tribal Council, www.nps.gov/jeff/learn/historyculture/cheyenne.htm (accessed 24 May, 2016).

6. http://rebelcherokee.labdiva.com/cheyenne.html (accessed 28 April, 2016).

7. Charmaine White Face, "Sacred Bear Butte Threatened," www.manatka.org/page278.html (accessed 28 April, 2016). As a native South Dakotan this author has hiked Bear Butte and can personally attest to its current use as an Indian sacred shrine.

8. Thom Hatch, *Black Kettle: The Cheyenne Chief Who Sought Peace But Found War* (Hoboken, NJ: John Wiley & Sons, 2004), 18; Charmaine White Face, "Sacred Bear Butte Threatened," www.manataka.org/page278.html (accessed 28 April, 2016). White Face says Sweet Medicine visited Bear Butte over 4,000 years ago, but the most common belief is that he lived around AD 1700. Some may claim Sweet Medicine was a god, but others dispute this; see Fr. Peter J. Powell, *Sweet Medicine: Continuing Role of the Sacred Arrows in the Sun Dance, and the Sacred Buffalo Hat in Northern Cheyenne History* (U. of Oklahoma Press 1998) II:433–42. It is not uncommon for nations to ascribe divinity to their earliest leaders; for example, in some Norse traditions the god Odin was their first king, Snorri Sturluson, *Heimskringla.* Also, many Indians of the Southwest, such as the Anasazi, believed their ancestors had emerged from the underworld through a cave.

White Face, the Lakota Sioux believed their ancestors had lived underground and had emerged on the earth's surface through Wind Cave.[9]

At some point, perhaps around 1750, while living in Dakota territory, the Cheyenne discovered a creature that would alter their lives forever. The Spanish Conquistadors had left horses in the Southwest, and the descendants of these horses had spread across the plains. At that time horses were unknown to the Indians of the east and the Great Lakes area, but Great Plains Indians used them extensively. The horse gave the Cheyenne mobility they had never known before, including the ability to transport large burdens. Gradually in the late 1700s and early 1800s, the Cheyenne gave up their sedentary lifestyle which included lodges about 40 feet in diameter made up of bark and earth and cultivating land, and opted for portable teepees and a hunting lifestyle that depended primarily upon bison, pronghorn, deer, and elk.

On their way westward in 1804, and again on August 21, 1806, while they were returning, Lewis and Clark met the Cheyenne on the Missouri in western Dakota Territory. Clark records in their journal that he "observed Several very white Lodge on the hill above the Town which the ricaras from the Shore informed me were Chyennes who had just arived." He related that "the Chiefs and brave men of the Ricaras & Chyennes formed a cercle around me, after takeing a Smoke of Mandan tobacco which the Big white Chief who was seated on my left hand furnished. . . ."[10] Clark continued,

> The Sun being very hot the Chyenne Chief envited us to his Lodge which was pitched in the plain at no great distance from the River. I accepted the invitation and accompanied him to his lodge which was new and much larger than any which I have seen. It was made of 20 dressed Buffalow Skins in the Same form of the Sceoux [Sioux] and lodges of other nations of this quarter about this lodges was 20 others several of them nearly the Same size. I enquired for the ballance of the nation and was informed that they were near at hand and would arive on tomorrow and when all together amounted to 120 Lodges.[11]

---

9. White Face, *op. cit.*

10. William Clark, *The Journals of Lewis and Clark* ed. Bernard DeVoto (Boston: Houghton Mifflin, 1806, 1953), 461. (Original spellings and capitalizations are preserved; spelling was not standardized at that time.)

11. Clark, 462.

Clark had invited the Cheyenne and Ricara to send members of their tribes with the expedition to see the eastern United States and meet the "great father" (the President), but the Chief informed him that "the Chyennes were a wild people and were afraid to go."[12] The next day, however, the Chief asked Clark to send traders to them, as beaver were plentiful in this area and trade would be an incentive for his people to learn how to catch beaver.[13] One gains a picture of a people who were in transition from a woodland environment to a plains existence and were learning to live in this new environment.

The Cheyenne continued to move westward, and as they did so they gave up their earth and bark lodges and began living in teepees that could more easily be moved as they traveled. Around 1832 they split into two groups, the Northern Cheyenne who live in Wyoming and Montana, and the Southern Cheyenne who live along the Arkansas River in Colorado and Oklahoma.

For the Cheyenne, religion and spirituality permeated all aspects of life. At the center of their worship and belief system was Heammawihio (shortened to Maheo), variously called the Creator, the Great Spirit, God, or the All Father. Maheo had created the earth, which the Cheyenne called Our Grandmother, and everything therein. Maheo had also created the Maheuno, the four Sacred Persons who guard the four corners of the cosmos, each of whom is represented by a different color: Esseneta'he (white) of the southeast and the sunrise who symbolizes light and life, Onxsovon (golden yellow) of the northwest and the sunset who symbolizes beauty, Sovota (red) of the southwest who provides warmth and rain, and Notamota (black) of the northeast who brings storms, blizzards, disease and death.[14]

Maheo had also created the Sacred Powers, called Maiyun, which serve the Sacred Persons. These are Heammawihio, the Wise One Above, and Ahtunowihio, who lives beneath the earth. The Sacred Powers are beneficial and provide food, shelter, clothing, and other necessities. At times they appear as animals or birds.[15]

Maheo also created man, and he created man with a spirit or soul, called the Ma'tasooma. At death the Ma'tasooma leaves the body and

---

12. Clark, 462.

13. Clark, 463.

14. Hatch, 17.

15. Hatch, 17.

soars across the Milky Way to live with Maheo and with the souls of the departed in a heavenly existence where they ride the fastest ponies through herds of buffalo and they can return to earth at times. Apparently the Cheyenne did not believe in hell,[16] but the spirits of those who had been scalped and strangled had to remain at earth level as ghosts, sometimes haunting their enemies. The hair was thought to be an extension of the soul, as it continued to grow throughout a person's lifetime. Mails explains that the Cheyenne believed one enters heaven exactly as one is on earth, with the same passions, needs, friendships, and enmities. One reason the plains Indians scalped their enemies, Mails says, was to prevent them from entering heaven and continuing their warfare against the Cheyenne.[17] Fear of ghosts was widespread, and for that reason grave-robbing was virtually nonexistent.

Mails also explains why the Great Plains Indians left material items like food, clothing, tools, and weapons at the graves of their departed loved ones:

> The Indians understood perfectly well that the dead did not actually take the material articles buried with them to the Great Hunting Ground, for some of the items were hung in plain view around the burial place. They did believe, however, that if the articles were allowed to remain with or near the body until the soul reached its paradise, the spirit of the dead man would have the use of a "spirit model" or duplicate of those articles. Accordingly, any article considered necessary in the future state, and which the dead man did not possess in life, was gladly supplied by relatives or friends, and often at considerable sacrifice.[18]

They wrapped the body in a buffalo robe and commonly entombed the body on a scaffold or in the branches of a tree. They preferred not to bury the body in the ground because that might separate the deceased person from Maheo.

Plains Indians had frequent celebrations of thanksgiving to the Creator. Sometimes these involved fasting, self-mutilation as an act of dedication, and/or penance, and sacrifice, although human sacrifice was

16. Hatch, 17.

17. Thomas E. Mails, *The Mystic Warriors of the Plains* (New York: Marlowe & Co., 1972, 1995), 177, 311–23.

18. Mails, 177. The "spirit model" sounds vaguely similar to Plato's doctrine of the "forms."

rare. Sometimes this fasting and self-mutilation, occasionally coupled with the use of peyote, was an attempt to put oneself in an altered state of consciousness in the hope of receiving a vision from Maheo or another god. To receive a vision one must be pure in body and spirit, so in preparation for a vision the plains Indians often practiced various rites of purification. The "sweat lodge" was more than just a health measure; it was a means of purification. As Curtis says, "With the Cheyenne the sweat bath is one of the most essential religious observances. Through its agency their purified minds and bodies are brought in accord with the supernatural powers. Even when it is employed in healing disease the thought is that the power of the spirits, not the steam, will expel the sickness."[19] The Cheyenne frequently sang hymns while using the sweat lodge, and would commonly begin with a prayer like the following:

> Spirits hear me; think especially of me, miserable man. Those that enter my sweat lodge for safety, going out may they leave behind all that is bad. Take thought of them; that good may come to them take thought. Let horses of different colors come to them. Ye spirits, my different wives I have given to you, that I might be permitted to speak to you. My wives from you I make no attempt to hide, that I might be permitted to speak to you. In your sweat lodge the search has been renewed. Stones of different colors they have heated; woods of different colors they have erected. Your pipe is filled; come and smoke. When they go out of my sweat lodge may some good go with them. To the place whence they came, may they all take good luck. May all their relatives receive good; their children let them embrace with joy. Let their way lie along the good road. Especially remember me, poor as I am; help me. That our patients may rise with ease, take thought of them; let them once more walk about with joy. Everywhere in divers manners I have tortured myself; may the spirits pity me. Who are ye that taught this custom? I do not claim to know anything; I am poor; I am far from knowing anything. Old men taught me this way, and if I make a mistake, turn it into good. Especially remember poor me. Everything I ask of you, grant me. Henahi![20]

19. Edward S. Curtis, *The North American Indian,* Vol. VI: 116; http://curtis.library.northwestern.edu/curtis/viewPage.cgi?showp=1&size=2&id=nai.06.book.00000182&volume=6#nav (accessed 28 April, 2016).

20. Curtis, VI: 119.

Note the reference to the pipe being full. Smoking the "peace pipe" was not just recreation; it was a religious ceremony. Smoking the peace pipe was thought to arrest evil powers, gain protection from enemies, bring game closer to the village, and invoke the blessing of supernatural powers on future undertakings. And apparently they had foreknowledge of the U.S. Surgeon General's 1964 report, for Mails tells us, "Ordinarily, young men were advised not to smoke, as it would make them short-winded."[21] Mails explains the theology of the pipe:

> There were several vital thoughts which undergirded the act of smoking. The pipestem was considered to be a connecting link with the supernatural. In the very process of filling and using the pipe, all wisdom, represented by the powers of the six directions, and all things, represented by the grains of tobacco, were drawn inward to a single focal point and placed in the bowl or heart of the pipe, so that when filled the pipe contained, or really became, the universe. But it was also men, for the one who filled and smoked the pipe united himself with it and brought the wisdom and power of the six directions of space within himself. By this gathering together he ceased to be separated from them, and in another way increased in holiness. In its sum, the general approach in smoking led the assembled Indians to patient actions and considered opinions.[22]

The leader of a pipe-smoking ceremony began by calling upon the Creator or Great Spirit to behold it, for, "The pipe smoke was the bearer of a heaven-sent voice, and all the wildlife and the six directions joined with the smokers in sending it. This showed that the Indians were thinking of the soul and of death, and was sure sign they were humiliating themselves before the Great Spirit, since they knew they were as dust before Him, who was everything and all-powerful!"[23]

Smoking the pipe was also like taking an oath that one was telling the truth. The straight stem was a reminder to "speak straight,"[24] and as the man prepared to smoke, a priest admonished him with words like:

---

21. Mails, 101.

22. Mails, 104.

23. Mails, 104.

24. Mails, 69.

> A man's mind should be straight. Accept this pipe, but remember that, if you smoke, your story must be as sure as the bowl in this pipe, and as straight as the hole through this stem. If so, our life shall be long and you will survive, but if you have spoken falsely your days are numbered.[25]

For similar reasons the "peace-pipe was smoked when persons entered into agreements with one another, and by chiefs when they solemnized a treaty." Writing around 1872, General George Armstrong Custer noted concerning the Cheyenne that "no matter how pressing or momentous the occasion, an Indian invariably declines to engage in a council until he has filled his pipe and gone through with the important ceremony of a smoke."[26] Some pipestems were thought to have special sacred power, and Pipestone National Monument in Minnesota is a site where stone for pipes was quarried and traded throughout much of North America.[27]

Cheyenne life featured many religious ceremonies, but three stand out as central: the Arrow Renewal, the Sun Dance (also called the New Life Lodge), and the Animal Dance. The reader will recall that when Sweet Medicine traveled to Bear Butte in South Dakota, Maheo entrusted him with four Sacred Arrows, two of which gave power over animals and the other two gave power over other men. The Cheyenne kept these Arrows in a medicine bundle with other sacred objects which symbolized their collective existence as a nation. Once a year, the ten bands of the Cheyenne would gather for four days of sacred rituals which were to cleanse and renew the power of the Arrows and thus renew the nation.[28]

The Sun Dance was an eight-day annual gathering which was to renew the spiritual life of the Cheyenne nation and which involved sacred observances of self-sacrifice, dance, and prayer.[29]

25. Mails, 106.

26. General George Armstrong Custer, *My Life on the Plains* (Lincoln: U. of Nebraska Press, 1872–74, 1966), 39.

27. Personal observations from numerous visits by the author to Pipestone National Monument, Pipestone, Minnesota.

28. www.okhistory.org/publications/enc/entry.php?entry=CH030 (accessed 16 May, 2016). The cleansing of the Sacred Arrows was spiritual and symbolic, not literal.

29. *Id.*

The Animal Dance was an annual five-day festival dedicated to silliness and fun and the only ceremony in which the women took part in the preparations. Men dressed up as animals and others hunted them.[30]

Plains Indians followed rules of etiquette which were appropriate for their mode of living. For example, one never passed between a person and the fire without an apology. The warmest spots in the teepee or lodge were reserved for guests. Young boys were told not to eat the softest buffalo meat because it would make their legs soft, but the real reason was that the softest meat was reserved for the elderly so they could chew it. One did not address another by his name, but rather by his relationship to you: father, mother, brother, sister, friend. And upon meeting a person, one should not ask his name or business; that would come out in due time as the relationship developed.[31]

Professor E. Adamson Hoebel describes the Cheyenne man:

> Reserved and dignified, the mature adult Cheyenne male moves with a quiet sense of self-assurance. He speaks fluently, but never carelessly. He is careful of the sensibilities of others and is kindly and generous. He is slow to anger and strives to suppress his feelings, if aggravated. Towards his enemies he feels no merciful compunctions, and the more aggressive he is, the better. He is neither flighty nor dour. Usually quiet, he has a lightly displayed sense of humor. His thinking is rationalistic to a high degree and yet colored with mysticism. His ego is strong and not easily threatened. He is serene and composed, secure in his social position, capable of warm social relations.[32]

The family was the basic unit of Cheyenne society, and most marriages endured for life. Although this was not true of all Indian nations, chastity was very important to the Cheyenne. Premarital sex was forbidden, and even brazen flirting was considered immoral. According to George Grinnell,

> The women of the Cheyennes are famous among all western tribes for their chastity. In old times it was most unusual for a girl to be seduced, and she who had yielded was disgraced forever. The matter at once became known, and she was taunted

30. *Id.*

31. Mails, 71–72.

32. Dr. E. Adamson Hoebel, quoted by Hatch, 7.

> with it wherever she went. It was never forgotten. No young man would marry her.[33]

Hatch writes,

> Cheyenne women exhibited many of the same characteristics as the men but were more artistically creative. The woman was by all means accomplished in domestic relations and was expected to care for the children and perform every household duty. Contrary to the customs of some Plains tribes, the relationship between the Cheyenne husband and the wife was an equal partnership—the women were not considered chattels—and most marriages endured for life. Women were the rulers of the camp and, although not permitted to participate in tribal councils, made their wishes known through their husbands, who obediently acted on any request, whether with respect to the tribe or to the family.[34]

A Cheyennne proverb recognizes the central role women play in shaping the spirit of the nation:

> A nation is not conquered
> Until the hearts of its women are on the ground.
> Then it is finished,
> No matter how brave its warriors
> Or how strong its weapons.[35]

The Cheyenne practiced private ownership of personal property, but their nomadic lifestyle made private ownership of real estate impractical. Rights to land were based on usage, not ownership. Most Plains Indians dealt with theft by requiring restitution,[36] but Mails says,

> Among the members of a given tribe, honesty was an absolute, and lying was sure to bring the direst consequences. The straight stem of the pipe a man smoked represented the need to speak straightly (or truthfully). In matters concerning the things in which he had no positive knowledge, he was exceedingly

33. George Grinnell, quoted by Hatch, 6.

34. Hatch, 7.

35. www.indians.org/welker/cheyenne.htm (accessed 28 April, 2016).

36. Mails, 82.

> careful to qualify his statements, so that it never might be said of him that "he had two tongues." Theft was virtually unknown in an Indian village and people could leave their goods unattended without fear. A lost piece of property was immediately delivered to the camp crier, who proclaimed the news of its discovery throughout the camp, so that the owner of the lost article might recover it. However, since it fitted his idea of proper defense, an Indian did not hesitate to take all the property he could from an enemy. Even then the usual loot was horses, and an enemy's village was seldom disturbed or ravaged.[37]

Among the Cheyenne the punishment for murder was banishment, which reduced the likelihood of blood feuds. But the banishment was not for life. Theoretically, banishment was to run for five or ten years, but in practice the ban was in the nature of an indeterminate sentence with commutation possible on a number of grounds, such as the murderer's past conduct, presence or absence of malice aforethought, repentance, or the feelings of the victim's next of kin.[38] Unlike some ancient societies in which banishment was like a death sentence, a banished Cheyenne was likely to be received by the Dakota or the Arapaho with no questions asked.[39]

The relatively lenient sentence for murder does not mean the Cheyenne regarded the offense lightly. On the contrary, murder had serious spiritual significance. The killing of one Cheyenne by another Cheyenne was a sin which bloodied the Sacred Arrows. Since the well-being of the Cheyenne nation depended on the purification and renewal of the Sacred Arrows which Maheo had entrusted to Sweet Medicine, murder endangered the Cheyenne people and was an offense against the nation. As Llewellyn and Hoebel explain,

> When murder had been done, a pall fell over the Cheyenne tribe. There could be no success in war; there would be no bountifulness in available food. "Game shunned the territory; it made the tribe lonesome." So pronounced Spotted Elk; so assent all Cheyennes.

---

37. Mails, 69.

38. K.N. Llewellyn and E. Adamson Hoebel, *The Cheyenne Way: Conflict and Case Law in Primitive Jurisprudence* (Norman: U. of Oklahoma Press, 1941), 132–51.

39. Llewellyn and Hoebel, 133.

> There is thus a branding synonym for "murder" in Cheyenne ...*putrid.* Such was the murderer's stigma. With murder a man began his internal corruption, a disintegration of his bodily self which perhaps contrition could stay, but never cure. About the killer clung the murderer's smell, an evil mantle eternally noisome to fellow men and the sought-after animal denizens of the plains. Though the tribe, after ridding itself of the murderer's presence through banishment, could purify itself by the sacred ritual of renewing the Medicine Arrows, the murderer was tainted beyond salvation. Hence, the immediate consequence of murder was a conference of the tribal chiefs—such were in the population of the band at the moment. By them a decree of exile was given.[40]

The renewing of the Sacred Arrows involved bringing the bands together for a four-day purification ceremony, so clearly the Cheyenne took murder very seriously. Even if the chiefs did not convict the killer because the act was accidental, or self-defense, or the result of provocation, the fact still remained that a Cheyenne had killed a Cheyenne, the Sacred Arrows had been bloodied, and for the well-being of the nation, the Arrows had to be cleansed.

Llewellyn and Hoebel describe a case in which a mother berated her daughter so severely that the daughter hanged herself. The Council decided that suicide is self-inflicted homicide and therefore constitutes a Cheyenne killing a Cheyenne, so the Sacred Arrows are bloodied and need to be purified. On the other hand, a warrior might announce that he is going into battle against the enemy in a way that is certain to result in death, and this type of "suicide" was justified and glorified.[41]

On another occasion an aborted unborn child was found in the vicinity of the camp. The war chiefs conducted an investigation by examining the breasts of the women in the camp. One girl showed symptoms, was charged, found guilty, and banished until the Sacred Arrows had been renewed. According to Llewellyn and Hoebel,

> Three salient points are to be noted here. First, that the unborn child had tribal status and insofar a legal personality; abortion, too, was murder which tainted the tribal medicine. Second, this was a situation wholly religious and criminal, for the violence

40. Llewellyn and Hoebel, 133.

41. Llewellyn and Hoebel, 158–68.

> had been done within the most intimate family unit possible. Blood-feud was precluded. Third, the murder was a secret crime demanding detection of the criminal—the only secret killing in the present material. A technique was ingeniously invented to meet the situation. Here, as throughout, one meets the Cheyenne legal elasticity—a quick adaptation and invention rare in any people, primitive or modern.
>
> Clearly, the military associations were well along toward establishment as a civil power and organ of government.[42]

The Cheyenne believed their system of government was revealed to them by the Creator, as Maheo imparted this wisdom to Sweet Medicine at Bear Butte.[43] The nation was divided into ten bands (the Cheyenne referred to them as bands rather than clans or tribes), each of which had four chiefs. In addition to the four chiefs of each of the ten bands, or a total of forty chiefs, there were four Priest Chiefs, and together these chiefs governed the Cheyenne nation as the Council of Forty-Four. The four special chiefs, plus a presiding chief who was called the Sweet Medicine Chief or the Prophet, constituted the supreme order within the Council. The hierarchy was as follows:

The Prophet or Sweet Medicine Chief

The four Priest Chiefs

Two Servant Chiefs, or Door Men

The Remaining Thirty-Seven Chiefs

Llewellyn and Hoebel say a Cheyenne chief had to be a "mature man, yet vigorous, who had been appointed to his station because he approached the ideal qualities of leadership—wisdom, courage, kindness, generosity, and even temper."[44] The Council of Forty-Four was a self-perpetuating body like a board of trustees; each chief served a ten-year term and then chose his own successor. A chief frequently chose his own son as his successor, but he was not required to do so. The Sweet Medicine Chief and the four Priest Chiefs were required to choose their

42. Llewellyn and Hoebel, 119.

43. Llewellyn and Hoebel, 69–73, offer an alternate tradition, that the Cheyenne derived their system of government from a captive maiden of another Indian nation who explained to them the governing system of her nation.

44. Llewellyn and Hoebel, 73.

successors from among the retiring Council chiefs, thus providing continuity and guaranteeing that the five Chiefs of the supreme order each had at least ten years of experience serving on the Council of Forty-Four. Chiefs were expected to be models of good conduct, but a chief could not be impeached for misconduct, although he could be banished temporarily for certain criminal offenses. Llewellyn and Hoedel further explain,

> The ritual of renewal of the chiefs was an event of great sacredness, the ceremony being connected in all its phases with Sweet Medicine and with the supernaturalism of Cheyenne cosmology. It was under the direction of the five priestly chiefs who served as the head chiefs of the tribe.[45]

The Council of Forty-Four governed during peacetime, but its inner workings were confidential.[46] The chiefs from each band governed the affairs of their respective bands, and their ways of governance may have varied from one band to another. They were also known as "peace chiefs," because they were not expected to go to war—perhaps because they were older men, or perhaps because civil and military authority were to be separated.

The Cheyenne wartime functions were controlled by "military societies," voluntary organizations that served not only as military units for both training and defense, but also were something like fraternities, with their own friendships, rites, secrets, protocols, and distinctive clothing and insignia somewhat comparable to the various branches of the armed forces or the military orders of medieval Europe, or the Order of the Eagle and Order of the Jaguar among the Maya and Aztecs. There were six military societies among the Cheyenne: (1) The Fox Soldiers (also known as the Kit Fox, Swift Fox, and Coyote), (2) the Elk Soldiers (aka Elk Horn Scrapers, Hoof Rattle, Crooked Lance, Headed Lance, and Medicine Lance), (3) the Shield Soldiers (aka Red Shield, Buffalo, Buffalo Bull, and Bull), (4) the Bowstring Society (aka Owl Man's Bowstring and Wolf Soldiers), (5) the Northern Crazy Dogs (aka Crazy Dogs and Foolish Dogs), and (6) largest and best known of all, the Dog Soldiers (aka Dogs and Dog Men).[47]

---

45. Llewellyn and Hoebel, 74, see generally, 74–76.

46. Llewellyn and Hoebel, 97–98.

47. Llewellyn and Hoebel, 99–100. Some dispute exists as to the number of military societies, possibly because some were known by more than one name. A once-popular belief, now largely discredited, is that the Cheyenne received their name when the Dog Soldiers came into contact with French explorers, as the French word for "dog" is *chien*.

Each military society was governed by "war chiefs" consisting of two headmen and two servants. Unlike the Council of Forty-Four, the war chiefs were subject to impeachment for misconduct or malfeasance. Members of military societies could serve as chiefs on the Council of Forty-Four, but no war chief could serve on the Council. Likewise peace chiefs could join military societies but could not serve as war chiefs at the same time. If a war chief was chosen for the Council of Forty-Four, he immediately retired as a war chief. Llewellyn and Hoebel write,

> The Cheyennes reiterate that the appointment of tribal chiefs is elevation to a position of responsibility to the entire tribe. We interpret the rule which separated the supreme tribal and the military chieftainships, preventing the vesting of the powers of the two types of office in any one individual, as a constitutional device designed to forestall undue accumulation of power by any special interest group. It served to guarantee the principle of checks and balances as between the military and civil branches of the social organization.[48]

Apparently the authority of the war chiefs expanded beyond military defense. Various military societies took charge of such activities as buffalo hunts, as firm discipline was needed to prevent premature attacks that might stampede the herd, and the routine police functions in the villages. They also undertook the resolution of disputes, as sometimes a firm hand was needed to enforce a settlement and keep the peace. Sometimes they forbade people to leave the camp if enemies might be near.[49] Llewellyn and Hoebel explain,

> The coercive authority of the military leaders bordered on the dictatorial in the hands of some of the fighting leaders. The function of fighting (and during the last two decades of their aboriginal existence the Cheyennes were fighting desperately) and policing in emergency lends itself readily to the development of summary power; and the qualities which brought a leader to the fore in Plains warfare were not exclusively those of balanced judgment and patient self-restraint. Nor is it clear that the ideological patterns of "As I struck the enemy, so I strike you" runs off without a vicious thrust toward striking "you" as

48. Llewellyn and Hoebel, 102.

49. Llewellyn and Hoebel, 108.

> "I" ought to strike the enemy. The ideological connection is, in any event, clear. The fact that some arrogant soldier chiefs "were just as mean to the enemy as they were to the people" is what caused them to be suffered. Willful leaders among them were not reluctant to use physical force. Cheyenne warriors submitted to whippings where it would have been inconceivable to a Comanche.[50]

The Cheyenne seem to have had few if any clear and binding rules to delineate the balance of power between the Council of Forty-Four and the military societies. The military societies seem to have been a later development after the Council, and they seem to have functioned primarily during the summer months. But their power seemed to increase as time progressed and as the Cheyenne came into conflict with other Plains nations and with the white man. Left unchecked, a serious power struggle could have erupted. But with the establishment of reservations came new forms of tribal government.

The most unique feature of the Cheyenne legal and governmental system is the entrustment to voluntary societies of clearly governmental functions, including national defense, law enforcement, and criminal investigation. But perhaps we regard this as unique because we are so acculturated to equate government with the State. It was not always so. Noah Webster's 1828 *American Dictionary of the English Language* offers twelve definitions of government, only five of which involve the state. Others include:

1. Direction; regulation. These precepts will serve for the *government* of our conduct.
2. Control; restraint. Men are apt to neglect the *government* of their temper and passions....
4. The exercise of authority by a parent or householder. Children are often ruined by a neglect of *government* in parents....
9. Manageableness; compliance, obsequiousness.
10. Regularity of behavior. *[Not in use.]*
11. Management of the limbs or body. *[Not in use.]*

50. Llewellyn and Hoebel, 104.

12. In *grammar*, the influence of a word in regard to construction, as when established usage requires that one word should cause another to be in a particular case or mode.[51]

If these early Americans can remind us that government is not solely the function of the State—that government includes personal self-discipline, family government, church government, and other forms of regulating human behavior—then the Cheyenne will have exercised a truly beneficial influence on American law and government.

Questions for Reflection, Discussion, and More Reflection

1. Although there is much variation, the Indian nations of North America seem to have enjoyed a much greater degree of personal freedom than those of Central America, even though their technological achievements are less spectacular and enduring. What might have caused this difference? Could the northern nations' wider spaces and greater mobility have been a contributing factor?
2. Does every society need a visible symbol like the Sacred Arrows to focus their attention on their traditions and values? What was the spiritual significance of the sweat lodge and the peace pipe?
3. Would you classify the Cheyenne as monotheists, polytheists, or henotheists? Is Maheo another name for the God worshipped by Christians and Jews, or an entirely different god?
4. What were the principal core values of the Cheyenne, and how did their legal system reflect these values?
5. How were the Cheyenne able to preserve law and order with such relatively mild punishments for criminal offenses? Can our society learn from their example?
6. Do you see a parallel between the ritual purification and renewal of the Sacred Arrows and the ritual cleansings of Old Testament

51. Noah Webster, *American Dictionary of the English Language* 1828 (San Francisco: Foundation for American Christian Education, 1967), "Government."

Israel? Do you see a parallel between Sweet Medicine ascending Bear Butte in South Dakota to receive instruction from the god Maheo, and Moses ascending Mt. Sinai to receive the Decalogue from Jehovah?

7. What significant legal points do you see in the case of the aborted unborn child which required the banishment of the child's mother until the Sacred Arrows were renewed and purified?
8. What was the function of the Council of Forty-Four, and what significance do you see in the way the Council was chosen and perpetuated?
9. Why did the Cheyenne so sharply separate the functions of the "war chiefs" and "peace chiefs"? Is this comparable to the way civilian and military authority is separated in Anglo-American societies?
10. What were the "military societies," and what functions did they fulfill in wartime and peacetime? Do they demonstrate that governmental functions which we normally assign to the State can be fulfilled by voluntary non-governmental entities?

Cheyenne Warriors. Edward S. Curtis, ca. 1905.

Iroquois Indians. William Alexander Drennan, 1914.

CHAPTER 11

IROQUOIS:
Early American Constitutionalism

Unlike the Incas, the Iroquois left no lasting pyramids or temples. Unlike the Maya, they left no written records of their history and accomplishments.[1] Unlike the Aztecs, they did not conquer or terrorize their neighbors.

But the Iroquois accomplished what the Incas, the Maya, and the Aztecs did not—a confederate republic which established order, security and justice, and yet preserved individual freedom and the autonomy of each tribe or republic. As Bruce Johansen says, few people today know that "a republic existed on our soil before anyone here had ever heard of John Locke, or Cato, the *Magna Charta*, Rousseau, Franklin, or Jefferson."[2]

The Iroquois consisted of, at first, five nations: the Mohawks, Oneidas, Onondagas, Cayugas, and Senecas, later joined by a sixth nation, the Tuscaroras. Around the year AD 1000, these five nations migrated to what is now New York. They lived by cultivating corn, beans, and squash, and by hunting, fishing, and gathering nuts, berries, and other wild foods. They did not build spacious palaces, but their bark-covered longhouses were functional and at least as warm and comfortable as the homes of the early Pilgrim and Puritan settlers.

Iroquois religious beliefs, like those of many North American Indians, stressed closeness to nature. They believed in a Creator known as Sky Holder and his companion Sky Woman, and in a host of other spirits, good and evil. They believed in a vital connection between the spirits of

1. The Iroquois did use wampum belts, long cords decorated with beads and other objects, which served as mnemonic (memory-aiding) devices. See William N. Fenton, *The Great Law and the Longhouse: A Political History of the Iroquois Confederacy* (Norman: U. of Oklahoma Press, 1998), 224–39.

2. Bruce E. Johansen, *Forgotten Founders: How the American Indian Helped Shape Democracy* (Boston: Harvard Common Press, 1982), xiv.

all humans and those of the objects and forces of nature. They believed, further, that each person has an inner spiritual power called *orenda*, that combated the powers of evil. Each person's *orenda* combined with those of his relatives to form a total *orenda* or power of the clan. When an individual died, the clan's total *orenda* was reduced.[3]

William N. Fenton, in his classic work *The Great Law and the Longhouse: A Political History of the Iroquois Confederacy*, identifies twenty core beliefs that arise out of the Iroquois cosmology:

1. The native earth. The earth, our mother, is living and expanding continually, imparting its life-giving force to all growing things on which our lives depend.
2. Renewal. The alternation of seasons and tasks is attuned to ecological time, as are the lives of plants and animals, which rest while the earth sleeps. Ceremonial obligations adhere to the same law.
3. "It is us women that count." A chain of kinship connects all members of society, running from the dead through mothers to the smallest child and reaching even those as yet unborn. Consequently, the Iroquois love their dead and cherish their children. The same concept underlies the chain of peace and friendship.
4. Paternity is secondary: *agadoni* comes after *ohwachira*. The fatherless boy becomes hero; rejected by his matrilineage, he may seek his father to learn. One's father's kin, or *agadoni*, are a second line of appeal in any enterprise.
5. Twins are lucky. They are creative, but sibling rivalry occurs. Only the pure who are "downfended," secluded, may succeed.
6. The law of the kettle. Hospitality is a right and duty to share. Throwing ashes is the negation of hospitality, sharing, friendship, peace, harmony, and accord; it is typically paranoid behavior that the culture seeks to guard against.
7. Home is where one customarily sits. The bench or bed is the place of rest, reflection, and council.
8. Do not oppose the forces of nature. Going to water, dip with the current when making medicine. When traveling, go around

3. Alvin M. Josephy, Jr., *500 Nations: An Illustrated History of North American Indians* (New York: Gramercy Books, 1994), 47.

natural objects such as fallen logs and part the brush. In ceremonial circuits, adhere to the "living way." Circuits are counterclockwise in life, clockwise in the hereafter.[4]

9. Three is a regular way. Life and customary procedures are fairly established. Protocol is vital.
10. *Orenda* (supernatural power). Adheres to inanimate and animate things, to aspects of the environment, and to sequences of behavior.
11. Equanimity. Restraint is important. One must not exert too much power and "spoil it." The equable person succeeds.
12. Impersonation. Acting the role is a means of taking on power.
13. *Kanonhenyonk*, or returning thanks from the earth to the sky. By continual and repeated greetings and thanks one must remember the hierarchy of spirit forces between the earth and the sky that the Creator appointed to assist people in the enjoyment of the earth. All of these must be remembered and balanced in the fulfillment of their appointed tasks.
14. Dreams compel fulfillment. Once the "word" that the soul desires is discovered, it must be fulfilled. Prescribed ceremonies, whether diverting the mind by games, dances, or something else, must be renewed during one's lifetime.
15. Sending up smoke. The column of smoke, which carried the gods back to the sky world, is also a vehicle for sending up words—prayers and incantations. Smoke itself symbolizes thought, desire, community, and government. The metaphorical column of smoke that arises from the central fire of the longhouse at Onondaga symbolizes the league itself. Tobacco is the word: committing it to the fire closes a contract with the spirit forces.
16. Earth shakers. These are friendly spirits such as Turtle, Thunder, Hadui, and "Our Uncles, the bigheads," the dream heralds of the midwinter ceremonies.
17. A man never refuses when asked, and he never shows fear.

4. This may be a recognition that whirlpools usually spin counter-clockwise north of the equator. The Iroquois probably did not know that whirlpools usually spin clockwise south of the equator. This is variously attributed to gravity, the earth's electro-magnetic field, or the "Coriolis Effect" of the earth's rotation.

18. Things go by twos and fours. Forked path, divided mind, sex, seasons, moieties, life/death, balance of forces, four tests, four ceremonies. Twenty has a capital value.
19. Reciprocity. This takes place between moieties for requickening life and faculties, for restoring society, and in all associations for renewal.
20. Mind. Culture is an affair of the mind. "Good mind" is prerequisite to welfare, whether personal, interpersonal, or social. It is essential for consensus and indispensable for peace.[5]

The family was the basic unit of Iroquois society, and extended families formed clans. The clan often lived together in a long house which was normally about 80 feet long but in some cases was up to 200 feet long, and about 25 feet wide, with partitioned space for each family. Each family section contained raised platforms covered with reed mats or pelts; these served as seats during the day and as beds at night. So much was the longhouse the center and symbol of Iroquois life that the Iroquois nations became known as the Hodenosaunee, or People of the Longhouse.

Life in an Iroquois village was structured. Men served as warriors and providers, while women owned the longhouses, did the housework, and cared for the children. For religious purposes the Iroquois nations had an organized priesthood of men and women called Keepers of the Faith who supervised religious rites.[6]

The Great Law of Peace, the basis for the Iroquois Confederacy, is of uncertain origin. According to Iroquois oral tradition, their people were brave warriors, and each clan believed itself responsible to avenge the death of one of their warriors. This led to constant warring and feuding among the various nations, until one day a Huron (some say Onondaga) elder named Daganoweda appeared among the Iroquois nations and preached a message of peace. He had observed that peace conferences frequently resolved wars and brought peace, but when the conference ended, the wars usually resumed. He concluded that the peace conference should become a permanent institution. He shared this proposal with a friend named Hayowentha, better known through Longfellow's poetry as Hiawatha, and together they developed a plan for a permanent

5. William N. Fenton, *The Great Law and the Longhouse: A Political History of the Iroquois Confederacy* (Norman: U. of Oklahoma Press, 1998), 49–50.

6. Josephy, 46–47.

confederation. Daganoweda preferred that the confederacy be open to any nation that wanted the benefits of perfect peace, but at Hiawatha's insistance it was limited to nations of Iroquois language and ethnicity. Their proposal received a cold reception from the Onondagas, but the Oneidas were much more receptive. A few years later a war led to a peace conference. There Daganoweda and Hiawatha presented their plan, there it was accepted, and there the Iroquois Confederacy began. The Tuscaroras joined the Confederacy around AD 1714.

The dating of the conference that began the Confederacy is uncertain. The Senecas' oral history says they adopted the Great Law of Peace shortly after a total eclipse of the sun. That led Paul Wallace to date the beginning around AD June 28, 1451, because a solar eclipse took place in that year. But Barbara Mann and Jerry Fields of Toledo University believe the Great Law coincided with the eclipse of AD August 31, 1142,[7] because the 1451 eclipse was total only in Pennsylvania rather than in New York Iroquois territory. Furthermore, the French explorer Jacques Cartier visited the Iroquois in the year AD 1535, and the Iroquois say this was during the tenure of the 33rd Chief Lord. Since the Chief Lord normally served a life term, 1142 would be a more likely date than 1451. If the Confederacy began in 1451 and there had been 33 Chief Lords by 1535, each of the 33 Chief Lords would have served an average of 2.5 years; if the Confederacy began in 1142, each would have served an average of 11.9 years.

The genius of Daganoweda and Hiawatha is shown in their creation of a republic that lasted for hundreds of years, enabled the Iroquois nations to deal effectively with each other, with other Indian nations, and eventually with the white man, without compromising their individual freedom and local autonomy. An outstanding feature of the Great Law is the way it apportions power, privilege, and responsibility among the various nations, factions, and interests within the Confederacy. The Longhouse was conceived as a metaphor for the entire Iroquois Confederacy, and just as each individual in the longhouse has his own special role, so each nation has its own special role in the Great Longhouse known as the Iroquois Confederacy. The Mohawks, meaning People of the Place of the Crystals, were the Keepers of the Eastern Door; that is, they protected the Confederacy from attackers from the east. The Oneida, People of the Erected Stone, and the Cayuga, People of the Great Pipe, were the Younger Brothers

7. Bruce E. Johansen, "Dating the Iroquois Confederacy," *Akwesasne Notes New Series* Fall 1995, I:3, 62–63, www.ratical.org/many_worlds/6Nations/DatingIC.html (accessed 28 April, 2016).

whose consent was required to pass a measure in council, whereas the Senecas and Mohawks were the Older Brothers who normally initiated proposals. The Onondaga, People of the Hills, were the Keepers of the Fire who were responsible for maintaining the fire in the center of the longhouse, or maintaining affairs in the interior of the Confederacy. The Seneca, People of the Great Hill, were the Keepers of the Western Door who protected the Confederacy against attacks from the west.[8]

The Great Law was passed down by oral tradition from generation to generation, and was also communicated by wampum belts which contained coded messages. In its Preamble, the Great Law is compared to a tree:

> 1. I am Dekanawidah and with the Five Nations' Confederate Lords I plant the Tree of Great Peace. I plant it in your territory, Adodarhoh, and the Onondaga Nation, in the territory of you who are Firekeepers.
>
> I name the tree the Tree of the Great Long Leaves. Under the shade of this Tree of the Great Peace we spread the soft white feathery down of the globe thistle as seats for you, Adodarhoh, and your cousin Lords.

The Great Law then extends an invitation to join the Confederacy:

> 2. Roots have spread out from the Tree of the Great Peace, one to the north, one to the east, one to the south and one to the west. The name of these roots is The Great White Roots and their nature is Peace and Strength.
>
> If any man or any nation outside the Five Nations shall obey the laws of the Great Peace and make known their disposition to the Lords of the Confederacy, they may trace the Roots to the Tree and if their minds are clean and they are obedient and promise to obey the wishes of the Confederate Council, they shall be welcomed to take shelter beneath the Tree of the Long Leaves.
>
> We place at the top of the Tree of the Long Leaves an Eagle who is able to see afar. If he sees in the distance any evil approaching or any danger threatening he will at once warn the people in the Confederacy.

8. http://syracusethenandnow.org/History/Early_History/IroquoisNations.html (accessed 13 May, 2016).

The purpose of the Confederacy was to provide a means by which the Five Nations could work together in matters of common interest, to provide a strong defense against outside nations, and to provide a means by which they could resolve differences among themselves without resorting to war. But they clearly never intended to strip the Nations of sovereignty in the management of their own internal affairs. The Great Law uses the symbol of a council fire for the transaction of business and often says, "the council fires are burning," meaning the Lords are in session or willing to come into session to hear the people's petitions. Paragraph 97 reads,

> 97. Before the real people united their nations, each nation had its council fires. Before the Great Peace their councils were held. The five Council fires shall continue to burn as before and they are not quenched. The Lords of each nation in [the] future shall settle their nation's affairs at this council fire governed always by the laws and rules of the council of the Confederacy and by the Great Peace.

In these council fires we may dimly discern a foretaste of the federalist design of the Framers of the United States Constitution, and particularly of the Tenth Amendment—that they may "form a more perfect Union," without intruding upon the sovereignty of the states.

Furthermore, each Nation within the Confederacy was entitled to keep its own unique religious practices:

> 99. The rites and festivals of each nation shall remain undisturbed and shall continue as before because they were given by the people of old times as useful and necessary for the good of men.

Just as each nation had its own role in the Confederacy, so each nation checked and balanced the others. A major proposal, such as a declaration of war, required the unanimous consent of all five nations, and in general the Confederacy strove for unanimity or at least consensus rather than bare majority will. Other proposals were first considered by the "Older Brothers," the Senecas and Mohawks. If approved, the proposal went to the "Younger Brothers," the Cayugas and Oneidas, for consideration. If the Older and Younger Brothers disagreed, the proposal was sent to the Onondagas, the Keepers of the Fire (interior affairs) to break the tie. If the Older and Younger Brothers agreed, the proposal was sent to the

Onondagas for confirmation. If the Onondagas confirmed the proposal, it was adopted. If the Onondagas rejected the proposal, it was sent back to the Older and Younger Brothers for reconsideration. If the Older and Younger Brothers both approved the proposal a second time, the Onondagas then had to accept it (Paragraphs 9–12). Johansen suggests that a rough comparison could be made to the United States Constitution. The Older and Younger Brothers are like the United States Senate and House of Representatives, who normally must agree before a bill can become law. The Keepers of the Fire (Onondagas) are like the President, who can veto a bill passed by both Houses of Congress, subject to being overridden by a two-thirds vote of both Houses of Congress.[9]

All nations were represented at the Grand Council, but the larger and more influential nations apparently had greater representation than others. The original Roll Call of the Chiefs/Lords seems to recognize nine Mohawk lords, nine Oneida lords, fourteen Onondaga lords, ten Cayuga lords, and eight Seneca lords, each with a distinct title.[10] One recalls that at the 1787 Constitutional Convention the larger states wanted proportional representation by population while the smaller states wanted every state to be represented equally—a dispute that resulted in the Sherman Compromise of a two-house Congress. One wonders whether a similar discussion occurred during the formulation of the Great Law.

Power is also divided between men and women, and while both sexes have substantial power in the Confederacy, the roles of men and women are sharply differentiated. In family life, the men were warriors and providers, while the women kept the household and raised the children. In the affairs of the Confederacy and of each nation within the Confederacy, only men could serve as lords and presiding lord—but only women could vote to elect them to office, although the men of the clan could disapprove the women's choice. The Great Law reads,

> 53. When the Royaneh women, holders of a Lordship title, select one of their sons as a candidate, they shall select one who is trustworthy, of good character, of honest disposition, one who manages his own affairs, supports his own family, if any, and who has proven a faithful man to the Nation.

9. Johansen, 25. The analogy is of course imperfect, but a good analogy nevertheless.

10. Fenton, 193–94.

> 54. When a Lordship title becomes vacant through death or other cause, the Royaneh women of the clan in which the title is hereditary shall hold a council and shall choose one from among their sons to fill the office made vacant. Such a candidate shall not be the father of any Confederate Lord. If the choice is unanimous the name is referred to the men relatives of the clan. If they should disapprove it shall be their duty to select a candidate from among their own number. If then the men and women are unable to decide which of the two candidates shall be named, then the matter shall be referred to the Confederate Lords in the Clan. They shall decide which candidate shall be named. If the men and the women agree to a candidate his name shall be referred to the sister clans for confirmation. If the sister clans confirm the choice, they shall refer their action to their Confederate Lords who shall ratify the choice and present it to their cousin Lords, and if the cousin Lords confirm the name then the candidate shall be installed by the proper ceremony for the conferring of Lordship titles.

Apparently the Iroquois recognized that, while men are often more natural leaders, women are often better able to discern the qualities that make men good leaders.

The power of women was asserted in another way—lineage and hereditary titles were traced through the female parent:

> 44. The lineal descent of the people of the Five Nations shall run in the female line. Women shall be considered the progenitors of the Nation. They shall own the land and the soil. Men and women shall follow the status of the mother.
>
> 45. The women heirs of the Confederated Lordship titles shall be called Royaneh (Noble) for all time to come.
>
> 46. The women of the Forty Eight (now fifty) Royaneh families shall be the heirs of the Authorized Names for all time to come....
>
> 47. If the female heirs of a Confederate Lord's title become extinct, the title right shall be given by the Lords of the Confederacy to the sister family whom they shall elect and that family shall hold the name and transmit it to their (female) heirs, but they shall not appoint any of their sons as a candidate for a title until

> all the eligible men of the former family shall have died or otherwise have become ineligible.

Iroquois women enjoyed freedom and power that were unknown to women in many other cultures, but they did not consider their household duties demeaning. In at least one respect the Great Law preserved a traditional role for women:

> 50. The Royaneh women of the Confederacy heirs of the Lordship titles shall elect two women of their family as cooks for the Lord when the people shall assemble at his house for business or other purposes.
>
> It is not good nor honorable for a Confederate Lord to allow his people whom he has called to go hungry.

The Great Law also recognized different responsibilities of leadership in time of peace and in time of war. While the Lords governed in peacetime, each Nation was to elect a War Chief who was ready to take command in time of war:

> 37. There shall be one War Chief for each Nation and their duties shall be to carry messages for their Lords and to take up the arms of war in case of emergency. They shall not participate in the proceedings of the Confederate Council but shall watch its progress and in case of an erroneous action by a Lord they shall receive the complaints of the people and convey the warnings of the women to him. The people who wish to convey messages to the Lords in the Confederate Council shall do so through the War Chief of their Nation. It shall ever be his duty to lay the cases, questions, and propositions of the people before the Confederate Council.
>
> 38. When a War Chief dies another shall be installed by the same rite as that by which a Lord is installed.
>
> 39. If a War Chief acts contrary to instructions or against the provisions of the Laws of the Great Peace, doing so in the capacity of his office, he shall be deposed by his women relatives and by his men relatives. Either the women or the men alone or jointly may act in such a case. The women title holders shall then choose another candidate.

Interestingly, the War Chief did not participate in the proceedings of the Confederate Council. Apparently they recognized that one might be a good military leader but lack the qualities for leadership in peace, such as mature judgment. Likewise they may have recognized that a good peacetime leader might, because of age or lack of strength or health, not be an effective military leader. However, the War Chiefs were to attend the Grand Council meetings and present their people's concerns there. Possibly one reason for this provision was to give the War Chiefs experience in Council affairs so that, when they became older, they might become Lords.

In this way the Great Law may have presaged another feature of American constitutionalism—subordination of military authority to civilian leadership. But as we have seen, this subordination was not absolute; the War Chiefs attended Council meetings and served as advocates for their Nations. Furthermore, Paragraph 79 provides that one War Chief "shall be vested with a double office, duty and with double authority. One-half of his being shall hold the Lordship title and the other half shall hold the title of War Chief." He played a prominent role in calling the Nations to war. "The warriors shall choose one of the five War Chiefs to lead the army into battle," and Paragraph 81 requires that this commanding War Chief shall "deliver an oration exhorting them with great zeal to be brave and courageous and never to be guilty of cowardice. At the conclusion of his oration he shall march forward and commence the War Song and he shall sing:

"Now I am greatly surprised
And, therefore I shall use it—
The power of my War Song.
I am of the Five Nations
And I shall make supplication
To the Almighty Creator.
He has furnished this army.
My warriors shall be mighty
In the strength of the Creator.
Between him and my song they are
For it was he who gave the song
This war song that I sing!"

Before going to war, the Iroquois were to try to arrange terms of peace. War was to be by formal declaration, so the enemy would know the reasons for the declaration of war and have the opportunity to try to make peace if they so desired. As Paragraph 88 says,

> 88. When the proposition to establish the Great Peace is made to a foreign nation it shall be done in mutual council. The foreign nation is to be persuaded by reason and urged to come into the Great Peace. If the Five Nations fail to obtain the consent of the nation at the first council, a second council shall be held, and upon a second failure, a third council shall be held, and this third council shall end the peaceful methods of persuasion. At the third council the War Chief of the Five Nations shall address the Chief of the foreign nation and request him three times to accept the Great Peace. If refusal steadfastly follows, the War Chief shall let the bunch of white lake shell drop from his outstretched hand to the ground and shall bound quickly forward and club the offending chief to death. War shall thereby be declared and the War Chief shall have his warriors at his back to meet any emergency. War must continue until the contest is won by the Five Nations.

Once the war was won, the defeated nation was disarmed of all weapons of war (Paragraph 87). The defeated nation then continued its existence as a conquered nation under Iroquois rule. The conquered nation continued its own system of internal government (Paragraph 84) but had no voice in the councils of the Iroquois Confederacy (Paragraph 86). Having disarmed these conquered nations, the Iroquois took upon themselves the military defense of those nations when they were attacked by others. As a result, the Confederacy found itself surrounded by a buffer of unarmed nations which often proved tempting bait to enemy attackers, but the combined forces of the Five Nations of the Confederacy were sufficient to overcome these attacks and often brought still another nation into the Iroquois sphere of influence.[11]

Foreign nations were allowed to enter the Confederacy, but only on a temporary basis and without the right to participate in government (Paragraphs 73–78). In language remarkably similar to Acts 17:26, Paragraph 73 declares,

---

11. W. J. Sidis, *The Tribes and the States* (Wampanoag Nation: 1935, 1982), IV:14, www.sidis.net/TSContents.htm (accessed 13 May, 2016).

> The Great Creator has made us of the one blood and of the same soil he made us and as only different tongues constitute different nations he established different hunting grounds and territories and made boundary lines between them.

The Confederacy was most insistent that its members not accept any foreign law. According to Paragraph 58, "...if at any time any one of the Confederate Lords chooses to submit to the law of a foreign people he is no longer in but out of the Confederacy, and persons of this class shall be called 'They have alienated themselves.' Likewise such persons who submit to laws of foreign nations shall forfeit all birthrights and claims on the Five Nations Confederacy and territory."

The Lords held their offices by the consent of their people, and the people could remove them if they were false to the trust reposed in them. Paragraph 19 provides that

> 19. If at any time it shall be manifest that a Confederate Lord has not in mind the welfare of the people or disobeys the rules of this Great Law, the men or women of the Confederacy, or both jointly, shall come to the Council and upbraid the erring Lord through his War Chief. If the complaint of the people through the War chief is not heeded the first time it shall be uttered again and then if no attention is given a third complaint and third warning shall be given. If the Lord is contumacious the matter shall go to the council of War Chiefs. The War Chiefs shall then divest the erring Lord of his title by order of the women in whom the titleship is vested. When the Lord is deposed the women shall notify the Confederate Lords through their War chief, and the Confederate Lords shall sanction the act. The women will then select another of their sons as a candidate and the Lords shall elect him. Then shall the chosen one be installed by the Installation Ceremony.

When a Lord is to be deposed, his War Chief shall address him as follows:

> "So you, __________, disregard and set at naught the warnings of your women relatives. So you fling the warnings over your shoulder to cast them behind you.
>
> "Behold the brightness of the Sun and in the brightness of the Sun's light I depose you of your title and remove the sacred

> emblem of your Lordship title. I remove from your brow the deer's antlers [symbol of authority], which was the emblem of your position and token of your nobility. I now depose you and return the antlers to the women whose heritage they are."

The War Chief shall now address the women of the deposed Lord and say:

> "Mothers, as I have now deposed your Lord, I now return to you the emblem and the title of Lordship, therefore repossess them."

Again addressing himself to the deposed Lord he shall say:

> "As I have now deposed and discharged you so you are now no longer Lord. You shall now go your way alone, the rest of the people of the Confederacy will not go with you, for we know not the kind of mind that possesses you. As the Creator has nothing to do with wrong so he will not come to rescue you from the precipice of destruction in which you have cast yourself. You shall never be restored to the position which you once occupied."
>
> Then shall the War Chief address himself to the Lords of the Nation to which the deposed Lord belongs and say:
>
>> "Know you, my Lords, that I have taken the deer's antlers from the brow of ____________, the emblem of his position, and token of his greatness."
>
> The Lords of the Confederacy shall then have no other alternative than to sanction the discharge of the offending Lord.

As we have already seen, references to the central role of the Creator are sprinkled throughout the Great Law of Peace, and He and His creation were to be recognized in the deliberations of the Confederacy:

> 7. Whenever the Confederate Lords shall assemble for the purpose of holding a council, the Onondaga Lords shall open it by expressing their gratitude to their cousin Lords and greeting them, and they shall make an address and offer thanks to the earth where men dwell, to the streams of water, the pools, the springs and the lakes, to the maize and the fruits, to the medicinal herbs and trees, to the forest trees for their usefulness, to the animals that serve as food and give their pelts for clothing,

> to the great winds and the lesser winds, to the Thunderers, to the sun, the mighty warrior, to the moon, to the messengers of the Creator who reveal his wishes and to the Great Creator who dwells in the heavens above, who gives all things useful to men, and who is the source and the ruler of health and life.

And the Lords of the Confederacy had a special responsibility to teach their people about the Creator and His ways:

> 26. It shall be the duty of all of the Five Nations Confederate Lords, from time to time as occasion demands, to act as mentors and spiritual guides of their people and remind them of their Creator's will and words. They shall say:
>
> > "Hearken, that peace may continue unto future days!
> >
> > "Always listen to the words of the Great Creator, for he has spoken.
> >
> > "United people, let not evil find lodging in your minds.
> >
> > "For the Great Creator has spoken and the cause of Peace shall not become old.
> >
> > "The cause of peace shall not die if you remember the Great Creator."
>
> Every Confederate Lord shall speak words such as these to promote peace.

The Great Law's open acknowledgment of the Creator should not be surprising when we recognize that in the Iroquois worldview, spirituality pervaded every aspect of life. As David Yarrow wrote,

> To Iroquois traditionalists the Great Law of Peace isn't merely a form of government, but religious practice of an ancient spiritual legacy. Peacemaker [the founder of the Confederacy] wasn't a military hero or social leader, but a messenger of the Creator. Following The Great Law is a spiritual practice, and those who follow the Longhouse tradition are "faithkeepers."

There's no separation of church and state in Iroquois society. Indeed, spirituality lies at the root of government and law.[12]

---

12. David Yarrow, "The Great Law of Peace: New World Roots of American Democracy," September, 1987, www.kahonwes.com/iroquois/document1.html (accessed 13 May, 2016).

The modern compartmentalization of spirituality and its radical separation from the rest of life would have seemed utterly foreign to the People of the Longhouse, as to others not steeped in modernity.

On July 4, 1744, a meeting took place between English colonial leaders and the Lords of the Confederacy. Canasstego, the speaker of the Grand Council, told the colonists,

> We have one Thing further to say, and that is, We heartily recommend Union and a good Agreement between you our Brethren. Never disagree, but preserve a strict Friendship for one another, and thereby you, as well as we, will become the stronger.
>
> Our wise Forefathers established Union and Amity between the Five Nations; this has made us formidable; this has given us great Weight and Authority with our neighbouring Nations.
>
> We are a powerful Confederacy and by your observing the same Methods our wise Forefathers have taken, you will acquire much Strength and Power; therefore, whatever befalls you, do not fall out with one another.[13]

Benjamin Franklin was familiar with the Great Law of Peace. In 1754, a congress convened in Albany, New York, to consider a plan for uniting the northern colonies and to formulate an alliance with the Iroquois against the French. Franklin commented favorably on the proposed union and pointed to "the strength of the League which has bound our Friends the Iroquois together in a common tie which no crisis, however grave, since its foundation has managed to disrupt."[14] Earlier Franklin had written,

> It would be a very strange thing if Six Nations of Ignorant Savages should be capable of forming a scheme for such an Union and be able to execute it in such a manner, as that it has subsisted Ages, and appears indissoluble, and yet a like union should be impracticable for ten or a dozen English colonies.[15]

Johansen, Sidis and others believe that the Framers of the United States Constitution drew their inspiration in part from the Great Law of Peace.

---

13. Fenton, 432; cf. Johansen, 61–62.

14. Johansen, 71.

15. Johansen, 66. Johansen notes that this comment might seem like a racial slur, but suggests that Franklin was actually insulting those colonists who erroneously thought the Iroquois were ignorant savages.

Lewis Henry Morgan, known as the "father of American anthropology," wrote in 1851 that

> The [six] nations sustained nearly the same relation to the [Iroquois] league that the American states bear to the Union. In the former, several oligarchies were contained within one, in the same manner as in the latter, several republics are embraced in one republic.... Their whole civil policy was averse to the concentration of power in the hands of any single individual, but inclined to the opposite principle of division among a number of equals.[16]

The points of comparison are substantial. In many ways the Great Law of Peace parallels or at least resembles the Articles of Confederation and the United States Constitution: federalism (power delegated to a united government with other powers reserved to the individual nations or states), limited powers, checks and balances, freedom for each nation to follow its own religious practices, local autonomy, two-house legislature, suffrage, subordination of the military to civilian leadership. But except for Benjamin Franklin (and Thomas Jefferson and Thomas Paine, who were not present at the Constitutional Convention), it is not clear that any of the other delegates were aware of the Great Law of Peace or considered it in their debates. The Iroquois Confederacy is not mentioned in Madison's *Notes on the Convention*, nor in the *Federalist Papers*.

And there are differences. The Iroquois Confederacy had no separation of powers like the Constitution provides. There was no executive branch comparable to that of the Constitution; the presiding Lord was more like a Speaker of the House than like the President. Nor did the Confederacy have an independent judiciary.

And similarities do not prove influence. The fact that two men are wearing blue neckties does not mean that either influenced the other's decision to wear a blue necktie. The Framers had plenty of Old World sources they could draw upon for their ideas: Locke, Blackstone, Montesquieu, the Council of Utrecht, the Anglo-Saxons, the Vikings, the Celts, the Greeks, the Romans, and of course, the twelve-tribe confederacy of ancient Israel, to name only a few.

16. Lewis Henry Morgan, *League of the Ho-de-no-sau-nee, or Iroquois* (1851); quoted by Johansen, 8–9.

The influence of the Iroquois Confederacy upon the United States Constitution has become a controversial issue. Unfortunately, on both sides the debate has degenerated to name-calling, and ideology and multicultural political correctness seem more important than objective scholarship. A good work arguing for Iroquois influence is *Exemplar of Liberty: Native America and the Evolution of Democracy* by Donald A. Grinde and Bruce E. Johansen (Los Angeles: American Indian Studies Center, UCLA, 1991). An equally fine work that is more skeptical of the Iroquois influence theory is Donald S. Lutz, "The Iroquois Confederation Constitution: An Analysis," *Publius: The Journal of Federalism* 28:2 (Spring 1998), pages 99–127.

Do parallels exist? Definitely, but so do differences. In fact, the Iroquois Confederacy bears more resemblance to the Articles of Confederation than to the U.S. Constitution.

Were the Framers aware of these parallels? Franklin was, but he didn't mention them at the Convention, and other delegates give no evidence of such awareness.

Did Franklin or other Framers consciously use the Iroquois Confederacy as their model? The evidence is, at best, inconclusive.

Consciously or unconsciously, were the Framers influenced by the Iroquois Confederacy? Maybe.

To what extent were they influenced? To answer that question, and to demonstrate a clear connection, more research is needed.

But the Indians were (so far as we know) the original Americans, and they certainly helped shape modern America's self-image. As Charles Sanford wrote, "The Indians presented a reverse image of European civilization which helped America establish a national identity that was neither savage nor civilized."[17] Felix Cohen noted that while Americans of European descent conquered the Indians militarily, "... in agriculture, in government, in sport, in education, and in our views of nature and our fellow men, it is the first Americans who have taken captive their battlefield conquerors."[18]

While historians "have seen America only as an imitation of Europe," Cohen wrote, "The real epic of America is the yet unfinished story of the Americanization of the white man."[19]

17. Charles Sanford, *The Quest for Paradise* (1961); quoted by Johansen, 119.

18. Felix Cohen, *American Scholar* (1952); quoted by Johansen, 7.

19. Cohen, 10.

11 Iroquois: *Early American Constitutionalism*

Questions for Reflection, Discussion, and More Reflection

1. Does the religion of the Iroquois constitute pantheism, henotheism, or monotheism? Does it involve "serving the creature more than the Creator" (Romans 1:25)? Or was the creator god Sky Holder a Supreme Being like the God of the Bible?
2. Do the core beliefs identified by Fenton arise out of the Iroquois cosmology, or are they part of the Law of Nature that has been written on the hearts of all people (Romans 2:14–15)?
3. Was the Iroquois Confederacy typical of North American Indians? Compare it to the Creek Confederacy, the Powhatan Confederacy, the Huron Confederacy, the Algonquin Confederacy, and others, and note the similarities and differences.
4. Explain how the Longhouse was significant in the life of the Iroquois, and how it serves as a microcosm of the Confederacy and of the world and the universe.
5. How did the Great Law of Peace balance the interests of large and small nations? Of war chiefs and peace chiefs? Of the Confederation verses the individual nations? Of men and women?
6. How do the Great Law's provisions for the declaration, conduct, and conclusion of war compare to the law of war of the Old World?
7. The Iroquois have been called the "Romans of America." How do the Iroquois and Rome compare? How do they differ? Is the Iroquois Confederacy more like the Roman Republic, or the Roman Empire? Note the similarity in the responsibility both assume for the defense of their conquered subjects.
8. What is the relationship between God and spirituality with law and government according to the Great Law of Peace? How does that compare to the colonial charters, or to the U.S. Constitution?

Questions continued on next page....

Questions *continued*

9. Except for statements of Ben Franklin, is there evidence that the Framers of the U.S. Constitution were familiar with the Iroquois Great Law of Peace and considered it when they drafted the U.S. Constitution? What similarities do you see between the Great Law and the Constitution? What differences? Does the Great Law more closely resemble the Constitution, or the Articles of Confederation?

10. Consider Cohen's statement that "The real epic of America is the yet unfinished story of the Americanization of the white man." Did the early settlers who came to America intend to create a replica of European culture, or did they intend something different? Is there something in the character of the American Indians that uniquely describes what the character of the American nation was to be—something free and untamed? Did the Indians of that era enjoy a freedom and vitality that Europeans had enjoyed a thousand years ago but that has all but vanished in Europe?

OBSERVATIONS ON ANCIENT LAW

Ancient Constitutionalism: Echoes of Eden?

If we have seen farther than others, it is because we have stood on the shoulders of giants.[1]

In Book I we have explored the systems of law and government of eleven civilizations in various parts of the world. We have seen that they were not merely primitive or stagnant. Rather, they laid the foundations on which we have built. Several striking features stand out.

Primitive?

First, human nature has changed very little, if at all, over the past four thousand years of recorded history. The judges and lawmakers in these civilizations faced the same issues and problems we face today. People committed crimes; others wanted vengeance. People embarked upon business ventures and entered into contracts with others; conditions changed, and these business associations had to be modified or dissolved. People married; people divorced. People knew they were going to die, so they made plans for the distribution of their estates. People disagreed, and they took their differences to the courts, and sometimes they lied. The courts had to decide whom to believe and whom to disbelieve, so they devised rules of evidence and penalties for perjury, and they established various levels of appeal to correct errors. As we read statutes, contracts, deeds, and testaments from ancient times, we are amazed at how similar they are to those of today.

On a national level, complex empires exist from the beginning of recorded history. People aspire to power, and to get it and keep it they sometimes oppress others. Stronger nations conquer weaker nations, and

1. This metaphor is commonly attributed to Sir Isaac Newton (*Letter to Robert Hooke*, 1673), but can be traced to John of Salisbury (*Metalogican*, AD 1159), who attributed it to Bernard of Chartres (d. AD 1124).

then try to govern them, while the conquered plan rebellion and aspire to independence. The architects of these empires face the same issues constitutional scholars and political scientists face today: how to separate legislative, executive, and judicial power so none become tyrannical; how to enable these branches and levels of government to check and balance one another; how to govern conquered nations. Few if any features of our present constitutional republic lack a counterpart somewhere in the ancient world.

Evolutionary Development?

Second, the world's legal systems do not reflect evolutionary development from the patriarchal (or matriarchal) family, or from the bartered exchange, or from the blood feud. At least as far as recorded history reveals, they begin as complex, sophisticated systems, well-planned to deal with human problems.

In some ways, legal systems degenerate with time. In Mesopotamia, as in other societies, the death penalty at first covers only a few offenses, but with time capital offenses proliferate. Early Mesopotamia, like Egypt, India, and the Iroquois, gave women substantial rights, but these rights were gradually curtailed as time went on. Slavery is rare in early Mesopotamia and in many early societies, including those of Central America, but slavery proliferates with time. In this respect Judeo-Christian civilization is a rare exception.

Certainly laws have proliferated and become more complex. Certainly governments have grown in size and function. As a general trend, laws multiply, governments grow, and government power increases and becomes more centralized. But more laws does not mean wiser laws, and growth of government often comes with a decrease in individual freedom.

Yes, we do stand on the shoulders of giants. We learn from their wisdom, and we learn from their mistakes. But if the course of history is any indication, we learn less than we should. We ignore their wisdom because we think we're wiser, and we learn from their mistakes only by repeating them.

C.S. Lewis spoke of a "chronological snobbery," which he explained by saying, "the uncritical acceptance of the intellectual climate common to our own age and the assumption that whatever has gone out of date is on that account discredited. You must find why it went out of date. Was it ever refuted (and if so by whom, where, and how conclusively) or did it merely die away as fashions do? If the latter, this tells us nothing about its truth or falsehood. From seeing this, one passes to the realization that our own age is also 'a period,' and certainly has, like all periods, its own characteristic illusions."[2]

Is ours truly the wisest generation in history? Or do we suppose ourselves the wisest solely because we are the most recent?

Higher Law?

Third, every civilization we have studied has believed that its laws were not simply manmade; they were given by a higher Source. The Babylonian King Hammurabi claimed that the god Bel, Lord of Heaven and Earth, gave him his famous legal code. The Persian kings believed their laws came from the supreme god Ahuramazda. The Egyptians believed their pharaohs were themselves gods, and that the laws of Egypt were the gift of the sun god Ra and the goddess Ma'at. The laws of India, the Code of Manu, came from the Self-existent Svayambhu. The Chinese ruled under the Mandate of Heaven. The Hawaiian laws were *kapus* pronounced by their gods. The Inca was a descendant of the sun god; his decrees reflected the divine original of the sun god. The Maya rulers were priests to the sun god and their laws and edicts were given in service of that god. The Aztecs were the servants of their god Huitzilopochtli, and their military and political achievements, as well as their bloody sacrifices, were to aid the sun god in his struggle against the forces of evil. The Cheyenne chief Sweet Medicine received the laws of his people from the supreme god Maheo at the sacred mountain Bear Butte. The Iroquois Confederacy was based upon the Great Law of Peace which the Creator gave to Daganoweda and Hiawatha.

Many of these civilizations spoke of a special power or condition that applied when man and his laws were in harmony with the higher laws of the Divine Being. The Mesopotamians called it *kittu* and *mesaru*; the Persians called it *kiten*, the Egyptians, *ma'at.* The sages of India related their laws to brahmin, *dharma,* and *karma.* The Chinese spoke of the Mandate of Heaven and the Tao, and Li and Lu as well as that cosmic *chi* energy which unites and invigorates the universe and all mankind. The Hawaiian chiefs ruled with a special divine power called *mana,* which the Maya called *ik,* the Zapotecs called *pi,* the Mixtecs called *yni* or *ini,* and

2. C.S. Lewis, *Surprised by Joy: The Shape of My Early Life* (Harcourt, Brace, Jovanovich 1955), 207.

the Aztecs called *tona,* and the Iroquois called *orenda.* These terms do not have precisely the same meaning in each of these societies, but they all recognized that their laws came from a higher, supernatural source.

Likewise, the Framers of the Declaration of Independence proclaimed that the American colonies were entitled to independence by "the laws of Nature and of Nature's God." This belief in an ancient Law of Nature, with its many variations, has been almost universal throughout history and in all parts of the world. Against this backdrop, the current idea that law is man-made and is simply the will of the State, is a modern aberration.

Why have people almost always believed that their laws come from a higher Source than man?

Some might suggest that cynical rulers have made this claim thinking it would enhance their power and enable them to govern with less resistance.

Others might say it represents a universal psychological longing, perhaps based upon Jungean archetypes.

But there is another possibility—that God really does exist, and that He (or She, or It, or They) has revealed His will to man in the form of Higher Law.

If we confront this possibility, then we might ask why that which is proclaimed to be Higher Law varies from one society to another (although the similarities far outweigh the differences). One explanation might be that the gods of each society have given them their own unique laws. Another might be that men originally worshipped the one true God and received His laws, and that in varying degrees they fell away from the knowledge of God and His laws. Still another possibility, not inconsistent with the second, is that God has revealed His law to man progressively as man has become ready to receive it. The running debate that threads through these chapters, as to whether man was originally monotheistic or polytheistic, thus becomes especially relevant and will be pursued further throughout this book.

Some readers might wonder why the great legal systems of northern Europe, the Celtic and the Germanic, have been omitted from this survey of ancient societies even though they had great impact upon English and American law. These will be covered in Book IV (Vol. II).

Others might ask why the cultural achievements of Greece and the politico-military accomplishments of the Romans have been left out. These will be covered in Book III (Vol. II).

And one might note a glaring omission—the Hebrew system that, some would say, has contributed more to our legal system than any other source. The laws of the ancient Hebrews will be the subject of Book II.

Book II

The Cornerstone:
The Hebrew Legal System

THE CORNERSTONE:
The Hebrew Legal System

John Adams, the second President of the United States, wrote in response to the Marquis de Condorcet's praise of Greek culture,

> As much as I love, esteem, and admire the Greeks, I believe the Hebrews have done more to enlighten and civilize the world. Moses did more than all their legislators and philosophers.[1]

And so we turn to the cornerstone of our legal foundation—the laws and institutions of ancient Israel. Not surprisingly, the Rabbi Joseph Telushkin called the Hebrew Bible "the most influential series of books in human history." He continued,

> Along with the Ten Commandments, the Bible's most famous document, no piece of legislation ever enacted has influenced human behavior as much as the Biblical injunction to *"Love your neighbor as yourself"* (Leviticus 19:18). No political tract has motivated human beings in so many diverse societies to fight for political freedom as the Exodus story of God's liberation of the Israelite slaves from their Egyptian masters. The law of *"Love your neighbor as yourself"* established the imperative of treating people with justice and compassion, and introduced the Golden Rule to the world; the Exodus narrative made clear that, despite the inequities of this world, God intends that ultimately people be free.
>
> The stories of the Bible are among the most timeless and moving narratives ever written about the human condition and about man's relationship to God. These stories have long shaped Jewish, Christian, and to a lesser degree, Muslim notions of

1. John Adams, handwritten comments on his copy of a book by the Marquis de Condorcet, *Outlines of an Historical View of the Progress of the Human Mind,* reprinted in Zoltan Haraszti, *John Adams and the Prophets of Progress* (Harvard U. Press, 1952), 246.

> morality, and continue to stir the conscience and imagination of believers and skeptics alike.[2]

And David de Sola Pool wrote,

> The law of ancient Egypt or that of ancient Assyria lives only in inscriptions known to the archaeologist. But the law of the ancient children of Israel has come down both directly and uninterruptedly through the ages in the tradition of the Jewish people, and indirectly through the culture of Christian peoples who guided their lives by the Bible. The church state of the Middle Ages drew not a little of its law from the Hebrew Bible, and early Puritan governments in this country before they had evolved their own constitutions and legal systems declared that their communities were to be bound and guided by the laws of Moses as contained in the Hebrew Scriptures which they called the Old Testament.[3]

And yet modern legal historians commonly ignore the Jewish contribution to Western law. If they go beyond the Renaissance and the Norman Conquest at all, they look to Greece and Rome as the sources of Western law, or, if they go back further, they look to Egypt and Babylon, or even India or China, but pass over Israel as unworthy of notice. Why this omission? Sir Henry Sumner Maine suggested that the majority of historians who studied the issue "were either influenced by the strongest prejudice against Hebrew antiquities or by the strongest desire to construct their system without the assistance of religious records."[4] John Adams put it more succinctly in responding to Condorcet's claim that genius had been suppressed by religious superstition:

> But was there no genius among the Hebrews? None among the Christians, nor Mahometans? I understand you, Condorcet. It is atheistical genius alone that you would honor or tolerate.[5]

---

2. Joseph Telushkin, *Biblical Literacy: The Most Important People, Events, and Ideas of the Hebrew Bible* (Morrow & Co., 1997), xxi.

3. David de Sola Pool, Foreword, George Horowitz, *The Spirit of Jewish Law: A Brief Account of Biblical and Rabbinical Jurisprudence with a Special Note on Jewish Law and the State of Israel* (Central Book Co., 1953), vii.

4. Henry Sumner Maine, *Ancient Law* (NY: Dorset Press, 1861, 1986), 101.

5. John Adams, reprinted in Haraszti, 250.

THE CORNERSTONE: *Laws of the Ancient Hebrews*

Though rejected by modern builders, Hebrew Law is the cornerstone of our legal system. In the ensuing chapters we will explore the sources, concepts, and principles of Hebrew Law; the institutions of the Hebrew republic and the later Hebrew monarchy; their influence on the development of Western law; and their use in American courts. But first, we will examine concepts of law as they are found in the early Hebrew thought even before the giving of the Law on Mount Sinai. We will look at the genesis of justice.

Cain and Abel. Titian, ca. 1542–1544.

CHAPTER 12

THE GENESIS OF HEBREW LAW: *Law Before the Law*

In the beginning was the Law. According to a rabbinical tradition, the Torah or Law always existed in the mind of God, long before Moses received the stone tablets on Mt. Sinai.

A literal interpretation of the Book of Genesis suggests that the human race lived for several thousand years before the Great Flood. Archbishop Ussher, in his classic work *The Annals of the World,* used the Genesis genealogy and other books of the Bible to date the creation of the world at 4004 BC. He calculated the date of the Flood as 2349 BC, leaving 1,651 years between Creation and the Flood.[1] Other Bible scholars gave similar but slightly different calculations. Still others believe there are gaps in the Biblical genealogies and that the earth, while relatively young, may be thousands of years older than Ussher believed.

Even if we assume the Flood[2] came only 1,651 years after Creation, that still leaves a long time for development and change. As we consider

1. Archbishop James Ussher, *The Annals of the World* (1658; Master Books, 2003), 17, 19. Ussher based his work not only on the Bible but also upon many other sources, some of which have been lost today. Without accepting Ussher's conclusions, Harvard paleontologist Stephen J. Gould called Ussher's work "the best scholarship in his time." This writer will not pass judgment upon Ussher's work except to say that a non-literal interpretation of Genesis is problematic. Many books of the Bible contain metaphors, allegories, and other figures of speech. But Genesis appears to be a precise account of origins. Repeatedly we are told that A lived X number of years, fathered B, and lived Y additional years and died, that Esau was the ancestor of the Edomites, Amalek of the Amalekites, or Benami of the Ammonites. The author appears to be communicating precise information about origins. One may refuse to accept the truth of Genesis, but it is difficult to spiritualize its meaning.

2. Some scholars believe that the Flood described in Genesis was local in the Middle East rather than worldwide; see, for example, William Ryan and Walter Pitman, *Noah's Flood: The New Scientific Discoveries About the Event That Changed History* (Simon & Schuster, 1998). Others believe the Flood covered the entire earth; see Alfred M. Rehwinkel, *The Flood in the Light of the Bible, Geology, and Archeology* (Concordia, 1951); John C. Whitcomb and Henry M. Morris, *The Genesis Flood: The Biblical Record and Its Scientific Implications* (Presbyterian and Reformed

how much change has taken place between AD 400 and AD 2000, we realize that it is simplistic to think of the antediluvian era as static. Consider, for example:

- The population may have grown exponentially. Genesis 6:1 tells us that "men began to multiply on the face of the earth." No statistics are given, but when we consider the population growth from AD 400 to the present, or when we consider the population growth in North America from AD 1600 to the present, the possibilities of population growth during the pre-Flood era are staggering.
- According to Genesis, people lived longer in those days—possibly because of a healthier diet and climate (Genesis 2:6), possibly because the genepool had not yet suffered the full effects of the Fall. Adam lived 930 years, Seth 912 years, Enos 905 years, Cainan 910 years, Mahalaleel 895 years, Jared 962 years, Enoch 365 years, Methuselah 969 years, Lamech 777 years, and Noah 950 years. After the Flood, lifespans begin to shorten: Abraham lived 175 years, Isaac 180 years, Jacob 147 years, Joseph 110 years. These longer lifespans would have given more time for procreation, as well as more time for study, reflection, experimentation, and intellectual growth.[3]

Publishing Co., 1961). This writer makes the following observations: (1) The plain language of Genesis is more compatible with a universal flood. God declares that he will "bring a flood of waters upon the earth, to destroy all flesh" (6:17); "And the waters prevailed exceedingly upon the earth; and all the high hills, that were under the whole heaven, were covered. Fifteen cubits upward did the waters prevail; and the mountains were covered. And all flesh died that moved upon the earth..." (7:19–21). (2) If the reason for the Flood were man's wickedness, it seems incongruous that the Flood would be limited to the Middle East. (3) If the Flood were merely local, it would make little sense for Noah to spend 120 years building an ark when he could have much more easily moved to another part of the world, such as the Alps or the Himalayas. (4) Although they differ on details, almost every indigenous tribe has a legend about a great deluge; Graham Hancock reports over 500 flood traditions (*Fingerprints of the Gods*, 193, citing Frederick A. Filby, *The Flood Reconsidered: A Review of the Evidences of Geology, Archaeology, Ancient Literature, and the Bible* [Pickering & Inglis, 1970], 58). The universality of Flood legends on every continent except Antarctica is evidence that these legends have a common basis in historical fact. (5) If the Flood were merely local, God's promise (9:13–16) that He will never again destroy the earth by flood would have little credibility, because there have been many local floods. (6) Throughout history there have been accounts of a structure high in the mountains of Ararat that resembles the ark; see Tim LaHaye and John Morris, *The Ark on Ararat* (Thomas Nelson, 1976). This structure has not been proven to be the ark, but no other explanation for its existence has been presented.

3. The Biblical claims concerning the longevity of our early ancestors may have some support in modern archeology and paleontology. Some suggest that paleolithic people may have been healthier and lived longer than those of the later mesolithic and neolithic eras, because their hunter/gatherer diet and lifestyle was healthier than the more sedentary lifestyles of those in the

- Genesis gives us hints of technological and cultural advancement. Chapter 4:19–22 relates the life of Lamech and his two wives. Lamech's wife Adah bore two sons: the first, Jabal, is described as *"the father of such as dwell in tents, and of such as have cattle,"* and the second, Jubal, was *"the father of all such as handle the harp and organ."* Here we see not only animal husbandry and the development of a tent or moveable home suitable to shepherding, but also both of the two major musical instrument groups, stringed instruments (the harp) and wind instruments (the organ). Lamech's other wife Zillah bore Tubal-cain, *"an instructor of every artificer in brass and iron."* This was not the Stone Age; this was at least the Bronze Age and the Iron Age.

We see an antediluvian world that may well have had a large population, intelligent people with great longevity, and substantially advanced technology. We should not be surprised, then, at the suggestion that this antediluvian world might have included law and government. We read in Genesis 4:17 that Adam's son Cain *"builded a city, and called the name of the city, after the name of his son, Enoch."* We do not know the size of this city, nor do we know how long it lasted. But no city of any size can function without some system of organization, government, and law.

God gave the Ten Commandments to Moses, carved in stone, around 1450 BC as recorded in Exodus 20. But the rudiments of the Ten Commandments appear much earlier than that, as natural law written upon the heart of man (Romans 2:14–15). Martin Luther declared,

> The Decalogue is not of Moses, nor did God give it to him first. On the contrary, the Decalogue belongs to the whole world; it was written and engraved in the minds of all human beings from the beginning of the world.[4]

Each of the Ten Commandments can be found in rudimentary form in the Book of Genesis. For example:

---

later periods. See Ward Nicholson, *Longevity & Health in Ancient Paleolithic vs. Neolithic Peoples: Not What You May Have Been Told* (1997, 1999) www.beyondveg.com/nicholson-w/angel-1984/angel-1984-1a.shtml (accessed 13 May, 2016); cf. Jeremy Adams, *Neolithic Europe* (The Teaching Company, 2000) Lecture 3 Study Guide, 14.

4. Martin Luther, quoted by Ewald M. Plass, *What Luther Says: A Practical In-Home Anthology for the Active Christian* (Concordia, 1959, 1994), 748.

- *"Thou shalt have no other gods before me"* describes the relationship God desired with Adam and Eve in the Garden of Eden in Genesis 2, and is violated in Genesis 3 when Eve and Adam chose to believe and obey Satan rather than God. It is portrayed in the covenant between God and Abraham (Genesis 17:1–8) and in Abraham's willingness to sacrifice his son Isaac at God's command (Genesis 22:1–14).
- *"Thou shalt not worship a graven image"* is implied in the fact that those who are faithful to God do not use graven images, even though idols are common among others. See Genesis 31, in which Rachel's theft of her father's idols creates an ongoing problem for Jacob.
- *"Thou shalt not take the name of the LORD thy God in vain"* is violated when Satan in the form of the serpent challenges the truth of God's words, asking *"Hath God said…"* (Genesis 3:1).
- *"Remember the sabbath day to keep it holy"* is rooted in Genesis 2:2–3: *"And on the seventh day God ended his work which he had made; and he rested on the seventh day from all his work which he had made. And God blessed the seventh day, and sanctified it: because that in it he had rested from all his work which God created and made."* This is the reason given for the sabbath command in Exodus 20:8–10.
- *"Honor thy father and thy mother"* is presaged in God's formation of the family unit by creating Adam and Eve in Genesis 2 and giving them children in Genesis 4. The obligation to respect one's parents is evidenced throughout the Book of Genesis, not least by Isaac's willingness to submit to Abraham's decision to sacrifice him to God (Genesis 22), the desire of Jacob and Esau for their father's birthright and blessing (Genesis 25–28), and the loyalty shown to Jacob by his twelve sons (Genesis 43–50).
- *"Thou shalt not kill"* was violated by Cain's murder of Abel (Genesis 4:8). God condemned Cain's crime (4:10–12) but also placed a value on Cain's life by protecting him from others' vengeance (4:13–15). God prescribed capital punishment for murder in Genesis 9:6: *"Whoso sheddeth man's blood, by man shall his blood be shed."* But the verse continues by saying that God's reason for

punishing murder is that human life is of infinite value: *"for in the image of God made he man."*

- *"Thou shalt not commit adultery"* is based upon the creation account in which God established a marital union of one man and one woman, saying, *"It is not good that the man should be alone; I will make him an help meet for him"* (2:18). And when God presented Adam's bride to him, Adam said, *"This is now bone of my bones, and flesh of my flesh: she shall be called Woman, because she was taken out of Man. Therefore shall a man leave his father and his mother, and shall cleave unto his wife: and they shall be one flesh"* (Genesis 2:23–24). While in captivity in Egypt, Joseph respected the marriage bond so highly that he refused to be seduced by Potiphar's wife, suffering imprisonment instead (Genesis 39:6–21). Abraham compromised his marriage obligations by sharing his wife Sarah with the Pharaoh of Egypt (Genesis 12) and later with Abimelech king of Gerar (Genesis 20), not telling them that she was his wife but instead telling them the half-truth that she was his sister. But God revealed to the Pharaoh and to Abimelech that Sarah was also Abraham's wife, and both of them strongly rebuked Abraham for almost causing them to sin. Interestingly, in this instance their morality, apparently learned through natural law, was higher than that of Abraham.
- *"Thou shalt not steal"* is preshadowed in the creation account, in which our first parents were given dominion over all of creation, except for the Tree of the Knowledge of Good and Evil which was forbidden to them (Genesis 1:28–30; 2:15–17). Private property and property rights are assumed throughout the Book of Genesis; see, for example, Genesis 13:2: *"And Abram was very rich in cattle, in silver, and in gold."* See also, Genesis 23, in which Abraham insists on paying for a burial plot for his wife Sarah.
- *"Thou shalt not bear false witness"* is attested by the truth of Scripture itself, and was challenged by the lie of Satan (3:4–5) in which he contradicted God: *"Ye shall not surely die: For God doth know that in the day ye eat thereof, then your eyes shall be opened, and ye shall be as gods, knowing good and evil."* It is challenged again when God asked Cain, *"Where is Abel thy brother?"* and Cain deceptively answered, *"I know not: Am I my brother's keeper?"* (4:9).

- *"Thou shalt not covet"* guards against the very first sin by which our first parents coveted the one fruit that God had withheld from them, the fruit of the tree of the knowledge of good and evil: *"And when the woman saw that the tree was good for food, and that it was pleasant to the eyes, and a tree to be desired to make one wise, she took of the fruit thereof, and did eat, and gave also unto her husband with her; and he did eat"* (Genesis 3:6). Covetousness led to Cain's murder of Abel (Genesis 4:5–8), Jacob's deceptive usurpation of the birthright and blessing (27, 28), and the jealousy of Joseph's brothers because of his favor with their father (Genesis 37:3–4).[5]

Let us now examine some legal issues and concepts that arise with the dawn of the human race.

Cain: A Study in Murder and Mercy

Genesis 4 tells us that after their expulsion from the Garden of Eden, Adam and Eve had two children, Cain and Abel. Cain made his living by raising crops, and Abel by tending flocks. When the time came to present sacrifices to God, Cain offered the grain that he had raised, and Abel offered an animal sacrifice. God looked with favor upon Abel's sacrifice and with disfavor upon Cain's—possibly because Abel offered his sacrifice in faith while Cain did not (Hebrews 11:4), possibly because Abel offered his sacrifice with a broken and contrite heart while Cain offered his with human pride (Psalm 51:17), possibly because Abel offered a blood sacrifice in accordance with God's command while Cain did not (Hebrews 9:22), possibly because the animal sacrificed on Abel's altar was a type of Christ's substitutionary death on the Cross while Cain's grain offering represented man trying to earn salvation by his own works (Ephesians 2:8–9).

Cain's disappointment and anger toward God turned into jealousy and resentment toward Abel, and Cain slew his brother—history's first murder. The Judge of the Universe pronounced sentence upon Cain:

> *And now art thou cursed from the earth, which hath opened her mouth to receive thy brother's blood from thy hand;*
>
> *When thou tillest the ground, it shall not henceforth yield*

5. For many of these concepts I am indebted to Attorney and Pastor Douglas Phillips, who presented some of them in a lecture at the Witherspoon School of Law and Public Policy in Fredericksburg, VA, 30 May 2008.

> *unto thee her strength; a fugitive and a vagabond shalt thou be in the earth.* (Genesis 4:11–12)

H. B. Clark suggested the following sequence of procedure in Cain's "trial":

1. Accusation (Thou has killed thy brother Abel)—*"Where is Abel thy brother?"*
2. Plea (Not Guilty)—*"I know not. Am I my brother's keeper?"*
3. Evidence—*"the voice of thy brother's blood crieth unto me from the ground."*
4. Judgment—Thou shalt be *"a fugitive and a vagabond in the earth."*
5. Petition for clemency—*"My punishment is greater than I can bear,"* for *"everyone that findeth me shall slay me."*
6. Judgment modified—*"the LORD set a mark upon Cain, lest any finding him should kill him,"* and decreed that *"whosoever slayeth Cain, vengeance shall be taken on him sevenfold."*[6]

Cain's punishment is significant. God did not impose the death penalty, even though death is clearly authorized for murder: *"Whoso sheddeth man's blood, by man shall his blood be shed: for in the image of God made he man"* (Genesis 9:6). Instead, God punished Cain by banishing him from that portion of the earth where his family dwelt, forcing him to live on less arable land, and making him a wanderer without a settled home.

The Book of Genesis does not explain why God did not sentence Cain to death, but Leupold offers several possible reasons:

> Yet in the face of later developments, especially 9:6 where the principle of the need of execution of murderers is laid down without exceptions, it seems strange that the first murderer should have been spared. A multitude of reasons can, however, be adduced why God should have spared Cain. Among those that have been offered the following stand out. The presence of this tragic figure, the "fugitive and the vagabond" among men, served as a more potent warning to men as to the enormity of

6. H.B. Clark, *Biblical Law, Being a Text of the Statutes, Ordinances, and Judgments Established in the Holy Bible—with Many Allusions to Secular Laws—Ancient, Medieval, and Modern—Document to the Scriptures, Judicial Decisions, and Legal Literature* (Lawbook Exchange, 1943, 2000; American Vision, 2010), 216.

> the curse of murder by the very misery of his existence. In addition, it must be admitted that banishment from God's presence was the heaviest punishment of all, heavier than the loss of life, and this heavier punishment Cain knows he has suffered. Then, too, there was a salutary lesson in this that God reserved for Himself the right to determine which life was to be terminated and which not; so God's supremacy as the Judge of all flesh was guarded, and a premium put on the value of human life. Then we may also consider the validity of the principle enunciated later, that it pleases the Almighty to let tares and wheat both grow together till the harvest. Closely allied to this is the other argument that God allows sin to run a free course and to develop to the full the potentialities that lie in it, so that the nature of evil as evil may be fully revealed in the historical development of mankind. To all these may yet be added the argument that the more rapid development of the human race, which had to be guaranteed in the days when men were few upon the earth, would certainly have been seriously checked if the first one of the sons of Adam had been put to death. However, it appears that one other argument perhaps ought not to be pressed, namely that God lengthened Cain's days that he might repent. True, God's mercy is displayed richly in His dealings with Cain as Yahweh, but it also has become very much apparent by this time that each successive advance of mercy resulted in a more rigid shutting of Cain's heart.[7]

This writer would advance several other possible reasons: (1) God's plan for civil law and government is that for a criminal law to have binding force to justify imposing punishment, that law must (a) be the will of God, and (b) be adopted by civil government in the form of a statute or ordinance, thus providing the consent of the people. (2) At this time there were only four people on earth (Adam, Eve, Cain, and the deceased Abel), so no institutions existed to give Cain a trial. (3) Cain's crime may have been more akin to manslaughter than to murder. As no person had ever died up until this time, Cain may not have fully comprehended that his act of violence against Abel would result in his brother's death. In fact, at that time Cain may have had only the dimmest understanding of what death was. (4) There might be a due process argument that Cain had not

7. H. C. Leupold, *Exposition of Genesis* (Baker Book House, 1942, 1977), 1: 212–213.

received notice that murder was a crime, although Psalm 19 and Romans 1 and 2 would militate against that position.

Cain should have been repentant and grateful for the mercy God extended to him, but he was not. Rather, Cain lamented,

> *My punishment is greater than I can bear.*
> *Behold, thou hast driven me out this day from the face of the earth; and from thy face shall I be hid; and I shall be a fugitive and a vagabond in the earth; and it shall come to pass, that every one that findeth me shall slay me.*
> (Genesis 4:13–14)[8]

Cain expressed not repentance, but self-pity and fear of punishment.[9] Nevertheless, God answered Cain,

> *Therefore whosoever slayeth Cain, vengeance shall be taken on him sevenfold. And the LORD set a mark upon Cain, lest any finding him should kill him.* (Genesis 4:15)

No one knows what the mark of Cain was, though many have speculated. The Hebrew text suggests that the mark was not *in* or *on* Cain, but rather *for* Cain. Whether it was a physical mark or something else, it was in some way a sign to men that God had reserved for Himself the sole authority to punish Cain, and that anyone who killed Cain would receive seven times the punishment that Cain deserved.

The judgment and mercy of God upon Cain is a reminder that the basic concept that "bloodshed demands blood in return 'is a principle of equity written on the heart of every man; and that Cain should see the earth full of avengers is just like a murderer, who sees avenging spirits ready to torture him on every hand.'"[10] It represents an early

---

8. Those who argue that this passage doesn't make sense because, with Abel's demise, there was no one left to slay Cain, need only look to the birth of Seth in Genesis 4:25 and the words of Genesis 5:4: *"And the days of Adam after he had begotten Seth were eight hundred years: and he begat sons and daughters."* This may also answer the sophists' question, where did Cain find his wife?

9. Not everyone interprets the passage this way. Shuckford argues that the Hebrew noun *aven* means "iniquity," not punishment, and that the Hebrew verb *nasha* means "to be forgiven," not to bear. He believes the passage thus reads "my iniquity is too great to be forgiven," and he therefore explains, "Upon Cain's being brought to a sorrow for his sin, God was pleased, in some measure, to pardon his transgression." Samuel Shuckford, *The Sacred and Profane History of the World Connected* (1727; 5th ed., 1824; reprinted by Tolle Lege Press, 2009), I: 6.

10. C.F. Keil and F. Delitzsch, *Commentary on the Old Testament* (Eerdmans, 1975), I: 115.

understanding that crime demands punishment, but that God may determine the punishment according to His sovereign will and purpose.

The Revenge of Lamech (Genesis 4:23–24)

Lamech was the great-great-great-grandson of Cain, and he appears to have been a man of violence:

> *And Lamech said unto his wives, Adah and Zillah, Hear my voice; ye wives of Lamech, hearken unto my speech: for I have slain a man to my wounding, and a young man to my hurt.*
>
> *If Cain shall be avenged sevenfold, truly Lamech seventy and sevenfold.*

Lamech's words are sometimes called his "Sword Song," and commentators have pictured him waving a sword, perhaps newly-forged by his son Tubal-Cain, and boasting to his wives of his manly power. As Leupold says, "It need not surprise us that this word was spoken to Lamech's wives. They are an audience that needs must listen, and boasting is most safely done at home before their ears. Whether Lamech really was the dangerous fellow that his words make him out to be we have no means of knowing."[11] The perfect tense in the Hebrew could be either a statement of fact that he has slain these two men for wronging him, or a statement of confident assurance that he will in fact slay anyone who injures him.[12]

Lamech's thirst for revenge arose out of a natural and justifiable desire for retributive justice, a deep-seated belief, rooted in an imperfect understanding of God's own justice, that crime creates a judicial imbalance, and that punishment is necessary to rebalance the scales of justice. But the concept of *lex talionis*, that the punishment should fit the crime and be proportionate to the crime, as in "an eye for an eye, and a tooth for a tooth" (Exodus 21:24, Leviticus 24:20, Deuteronomy 19:21, Matthew 5:38) seems to have eluded Lamech. Rather, he will inflict death for the slightest offense, and his 77-fold vengeance shall be eleven times greater than God's 7-fold vengeance upon anyone who slays Cain. With my fist and my sword, boasted Lamech, I shall be a far harsher avenger than God.

---

11. Leupold, *Exposition of Genesis* (Baker Book House, 1942, 1977) I: 223.

12. Leupold, I: 223.

Tyranny and the Tower (Genesis 11:1–9)

And the whole earth was of one language, and of one speech.

And it came to pass, as they journeyed from the east, that they found a plain in the land of Shinar; and they dwelt there.

And they said one to another, Go to, let us make brick, and burn them thoroughly. And they had brick for stone, and slime had they for morter.

And they said, Go to, let us build us a city and a tower, whose top may reach unto heaven; and let us make us a name, lest we be scattered abroad upon the face of the whole earth.

And the Lord came down to see the city and the tower, which the children of men builded.

And the Lord said, Behold, the people is one, and they have all one language; and this they begin to do: and now nothing will be restrained from them, which they have imagined to do.

Go to, let us go down, and there confound their language, that they may not understand one another's speech.

So the Lord scattered them abroad from thence upon the face of all the earth: and they left off to build the city.

Therefore is the name of it called Babel, because the Lord did there confound the language of all the earth: and from thence did the Lord scatter them abroad upon the face of all the earth.

Why was this tower displeasing to God? First, the tower was a picture of man trying to gain heaven by his own works rather than by God's grace. Second, the tower was the prototype of the later Babylonian ziggaurats, towers which were used for astrology and other pagan practices. Third, God had commanded the people to disperse across the earth and form separate nations. Each nation was to be a check on the power of other nations; a world government in the hands of sinful men would have unlimited potential for evil. The tower represented man's rebellion against God's command.

Genesis 10:8–10 speaks of Nimrod, the great-grandson of Noah through his son HAM:

> *And Cush begat Nimrod: he began to be a mighty one in the earth.*
>
> *He was a mighty hunter before the LORD: wherefore it is said, Even as Nimrod the mighty hunter before the LORD.*
>
> *And the beginning of his kingdom was Babel, and Erech, and Accad, and Calneh, in the land of Shinar.*

The name *Nimrod* literally means "we will revolt," and he is called a "mighty one," that is, "a man who makes himself renowned for bold and daring deeds."[13] He is called a "mighty hunter," but this literally means "mighty killer" and could refer to a killer of men rather than of animals, "a trapper of men by stratagem and force."[14] Genesis does not directly identify Nimrod with the Tower, but it does say the beginning of his kingdom was Babel in the land of Shinar (Babylonia). However the Jewish historian Flavius Josephus, writing about AD 70, connected the building of the tower to Nimrod and described it as an act of disobedience against God:

> Now it was Nimrod who excited them to such an affront and contempt of God. He was the grandson of Ham, the son of Noah,—a bold man, and of great strength of hand. He persuaded them not to ascribe it to God, as if it was through his means they were happy, but to believe that it was their own courage which procured their happiness. He also gradually changed the government into tyranny,—seeing no other way of turning men from the fear of God, but to bring them into a constant dependence upon his power. He also said he would be revenged on God, if he should have a mind to drown the world again; for that he would build a tower too high for the waters to be able to reach! And that he would avenge himself on God for destroying their forefathers![15]

13. Keil & Delitszch, I: 165.

14. Keil & Delitszch, I: 166.

15. Flavius Josephus, *The Antiquities of the Jews,* AD 70; translated and reprinted as *Complete Works of Flavius Josephus* (William P. Nimmo, Edinburgh, Scotland, 1867; reprinted by Kregel Publications, 1960), 30. The writings of Josephus, while highly respected, should not be

Inevitably, governments and legal systems must have arisen shortly after the Flood. And if Nimrod changed the government into tyranny, it must originally have been something other than tyranny. And notice Nimrod's reason for imposing tyranny—to make people dependent upon government and thereby wean them away from the fear of God. Nimrod may have been the world's first empire-builder, his empire encompassing Sumeria, Babylonia, and maybe Assyria. Giles of Rome (AD 1243–1316), in his treatise *On Ecclesiastical Power,* noted that "... Nimrod, of whom we read that he was the first king, whose reign began in Babylon [as can be gathered from Genesis 10:8–12], made himself a king by invasion and usurpation; and so it is said of him in the same place that he began to be mighty on earth: he acquired his kingdom through civil might and not through justice."[16]

But Nimrod's ambitions may have transcended worldly empire. His desire to reach the heavens may have found fruition, either during his lifetime or afterward, with his deification as Marduk, chief of the Babylonian gods,[17] and his wife, unnamed in Scripture but known in tradition as Semirami (Queen of Heaven),[18] became Astarte, queen of the Babylonian pantheon of gods. Alexander Hislop, in his classic work *The Two Babylons,*[19] concluded that Nimrod and Semirami, along with the Babylonian pantheon, served as the prototype for other nations' pagan deities: Marduk and Astarte become Osiris and Isis for the Egyptians, Zeus and Hera for the Greeks, Jupiter and Juno for the Romans, Wotan and Frigg for the Germans.

The oft-overlooked lesson of Nimrod and the Tower of Babel is that man, because of his sinful nature, cannot be trusted with absolute centralized power. God therefore ordered Noah's descendants to disperse and replenish the earth as separate nations that would serve as checks on each other's power. Nimrod represents man's countervailing tendency toward

---

considered the equivalent of the Biblical text.

16. Giles of Rome, *On Ecclesiastical Power,* reprinted in Oliver O'Donovan and Joan Lockwood O'Donovan, editors, *From Irenaeus to Grotius: A Sourcebook in Christian Political Thought* (Eerdmans, 1999), 366.

17. Edward Mack, "Nimrod," *International Standard Bible Encyclopedia* (Eerdmans, 1939), IV: 2147.

18. Bryce Self, *Nimrod, Mars and the Marduk Connection,* http://ldolphin.org/Nimrod.html (accessed 13 May, 2016), traced the Semirami legend to the first century BC Greek historian Diadorus Siculus and suggested that Diodorus may have based his account on earlier legends.

19. Alexander Hislop, *The Two Babylons* (1853; expanded 1858; reprinted 1903; reprinted Cosimo, Inc., 2009), 23–38ff.

centralization, empire, state-worship, and emperor-worship—related tendencies that will be repeated over and over in human history.

If Josephus is correct, Nimrod was the first man who wanted to rule a world government. If Hislop is correct, Nimrod was also the first man who wanted to be worshipped as a god.

But God confounded Nimrod's plan—at least temporarily.

Abraham Bargains with God for Sodom and Gomorrah (Genesis 18:20–33)

Nine generations after Noah and the Flood, Abraham received a call from God to go west of Ur of the Chaldees to a land God would give to Abraham. Abraham obeyed God's command and traveled to the land, along with other members of his family. Once they were settled in the land, Abraham and his nephew Lot divided the territory between themselves; Lot chose to dwell in the pagan cities of Sodom and Gomorrah, while Abraham remained in the rural areas with his flocks.

We know very little of the system of law and government that prevailed in Sodom and Gomorrah, but Abraham came into direct contact with some of the greatest empires of the ancient world. Genesis 14 informs us that "Amraphel king of Shinar, Arioch king of Ellasar, Chedorlaomer king of Elam, and Tidal king of nations" made war with the kings of Sodom, Gomorrah, and other cities of the Valley of Siddim near the Dead Sea. These cities of the Valley submitted to the rule of these kings for twelve years, but in the thirteenth year they rebelled, and the conquering kings attacked to subdue the rebellion. During a raid upon Sodom they took Lot captive. Abraham armed 318 of his servants, and in a daring commando raid he secured the release of Lot and other captives, thereby winning a great battle in the first recorded war in human history and also winning the respect of the king of Sodom and likewise of Melchizedek king of Salem.

Who was *Amraphel* of Genesis 14:1, 9? *Shinar* clearly means Babylonia. The only Babylonian king who reigned around the time of Abraham (circa 2000 BC) with a name remotely similar to Amraphel was Hammurabi. If Amraphel is in fact a Hebraic form of Hammurabi (note the parallel syllables "Am" with "Ham," and "raph" with "rab"), then Abraham came into contact and conflict with one of the greatest lawgivers of the ancient world.[20] Note also that Ur of the Chaldees, out of which Abraham had come, was part of Hammurabi's Babylonia. During this encounter, and also during his encounter with the Egyptian Pharaoh (Genesis 12:9–20), Abraham dealt directly with the heads of some of the greatest legal systems of his day. Likewise, in Genesis 21 Abraham dealt with and made a treaty with Abimelech, the King of the Philistines.

Later, in Genesis 18, God visited Abraham in the person of two angels in the form of men, and He announced His plan to destroy Sodom and Gomorrah. Abraham pleads with God for the lives of Lot and his family:

> *And the Lord said, Because the cry of Sodom and Gomorrah is great, and because their sin is very grievous;*
>
> *I will go down now, and see whether they have done altogether according to the cry of it, which is come unto me; and if not, I will know.*
>
> *And the men turned their faces from thence, and went toward Sodom: but Abraham stood yet before the Lord.*
>
> *And Abraham drew near, and said, Wilt thou also destroy the righteous with the wicked?*
>
> *Peradventure there be fifty righteous within the city: wilt thou also destroy and not spare the place for the fifty righteous that are therein?*
>
> *That be far from thee to do after this manner, to slay the righteous with the wicked: and that the righteous should be as the wicked, that be far from thee: Shall not the Judge of all the earth do right?*
>
> *And the Lord said, If I find in Sodom fifty righteous within the city, then I will spare all the place for their sakes.*

---

20. T.G. Pinches, writing in *The International Standard Bible Encyclopedia* (Eerdmans, 1939) "Amraphel" I: 126, makes this identification persuasively and with considerable certainty; Arno C. Gaebelein, *The Annotated Bible* (Loizeaux, 1970), I: 45, concurs with this identification, as does J. Vernon McGee, *Thru the Bible* (Thomas Nelson, 1981), I: 63. Leupold, *Exposition of Genesis* I: 447 is more skeptical, as is Clyde T. Francisco, *The Broadman Bible Commentary* (Broadman, 1969, 1973) I: 161. Gabriel Oussani, writing in *The Catholic Encyclopedia* (Gilmary Society, 1913) "Amraphel" I: 441, says "The identity of Amraphel and Hammurabi is now unanimously accepted by Assyriologists and Biblical critics," and "Phonetically, the two names are identical."

> *And Abraham answered and said, Behold now, I have taken upon me to speak unto the Lord, which am but dust and ashes:*
>
> *Peradvanture there shall lack five of the fifty righteous: wilt thou destroy all the city for lack of five? And he said, If I find there forty and five, I will not destroy it.*
>
> *And he spake unto him yet again, and said, Peradventure there shall be forty found there. And he said, I will not do it for forty's sake.*
>
> *And he said unto him, Oh let not the Lord be angry, and I will speak: Peradventure there shall thirty be found there. And he said, I will not do it, if I find thirty there.*
>
> *And he said, Behold now, I have taken upon me to speak unto the Lord: Peradventure there shall be twenty found there. And he said, I will not destroy it for twenty's sake.*
>
> *And he said, Oh let not the Lord be angry, and I will speak yet but this once: Peradventure ten shall be found there. And he said, I will not destroy it for ten's sake.*
> (Genesis 18:20–32)

On the surface this sounds like an attempt by Abraham to engage in plea-bargaining with the Supreme Judge. Harvard Law Professor Alan M. Dershowitz, in his fascinating book *The Genesis of Justice,*[21] suggests that Abraham actually called upon God to be just in His dealings with men and almost accused God of injustice.[22] But this writer suggests that

21. Alan M. Dershowitz, *The Genesis of Justice* (Warner Books, 2000).

22. Dershowitz, 69–93. Jeffrey Brauch, Dean of Regent University Law School, and Professor Robert Woods of Arbor University question this assertion in an article titled "Faith, Learning and Justice in Alan Dershowitz's *The Genesis of Justice:* Toward a Proper Understanding of the Relationship Between the Bible and Modern Justice," 36 *Valparaiso University Law Review* 1 (Fall 2001). They applaud Dershowitz's use of Genesis to find early principles of law, but they contend that Dershowitz failed to employ sound principles of Biblical hermeneutics. He failed to distinguish between Biblical descriptions of what is and Biblical imperatives of what should be (the is/ought fallacy), depicts God as angry and unjust instead of trying to understand the principles of God's justice, tries to hold God to man's standards of justice instead of judging man's justice by God's standards, treats other Jewish works such as the midrash as comparable to the Bible in authority, and fails to fully appreciate man's sinful nature as a reason for God's redemptive justice. Dershowitz's book is a valuable contribution, but as Brauch and Woods suggest, it should be read as "the beginning, not the end, of your study of the integration of Biblical and legal principles." Brauch and Woods, 70–71.

Abraham's question, *"Shall not the Judge of all the earth do right?"* is actually rhetorical. Abraham knew that God is perfectly just, and he employed that premise to argue that the destruction of wicked Sodom would necessarily include the destruction of righteous Lot and his family, and this would be contrary to God's principles of justice. He asked the Lord, *"Wilt thou also destroy the righteous with the wicked?"*

Abraham has reasoned, perhaps on the basis of natural law, that while it is wrong to allow guilty persons to go unpunished, it is also wrong, perhaps more wrong, to punish innocent persons. Sir William Blackstone forcefully stated that it is better that ten guilty persons go free rather than that one innocent person be wrongfully convicted and punished.[23]

A criminal justice system tries to draw a balance between punishing the guilty and protecting the innocent. If a system is weighted so heavily in favor of making certain that no guilty person escapes justice, many innocent persons will be wrongly convicted and punished. But if the system is weighted heavily in favor of making certain that no innocent person is ever wrongly convicted, it is likely that more guilty persons will go free.

Where should the balance be drawn? Do we agree with Blackstone that it is better that ten guilty murderers go unpunished than that one innocent person be punished? What about 100? Or 1,000? 100,000?

Let's add another factor to the equation: Does it matter that of those 100 murderers who go free, about 70% may be recidivists who will murder 70 more innocent persons? Should that change our evaluation of this dilemma? Or is a system in which an innocent person is convicted and punished categorically wrong, regardless of the consequences? Jurists have searched for thousands of years for answers to these questions, and are probably no closer to an answer than was Abraham four thousand years ago.[24]

23. William Blackstone, *Commentaries on the Laws of England* IV: 358, quoted by Alexander Volokh, "*n* Guilty Men" 146 *University of Pennsylvania Law Review* 173 (1997).

24. Alexander Volokh has written a most informative and thought-provoking article on this subject, "*n* Guilty Men," 146 *University of Pennsylvania Law Review* 173 (1997). He closes by saying, "The story is told of a Chinese law professor, who was listening to a British lawyer explain that the Britons were so enlightened, they believed it was better that ninety-nine guilty men go free than that one innocent man be executed. The Chinese professor thought for a second and asked, 'Better for whom?'"

As it turned out, Sodom contained only four righteous persons—Lot, his wife, and their two daughters. God solved the dilemma by destroying Sodom but allowing Lot and his family to escape.[25]

And possibly we are not condemned to constantly watch the pendulum swing between a criminal justice system that is so prosecution-oriented that innocent persons get convicted and one that is so defense-oriented that guilty persons escape justice. Modern technology may help us avoid that dilemma. Fingerprinting, DNA, and other forensic evidence seems to have great potential to both prove the guilt of criminals and exonerate those who are falsely accused.

The Incest of Lot's Daughters: The Defense of Necessity? (Genesis 19:30–38)

After God destroyed Sodom and Gomorrah by brimstone and fire from heaven, He provided a way of escape for Lot and his family. He commanded that they not look back upon the city; but Lot's wife looked back, apparently because she still longed for the city and its sinful lifestyle, and she became a pillar of salt (Genesis 19:15–26).

And so the narrative resumes,

> *And Lot went up out of Zoar, and dwelt in the mountain, and his two daughters with him; for he feared to dwell in Zoar: and he dwelt in a cave, he and his two daughters.*
>
> *And the firstborn said unto the younger, Our father is old, and there is not a man in the earth to come in unto us after the manner of all the earth:*
>
> *Come, let us make our father drink wine, and we will lie with him, that we may preserve seed of our father.*
>
> *And they made their father drink wine that night: and the firstborn went in, and lay with her father; and he perceived not when she lay down, nor when she arose.*
>
> *And it came to pass on the morrow, that the firstborn said unto the younger, Behold, I lay yesternight with my father:*

25. Rev. Carey Gordon correctly notes that although Abraham may have thought he was plea-bargaining with God, from the beginning God Himself had no doubt as to what He was going to do. In fact, no innocent person was destroyed and no guilty person was spared—and this was God's plan all along. Carey Gordon, lecture series *The Doctrine of... Divine Law,* available in CD album from Cornerstone Church, Sioux City, Iowa.

> *let us make him drink wine this night also; and go thou in, and lie with him, that we may preserve seed of our father.*
>
> *And they made their father drink wine that night also: and the younger arose, and lay with him; and he perceived not when she lay down, nor when she arose.*
>
> *Thus were both the daughters of Lot with child by their father.* (Genesis 19:30–36).

The Bible clearly forbids incest (Leviticus 18:17; 20:14; II Samuel 13:14); yet Lot and his daughters were not punished for this offense. Lot might be excused because in his intoxicated state he didn't know what he was doing;[26] but what about his daughters? One possible defense might be that although incest was always a violation of God's moral law, it had not yet been proclaimed a crime, so Lot's daughters lacked the notice that is an essential element of due process of law.

But Professor Dershowitz suggests another explanation. Lot's daughters were not punished for incest, he says, because of a legal defense known as "necessity." The law recognizes higher values than technical obedience to a criminal statute. If it is necessary to violate a criminal statute in order to accomplish a higher good, like the saving of human life, that criminal violation can be excused.[27] For example, if one is lost in a blizzard and breaks into a cabin to find shelter from the storm, he has a defense to a charge of breaking and entering, because that act was necessary to preserve human life.[28]

Dershowitz suggests that as Lot's daughters witnessed the destruction of Sodom and Gomorrah, they concluded that, except for their father, *"there is not a man in the earth to come in unto us after the manner of all the earth"* (19:31), and therefore they needed to lie with him *"that we may preserve seed of our father"* (19:32). They believed that

26. Voluntary intoxication normally is not a defense to a criminal charge, but involuntary intoxication may be a defense. Wayne R. LaFave, *Criminal Law* 3d (West, 2000) § 4.10 Intoxication, 411–24. The Genesis 19 account suggests that Lot's intoxication may have been, at least in part, involuntary.

27. LaFave, § 5.4 Necessity, 476–86.

28. Those who have been charged with criminal trespass for blocking entry to abortion clinics have sometimes used the defense of necessity, arguing that their criminal trespass was necessary to accomplish a higher good, saving the life of the innocent unborn child. Most courts have been reluctant to accept this defense, because the "higher good" to be preserved must be recognized as a higher good by law, and abortion has been declared (wrongly, in the opinion of this writer) to be a constitutional right; *Roe v. Wade,* 410 U.S. 113 (1973).

the entire human race, or at least their father's family, had been extinguished by God's judgment upon Sodom and Gomorrah, and therefore it was necessary for them to lie with their father to prevent the human race, or at least their portion of it, from becoming extinct. Preserving the race was a higher value than abstaining from incest, so their incest with their father was justified by the defense of necessity.[29] Under modern law they would be entitled to this defense even though they were mistaken, at least as to the extinction of the entire human race, if they could convince the court that their belief was sincere and reasonable.

Although God did not punish Lot or his daughters, their incest had long-term consequences. Lot's older daughter gave birth to Moab, who became the ancestor of the Moabites, a nation that was at times the ally and at times the enemy of Israel. And Lot's younger daughter gave birth to Benammi, the progenitor of the Ammonites, enemies of Israel in centuries to come. Later Hebrew Law would provide that *"The fathers shall not be put to death for the children, neither shall the children be put to death for the fathers: every man shall be put to death for his own sin"* (Deuteronomy 24:16). But whether or not criminal punishment is imposed, the natural consequences of sin may persist for future generations.

And so, even in these early days of Genesis, men recognized that obedience to law, while highly important, was not always supremely important. Circumstances could arise in which God might excuse disobedience.

Or, as we shall see later, even command it.

The Case of Jacob v. Laban: The Deceiver Is Deceived (Genesis 25–31)

Abraham's son Isaac married Rebekah. The twin sons of Isaac and Rebekah were born under unusual circumstances: *"the children struggled together"* within Rebekah's womb; Esau was born first, Jacob came out of the womb grasping Esau's heel. The name *Jacob* means "cheater" or "supplanter," and Esau and Jacob were bitter rivals until they finally reconciled much later in life (Genesis 33).

Primogeniture, the system under which the oldest son received the birthright, which was all of his father's inheritance (or sometimes a double portion compared to the other sons), was common at that time. It preserved family estates from being subdivided, provided an orderly means

29. Dershowitz, 94–102.

of transition, and enabled the eldest son to assume the role of family patriarch; however, he also assumed the responsibility of care for other members of his family, widows, and unmarried sisters. As the eldest son, the birthright properly belonged to Esau; but Jacob tricked Esau into trading his birthright for a meal, indicating that the birthright could be altered or exchanged (Genesis 25:27–34).

Years later, when Isaac was old and nearly blind, he determined to give his blessing to Esau.[30] Jacob impersonated Esau and tricked his father into giving him the blessing instead of Esau, speaking these words to Jacob:

> *Therefore God give thee of the dew of heaven, and the fatness of the earth, and plenty of corn and wine:*
>
> *Let people serve thee, and nations bow down to thee: be lord over thy brethren, and let thy mother's sons bow down to thee: cursed be every one that curseth thee, and blessed be he that blesseth thee.* (Genesis 27:28–29)

When Isaac realized that Jacob had impersonated Esau, he was very upset. When Esau asked plaintively, *"Hast thou not reserved a blessing for me?"* Isaac told him he had already blessed Jacob and said, *"I have made him thy lord,"* but he did give Esau a lesser blessing:

> *Behold, thy dwelling shall be the fatness of the earth, and of the dew of heaven from above;*
>
> *And by thy sword shalt thou live, and shalt serve thy brother; and it shall come to pass when thou shalt have the dominion, that thou shalt break his yoke from off thy neck.* (Genesis 27:39–40)

The birthright involved a major portion of the father's estate, and while that normally passed to the eldest son, that custom was subject to change. But the blessing, although pronounced by the father, was actually the blessing of God, and therefore Isaac was powerless to change it.

---

30. The birthright involved a major portion of the father's estate. The blessing was a benediction invoking God's special care for the son and for his future descendants. Normally they were both bestowed on the same son. "The birthright consisted afterwards in a double portion of the father's inheritance (Deut. xxi.17); but with the patriarchs it embraced the chieftainship, the rule over the brethren and the entire family (xxvii. 29), and title to the blessing of the promise (xxvii. 4,27–29), which included the future possession of Canaan and of covenant fellowship with Jehovah (xxviii.4)." Keil & Delitzsch, I: 268–69.

The blessing, however, was not unmixed. Along with the blessing, Jacob also incurred the hatred of his brother Esau, and for his own safety he had to leave home. And so Jacob traveled to Padan-aram to find a wife from among the daughters of Laban, the brother of Jacob's mother Rebekah. And there he met the love of his life, Laban's daughter Rachel.

In keeping with the custom of the time, Jacob and Laban reached an agreement that Jacob would work for Laban for seven years, at which time Laban would give his daughter to Jacob in marriage. Laban fulfilled his bargain—but not as Jacob expected. After the wedding festivities were over, Jacob discovered that his veiled bride was not Rachel but her older sister Leah. Laban justified his deception by noting his people's custom that the younger sister could not be married before the older sister, and to gain Rachel as his bride, Jacob had to work another seven years.[31]

The lesson Jacob's life leaves to us is that *"they that plow iniquity, and sow wickedness, reap the same"* (Job 4:8; cf. Galatians 6:7). Laban's deception of Jacob, disguising Leah as Rachel, is strikingly similar to Jacob's own deception of his father Isaac, pretending to be Esau to receive his father's blessing. Jacob tended Laban's flocks and negotiated an agreement with Laban whereby part of the flock would be his; but by selective breeding he arranged that the stronger livestock would be his and the weaker livestock would be Laban's (Genesis 30:27–43). Much later, Jacob's own sons deceived him into believing his favorite son Joseph had been killed by wild beasts (Genesis 37), and only later still did Jacob learn that the man who was acting as prime minister of Egypt during the great famine was in fact his long-lost son Joseph (Genesis 44–50). All of this brings to mind the maxim that guides courts of equity, "He who comes into equity must come with clean hands."[32]

Joseph in Egypt (Genesis 39–50)

Jacob had twelve sons, out of whom came the twelve tribes of Israel. But Joseph and Benjamin, his sons by Rachel, were his favorites, and this favor engendered resentment by the older brothers, so they sold Joseph into slavery in Egypt. But in Egypt Joseph rose from slavery to a position

31. The Old Testament nowhere approves polygamy, but in the early days of Israel's history the practice seems to have been tolerated. Genesis 2:18–24 suggests that God's plan for the human race has always been monogamy, and in the New Testament, 1 Timothy 3:2 and Titus 1:6 require that a church bishop or elder must be "the husband of one wife."

32. *American Jurisprudence 2d* 27:666 "Equity" § 136.

of great influence. With God's help he had interpreted a dream to mean there would be seven years of bountiful harvests followed by seven years of famine, and as a result, the Pharaoh made him prime minister:

> *And Pharaoh said unto Joseph, See, I have set thee over all the land of Egypt.*
>
> *And Pharaoh took off his ring from his hand, and put it upon Joseph's hand, and arrayed him in vestures of fine linen, and put a gold chain about his neck;*
>
> *And he made him to ride in the second chariot which he had; and they cried before him, Bow the knee: and he made him ruler over all the land of Egypt.*
>
> *And Pharaoh said unto Joseph, I am Pharaoh, and without thee shall no man lift up his hand or foot in all the land of Egypt.* (Genesis 41:41–44)

During the seven years of abundance, Joseph established storehouses for the surplus grain. Then, when the famine struck the area and people throughout the Middle East faced starvation, there was enough grain to feed not only Egypt but other nations as well. And so, Jacob was able to provide food for his brothers when they came down to Egypt, and the family was reconciled at last.

In Part One we saw the amazing accomplishments of ancient Egypt—the well-organized court system, the executive department that managed the economy and even used a "nilometer" to gauge the level of the Nile River and thereby estimate the rainfall upstream and predict the harvest. Did Joseph learn the art of government from the Egyptians? Or did the Egyptians learn from him?

In either event, the Pharaoh would not have appointed Joseph to such a critical office if he had not respected Joseph's character and ability. And in either event, Joseph emerged from this experience as a seasoned statesman and skilled administrator.

And centuries later, from 1380–1362 BC, Egypt would be ruled by a Pharaoh who led his people to the worship of only one God, even though only briefly. Was Amenhotep's monotheism a vestige from Joseph? Or from Moses?

And in Conclusion...

And so, thousands of years before Moses received the Ten Commandments on Mt. Sinai, people understood the need for law and government. Perhaps they understood basic principles of natural law by means of human reason and conscience, or by observing nature (Psalm 19:1–14; Romans 1:18–20; 2:14–15). Or possibly they understood certain principles of law by God's direct and special revelation.

But some of the children of Abraham wanted something more. They wanted a complete system of law and government, given to them directly by God Himself.

The system they received is the subject of the coming chapters.

Questions for Reflection, Discussion, and More Reflection

1. How does the Book of Genesis Chapters 1–6 describe the world condition prior to the Flood? Could there have been a substantial population, technology, and level of civilization? Might this indicate a system of law and government at that time?
2. Are the Ten Commandments found in various forms in Genesis? How did people know the Commandments before they were given on Mt. Sinai? Direct revelation from God? The Law of God written on men's hearts (Romans 2:14–15)? Is the law found in Genesis evidence of a universal Law of Nature known in the early years of the human race?
3. Why did God not pronounce the death penalty on Cain in Genesis 4?
4. Explain the Covenant between God and Noah after the Flood in Genesis 9. Who was covered by this Covenant, and for what duration? What kinds of law, government, and criminal punishments are authorized by this Covenant?
5. Why was the Tower of Babel (Genesis 11) offensive to God? Was Nimrod the world's first tyrant? What does the narrative of Nimrod and the Tower tell us about the nature of absolute government power? Does the existence of a multitude of nations constitute a check on tyranny, as each nation serves as

a check on other nations' power? Why does pagan mythology deify Nimrod and his queen? Is Nimrod the origin of all pagan mythology?

6. What are the Ebla Tablets, and what do they reveal about the City of Ur and about Abraham and his family?
7. What lessons do we see in Abraham's "plea-bargaining" with God over Sodom and Gomorrah? Does this narrative involve the underlying issue of the innocent suffering along with the guilty? In criminal justice, where should our legal system draw the line between interests of the state and the rights of the accused?
8. If you were serving on a jury would you acquit Lot's daughters of incest based upon their "necessity" defense (Genesis 19)? Do the progeny of Lot's daughters, the Moabites and the Ammonites and their conflicts with Israel, demonstrate that violations of the Laws of Nature sometimes have long-term consequences?
9. Explain the difference between a "birthright" and a "blessing" (Genesis 25 and 27). Considering Jacob's character as a deceiver, why does Malachi say God loved Jacob but hated Esau (Malachi 1:2–3)?
10. After Joseph and his brothers are reconciled in Egypt, Joseph tells them concerning their act of selling him into slavery, *"Ye thought evil against me; but God meant it unto good..."* (Genesis 50:20). What does this tell us about God's directive, permissive, and overruling will, and the way He works through history in the affairs of men?

Hear O Israel,... John W. Van Leeuwen. ca. 1876.

Chapter 13

The Documents of Hebrew Law: *Preserving God's Law, or Evolving God's Law?*

Even in ancient times, the Hebrews were known as the "People of the Book."

Their laws, rituals, history, and prophecy were stored not only in the minds of prophets, priests, and kings. They were written in scrolls (the form of books at that time), and they were widely available. Hebrew families held rituals in their homes, in which the eldest son read from those sacred scrolls. As the command is given in Deuteronomy 6:4–7,

> *Hear, O Israel: The LORD our God is one LORD:*
>
> *And thou shalt love the LORD thy God with all thine heart, and with all thy soul, and with all thy might.*
>
> *And these words, which I command thee this day, shall be in thine heart:*
>
> *And thou shalt teach them diligently unto thy children, and shalt talk of them when thou sittest in thine house, and when thou walkest by the way, and when thou liest down, and when thou risest up.*

For this reason, the Hebrews were one of the most literate societies of the entire ancient world. Until about 200 BC, Hebrew education took place mostly in the home. Generally the parents were the instructors, although wealthier families might employ tutors. The Levites, who had been specially set aside for religious vocations and who dwelt among the twelve tribes, apparently played a prominent role in the instruction of adults and perhaps of children as well, as did the scribes and Pharisees in later times. As the rabbinical era arose, the synagogue began to play a greater role in education, but it never replaced the home as the basic educational institution. Education consisted of religious and moral training, the history of the Jewish people, and basic literacy and mathematics, as well as occupational training for boys and homemaking for girls. The important role that mothers played in the education of their children suggests that literacy was widespread among women as well as among men: "We should bear in mind, moreover, that the understanding of the sacred oracles was not the peculiar prerogative of the priestly order, but was enjoined upon every Israelite.... Now, when we consider that the education of the Hebrew children depended upon the parents, it becomes self-evident that the Hebrews must have been, while residents of Canaan, a universally educated people."[1] Edersheim wrote,

> The first education was necessarily the mother's. Even the Talmud owns this, when among the memorable sayings of the sages, it records one of the School of Rabbi Jannai, to the effect that knowledge of the Law may be looked for in those, who have sucked it in at their mother's breast (Ber. 63 b)....
>
> There could not be national history, nor even romance, to compare with that by which a Jewish mother might hold her child entranced....
>
> It was, indeed, no idle boast that the Jews "were from their swaddling-clothes...trained to recognize God as their Father, and as Maker of the world;" that, "having been taught the knowledge (of the laws) from earliest youth, they bore in their souls the image of the commandments" (*Philo,* Legat. Ad Cajum, sec. 16.31); that "from their earliest consciousness they learned the laws, so as to have them, as it were, engraven upon the soul" (*Jos.* Ag. Apion ii. 19); and that they were "brought up in learning," "exercised in the laws," "and made acquainted with the acts of their predecessors in order to their imitation of them" (*Jos.* Ag. Apion ii 26; comp. i . 8. 12; ii. 17).
>
> But while the earliest religious teaching would, of necessity, come from the lips of the mother, it was the father who was

1. *The Cyclopaedia of Education: A Dictionary of Information for the Use of Teachers, School Officers, Parents, and Others, 3rd Ed.,* Henry Kiddle and Alexander Jacob Schem, ed. (E. Steiger and Co., 1876, 1883), 411; cf. H.H. Meyer, "Education," *International Standard Bible Encyclopedia* (Eerdmans, 1939), II: 900–05; Ron Moseley, "Jewish Education in Ancient Times" https://sites.google.com/site/educationinjesustime/ (accessed 13 May, 2016); James L. Crensaw, *Education in Ancient Israel: Across the Deadening Silence* (Anchor Bible, Double Day, 1998); Bruce Waltke, *The Book of Proverbs* (Eerdmans, 2004), 61–63; E.A. Pace, "Education" *Catholic Encyclopedia* V: 298–99. These sources agree that literacy was widespread in ancient Israel, but they do not agree as to *how* widespread it was; some believe literacy was nearly universal, but others believe it was widespread but far from universal.

> "bound to teach his son" (Kidd. 29 a). To impart to the child knowledge of the Torah conferred as great spiritual distinction, as if a man had received the Law itself on Mount Horeb (Sanh. 99 b). Every other engagement, even the necessary meal, should give place to this paramount duty (Kidd. 30 a)....
>
> The regular instruction commenced with the fifth or sixth year (according to strength), when every child was sent to school (Baba B. 1a; Keth. 50 a). There can be no reasonable doubt that at such time [the first century AD during the lifetime of Jesus] such schools existed throughout the land. We find references to them at almost every period; indeed, the existence of higher schools and Academies would not have been possible without such primary instruction.... Later on, tradition ascribes to Joshua the son of Gamala the introduction of schools in every town, and the compulsory education in them of all children above the age of six (Baba B. 21 a).... To pass over the fabulous number of schools supposed to have existed in Jerusalem, tradition had it that, despite of this, the City only fell because of the neglect of the education of children (Shabb. 119 b). It was even deemed unlawful to live in a place where there was no school (Sanh. 17 b). Such a city deserved to be either destroyed or excommunicated (Shabb. u.s.).
>
> Roughly classifying the subjects of study, it was held, that, up to ten years of age, the Bible exclusively should be the textbook; from ten to fifteen the Mishnah, or traditional law; after that age, the student should enter on those theological discussions which occupied the time and attention in the higher Academies of the Rabbis (Ab. v. 21)....
>
> The teaching in school would, of course, be greatly aided by the services of the Synagogue, and the deeper influences of home-life.[2]

Those who desired higher education associated together in the "schools of the prophets," referred to briefly in 1 Samuel 10:5–10; 19:18–20; 2 Kings 2:3–7, 15–18; 4:38–41; 6:1–2. Little is known about these schools. Many believe they were simply traveling bands, perhaps similar to Socrates and his pupils; but 1 Samuel 19:18–19 suggests that at least the school of Samuel had habitations or buildings.[3]

2. Alfred Edersheim, *The Life and Times of Jesus the Messiah* (1883; reprinted by MacDonald), 106–09.

3. Leon J. Wood, *The Prophets of Israel* (Baker, 1979), 164–66.

Moseley speaks of a *Bet Midrash* (House of Study) which was the main place for the study of the Law and all interests that surrounded its investigation. The sanctity of the *bet midrash* was considered greater than that of the synagogue (*bet Knesset*), and rabbis often preferred to pray in the *bet midrash* rather than the synagogue (Ber. 8a). It was here that senior students spent most of their day, either in individual study or under the discipline of a *rosh yeshivah* (elder rabbi, later known as the academy head). The *bet midrash* was also a popular place for general study. Almost all those who attended the synagogue for prayer would usually spend some time before or afterwards in the *bet midrash.* It served as the communal library with the best of the literature concerning the Law and sages.

> According to Jewish tradition, the antiquity of the institution goes back to the *bet midrash* established after the flood by Shem and Eber, where the Patriarchs are said to have studied.[4]

As in more recent societies, the widespread literacy of ancient Israel helped make republican government possible.

THE HEBREW BIBLE

The primary document of Hebrew Law is the first thirty-nine books of the Bible, which Jews call the Tanakh and Christians call the Old Testament, and which we will call the Hebrew Bible.

The Hebrew Bible contains the same 39 books that Christians call the Old Testament, but they are organized differently. 1 and 2 Samuel are combined as simply Samuel in the Hebrew Bible, as are 1 and 2 Kings and 1 and 2 Chronicles. The twelve Minor Prophets (Hosea, Joel, Amos, Obadiah, Jonah, Micah, Nahum, Habakkuk, Zephaniah, Haggai, Zechariah, and Malachi) are combined into a book called the Twelve.

The Hebrew Bible is divided into three parts:

(1) **The Torah**, consisting of the first five books, Genesis, Exodus, Leviticus, Numbers, and Deuteronomy. *Torah* literally means "instruction," and it comes from the word *yarah* which means "to point out" or "to direct and lead." Barry states that Torah represents the law's "moral authority as teaching truth and guiding in the right way."[5] Judaism has

4. Moseley, 1.

5. Rev. Alfred Barry, *Smith's Dictionary of the Bible* II: 1000 "Law" (Baker, 1869, 1971); Dr. William Smith's *Dictionary of the Bible* II: 1601 "Law" (Hurd & Houston, 1869).

traditionally taught that Moses wrote the Torah under divine inspiration. The Torah is sometimes called the "Five Books of Moses," the *Chumash* (Hebrew for "fivesome"), and the Pentateuch (Greek term meaning "five scroll-cases"). The Torah contains the basic laws of the Hebrews, but it also contains considerable history and some prophecy. Occasionally the term Torah is used for the entire Hebrew Bible, but this writer will use the term in the more common and more restrictive sense.

(2) **The Nevi'im**, or "Prophets," consisting of the books of Joshua, Judges, Samuel, Kings, Isaiah, Jeremiah, Ezekiel, and the Twelve (Minor Prophets). Joshua, Judges, Samuel, and Kings are primarily historical narratives, but they contain some exhortation as well. Isaiah, Jeremiah, Ezekiel, and the Twelve contain prophecy, both in the "foretelling" sense of predicting the future and in the "forthtelling" sense of exhortation. They are not primarily law books, but they do contain exhortations to judges and rulers, calling upon them to interpret and administer the law justly and often reproving them for accepting bribes, perverting law and judgment, accepting bribes, and ignoring the causes of the poor, widows, orphans, and sojourners.

(3) **The Ketuvim**, or "Writings" or "Scriptures," consisting of the books of Psalms, Proverbs, Job, Song of Songs (Song of Solomon in most Christian Bibles), Ruth, Lamentations (of Jeremiah), Ecclesiastes, Esther, Daniel, Ezra (which includes Nehemiah), and Chronicles. The Writings include "wisdom literature" such as Psalms, Proverbs, Job, Song of Songs, and Ecclesiastes; history such as Chronicles, narratives such as Esther and Ezra, and Daniel which contains both history and prophecy. They are not primarily law books, but much of their content is relevant to law and government. Many of the Psalms and Proverbs are directed to rulers and judges. Ruth is instructive in the use of the levirate law concerning a man's duty to marry his kinsman's widow. Ezra, Nehemiah, and Esther involve the responsibilities of government officials, and Daniel serves as a role model for a believer who lives in a secular or pagan empire.

We will draw upon the Prophets and the Writings where relevant, but our primary focus will be upon the Torah or Pentateuch.

THE TORAH OR PENTATEUCH

The Authorship of the Pentateuch

As noted above, Judaism has traditionally taught that Moses wrote the Torah under divine inspiration, and this has also been the traditional view of the Christian Church. Moses served as a prophet, priest, and judge of Israel from the Exodus from Egypt through the wandering in the wilderness until just before Israel's conquest of Canaan. The Exodus is commonly dated at 1446 BC,[6] although some date it as late as the 1200s BC. Moses probably wrote these five books over a long period of time during his 120-year lifespan. This does not foreclose the possibility that Moses may have drawn upon earlier writings or oral traditions, nor does it preclude the possibility that a later writer (possibly Joshua) may have added the account of Moses' death in Deuteronomy 34.

In the 1700s the Mosaic authorship of the Torah came under challenge, and in the 1800s an alternative theory developed. This view, known as the Graf-Wellhausen theory because of its primary authors, or the documentary hypothesis, or the JEDP theory, began to fall into disfavor as the twentieth century progressed, but it still has its adherents in academia and among liberal Christians and Jews. Various works of Biblical scholarship discuss the theory at great length,[7] but when legal scholars write about Hebrew Law, they commonly parrot the JEDP theory as though it were established fact.

Some readers might wonder why so much space is devoted to an analysis and critique of the JEDP theory. But higher criticism[8] affects the origin, authority, and interpretation of the books of the Hebrew Law, and therefore we must give it a thorough analysis.

The documentary hypothesis held that the Torah was not the work of Moses; rather, it was composed by four different writers over several

---

6. Leon Wood, *A Survey of Israel's History* (Zondervan, 1970), 88.

7. Two of the best works of Biblical scholarship that address the documentary hypothesis are Josh McDowell, *The New Evidence That Demands a Verdict* (Thomas Nelson, 1999), 389–533, and Robert Dick Wilson, *Is the Higher Criticism Scholarly? Clearly Attested Facts Showing That the Destructive "Assured Results of Modern Scholarship" Are Indefensible* (The Sunday School Times Company, 1922, 1923), 1–62.

8. The term "higher criticism" refers to a school of Biblical scholarship that questions whether the books of the Bible were really written by the authors to whom they are attributed, at the times they have been thought to have been written, and in the form in which we have them today. The term is used in contrast to "lower criticism" that seeks to determine the true meaning of the Bible texts without questioning the authority of the original manuscripts.

centuries, commencing in the 900s BC and being completed after the Babylonian Exile in the 500s BC. Those who promulgated the documentary hypothesis observed that various portions of the Pentateuch use different Hebrew terms for God. Sometimes God is referred to as *Jehovah* or *Yahweh* (The *J* and *Y* are the same in Hebrew, as are *V* and *W*, and Hebrew had no vowels until about AD 600). In other passages the term *Elohim* is used for God. The use of these two different terms, they reasoned, suggests two different authors.

They also observed that the Pentateuch contains repetitious accounts. Genesis Chapter One and Genesis Chapter Two, they say, contain two creation accounts, and they differ markedly—for example, in Chapter One the creation of man is the culmination of God's creative activity, whereas Chapter Two begins with the creation of man. Furthermore, God gave the Ten Commandments to Moses on Mount Sinai in Exodus 20, but that event is repeated in Deuteronomy 5. Much of the Law that is given elsewhere in Exodus is repeated in Deuteronomy.

These and other considerations led these scholars to conclude that the five books of the Pentateuch were not the work of Moses. Rather, they were actually several different accounts that were later woven together. Certain portions of the Pentateuch were attributed to a writer who lived in the southern kingdom of Judea after the division of the kingdom in 922 BC. He is called the *J* writer because he uses the term Jehovah for God. His writings include some of the law but also much epic narrative about the establishment of Israel as a special nation chosen by Jehovah.

Around the same time period, another writer in the northern kingdom wrote other portions of the Pentateuch, including much about the traditions of the twelve tribes of Israel. He is called the *E* writer because he refers to God as Elohim.

A third strain is the legal corpus found in Deuteronomy and elsewhere in the Pentateuch. This, the higher critics concluded, is the work of a writer identified as *D*; when he lived and wrote is uncertain but probably before the reign of Josiah in the 600s BC.

And a fourth writer is called the *P* source because he recorded the priestly tradition. He supposedly lived and wrote during or after the Babylonian exile (roughly 606–536 BC), and he edited, reorganized and redacted the works of J, E and D and developed the Pentateuch roughly into the form we know it today.

A distinguishing feature of the documentary hypothesis is the dogmatism and tenacity with which its adherents cling to it and present it. Gottwald's approach is typical:

> One of the certain results of modern Bible study has been the discovery that the first five books of the Old Testament were not written by Moses. The present Pentateuch ('five scrolls') was constructed from anonymous sources (commonly designated J, E, D, and P) only at a relatively late date.[9]

In fact, the documentary hypothesis has never enjoyed general acceptance, and it is far less popular today than it was 100 years ago. Even among its adherents, the theory has morphed greatly; JEDP theorists now commonly claim there were (at least) two E writers, and some think the four anonymous sources are not specific writers but traditions that arose in various areas. Others say the P writer was not the final editor; rather, he was a fourth source of original material, and the editor/redactor was a fifth source identified as R.

The following observations about the authorship of the Pentateuch are in order:

1. Different names for God do not indicate multiple authorship. The same writer might refer to a person by different names. John Smith might call his wife "Dear Mary" in a personal letter, "Mary Anne Smith" in a legal document such as a will, "Mary Anne Wilson" if he is writing about something that happened before their marriage, or a host of other combinations.

"Jehovah *(YHVH)"* is God's name. It is used when speaking specifically of the God of Israel and emphasizing His attributes and His role in the history of Israel. "Elohim" is a generic term for God or gods.[10] The Pentateuch uses the term Elohim when speaking of God's relations with other nations or when a more general reference to God is desired. The term elohim could be used for pagan gods; no Jew would ever call a pagan god Jehovah. It is not at all surprising that Moses, writing at various times and in various places and with various purposes, would use more than one legitimate term for God.

---

9. Norman K. Gottwald, *A Light to the Nations* (Harper & Row, 1959), 103.

10. The "im" ending of Elohim indicates the plural form. The Pentateuch commonly uses this plural form for God either to emphasize His greatness (the "plural of majesty") or, Christians believe, as a foreshadowing of the Trinity.

2. No manuscript has ever been discovered that contains only the J, E, D, or P writing. All ancient manuscripts of the Pentateuch show a fully integrated document as though it were written by Moses.

3. Not one ancient Jewish writer, nor any other ancient author writing about the Jews, ever suggested in any way that the Pentateuch is the work of anyone but Moses.

4. The Pentateuch itself repeatedly claims that Moses is its author: Exodus 17:14; 24:4–7; 34:27; Numbers 33:2; Deuteronomy 31:9, 22, 24, and many others.

5. Other Old Testament writers attribute the Pentateuch to Moses: Joshua 1:7–8; 8:32–34; Judges 3:4; 1 Kings 2:3; 2 Kings 14:6; 21:8; 2 Chronicles 25:4; Ezra 6:18; Nehemiah 8:1; 13:1; Daniel 9:11–13. The Jews of Old Testament Israel were the "people of the Book." They believed the Hebrew Bible was authoritative because it was given by Divine inspiration. If JEDP theorists are correct, the various portions of the Pentateuch were being compiled at the time Ezra, Nehemiah, Daniel, and others were living and writing. Surely they, and other prophets and priests of that time, would have noted that someone other than Moses had a hand in writing the Pentateuch, if that were truly the case. And yet, none of the authors of other books of the Old Testament, nor any other Jewish writers during the Old Testament era, ever attribute the Pentateuch to anyone else but Moses.

6. In the New Testament, Jesus frequently quoted from the Pentateuch and attributed it to Moses: Matthew 8:4; 19:7–8; Mark 7:10; 12:26; Luke 16:31; 24:27, 44; John 5:46–47; 7:19. Never did He attribute the Pentateuch to anyone else but Moses.[11]

7. Other New Testament writers attribute the Pentateuch to Moses: John 1:17; Acts 6:14; 13:39; 15:5; 1 Corinthians 9:9; 2 Corinthians 3:15; Hebrews 10:28. No New Testament writer attributed the Pentateuch to anyone else but Moses.

8. The Mosaic Law was already in existence in the days of King Josiah (circa 638 BC; 2 Kings 22); in fact, the Mosaic Law had been virtually forgotten in the days of King Manasseh and King Amon and was rediscovered during King Josiah's revival. Likewise, the Law was well-known

11. Jesus' attribution of the Pentateuch to Moses presents a serious problem for a JEDP adherent who believes Jesus to be the Son of God and the Second Person of the Trinity. If Moses did not write the Pentateuch, the JEDP adherent is left with two possibilities: Either (1) Jesus mistakenly believed that Moses wrote the Pentateuch, in which case Jesus cannot be omniscient; or (2) Jesus claimed that Moses wrote the Pentateuch even though He knew that was not true, in which case Jesus was not truthful.

during the Babylonian Exile (Daniel 6:5; 9:10–13; Ezra 7:12–26; Nehemiah 1:7–9).

9. Ezra, the post-exilic governor of Judea, reinstated the entire Mosaic Law, including the sacrifices and offerings, and even required those who had married foreign wives to separate from them (Ezra 9; 10:1, 3, 16–17). Upon their return from Babylon, the Law was read to the people for many days, and 23 priests, 17 Levites, and 44 tribal chiefs affixed their seals reaffirming the Mosaic covenant (Nehemiah 8:18, 9:38, 10:1–29). No wise governor would have imposed such stringent requirements upon a people just returning from exile, unless those requirements were enacted pursuant to an ancient law of unquestioned authority.

10. During the reign of the Persian King Ahasuerus (486–465 BC), even the Jews who lived in Persia accepted the Mosaic Law. Haman complained to the king that *"There is a certain people scattered abroad and dispersed among the people in all the provinces of thy kingdom; and their laws are diverse from all people; neither keep they the king's laws: therefore it is not for the king's profit to suffer them"* (Esther 3:8). It seems unlikely that the Jews dispersed in foreign lands would have followed the Mosaic Law if it were not of ancient and unquestioned authority.

11. The Samaritans were a people who lived between Judea and Galilee after the Babylonian exile, of mixed Babylonian and Jewish ancestry. They and the post-exilic Jews were bitter enemies, yet the Samaritans accepted the Mosaic Law. They would not have done so, were the Mosaic Law not of unquestionable ancient authority.

12. Karl Graf and Julius Wellhausen, the primary authors of the documentary hypothesis, assumed that in Moses' time the Hebrews were an illiterate society. That seems very unlikely. Abraham came out of the City of Ur of the Chaldees around 2000 BC. The Ebla tablets, thousands of stone tablets found in the vicinity of Ur dating back to 2000 BC and before, demonstrate that writing was a highly developed art at that time. The tablets include business contracts and other legal documents, and they contain names such as "Abram."[12] Later the descendants of Abraham sojourned 400 years as slaves in Egypt. The Egyptians had a well-developed

12. Randall Price, *The Stones Cry Out: What Archaeology Reveals About the Truth of the Bible* (Harvest House, 1997), 83–85; Werner Keller, *The Bible as History* 2d (Bantam, 1982), 83; Clifford Wilson, *Ebla Tablets: Secrets of a Forgotten City* (Master Books, 1979, 1981). The finding of these names on the Ebla tablets does not prove that Abraham (Abram) was a historical figure, as it could have been a common name. But it is consistent with the hypothesis that Abraham was a historical figure.

system of writing before 2000 BC, and education in ancient Egypt was of high quality and was widely available to people of all classes.[13] One need not stretch the imagination too much to conclude that Moses, who was raised as a prince in the palace of the Pharaoh, not only knew how to read and write but received the best education and training that Egypt had to offer to a prince. The British Assyriologist A.H. Sayce wrote that

> [T]his supposed late use of writing for literary purposes was merely an assumption, with nothing more solid to rest upon than the critic's own theories and presuppositions. And as soon as it could be tested by solid fact it crumbled into dust. First Egyptology, then Assyriology, showed that the art of writing in the ancient East, so far from being of modern growth, was of vast antiquity, and that the two great powers which divided the civilized world between them were each emphatically a nation of scribes and readers. Centuries before Abraham was born, Egypt and Babylonia were alike full of schools and libraries, of teachers and pupils, of poets and prose-writers, and of the literary works which they had composed....
>
> The Babylonia of the age of Abraham was a more highly educated country than the England of George III.[14]

The Cyclopaedia of Education observes that

> During the Egyptian bondage, the Hebrews probably enjoyed some educational advantages, but to what extent does not clearly appear from the records. Moses himself had been carefully trained, and was competent not only to lead but also to instruct the people of God, during their wanderings in the wilderness. At that time, the Hebrews must have been more or less subject to mental as well as to religious training. They must have been able to read and write; for they were commanded of God to write the precepts of the Law upon their doorposts

13. S.S. Laurie, *Historical Survey of Pre-Christian Education* (Longmans, Green, & Co., 1915) 8; Frank P. Graves, *A History of Education Before the Middle Ages* (MacMillan Co. 1918), 35; Heinrich Brugsch, *A History of Egypt Under the Pharaohs* (John Murray 1881) 28–29; Adolf Erman, *Life in Ancient Egypt,* Vol. 2 (MacMillan Co. 1894), 328; cited by Elijah Brown, "Liberal Education and the Civil Establishment of Thought: The Liberty Interests of Parent, Child, and State in Conflict," Senior Seminar Paper for Oak Brook College of Law & Government Policy submitted December 2009, 5–6.

14. A.H. Sayce, *Monument Facts and Higher Critical Fancies* (The Religious Tract Society, 1904), 28–29, 35; quoted in Josh McDowell, *The New Evidence That Demands a Verdict* (Thomas Nelson, 1999), 431, 432; cf. Price, *The Stones Cry Out.*

> and gates; and they were, moreover, required to *write* the injunctions upon great stones "very plainly," immediately upon crossing the Jordan, so that they might easily be *read* by every Israelite.[15]

Furthermore, "In the days of the Judges we read of a *kiriath-sepher,* the 'city of books' (Joshua 15:15; Judges 1:11), a name which seems to indicate the seat of some scholastic establishment that had been founded by the Canaanites."[16] All of this demonstrates that Israel in the days of Moses, like other nations of the Middle East, was a literate society.

In fact, the evidence of archeology since the development of the documentary hypothesis has confirmed the accuracy of the first five books of the Bible. As Sayce observes, "Time after time the most positive assertions of a sceptical criticism have been disproved by archaeological discovery, events and personages that were confidently pronounced to be mythical have been shown to be historical, and the older writers have turned out to have been better acquainted with what they were describing than the modern critic who has flouted them."[17] And yet, as R.K. Harrison says,

> Wellhausen took almost no note whatsoever of the progress in the field of oriental scholarship, and once having arrived at his conclusions, he never troubled to revise his opinion in the light of subsequent research in the general field.[18]

13. The critics' claim that the Pentateuch contains various accounts that duplicate and at times contradict each other does not stand up to careful scrutiny. If Genesis 1 and Genesis 2 do in fact contain contradictory accounts of creation, is it not strange that no one noticed this until about two hundred years ago? In a more Biblically literate age, readers knew that Genesis 1 and 2 describe consecutive phases of creation. Genesis 1 describes God's general creation of the heavens and the earth, followed by the creation of plants, animals, and ultimately man. Genesis 2 describes God's special creation of the Garden of Eden, beginning with Adam and proceeding to the animals that are under his dominion.

---

15. *The Cyclopaedia of Education,* 411 (emphasis original).

16. *The Cyclopaedia of Education,* 411 (emphasis original).

17. Sayce, 23.

18. R.K. Harrison, *Introduction to the Old Testament* (Eerdmans, 1969), 509.

As noted earlier, Deuteronomy repeats much of the law that is set forth in Exodus. But the purpose is different. In Exodus, God gives the law to His people Israel. But as Attorney Howard B. Rand observed,

> Deuteronomy is the codification of the law of the Lord by Moses, a system of laws which he admonished Israel to administer at all times. In this book there are no laws of ordinance or ritual. In chapter after chapter for over 600 verses there are set forth statutes and laws for individual, national, and economic well-being. Fifteen verses only of this book cover the Ten Commandments, the perfect moral code which men have continually acknowledged.[19]

The Pentateuch does contain repetition, but the repetition always has a purpose. Exodus is an historical account of the reception of the law. Deuteronomy is a systematic recounting and codification of the law. And the repetitions and apparent inconsistencies would certainly suggest that the P redactor, if he existed, did a very sloppy job of editing the J, E and D materials and putting them together.

14. Robert Dick Wilson, Professor of Semitic Philology at Princeton Theological seminary, observed that "The almost universal inaccuracy and unreliability of the Greek and Arab historians with reference to the kings of Egypt, Assyria, and Babylon is in glaring contrast with the exactness and trustworthiness of the Hebrew Bible. It can be accounted for, humanly speaking, only on the grounds that the authors of the Hebrew records were contemporaries of the kings they mention, or had access to original documents; and secondly, that the Hebrew writers were good enough scholars to transliterate with exactness; and thirdly, that the copyists of the Hebrew originals transcribed with conscientious care the text that was before them."[20] Professor Wilson also posed some piercing questions of JEDP theorists that have never been satisfactorily answered:

> First, if Exodus 20–24 and Deuteronomy were written in the period of the kingdoms of Israel and Judah, how can we account

19. Howard B. Rand, *Digest of the Divine Law* (Destiny Publishers, 1943, 1983), 39.

20. Robert Dick Wilson, *Is the Higher Criticism Scholarly? Clearly Attested Facts Showing that the Destructive "Measured Results of Modern Scholarship" Are Indefensible* (Sunday School Times Company, 1922).

for the fact that the king is referred to but once (Deuteronomy 17), and that in a passage difficult to read and explain and claiming to be anticipatory? And why should this passage make no reference to the house of David, and place its emphasis on a warning against a return to Egypt?

Second, why should the law never mention Zion, or Jerusalem, as the place where men ought to worship, if these laws were written hundreds of years after the Temple had been built?

Third, why should the Temple itself receive no consideration, but be set aside for a "mythical" tabernacle whose plan to the minutest particular has been elaborated with so much care? And why, if this plan were devised at Babylon in the fifth century BC, should it in its form and divisions show more resemblance to an Egyptian than to a Babylonian house of God?

Fourth, if the laws of the Priest-code were made at Babylon, how does it come about that the main emphasis in these laws is upon the shedding of blood and that the principal offerings are bloody offerings; whereas, in the Babylonian religion it is doubtful if any reference is ever made to the importance of the blood and no word corresponding to the Hebrew word for altar *(misbeach)* has ever yet been found in the Babylonian language? How is it, also, that almost the entire vocabulary bearing upon the ceremonial observances is different in Babylonian than it is in Hebrew? The Hebrew names for the various articles of clothing worn by the priests, for the stones of the breastplate, for the sacrifices, for the altar and the many spoons and other implements used in its service, for the festivals, for the ark and the multifarious articles used in its construction, for sins and removal of sins, and for nearly all the gracious acts of God in redemption, differ almost entirely from the Babylonian. How to account for all this, if the ceremonies of the second temple were first conceived by the rivers of Babylon under the shadow of the tower of Bel?

Fifth, if the ceremonial law were written between 500 and 300 BC, at a time when the Persian power was supreme, how to account for the entire absence of Persian words and customs from the priestly document? Why should Ezra and his contemporaries have used so many Persian words in their other com-

> positions and have utterly eschewed them in the lengthiest of their works? Not one Persian word, forsooth! How careful they must have been to camouflage their attempt to foist their work on Moses!...
>
> Sixth, if the Israelitish religion is a natural development like that of the nations that surrounded them, how does it happen that the Phoenicians who spoke substantially the same language have an almost entirely different nomenclature for their ceremonial acts, for sacrifices and the material of sacrifice; and that the Phoenicians and Carthaginians and their colonies remained polytheistic to the last?
>
> Seventh, if the ceremonial law were written after the exile, when all the Jews, from Elephantine in Egypt on the west to Babylon on the east, were speaking and writing Aramaic, how did it come to pass that the law was written in a Hebrew so different that almost every word used in it required to be translated in order to make it understood by the Aramaic-speaking Jews? Are we to suppose that the exiled Hebrews invented their religious vocabulary arbitrarily after their language had ceased to be spoken by any great body of living men?...
>
> Eighth, how is the fact to be explained that the Aramaic of the Targum and Talmud has taken over so many roots and vocables from the Hebrew of the Old Testament?...[21]

15. JEDP theorists seem to start with the presupposition that miracles do not happen and therefore accounts of miracles must be early superstition, and that prophecy is not possible, and therefore prophecies in the Pentateuch must have been written much later after the "prophecies" had come to pass. Such presuppositions skew the results of research. They are not the presuppositions of traditional Judaism and Christianity.

16. In the face of such objections, how could the documentary hypothesis have taken hold? Herbert F. Hahn made a revealing observation:

---

21. Wilson, *op. cit.* After the Jews returned to Judea around 536 BC at the close of their exile in Babylon, they no longer spoke Hebrew but rather spoke Aramaic. Hebrew and Aramaic are both Semitic languages, but they are substantially different. Professor Wilson suggested that if the Pentateuch was in fact set in final form after the Babylonian Exile by the P redactor, it would have been in Aramaic rather than in Hebrew.

> The conception of historical development was the chief contribution of the liberal critics to the exegesis of the Old Testament. It is true, of course, that this conception did not grow merely from an objective reading of the sources. In a larger sense, it was a reflection of the intellectual temper of the times. The genetic conception of Old Testament history fitted in with the evolutionary principle of interpretation prevailing in contemporary science and philosophy. In the natural sciences, the influence of Darwin had made the theory of evolution the predominant hypothesis affecting research. In the historical sciences and in the area of religious and philosophical thought, the evolutionary concept had begun to exercise a powerful influence after Hegel had substituted the notion of "becoming" for the idea of "being."... In every department of historical investigation the conception of development was being used to explain the history of man's thought, his institutions, and even his religious faiths. It was not strange that the same principle should be applied to the explanation of Old Testament history.[22]

Hahn said the documentary hypothesis was not based strictly upon scholarly research; rather, it was the result of a Darwinian worldview. He said concerning Wellhausen:

> He consciously based his exposition on the evolutionary view of history.... From the evolutionary point of view, which assumed that development invariably took place from lower to higher forms, it was inconceivable that the nomadic ancestors of the Israelites could have held the lofty, monotheistic conceptions ascribed to Abraham....[23]

Hahn explained further,

> The theory that Hebrew religious conceptions were derived in fully developed form from a highly mature intellectual background at the very beginning of Old Testament history ran counter to the evolutionary interpretation of religious history

---

22. Herbert F. Hahn, *The Old Testament in Modern Research* (Fortress Press, 1954, 1966), 9–10.

23. Hahn, 12. The reader will recall from Part I of this book that the modern view that legal systems evolve from the simple to the complex—a view refuted by the historical evidence—is also based upon Darwinian presuppositions, as is the belief that human societies begin polytheistic and evolve into monotheism.

> popularized by both the critical and the anthropological schools of Old Testament study.[24]

If humans are merely another species of animal and the result of an evolutionary process, then human society, human law, and human religion evolves as the species evolves physically:

> Behind this methodology was not only the hypothesis that religion, like other aspects of human culture, had evolved from elementary forms of belief and practice to higher and more complete forms, but also the assumption that cultural evolution was a uniform process that went through the same stages everywhere. This assumption, of course, was not peculiar to the anthropologists. But, for more than a generation after Herbert Spencer had popularized the notion that biological evolution had an analogue in the cultural history of mankind, the ideas of unilinear evolution and parallel development dominated anthropological research.[25]

The controversy over the authorship of the Pentateuch, then, is not just an academic debate over who wrote those books and when. It affects one's view of Old Testament history as a whole. A belief in Mosaic authorship of the Pentateuch leads to the conclusion that God revealed Himself to Adam and Eve, Noah, and later to Abraham, Isaac, Jacob, and Joseph, and later to Moses, and that throughout Old Testament history faithful Jews have striven to keep God's revelation pure from corrupting influences. The documentary hypothesis points to the opposite conclusion—that man has evolved from an apelike ancestor, that as his brain evolved he began to develop notions of animism, then polytheism, then henotheism, and eventually monotheism. Abraham, in this view, was a polytheist who lived in the City of Ur and who came to believe that this one God named Jehovah (an anachronism according to JEDP theorists) had specially called him to a new land. Jehovah, in Abraham's primitive thought, was only one of many gods, but He happened to be Abraham's personal God. Gradually, as Abraham's descendants evolved, they came to believe that Jehovah was the greatest of all gods, and eventually after the Babylonian Exile they came to recognize that He was the only true God. As Hahn says,

---

24. Hahn, 91.

25. Hahn, 46–47.

> The transfer of the "Mosaic law" from the beginning [Mount Sinai] to the end of the history [after the Babylonian Exile] did away with all theories based on the supposition that the religious institutions of the Levitical legislation were characteristic of the age of Moses. With these elaborate institutions shifted to the end, the history of Israel's religion no longer appeared as a continual struggle to maintain an ideal system established at the beginning; instead, it took on the character of gradual growth from the simple to the complex, with the Levitical institutions as the climax of the whole development.... The evolutionary conception proved of great value in ordering and explaining various phenomena of this sort which had puzzled earlier scholars. Now the characteristic ideas and institutions of each age could be understood as parts of the continuous process of development through which Israel's religion had gone.[26]

17. The documentary hypothesis followed the intellectual fad of the times in another way—it was developed at a time when multiple authorship was the trend in literary criticism. During this time the medieval epic *Beowulf* was thought to have been the work of six different sources and the *Niebelungenlied* was thought to have originally been 20 different songs. Literary scholarship has generally moved away from that form of analysis:

> In field after field, theories of composite authorship, earlier versions, different strata, have been discarded. The kind of analysis which was once thought to have been the particular duty of literary criticism is now markedly out of fashion. The assumption today is more and more in favour of single authorship, unless there is clear external evidence to the contrary.[27]

And yet, JEDP theorists cling to their position. As the Jewish scholar Cyrus Gordon said, "I have heard professors of Old Testament refer to the integrity of JEDP as their "conviction." They are willing to countenance modifications in detail. They permit you to subdivide (D1, D2, D3, and so forth) or combine (JE) or add a new document designated by

26. Hahn, 8.

27. Helen Gardner, *The Business of Criticism* (Oxford, 1959), 97.

another capital letter but they will not tolerate any question of the basic JEDP structure."[28]

Why? Gordon suggested "intellectual laziness or inability to reappraise."[29] Jewish author Herman Wouk added, "It is a hard thing for men who have given their lives to a theory, and taught it to younger men, to see it fall apart."[30] But this writer would suggest another explanation: the JEDP theory fits their theological presuppositions, while Mosaic authorship does not.

This writer concludes that no valid reason exists to contest the claim of Scripture that Moses was the author of the first five books of the Bible, and this book will proceed upon that assumption.[31] This writer observes, further, that the higher critics, in their attempts to undermine the authority of the Old and New Testaments, have handed Islam a notable weapon to use against Judaism and Christianity.[32]

The Content of the Pentateuch

The Pentateuch contains five books:

28. Cyrus Gordon, "Higher Critics and Forbidden Fruit," *Christianity Today* IV:131, November 23, 1959.

29. Gordon, 131.

30. Herman Wouk, *This Is My God* (Doubleday, 1959), 318.

31. An amusing and insightful essay, "New Directions in Pooh Studies: Uberlieferungs- und religionsgeschichtliche Studien zum Pu-Buch" appears in *On the Way to the Postmodern: Old Testament Essays 1967–1998* Vol. 2 (Sheffield Academic Press, 1998), 830–39. Satirizing the methodology and terminology of JEDP theorists, the tongue-in-cheek essay proposes multiple authorship of *Winnie the Pooh* and declares that "the dogma of unitary authorship for works of literature must be abandoned," and "the Pooh corpus (viz. Winnie-the-Pooh, hereafter abbreviated W, containing traditions of higher antiquity than the Deutero-Pooh book, *The House at Pooh Corner,* hereby abbreviated H) to be of composite origin." Even if A. A. Milne was an historical person, "His name does not appear once within the narratives themselves, and we can hardly be expected to take a title-page, manifestly a later addition, seriously." The essay observes the different names used for Winnie the Pooh, i.e., Pooh Pooh, Winnie-the-Pooh, Pooh-Bear, Sir Pooh de Bear, all of which are "a plain indication of the interweaving of a number of sources." The book contains contradictory accounts: "'Oh, help!' said Pooh, 'I'd better go back.' But according to the second source: 'Oh, bother!' said Pooh, 'I shall have to go on.' The redactor has simply set down these two contradictory statements side by side, and then has attempted to harmonize them . . . : 'I can't do either!' said Pooh. 'Oh, help and bother!'" Through this reduction to absurdity, the essay demonstrates the foolishness of the documentary hypothesis.

32. Uwe Siemon-Netto, "Faith Matters: Are Christians to Blame for Muslim Hate?" www.messianicassociation.org/ezine26-usn.are-christians2blame.htm (accessed 13 May, 2016). Dr. Siemon-Netto notes that until the eighteenth century, few Muslim theologians questioned the authenticity of the Old and New Testaments, but the higher critics' attempts to undermine the authority of Scripture has led prominent Islamic leaders to echo similar conclusions.

(1) **Genesis**, so named from the Greek word for "beginning" and in the Hebrew called *Breishit,* begins with Creation and the Fall of man, followed by the judgment of the Flood and the replenishment of the world. It narrates the lives of four great patriarchs—Abraham, Isaac, Jacob, and Joseph. At the close of the book, Jacob and his sons are reconciled to Joseph and go down to Egypt to join him there. Finally Joseph died, was embalmed apparently according to Egyptian methods, and was placed in a coffin which, 400 years later, the Hebrews would carry with them as they left Egypt, wandered in the wilderness, and entered the Promised Land. But that comes in the Book of Exodus. The downward direction of history is illumined by the way Genesis begins with God creating the heavens and the earth, and ends in a coffin in Egypt.

The giving of the Law does not take place until the Book of Exodus, but as we saw in Chapter 12, certain elemental principles of natural law are found in the Book of Genesis, as are the great covenants that God made with Noah, Abraham, and Jacob.

(2) The name **Exodus** comes from a Greek term meaning "exit" or "departure," referring to the Hebrew exodus from Egypt. In the Hebrew the book is called *ve'elleh shemot,* from the first words of Exodus 1:1, *"Now these are the names."* The book begins about 400 years after the close of Genesis. The descendants of Jacob had settled in Egypt, but a Pharaoh arose who *"knew not Joseph"* (1:8) and who enslaved the Hebrew people. The book records the birth and early life of Moses, his wandering in the wilderness, his encounter with Jehovah in the burning bush, his return to Egypt, the way Jehovah used him to deliver the Hebrews out of Egypt, and their wandering in the wilderness. In Chapter 18 Moses' father-in-law, Jethro the Midianite, proposed that Moses decentralize the judicial system by selecting various tiers of judges, laying the groundwork for the Hebrew republic.

In Chapter 19 we read that Moses ascended Mt. Sinai to receive the Law from Jehovah, and in Chapter 20 Jehovah revealed the Ten Commandments to him on tablets of stone. In the remaining chapters of Exodus we see the additional provisions of the Law, the tabernacle and the priesthood, Jehovah's covenant with Israel, Israel's unfaithfulness to the covenant, Moses' intercession for Israel, and God's renewal of the covenant.

(3) **Leviticus** is the title given to the third book by the Greek Septuagint.[33] The title means "that which pertains to the Levitical priesthood," the

33. The Septuagint is a translation of the Hebrew Bible into Greek by a team of 72 Jewish

priests being descendants of Jacob's son Levi; but the Hebrew title for the book is *wayyiqra*, taken from the first words of the book: *"And he called...."*

The central theme of Leviticus is the holiness of God and Israel's approach to God through the Levitical priests and the sacrifices. It contains the laws of acceptable approach to God (Chapters 1–7), the laws pertaining to the priesthood (8–10), the laws concerning cleansing and purity (11–15), the laws concerning national atonement (16–17), the laws of sanctification for the people (18–20), the laws of sanctification for the priesthood (21–22), the laws concerning worship (23–24), the laws concerning sanctification of the land of Israel (25–26), and the laws concerning vows and consecration to the Lord (27).

Most of what we commonly call the "ceremonial law"—the feasts, the sacrifices, the offerings, the Sabbaths—is found in Leviticus. Note that expressions like *"And the LORD called unto Moses, and spake unto him...."* occur no less than 56 times in Leviticus.

(4) **Numbers** is so named because the book records the numbering of the people of Israel, first in Chapter One at Mt. Sinai, and then again on the plains of Moab in Chapter 26. The Hebrew name for the book is *bemidbar*, from the phrase of Ch 1 v. 1, *"in the wilderness."* The book records the Hebrews' wanderings in the wilderness for 40 years, from approximately 1444–1405 BC. Throughout the book, phrases like *"The LORD spoke unto Moses"* occur no less than 80 times.

The first enumeration was for military purposes, and it led into the organization of the tribes and their respective armies (Chapters 1–4), and the sanctification of Israel through separation from other nations, through vows, through worship, and through Divine guidance (5–10). Israel then wandered in the wilderness for 40 years, because after their rebellion, God had vowed that that generation would never enter the Promised Land. The book then chronicles the wandering of Israel in the wilderness, their various rebellions against God and against Moses, their various wars against other nations, their preparations for entering the Promised Land, and God's disciplining and preparation of Israel to be His people, chosen by Him for the special purpose of bearing His Word to the world.

The second enumeration, this time involving a new generation, took place on the plain of Moab in Chapter 26 for the purpose of conquering and dividing the Promised Land. Throughout the Book of Numbers we

---

scholars around 200 BC. Bible scholars value the Septuagint because it helps us understand how the Jews interpreted the Hebrew Bible at that period of their history.

see various laws set forth, but the basic theme of the book is that God's people can move forward only as they are faithful to Him.

(5) **Deuteronomy** comes from the Greek words *deuteros* meaning second and *nomos* meaning law, for Deuteronomy is the second statement of the law. The Hebrew name for the book is *Devarim,* meaning "things." Throughout the book there are at least 40 claims that Moses was its author. Deuteronomy does not contradict Exodus, but it restates and expands the commands of Exodus. It presents the Ten Commandments as a covenant with Jehovah the Great King (Ch. 5), and there follows an exposition of the ceremonial laws (12–16), an exposition of the civil laws (16–20), and an exposition of the social laws (21–26), along with the prescribed punishments for their violation.

At the close of the book, Moses commissioned Joshua as his successor to lead and judge Israel. God then led Moses to Mt. Pisgah, from which he could see the Promised Land that he was not allowed to enter. Moses then died on the mountaintop, and God buried him, *"but no man knoweth of his sepulcher unto this day"* (34:6).[34] Critics insist that Moses could not have written Deuteronomy because Chapter 34 records his death. Those who accept Mosaic authorship of Deuteronomy respond that either (1) God through divine inspiration led Moses to write prophetically about his death; or (2) Moses wrote the basic book of Deuteronomy but another writer, possibly Joshua, added the last chapter.

These five books comprise the Torah, the basic statement of Hebrew Law. We will examine the Torah's legal precepts in Chapter 15.

THE NEVI'IM OR PROPHETS

Jews commonly call this division of the Hebrew Bible "the Prophets," but they contain much history as well as prophecy.

Joshua begins where Deuteronomy left off, with the death of Moses and the passing of the mantle of leadership to Joshua, from around 1405 BC to around 1390 BC. Chapters 1–12 chronicle the conquest of Canaan,[35] and chapters 13–24 describe the division of Canaan among the tribes of Israel after the conquest was complete, and the apportionment of 48 cities for the Levites, who were given no territory of their own because they

34. A likely reason God left Moses' gravesite unknown is to prevent the Jews from making his body or his tomb an object of worship; cf. Jude 9.

35. A good discussion of Israel's warfare from a military standpoint is found in Chaim Herzog and Mordechai Gichon, *Battles of the Bible* (Stackpole Books, 1978, 1997).

were set apart for priestly service. Joshua 20 also records the establishment of the *cities of refuge,* cities to which a person accused of a crime could flee and dwell therein safely until there was a trial and an adjudication of guilt or innocence.

Judges describes Israel after the conquest but before the establishment of the Hebrew monarchy. We are told repeatedly that *"In those days there was no king in Israel: every man did that which was right in his own eyes"* (17:6; 18:1; 19:1; 21:25). Although this might ideally sound like a state of perfect freedom, it actually describes a chaotic scene, in many ways like that of the American states under the Articles of Confederation after the War for Independence. In this book we see Israel's government under the judges, in which each tribe was largely self-governing with little central authority. Each tribe also had its own militia, consisting of the able-bodied men of the tribe, but when an enemy nation threatened the territory of one of the tribes, that tribe could count on little help from the other eleven. The book provides some information about the administration of government and the administration of justice during this period.

Samuel, which is divided into 1 Samuel and 2 Samuel in the Christian Bible, is named after the great prophet and judge of Israel who, according to tradition, was also the author of the book. 1 Samuel 1–7 narrates the early life of Samuel and his tenure as the last judge over all Israel. Chapters 8–12 relate the people's demand for a king (cf. Deuteronomy 17:15–20), and the selection and accession of Saul as Israel's first king. Chapters 13–31 describe the early successes and later failures of King Saul, the conflict between Saul and David, and finally the death of Saul.

2 Samuel begins with the accession of Israel's greatest king, David, to the throne, his triumphs over Israel's enemies, his sins, repentance, judgment, and restoration to God's favor. 1 and 2 Samuel give much insight into the institution of the judges and of the monarchy.

Kings, which is divided into 1 Kings and 2 Kings in the Christian Bible, begins where Samuel left off, with David as an aging and dying king and his son Solomon as his successor. Under Solomon's rule we see the limited kingship of Saul and David grow into a full-blown monarchy, complete with impressive public works financed by heavy taxation and forced labor. Despite his beginning with divinely-given wisdom (Chapter 3), Solomon turned away from God and began worshipping idols with his many pagan wives (5–11), although the Book of Ecclesiastes leads us to believe Solomon repented and returned to the Lord late in life.

After the death of Solomon, the kingdom was divided, with the tribes of Judah and Benjamin following Solomon's son King Rehoboam in the south (called Judea) and the other ten tribes following Rehoboam's rival King Jeroboam in the north (called Israel) (Chapters 12–14). Despite a good beginning, the northern kingdom quickly degenerated into paganism until its people were conquered and taken captive by the Assyrians around 721 BC. The southern kingdom also degenerated, but less rapidly as several kings led periods of revival, until they are taken captive by the Babylonians around 605 BC. In the midst of this apostasy and degeneracy, two faithful prophets, Elijah and Elisha, called the people to return to the God of their fathers.

Isaiah, named after the prophet whose writings comprise the book,[36] records events in Judea and Israel during Isaiah's ministry from around 740–680 BC. Isaiah's prophecies include judgments upon the many pagan nations that surround Judea, but also upon Judea itself (Chapters 22, 29), but these are followed by God's restoration of Israel (40–66).

Chapter 38 narrates the critical illness of Judea's King Hezekiah, and his recovery after praying to the Lord. Then, in Chapter 39, as an act of diplomacy, King Merodoch-Baladan of Babylon[37] sent messengers with gifts for King Hezekiah, and Hezekiah naively gave them a tour of his palace, including the vault which contained his treasures and sacred vessels. Isaiah perceives the Babylonians' true intent, and he prophesies that the day will come when those treasures and sacred vessels will be pillaged and carried off to Babylon, along with the finest young men of Jerusalem as hostages. This prophecy came to pass about 115 years later in Daniel 1: 1–6. But as we read in Daniel 5, about 70 years later, when Babylonian King

---

36. The same presuppositions which led critical scholars of the 1800s to postulate the documentary hypothesis for the multiple authorship of the Torah, also led critical scholars to theorize that Isaiah, or at least chapters 40–66 of Isaiah, were in fact written much later by a different author identified as "Deutero-Isaiah" (Second Isaiah), or even a third author identified as Trito-Isaiah. Space will not permit a detailed refutation of these theories, as they apply not only to Isaiah but also to Daniel and other prophetic books. Suffice it to say that this writer considers these theories to be groundless and will treat these prophetic books with the assumption that they were written by their claimed authors. For a good refutation of these theories, see *Catholic Encyclopedia* "Isaiah;" Josh McDowell, *Daniel in the Critics' Den* (Campus Crusade for Christ International, 1979).

37. Babylon at this time was still under Assyrian rule, but Assyria was weakening and the Babylonians or Chaldeans were seeking to throw off the Assyrian yoke and restore the old Babylonian Empire. Merodoch-Baladan had proclaimed himself king of Babylon but did not really have control of Babylon at this time. His name is an interesting combination of two pagan gods, Marduk and Baal.

Belshazzar staged a wild orgy and used the sacred vessels of Jerusalem to drink toasts to pagan gods, the handwriting on the wall appeared and God judged and destroyed Babylon that night by giving them over into the hands of the Medes and the Persians. In these events we see the Jewish view of God's hand in history, protecting Israel but using pagan empires to judge and discipline Israel when his people have become apostate.

Isaiah also proclaimed the timeless, absolute, and unchanging standard of God's righteousness, and he pronounced a curse upon those who pervert God's righteousness by calling good what God calls evil and by calling evil what God calls good:

> *Woe unto them that call evil good, and good evil; that put darkness for light, and light for darkness; that put bitter for sweet, and sweet for bitter!*
>
> *Woe unto them that are wise in their own eyes, and prudent in their own sight!* (5:20–21)

Isaiah's theology made little room for moral relativism, postmodern morality, language deconstruction, or tolerance for that which God has declared to be sin.

Jeremiah was written in the late 7th century and early 6th century BC by the prophet after whom the book is named (1:1). Sometimes called the "weeping prophet," Jeremiah wrote from Jerusalem to call his people to repentance, and he predicted that they would incur God's judgment and be taken captive to Babylon. Despite his condemnation of Judah's sins, Jeremiah's love for his people was obvious, and he predicted that God will make a new covenant with His people.

Although Jeremiah is not a law book, the prophet sometimes addressed legal subjects. He condemned the judicial system of his day, declaring that *"they that handle the law knew me [God] not"* (2:8). Jeremiah's condemnations of Judah's sin were so strong that, even today, a scathing denunciation is called a "jeremiad."

Jeremiah's denunciations earned him the wrath of the Jewish authorities, and they cast him into a cistern (Ch 38)—apparently because there were no prisons in Judah, as the Mosaic Law did not prescribe imprisonment as a criminal punishment. Jeremiah predicted that the people of Judah would spend 70 years in captivity in Babylon, but he exhorted his people to be good citizens of Babylon during this captivity:

> *Thus saith the* L*ORD of hosts, the God of Israel, unto all that are carried away captives, whom I have caused to be carried away from Jerusalem unto Babylon;*
>
> *Build ye houses, and dwell in them; and plant gardens, and eat the fruit of them;*
>
> *Take ye wives, and beget sons and daughters; and take wives for your sons, and give your daughters to husbands, that they may bear sons and daughters; that ye may be increased there, and not diminished.*
>
> *And seek the peace* [*shalom*, meaning peace, welfare, or benefit] *of the city whither I have caused you to be carried away captives, and pray unto the* L*ORD for it: for in the peace* [*shalom*] *thereof shall ye have peace.* (29:4–7)

Jeremiah's timeless words are good advice for believers who find themselves living in a secular or pagan society.

Ezekiel was written by Jeremiah's contemporary, the prophet Ezekiel, who was taken captive to Babylon during Jerusalem's second fall to King Nebuchadnezzar around 577 BC. Like Jeremiah, he denounced the sins of his people and predicted God's judgment upon them, but he also prophesied that God would restore Judah, most famously in his vision of the valley of dry bones (37:1–14). Through Ezekiel's prophecies of judgment and restoration we learn of God's justice, both in the history of nations and in the lives of individual people.

The Twelve is the Jewish title for 12 shorter works of prophecy. Christians treat them as 12 separate books and call them collectively "The Minor Prophets," emphasizing that they are "minor" only in their relative lengths and not in the importance of their messages.

The Minor Prophets' messages are not law texts; they consist largely of exhortations to righteousness and faithfulness to God, condemnations of sin and apostasy, and, as interpreted by Christians, prophecies concerning the coming of the Messiah. But their exhortations and condemnations are sometimes directed toward kings and judges, and they are therefore relevant to our understanding of Hebrew Law and government.

Hosea compared his adulterous wife Gomer to Israel's unfaithfulness to God, and he observed that *"My people ask counsel at their stocks"* (4:12); that is, the Jews, like people everywhere, are interested in learning

God's law only when they are being disciplined for disobeying it. Without downgrading the importance of the sacrificial offerings, Hosea declared that God *"desired mercy, and not sacrifice; and the knowledge of God more than burnt offerings"* (6:6).

Joel denounced the sins of Judah, declaring that his people had become so corrupt that they even sold their own people into slavery. He charged them with having *"given a boy for a harlot, and sold a girl for wine"* (3:2, 3); he declared that they had sold their fellow Jews to *"the Grecians, that ye might remove them far from their border"* (3:6); and he prophesied that God would *"raise them out of the place whither ye have sold them, and will return your recompense upon your own head"* (3:7). Selling their people into slavery violated the law of Moses (Exodus 21:2–8), and Joel emphasized that Judah's defiance of God's law would have devastating, if not immediate consequences.

Amos, one of the earliest of the prophets, was a sheepherder from Tekoa in the Southern Kingdom (Judea), but he prophesied mostly to the Northern Kingdom (Israel). He singled out the judges for special condemnation: *"They afflict the just, they take a bribe, and they turn aside the poor in the gate*[38] *from their right"* (5:12). He called upon Israel to *"Hate the evil, and love the good, and establish judgment in the gate: it may be that the Lord God of hosts will be gracious unto the remnant of Joseph"* (5:15). His passion for justice is revealed in his clarion call, *"let judgment run down as waters, and righteousness as a mighty stream"* (5:24).

Obadiah's prophecy was directed against the nation of Edom, an oppressor of Israel. The day will come, Obadiah declared, that God will judge Edom, and *"as thou hast done, it shall be done unto thee: thy reward shall return upon thine own head"* (v. 15).

Jonah was called by God to preach to Nineveh, the capital of the Assyrian Empire. Knowing the cruelty of the Assyrians toward foreign peoples, Jonah fled in the opposite direction, to Joppa, where he boarded a Phoenician ship to Tarshish on the west coast of Spain. However, a storm arose, and he was cast overboard and was swallowed by a sea creature,[39]

38. The term "the gate" commonly refers to the courts, as in the ancient Middle East the court proceedings usually took place by the city gate. For example, the statement in Daniel 2:49 that "Daniel sat in the gate of the king" means that Daniel served as a Babylonian judge.

39. Some claim Jonah contradicts Matthew because in the King James Version Jonah speaks of this creature as a "great fish" while Matthew calls it a "whale." But the Hebrew term *dag* (Jonah 1:17) literally means "sea creature," as does the Greek term *ketos* (Matthew 12:40). There is no

and he then obeyed God's calling and journeyed to Nineveh, where he preached, *"Yet forty days, and Nineveh shall be overthrown"* (3:4). Much to Jonah's surprise and consternation, the people of Nineveh heeded his warning and repented of their sins, and God did not destroy them. Jonah was angry at God for not destroying Ninevah, but God said to Jonah,

> *And should not I spare Nineveh, that great city, wherein are more than sixscore thousand persons that cannot discern between their right hand and their left hand; and also much cattle?* (4:11)

God's mention of 120,000 persons who cannot distinguish between their left hand and their right hand seems to refer to small children who have not reached an age of accountability when they are mature enough to be held responsible for their sins. The common law presumed that children age seven and under are not capable of forming criminal intent and therefore cannot be prosecuted for their crimes, and our juvenile court system treats juvenile offenders as less hardened than adult criminals and therefore focuses on rehabilitation rather than punishment.

Micah condemned his people for punishing criminals with excessive cruelty by flaying the skin off them and breaking their bones (3:3), and he declared that *"The heads thereof judge for reward"* (3:11). He exhorted Judah to follow the higher law of God, *"for the law shall go forth of Zion, and the word of the LORD from Jerusalem"* (4:2). His exhortation in 6:8 is worthy of remembrance for judges and lawyers throughout all time:

> *He hath shewed thee, O man, what is good; and what doth the LORD require of thee, but to do justly, and to love mercy, and to walk humbly with thy God?*

Nahum assured his people that even though they were oppressed by many pagan nations, *"The LORD is good, a strong hold in the day of trouble; and he knoweth them that trust in him"* (1:7). Further, Nahum declared to Israel's pagan enemies, *"Behold, I am against thee, saith the LORD of hosts"* (2:13), and He will judge those nations and bring them to ruin.

Habakkuk, speaking during the days of Judah's decline shortly before the Babylonian captivity, condemned the legal system of his day:

---

contradiction in the original languages. The sea creature could have been a mammal, a fish, or another creature specially created by God.

> *Therefore the law is slacked, and judgment doth never go forth: for the wicked doth compass about the righteous; therefore wrong judgment proceedeth* (1:4).

Because *"the law is slacked,"* that is, because the law is not interpreted and applied strictly, the law has lost its hold, and Judah has become a nation of men rather than of law, each judge doing what seems right in his own eyes. And perverted interpretations of the law lead to bad decisions and perversions of justice.

Zephaniah prophesied during the period of reform and revival under King Josiah. Even though Josiah attempted to lead his people back to the service of God and obedience to the Law of Moses, the nation was decadent and its judicial system corrupt and oppressive: *"Her princes within her are roaring lions; her judges are evening wolves; they gnaw not the bones till the morrow"* (3:3). Zephaniah prophesied that God will judge this apostate nation, but He will preserve the remnant within the nation who are faithful to Him:

> *The LORD thy God in the midst of thee is mighty; he will save, he will rejoice over thee with joy; he will rest in his love, he will joy over thee with singing.*
>
> *I will gather them that are sorrowful for the solemn assembly, who are of thee, to whom the reproach of it was a burden.* (3:17–18)

Haggai likewise prophesied of God's judgment, but he emphasized that God *"will shake the heavens, and the earth, and the sea, and the dry land; And I will shake all nations"* (2:6–7); and that God *"will overthrow the throne of kingdoms, and I will destroy the strength of the kingdoms of the heathen"* (2:22). God and His Law are eternal, universal, and supreme over all of the laws and judges and rulers of all of the nations on earth.

Zechariah exhorted his people to rebuild the Temple and to rely upon the higher power of the Spirit of God, and he also commanded judges to

> ...*Execute true judgment, and shew mercy and compassions every man to his brother.*
>
> *And oppress not the widow, nor the fatherless, the stranger, nor the poor; and let none of you imagine evil against his brother in your heart.* (7:9–10)

And *Malachi*, the last of the prophets, recounted God's love for His people and His provision for them, but he declared that Judah had departed from God and His truth. The priests should teach the true law, *"But ye are departed out of the way; ye have caused many to stumble at the law; ye have corrupted the covenant of Levi, saith the LORD of hosts"* (2:8). The day is coming when the Lord will judge unrighteousness:

> *And I will come near to you to judgment; and I will be a swift witness against the sorcerers, and against the adulterers, and against false swearers, and against those that oppress the hireling in his wages, the widow, and the fatherless, and that turn aside the stranger from his right, and fear not me, saith the LORD of hosts.*
>
> *For I am the LORD, I change not; therefore ye sons of Jacob are not consumed.*
>
> *Even from the days of your fathers ye are gone away from mine ordinances, and have not kept them. Return unto me, and I will return unto you, saith the LORD of hosts.* (3:5–7)

In a world of change and decay, God and His Law stand unchanged as man's only hope for order and stability: *"Remember ye the law of Moses my servant, which I commanded unto him in Horeb for all Israel, with the statutes and judgments"* (4:4).

THE KETUVIM OR WRITINGS

The Ketuvim include various books that Christians call "Wisdom Literature" (Psalms, Proverbs, Job, Song of Songs, and Ecclesiastes), books of history (Chronicles, Esther, Ezra, and Daniel), Ruth, and the Lamentations of Jeremiah. Like the Nevi'im, they are not primarily law books, but they do address law and government and provide insight into Hebrew Law.

Ruth is set in the period of the judges, before the institution of the monarchy, and gives us a picture of the Mosaic Law in practice. Ruth was a Moabite, and the young widow of an Israelite man. After her husband's death, Ruth lived by gleaning in the fields, for the Mosaic Law (Deuteronomy 24:19–21) provided that after a farmer had finished harvesting his crop, he must allow widows, orphans, and strangers to collect what remains in the field. The Mosaic Law (Deuteronomy 25:5–10) also provided that a childless widow was entitled to demand that a surviving brother of her deceased husband marry her. However, if the brother refused to marry the widow, she was free to marry another. This was called the levirate law (from the Hebrew word *levir* meaning husband's brother), and its purpose was to ensure that widows were properly cared for.

Ruth and her mother-in-law Naomi traveled to Bethlehem to the home of Boaz, a relative of Naomi's late husband. When Boaz learned that Ruth wanted him to marry her, he was overjoyed, but there was a problem: Ruth had a brother-in-law, and as a closer relative he had the first right to marry Ruth. So Boaz met Ruth's brother-in-law at the city gate, where the court held session, and asked him in the presence of witnesses whether he intended to marry Ruth. When the brother-in-law gave a clear refusal, ratified by the appropriate legal forms of the period, Boaz was then free to marry Ruth. He did so, and they became the great-grandparents of King David, and therefore also ancestors of Jesus Christ.[40]

Chronicles, divided into 1 and 2 Chronicles in the Christian Bible, records the events that took place during the reigns of the kings of Israel and Judah, their apostasies, and their periods of revival. Especially interesting is the account in 2 Chronicles 19 of King Jehoshaphat's effort to reconstruct the kingdom with an institutional separation of the civil and the religious authority:

> *And he [Jehoshaphat] set judges in the land throughout all the fenced cities of Judah, city by city,*
>
> *And said to the judges, Take heed what ye do: for ye judge not for man, but for the Lord, who is with you in the judgment.*
>
> *Wherefore now let the fear of the Lord be upon you; take heed and do it: for there is no iniquity with the Lord our God, nor respect of persons, nor taking of gifts.*
>
> *Moreover in Jerusalem did Jehoshaphat set of the Levites, and of the priests, and of the chief of the fathers of Israel, for the judgment of the Lord, and for controversies, when they returned to Jerusalem.*
>
> *And he charged them, saying, Thus shall ye do in the fear of the Lord, faithfully, and with a perfect heart.*

40. Boaz is described in 4:14–15 as a kinsman and as a restorer of life, or "kinsman-redeemer." Christians therefore view the relationship of Boaz and Ruth as a type of Christ and His Church.

> *And what cause soever shall come to you of your brethren that dwell in their cities, between blood and blood, between law and commandment, statutes and judgments, ye shall even warn them that they trespass not against the LORD, and so wrath come upon you, and upon your brethren: this do, and ye shall not trespass.*
>
> *And behold, Amariah the chief priest is over you in all matters of the LORD; and Zebadiah the son of Ishmael, the ruler of the house of Judah, for all the king's matters: also the Levites shall be officers before you. Deal courageously, and the LORD shall be with the good.* (2 Chronicles 19:5–11)

Notice that the separation instituted by King Jehoshaphat was an *institutional* separation. Amariah the chief priest was the supreme human authority in *"matters of the LORD,"* and Zebadiah of the house of Judah was supreme in *"all the king's matters."* But both received their authority from God, and both were subject to the law of God; the judge judges *"not for man, but for the LORD, who is with you in the judgment."*

After Judah was taken captive to Babylon, the Babylonian Empire began to decay, and in 539 BC Babylon had fallen to the Persians. In 536 BC the Persian King Cyrus decreed that the captive Jews could return to their homeland. This is consistent with general Persian policy, which was to allow conquered nations considerable autonomy in their domestic affairs.

Many Jews returned to Judea, but many others stayed in Babylon, which by then had become a Persian province. Among those who remained in Babylon, or who stayed in other parts of the Persian Empire, were the subjects of three books of the *Ketuvim:* **Ezra, Nehemiah,** and **Esther.**

The Book of **Ezra** concerns the rebuilding of the Temple of Jerusalem. Some of those who returned to Judea began to rebuild the Temple, but their adversaries persuaded the Persian King Artaxerxes I that if the Jews were allowed to rebuild, they would become rebellious as in the past. King Artaxerxes therefore halted the rebuilding of the Temple, and it ceased until the reign of King Darius II.

Not long after Darius II began to reign, Jewish leaders told him King Cyrus the Great had issued a decree that the Temple should be rebuilt. King Darius ordered a search of the records, and the decree of King Cyrus was found. King Artaxerxes therefore issued a decree authorizing a scribe named Ezra and others to return to Jerusalem to rebuild the Temple, and to bring with them the sacred silver and gold vessels that the Babylonians had taken when they conquered Jerusalem around 605 BC. Artaxerxes' decree gave Ezra authority to govern according to the Law of God and the law of Persia:

> *And I, even I Artaxerxes the king, do make a decree to all the treasurers which are beyond the river, that whatsoever Ezra the priest, the scribe of the law of the God of heaven, shall require of you, be it done speedily,...*
>
> *And thou, Ezra, after the wisdom of thy God, that is in thine hand, set magistrates and judges, which may judge all the people that are beyond the river, all such as know the laws of thy God; and teach ye them that know them not.*
>
> *And whosoever will not do the law of thy God, and the law of the king, let judgment be executed speedily upon him, whether it be unto death, or to banishment, or to confiscation of goods, or to imprisonments.* (Ezra 7:21, 25–26)

"Ezra had prepared his heart to seek the Law of the Lord, and to do it, and to teach in Israel statutes and judgments" (7:10). By his strong adherence to the Law of Moses, Ezra set the tone for future generations of rabbis who would devote themselves to the faithful study and observance of the Law. He and others desired to rebuild the Temple of Jerusalem and to restore the Law of Moses to Judea. He served as governor of Judea, and is believed by some to have been the author of 1 and 2 Chronicles as well as the Book of Ezra. It is especially interesting to see that the King of the Persian Empire issued a decree authorizing the government of Judea under both Persian law and Biblical Law.

Nehemiah, another Jew who had initially remained in Persia after the Exile ended, served as "cupbearer" to the Persian king—a position of great authority, because a common means of assassinating a Persian king was to poison his wine. When Nehemiah learned that the walls of Jerusalem were in disrepair, he prayed and fasted and asked King Artaxerxes for permission to lead a few men to Jerusalem to repair the wall. The King granted letters of authority to govern to Nehemiah, that he could show to the various governors whose territory he passed through on his way to Jerusalem. Significantly, although Nehemiah knew it was God's will that he rebuild the walls of Jerusalem, he sought and received authority from the Persian king as well.

As Nehemiah organized the people of Jerusalem and began rebuilding the walls, hostile tribes plotted to destroy the walls as they were being rebuilt. Through good intelligence Nehemiah learned of their plans and armed his men to defend against attack (4:7–15). As the threat diminished, Nehemiah placed half his men on reserve status so they could continue the building but have their weapons ready, while the others remained on active duty in defense of the walls (4:16–23). Because Nehemiah and his men were informed and prepared, the attack was deterred.

Nehemiah also served 12 years as governor of Jerusalem (5:14), and during his reign he continually exhorted his people to follow the Law of God as revealed through Moses.

Esther, a beautiful young Jewish woman, became the wife of King Ahasuerus and therefore a Queen of Persia. Mordecai, who was Esther's uncle and had raised her after her parents died, *"sat in the king's gate"* (2:19) as a Persian judge. Mordecai learned that two chamberlains were planning to assassinate the king, and he made this known to the king through Esther. The king conducted an inquisition (2:21–23) and the charges were proven to be true and the chamberlains were hanged.

Shortly thereafter, a high Persian official named Haman became angry about the strong Jewish presence in Persia. Mordecai's refusal to bow before Haman (3:2) (because a devout Jew could bow before no one except God) particularly infuriated him, and he planned to destroy the Jews. Mordecai learned of the plot, communicated it to Esther, and entreated her to convey the information to the king. Esther hesitated, because under Persian law it was a capital offense to come before the king without being summoned, and anyone who did so would be put to death unless the king extended to that person his golden scepter as a gesture of pardon (4:11). Mordecai sent this message to Esther:

> *Think not with thyself that thou shalt escape in the king's house, more than all the Jews.*
>
> *For if thou altogether holdest thy peace at this time, then shall there enlargement and deliverance arise to the Jews from another place; but thou and thy father's house shall be destroyed: and who knoweth whether thou art come to the kingdom for such a time as this?* (4:13–14)

Emboldened by her uncle's exhortation, Esther sent an answer to Mordecai:

> *Go, gather together all the Jews that are present in Shushan [the Persian capital], and fast ye for me, and neither eat nor drink three days, night or day: I also and my maidens will fast likewise; and so will I go in unto the king, which is not according to the law: and if I perish, I perish.* (4:16)

On the third day Esther approached the king, and he extended to her the golden scepter. Haman's plot against the Jews was thus exposed, and he was hanged on the very scaffold he had prepared for Mordecai. Mordecai eventually became the king's chief advisor (10:1–3).

Throughout the centuries, the Jews have looked upon Ezra, Nehemiah, and Esther as examples of Jews living in foreign and pagan lands. Through these examples they learned the proper role of citizenship in a foreign country and the value of having their people in high places to intercede for them when necessary.

Next we come to **Job**, believed by many to be the oldest book in the Bible.[41] Job addresses one of the most basic human questions: Why would a righteous, just, and loving God allow human suffering? The story features a man whom Satan afflicted with grievous disasters: boils, loss of property, death of family members. Job didn't know it at the time, but God allowed Satan to torment Job in this manner to prove a judicial point: that a man created lower than the angels could remain faithful to God despite grievous afflictions, and therefore God could justly punish Satan for his rebellion.

While Job was thus tormented, his friends visited him and told him he must have sinned against God, or God would not have allowed this to

---

41. Reasons for believing Job to be the oldest book in the Bible include the following: (1) Job's age was consistent with that of the patriarchs, Abraham, Isaac, and Jacob, who lived around 2000 BC. When Job's trial took place he already had adult children, and after this trial he lived 140 years (42:16). (2) Job was written in an old form of Hebrew; it contains at least 113 *hapax logenami* (words that appear only once in the Hebrew Testament). (3) The book describes creatures like *behemoth* (40:15), *unicorn* (39:9–10), and *leviathan* (41:1) that do not match any animals known to exist today. (4) The invading tribes, the Sabeans (1:15) and the Chaldeans (1:17), match tribes known to exist in the area around 2000 BC. (5) The land of *Uz* (1:1) existed around 2000 BC in what was later known as Edom; at that time it was range country for cattle and sheep (1:3). (6) Job's wealth was measured in cattle, sheep, camels, and donkeys (1:3), indicating that these events took place before the institution of money as a means of exchange. (7) Job acted as priest for his family, sanctifying them and sacrificing for them, indicating that Job lived before the institution of the Levitical priesthood.

happen to him. Job insisted that he had not sinned, but he was mystified and frustrated by these afflictions—why would God allow this to happen to a man who has been His faithful servant? At one point (Ch. 23) Job even expressed a wish to bring God to court, confront Him, and compel Him to explain why He had treated Job in this manner. But throughout the ordeal Job remained faithful, expressing confidence in God's ultimate deliverance:

> *For I know that my redeemer liveth, and that he shall stand at the latter day upon the earth:*
>
> *And though after my skin worms destroy this body, yet in my flesh shall I see God.* (19:25–26)

In the end, God appeared to Job in the whirlwind and asked Job pointed questions about the mysteries of creation and nature. As Job had no answers to these questions, he could not possibly understand God's reasons for allowing human suffering. Sometimes suffering comes to us as a result of sin, but not always. Sometimes, at least in this life, God allows the guilty to escape judgment, and He also allows those who are relatively innocent to suffer. Job came to understand that even though he had not committed any outstanding heinous sin that would bring upon him this kind of affliction, he was a sinner nevertheless: *"Wherefore I abhor myself, and repent in dust and ashes"* (42:6). The message of Job for those who suffer and ask "Why me?" is "Why not you? What is it about you that is so special that you should be exempt from the suffering that is endemic to the entire human race?" And although Job never understood the reason God allowed him to suffer in this way, he could finally rest in the confidence that God in His infinite wisdom had a reason, and that knowledge had to be sufficient to give him peace.

The **Psalms** are poems or songs written in praise of God, expressing the deepest of human emotions. Approximately half of them were written by King David; the others are the work of various authors. Many passages from the Psalms are relevant for law and government.

Psalm 1:2 tells us that the blessed man's *"delight is in the law of the LORD; and in his law doth he meditate day and night."* And a nation must be based upon a moral foundation: *"If the foundations be destroyed, what can the righteous do?"* (11:3).

Psalm 19 speaks of the natural revelation by which all men know of God:

> *The heavens declare the glory of God; and the firmament sheweth his handywork.*
>
> *Day unto day uttereth speech, and night unto night sheweth knowledge.*
>
> *There is no speech nor language, where their voice is not heard.* (19:1–3)

Then, in verse 7, David moves from God's general revelation of Himself to His special revelation of His Law:

> *The law of the LORD is perfect, converting the soul: the testimony of the LORD is sure, making wise the simple.*
>
> *The statutes of the LORD are right, rejoicing the heart: the commandment of the LORD is pure, enlightening the eyes.*
>
> *The fear of the LORD is clean, enduring for ever: the judgments of the LORD are true and righteous altogether.*
>
> *More to be desired are they than gold, yea, than much fine gold: sweeter also than honey and the honeycomb.* (19:7–10)

King David must have had considerable knowledge of lawyers and judges, for 1 Chronicles 23:4 tells us that he appointed 6,000 Levites as officers and judges. And yet, David would prefer that the Lord act as his advocate and judge:

> *Plead my cause, O LORD, with them that strive with me: fight against them that fight against me....*
>
> *False witnesses did rise up; they laid to my charge things that I knew not....*
>
> *Judge me, O LORD my God, according to thy righteousness; and let them not rejoice over me.* (Psalm 35:1, 11, 24)

Psalm 82 speaks of gods; but it is generally understood that this Psalm is addressing judges and other leaders:

> *God standeth in the congregation of the mighty; he judgeth among the gods.*
>
> *How long will ye judge unjustly, and accept the persons of the wicked? Selah.*
>
> *Defend the poor and fatherless: do justice to the afflicted and needy.*
>
> *Deliver the poor and needy: rid them out of the hand of the wicked.*
>
> *They know not, neither will they understand; they walk on in darkness: all the foundations of the earth are out of course.*
>
> *I have said, Ye are gods; and all of you are children of the Most High.*
>
> *But ye shall die like men, and fall like one of the princes.*
>
> *Arise, O God, judge the earth: for thou shalt inherit all nations.* (82:1–8)

The judges are called "gods" *(elohim)* because God, Who has absolute authority to judge and punish, has delegated a portion of that authority to civil magistrates (Romans 13). God's authority is original and absolute; the authority of judges is derivative and limited. However, Israel's judges have betrayed their trust; they have not defended the poor and fatherless; rather, they have perverted judgment in favor of the wicked.[42] God therefore reminds them that even though He has given them divine authority, they are really only human and they will *"die like men."*

In contrast to these unrighteous and arrogant judges, the godly judge or king takes his duties seriously and endeavors to do justice: *"The king's strength also loveth judgment; thou dost establish equity, thou executest judgment and righteousness in Jacob"* (99:4).

The **Proverbs** are words of wisdom for dealing with the problems of everyday life relating to God, parents, children, neighbors, and government. The primary author appears to have been Solomon, but he may have learned many of these proverbs from his father David.

42. God has not commanded the judges to show favoritism to the poor (Exodus 23:3: "Neither shalt thou countenance a poor man in his cause."); rather, they were to dispense equal justice to all. The judges often showed favoritism to the rich and ignored the poor, because the rich paid them bribes. The poor were less likely to bribe the judges, not because they were more virtuous, but because they had less money with which to pay bribes.

Proverbs 18:17 tells us that *"He that is first in his own cause seemeth just; but his neighbor cometh and searcheth him."* This is the reason courts require witnesses to undergo cross-examination: the witness may sound very persuasive until cross-examination brings out the weaknesses of his testimony. And *"A false witness shall not be unpunished; and he that speaketh lies shall not escape"* (19:5). A court cannot do justice without knowing the truth; therefore, the Jewish legal system imposed severe punishments for perjury (Exodus 20:16; 23:1; Deuteronomy 19:15–21).

Righteousness and justice were a national as well as an individual responsibility: *"Righteousness exalteth a nation: but sin is a reproach to any people"* (Proverbs 14:34). It was therefore essential that those who hold public office be, above all, persons of integrity: *"When the righteous are in authority, the people rejoice: but when the wicked beareth rule, the people mourn"* (29:2). For:

> *The king by judgment establisheth the land: but he that receiveth gifts overthroweth it....*
>
> *The king that faithfully judgeth the poor, his throne shall be established for ever.* (29:4,14)

Anything that might interfere with the king's or judge's impartial judgment was to be condemned. Therefore Solomon says,

> *It is not for kings, O Lemuel, it is not for kings to drink wine; nor for princes strong drink:*
>
> *Lest they drink, and forget the law, and pervert the judgment of any of the afflicted.* (31:4–5)

The judge must base his decisions upon the law and the facts, not upon his personal prejudices or his favor or disfavor for the individual parties: *"It is not good to have respect of persons in judgment"* (24:23b).

The balance and timing commended by **Ecclesiastes** 3 can enhance the practice of law or of any profession. Solomon also tells us that obedience to God includes obedience to the law of the land, because God has ordained civil government: *"I counsel thee to keep the king's commandment, and that in regard of the oath of God"* (Ecclesiastes 8:2). And he also recognized a fundamental truth about criminology that we seem to have forgotten in our day of delayed trials, plea bargains, and endless appeals:

"Because sentence against an evil work is not executed speedily, therefore the heart of the sons of men is fully set in them to do evil" (Ecclesiastes 8:11).

The **Song of Solomon**, or **Song of Songs**, tells of a king's romance and reveals that even a king like Solomon has the same human emotions as all the rest of us. Many believe the book is also a picture of God's love for us.

The **Lamentations**, probably written by Jeremiah, mourn the destruction of Jerusalem and the Babylonian captivity of the Jews. They stand as a stark reminder that all earthly cities are temporal and subject to God's judgment, that we should love and pray for our earthly kingdoms but always remember that our ultimate citizenship is in heaven. And for the Jews, the Lamentations remind them that although they were suffering affliction because of their sins and those of their fathers,

> *It is of the LORD's mercies that we are not consumed, because his compassions fail not.*
>
> *They are new every morning: great is thy faithfulness.* (3:22–23)

Millennia later, suffering even greater affliction, faithful sons of Israel would remember these words.

And finally we come to **Daniel.** The first six chapters of Daniel are history, and the last six chapters are prophecy. Both deal with law and government; in fact, no book of the Bible encompasses such a vast panorama of nations and empires, and Daniel is the ideal model of a believer living in a pagan society who fulfills his duties of citizenship and yet is faithful to God.

The Book of Daniel opens around 605 BC, as Babylonian King Nebuchadnezzar conquered Jerusalem and took various teenage boys of the aristocracy captive to Babylon. This was consistent with Babylonian policy toward conquered nations, which was to break down their national identity and amalgamate them into the Babylonian Empire, in contrast to the Persian policy of respecting the customs and practices of conquered nations. Daniel and the other Jewish youths were subjected to a three-year education which was designed to break down their identity as Jews and to teach them the language, manners, customs, and religion of Babylon (1:1–7).

Daniel, however, resisted the Babylonian indoctrination and refused to follow the King's diet, perhaps because it violated Jewish dietary laws. Rather than force a confrontation, Daniel spoke respectfully to the captain of the guard, and they agreed to a 10-day test of the Jewish diet. At the end of the 10 days, Daniel and his friends were the healthiest of the captives, and so they were allowed to continue their Jewish diet (1:8–16). At the end of the three years, Daniel and his friends excelled in their oral examinations before the King, and they became officials of the Babylonian government.

In Chapter 2, King Nebuchadnezzar had a disturbing dream of a great image of a man with a head of gold, shoulders and chest of silver, belly and thighs of brass, legs of iron, and feet of mixed iron and clay, which was destroyed by a great stone. The King's royal cabinet, which consisted of magicians, astrologers, and sorcerers (all of which represented the epitome of Babylonian wisdom and scholarship) were unable to interpret the dream, but with God's help Daniel did so. He advised the King that the image represented four great empires that would rule the known world: The head of gold represented Nebuchadnezzar's kingdom, and the breast and arms of silver, belly and thighs of brass, and legs and feet of iron and clay represented three kingdoms that would arise after.[43] The stone was the Kingdom of God which would eventually destroy and subsume all earthly kingdoms (2:1–45).

Daniel's message to King Nebuchadnezzar was that God is sovereign and eternal; *"he removeth kings, and setteth up kings"* (2:21). God has given Nebuchadnezzar the Kingdom of Babylonia, and He desires to use King Nebuchadnezzar in this capacity to bring peace and stability to millions of people. But Babylonia is only a temporary kingdom; it will be replaced by another, and another, and another, until the eternal Kingdom of God rules over the entire world.

In Chapter 3, the King has built a huge golden image. Unlike the image in the dream of Chapter 2, Nebuchadnezzar's image was gold from head to toe and officials throughout the realm were commanded to assemble and

43. Although Daniel in Chapter 2 does not name these nations, higher critics point to these and other prophecies as evidence that the Book of Daniel must be of later origin, because Daniel in the 6th century BC could not possibly have known that Greece and Rome would arise hundreds of years later. That is a common interpretation of the passage, and Greece and Persia are specifically named in 8:20–21. These critics dismiss or ignore the possibility of divine revelation. For an excellent refutation of the higher critical view of the origin of the Book of Daniel, see Josh McDowell, *Daniel in the Critics' Den* (Campus Crusade for Christ, 1979).

bow down before it. This image represented state-worship and emperor-worship, a common pagan practice, but a practice strictly forbidden by the Decalogue's command against worshipping graven images (Exodus 20:4–6). Daniel's three friends Shadrach, Meshach, and Abednego refused to bow before the image and were cast into a fiery furnace from which they were delivered by the power of God. From this episode Jews learn that human authority is to be respected but never worshipped; worship belongs only to God. God has established human government, but human government is not God.

In Chapter 4 King Nebuchadnezzar had another dream, this time of a great tree that provides shelter for many but is cut down. With God's help Daniel interpreted the dream to mean that Nebuchadnezzar was a great king, but because of his pride God would cut him down and cause him to lose his kingdom for a period of seven years, until he learned that *"the most High ruleth in the kingdom of men, and giveth it to whomsoever he will"* (4:25b).

And the prophecy came to pass. As King Nebuchadnezzar walked through his palace, he took credit for the empire he had built:

> *Is not this great Babylon, that I have built for the house of the kingdom by the might of my power, and for the honour of my majesty?* (4:30)

God's judgment immediately fell upon him, and he was removed from the throne and forced to live as an animal for seven years. At the end of that time he bowed before God and acknowledged His sovereignty, and his kingdom was restored to him. As he declared,

> *And at the end of the days I Nebuchadnezzar lifted up mine eyes unto heaven, and mine understanding returned unto me, and I blessed the most High, and I praised and honoured him that liveth for ever, whose dominion is an everlasting dominion, and his kingdom is from generation to generation:*
>
> *And all the inhabitants of the earth are reputed as nothing: and he doeth according to his will in the army of heaven, and among the inhabitants of the earth: and none can stay his hand, or say unto him, What doest thou?*

> *At the same time my reason returned unto me; and for the glory of my kingdom, mine honour and brightness returned unto me; and my counsellors and my lords sought unto me; and I was established in my kingdom, and excellent majesty was added unto me.*
>
> *Now I Nebuchadnezzar praise and extol and honour the King of heaven, all whose works are truth, and his ways judgment: and those that walk in pride he is able to abase.* (4:34–37)

Daniel's prophecy that the head of gold, Babylon, would rule for a time and then be replaced by another kingdom, came to pass. After Nebuchadnezzar died, the Empire quickly withered, while the Persian Empire was rising in the east. Chapter 5 opens in 539 BC with a great Babylonian feast held by King Belshazzar,[44] while Persian armies besieged the City. During this drunken orgy, King Belshazzar brought forth the sacred vessels which the Babylonians had seized from Jerusalem (1:2; cf. Isaiah 39). At this supreme act of blasphemy, God announced His judgment upon Babylon through the *handwriting on the wall* (5:5–7), and the Persians conquered Babylon that very night. Thus the spotlight of history passed from the head of gold to the chest of silver, and Persia ruled the known world.

Chapter 6 opens shortly after 539 BC. Babylon has become a Persian province, and King Cyrus the Great of Persia has appointed Darius the Mede as his vassal king of Babylon. In keeping with Persian principles of government, Darius has divided Babylon into 70 districts or satrapies, and over each of these he has appointed a governor or satrap. He has also appointed three presidents to oversee these governors, and the first of these was Daniel. Daniel, who by this time was at least 80 years old and a seasoned statesman, governed so well that Darius considered making him prime minister over all of Babylon. However, other presidents and satraps

44. Critics used to claim that Daniel Chapter 5 was a myth because there was never a Babylonian King Belshazzar, since the Babylonian line of kings ended with Nabonidus. However, in 1854 Sir Henry Rawlinson discovered Babylonian tablets that reveal that Nabonidus effectively retired as king and left the Empire in the hands of the crown prince, his son Belshazzar, the Babylonian. This explains why Belshazzar offered to make Daniel only the "third ruler in the kingdom" (5:16) if he would interpret the handwriting on the wall: Belshazzar was only the second ruler in the kingdom; his father Nabonidus was the first ruler. Once again, archeology has demonstrated that the Bible is right and the critics are wrong. McDowell, *Daniel in the Critics' Den,* 59–67; *International Standard Bible Encyclopedia* I: 433 "Belshazzar."

became jealous of Daniel. They tried to find a scandal with which they could smear Daniel's reputation, but they could find nothing; so they declared, *"We shall not find any occasion against this Daniel, except we find it against him concerning the law of his God"* (6:5). So they concocted a scheme to force Daniel to choose between obeying the law of the realm or obeying God. They drafted a decree that for the next 30 days no one may ask anything of any man or any god except this king, and Darius signed the decree (6:6–9).

When Daniel learned of the decree, he went to his chamber; and with his window open and knowing his enemies were watching, he prayed to God in keeping with his lifelong practice (6:10–11). When his enemies reported this to Darius, the king immediately saw the folly of his decree, but Daniel's enemies repeatedly remind him of *"the law of the Medes and Persians, which altereth not"* (6:8b) and *"Know, O king, that the law of the Medes and Persians is, That no decree nor statute which the king establisheth may be changed"* (6:15b). This was a unique feature of Persian law; in keeping with other Indo-European peoples, they believed that no one, including the king, is above the law. If King Nebuchadnezzar of Babylon had signed a law like this one, he could have immediately nullified it; but Darius did not have that kind of authority.

As the decree required, Darius placed Daniel in the den of lions, but God delivered Daniel from the lions (6:16–24), and through this experience King Darius, like Nebuchadnezzar before him, learned to respect the power of Daniel's God (6:25–28).

The remaining six chapters of Daniel are mostly prophecy, but his prophecies concern the nations that shall rule the earth. The basic theme of Daniel, in fact, is God's sovereign rule over the nations throughout history. Through Daniel the Jews saw the value of citizenship and governmental service, so long as one was, first and foremost, faithful to God and His Law.

In the **Torah** the Jewish people read the Law of God. In the **Nevi'im** and the **Ketuvim** they saw the Law of God in practical application. Together they form the **Tanach** or Hebrew Bible.

THE TALMUD

The Hebrew Bible contained the Law of God, but the Jews believed they needed guidelines to interpret that Law. Besides the "written law" found in the Torah, the Jews also used the "oral law" which is now found in the *Talmud*, which literally means "teaching" or "study."

The *Talmud* is called the oral law because it was not reduced to writing until about the time of Christ and in centuries thereafter. Orthodox Jews generally believe God gave the oral law, or at least the principles that underlie it, to Moses on Mt. Sinai. Moses passed it orally to Joshua, Joshua to the Jewish elders, and the elders to succeeding generations as oral tradition. More liberal Jews believe the oral law has evolved and changed with time. Orthodox Jews believe the oral law, like the written law, is perfect and therefore cannot be changed. More liberal Jews believe that morality changes with time, and that sometimes provisions of the *Talmud* that are harsh or strict when compared with today's morality must be discarded or changed.

Of the Tribes of Israel, the Levites (descendants of Jacob's son Levi) were set aside to be priests. Moses established the Aaronic priesthood among those Levites who were descended from Moses' brother Aaron. The Aaronic priests were responsible for the sacrifices, supervising the feasts and offerings, performing the Temple rituals, and instructing the people in the Law of Moses.

During and after the Babylonian Exile in the 500s BC, the Jewish people did not have access to the Temple of Jerusalem until it was rebuilt 538–515 BC. The priests, the sacrifices, and the Temple therefore declined in importance, while because of the leadership and influence of men like Ezra and Nehemiah, the Law of Moses became increasingly important in defining Judaism. A class of teachers and scholars arose known as rabbis, who assumed most of the responsibility for teaching the Law even though they were not necessarily descendants of Levi or Aaron. As they expounded the Torah, they used the sayings of the oral law or *Talmud* to explain them. Because the Torah and the *Talmud* were the basic civil and criminal law as well as the moral and religious law, the rabbis functioned much as lawyers do today. However, rather than issuing individual interpretations of the Law, they acted in councils. Their interpretations and opinions had greater authority when they were issued by a corporate body.

The opinions or rulings issued by these rabbinical councils, first orally and later in writing, became known as *Midrash* or "interpretation." *Midrash* gradually multiplied into a large body of oral tradition, although the Orthodox would insist that the rabbinical counsels simply articulated the oral tradition God gave to Moses on Mt. Sinai. Frequently each

Midrash began with a statement from the Hebrew Bible, followed by interpretation. *Midrash* that dealt with legal subjects was called *Halakha* (from *halak*, meaning "to walk"), and that which dealt with other subjects was called *Haggada* (from *'agada*, meaning "narration").[45]

As the rabbis and priests differed on their interpretations of Torah, various sects arose. The "Pharisees" believed in a strict literal interpretation of the law, while the "Sadducees" believed the law should be interpreted more liberally. The Pharisees accepted the oral law as well as the written law; the Sadducees rejected the oral law. The Pharisees believed strongly in a resurrection and in God's judgment for sin; the Sadducees did not believe in life after death. The Pharisees were much less willing to cooperate with the Greeks and Romans and adopt to Hellenistic culture than were the Sadducees. These two sects battled for influence in Judea, and eventually the Pharisees became the dominant sect.

Shortly after the time of Christ, the rabbis, and particularly the Pharisees, became convinced that because they were few in number, in order to preserve the *Talmud* from corrupting influences, it must be committed to writing. Rabbi Judah the Prince began the organization and recording of the oral law around AD 166. He and those who worked with him organized the oral law into 62 (some say 63) tractates, and this work, known as the *Mishnah* or "teaching," was completed around AD 200. It consists largely of terse statements of rabbis and rabbinical courts about various subjects of the law. Much of the *Midrash* thus became the *Mishnah*. Other portions of the *Midrash* that did not become part of the *Mishnah* are called Baraitah, meaning "outside" because they were outside the six orders of the *Mishnah*.

As rabbis discussed and debated the interpretation of the *Mishnah*, a body of scholarly commentary developed which is known as the *Gemarah*, which literally means "completion." The *Gemarah* consists of lengthy commentaries elucidating and elaborating on the *Mishnah*. Roughly speaking, lawyers might say the Torah is like the United States Code, the *Mishnah* is like the case law summarized in the United States Code Annotated, and the *Gemarah* is like a collection of lengthy law review articles. Two bodies of *Gemarah* developed, the *Jerusalem Gemarah* which was completed around AD 350 and the *Babylonian Gemarah* which was completed around AD 550. As each of these was combined with the *Mishnah*, they became known as the *Jerusalem Talmud* and the *Babylonian Talmud*. The

45. Many of these Hebrew terms have variant spellings as they are transliterated into English.

Babylonian Talmud is generally considered more authoritative than the *Jerusalem Talmud*, because Babylon had become an important center of Judaism after the Roman conquest and destruction of Jerusalem and the diaspora in AD 70; the *Babylonian Talmud* was finished later and was therefore more complete, and the *Babylonian Talmud* is better organized and more accessible.

The *Mishnah* is divided into six volumes or *sedarim*: (1) *Zera'im* or "Harvest," containing eleven tractates on the cultivation of the soil and its products, which parts of fields must be left for gleaning by the poor, and which firstfruits must be brought to the Temple. (2) *Mo'ed* or "Feasts," twelve tractates concerning the Sabbath and other feasts and holy days, taxes for the maintenance of divine service in the Temple, the kinds of work permitted on festival days, and pilgrimages to Jerusalem. (3) *Nashim* or "Women," seven tractates concerning betrothal, marriage, divorce, annulment, and marriage settlements. (4) *Neziqin* or "Damages," eight tractates on civil and criminal law, damages and punishments. (5) *Qodashim* or "Sacred Things," twelve tractates about sacrifices and Temple services. (6) *Tohorot* or "Purifications," twelve tractates about ritual uncleanness and purification or cleansing.

To illustrate the interrelationship of the Torah to the *Mishnah* and the *Gemarah*, consider the Sabbath command of Exodus 35:3: *"Ye shall kindle no fire throughout your habitations upon the sabbath day."* This appears to mean there can be no fires on the Sabbath even if that means people have to sit in the cold and in the dark. But the Jews came to interpret this to mean one may not *start* a fire on the Sabbath, but if a fire is started on Friday, one may be warmed and illumined by it throughout the Sabbath day so long as one does not add to the fire. But the Jews were also careful to avoid situations which might tempt them to sin. And so, the *Mishnah* stated that "one shall not read by the lamplight" on the Sabbath, because if one were to do so, he might be tempted to adjust the lamp and thereby violate the basic commandment.

The following excerpt from the *Babylonian Talmud* illustrates its nature:

> MISHNA I: There are four principal causes of tort (expressly mentioned in the Scripture): the ox; the (uncovered) excavation; the mabeh (the pasture of one's cattle in another's field); and the fire. The measure of the damages done by the ox is different from that of the damages done by the mabeh, and *vice versa;* and that of both, which are animated beings is not like that of

the damages caused by the fire, which is not animated. And the measure of damages caused by the three last mentioned, which are movable, is different from that of the damages caused by the (uncovered) excavation, which is stationary. One thing, however, is common to all, and that is, that they are all likely to do damage, which must be guarded against, and if damage is done, the one responsible for it must make good from his best estates.

GEMARA: If the Mishna states that there are "principals" there must be derivatives. Are those derivatives as their principals or not? Said R[abbi] Papa: "Some of them are and some of them are not" (as explained further on). The rabbis taught: "It was said of the ox that he has three principals, the horn, the tooth, and the foot. Of the horn the rabbis taught: It is written [Ex. Xxi. 28]: *"If an ox gore," and goring is only with the horn, as it is written* [Deut. Xxxiii. 17]" *"And his horns are like the horns of reem; with them shall he push (gore),"* etc. What is the derivative of the horn? Hurting, biting, lying upon, and kicking; (because they are usually done intentionally, as goring). Why is "goring" called a principal? Because it is written [Ex. Xxi. 28]: *"If an ox gore?"* Let also hurting be a principal, because it is written...: *"And if a man's ox hurt."* That hurting means goring, as we have learned in the following Boraitha: "It starts out with hurting, and it ends with goring, to teach thee that the hurting mentioned here means goring."... [And the discussion of this Midrash continues for 14 pages].[46]

Or consider another example:

MISHNA I: If one has robbed an edible article and used it for his family, or he left the article as it was, his heirs are free from payment. If, however, it was an article of responsibility, they are obliged to pay....

GEMARA: Said R[abbi] Hisda: "If one has robbed an article of which the owner did not renounce the hope of gaining it, and another one came and took it away from him, the owner may collect it from any one of them he chooses. Why so? Because as

46. Michael L. Rodkinson, *New Edition of the Babylonian Talmud: Original Text, Edited, Corrected, Formulated, and Translated into English* (New Talmud Publishing Company, 1896, 1903) V: Tract Baba Kama (The First Gate) Ch. 1, 1–2.

> long as the owners did not renounce their hope, it is considered as it were still under their control."...
>
> *"Or he left the article,"* etc. Said Rami bar Hama: "From this statement is to be inferred that the control of an heir is the same as the control of a buyer (*i.e.*, as the Mishna speaks of a case where the hope of regaining it is renounced, the change of control gives title, and the control[47] of the heirs after the death of the robber is also considered a change as if it would be bought by somebody else)." R[abbi] Rabha, however, said: "It is not so, and our Mishna, which makes them free, treats of a case where the heirs have already consumed the article after the death of their father." But from the latter part of our Mishna, which states that "if there was a responsibility," etc., it must be said that the first part treats of the robbed article still in existence....
>
> The rabbis taught: "If one robbed an edible article and he used it for his children, the children are free from payment; if however, the article is yet in existence after the death of the robber, and the children are grown up, they must pay; but if they are still minors, they are free; and even when they are grown up, if they say: 'We know the accounts of our father with you, and he owes you nothing,' they are free."

The *Talmud* has undergone reorganizations and revisions many times in the last fifteen centuries. Some might regard new editions as corruptions of the originals; others might regard them as part of a continuous unfolding of the oral tradition. One of the most significant is the reorganization and commentary on the *Mishna* by Rabbi Moses ben Maimon (Maimonides), AD 1135–1204, a Talmudist, philosopher, astronomer, physician, and jurist and one of the towering intellects of the Middle Ages. Maimonides took materials from both the *Jerusalem Talmud* and the *Babylonian Talmud*, organized them into a more systematic body, and removed some materials dealing with wizardry and amulets that Maimonides considered contrary to true Judaism. As we shall see in Volume II, Book IV, Chapter 24, Maimonides' code had considerable influence upon the development of medieval European law.

Most Jews consider the *Talmud* to be second only to the Hebrew Bible in its inspiration and authority; some would say it is of equal authority, and

47. Rodkinson, VI: Chapter X, 251–52.

some would say it is more significant than the Hebrew Bible in defining Judaism. Most Christians do not consider the *Talmud* to be the inspired Word of God as only the Bible is inspired, but they would agree that the *Talmud* is worthy of study for its wisdom and for the insight it provides into Jewish interpretation of the Hebrew Bible during the rabbinic era and the time of Jesus Christ.

We will now examine the governmental institutions and legal precepts that were built upon this foundation.

Questions for Reflection, Discussion, and More Reflection

1. How important was the Hebrews' high level of literacy to the Hebrew republic? Is republican government possible without a literate populace? Why have some assumed the Hebrews were illiterate despite convincing evidence to the contrary?
2. What are the Torah, the Nevi'im, and the Ketuvim? Contrast them with the *Talmud*, the *Mishnah* (both *Halakha* and *Haggada*), the *Targums*, and the *Gemarah*.
3. What is the documentary hypothesis, also called the Graf/Wellhausen theory and the JEDP theory? To what extent is the theory driven by Darwinist assumptions? Why does the author devote so much space to a refutation of this theory? Why is the dating and authorship of the Pentateuch so important to a proper understanding of the Law?
4. Why do we find repetition in the Pentateuch? For example, why are the Ten Commandments and much of the Mosaic Law found first in the Book of Exodus, and then found again in Deuteronomy? What different purposes do those two books serve? What is meant by the terms "inspiration," "inerrancy," and "infallibility"? Could the Pentateuch be inspired but not inerrant or infallible?
5. What are the common arguments for and against multiple authorship and late dating of Isaiah and Daniel? What was the

Biblical definition of the term "prophet"? Can prophecy be understood apart from divine inspiration? What relevance do the "minor prophets" have to our understanding of the Mosaic Law?

6. Among the books classified as Ketuvim or Writings, Ruth narrates a beautiful love story involving an ancestor of Jesus Christ, and also presents a picture of God's love for man. Explain the levirate law, and how, according to the Book of Ruth, the levirate law was satisfied, and Boaz was freed to marry Ruth.

7. Did Queen Esther disobey Persian law by coming before the King without being summoned? Did Daniel disobey King Darius by praying in Daniel 6? If so, was this disobedience justified? What does this tell us concerning our obligation to obey or disobey the law of the land?

8. Job is thought by many to be the oldest book of the Bible. Give reasons for and against that conclusion. Some say Job is the deepest book of the Bible. What basic question does the book raise, and how is the question answered?

9. In what sense are judges called "gods" in Psalm 82? What does this tell us about the nature and source of governmental authority?

10. What is the *Talmud*? When, how, and by whom was it composed? What is its authority in relation to the Torah?

Jethro advises Moses on representative government.
Jethro and Moses by James Tissot, 1896–1900.

CHAPTER 14

THE INSTITUTIONS OF HEBREW LAW: *Confederacy, Republic, Then Monarchy*

Viewed over two millennia, the institutions of Hebrew[1] law follow the nearly-universal trend of human government toward centralization and expanded power. But they also reflect some of the constancies of Hebrew legal and political thought.

We have already seen in Chapter 13 that some kind of law and governmental structure must have existed before the Flood of Genesis 6–8. After the Flood, we read in Genesis 9 that God established His covenant with Noah. The Noahic Covenant, which included Noah and all of his descendants (9:9), all other living creatures (9:10), and all future generations (9:12), contained the following provisions:

- God promised that He would never again destroy the entire earth by flood (9:11–16).
- Noah's descendants were to be fruitful and multiply and replenish the earth (9:1,7).
- Humans were to have dominion over the animals of the earth, air, and sea, including the right to use animals for food, clothing, and

1. The terms *Hebrew, Israelite,* and *Jew* are often used interchangeably, but the terms have different shades of meaning. Abraham was called a Hebrew (Genesis 14:13), possibly after his ancestor Eber (Genesis 10:21, 11:16–17) or possibly from the term's literal meaning "to come from beyond" or "to pass over (as a river)." Joseph called Canaan the "land of the Hebrews" (Genesis 40:15), and the Canaanites called their invaders Hebrews as people coming from beyond the Jordan River. God changed Jacob's name to Israel (Genesis 32:28), and his descendants were therefore called Israelites. The names Hebrew and Israelite are often used interchangeably, although no one before Jacob's time could be called an Israelite. Jacob was a Hebrew as well as an Israelite, while Abraham and Isaac were Hebrews but not Israelites.

The term Jew has a more distinctive meaning. Jews were descendants of Judah who lived in the Southern Kingdom, Judah or later Judea. The term Jew should not be used for a member of the ten northern tribes who made up the Northern Kingdom of Israel, nor for Moses who was a Levite. One could say that all Jews were Hebrews/Israelites, but not all Hebrews/Israelites were Jews.

other purposes (9:2–3); however, they were not to drink blood (9:4).

- Because humans were created in God's image and were therefore of infinite value, murder was prohibited and was to be punished by death.

Taken together, these commands from the Noahic Covenant convey a duty to spread humanity throughout the earth and establish civil governments complete with structures and statutes. In Chapter 12 we saw that shortly after the Flood, the earth's inhabitants, probably inspired by Nimrod, began the construction of the Tower of Babel, *"lest we be scattered abroad upon the face of the whole earth"* (11:4). God's command was to spread humanity throughout the earth under decentralized governments, probably because human nature, corrupted by the Fall with original sin, would quickly turn centralized government into tyranny and state-worship. But the Tower represented concentrated power under centralized government, and God intervened to stop the construction by confounding the language of the people.

As the world once again sank into polytheism, idolatry, and immorality, God intervened in human history to found a unique nation that would worship Him only and would be a light to the nations of the world. He did so beginning with Abraham.

Government Under the Patriarchs

The era of the patriarchs began around 2000 BC with Abram (later Abraham[2]), an eleventh-generation descendant of Noah. Abraham had lived in Ur of the Chaldees, a Babylonian city in what is now Iraq, midway between Baghdad and the Persian Gulf. Archeology has revealed that a magnificent civilization existed in Ur at that time, including temples, towers, a large building titled the "Hall of Justice," and canals and dykes, and the Ebla tablets have revealed a sophisticated writing system and active commerce.

Abraham's father Terah had taken Abraham, Abraham's wife Sarai (later Sarah), and Abraham's nephew Lot to Haran (Harran), a city in what is now southeastern Turkey. While they were there, Genesis records that God commanded Abraham,

---

2. In Genesis 17:5, God changed this man's name from Abram (*honored father*) to Abraham (*father of nations*). We will use the name Abraham throughout this book.

14 The Institutions of Hebrew Law

> *Get thee out of thy country, and from thy kindred, and from thy father's house, unto a land that I will shew thee:*
>
> *And I will make of thee a great nation, and I will bless thee, and make thy name great; and thou shalt be a blessing:*
>
> *And I will bless them that bless thee, and curse him that curseth thee: and in thee shall all families of the earth be blessed.* (Genesis 12:1–3)

In obedience to God's command, Abraham, Sarah, and Lot traveled south to Canaan, in what is now Israel.

Abraham was a wealthy man (13:2), and because of the widespread literacy in Ur, it is reasonable to assume that he was literate and familiar with the laws and customs of Ur, Babylon, and surrounding cities. Ur was essentially a city-state under the suzerainty of the Babylonian Empire. The Babylonian lawgiver Hammurabi was likely a contemporary of Abraham, and as we saw in Chapter 12, Abraham may well have had contact with him. Very likely, the law by which Abraham governed himself, his family, and his dealings with others was mostly Babylonian law.

After leaving Ur and Haran, Abraham and his family and servants lived in the countryside. As the patriarch of this family unit, Abraham probably governed his family and servants as a virtual head of state, combining all three functions of government into one as he gave commands, made rules, settled disputes, and provided executive leadership. The patriarchs who followed Abraham, his son Isaac and Isaac's son Jacob (later Israel), probably governed in much the same way, although their personalities were very different.

Even so, common law and custom governed their relationships with other people as they bought and sold, divided and made use of land, traveled across others' lands, and practiced diplomacy with other heads of state. These could vary somewhat depending on the locale, the two major powers being Babylon to the east and Egypt to the southwest, and lesser powers such as Aramaea and Canaan. Abraham, Isaac, and Jacob must have been familiar with laws and customs in these areas and followed them to the extent necessary. In keeping with local custom, Abraham married his half-sister Sarah. After his victory over the local kings who had captured Lot, Abraham received bread and wine from Melchizedek the king of Salem and received Mechizedek's blessing (14:18–20). He returned the persons but refused an offer from the king of Sodom to keep the captured goods because he did not want to become indebted to him (14:21–24). Following Babylonian custom, when Abraham's wife Sarah could not conceive a child, she urged Abraham to impregnate her servant Hagar, who conceived and bore Ishmael. At first Abraham received Ishmael into his family, but after Sarah conceived and bore Isaac, Abraham at her insistence sent Hagar and Ishmael away with provisions. As was the nearly universal custom of the Middle East, he showed hospitality to the strangers who visited his tent, not knowing that they were angels. Abraham settled a property dispute with Abimelech over a well and livestock (21:22–34). When Sarah died, Abraham claimed his right as a stranger and sojourner to a burying place for his wife's body. Clearly, law and custom existed at that time, and Abraham knew it and followed it.

In the days of Abraham and Isaac, one man could rule his family. Wines says,

> Abraham, Isaac, and Jacob governed their families with an authority well nigh unlimited. Their power over their households was little short of a sovereign dominion. They were independent princes. They acknowledged no subjection, and owed no allegiance, to any sovereign. They formed alliances with other princes [Genesis 21:22–32]. They treated kings on a footing of equality [Genesis 14:17, 34:6–19]. They maintained a body of servants, trained to the use of arms; were the chiefs who led them in war; and repelled force by force [Genesis 14:13–16]. They were the priests, who appointed festivals, and offered sacrifices [Genesis 8:20, 22:13; Job 1:5]. They had the power of disinheriting their children [Genesis 49:3–4; 1 Chronicles 5:1], of sending them away from home without assigning any reason [Genesis 21:14], and even of punishing them capitally [Genesis 38:24].[3]

But in Jacob's later years, with his twelve sons and their many descendants, the tribes had increased to the point that each of Jacob's twelve sons probably exercised authority over their families under the overall authority of Jacob. Jacob's favorite son, Joseph, incurred the jealousy and wrath of his brothers, and they threw him into a pit from which Midianite traders drew him and sold him into slavery in Egypt. In Egypt Joseph gained influence and favor, and when the Middle East was stricken with severe

3. E.C. Wines, *Commentaries on the Laws of the Ancient Hebrews* (Geo. P. Putnam & Co., 1853; American Vision, 2009), 491.

famine, the Pharaoh appointed Joseph prime minister, and he managed the economy and saved Egypt from famine. His brothers in Canaan also suffered from the famine, and when they came to Egypt to buy food, they were reconciled with Joseph, and all of them including their father Jacob came to Egypt to live. But they never wholly lost their identity as Hebrews, and they always retained a desire to return to their homeland. On his deathbed, Jacob asked that he be buried with his fathers in the land of Canaan (Genesis 49:29–32). The Hebrews placed his body in a coffin (presumably preserved by Egyptian-style embalming), and eventually Joseph fulfilled his father's dying request; and when he was old he made the same last request, that his people *"carry up my bones from hence"* (50:25). The Book of Genesis concludes by telling us, *"So Joseph died, being an hundred and ten years old: and they embalmed him, and he was put in a coffin in Egypt"* (50:26).

At this time, Wines says,

> Each of the Israelitish tribes formed a separate state, having a local legislature and a distinct administration of justice. The power of the several states was sovereign within the limits of their reserved rights. Still, there was both a real and a vigorous general government. The nations might have been styled after the united tribes, provinces, or states of Israel.[4]

THE HEBREWS IN BONDAGE IN EGYPT

Grateful to Joseph for rescuing Egypt from starvation, the Egyptians treated the Israelites with great favor, and in Egypt their numbers grew rapidly (Exodus 1:7). But gratitude is often short-lived, and eventually *"there arose up a new king over Egypt, which knew not Joseph"* (1:8). Fearful of the Hebrews' growing power and influence, this Pharaoh placed them in slavery, and they remained slaves for hundreds of years. *"But the more they afflicted them, the more they multiplied and grew"* (Exodus 1:12), so a later Pharaoh ordered the midwives who served the Hebrew community to kill all male Hebrew babies at birth (Exodus 1:16). But the midwives, because of their fear of God, refused to obey the Pharaoh's command (Exodus1:16–21). The Pharaoh then extended his command, ordering all

4. *Id.*, 490. Interestingly, the Ishmaelites, descendants of Abraham through his son Ishmael, were also organized into twelve tribes after Ishmael's twelve sons and governed by twelve princes (Genesis 25:13–16).

of his people to cast first-born male Hebrew babies into the river (Exodus 1:22).

When Moses was born, his parents protected him from the Egyptians by hiding him in a woven basket in the bulrushes of the Nile (Exodus 2:1–4). The Pharaoh's daughter came to the Nile to wash herself and found Moses in the basket, brought him to the palace, named him Moses, and raised him in royalty. But Moses identified with his Israelite kinsmen, and when he came upon an Egyptian taskmaster whipping a Hebrew slave, he killed the taskmaster and buried him in the sand. But some of the Hebrews had settled into the role of slaves and preferred to remain in slavery rather than upset their masters. When Moses tried to stop a quarrel between two Hebrew slaves, one of them said to him,

> *Who made thee a prince and a judge over us? intendest thou to kill me, as thou killedst the Egyptian?* (2:14)

Realizing that it was unsafe to remain in Egypt, Moses fled to Midian east of the Persian Gulf. There he married Zipporah, the daughter of the Midianite priest Jethro. He remained there for forty years while, unbeknown to him, God was preparing him to lead the Hebrew slaves out of Egypt into freedom.

As slaves, the Hebrews were under the authority of Egypt's rulers, who assigned Egyptian taskmasters to oversee them. But they apparently retained some authority structure of their own, as is common with slave populations and in prisoner of war camps. When God spoke to Moses through the burning bush, He told Moses to *"Go, and gather the elders of Israel together, and say unto them..."* (Exodus 3:16). They must have retained their system of government by tribal elders, and perhaps the elders served as intermediaries between the people and their Egyptian overlords—as Wines says, an *imperium in imperio,*[5] or government independent of the official general government. Besides the tribal elders, Wines wrote, another order of officers arose during the Egyptian captivity, called *shoterim.* Wines says the role of the *shoterim* was to keep genealogical records of births, marriages, and deaths.[6] The Egyptians may have assigned to them the additional duty of ensuring that each Israelite made and delivered the requisite number of bricks, considering it more efficient

5. *Id.,* at 492.

6. *Id.,* 493–94.

and effective, when possible, to work through the slaves' own governing structure.

When, in Exodus 12–13, Pharaoh relented and commanded the Hebrews to leave Egypt, they immediately fell into ranks according to their tribes and families and commenced their exodus. They could not have organized so quickly, had they not preserved their genealogies and tribal identities during their bondage in Egypt.

To what extent did the Hebrews retain the knowledge of the God of their fathers? Did they forget Him during their captivity? We read that when the Pharaoh ordered the midwives to kill the male Hebrew children, *"the midwives feared God, and did not as the king of Egypt commanded them, but saved the men children alive"* (Exodus 1:17). The Israelites in captivity apparently kept some religious observances, including sacrifices (Exodus 8:25–28), circumcision (Exodus 4:24–26, Joshua 5:5), and shortly after their captivity, the Sabbath (Exodus 16:22–30). Whatever they may have forgotten, we are told that when Moses and Aaron spoke to the elders of Israel, *"the people believed: and when they heard that the LORD had visited the children of Israel, and that he had looked upon their affliction, then they bowed their heads and worshipped"* (Exodus 4:31). Edersheim believes that, although direct revelation from God apparently ceased during the centuries of Hebrew slavery in Egypt, the Israelites nonetheless retained much of their traditional religion while they were slaves in Egypt, and much of their traditional social and governmental structure as well.[7]

And when God spoke to Moses through the burning bush, He identified Himself as *"the God of thy father, the God of Abraham, the God of Isaac, and the God of Jacob"* (Exodus 3:6). Even though Abraham, Isaac, and Jacob lived about four centuries before the time of Moses, he did not have to ask who they were. Moses obviously knew his ancestry, and he knew Who the God of Abraham, Isaac, and Jacob was, even if he did not know His name.

During the Exodus, as the Hebrews left Egypt, and as they wandered through the wilderness seeking their Promised Land, they followed Moses as their supreme commander in war and peace alike. Flanked by Aaron and Joshua as lieutenants, Moses arranged the people to live and travel with their respective tribes, following their tribal leadership. Clearly, they

---

7. Alfred Edersheim, *Old Testament Bible History* (1876–87, 1890, reprinted by Eerdmans, 1982), II:24–34.

had not forgotten their identity as descendants of Jacob, nor had they forgotten their special ancestry through Jacob's twelve sons.

THE HEBREW THEOCRACY

One cannot fully understand the Hebrew institutions of government without appreciating, first, that it was a theocracy. It was also a republic and later a constitutional monarchy, and in a very real sense it separated the functions of church and state. But first and foremost it was a theocracy.

"Theocracy" does not mean the church rules the state, or the state rules the church. Theocracy comes from two Greek words, *theos* meaning God and *kratos* meaning ruler. It means God—not the judge, not the king, not the prophet, not the priest—is the Head of state.

The Hebrew theocracy arose under unique circumstances. The world, and particularly the Middle East, had degenerated from original monotheism into polytheism, paganism, and immorality. Immorality and cruelty were consecrated vices among these pagan nations. As Wines says,

> Incredible as it may seem, uncleanness formed a part of the religious worship paid to the gods. Persons of both sexes prostituted themselves in honor of Venus, Priapus, Astarte, Baal-peor, and other filthy and loathsome deities. Of these obscene rites, as constituting a part of the religion of idolators, we have the clearest proofs in authors of undoubted credit. Strabo informs us, that a single temple at Corinth maintained more than a thousand religious prostitutes. Herodotus tells us, that women of this description abounded among the Phoenicians, Babylonians, and other eastern nations. He even says, that by an express law, founded on an oracle, it was ordained, that all the women of Babylon should, at least once in their lives, repair to the temple of Venus, and prostitute themselves to strangers.... It is further evident from a law of Moses, forbidding a father to prostitute his daughter, *"to cause her to be a whore"* [Leviticus 19:29]. This law must be understood as prohibiting the exposure of a daughter as an act of religion, for surely no man, not even the vilest and most abandoned, could prostitute a child to purposes of common whoredom.[8]

Wines continues,

8. Wines, 476–77.

> Herodotus attributes to Solon, in his interview with Croesus, the formal declaration,—"The gods envy the happiness of men."... The sage Artabanus warns Xerxes that even the blessings which the gods bestow, are derived from an envious motive....
>
> As a necessary consequence, almost the whole of the religion of the ancient pagan world consisted in rites of deprecation. Fear was the leading feature of their religious impressions. Hence arose that most horrid of all religious ceremonies—the rite of human sacrifice. Of this savage custom, archbishop Magee, in one of the notes appended to his *Discourses on Atonement and Sacrifice* [I: 89–109], asserts and proves, that there is no nation mentioned in history, which we cannot reproach with having, more than once, made the blood of its citizens to stream forth, in holy and pious ceremonies, to appease the divinity, when he appeared angry, or to move him, when he appeared indolent.
>
> "Conformably with this character of their gods," adds the same learned prelate, "we find the worship of many of the heathen nations to consist in suffering and mortification, in cutting their flesh with knives, and scorching their limbs with fire. The cruel austerities of the gymnosophists, both of Africa and India; the dreadful sufferings of the initiated votaries of Mithra and Eleusis; the frantic and savage rites of Bellona; and the horrid self-mutilations of the worshippers of Cybele—but too clearly evince the dreadful views entertained by the ancient heathens of the nature of their gods."
>
> Undoubtedly, then, it became the wisdom, the justice, and the goodness of the one true God, to check these spreading and direful evils; to bring men back from their polytheistic follies to the belief and worship of himself....[9]

The Hebrews believed that God unfolded a plan to bring the world back to the true worship of Him. He called Abraham out of the City of Ur of the Chaldees, and Abraham traveled west to Canaan. God preserved Abraham's descendants through four centuries of slavery in Egypt, and then He commissioned Moses to lead them out of Egypt into freedom.

God's deliverance of Israel from Egyptian bondage was a frontal assault upon the pagan world-system. The ten plagues upon Egypt were sent not simply to make the Egyptians so miserable they would have to release

9. *Id.*, 478–79.

the Hebrews, but to demonstrate God's superiority over every aspect of Egyptian religion, a religion consisting of the worship of false gods and reverence for creatures rather than the Creator:

- The Egyptians worshipped serpents, so God changed Aaron's rod into a serpent that swallowed the serpents produced by the Egyptian priests (Exodus 7:1–13).
- The Egyptians worshipped the Nile River as a source of life, so as the first plague God turned the waters of the Nile into blood (Exodus 7:14–25).
- The Egyptians held their magicians in great esteem. As the second plague God caused frogs to come up out of the Nile and infest the land, and He confounded the magicians who were unable to undo the plague (Exodus 8:1–15).
- The Egyptians trusted their priests to officiate in the temples on their behalf, but the priests were not allowed to minister before the gods in an impure, diseased, or blemished condition. As the third plague God caused the dust of the earth to form into lice which infested every man and beast (Exodus 8:16–19). The lice-infested priests were unable to officiate in the temples. The Egyptian system of worship had to come to an abrupt halt.
- The Egyptians worshipped animals, particularly livestock, so as the fourth plague God caused the land to be corrupted by a swarm of flies (Exodus 8:20–32). The flies' torment of the livestock was an object lesson to the Egyptians, that they might see how helpless these livestock were before flies sent by the true God.
- The fifth plague, like the fourth, was aimed at animal worship, causing a terrible disease to fall upon the livestock, killing them by the thousands (Exodus 9:1–7). One might think this would cause the Egyptians to reconsider their worship of animals as gods, as they obviously could not stand before the God of Israel.
- The Egyptians also believed in an evil god called Typho, and they tried to appease his wrath by burning human sacrifices. Faced with the previous plagues, the Egyptians naturally tried to appease Typho by burning human sacrifices, but as the sixth plague the ash from these sacrifices caused boils to break out upon the Egyptians.

(Exodus 9:8–12) God turned even their sacrifices to Typho into a curse upon them, demonstrating once again the utter futility of Egyptian religion.

- Next God turned to the vegetable kingdom, for the Egyptians believed in and worshipped tree-gods and held other plants in superstitious veneration. As the seventh plague, God caused a severe storm with lightning, thunder, hail, and rain, and *"the hail smote every herb of the field, and brake every tree of the field"* (Exodus 9:22–35, esp. 25). The Egyptian pantheon of creature-worship was devastated.

- One Egyptian god, Serapis, served to protect Egypt from locusts. As the eighth plague, God sent a swarm of locusts, so numerous that they filled the sky and the earth was darkened, and they consumed every vegetable that had not been destroyed by the hail (Exodus 10:1–20). By this time the Egyptians should have realized that the gods they worshipped were crumbling before the onslaught of the true God.

- But one class of Egyptian deities still remained untouched—the sun, moon, and star gods. As the ninth plague, God caused three days of darkness so thick that the people could not see one another (Exodus 10:21–29). Even the heavenly luminaries had fallen in defeat before the God of Israel.

- Stripped of the protection of all their gods, the Egyptians now stood alone. And then, as the tenth plague, even their human hopes for the future, the first-born sons, were stricken and killed (Exodus 11:1–10).[10] And Pharaoh finally relented and ordered the Hebrews to depart from the land. The Egyptians and their gods had finally conceded defeat.

Now God prepared Moses to lead His people to the Promised Land, where the Hebrew theocracy would restore the worship of the one true God and obedience to His commands. And under God's theocratic rule, Israel developed a constitutional system of government that was highly republican in character.

In an era in which we are accustomed to thinking of constitutions as written political documents, it may seem strange to speak of the "Hebrew

10. Wines explains the significance of these plagues in greater detail, 237–55.

constitution." But written constitutions like that of the United States are modern phenomena. The principles of government embodied in the United States Constitution and many other nations today would, in other times, have been embodied in customs, traditions, decrees, statutes, court decisions, and other sources of authority.[11] But even in that disjointed form, they were nonetheless constitutions.[12]

Again, the central feature of the Hebrew theocracy is that God is Israel's king. At first He reigns with Moses as His vice-regent, then with a series of judges, and then through human kings as limited constitutional monarchs. But this judge or king, God's chief executive officer, worked in conjunction with other branches of government. According to Wines,

> The bond of political union between the sovereign states appears to have been fourfold. In other words, there were four departments of the Hebrew government: viz. the chief magistrate, whether judge, high priest, or king; the senate of princes; the congregation of Israel, the popular branch of the government; and the oracle of Jehovah, a most interesting and singular part of the political structure.[13]

Moses, Israel's first chief executive, organized the other departments of government. In doing so, he may have relied in part upon officers who were already in place.

MOSES ORGANIZES THE SENATE

The Book of Numbers records that God commanded Moses to establish a deliberative body known as the council of elders:

> *And the* L*ORD* *said unto Moses, Gather unto me seventy men…,* [of] *the elders of the people, and officers over them; and bring them unto the tabernacle of the congregation, that they may stand there with thee.*
>
> *And I will come down and talk with thee there: and I will take of the spirit which is upon thee, and will put it upon*

11. Charles Howard McIlwain, *Constitutionalism: Ancient and Modern* (Cornell University, 1940; Liberty Fund, 2007).

12. One is tempted to suggest that a written constitution would be followed more strictly than an unwritten constitution, but the past century of American constitutional history makes that proposition difficult to defend.

13. Wines, 490.

> *them; and they shall bear the burden of the people with thee, that thou bear it not thyself alone.* (Numbers 11:16–17; cf. 11:24–25)

This council of seventy elders may have functioned as a senate, an advisory council or cabinet, or both. As Moses formed this senate at God's command, it is reasonable to assume that the senate continued after Moses' demise, but the manner of its selection is unstated. Some believe this council of elders continued to function during the monarchy as a senate; others suggest that it may have developed into the Sanhedrin of the time of Christ. Wines believed this representative body functioned as a provisional senate even before the Exodus out of Egypt, noting that Moses addressed the judges not as princes of particular tribes but as elders of Israel (Exodus 3:16, 4:29, 12:21).[14] This author believes the seventy elders functioned in a manner similar to the House of Lords in England.

This upper house or senate seems to have been a council of princes and sages, respected for their age, wisdom, and dignity. Originally these were the seventy chosen by Moses in Numbers 11. Subsequently, the senate consisted of 58 men chosen at large, plus the heads or princes of each of the twelve tribes (Numbers 26:1–65). Their role seems to have been to advise the judge or king and to curb the rashness of the general assembly. In a sense they were a buffer between the king and the assembly. They were chosen by God, but He made His choice known through the king or judge, subject to ratification by their respective tribes. They proposed legislation, the assembly adopted it, and the judge or king carried it out. They also served as a supreme court to help the judge or king decide the most difficult legal cases.

MOSES INSTITUTES THE GENERAL ASSEMBLY

Wines also believed that, in addition to this provisional senate, there was a popular assembly similar to England's House of Commons or the United States House of Representatives. It was variously called the congregation, the congregation of Israel, all the assembly, all the children of Israel, and the whole congregation of the Lord. He cited Numbers 10:2–4:

14. Wines, 576.

> *Make thee two trumpets of silver; of a whole piece shalt thou make them: that thou mayest use them for the calling of the assembly, and for the journeying of the camps.*
>
> *And when they shall blow with them, all the assembly shall assemble themselves to thee at the door of the tabernacle of the congregation.*
>
> *And if they blow but with one trumpet, then the princes, which are heads of the thousands of Israel, shall gather themselves unto thee.*

The references to the general assembly, Wines believed, refer to this lower house of the legislature similar to the English House of Commons or the American House of Representatives. The Hebrews now numbered several million souls, and it would have been impossible for the entire population to assemble together, or for Moses or a later judge to address the entire population at once. Numbers 1:16 also refers to the *"renowned of the congregation, princes of the tribes of their fathers, heads of thousands in Israel."* Numbers 16:2 refers to *"certain of the children of Israel, two hundred and fifty princes of the assembly, famous in the congregation, men of renown."*

The general assembly seems to have had the authority to ratify the succession of judges and even kings. In Numbers 27:15–23 we read of instructions that at the death of Moses, Joshua was to be set before *"all the congregation"* that they might ratify this choice. The assembly also approved the choice of Saul to be king (1 Samuel 10:17–27), and later did the same for Solomon (1 Chronicles 29:22–23).

The assembly also performed a legislative function, deciding issues of general application to all Israel. For example, the daughters of Zelophehad brought before the assembly the question of female succession in default of male heirs. They alleged that their father had died without male heirs, and they asked that they be designated his heirs. The assembly agreed, and established a statute that daughters could inherit if the father left no sons, thus settling the question for future ages (Numbers 27:1–9).

They also exercised a limited role in foreign policy. During the conquest of Canaan, when Joshua agreed to spare the Gibeonites and the princes of Israel agreed, the congregation of Israel strongly disapproved this agreement and complained against both Joshua and the princes. When they discovered that the Gibeonites had deceived them into agreeing to spare them, they still honored their agreement but on the condition that the Gibeonites be their servants (Joshua 9:1–27).

THE ORACLE OF JEHOVAH

The oracle of Jehovah is a unique feature of the Hebrew theocracy. It was a special means by which God revealed His will to the people and their leaders, but the manner in which the oracle revealed God's will is unclear.

Among the Greeks, the oracle was a person. Among the Hebrews, the oracle was the *"holy of holies"* in the Temple (1 Kings 6:16, 19–23), the sacred area behind the veil from where God communicated with the high priest. Normally, only the high priest could consult the oracle, but unlike the oracle at Delphi and other pagan oracles, the high priest never received any compensation for consulting the oracle, and he could consult the oracle at any time.

Most commonly, the oracle revealed God's will to the high priest through the Urim and Thummim that were put into the breastplate of the high priest on the front of which were set twelve precious stones engraved with the names of the twelve tribes. The Urim and Thummim are mentioned in Exodus 28:30, Leviticus 8:8, Numbers 27:21, Deuteronomy 33:8, 1 Samuel 28:6, Ezra 2:63, and Nehemiah 7:65; and they may have played a role in other instances in which Israel's leaders sought to know God's will. How they functioned is a mystery, and many theories have been advanced from electricity to computers to cosmic energy to contact with extraterrestials. The most common explanation is that by some miraculous means the stones radiated light in a way that showed God's will.

Wines describes the probable manner of the consultation with the oracle:

> The opinion of learned and judicious authors, as to the manner of taking the sense of the oracle, is this: The high priest clothed in his pontifical garments, and having on the breastplate of judgment, in which were the mysterious urim and thummim, symbolical of the clearness and fulness of the oracular responses, presented himself before the veil of the tabernacle, over against the mercy seat—the immediate residence of the Divine presence. The magistrate, who came to consult the oracle, stood directly behind him [the high priest], and propounded the question, which was repeated by the priest. The answer

> was returned in an audible voice, in terms explicit, direct, and unambiguous. This explains the reason why the holy of holies, where the mercy seat stood, is so often called the oracle. It was because from thence, God returned answers to those, who came to ask counsel of him, on behalf of the public conscience, or the public administration.[15]

The oracle was sometimes consulted in matters of foreign policy, and sometimes in legal cases, either in the first instance or on appeal. According to Wines,

> The oracle was the institution of all others, adapted to the mental condition, habits, and needs of the Hebrew people. It operated as a salutary check to the ignorance and rashness of both rulers and people.[16]

Though not a human person, the oracle was nevertheless a very real institution in a theocratic government under the rulership of God. This does not necessarily mean God is the ruler of nations in the same sense today. Israel was God's uniquely chosen nation, God's chosen instrument for calling the nations back to Himself.

MOSES INSTITUTES THE JUDGES

Besides serving as a commander and chief executive, Moses personally exercised the judicial function. When his father-in-law, Jethro the Midianite, came for a visit, he found Moses overextended as he judged cases:

> *And it came to pass on the morrow, that Moses sat to judge the people: and the people stood by Moses from the morning unto the evening.*
>
> *And when Moses' father in law saw all that he did to the people, he said, What is this thing that thou doest to the people? why sittest thou thyself alone, and all the people stand by thee from morning unto even?*
>
> *And Moses said unto his father in law, Because the people come unto me to enquire of God:*

15. *Id.*, 600–01.

16. *Id.*, 606–07.

When they have a matter, they come unto me; and I judge between one and another, and I do make them know the statutes of God, and his laws.

And Moses' father in law said unto him, The thing that thou doest is not good.

Thou wilt surely wear away, both thou, and this people that is with thee: for this thing is too heavy for thee; thou art not able to perform it thyself alone.

Hearken now unto my voice, I will give thee counsel, and God shall be with thee: Be thou for the people to God-ward, that thou mayest bring the causes unto God:

And thou shalt teach them ordinances and laws, and shalt shew them the way wherein they must walk, and the work that they must do.

Moreover thou shalt provide out of all the people able men, such as fear God, men of truth, hating covetousness; and place such over them, to be rulers of thousands, and rulers of hundreds, rulers of fifties, and rulers of tens:

And let them judge the people at all seasons: and it shall be, that every great matter they shall bring unto thee, but every small matter they shall judge: so shall it be easier for thyself, and they shall bear the burden with thee.

If thou shalt do this thing, and God command thee so, then thou shalt be able to endure, and all this people shall also go to their place in peace.

So Moses hearkened to the voice of his father in law, and did all that he had said.

And Moses chose able men out of all Israel, and made them heads over the people, rulers of thousands, rulers of hundreds, rulers of fifties, and rulers of tens.

And they judged the people at all seasons: the hard causes they brought unto Moses, but every small matter they judged themselves.

And Moses let his father in law depart; and he went his way into his own land. (Exodus 18:13–27)

And so, with these austere beginnings among desert nomads began a judicial system that for more than three millennia has influenced the world more than any other. Notice the special features of the system:

- The qualifications Moses was to look for in these judges were that they fear God, they seek the truth and judge accordingly, they hate covetousness and are therefore not susceptible to bribery or blackmail, and they are able. Graduation from an approved law school and passing a bar exam are not listed among these qualifications. Competence was a requirement, but the most important qualities were fear of God, character, and integrity.
- The system was decentralized, with justices of the peace serving over ten families, district judges over fifty families, county judges over a hundred families, appellate judges over a thousand families, and Moses as the supreme court. Most likely these divisions were approximate; the judicial districts did not alter every time someone was born or died.
- Moses was to seek wisdom from God and to speak as His voice, because in the Hebrew view all true and just law is from God.
- Moses was to teach God's ordinances and laws to the people. The judiciary played an educational function, and through such education the people become more law-abiding and easier to govern.
- The judges apparently performed an executive as well as a judicial function, and possibly, in concert with other judges, a legislative function as well.
- Seeking God's wisdom, Moses selected the initial judges. After that, the people of the twelve tribes chose their judges' successors. Moses told the people of Israel, *"Take you wise men, and understanding, and known among your tribes, and I will make them rulers over you"* (Deuteronomy 1:13). And Moses further instructed the people, *"Judges and officers shalt thou make thee in all thy gates, which the Lord thy God giveth thee, throughout thy tribes: and they shall judge the people with just judgment"* (16:18).

This pattern continued throughout much of Israel's history. When Israel took possession of the land of Canaan and prepared to divide that land among the twelve tribes, Moses' successor Joshua told the people, *"Give out from among you three men for each tribe: and I will send them"* (Joshua 18:4). Wines, in his classic work *Commentaries on the Laws of the Ancient Hebrews,* observes that the phrase *"give out from among you"* literally means "select or choose for yourselves."[17]

The Book of Judges records, *"The men of Israel said unto Gideon, Rule thou over us"* (8:22). Likewise 9:6: *"The men of Shechem... made Abimelech king."* And in 11:11: *"[T]he people made him [Jephthah] head and captain over them."*

The method by which the judges and elders were selected is uncertain. It is tempting to suggest, with Wines and others, that they held popular elections, and this is possible. But at the very least, as these and other passages of Scripture make clear, the judges and elders of the tribes of Israel definitely received their authority from God through the consent of the people.

Whether these judges constituted another branch of government, or whether they along with the *shoterim* (translated "officers") and elders constituted the general assembly, is uncertain. The latter is more likely because, as noted, they appear to have performed legislative and executive as well as judicial functions.

THE TRIBES

As noted earlier, each of the twelve tribes had its own princes, elders, *shoterim,* and judges, much as each of the thirteen states after independence from England retained its own governor, legislature, judiciary, and militia. Also, like the states in the American system, and in keeping with a virtually universal trend toward centralization, as time progressed the national government of Israel grew stronger and the tribes gradually lost much of their sovereignty.

17. Wines, 407.

THE ERA OF THE CHIEF JUDGES: THE HEBREW REPUBLIC

Before the institution of the monarchy, Moses and a succession of judges served as the chief executive officers of Israel. The author of the Book of Judges pronounced this benediction on the era:

> *In those days there was no king in Israel: every man did that which was right in his own eyes.* (Judges 21:25)

This sounds like an idyllic state of freedom. But from the context we may infer that this was also a time of confusion and discord. The government was decentralized to the extent that a common faith and ancestry, rather than a centralized government, held the nation together.

Although these chief executives were called judges, the term "judge" appears to denote a person who had executive as well as judicial authority. At any given time one particular judge seems to have been supreme over the others and governed all or part of Israel, while local judges (sometimes called governors or princes) and elders governed each of the twelve tribes.

We may draw several conclusions about these chief judges:

- Unlike the later kings, the office of chief judge was not hereditary. In fact, while all of the kings except Saul were from the tribe of Judah, the chief judges arose from different tribes: Moses was of the Tribe of Levi; Joshua, of Ephraim; Othniel, of Judah; Ehud, of Benjamin; Deborah, of Naphtali; Gideon, of Manasseh; Samson of Dan; and Samuel, of Ephriam.
- The chief judge was elected to office. How the vote was conducted is unclear, but he governed by the consent of the people. This may have been by popular election, or it may have been by vote of the senate and the general assembly. Gideon was chosen by the people (Judges 8:22), likewise Jephthah (Judges 11:5-11) and Samuel (1 Samuel 7:5–8). The manner of their choosing was probably true of others as well.
- Once elected, the chief judge may have held office for life. We read nothing that says he ever stood for re-election.

- The chief judge's duties were both executive and judicial; he governed in peace and commanded in war, and he also adjudicated cases.
- The chief judge's authority, while substantial, was not absolute. He could punish those who disobeyed him, even by death (Joshua 1:18; Deuteronomy 17:12), but his authority was tempered by the oracle, by the senate, by the general assembly, and by the law.

During the era of the chief judges, each of the twelve tribes managed its own internal affairs, and to a large extent its defense and foreign policy. And when a foreign nation threatened one of the tribes, that tribe could count on very little help from the others. Jephthah's leadership of the Tribe of Gad is a case in point.

Gad occupied the land known as Gilead, east of the Jordan River and the Dead Sea. A hostile nation to the east of them, the Ammonites, threatened to make war upon Gilead, claiming the land occupied by the men of Gad was rightfully theirs. The men of Gilead looked for a military leader and settled upon Jephthah. Jephthah was something of an outcast because his mother was a harlot, but the men of Gilead knew he was a *"mighty man of valor"* (Judges 11:1) and asked him to lead them in battle. He agreed to be their battle captain, provided they make him their permanent judge in peace as well as in war.

Jephthah's exchange with the Ammonite king, recorded in Judges 11:12–27, provides a fascinating glimpse of ancient Middle Eastern diplomacy. Jephthah sent messengers to ask the Ammonite king why they were making war upon Gilead. This illustrates the historic reason in international law for a declaration of war; it enables the nation under attack to know the reasons for the attack and what it can do to end the attack and rectify the situation. The king answered that Israel had taken Ammonite land when they came up out of Egypt. Jephthah denied that Israel had taken Ammonite land. Rather, he said the Edomites and the Moabites had taken that land from Ammon long before the Exodus. As the Israelites traveled from Egypt to the promised land of Canaan, they requested permission to cross the land peaceably, but the Edomite and Moabite kings refused. Israel then crossed the land, the Edomites and Moabites attacked, and the Lord Jehovah gave Israel a great victory. Jephthah then asked the Ammonite king, if your god Chemosh gave land into your hands, would you not keep it? Our God Jehovah, a far greater god than Chemosh, gave this land into our hands, and we're going to keep it.

And then in verse 26 he raised the legal defense of "laches," that a claim becomes invalid when not asserted within a reasonable time:

> *While Israel dwelt in Heshbon and her towns,... and in all the cities that be along by the coasts of Arnon, three hundred years? why therefore did ye not recover them within that time?* (Judges 11:26)

Jephthah's point is that the conquest happened 300 years ago, and by not contesting Israel's possession at that time or shortly thereafter, the Ammonites have forfeited any claim to them, and they belong to Israel by adverse possession. The exchange gives us some insight into Israelite warfare, Israelite diplomacy, and Israel's use of and recognition of certain principles of international law that were recognized at that time.

Jephthah's answer notwithstanding, the Ammonites attacked, and Jephthah led the men of Gad to a great victory. Jephthah served as judge over Gilead for the remaining six years of his life (Judges 11:28–12:7).

Apparently Gilead received no help from the other tribes of Israel, nor did they expect any help. This illustrates a downside of decentralized government. At times, though, the various tribes of Israel did cooperate in the common defense, as in the days of Gideon (Judges 6–9). As parts of Israel were under attack from the Midianites to the northeast, Gideon called for help from the northern tribes of Ephraim, Naphtali, Asher, and Manasseh, and they responded to his call. After his victory, "*the men of Israel said unto Gideon, Rule thou over us, both thou, and thy son, and thy son's son also: for thou hast delivered us from the hand of Midian*" (8:22). This was a clear invitation to establish a hereditary monarchy by popular consent, but Gideon refused: *"I will not rule over you, neither shall my son rule over you: the Lord shall rule over you"* (8:23). God Himself was king over Israel; the judges administered justice and the affairs of state in His Name.

This decentralized system of government under the judges continued from the time of Moses (circa 1462 BC) until the establishment of the monarchy around 1064 BC. As noted above, it was a time of substantial individual liberty, but occasionally also a time of confusion and disorder. Wines says concerning the era of the chief judges,

> If any one will attentively read over the book of Judges, and take the trouble to compare the times of oppression and adversity with those of independence and prosperity, he will find the duration of the former less than one-fourth that of the latter. The entire history of one hundred and twenty years of this period is contained in these two brief records:—*"The land had rest forty years"* [Judges 3:11]; *"the land had rest fourscore years"* [Judges 3:30]. Surely, Othniel, Ehud, and Shamgar must have governed with prudence and ability, since all the time of their administration was prosperous and peaceable, both within and without. It is quite apparent, therefore, that the Israelites experienced much more of prosperity than of adversity in the time of the judges. Under their government, the nation enjoyed periods of repose, happiness, and plenty, of which the history of other ancient nations affords but few examples. Wherefore, then, change the republican to the regal form? Pride and folly prompted the revolution; a revolution, soon repented of with bitter but unavailing regrets; a revolution, in which lay buried the seeds of despotism and ultimate dissolution.[18]

THE ERA OF THE UNIFIED MONARCHY

The last supreme judge over Israel was Samuel, who judged Israel from about 1084–1063 BC. Samuel was noted not only for his military leadership in turning back the Philistine incursions into Israel (1 Samuel 7:13–14; 12:11) but also for his judicial leadership (1 Samuel 7:15–8:3). However, his sons took positions as lesser judges, and they were Samuel's likely successors. They were corrupt and took bribes, and this gave people an excuse to change the form of government, because free republican government can endure only if its leaders and the general populace have a strong moral foundation that shapes not only their laws and institutions but also their character. The elders of Israel approached Samuel and said,

> *Behold, thou art old, and thy sons walk not in thy ways: now make us a king to judge us like all the nations.*
> (1 Samuel 8:5)

Interestingly, the elders' excuse for wanting a king was the corruption of Samuel's sons, but their real reason was exactly that which Moses

18. Wines, 547–48.

had predicted four centuries earlier in Deuteronomy 17:14: to be *"like as all the nations that are about"* Israel. Samuel interpreted their request personally as a rejection of his leadership, but when he took their request to God in prayer, God told him *"they have not rejected thee, but they have rejected me, that I should not reign over them"* (1 Samuel 8:7). God told Samuel to grant their request but also to warn them that a king would rob them of their basic liberties by taking their children to be his servants, confiscating their lands, crops, and livestock, and taxing their income (1 Samuel 8:10–18). But the people were adamant in their demand for a king.

Moses foresaw that the day would come when Israel would demand a king, and he did not forbid it. The institution of the monarchy did not constitute an end to the Hebrew theocracy; it simply meant that God's vice-regent, the chief executive officer was now a constitutional monarch instead of a judge. This was not ideal, but it was permissible under certain conditions:

> *"When thou art come unto the land which the LORD thy God giveth thee, and shalt possess it, and shalt dwell therein, and shalt say, I will set a king over me, like as all the nations that are about me;*
>
> *Thou shalt in any wise set him king over thee, whom the LORD thy God shall choose: one from among thy brethren shalt thou set king over thee: thou mayest not set a stranger over thee, which is not thy brother.*
>
> *But he shall not multiply horses to himself, nor cause the people to return to Egypt, to the end that he should multiply horses: forasmuch as the LORD hath said unto you, Ye shall henceforth return no more that way.*
>
> *Neither shall he multiply wives to himself, that his heart turn not away: neither shall he greatly multiply to himself silver and gold.*
>
> *And it shall be, when he sitteth upon the throne of his kingdom, that he shall write him a copy of this law in a book out of that which is before the priests the Levites:*
>
> *And it shall be with him, and he shall read therein all the days of his life: that he may learn to fear the LORD his God,*

> *to keep all the words of this law and these statutes, to do them:*
>
> *That his heart be not lifted up above his brethren, and that he turn not aside from the commandment, to the right hand, or to the left: to the end that he may prolong his days in his kingdom, he, and his children, in the midst of Israel."* (Deuteronomy 17:14–20)

Observe the restrictions:

- The king must be *"from among thy brethren";* he is to be one of the people so the people will not worship him as a god, as did the pagan nations surrounding Israel.
- The king must not *"multiply horses,"* because God did not want Israel to be dependent upon Egypt which was the main source of cavalry horses, and because cavalry would be useful only for offensive warfare, and once the conquest of Canaan was completed Israel was not to engage in offensive warfare against neighboring nations.
- The king must not *"multiply wives to himself, that his heart turn not away,"* a recognition that foreign wives could lead the king into pagan idolatry, as happened with Solomon (1 Kings 11:1–11).
- The king must not *"greatly multiply to himself silver and gold,"* either through enriching himself or through oppressive taxation.
- The king must write out a copy of the Mosaic Law, must read from it every day, and must follow it throughout his reign. Israel was to be a government of laws, not of men, and even the king was not above the law.

If these conditions were honored, the king and his descendants would reign successfully, and the people would be blessed with good government thereunder.

And yet, God told Samuel that *"they have not rejected thee, but they have rejected me, that I should not reign over them"* (1 Samuel 8:7). Their rejection of God consisted not so much in wanting a king, but in wanting a king for the wrong reasons—so they could be like the pagan nations around them. And in 1 Samuel 12:19 the people recognized their sin in demanding a king—but too late, because the kingship was firmly entrenched.

Saul, a Limited Monarch

1 Samuel 9–12 describes how God led Samuel to choose Saul to be Israel's first king. The choice was God's; He revealed His choice through Samuel; but the choice did not become effective until it was ratified by the people:

> *And Samuel said to all the people, See ye him whom the LORD hath chosen, that there is none like him among all the people? And all the people shouted, and said, God save the king.* (1 Samuel 10:24)

This illustrates a basic principle of Hebrew republican thought: God chooses those who are to serve in public office, but the people ratify God's choice. They may do so through elections, through confirmation by a body of chosen leaders, or, as in Saul's case, by public acclamation: *"God save the king."*

Saul had many good qualities: he was, at least at first, a humble man (1 Samuel 9:21); he never demanded great wealth or luxury or power for himself; he was a good and faithful husband and father; and he was a brave and capable soldier. He began his reign with worship and sacrifices to God and with generosity toward his opponents; refusing the demands of his supporters that his opponents be put to death, he declared,

> *There shall not a man be put to death this day: for to day the LORD hath wrought salvation in Israel.* (1 Samuel 11:13)

Saul was a limited monarch. On a day of battle with the Philistines, Saul had commanded that no one should eat until evening, but his son Jonathan had not heard the order, and ate. Saul prepared to execute Jonathan in accordance with his order. But the people loved Jonathan and interceded:

> *And the people said unto Saul, Shall Jonathan die, who hath wrought this great salvation in Israel? God forbid: as the LORD liveth, there shall not one hair of his head fall to the ground; for he hath wrought with God this day. So the people rescued Jonathan, that he died not.* (1 Samuel 14:45)

This again demonstrates that according to Hebrew political philosophy, the king's authority comes from God through the people, and the people have a right to countermand the king's decisions. The reference to the "people" probably refers to the common assembly, as the common assembly and the senate seem to have functioned during the era of the monarchy much as they had during the era of the judges. The assembly exercised a power commonly known as "interposition," by which a lesser official places himself between the higher official and the people when the higher official exercises his powers in a tyrannical manner. The incident may also illustrate a basic principle of law that lack of knowledge of a criminal statute may be a defense or a mitigating factor.

But Saul's character flaws led to problems during his reign. He refused to accept the limits of his authority, usurping the functions of the priesthood by performing sacrifices that only priests were authorized to perform (1 Samuel 15). His admirable desire to reign by the consent of the governed degenerated into an obsession about his popularity. After David slew Goliath, Saul admired his courage and valor and made him a commander. But after Saul and David returned to the capital victorious over the Philistines, the women filled the streets of the city, singing *"Saul hath slain his thousands, and David his ten thousands"* (1 Samuel 18:7). Saul became insecure and jealous, and instead of promoting David to chief of his general staff and thereby benefiting from David's victories, he tried to undercut David, thereby plunging Israel into a civil war. And as Saul's reign came to a close, his earlier victories in battle were reversed, foreign enemies began closing in and winning victories while Saul was engulfed in a civil war with David, and Saul turned in desperation to the occult and visited a witch. As predicted, he died in battle the next day, and David his successor, to his great credit, had him buried with full military honors.[19]

David, Israel's Greatest King

Despite his numerous sins and failures, David is called *"a man after his [God's] own heart"* (1 Samuel 13:14), because his heart was devoted to God and he continually sought God's counsel. He reigned over Israel

19. God knew that Saul, despite his good beginning, would end his reign in tragic failure. Why, then, did God choose Saul to be Israel's first king? One possible explanation is that God chose Saul to show Israel how monarchy degenerates into tyranny and to lead Israel back to its republican foundations. Unfortunately, Israel did not heed God's warning. People seldom do.

for 40 years, from 1011–971 BC, at first reigning in his native Judea and shortly thereafter consolidating his reign over all Israel. A great soldier and officer, he turned back the Philistine incursions and also defeated the forces of Moab, Edom, Damascus, Zobah, Hamath, and Ammon. Like the United States from the time of the War Between the States to World War I, David reorganized the army into twelve companies of 24,000 men each, for a total force of 288,000. Each company of 24,000 served one month of active duty each year, so at all times David had a standing army of 24,000 and a much larger reserve force that he could call to active duty when needed (1 Chronicles 27:1–15).

David also made Jerusalem his capital, a wise choice because of its central location and lack of tribal affiliations. He kept the tribal governments intact but appointed general supervisors to oversee most of them (1 Chronicles 27:16–22). He also established various departments, including the treasury, storehouses, and types of agriculture, and appointed supervisors over them (I Chronicles 27:25–31). Leon Wood suggests that under David Israel became an empire with foreign conquests, but that all this was at the cost of higher taxes, as well as foreign tribute,[20] and also with the use of foreign conscript labor (2 Samuel 20:23).

Solomon, Israel's Glorious King

David's son Solomon was different from his predecessors. Saul had been a rustic farmer and soldier and was probably never fully comfortable with royalty. David likewise had been a shepherd and a soldier, and he could feel at home either in a king's palace or in a soldier's tent. But Solomon was raised in the palace and was thoroughly urbanized. David led soldiers in battle, but Solomon preferred to stay in the palace. He expanded the royal palace and other buildings of the capital far beyond anything Saul or David had ever imagined, and he built Jerusalem into a showplace capital that was the envy of other Middle Eastern kings.

During his 40-year reign (971–931 BC), Solomon engaged in foreign trade and diplomacy to a far greater extent than did his predecessors. His 600 wives and 300 concubines were, in many instances, a means of securing alliances with foreign powers (1 Kings 3:1). Because David had conquered territory as far south as the Gulf of Aqaba, Solomon was able to send fleets of trading ships into the Indian Ocean. Among his foreign visitors was the

20. Leon Wood, *A Survey of Israel's History* (Zondervan, 1970, 1986), 227.

Queen of Sheba,[21] who came to test his wisdom with difficult questions; he impressed her with his answers beyond expectation. She gave him great tribute of gold, abundant spices, and precious stones (1 Kings 10:1–13).

All of this required bureaucracy. Solomon divided Israel into twelve districts that did not always conform to the old tribal boundaries, and each district was required to furnish provisions for Solomon's court for one month of the year (1 Kings 4:7–28). He expanded the foreign conscript labor begun by David, and he also conscripted Israelites into temporary forced labor to support his projects (1 Kings 5:13). This created a core of dissatisfaction, which led to the division of the kingdom after his death. Jeroboam, an official who had turned against Solomon and was forced to flee to Egypt, was waiting in the wings to exploit that dissatisfaction.

The Divided Kingdom

After Solomon died, his son Rehoboam assumed the throne. The congregation of Israel, led by Jeroboam who had secretly returned from Egypt, approached Rehoboam and asked for relief from Solomon's oppressive policies:

> *And they sent and called him [Rehoboam]. So Jeroboam and all Israel came and spake to Rehoboam, saying,*
>
> *Thy father made our yoke grievous: now therefore ease thou somewhat the grievous servitude of thy father, and his heavy yoke that he put upon us, and we will serve thee.*
>
> *And he said unto them, Come again unto me after three days. And the people departed.* (2 Chronicles 10:3–5)

Rehoboam then consulted with the older advisors who had served Solomon, and they advised him to grant some relief: *"If thou be kind to this people, and please them, and speak good words to them, they will be thy servants for ever"* (2 Chronicles 10:7). But then he spoke with the younger advisors who had grown up with him, and they rashly told him to take a hard approach. And when the congregation of Israel returned, Rehoboam told them,

21. Sheba is thought to have been in the vicinity of what is now Yemen, though some place it in or near Ethiopia. Throughout history Yemen has maintained a Jewish community, and for at least part of the period between AD 70 and AD 620 Yemen was ruled by Jewish kings. Could the Jewish presence in Yemen go back to the Queen of Sheba?

> *My father made your yoke heavy, but I will add thereto: my father chastised you with whips, but I will chastise you with scorpions....*
>
> *And when all Israel saw that the king would not hearken unto them, the people answered the king, saying, What portion have we in David? and we have none inheritance in the son of Jesse: every man to your tents, O Israel: and now, David, see to thine own house. So all Israel went to their tents.*
>
> *But as for the children of Israel that dwelt in the cities of Judah, Rehoboam reigned over them.*
> (2 Chronicles 10:14, 16–17)

From that point on, the kingdom was divided. The ten northern tribes seceded from Rehoboam's kingdom and formed a confederacy known as Israel, and Jeroboam became their first king. The large tribe of Judah, to which David, Solomon, and Rehoboam belonged, remained loyal to Rehoboam, and the neighboring small tribe of Benjamin stayed with Judah.

Several observations are appropriate. First, it would be difficult for Rehoboam, or any of the kings or judges before or after him, to address the entire populace of Israel, which probably consisted of about 4 million people at that time. Accordingly, many believe the reference to *"all Israel,"* or in many other passages the *"congregation of Israel,"* refers to the common assembly body consisting of judges and elders from each of the twelve tribes. The advisors Rehoboam consulted may have been senators.

Second, the action of the assembly in appealing to King Rehoboam and then breaking away from him when he refused their appeal, is often cited as justification for the power of interposition, previously defined as a lesser authority resisting a higher authority when the higher authority has become tyrannical. But the fact that the northern tribes seceded from the kingdom does not mean they did so with God's approval, and the northern kingdom's subsequent apostasy may cause one to question whether they were truly in God's will. However, when Rehoboam gathered 140,000 warriors to subdue the northern kingdom, God made His will known:

> *But the word of the LORD came to Shemaiah the man of God, saying,*

> *Speak unto Rehoboam the son of Solomon, king of Judah, and to all Israel in Judah and Benjamin, saying,*
>
> *Thus saith the Lord, Ye shall not go up, nor fight against your brethren: return every man to his house: for this thing is done of me. And they obeyed the words of the Lord, and returned from going against Jeroboam.* (2 Chronicles 11:2–4)

In some way at least, God did approve the northern tribes' secession from Rehoboam's kingdom.

The Era of the Divided Kingdoms

From 931 BC Israel was divided into two kingdoms. The southern tribes of Judah and Benjamin remained loyal to Rehoboam, and they were called Judea. The ten northern tribes were called Israel, and Jeroboam was their first king. The Hebrew commons confirmed Jeroboam as king of the ten northern tribes (1 Kings 12:20), indicating that this representative body continued to function in the north after the separation.

The Northern Kingdom (Israel)

Between 931 BC and 721 BC nineteen kings ruled over Israel. Some, like Jeroboam and Omri, appear to have been quite capable. However, all of them, with the partial exception of Jehu,[22] were apostate in the eyes of the Old Testament narratives.

Jeroboam began his reign well, rebuilding the northern city of Shechem and making it his capital. But problems began when the time came for the priests to offer sacrifice at Jerusalem. Jerusalem, however, was the capital of the southern kingdom, so Jeroboam prohibited the priests from traveling to the south and decreed that sacrifices would be offered thereafter at two northern cities, Bethel and Dan. But the priests adamantly insisted

---

22. Jehu (841–814 BC) is a most intriguing historical figure. He was a commander in the army of Israel, when the prophet Elisha informed him that he was God's choice to be king of Israel and anointed him to that purpose. Jehu therefore killed King Joram and the older queen mother, Jezebel, who had long been a force for paganism in Israel (2 Kings 9:21–37).

Jehu knew, however, that before Israel could experience renewal, he had to break the power of the priests of the pagan fertility god Baal. He did so by convening the Baal priests into a great temple, ostensibly to offer Baal worship, and then barricaded the temple and sent armed guards to massacre all of the Baal priests (2 Kings 10:18–30). However, despite Jehu's hostility toward Baal worship, he did not embrace the true worship of Jehovah but rather adhered to the syncretistic religious practices of Jeroboam (2 Kings 10:31). His reign, therefore, must be considered at best a mixed blessing to Israel.

that the sacrifices must take place in Jerusalem. Jeroboam then appointed new priests who were not of the tribe of Levi, and he established a syncretistic system of worship that combined the Hebrew worship of Jehovah with elements of Canaanite pagan religions.

Thereafter, the northern kingdom degenerated spiritually and politically, despite attempts by King Omri (885–874 BC) to restore the kingdom to its former strength by establishing Samaria as its new capital. But his son King Ahab (874–852 BC) sunk the kingdom to new depths of tyranny and idolatry. To cement an alliance with the Phoenicians, he married the Phoenician princess Jezebel (1 Kings 16:29–33). Ahab still had some understanding of the restrictions on an Israelite king's power, but Jezebel came from Phoenicia where king-worship and absolute monarchy were the norm and where child-sacrifice and the worship of the fertility gods were the accepted form of religion. As queen, Jezebel made war upon the prophets of Jehovah, many of whom were slain and others forced into hiding.

The contrast between Israel's limited monarchy and Jezebel's Phoenician absolutism is seen in the travesty of Naboth's vineyard:

> *And it came to pass after these things, that Naboth the Jezreelite had a vineyard, which was in Jezreel, hard by the palace of Ahab king of Samaria.*
>
> *And Ahab spake unto Naboth, saying, Give me thy vineyard, that I may have it for a garden of herbs, because it is near unto my house: and I will give thee for it a better vineyard than it; or, if it seem good to thee, I will give thee the worth of it in money.*
>
> *And Naboth said to Ahab, The* Lord *forbid it me, that I should give the inheritance of my fathers unto thee.* (1 Kings 21:1–3)

Ahab returned to the palace unhappy and frustrated by his failure to obtain the vineyard from Naboth, but he seemed to recognize Naboth's legal right to refuse to part with it. Not so with Jezebel. When he told her of Naboth's refusal, she asked sarcastically, *"Dost thou now govern the kingdom of Israel?"* (1 Kings 21:7) She had been raised in the palace of Phoenicia, where no commoner would dare refuse a king's demand. And she declared, *"[A]rise, and eat bread, and let thine heart be merry: I will give thee the vineyard of Naboth the Jezreelite"* (1 Kings 21:7). Jezebel then forged Ahab's signature to false charges of blasphemy and treason, and at her command two *"sons of Belial [Satan]"* falsely accused Naboth of these charges and promptly dragged him out and stoned him to death without a trial, and his vineyard was then forfeited to the king (1 Kings 21:8–16). But Elijah the prophet condemned the royal couple for this act of tyranny, and prophesied to Ahab that *"Thus saith the LORD, In the place where dogs licked the blood of Naboth shall dogs lick thy blood, even thine"* (1 Kings 21:19), and *"of Jezebel also spake the LORD, saying, The dogs shall eat Jezebel by the wall of Jezreel"* (1 Kings 21:23). Elijah's prophesy of Ahab's death was fulfilled shortly thereafter during a battle with Syria (1 Kings 22:34–38), and his prophesy of Jezebel's death was fulfilled at the command of Jehu (2 Kings 9:30–37).

By 732 BC, when Israel's last king Hoshea took the throne, Israel had become a vassal state of the Assyrian Empire. Hoshea chose to reject Assyrian dominance, possibly because Egypt appeared to be rising as a rival to Assyria. King Shalmaneser V therefore besieged Samaria, and in 722 BC Israel surrendered to Assyria. In keeping with Assyrian policy of conquest, many of the people of the northern kingdom were deported to various places throughout the Assyrian Empire.[23] Others remained, but the Assyrians moved people of other Middle Eastern nationalities into Israel. They intermarried with the Israelites, and their descendants became known as the Samaritans, people who are a mixture of Jew and Gentile.

The Southern Kingdom (Judea)

The Southern Kingdom also declined, but not as rapidly as the Northern Kingdom. Several godly kings led revival, notably Asa (911–870 BC), Jehoshaphat (870–848 BC), Joash (835–796 BC), Hezekiah (729–686 BC), and Josiah (640–609 BC). Asa rebuilt Judea's fortifications and led Judea successfully in battle. Jehoshaphat reorganized Judea's government and especially revitalized the judiciary, placing judges in the fortified cities and creating a supreme court that consisted of priests and other judges, headed by Amariah the chief priest and Zebadiah who served like a prime

23. What happened to the lost ten tribes of Israel? This has been the subject of much speculation, sometimes based on religious doctrine. Some believe they became the nations of Western Europe, others that they came to the Western Hemisphere. Others think it more likely that they intermarried with the Assyrians or with other people in the Middle East. DNA research might provide some answers to these questions.

minister. Hezekiah reorganized the priesthood in accordance with the Mosaic Law, and with the encouragement of Egypt he rebelled against Assyrian domination. The Assyrian King Sennacherib besieged Jerusalem in 701 BC, but Jerusalem was spared by divine deliverance. However, the kings who followed Hezekiah—Manasseh and Amon—returned Judea to pagan Baal-worship.

King Josiah tried to lead Judea back to the worship of God, purged the kingdom of pagan worship, and renovated the Temple in Jerusalem, and restored observance of the Law of Moses (2 Kings 22).[24] But after he was killed in battle against the Egyptians, the kingdom degenerated further under Jehoahaz, Jehoiakim, Jehoiachin (also known as Jeconiah and Coniah), and Zedekiah. Meanwhile, the Babylonians had replaced Assyria as the leading power in the Middle East, and King Nebuchadnezzar took the Judeans captive to Babylon in various stages from 605–586 BC.[25] They remained in captivity in Babylon 70 years. Then, in 539 BC, the Persians conquered Babylon. In keeping with the Persian policy of allowing conquered peoples to remain in their homelands and keep their local customs, in 538 BC King Cyrus the Great of Persia decreed that the Jews could return to their homeland. Many returned to Judea, although some chose to remain in Babylon.[26]

Judea After the Babylonian Exile (538 BC and After)

After their return from exile, the Judeans became a vassal state of Persia, ruled by a series of governors appointed by the Persian kings. One such governor, Nehemiah, with permission from the Persian King Artaxerxes I, returned to Judea to rebuild the walls of Jerusalem. When neighboring tribes threatened to prevent the rebuilding, Nehemiah armed his men and commanded them to stand guard on the walls. After the danger subsided, he kept some of his men on active duty and placed others

24. 2 Kings 22 records that while the workers were renovating the Temple, they discovered a scroll. They gave it to the priests, who discovered that it was a copy of the Law of Moses. They brought the scroll to King Josiah, who immediately ordered national repentance and observance of the law. It might seem strange that the discovery of the Law of Moses in the Temple would create such consternation. It demonstrates how quickly a nation's spiritual heritage can be erased from memory.

25. The captivity of Daniel, Shradrach, Meshech, and Abednego, as recorded in the Book of Daniel, took place during this period and shortly thereafter.

26. Clay tablets from this period record business contracts with Jewish names, indicating that some of them were quite successful in Babylon.

on reserve status, building with one hand and holding a weapon with the other (Nehemiah 4:17). Nehemiah then reorganized the government, reestablished the priesthood, launched economic reforms, and reaffirmed the Jews' covenant with God. The Books of Nehemiah, Ezra, and Malachi describe events during this period.

The Persian Empire dominated the Middle East until about 330 BC, at which time Persia fell to Alexander the Great of Greece. After Alexander's death in 321 BC, his empire was divided among four of his generals. Two of these generals, Seleucus of Syria and Ptolemy of Egypt and their descendants, were constantly at war with one another, and Judea was a buffer zone between them. Internally, the Judeans were divided between the Hellenizers who wanted to adopt Greek culture, and the Hasidim and other traditional Jews who resisted Hellenization. Finally, in 167 BC, during the oppressive reign of Antiochus Epiphanes, a priest named Mattathias and his sons led a revolt against the Seleucid Greeks, and after three years of guerrilla warfare, in December 164 BC (celebrated in Judaism as Hanukkah), his son Judas Maccabeus rode in triumph into Jerusalem and restored traditional Hebrew worship according to the Law. Judas and his descendants then ruled Judea as the Hasmonean dynasty, which began well but degenerated into apostasy and corruption in the course of time.

JUDEA DURING THE TIME OF CHRIST

Kings and Governors

The Hasmonean or Asmonean kings ruled Judea, albeit weakly, until the coming of the Romans, and after a power struggle the Herodian kings took power and served as limited monarchs or governors at the sufferance of Rome. As Henry Dosker says,

> The history of the Herodian family is not lacking in elements of greatness, but whatever these elements were and in whomsoever found, they were in every case dimmed by the insufferable egotism which disfigured the family, root and branch. Some of the Herodian princes were undeniably talented; but these talents, wrongly used, left no marks for the good of the people of Israel. Of nearly all the kings of the house of Herod, it may truly be said that at their death "they went without being desired,"

> unmissed, unmourned. The entire family history is one of incessant brawls, suspicion, intrigue, and shocking immorality.[27]

The Herodian kings began their rule by exterminating the Hasmonean descendants of the Maccabees, thus eliminating rivals to the throne but also incurring the incessant hatred of Jewish loyalists. Antipas reigned from 47–43 BC, and after an interlude of instability his son Herod the Great reigned from 37 BC–AD 4, chiefly remembered for his inquiry of the Magi as to the birthplace of the Messiah (Matthew 2:1–21). After his death his son Herod Archelaus ruled Judea and his other son Herod Antipas ruled Galilee until AD 39; he it was who beheaded John the Baptist on the demand of his stepdaughter Salome (Matthew 14:3–12) and before whom Jesus appeared during His trial (Luke 23:7–12). There followed Herod Agrippa I (AD 39–44) and Herod Agrippa II who died in AD 100, his kingdom having practically ceased to exist after the fall of Jerusalem in AD 70.

But despite all their ego and pomp, the Herodian kings ruled only at the sufferance of Rome and could exercise no powers other than those allowed them by Rome.

To understand the relationship between the Herodian kings and the Roman governors or procurators such as Pontius Pilate, one might look to the American judicial system and compare the federal district courts to the 50 state judicial systems. State judges and justices are elected by the people of their states or appointed by state officals, while federal judges are nominated by the President and confirmed by the U.S. Senate.

State courts follow state law but sometimes have to yield to the supremacy of the U.S. Constitution and federal law. Federal courts follow federal law but sometimes, as in contract matters, recognize the law of the state in which the transaction took place. Federal courts are under the U.S. Courts of Appeal, which in turn are under the United States Supreme Court. Relations between federal and state courts are usually harmonious, but sometimes they can be strained, as during the Reconstruction Era in the South.

The Herodian kings and their administrations were similar to state judicial systems. They came to power independently of Rome, although

27. Henry E. Dosker, *International Standard Bible Encyclopedia*, "Herod." James Orr, *The International Standard Bible Encyclopedia* (Howard-Severance, 1915), III: 1378.

they were not really Jewish but Idumean,[28] but Rome could eliminate or replace them at will. For example, Herod Archelaus incurred such animosity because of his oppressive rule and his conflicts with the Pharisees that, in a rare display of unity, Jews and Samaritans petitioned to Rome for his removal, and Rome removed him in AD 6.

By contrast, Pilate and other procurators were appointed by Rome and governed the Roman province of Judea, under the larger province of Syria. They were answerable to Rome, not to Judea; however, Rome wanted a peaceful empire and would not look kindly upon a Roman governor who could not get along with his Jewish subjects. The procurator's responsibilities were to maintain law and order through military power, collect taxes, supervise the administration of the province, and administer justice. Procurators followed primarily Roman law but also occasionally recognized local law, as when Pilate, following Jewish custom, allowed the Jews to choose one prisoner for release on the Passover, hoping they would choose Jesus rather than Barabbas (Luke 23:13–25).

The Sanhedrin

The Sanhedrin was a governing body, perhaps similar to the English House of Lords. Its origin may be found in the Council of Seventy Elders established by Moses (Numbers 11:16) and reconstituted by King Jehoshaphat (2 Chronicles 19:8), but its function varied over the centuries.

The Sanhedrin was composed of seventy-one judges, including the presiding High Priest, and they consisted of scribes and priests known for their knowledge of Jewish law. They were divided into three smaller sanhedrins of 23 judges each, which carried out more specialized functions, and when they met together they were known as the Great Sanhedrin. They passed judgment on religious matters and also on civil and criminal cases, and may have functioned as a senate or lawmaking body as well. They had the power to order arrests and had their own officers to carry out those arrests. After the Romans came to power in Judea, the Sanhedrin no longer had the power to sentence a person to death without the approval of the Roman procurator (John 18:31).

The Sanhedrin employed procedures that protected the rights of the accused, many of which were from Old Testament law. One member of the Sanhedrin was directed to present the evidence and arguments for his

28. The Idumeans or Edomites were descendants of Esau, son of Isaac and Rebecca and brother of Jacob. They lived in the land of Edom which was southeast of Judea.

guilt, another the evidence and arguments for his innocence. The accused was not required to incriminate himself, and he could not be convicted except on the testimony of two or three witnesses whose testimony did not contradict one another. If a witness committed perjury, he was subject to the same punishment the accused could have received if he had been found guilty; perjury in a capital case could be punished with death. A guilty verdict in a capital case had to be unanimous, and the Sanhedrin was required to deliberate again the following day. Between the two deliberations a crier was sent out to proclaim, "__________ has been found guilty of ____________; if anyone knows anything to clear him, let him come forward and declare it!"[29] Unlike many judicial systems, the Hebrew system was prepared to discover its errors and correct them.

The Sanhedrin was a tool used by the procurators and tetrarchs to administer justice, but it also served as a check on the rulers' power. For example, after Herod Archelaus murdered a large group of Pharisees, he was arraigned before the Sanhedrin, but he managed to intimidate most of the Sanhedrin with his royal power.

The Religious Authorities

Israel was, so far as this author is able to determine, the first nation in world history to practice separation of church[30] and state in the proper sense of the term, that is, as separate institutions. In most other nations the state was considered divine and kings were gods or demigods or descended from gods. But the Jews believed differently: the state was ordained by God, but the state was not god itself. That distinction is vital to a proper understanding of Jewish and Christian political theory.

Israel's kings came from the Tribe of Judah and the priests came from the Tribe of Levi. King Saul's line was cut off from the kingship of Israel because he usurped the function of the priesthood by offering sacrifices himself instead of waiting for the priest Samuel to do so (1 Samuel 15). King Uzziah was smitten with leprosy because he entered the sanctuary of the Temple and offered sacrifices, seemingly exercising his royal prerogative but actually usurping the function of the priests (2 Chronicles 26:16–22).

---

29. J. Oscar Boyd, *International Standard Bible Encyclopedia,* "Sanhedrin" James Orr, *The International Standard Bible Encyclopedia* (Howard-Severance, 1915), IV: 2690.

30. The term *church* is used in the loose sense to denote religious authorities and institutions.

But the separation was not absolute. The first chief judge of Israel, Moses was a priest from the Tribe of Levi. King David divided the priests into 24 courses, each of which served a two-week period in the Temple each year (1 Chronicles 24).[31] It appears from 1 Chronicles 29:22 that the general assembly chose the high priest. King Jehoshaphat reformed both the civil government and the priesthood. He appointed new judges and told them, *"Take heed what ye do: for ye judge not for man, but for the Lord, who is with you in the judgment. Wherefore now let the fear of the Lord be upon you; take heed and do it: for there is no iniquity with the Lord our God, nor respect of persons, nor taking of gifts"* (2 Chronicles 19:6–7). He also reconstituted the priesthood and gave them judicial functions (2 Chronicles 19:8–10), and he declared,

> *And behold, Amariah the chief priest is over you in all matters of the Lord; and Zebadiah the son of Ishmael, the ruler of the house of Judah, for all the king's matters: also the Levites shall be officers before you. Deal courageously, and the Lord shall be with the good* (2 Chronicles 19:11).

The very fact that the king establishes the judges and priests demonstrates that the separation is not complete, but it is clear: Amariah the chief priest is in charge of religious matters, and Zebadiah of the house of Judah is in charge of the king's matters.

The Priests

The priests were limited to descendants of Aaron, who was in turn descended from Levi. Their functions were to take care of the tabernacle (later the Temple) and its furniture, to offer sacrifices to God on behalf of the people, to bestow God's blessings upon the people, to lead in congregational worship, and to teach the people about God and his precepts. At times they also performed judicial functions, not surprisingly because the civil and criminal law was the Law of God.

In all of these ways, the priests served as mediators between God and His people, a conduit through which God bestowed His blessings upon

31. Noting that Zacharias was a priest after the order of Abia (Luke 1:5), that a vision came to him during his Temple service that his wife Elizabeth would conceive, and that Jesus was conceived during the sixth month of Elizabeth's pregnancy with John the Baptist, some believe it is possible to ascertain the approximate date of Christ's birth by looking to the courses of the priesthood.

the people. By delegating these functions to the priests rather than to the kings and their deputies, the Mosaic system made the priesthood into a check upon the power of the state. Throughout history, the two kingdoms concept of separation of church and state has been a limit upon state power.

The Prophets

In civil matters, power was separated between the king and the legislative institutions such as the Sanhedrin and the Congregation of Israel, and between the national government of Israel and the governments of the twelve tribes. In religious matters, power was separated between the priests and another institution, the prophets.

We commonly think of prophets as those who can foretell the future, but in Scripture prophecy also has the function of "forthtelling" or exhortation to righteousness. Unlike the priests who received their offices by inheritance, prophets were called by God regardless of their family or ancestry.

The prophets preached to the people about God's righteousness. In this way their function overlapped with that of the priests; but whereas the priests' preaching and teaching was fairly routine, the prophets focused upon particular sins of the people. Prophets often singled out influential people for their special exhortations, such as Samuel with King Saul (1 Samuel 15), Nathan with King David (2 Samuel 12), or Isaiah to King Hezekiah (Isaiah 39), and their messages were sometimes creative, symbolic, or inflammatory. They generally supported the priests, but they could be critical of priests who had become corrupt, heretical, or apostate. They could even be critical of their fellow prophets: *"The heads thereof judge for reward, and the priests thereof teach for hire, and the prophets thereof divine for money…"* (Micah 3:11); *"For both prophet and priest are profane; yea, in my house have I found their wickedness, saith the LORD"* (Jeremiah 23:11).

The Rabbis

During the Babylonian Captivity (appr. 605–535 BC), the Temple sacrifices ceased because the Jews no longer had access to the Temple in Jerusalem. After the Jews returned from Babylon, the sacrifices resumed, but the priests had lost much of their earlier authority. A class of teachers arose known as rabbis, and they assumed most of the responsibility for teaching the Law even though they were not necessarily priests or descendants of Levi. The term *rabbi* can refer to one who was ordained into a special class of rabbis, but more broadly it can be used for any respected teacher of the Law. The Torah and the *Talmud* were the basis for the civil and criminal law, so the rabbis functioned both as lawyers and as theologians and were often called scribes.

Some rabbis, because of their expert knowledge of the Law, were referred to as *nomikos;* one such lawyer asked Jesus, *"Master, what is the great commandment in the law?"* (Matthew 22:35–36). In Luke 11:45–52 Jesus condemned the *nomikos* for burdening the people with the extra-Biblical commands of the *Talmud* and hindering them from the true knowledge of God. In Titus 3:13 Paul mentions another *nomikos* as a follower of Christ. These lawyers were teachers of the Law and also served as judges to decide questions of the Law in rabbinical councils.

As noted in Chapter 14, the scribes and lawyers often disagreed on the interpretation of the Law. Out of these disagreements arose two schools, that of the Pharisees and that of the Sadducees. The Pharisees believed the Law should be interpreted literally, while the Sadducees favored a more loose or liberal interpretation. The Pharisees believed in a resurrection and judgment after death; the Sadducees did not believe in life after death. The Pharisees wanted to maintain Jewish culture and tradition and opposed Hellenization or accommodation to Greek culture; the Sadducees were enamored of Greek culture and sought absorption into Hellenistic ways. The Pharisees and Sadducees struggled for control of the Sanhedrin and, even more, for the hearts and minds of the Jewish people.

The essence of the Hebrew system was, "no king in Israel but God Himself." God and His Law were supreme in the Hebrew vision, and no man or human institution could be allowed to usurp the place of God and His Law. Unlike the totalitarian monarchies that surrounded Israel, the Hebrews established a decentralized republic of twelve confederated tribes. Over time, it is the nature of human institutions to centralize power, and the Hebrews' confederate republic became a more centralized monarchy which grew in power. Even so, the system contained checks and balances to restrain power: Civic and religious institutions were separated though not completely so. Religious authority was shared by priests and prophets; the king's civil powers were checked by the twelve tribal governments represented in the Congregation of Israel. And among all of these institutions stood the Great Sanhedrin.

The corruptions of human nature will inevitably corrode any system of government, and the Hebrew system was no exception. But thirty-four centuries have passed since Moses received God's Law on Mt. Sinai and taught His precepts to His people, and during this time, even during dispersion and under foreign domination, the Jews have preserved their identity and remained a free people under God. In this none has surpassed them. Few have even come close.

Questions for Reflection, Discussion, and More Reflection

1. Explain in what ways Israel followed the universal trend toward centralization of power. As you look at history, are there any nations that are exceptions to this trend? If so, how did they manage to resist it?
2. What kind of government do we see among the patriarchs of Israel, Abraham, Isaac, and Jacob? What evidence do we have of the laws and customs that prevailed in the Middle East at that time?
3. How much of their knowledge of God, their Jewish laws and customs, and their structure of government did the Israelites retain while they were slaves in Egypt?
4. What does the term *theocracy* mean, and in what sense was Israel a theocracy? Why did God establish Israel as a theocracy? Is it His intent that every nation should be a theocracy, or was Israel unique in this regard?
5. How were the legislative, executive, and judicial functions of government apportioned during the era of the judges? How did this change during the era of the kings? In what ways was Israel better off under the republic? Under the monarchy? Do you believe it was God's will that Israel have a king?

6. Trace the events that lead to the secession of the northern tribes under Jeroboam. What is meant by the term *interposition?* Is it ever justified? Was it justified in the instance of Jeroboam and the ten northern tribes of Israel?
7. In the history of Israel and Judah, why do liberty and order seem to go hand-in-hand with godliness, while tyranny and violence accompany apostasy and idolatry?
8. After the ten northern tribes of Israel were taken captive to Assyria in 721 BC, what do you think happened to them? After the people of Judah were taken captive to Babylon in 605 BC and then allowed to return to Palestine around 538 BC, how was their system of government changed?
9. Explain the rise of the Herodian kings. What was their relationship to the Romans and to the Roman governors such as Pontius Pilate?
10. What was the Sanhedrin, and how did its criminal trials protect the rights of the accused? How was their authority limited by the Roman governors? Explain the rise of the rabbis and their relationship to the Levitical priesthood. Who were the Pharisees and Sadducees, and how did they differ?

Moses receives the Law of God.
F. W. McCleave & Co., ca. 1877.

CHAPTER 15

THE PRECEPTS OF HEBREW LAW: *One God = One Law*

We have looked at the genesis or beginnings of Hebrew Law, the documents in which Hebrew Law is found, and the institutions which implemented and enforced Hebrew Law. Now we will examine the Hebrew Law itself,[1] as it is found in the Torah.[2]

Like most ancient societies, the Hebrews attributed their laws to a higher source, i.e., to the God Jehovah who revealed them to Moses. But unlike most others, the Hebrews believed Jehovah is a God of perfect justice and perfect righteousness. His laws are not just arbitrary and capricious

1. Several legal scholars have examined the Old Testament law in detail, and their writings have been helpful. E. C. Wines's classic work, *Commentaries on the Laws of the Ancient Hebrews* (1853; reprinted by American Vision, 2009), has already been noted. H.B. Clark, in *Biblical Law, Being a Text of the Statutes, Ordinances, and Judgments Established in the Holy Bible–with Many Allusions to Secular Laws–Ancient, Medieval, and Modern–Documented to the Scriptures, Judicial Decisions, and Legal Literature* (1943; reprinted by American Vision, 2010), organized his discussion along modern legal categories such as political law, civil law (property, contracts, trespass, and domestic relations), economics and welfare, general laws, penal law, procedure and administration. Edward J. White, in *The Law in the Scriptures, with Explanations of the Law Terms and Legal References in Both the Old and the New Testaments* (Law Book Exchange: 1935, 2000), examined each book of the Bible from Genesis through Revelation and explained the legal concepts found in each. J.W. Erlich, in *The Holy Bible and the Law* (Law Book Exchange, 1962, 2002), examined specific statutes of the Old Testament law, arranging them alphabetically. George Horowitz, in *The Spirit of Jewish Law: A Brief Account of Biblical and Rabbinical Jurisprudence with a Special Note on Jewish Law and the State of Israel* (Central Book Co., 1953), examined both the Old Testament Scriptures and the rabbinical traditions and scholarship from Biblical times to the present. And R. J. Rushdoony's 3-volume *Institutes of Biblical Law* (Presbyterian & Reformed Pub. Co., 1973), ably presents a Calvinist and Christian Reconstructionist approach to Biblical Law. All of these works and others have been helpful in developing this chapter.

2. Some contend that Jewish law has continued to unfold and develop through the ages, and that the Torah represents only the beginning of Jewish law. The focus of this section of this book is upon Hebrew Law as it is found in the first five books of the Bible, so the development of Jewish law after the completion of the Torah will not be considered here. Two works that trace the subsequent development of Jewish law are George Horowitz, *The Spirit of Jewish Law,* described in footnote 1 above; and John Henry Wigmore, *A Panorama of the World's Legal Systems* (West Publishing Co., 1928), I: 98–134.

commands; they reflect His just and righteous character. David said *"The law of the LORD is perfect, converting the soul," "The statutes of the LORD are right, rejoicing the heart,"* and *"the commandment of the LORD is pure, enlightening the eyes"* (Psalm 19:7, 8). Paul declared that the law and the commandment are *"holy, and just, and good"* (Romans 7:12). Each of His laws reflects and teaches us something of His righteous and just character. Hebrew Law is thoroughly infused with an ethical dimension.

PREMISES OF HEBREW LAW

All legal systems are based upon fundamental premises or assumptions. The following assumptions underlie the Hebrew legal system:

1. **God exists, and He is one God, omnipotent, omniscient, omnipresent, righteous, just, truthful, immutable, and loving.** E. C. Wines, in his classic *Commentaries on the Laws of the Ancient Hebrews,* described this principle as the "**unity of God**,"[3] and it has profound implications for law and government. Unlike pagan and polytheistic systems in which different gods might issue different and conflicting laws or commands, the unity of God means that His laws will be consistent and harmonious with one another. Wines wrote,

> All the ancient lawgivers called in the aid of religion to strengthen their respective polities. Thus did Menes in Egypt; Minos in Crete; Cadmus in Thebes; Lycurgus in Sparta; Zaleucus in Locris; and Numa in Rome.
>
> But the procedure of Moses differed fundamentally from that of these heathen legislators. They employed religion in establishing their political institutions, while he made use of a civil constitution as a means of perpetuating religion. Thus Moses made the worship of the one and only God the fundamental law of his civil institutions. This law was to remain forever unalterable, through all the changes, which lapse of time might introduce into his constitution.[4]

3. Wines, 393ff. The Jewish concept of the unity of God does not conflict with the Christian doctrine of the Trinity, which teaches that God is three in personality (Father, Son, and Holy Spirit) but one in essence. Many Christians believe the doctrine of the Trinity is foreshadowed, though not expressly stated, in the Old Testament by the use of the plural *Elohim* for God and by references to the Redeemer (Job 19:25) and to the Spirit of God (Genesis 1:2).

4. Wines, 394–95.

Having brought the Hebrews out of bondage in Egypt and having led them into a land flowing with milk and honey that He gave them (Exodus 3:8), God was rightfully the Hebrews' king. As such, apostasy and blasphemy against Him were akin to treason. The late mythologist Joseph Campbell stated the difference succinctly: To the pagans, the gods were *symbols;* to the Hebrews, God was a *fact.*[5]

2. **God is the Source of all true law.** (Isaiah 33:22: *"For the Lord is our judge, the Lord is our lawgiver, the Lord is our king; he will save us."*) This premise, closely related to the first, implies that any law or command which is contrary to the law of God is invalid. In Ezekiel 20:24, 25, God says of His people, *"Because they... had despised my statutes," "I gave them also statutes that were not good."* But this should be interpreted in the sense of God's permissive will rather than His directive will; Rotherham translates this passage, "I myself indeed suffered them to walk in statutes which were not good."

3. **Law reflects the will and character of God.** (Psalm 19:7: *"The law of the Lord is perfect, converting the soul: the testimony of the Lord is sure, making wise the simple."*) Laws issued by pagan gods might be arbitrary, capricious, whimisical, and unreasonable, but God's laws reflect His character of truth, righteousness, and justice.

4. **God's justice requires punishment for sin.** (Ezekiel 18:4, 20: *"The soul that sinneth, it shall die."*) Because God's attributes include perfect righteousness and perfect justice, He does not simply overlook sin. His law requires punishment. In Old Testament Israel, the Levitical priests offered sacrifices as substitutionary atonement for sin. New Testament Christianity teaches that Jesus Christ died on the Cross as our substitutionary atonement. In this way sacrifice in Christianity and Judaism is fundamentally different from sacrifice in other religions. In most religions the purpose of sacrifice is to gain the favor of the gods or to appease their anger. In Christianity and Judaism the purpose of sacrifice is to satisfy God's justice.

5. **Man is created in God's image.** (Genesis 9:6: *"Whoso sheddeth man's blood, by man shall his blood be shed: for in the image of God made he man."*) Because he is created in God's image, he has human dignity, and his life has infinite value. (Psalm 8:5: *"For thou hast made him a little lower than the angels, and hast crowned him with glory and honour."*) Man's

5. Joseph Campbell, *The World of Joseph Campbell: Transformations of Myth Through Time* (HighBridge Productions, 1990), Vol. II Lecture 3.

creation in the image of God is a basis for the doctrine of human rights, because that which is created in God's image possesses human dignity, and certain rights go naturally with that dignity.

6. **Ever since the Fall, man has been and continues to be sinful.** (Psalm 51:5: *"Behold, I was shapen in iniquity; and in sin did my mother conceive me."* Isaiah 53:6: *"All we like sheep have gone astray; we have turned every one to his own way; and the LORD hath laid on him the iniquity of us all."*) While there is variation within Jewish thought just as there is within Christian thought, modern Judaism generally teaches that sin involves missing the mark or coming short of God's standards of righteousness. The Hebrew concept of sin generally has not fully embraced the Christian doctrine of original sin (that all men since Adam and Eve have been born with a sinful nature). But the Hebrews were fully cognizant of man's imperfections, and this doctrine profoundly affects the Hebrew concept of law and government. Hebrew thought would reject utopian schemes based upon the perfectibility of human nature, just as it would reject totalitarian systems built upon the absolute power of one imperfect ruler.

7. **God has established human government to punish crime and preserve order** (Romans 13:1–7).[6] The function of government is not to engage in social engineering or income redistribution. The function of government is to protect ordered liberty against foreign invasion and domestic crime. Israel enjoyed such protection under the judges and under the limited monarchy of Saul and David, but government veered toward absolutism under Solomon and the kingdom was divided thereafter.

8. **Before government may punish crime, great precautions must be taken to ensure that no one is wrongly convicted.** In most pagan systems, the individual person is of miniscule value compared to that of society and the state. As rulers seek to advance the public interest, which they commonly identify with their own interests, it matters little if individual lives are sacrificed in the process. Likewise, as judges try to preserve law and order by punishing criminals, they care little if innocent persons are convicted and innocent lives are ruined in the process.

But the Hebrew view was and is different. Because all men, criminals included, are created in God's image, all men possess human dignity

6. Although Paul (formerly called Saul) was a New Testament writer, he had been a lawyer or Pharisee thoroughly trained in the Jewish law, having been educated in the highly prestigious law school of the Rabbi Gamaliel (Acts 22:3).

and infinite value. For this reason, the law must be exceedingly careful to ensure that innocent persons are not wrongly convicted, and the human dignity even of guilty persons must be respected. As will be seen later in this chapter, the Hebrew system of criminal justice therefore provided protections for criminal defendants far beyond those of nearly any other system in the world.[7]

9. **Once a defendant's guilt is proven, punishment is appropriate.** But even the guilty defendant was entitled to certain protections because of the dignity that resulted from his creation in the image of God, and punishment had to be appropriate for the crime.

10. **The Hebrews were a unified people.** Even though they were divided into twelve tribes, each person regardless of tribe was an equal citizen of the Hebrew republic. Unlike most pagan societies, theoretically at least there were no class distinctions among the Hebrew people. The Levitical priests were set aside for religious purposes, but they were not considered to be a superior or privileged class. The law applied to all classes equally, and no one was above the law (Leviticus 24:22). According to John Bright, "Israel's law in no way reflects the stratification of Canaanite feudal society."[8]

11. **The family was the basic unit of society.** The family unit begins with Adam and Eve and their children, and the commandments *"Honour thy father and thy mother"* and *"Thou shalt not commit adultery"* reenforce the family unit. Strong penalties were attached to smiting (Exodus 21:15) or disobeying (Deuteronomy 21:18–21)[9] a parent, and the law also imposed strong obligations upon parents toward their children (Deuteronomy 6:3–9). Many have argued that all governmental authority stems from delegated parental authority.

7. As we shall see later, the Anglo-Saxon system of criminal justice also provided strong protections for the criminal defendant, even though the pre-Christian Anglo-Saxons lacked a theological and philosophical basis for protecting individual rights. The common law that we cherish resulted from a fusion of Biblical theology and Anglo-Saxon law based upon ancient principles of the Law of Nature.

8. John Bright, *A History of Israel 4th Ed.* (Westminster John Knox Press, 2000), 173.

9. Stoning a child for disobedience sounds severe, but (1) the text implies continual and habitual disobedience, not a single disobedient act; (2) the reference to the child being a *"glutton and a drunkard"* suggests that the child is a young adult, not a small child; (3) the father and mother must agree on this course of action; (4) the parents must have first chastised the child to no avail; and (5) the parents must bring the child to the tribunal. This passage of Scripture provides no basis for the state to intervene in family relations except to support and buttress parental authority. Also, many believe this penalty was seldom if ever actually carried out.

12. **Government was by the consent of the governed.** After descending from Mount Sinai, Moses read the laws of God to the Hebrew people. They ratified this system of laws by saying, *"All that the LORD has spoken will we do"* (Exodus 19:8). As Wines said, "The Hebrew constitution was adopted by the Hebrew people, as truly as the American constitution was adopted by the American people."[10]

Likewise, those who held public office, from the highest to the lowest, were responsible to the people. At the close of his judgeship, as Samuel prepared to hand the reins of government over to King Saul, he addressed the congregation of Israel:

> *And Samuel said unto all Israel, Behold, I have hearkened unto your voice in all that ye said unto me, and have made a king over you.*
>
> *And now, behold, the king walketh before you: and I am old and grayheaded; and, behold, my sons are with you: and I have walked before you from my childhood unto this day.*
>
> *Behold, here I am: witness against me before the LORD, and before his anointed: whose ox have I taken? or whose ass have I taken? or whom have I defrauded? whom have I oppressed? or of whose hand have I received any bribe to blind mine eyes therewith? and I will restore it you.*
>
> *And they said, Thou hast not defrauded us, nor oppressed us, neither hast thou taken ought of any man's hand.*
>
> *And he said unto them, The LORD is witness against you, and his anointed is witness this day, that ye have not found ought in my hand. And they answered, He is witness.* (1 Samuel 12:1–5)

In part, Samuel may have been trying to reassure himself that the people had not rejected him in choosing a king. But in a larger sense his statement was a recognition that he governed by popular consent[11] and he was accountable to the people.

---

10. Wines, 407.

11. cf. U.S. Declaration of Independence (1776), "derived their just powers from the consent of the governed. . . ."

13. **The Hebrews respected the dignity of labor.** In the pagan societies that surrounded Israel, aristocrats felt no compunction to engage in labor, and they looked down upon those who performed labor. In contrast, the Hebrews respected labor, particularly agricultural labor, because all true wealth ultimately comes from the land or the sea. The prophet Amos declared, *"Woe to them that are at ease in Zion, ... [t]hat lie upon beds of ivory, and stretch themselves upon their couches, ..."* (Amos 6:1, 4). In the Book of Proverbs the *"sluggard"* is repeatedly admonished to correct his ways (6:6, 6:9, 10:26, 13:4, 20:4, 26:16).

14. **The Hebrews placed high value on education.** We saw in Chapter 13 that the Hebrews were considered the "people of the Book," that literacy was widespread among them, and that education centered around the books of the Bible. For adults, education included the public reading of the Mosaic Law every seventh year (Deuteronomy 31:12–13), covenant renewal enactments (Deuteronomy 29–30; Joshua 23–24), and periodic national festivals in which Israel's history and traditions were taught. The Hebrews knew that an educated populace made free republican government possible.

15. **The Hebrews valued liberty, and their legal institutions were designed to promote and protect liberty.** *"Proclaim liberty throughout all the land unto all the inhabitants thereof"* (Leviticus 25:10). As Wines stated,

> ... nowhere, without the limits of Palestine, was there to be found a rational, well-poised and well-guarded public freedom; and ... all antiquity does not afford an example of a state, where the people enjoyed any just influence in the government, till we come to the Jewish republic.[12]

As it is used in the Old Testament, the term liberty has various contexts: national independence as when Israel was led out of bondage in Egypt to freedom as an independent state, freedom from servitude in the year of Jubilee, and freedom from oppressive burdens. Liberty is also found in the commands of the Mosaic Law, which are mostly negative: the positive command "thou shalt" obligates one to do exactly what is commanded and nothing else; the negative command "thou shalt not" means the hearer is free to do anything except the one thing that is prohibited.

12. Wines, 341–42.

But the modern idea that freedom means doing whatever you want to do would have been utterly foreign to the Hebrews, as to most people throughout history. James Orr wrote,

> ...liberty consists, not simply in external freedom, or in possession of the formal power of choice, but in deliverance from the darkening of the mind, the tyranny of sinful lusts, and the enthrallment of the will, induced by a morally corrupt state. In a positive respect, it consists in the possession of holiness, with the will and ability to do what is right and good. Such liberty is possible only in a renewed condition of soul, and cannot exist apart from godliness.[13]

Western jurisprudence is generally divided into criminal law and civil law. Modern criminal law involves crimes against the state, which the state must punish to establish justice, to keep criminals under restraint, to rehabilitate criminals, and to deter others from committing similar crimes. Civil law usually involves acts that have injured other people, often by negligence rather than by deliberate intent, and the goal of the court is to do justice by providing restitution to the injured party. Restitution is usually defined as putting the injured party in the same position he would have been, had the injury not occurred.

In Hebrew jurisprudence the distinction between criminal law and civil law is less clear, because the common penalty for most offenses is restitution. Nevertheless, some criminal offenses are found in the Hebrew system, and they involve distinctive punishments and procedures.

HEBREW CRIMINAL JURISPRUDENCE

Because man is created in God's image, he possesses human dignity even though he has fallen into sin. For this reason, great caution must be taken to ensure that he is not punished unjustly for a crime he did not commit, and in some respects his dignity must be respected even if he is found guilty.

Responsibility for sin is both an individual and a corporate responsibility, in that the entire nation may be held responsible for the sin of one person, and the entire nation may reap the natural or divinely-caused

---

13. Orr, James, "Liberty," *International Standard Bible Encyclopedia* (Eerdman, 1939), III: 1881.

consequences of sin. But criminal punishment was meted out by the Hebrew judicial system, only upon the individual who committed the crime:

> *The fathers shall not be put to death for the children, neither shall the children be put to death for the fathers: every man shall be put to death for his own sin.*
> (Deuteronomy 24:16)

As G. Ernest Wright explains,

> Such a law as this seems superfluous in modern society when the individual is the primary unit and the sense of community solidarity is weak or entirely lacking. In patriarchal and semi-nomadic life, however, the sense of community responsibility was very strong, particularly that of the family. A nomadic blood feud could annihilate a whole family for a crime of one of its members.[14]

Protections for Criminal Defendants

Because punishment for crime must not be administered without individual guilt, the Hebrew system required strict procedures for determining guilt. First, six *cities of refuge* were established, three on each side of the River Jordan, to which homicide suspects could flee and in which they could reside until their guilt or innocence was determined (Numbers 35; Deuteronomy 19:1–13; Joshua 20). These were necessary because the common custom in the ancient world was that if a person were murdered, that person's nearest relative had a duty to avenge their kinsman by slaying the murderer. The *cities of refuge* ensured that no vengeance could be taken before the suspect had the benefit of due process of law.

Judges must be honest and not take bribes (Exodus 23:1–8). Despite this command, the prophets repeatedly condemned the judges for violating it (Amos 5:12; 1 Samuel 8:3).

14. G. Ernest Wright, "Deuteronomy," *Interpreter's Bible,* II: 476f. We may think of the example of Achan (Joshua 7), whose entire family was stoned to death with him because he had kept certain spoils from the conquered city of Jericho in violation of God's command to destroy everything. However, as R.J. Rushdoony notes, Achan had kept these spoils in the family tent, meaning the entire family must have been accomplices to this offense (Rushdoony I: 269). Others see the execution of Achan and his family as a ritual cleansing whereby Israel put uncleanness out from among them.

Testimony must be corroborated (2 or 3 witnesses) (Deut. 17:6; 19:15; Numbers 35:30). If two or more witnesses agree, the likelihood of error is reduced; two or more witnesses could also lie or be mistaken, but requiring two or more witnesses to testify consistently lessened the possibility of error.

The penalty for perjury was the penalty the accused would have received had he been found guilty. If the accused was on trial for a capital offense, the penalty for perjury was death (Deut. 19:16–21).

Extra-Biblical Jewish law provided further protections: the court had a quorum requirement; the accused had a right to counsel; the accused was entitled to the privilege against self-incrimination. If the court adjudged the death penalty, they had to deliberate again on another day to ensure that was still their decision.

The Hebrew Concept of Criminal Guilt

As in Anglo-American law, Hebrew Law normally required both a *mens rea* (guilty mind) and an *actus reus* (guilty act) as prerequisites for a crime. In other words, the criminal defendant normally could not be found guilty unless he had a criminal intent as well as a criminal act. One might contemplate a crime in his mind and even decide to commit the crime, but he could not be guilty of a crime unless he acted upon that intent in some way.[15]

Conversely, an act without criminal intent might constitute a tort and provide the basis for a civil lawsuit, but it is not sufficient to justify a criminal condition. An accidental killing, if it involves negligence, might result in a lawsuit for damages,[16] but it does not constitute murder. However, extreme negligence, sometimes defined as a reckless, wanton, man-endangering state of mind, can provide the basis for a criminal conviction

15. However, one need not have completed the crime to satisfy the *mens rea* element. An intent to commit murder, coupled with carrying out certain steps toward the completion of the murder, might be sufficient to constitute attempted murder. Asking someone to commit the murder for you might constitute solicitation of murder, and planning with others to commit murder, coupled with some step toward completion, may constitute conspiracy to commit murder. In the opinion of this writer, the comparatively recent doctrine of strict liability, by which one can be guilty of certain crimes without criminal intent or even negligence, has no place in Anglo-American law.

16. A damage award in a civil lawsuit is intended to compensate the injured party for the damages he has suffered due to the defendant's negligence, and to put the plaintiff in the position he would be had the defendant's negligent act not occurred. Punitive and exemplary damages are an exception to this principle and, in the opinion of this writer, belong in the criminal courts rather than the civil courts.

for a lesser offense such as second-degree murder, manslaughter, or negligent homicide. Consider Exodus 21:28–29:

> *If an ox gore a man or a woman, that they die: then the ox shall be surely stoned, and his flesh shall not be eaten; but the owner of the ox shall be quit [acquitted].*
>
> *But if the ox were wont to push with his horn in time past, and it hath been testified to his owner, and he hath not kept him in, but that he hath killed a man or woman; the ox shall be stoned, and his owner also shall be put to death.*

Even though the ox gored a person to death, the owner is not liable if he had no reason to believe the ox was dangerous. But if the ox has gored people on previous occasions, and the owner knows this, his failure or refusal to restrain the ox constitutes such reckless indifference to the lives and safety of others that it is punishable criminally.[17]

Likewise, Deuteronomy 22:8 provides that

> *When thou buildest a new house, then thou shalt make a battlement [fence] for thy roof, that thou bring not blood upon thine house, if any man fall from thence.*

Houses in ancient Israel had flat roofs, and people often used their roofs for sleeping and other activities. One therefore had a duty to provide for the safety of others by putting a fence on his roof. If he failed to do so and someone fell off his roof, he might be liable for civil damages in a tort lawsuit.

The degree of criminal guilt could vary with circumstances:

---

17. The stoning of the ox may seem strange to modern readers but must be understood in light of the special features of the Hebrew ceremonial law concerning ritual uncleanness (Numbers 35:33). Although not exactly guilty of a crime, the ox was considered *"unclean"* because of its involvement in the killing, and therefore the ox had to be removed from Israel, or Israel would be defiled by its presence. This may be the origin of the modern practice of civil forfeiture of the instrumentalities of a crime, e.g., a vehicle used to transport illegal drugs. An animal or object that was used to cause the death of another was called a "bane" or a "deodand," from the Latin *deo dandum,* meaning "to be given to God." Leonard W. Levy, *A License to Steal: The Forfeiture of Property* (U. of NC Press, 1996); Fletcher N. Baldwin, Jr., "United States and Civil *in rem* Forfeiture: The History and Its Ancient Roots," *Journal of Money Laundering Control* 2000:3:3, 204–213. Keil & Delitzsch contend that because this crime involved carelessness rather than intentional crime, the owner "was allowed to redeem his forfeited life by the payment of expiation money… 'according to all that was laid upon him,' sc. by the judge," 21: 31–32. C.F. Keil and F. Delitzsch, *Commentary on the Old Testament* (Eerdmans, 1975), I: 135–36.

> *If a thief be found breaking up, and be smitten that he die, there shall no blood be shed for him.*
>
> *If the sun be risen upon him, there shall be blood shed for him; for he should make full restitution; if he have nothing, then he shall be sold for his theft.* (Exodus 22:2–3)

Common law usually distinguished between burglary in the night-time and burglary in the daytime. Breaking into a house at night is a more serious offense than during the day, because it involved greater danger: the occupants may be startled in their sleep and believe themselves to be in physical danger of violence. The occupant may therefore kill a thief who breaks in at night and will not be liable for doing so. But *"if the sun be risen upon him,"* the occupant may not kill the thief, because man is created in God's image and human life is of greater value than property.

Capital Murder

An intentional and unjustified killing of a person constituted murder and was punishable by death. This precept preceded the Mosaic Law. The Noahic covenant of Genesis 9 provided in v. 6, *"Whoso sheddeth man's blood, by man shall his blood be shed: for in the image of God made he man."* The reason for the command is that human life is precious because man was created in the image of God. The Mosaic Law restates this commandment: *"He that smiteth a man, so that he die, shall be surely put to death"* (Exodus 21:12).[18]

Other capital offenses in Scripture include the following:

- Man-stealing (kidnapping and selling into slavery) (Exodus 21:16).
- Striking and reviling a parent (Exodus 21:15–17).
- Rape (Deuteronomy 22:25).
- Incest and other unnatural sex (Exodus 22:19; Leviticus 20:11, 14, 16).
- Some forms of unchastity (Deuteronomy 22:21–24).
- Witchcraft and other occult practices, including false prophecy (Exodus 22:18; Leviticus 20:27).

---

18. Some would argue that the Noahic Covenant applies universally to all humanity, while the Mosaic Covenant applies only to Israel, and therefore the Bible provides continual justification of capital punishment for murder based upon Genesis 9:6, but not necessarily for other offenses made capital by the Mosaic Law. See Herbert W. Titus, *God, Man, and Law: The Biblical Principles* (Institute in Basic Life Principles, 1994), 47–52.

- Idolatry (Leviticus 20:2; Deuteronomy 13:6–10; 17:2–7).
- Blasphemy (Leviticus 24:14–16, 23).
- Sabbath-breaking (Exodus 31:14; 35:2).
- Perjury in capital cases (Deuteronomy 19:16–19).

Wines listed seventeen capital offenses in Old Testament Israel, whereas the English law code of the 1600s made 148 offenses capital, including petty theft and trespass upon property.[19]

Some of these offenses, such as blasphemy, may seem minor to those for whom God is merely an abstract concept. But the Hebrews believed that Jehovah is very real, that His wrath is real, and that blasphemy against His Name could bring down His wrath upon the nation. They therefore employed the criminal justice system against blasphemy for their own protection.

The most common method of execution in Israel was stoning. This method involved the entire community and made the people realize the seriousness and somberness of what they were doing. The accusers and complaining witnesses were required to cast the first stones, followed by the rest of the community. Even though the condemned person may deserve death, the people were not to forget that they were taking the life of a fellow human being who, like them, had been created in the image of God.

Noncapital Offenses

Noncapital offenses were punished in a variety of ways, including by forfeiture of property for refusal to obey a governor's command to assemble (Ezra 10:8) and scourging with a limit of forty stripes (Deuteronomy 25:3) for miscellaneous offenses including some forms of fornication (Leviticus 19:20; Deuteronomy 22:18; 25:2).[20] The scourging was to take place at the direction of the judge and in the presence of the judge. The reason for the 40-stroke limit is clearly stated: *"Lest, if he should exceed, and beat him above these with many stripes, then thy brother should seem vile unto thee."* Excessive corporal punishment would have a dehumanizing effect on both parties. As Matthew Henry wrote,

19. Wines, 263.

20. The *Jamieson-Fausset-Brown Bible Commentary* suggests that scourging was the most common form of punishment in noncapital cases.

> Every punishment should be with solemnity, that those who see it may be filled with dread, and be warned not to offend in like manner. And though the criminals must be shamed as well as put to pain, for their warning and disgrace, yet care should be taken that they do not appear totally vile. Happy those who are chastened of the Lord to humble them, that they should not be condemned with the world to destruction.[21]

But the most common punishment for noncapital offenses was restitution. The *lex talionis* (law of like punishment) was stated simply, *"life for life, eye for eye, tooth for tooth, hand for hand, foot for foot, burning for burning, wound for wound, stripe for stripe,"* (Exodus 21:23–25; see generally Exodus 21–22). Some may think this sounds severe, but the principle was humane and fair: Let the punishment fit the crime. *"Life for life"* meant that murder was punishable by death, but the rest of the passage does not require amputation of eyes, teeth, hands, or feet. Rather, the law required the wrongdoer to reimburse the victim for the value of that which the wrongdoer had stolen, damaged, or destroyed. If the wrongdoer was unable to reimburse the victim, he could become the victim's bondservant until the next year of Jubilee (the year after every seventh sabbath year, or every 50th year). In this way the victim was made whole, insofar as possible, and the wrongdoer was given the opportunity to regain his dignity by making restitution to his victim.

---

21. *Matthew Henry's Concise Commentary on the Whole Bible,* Deuteronomy 25:1–3; www.biblestudytools.com/commentaries/matthew-henry-complete/deuteronomy/25.html (accessed 13 May, 2016). *Matthew Henry's Commentary on the Whole Bible in One Volume,* Deuteronomy 25:1–4 (Zondervan, 1961) states on page 105:

> A direction to the judges in scourging malefactors, v. 1–3.... A great many precepts we have met with, which have not any particular penalty annexed to them, the violation of most of which, according to the constant practice of the Jews, was punished by scourging,... The directions here given for the scourging of criminals are, 1. That it be done solemnly; not tumultuously through the streets, but in open court before the judge's face, and with so much deliberation as that the stripes might be numbered. The Jews say that while execution was in doing, the chief justice of the court read with a loud voice Deut. xxviii. 58, 59, and xxix. 9, and concluded with those words (Ps. lxxvii. 38). *But he, being full of compassion, forgave their iniquity.* Thus it was made a sort of religious act, and so much the more likely to reform the offender himself, and to be a warning to others. 2. That it be done in proportion to the crime.... 3. That how great soever the crime was the number of stripes should never exceed *forty,* v. 3. Forty *save one* was the common usage, as appears, 2 Cor. xi. 24.... They abated one either for fear of having miscounted... or because they would never go to the utmost rigour, or, because the execution was usually done with a whip of three lashes, so that thirteen stripes (each one being counted for three) made up thirty-nine, but one more by that reckoning would have been forty-two [emphasis original].

In some instances multiple restitution is required. Exodus 22:1 says, *"If a man shall steal an ox, or a sheep, and kill it, or sell it; he shall restore five oxen for an ox, and four sheep for a sheep."* In Leviticus 5:15–16 we read, *"If a soul commit a trespass, and sin through ignorance, in the holy things of the LORD; then he shall bring for his trespass unto the LORD a ram without blemish out of the flocks, with thy estimation by shekels of silver, after the shekel of the sanctuary, for a trespass offering: And he shall make amends for the harm that he hath done in the holy thing, and shall add the fifth part thereto."* He had to pay for what he had damaged and 20% in addition. We see the same principle in Exodus 22:7, Leviticus 6:4–5, Leviticus 24:21, Numbers 5:5–7, and 2 Samuel 12:6. Multiple restitution seems to have been required when the theft interfered with the victim's ability to pursue his occupation and make a living, like the theft of livestock, or theft of or damage to goods that were to be offered to God (Luke 19:8). Livestock breed and multiply, so theft of livestock deprived the owner of more than just the individual animal but the animal's progeny as well; theft of livestock therefore required multiple restitution.

Although there were exceptions, punishment was usually mandatory in Old Testament Israel:

> *Thou shalt not consent unto him, nor hearken unto him; neither shall thine eye pity him, neither shalt thou spare, neither shalt thou conceal him:*
>
> *But thou shalt surely kill him; thine hand shall be first upon him to put him to death, and afterwards the hand of all the people.*
>
> *And thou shalt stone him with stones, that he die....* (Deuteronomy 13:8–10; cf. 19:12–13, 21; 25:11–12)

The purposes for punishing criminals in Israel are similar to the reasons advanced for criminal punishment today:

Justice, or as some call it, retribution. When one commits a crime against another, an injustice has been done, and the scales of justice are imbalanced. To rebalance them, punishment is required. Paul says in Romans 13:4b that the civil ruler is the *"minister [servant] of God, a revenger to execute wrath upon him that doeth evil."*

Deterrence, that is, discouraging others from committing crimes. The knowledge that criminals are punished tends to discourage others from committing crimes. Although some say deterrence was not a reason for punishment in Jewish thought, Moses clearly says that a reason for punishing criminals is that *"all Israel shall hear, and fear"* (Deuteronomy 17:13, 21:21). Likewise Paul states in Romans 13:3 that *"rulers are not a terror to good works, but to the evil."*

Rehabilitation, that is, correcting criminal behavior so the wrongdoer will reform and become a law-abiding member of society. This writer has found no Scripture passage stating that rehabilitation is a purpose of criminal punishment, but many passages in Proverbs speak of disciplining a child for the purpose of correction (13:24; 22:15; 23:13, 14), so a similar principle might apply in criminal justice as well. One salient feature of Hebrew Law was that once the criminal's punishment was complete, he was welcomed as a fully-restored member of society—a refreshing contrast to today's system of criminal justice in which the convict's criminal record follows him for the rest of his life and frequently bars him from some types of employment and various civic rights.

Restraint. When criminals are executed, jailed,[22] shackled, or banished from the community, they cannot commit crimes upon innocent people. *"[S]o shalt thou put evil away from among you"* (Deuteronomy 21:21; cf. 17:7; 17:12).

Prevention of private vengeance. The principle of retribution, or vengeance, is so instilled in the human heart that if there were no criminal justice system, crime victims or their surviving relatives would seek to avenge their kinsmen, perhaps without affording a trial to determine guilt or innocence, leading to blood feuds that could last for generations. The *cities of refuge*, that we read about in Numbers 35:25–28 and other passages, were established as a haven of refuge to which those suspected of crimes could flee and remain safely until a court could determine guilt or innocence.

HEBREW CIVIL LAW

Just as the criminal law was concerned with punishing wrongdoers and protecting the innocent, the civil law sought to stabilize interpersonal

22. Interestingly, jails and prisons are utterly foreign to the Mosaic Law. Prisons are mentioned in the Bible but as institutions introduced by foreign powers. Joseph was jailed in Egypt and Jeremiah was confined in a cistern, apparently because there were no prisons in Judea. Micaiah was put in prison by the apostate King Ahab (1 Kings 22:27) and Hanani by King Asa (2 Chronicles 16:10), but this practice seems to have been adopted from foreign countries. In the New Testament, prisons are a Roman institution.

relations and ensure that people's rights and interests were protected. The civil law covered many aspects of life, so we will examine it category by category.

Property

The Hebrews believed they were in a unique covenant relationship with God, set forth in the covenant God made with Moses on behalf of his people, and that by this covenant God gave the land of Palestine to the Hebrew people, to be divided among the twelve tribes and further subdivided among the various clans and families that made up the twelve tribes. For this reason, individual ownership of real estate in Palestine was subject to certain conditions to ensure that title to land remained in the hands of the original tribes and families.

Just as every seventh day was the sabbath day for personal rest, every seventh year was the sabbath year during which the land was to lie fallow and rest. And after every seventh sabbath year, that is, after every 49th year, came the 50th year, the Year of Jubilee. *"The land shall not be sold forever: for the land is mine [God's]"* (Leviticus 25:23); in the Year of Jubilee all debts were canceled, all bondservants were set free, and all land reverted to its original family owners. One who was not of the original family could not purchase clear title to real estate; he could purchase only a conditional title subject to reversion in the Year of Jubilee, and it is reasonable to assume that the cost of purchasing such an interest varied according to the length of time until the next Year of Jubilee.

Personal property, however—livestock, grain, timber, clothing, jewels, and all other property except real estate—was subject to individual ownership and could be bought and sold much the same as in any free economy today.

Wills and Estates

> *"A good man leaveth an inheritance to his children's children"* (Proverbs 13:22), and *"he that shall come forth out of thine own bowels shall be thine heir"* (Genesis 15:4b).

At God's command, Moses set forth the laws concerning the distribution of an estate after a person's death:

> *If a man die, and have no son, then ye shall cause his inheritance to pass unto his daughter.*
>
> *And if he have no daughter, then ye shall give his inheritance unto his brethren.*
>
> *And if he have no brethren, then ye shall give his inheritance unto his father's brethren.*
>
> *And if his father have no brethren, then ye shall give his inheritance unto his kinsman that is next to him of his family, and he shall possess it: and it shall be unto the children of Israel a statute of judgment, as the LORD commanded Moses.* (Numbers 27:8–11)

Western codes commonly include laws of intestate succession, that is, laws that govern the distribution of an estate if a person dies without leaving a will. However, with some limitations, if the deceased leaves a last will and testament, that will takes precedence over the laws of intestate succession. But written wills seem to have been unknown in ancient Israel, though they did occur in Egypt and were common among the Romans. As Clark explained,

> The ancient ceremony or proceeding in which the head of a family, believing himself about to die, designated his eldest son—or possibly a younger son or some other member of the family—to be his successor, constituted the primitive form of will. In this manner the aged patriarch transferred his authority over the household. Originally he could make no will in respect of property, for the property belonged not to him but to the family as a sort of corporation. In the Scriptures the succession ceremony is called a *"blessing."* In the blessing of Jacob, who had impersonated his elder brother Esau, their father Isaac declared that he should *"be lord over thy brethren, and let thy mother's sons bow down to thee."* [Genesis 27:29] Subsequently, when Jacob had become old and was upon his death bed, he conferred his blessing upon his fourth son Judah, rather than upon his firstborn son Reuben, saying: *"thou art he whom thy brethren shall praise;... thy father's children shall bow down before thee."*
>
> ...Mosaic law originally contemplated that a man should dispose of his property during his lifetime; otherwise that

> it should pass at the time of his death according to the rules of descent or succession. But in later times the testamentary disposition of property was allowed when all of the kindred entitled to inherit under Mosaic law had failed or were undiscoverable. Wills were commonly recognized and understood by the beginning of the Christian era, and those of Christians were often deposited in churches for safekeeping.[23]

Normally, only legitimate children inherited from their parents, for several likely reasons: The stigma attached to illegitimacy, the danger of false claims of paternity, and the likelihood that the persons who raise the illegitimate child will provide for him. Gilead's illegitimate son Jephthah, who grew up to become a mighty military commander and a judge, was cast out by Gilead's legitimate children, saying, *"Thou shalt not inherit in our father's house; for thou art the son of a strange woman"* (Judges 11:2). Of course, during his lifetime a father could bestow a gift upon his illegitimate child if he chose to do so.

The eldest son commonly received a double portion of the estate, that is, twice as much as his brothers (Deuteronomy 21:17). This may have served the purpose of keeping the family estate together, and it could also constitute recognition of the fact that the eldest son will become the head of the family and will incur obligations toward other family members. The firstborn son's headship and double portion was called the *birthright.* The father could give the birthright to a different son, as Jacob/Israel did (Genesis 48:22; 49:3–4; 1 Chronicles 5:1–2) and as in the case of Shimri (1 Chronicles 26:10), but he could not do so just because the younger son's mother was more loved than the mother of the firstborn (Deuteronomy 21:15–17). Apparently the oldest son could sell his birthright to a younger son, as Esau did (Genesis 25:29–34). The birthright should be distinguished from the *blessing* that a father gave to his firstborn son, which placed the son in a close and favored covenant relationship with God.

Under American law, if the deceased left no last will and testament and no close relatives can be located, the property of the deceased becomes the property of the state, although this happens very rarely. Clark says, "There is nothing in Jewish law to warrant the belief that the King or the State had any right to inherit property upon the death of the owner

23. Clark, 78. Clark also cites Genesis 31:16 in which Rachel and Leah declared that the riches acquired by their husband Jacob from their father Laban *"is ours and our children's."*

without lawful heirs."[24] Although the corrupt King Ahab, at the instigation of his Phoenician wife Queen Jezebel, ordered the execution of Naboth so he (Ahab) could seize Naboth's vineyard, this was completely illegal and was condemned by the prophet Elijah (1 Kings 21:1–29).

Contracts

Agreements by which people contract to do certain things or sell or buy certain things were common in the ancient world. In fact, it is difficult to imagine a society without contracts.

Not surprisingly, many contracts appear in the Bible. Abraham and Lot reached an agreement for the division of their lands, herds, and flocks (Genesis 13:5–11). Other contracts occur between Isaac and Abimelech (Genesis 21:23), between Jacob and Laban (Genesis 29:19–20, 26, 30), between Joshua's spies and Rahab (Joshua 2:12–21), and between David and Jonathan (1 Samuel 18:3; 20:16; 23:18). These contracts may have been oral, that is, by word of mouth only, but King Solomon and King Hiram of Tyre entered into an agreement whereby Hiram furnished cedars for building materials for the Temple, in return for wheat, barley, wine, and oil (1 Kings 5:1–11; 2 Chronicles 2); this agreement appears to have been in writing (2 Chronicles 2:11).

Sometimes people required sworn oaths that the terms of the agreement would be fulfilled: *"Thou shalt…swear by his [God's] name"* (Deuteronomy 6:13; 10:20). Realizing that David would become king after his (Saul's) death, Saul asked David to *"Swear now therefore unto me by the LORD, that thou wilt not cut off my seed after me, and that thou wilt not destroy my name out of my father's house. And David sware unto Saul"* (1 Samuel 24:21–22). Sometimes the oath was accompanied by a symbolic gesture. Consider Jacob [Israel] and his son Joseph:

> *And the time drew nigh that Israel must die: and he called his son Joseph, and said unto him, If now I have found grace in thy sight, put, I pray thee, thy hand under my thigh, and deal kindly and truly with me; bury me not, I pray thee, in Egypt:*
>
> *But I will lie with my fathers, and thou shalt carry me out of Egypt, and bury me in their buryingplace. And he [Joseph] said, I will do as thou hast said.*

24. Clark, 78, quoting 12 Gr.B. (1900).

> *And he said, Swear unto me. And he sware unto him.* (Genesis 47:29–31; cf. Genesis 24:2–4, 9)

Sworn or unsworn, contracts were sacred obligations: *"Ye shall not steal, neither deal falsely, neither lie one to another. And ye shall not swear by my name falsely, neither shalt thou profane the name of thy God: I am the LORD"* (Leviticus 19:11–12). Proverbs 12:22 declares that *"Lying lips are abomination to the LORD: but they that deal truly are his delight."* And one may not abrogate an agreement solely because changed circumstances render the agreement no longer to his advantage; Psalm 15:4 commends *"He that sweareth to his own hurt, and changeth not."*

The Hebrew system also provided for the loans of money or other property, and the lender might require the borrower to deposit goods as a pledge or security, subject to some restrictions:

> *When thou dost lend thy brother any thing, thou shalt not go into his house to fetch his pledge.*
>
> *Thou shalt stand abroad, and the man to whom thou dost lend shall bring out the pledge abroad unto thee.*
>
> *And if the man be poor, thou shalt not sleep with his pledge:*
>
> *In any case thou shalt deliver him the pledge again when the sun goeth down, that he may sleep in his own raiment.* (Deuteronomy 24:10–13; cf. Exodus 22:26)

Lending to a poor person was considered an act of charity: *"A good man sheweth favour, and lendeth"* (Psalm 112:5); *"He that hath pity upon the poor lendeth unto the LORD"* (Proverbs 19:17). But a loan was not a gift; the poor person had a duty to repay it, if possible; *"The wicked borroweth, and payeth not again"* (Psalm 37:21).

Lending money at interest is problematic in the Hebrew Scriptures:

> *If thou lend money to any of my people that is poor by thee, thou shalt not be to him as an usurer, neither shalt thou lay upon him usury.* (Exodus 22:25)
>
> *Thou shalt not lend upon usury to thy brother; usury of money, usury of victuals, usury of any thing that is lent upon usury:*

> *Unto a stranger thou mayest lend upon usury; but unto thy brother thou shalt not lend upon usury....*
> (Deuteronomy 23:19–20)

But the meaning of the term *usury* is unclear. Clark says that "In early times, 'usury' and 'interest' were synonymous, but later interest came to signify a moderate and lawful charge, and usury an excessive and unlawful charge, for the use of money."[25] Over the centuries, the prohibition against *usury* has been defined in at least three ways:

- The prohibition was against all interest, which was the interpretation of many early and medieval Churchmen.
- The prohibition was against lending money at interest to widows, orphans, the poor, or sojourners in the land. This was considered an act of charity, and one should not profit from such charity but should consider oneself fortunate to be repaid at all. By this interpretation, which was common among medieval Jews, it was permissible to charge interest when lending money to strangers in arms-length transactions.
- The prohibition was against lending money at excessive rates of interest. This has been the interpretation of many Protestants.

Marriage and the Family

Hebrew Law recognized the family as the most basic of human institutions. From the beginning, marriage was considered a sacred institution. God said, *"It is not good that the man should be alone; I will make him an help meet for him"* (Genesis 2:18):

> *And Adam said, This is now bone of my bones, and flesh of my flesh: she shall be called Woman, because she was taken out of Man.*
>
> *Therefore shall a man leave his father and his mother, and shall cleave unto his wife: and they shall be one flesh.*
> (Genesis 2:23–24)

25. Clark, 152 fn 22. He further notes on p. 154 that "Out of respect for Mosaic law, primitive Christians took no interest," and that until the 16th century the common law forbade interest.

This and other passages (Proverbs 5:18; Ecclesiastes 9:9) demonstrate a preference for monogamy, although instances of polygamy are found in Scripture: Lamech (Genesis 4:19), Jacob (Genesis 29:30), Elkanah (1 Samuel 1:1–2), Esau (Genesis 26:34; 28:9; 36:2), Gideon (Judges 8:30), Abijah (2 Chronicles 13:21), Rehoboam (2 Chronicles 11:21), and Solomon (1 Kings 11:3), etc.; also, there are instances of concubinage (Genesis 25:6; 35:22; 36:12; Judges 8:31; 2 Samuel 5:13; 1 Kings 11:3; 2 Chronicles 11:21). But we need to beware the "is/ought" fallacy; the fact that the Bible records certain conduct does not mean the Bible sanctions such conduct.

The Scriptures encourage marriage: *"Whoso findeth a wife findeth a good thing, and obtaineth favour of the LORD"* (Proverbs 18:22). Marriages were solemnized before various officials (Ruth 4:2), and were accompanied by feasting and celebrations that could last several days (Genesis 29:22, 28). A newly-married man was given a one-year exemption from military service (Deuteronomy 24:5).

The Mosaic Law prohibited incestuous marriages and incestuous relationships: *"Cursed be he that lieth with his sister, the daughter of his father, or the daughter of his mother"* (Deuteronomy 27:22).[26] However, under the levirate law, if a married man died leaving a widow and no children, the man's brother had a legal duty to marry his brother's widow, and the firstborn child of that couple was considered the heir of the deceased brother.[27] Also, in the early history of the human race as recorded in Genesis, incestuous marriages appear to have been tolerated, if not approved, because of the lack of alternatives. Abraham married his half-sister Sarah (Genesis 20:12), and Amram married his father's sister Jochebed, and she bore to him Aaron, Miriam, and Moses (Exodus 6:20).

HEBREW CEREMONIAL LAW

Most Christians believe the Hebrew ceremonial law applies uniquely to Israel and is not binding on the Church or on Gentile nations, basing this position on Galatians 3:10–14, Colossians 2:16, Hebrews 10:8–10,

26. See also Leviticus 18:6–29; 20:11–17; Deuteronomy 27:20; compare Matthew 14:4; Mark 6:18.

27. Deuteronomy 25:5–10; cf. Ruth 4. In some circumstances, the brother could be excused from that duty. Commentators disagree among themselves as to whether the levirate law applied to a surviving brother who was already married; compare *The MacArthur Study Bible* ("Obviously, this required that the brother be unmarried. . . .") to *The Reformation Study Bible* ("The limitation to brothers 'living together' may indicate that it applied to an unmarried brother, but it is doubtful that this limitation held in practice.")

and other New Testament passages. Nevertheless, the ceremonial law composes substantial portions of Exodus, Leviticus, Numbers, and Deuteronomy. Portions of the ceremonial law of the Hebrew Scriptures inculcate moral lessons, and many Christians believe portions of the ceremonial law are types of Christ.

The ceremonial law includes:

- Prescriptions for sacrifices and offerings of lambs and other animals as atonements for sin. Some of these were regular and periodic; others were one-time sacrifices for particular sins (Numbers 15:27). Many Christians believe that the Hebrew animal sacrifices were types that foreshadowed the Sacrifice of Jesus Christ on the Cross, that the Hebrews, as they looked upon the sacrifice of the lamb on the altar, saw it as a picture of the coming Messiah, and that these sacrifices were efficacious only to the extent that the Hebrew worshipper placed his faith in the coming Messiah.

- Directions concerning the tabernacle, and, later, the Temple. These pertain to the manner in which God is to be worshipped.

- Sabbatarian laws concerning what activities could or could not be engaged in on the Sabbath. Some disagreement exists as to whether the sabbatarian laws are moral or ceremonial, and we need to remember that the Scriptures do not sharply distinguish these categories of civil, moral, and ceremonial law. The sabbath laws certainly concern respect for and worship of God, but they also satisfy man's need for periodic rest.

- Dietary laws, found especially in Leviticus 11, Leviticus 20, and Deuteronomy 14, such as the prohibition against eating pork, shellfish, and other foods. Some believe the purpose of these provisions was to protect the health of the people, because, for example, improperly cooked pork can cause trichinosis. Others attribute these prohibitions to the fact that the Hebrews should look upon their food with a view to what God would and would not accept as sacrifice, and also to impress upon them that they were a people distinct from other nations. Others suggest that the dietary restrictions were an exercise in self-discipline whereby the observant demonstrated that he was not a slave to his appetites (unlike Esau; Genesis 25:29–34), but rather that he valued obedience to the Lord's commands above the eating of certain foods that he might want from time to time.

- Periodic feasts and rituals observed to teach certain principles to the people, and especially to impress them upon the younger generations. Among these are Rosh Hashanah, the Jewish new year; Yom Kippur, the day of atonement for sins between man and God; Sukkoth, the seven-day holiday commemorating the dwelling of the Hebrew people in booths during their travels in the desert; Hanukkah, the Festival of Lights celebrating the Maccabees' victory over the Greeks in 167 BC and the cleansing and rededication of the Temple; Purim, commemorating the defeat of Haman's plot to destroy the Jews of Persia as narrated in the Book of Esther; and Pesach or Passover, the eight-day celebration of the deliverance of the Hebrews from Egypt.
- Miscellaneous provisions that may not actually involve immoral acts but impress an important principle upon the people. The commandment, *"Thou shalt not seethe a kid [baby goat] in his mother's milk"* (Exodus 23:19, 34:26; Deuteronomy 14:21) was intended to impress a principle of kindness and avoiding cruelty; boiling a baby goat in its mother's milk adds insult to injury, like requiring the parents of a condemned murderer to furnish the rope for his hanging. The prohibition against wearing garments of the opposite gender (Deuteronomy 22:5) was intended to re-enforce gender roles which, the Hebrews believed, had been assigned by God. The prohibition against mixed garments, *"neither shall a garment mingled of linen and woollen come upon thee"* (Leviticus 19:19; cf. Deuteronomy 22:11), was to impress upon the Jewish people that they were a unique people, set apart from all others, and that they were to keep their culture pure. The prohibition against sowing a field with mixed seed (Leviticus 19:19; Deuteronomy 22:9) served a similar purpose. *"For thou art an holy people unto the LORD thy God, and the LORD hath chosen thee to be a peculiar people unto himself, above all the nations that are upon the earth"* (Deuteronomy 14:2). Additionally, as Wines demonstrated, all of these practices—boiling a kid in its mother's milk, wearing garments of

the opposite gender, and wearing garments of mixed cloth—were customs and rituals of pagan nations.[28]

These laws and institutions enabled the preservation of the Hebrews as a unique people, or as the Scriptures describe them a *"peculiar people"* (Exodus 19:5; Deuteronomy 14:2, 26:18; Psalm 135:4) with a special identity and mission from God, for 4,000 years. Through these laws and institutions, the Hebrews were preserved as a free and godly people, though far from a perfect people, from the days of Abraham through the present. And as we shall see in the next chapter, through these laws and institutions the Hebrews have influenced the world more than any other people.

> *"O how I love thy law! It is my meditation all the day."* (Psalm 119:97)

Questions for Reflection, Discussion, and More Reflection

1. How does the Hebrew doctrine of the unity of God affect one's view of law? Does the Christian doctrine of the Trinity conflict at all with Hebrew monotheism?
2. How does the Hebrew belief that man was created in the image of God provide a basis for a belief in human rights?
3. How are the sacrifices in Judaism and Christianity different from sacrifices in other religions? How is the sacrifice of Christ in Christianity different from the sacrifices of Judaism?
4. How does the concept of sin in Judaism and Christianity affect the Jewish and Christian view of law and government? How does the Christian doctrine of sin differ from that of Judaism?
5. Where in Scripture do we find the concept of government by the consent of the governed?

28. Wines, 461–64.

6. What are the various meanings attached to *liberty* in Scripture? Are those concepts consistent with popular views of liberty today?
7. How and why is the requirement of *mens rea* or criminal intent a part of the Hebrew Law? By the adoption of "strict liability" crimes, are we moving away from the *mens rea* requirement today? Is that a good thing?
8. Does the fact that an act is made criminal in Scripture for ancient Israel necessarily mean it should be a crime in modern legal codes? Does the fact that the Scriptures prescribe the death penalty (or another penalty) for a crime mean that our legal system today should impose the same penalty? Why, or why not? Does the fact that capital punishment for murder is justified by the Noahic Covenant (Genesis 9:6) mean that it is applicable today?
9. Why did the Mosaic Law impose restraints on the sale of real estate in Israel? How does this relate to the covenant by which God gave that land to Israel? Should real estate law today be the same as it was in Israel?
10. What were the purposes of criminal punishment in the Mosaic Law? Which of those punishments are still valid today? Are there additional reasons for punishment today? Which of these purposes are still valid today?

Moses, Lawgiver to the World.
Henry Schile, ca. 1874.

CHAPTER 16

THE INFLUENCE OF HEBREW LAW: *Moses, Lawgiver to the World*

John Adams was perhaps the finest scholar ever to occupy the White House. His library is fascinating, not only for the volumes it contains, but especially for Adams's interaction with it. By notes in the margins, he carried on a running dialogue with the authors whose books he read.

One such volume was *Outlines of an Historical View of the Progress of the Human Mind,* by the French enlightenment thinker the Marquis de Condorcet. As the Marquis glowingly praised the accomplishments of Greek civilization, Adams wrote in the margin:

> As much as I love, esteem and admire the Greeks, I believe the Hebrews have done more to civilize the world. Moses did more than all their legislators and philosophers.[1]

In a similar vein, Adams wrote to Judge F. A. Van der Kamp February 16, 1809:

> The Hebrews have done more to civilize men than any other nation ... [God] ordered the Jews to preserve and propagate to all mankind the doctrine of a supreme, intelligent, wise, almighty sovereign of the universe... [which is] to be the great essential principle of morality, and consequently all civilization.[2]

And in a further expression of appreciation for Hebrew thought, Adams wrote to F. A. Van der Kamp in 1816, "The Hebrew unity of Jehovah,

1. John Adams, handwritten comments on his copy of *Outlines of an Historical View of the Progress of the Human Mind;* reprinted in Zoltan Haraszti, *John Adams and the Prophets of Progress* (Harvard University Press, 1952), 246.

2. John Adams, letter to F. A. Van der Kamp, February 16, 1809; reprinted in Norman Cousins, *"In God We Trust": The Religious Beliefs and Ideas of the American Founding Fathers* (Harper, 1958), 102–03.

the prohibition of all similitudes, appears to me the greatest wonder of antiquity."[3]

Adams understood that Hebrew monotheism was far more than just a belief in one God. In Hebrew thought, Jehovah brought together all qualities of truth and righteousness. All just law emanated from Him, and any law contrary to His law was unjust, invalid, and nonbinding.

His son also understood the value of Hebrew Law. Wines related,

> Here I cannot but recall a conversation which I had some years ago, with that eminent scholar and statesman, the late John Quincy Adams. In it, he drew, with a luminousness and power peculiar to himself, a contrast between the Hebrew government and the other ancient oriental polities. Point by point, did he unfold, with copious eloquence, the differences between them. But that which he chiefly insisted on, was the fact, that all the rest were founded on force, this only on consent. I have regretted since, that I did not ask him to commit those views to writing; and I cannot but indulge the hope, that the subject will somewhere be found alluded to at least, if not handled at length, in his posthumous papers.[4]

And Moses foresaw that his laws would be a model and inspiration for other nations:

> *Behold, I have taught you statutes and judgments, even as the LORD my God commanded me, that ye should do so in the land whither ye go to possess it.*
>
> *Keep therefore and do them; for this is your wisdom and your understanding in the sight of the nations, which shall hear all these statutes, and say, Surely this great nation is a wise and understanding people.*
>
> *For what nation is there so great, who hath God so nigh unto them, as the LORD our God is in all things that we call upon him for?*

---

3. John Adams, letter to F. A. Van der Kamp, December 27, 1816; reprinted in Norman Cousins, *"In God We Trust"* (Harper, 1958), 104.

4. E.C. Wines, *Commentaries on the Laws of the Ancient Hebrews* (1853; American Vision, 2009), 49–50.

> *And what nation is there so great, that hath statutes and judgments so righteous as all this law, which I set before you this day?* (Deuteronomy 4:5–8)

This does not mean that other nations were to enact the Mosaic Law into statutes and follow them literally. Some have done so, most notably the Anglo-Saxon rulers of England and the New England colonies in the 1600s, but most have looked to its principles but not copied the letter. As Wines wrote, a literal application of the Mosaic Law "overlooks a material distinction—the distinction between laws intrinsically the wisest, and laws which are the wisest only when viewed as relating to times and circumstances. Laws may be perfectly wise, when framed with reference to one state of society, which would be unwise and absurd, if framed with reference to another condition of things."[5] Wines continued:

> Civil laws, whatever be their source, to be adopted to the wants of any given community, must arise out of circumstances, and be relative to certain specific ends; which ends, under other circumstances, it might be the height of folly to pursue. When Solon was asked whether he had given the best laws to the Athenians, he replied: "I have given them the best that they were able to bear." Sage response! Is it not of much the same nature with that declaration of divine wisdom to the Jews, which has so perplexed Biblical inquirers,—"*I gave them also statutes that were not good,*" [Ezekiel 20:25] that is, laws not absolutely the best, though they were relatively so. Montesquieu, with that penetration which belongs to all his philosophical reflections, has observed, that the passage, cited above, is the sponge that wipes out all the difficulties, which are to be found in the law of Moses. This view of the meaning and force of the passage is confirmed by the words of our Savior. He has told us, that Moses tolerated divorce among the Jews, because of the hardness of their hearts. [Matthew 19:8; Mark 10:5] It is reasonable to conclude that he permitted the continuance of other social evils on the same principle. It is implied in our Lord's declaration, that, if the Jews of Moses' time had been less hard-hearted, that is, less prejudiced, less wedded to old notions and usages, several of his statutes would have been different from what they were. Is it not also involved, that the

5. Wines, 118.

> excellence, which Moses claims, and most justly, as belonging to his laws, is, as it respects some of them at least, a relative rather than an absolute excellence? Considerations of political expediency were often of prevailing force with him in framing his laws.
>
> A wise legislator, whether divine or human, in framing a new code of laws for a people, will give attention to considerations of climate, of religion, of existing institutions, of settled maxims of government, of precedent, of morals, of customs, and of manners. Out of all these there arises a general tone, or habit, of feeling, thinking, and acting, which constitutes what may be called the spirit of the nation. Now, a lawgiver shows himself deficient in legislative wisdom, who makes laws which shock the general sentiment of the people, laws which are at war with prevalent notions and rooted customs, laws which strip men of long-established and favorite rights. Nations in general cling tenaciously to what is old. True legislative wisdom, therefore, will abide by established laws, when it can, even though satisfied, that other laws are better in themselves, and, but for the force of custom in favor of the old, would be more expedient. A wise lawgiver, who desires to see ancient usages replaced by new and different ones, will not attempt to change such customs at once, by direct legal enactments, but will seek, by the introduction of judicious provisions into his code, to lead the people to change them themselves....
>
> The principle that laws must be relative to circumstances, that they must grow out of the state of society, and be adopted to its wants, is founded in reason, and confirmed by experience.[6]

Divorce laws are a good example. God's will is that marriage be permanent, and in Malachi 2:15–16 we read, "*...let none deal treacherously against the wife of his youth. For the* Lord, *the God of Israel, saith that he hateth putting away [divorce]:...*" But the Mosaic Law allowed divorce:

> *When a man hath taken a wife, and married her, and it come to pass that she find no favour in his eyes, because he hath found some uncleanness in her: then let him write her a bill of divorcement, and give it in her hand, and send her out of his house.* (Deuteronomy 24:1)

6. Wines, 118–121.

The Jews in Christ's time disagreed among themselves as to the proper interpretation of this passage. Some understood the term *"uncleanness"* to mean adultery and argued that unfaithfulness was the only valid ground for divorce; others thought it could embrace all kinds of reasons. And so the Pharisees, who normally gave the Mosaic Law a strict interpretation, put the question to Jesus:

> *The Pharisees also came unto him, tempting him, and saying unto him, Is it lawful for a man to put away his wife for every cause?*
>
> *And he answered and said unto them, Have ye not read, that he which made them at the beginning made them male and female,*
>
> *And said, For this cause shall a man leave father and mother, and shall cleave to his wife: and they twain shall be one flesh? Wherefore they are no more twain, but one flesh. What therefore God hath joined together, let not man put asunder.*
>
> *They say unto him, Why did Moses then command to give a writing of divorcement, and to put her away?*
>
> *He saith unto them, Moses because of the hardness of your hearts suffered you to put away your wives: but from the beginning it was not so. And I say unto you, Whosoever shall put away his wife, except it be for fornication, and shall marry another, committeth adultery: and whoso marrieth her which is put away doth commit adultery.* (Matthew 19:3–9; cf. Matthew 5:31–32; Mark 10:2–9; Luke 16:18)[7]

Jesus explained that the Mosaic Law allowed for divorce, not because God approved divorce, but because of the hardness of the Hebrews' hearts. Human nature being what it was (and still is) at the time, a total prohibition of divorce would have been unworkable. Moses therefore provided for divorce as a reluctant concession to human nature.

7. This writer will not fully address the question whether adultery is a valid ground for divorce, except to note that the word *pornea*, translated "fornication" in Matthew 19:9 above, is different from the word *moichetai* which is translated "adultery," and that the supposed fornication exception does not appear in the Matthew 5, Mark 10, and Luke 16 passages.

Wines also noted that changed conditions in Israel could result in changes in the law:

> The purely civil laws of Moses could be repealed or changed, as the altered state of the commonwealth required or justified, even during the continuance of the Mosaic government. For example, Moses's first law against usury forbade the taking of interest from the poor Israelites only [Exodus 22:25]; his second law on the subject extended the same prohibition to the whole nation [Deuteronomy 23:19]. His statute, forbidding to kill animals for food in private, and enjoining to bring all such to the altar and offer them to Jehovah [Leviticus 17:3–7], remained in force only during the abode in the wilderness. It was formally repealed on entering the promised land [Deuteronomy 12:20–21]. The punishments originally annexed to the violation of laws, must be increased in severity, when, as often happens in the progress of society and of crime, they become too mild to secure obedience to the civil rule. Hence the penalty for theft, which Moses had fixed at a fourfold or fivefold restitution [Exodus 22:1], was increased to a sevenfold restitution in the time of Solomon [Proverbs 6:30–31]. The highest fine imposed by Moses in punishment for crime, was about fifteen dollars. What would that be, when the increasing wealth of the nation had proportionately diminished the value of gold and silver?[8]

Occasionally Moses left in place old laws and customs temporarily, recognizing that change sometimes takes time. At first the Hebrews followed the old custom that only the sons inherited from their parents, daughters being provided for by their husbands and their husbands' inheritances. But in Numbers 27 the daughters of Zelophehad sought to change the law:

> *And they stood before Moses, and before Eleazar the priest, and before the princes and all the congregation, by the door of the tabernacle of the congregation, saying,*
>
> *Our father died in the wilderness, and he was not in the company of them that gathered themselves together against the LORD in the company of Korah; but died in his own sin, and had no sons.*

8. Wines, 123.

> *Why should the name of our father be done away from among his family, because he hath no son? Give unto us therefore a possession among the brethren of our father.*
>
> *And Moses brought their cause before the Lord.*
>
> *And the Lord spake unto Moses, saying,*
>
> *The daughters of Zelophehad speak right: thou shalt surely give them a possession of an inheritance among their father's brethren; and thou shalt cause the inheritance of their father to pass unto them.*
>
> *And thou shalt speak unto the children of Israel, saying, If a man die, and have no son, then ye shall cause his inheritance to pass unto his daughter.*
>
> *And if he have no daughter, then ye shall give his inheritance unto his brethren.*
>
> *And if he have no brethren, then ye shall give his inheritance unto his father's brethren.*
>
> *And if his father have no brethren, then ye shall give his inheritance unto his kinsman that is next to him of his family, and he shall possess it: and it shall be unto the children of Israel a statute of judgment, as the Lord commanded Moses.* (Numbers 27:2–11)[9]

The principle didn't change, but changed circumstances required a change in the application of the principle.

The same may be true of various social evils. Slavery is contrary to the basic principles of the Bible, the value of liberty and the equality and dignity of all persons as a result of their creation in the image of God. But the Mosaic Law did not explicitly abolish or prohibit all forms of servitude, possibly because the world was not ready to receive that truth at that time. The same might be said of polygamy, which is never sanctioned in the Bible but which was practiced early in Israel's history, although Jesus said monogamous marriage was God's will from the beginning (Matthew 19:3–9).

9. The new Mosaic statute is similar to the laws of intestate succession in many jurisdictions today.

Likewise the Hebrew theocracy—which was a republic under the rulership of God, not a despotism under the rulership of kings or priests—was instituted for a unique people in a unique place and time. In a world which had fallen away from the worship of the one true God and had embraced pagan polytheism and all its attendant evils, God called Abraham out of the city of Ur of the Chaldees to a new land, and then, after four centuries of bondage in Egypt, God called Moses to lead the children of Abraham out of slavery into freedom. He called them into Canaan, a land of paganism, temple prostitution, and human sacrifice, there to restore them to Himself. He therefore reigned Himself as their king, with Moses and the judges as His vice-regents. Because God was Israel's true King, blasphemy and idolatry were comparable to acts of treason.

But God had a unique plan for Israel, and the theocratic rule that He deemed necessary for Israel may not have been His plan for other nations. Again, the principles do not change, but the application does.

An 1874 case in New South Wales, Australia, is most instructive. The Court stated:

> We, the colonists of New South Wales, "bring out with us" (to adopt the words of Blackstone) this first great common law maxim distinctly handed down by Coke and Blackstone and every other English judge long before any of our colonies were in existence or even thought of that "Christianity is part and parcel of our general laws, and that all the revealed or divine law, so far as enacted by the Holy Scriptures to be of universal obligation," is part of our colonial law—as clearly explained by Blackstone Vol. 1 pp. 42–43 and Vol. 4 pp. 43–60.[10]

The Court recognized, with Blackstone and Coke, that Christianity was part of the common law of colonial New South Wales, as were those portions of Scripture that were intended to be of universal obligation. The Court acknowledged, with Blackstone and Coke, that some parts of Biblical Law were of "universal obligation" and some were not.

Similarly, Martin Luther spoke of natural law *(gesetz)* and natural justice *(recht)* as having universal obligation, and the Ten Commandments were part of this universal natural law. However, Luther believed that much of the Jewish law was *Sachsenspiegel,* laws unique to Israel that are

10. *Ex parte Thackeray,* 13 S.C.R. 1, 61 (N.S.W., 1874); cited by Joshua Reimer, "Church-State Relations in America and Australia: Why Australia Should Not Follow the American Example," Senior Seminar Paper, Oak Brook College of Law and Government Policy, December 10, 2009.

no more binding on civil governments today than the laws of France are binding in Germany.[11]

Even though they usually did not codify the Mosaic Law exactly as written, nations throughout the world have looked to the Law of Moses as a model.

The influence of Hebrew Law upon later civilizations is well demonstrated in Max I. Dimont's 1962 book *Jews, God, and History:*

> The Mosaic code... was the first truly judicial, written code, and eclipsed previously known laws with its all-encompassing humanism, its passion for justice, its love of democracy. It also helped to establish a new Jewish character and directed Jewish thinking into new paths which tended to set the Jews further apart from their neighbors.
>
> The ideological content of these Mosaic laws is of great interest. Here we find the Jewish concept of the state and philosophy of law. These laws were essentially divided into three categories: those dealing with man's relation to man, those dealing with man's relation to the state, and those dealing with man's relation to God.
>
> ... The lofty framework of these laws permitted the emergence of a democratic form of government virile enough to last eight hundred years until the Prophets in turn renovated them....
>
> The Mosaic Code laid down the first principles for a separation of church and state, a concept not encountered in world history until three thousand years later, during the Enlightenment in the eighteenth century of our era. [Note: Dimont is referring to the commands of Mosaic law that the kings or civil authority come from the Tribe of Judah while the priests or religious authority come from the Tribe of Levi.] In the Mosaic Code the civil authority was independent of the priesthood. Though it is true that the priesthood had the right to settle cases not specifically covered by Mosaic law (Deuteronomy 17:8–12), that did not place it above the civil government. The priesthood was charged with the responsibility of keeping this government within the framework of Mosaic law, just as the United States Supreme Court is not above the federal government but

11. Heinrich Bornkamm, *Luther's World of Thought* trans. Martin H. Bertram (St. Louis: Concordia, 1958, 2005), 203–04.

is, nevertheless, charged with the responsibility of keeping it within the framework of the Constitution. Moses also laid the foundation for another separation, which has since become indispensable to any democracy. He created an independent judiciary.

There is a curious resemblance between the philosophic outlook of American constitutional law and that of Mosaic law. The federal government has only the powers specifically-granted to it by the Constitution. The individual states can do anything not specifically denied to them. In essence, the Mosaic law also established the principle that the Jews could do anything not specifically denied to them. Instead of saying, "Do such and such a thing," the laws of Moses usually say "Don't do this or that." Even where the Mosaic law makes a positive statement, it is often either an amendment to a negative commandment or else hemmed in by a negative admonition, saying, in effect, "When you do this, then don't do that." The Ten Commandments, for instance, list only three *do*'s but seven *don't*s. The three positive commandments are *"I am the LORD thy God"*; observe the Sabbath; and honor your parents. The seven *don't*s leave little doubt as to what one is not supposed to do. By fencing in only the negative, Moses left an open field for positive action. This allowed the Jews great flexibility. As long as they did not do anything specifically prohibited, they could, like the individual American states, do anything they wanted to do. This type of thinking led Jewish philosophers into stating their maxims in negations.

We can see this gulf in thinking interestingly illustrated in a maxim attributed by Christians to Jesus and by Jews to Hillel, one of the great teachers of Judaism. According to the Christians, Jesus said, *"Do unto others what you want others to do unto you."* According to the Jews, Hillel, who lived 100 years before Jesus, said, *"Do not do* unto others what you *don't want* others to do unto you." There is a world of difference between these two expressions, and the reader is invited to ponder on them and reason out why he would prefer one to the other as applied to himself.[12]

12. Max I. Dimont, "On Mosaic Law," *Jews, God and History* (1962), reprinted in *Law: A Treasury of Art and Literature,* ed. Sara Robbins (New York: Macmillan, 1990): 27–29. Dimont used the Jewish numbering of the commandments; by the other numbering systems there are only two positive commands.

The Phoenicians, the mariners of the ancient world, were a Semitic people closely related to the Hebrews, and their language was almost as similar to Hebrew as German is to Dutch or Spanish is to Portugese.[13] Through their interaction with the Hebrews, their voyages and their colonies, they transported Hebrew ideas to many parts of the ancient world.[14]

Moses, the consummate lawgiver, deliverer, statesman, judge, commander, prophet, and priest, created a constitutional framework and legal code that birthed a great nation and has influenced other nations for thousands of years. Let us examine a few of these:

Egypt

Some have argued that the Hebrews learned their laws and institutions from the Egyptians. But as we saw in Chapter 13, this theory is based on the false assumption that the Hebrews were an illiterate people and that the Hebrew legal system was developed much later than it was in fact. And while Moses may have learned from some of the Egyptian institutions,[15] the differences between Egyptian and Judean systems are substantial. Wines continued,

> ... in their fundamental principles, the two constitutions were the antipodes of each other. Egypt was a despotism; Judea a republic. The people of the former were slaves; the people of the latter, freemen. In Egypt the prince governed, or the priesthood through the prince; in Palestine the nation. The Egyptian government was founded on force; the Hebrew government on consent. The former was a government of will; the latter, a government of law. In Egypt an iron system of caste crushed every opening faculty and every generous aspiration of man's nature; on the banner of Palestine flamed, in living letters, liberty, equality, fraternity.[16]

But the Hebrews may have influenced the Egyptian legal system. Genesis 41 records that the Pharaoh of Egypt dreamed of seven fat cattle and

---

13. George Rawlinson, *The Story of Phoenicia* (G.P. Putnam's Sons, 1891), 24.

14. Rawlingson, 89–117, 327–28.

15. The idea that Moses might have learned from Egyptian institutions is not necessarily inconsistent with the idea of divine inspiration. God could have drawn Moses' attention to oral traditions, institutions of other nations, or other sources to inspire his writing of the Torah.

16. Wines, 138.

seven lean cattle, and Joseph interpreted this dream to mean that Egypt would experience seven years of abundant crops and seven years of famine. The Pharaoh then said to Joseph, *"See, I have set thee over all the land of Egypt"* (Genesis 41:41), and Joseph developed a system for gathering and storing food during the time of abundance and rationing the food during the famine. As Wines wrote, "For eighty successive years Joseph swayed the destinies of that empire; and an inspired writer has told us, that he taught her senators wisdom [Psalm 105:22]. It cannot be doubted, therefore, that many of the wisest maxims of Egyptian policy were due to the genius of that illustrious minister, and to the special divine guidance vouchsafed to him in his administration."[17]

Greece

Greek legal thinking, as we will see in Chapter 19, was a mixture of noble and ignoble concepts. Some view Greece as the fountain of modern thinking and the birthplace of democracy. But the Hebrew republic flourished a thousand years before the Golden Age of Athens and evinced a stability that was forever lacking in Greece. Solon (638–558 BC), the great lawgiver of Athens, traveled around 590 BC throughout Egypt and the Middle East to gain wisdom for legislation. During his travels he may have come into contact with Hebrew thought, even though many of the Judeans were in captivity in Babylon from 605–536 BC. Others, including Thales, Anaximander, Anaxagoras, Pherecydes, Pythagoras, Plato, and Herodotus traveled and resided in Egypt, Chaldea (Babylon), and Phoenicia, where they may have learned of the wisdom of the Hebrews.[18] Clement of Alexandria and others insisted that Plato borrowed extensively from Hebrew thought, and that Moses was Plato's ideal philosopher king.[19] Wines wrote that "The similitude between the Grecian and Mosaic laws has been noticed by many learned men besides Grotius; as Josephus, Clemens Alexandrinus, Augustine, Selden, Gale, Cunnaeus, Serranus, Sir Matthew Hale, and Archbishop Potter. Potter wrote:

---

17. Wines, 137. Daniel Chapter Four suggests that during the period of King Nebuchadnezzar's insanity, Daniel governed the Babylonian Empire in his name.

18. Wines, 332–33.

19. Clement of Alexandria, *Stromateis,* Book 1, reprinted by Oliver O'Donovan and Joan Lockwood O'Donovan, *From Irenaeusto Grotius: A Sourcebook in Christian Political Thought* (Eerdmans, 1999), 30–38. Clement quoted Numenius of Apamea as calling Plato the "Atticizing Moses" [a reference to Attic Greek].

The Athenians had a prescribed bill of divorce, and so had the Jews. Among the Jews, the father gave names to the children; and such was the custom among the Greeks. The purgation oath among the Greeks, strongly resembled the oath of jealousy among the Hebrews. The harvest and vintage festival among the Greeks, the presentation of the best of their flocks, and the offering of their first fruits to God, together with the portion prescribed to the priests, the interdiction against garments of divers colors, protection from violence to the man who had fled to their altars, would seem to indicate that the Greeks had cautiously copied the usages of the Jews. And whence was it, that no person was permitted to approach the altar of Diana, who had touched a dead body, or been exposed to other causes of impurity, and that the laws of Athens admitted no man to the priesthood who had any blemish on his person, unless from the institutions of Moses? And has not the agrarian law of Lycurgus its prototype, though none of its defects, in the agrarian law of the Hebrews? Many of the Athenian laws in relation to the descent of property and the prohibited degrees of relationship in marriage, seem to have been transcribed by Solon from the laws of Moses. Sir Matthew Hale, in his *History of the Common Law* of England, affirms, "that among the Grecians, the laws of descent resemble those of the Jews."[20]

Rome

Roman law, which we will examine in Chapter 20, was based in part on Grecian law, and therefore may have been influenced indirectly by Hebrew law. And as Hugo Grotius (AD 1583–1645) wrote, "The most ancient Attic laws, whence in after times the Roman were derived, owe their origin to Moses's laws."[21] Grotius also asked, "Who may not believe, that, seeing the law of Moses had such an express image of the divine will, the nations did well in taking their laws thence? Which that the Grecians did, especially the Attics, is credible. Whence the Attic laws and the Roman twelve tables, which sprang thence, bear so much similitude with the Hebrew laws."[22]

20. Archbishop Potter; quoted by Wines, 335–36.

21. Hugo Grotius, *The Truth of the Christian Religion;* quoted by Wines, 335.

22. Hugo Grotius, *The Right of War and Peace;* quoted by Wines, 335. Around 500 BC the Decemviri also traveled throughout the Middle East to learn about legal systems and may have

Ireland

Hebrew Law also influenced the development of Irish law. Early Celtic jurisprudence was in the hands of Druid Brehon priests, who adjudicated disputes according to the unwritten Brehon laws passed down by oral tradition. In the fifth century AD, St. Patrick evangelized Ireland, and according to Marshall Foster,

> ... wherever he set up a church he left his converts with an old Celtic law book, *Liber ex Lege Moisi* (The Book of the Law of Moses), along with the books of the Gospel. The Liber begins with the Ten Commandments, and continues with selections from Exodus, Leviticus, Numbers, and Deuteronomy. From that time forward, this book became the basis of all social organization, including family, economics, welfare, and government. The Liber is the first essential document of liberty that led Christian civilization to far surpass the Roman Empire. The decentralized, God-centered worship of the Christian Celtic peoples avoided hierarchy and gave glory to God.[23]

Later in the 5th century, the High King of Ireland commissioned St. Patrick and a commission of bishops, Druids, and lesser kings to draft a written law code for Ireland. They composed the *Senchus Mor* or written legal code for Ireland, the introduction to which states:

> What did not clash with the Word of God in the written law and in the New Testament, and with the consciences of the believers, was confirmed in the laws of the Brehons by Patrick and by the ecclesiastics and the chieftains of Erin; for the law of nature had been quite right, except the faith, and its obligations. And this is the Senchus Mor.[24]

---

encountered the Hebrew system during their travels.

23. Marshall Foster, "Saint Patrick's Contributions to Western (Christian) Civilization," March 13, 2009, Publisher's Corner, Nordskog Publishing, http://nordskogpublishing.com/saint-patricks-contributions-to-western-christian-civilization/ (accessed 13 May, 2016); see also, Marshall Foster and Ron Ball, *Christian Home Learning Guide* (Zane Publishing, 1997), 58; see also, Leslie Hardinge, *Review: The Celtic Church in Britain,* www.giveshare.org/churchhistory/celticchurch.html (accessed 13 May, 2016). Also, an AD 1171 manuscript titled *The Leabhar Gabhala [The Book of Conquests of Ireland* or *The Book of Invasions]* claims that the ancestors of the Irish migrated westward from Scythia and brought with them the Mosaic Law; see also, Louis Hyman, *The Jews of Ireland* (Jerusalem, 1972).

24. Reprinted in Seumas McManus, *The Story of the Irish Race* (Old Greenwich, Connecticut, 1921, 1990), 133ff.

England

The Mosaic Law played a foundational role in the development of English common law. John C. H. Wu, Professor of Law at Seton Hall, after a detailed study, concluded that "... while the Roman law was a death bed convert to Christianity, the common law was a cradle Christian."[25] Concluding that the common law "was Christian from the very beginning" (p. 64), Wu continued:

> ... in preparing this study, I have gone to the very origins, and have been thrilled to find that many sages of the common law are also saints of the Church. King Ethelbert is a saint; and it is well known that up to the days of Henry VIII [when England broke away from the Roman Catholic Church], a light was always kept lighted before his tomb. It was St. Theodore who planted the Christian law of marriage on the soil of England. Edward the Confessor was noted not only for his laws but for his just administration, which caused him to reign in the hearts of his people. His selfless devotion to the welfare of the people made them love his law and government. He has been described as "a man by choice devoted to God, living the life of an angel in the administration of his kingdom, and therefore directed by Him." "The laws and customs of good King Edward" became a household saying for all succeeding generations. His life illustrates the truth that "love therefore is the fulfillment of the law." My impression is that the common law was not only founded on justice, but, what is more important, rooted in grace. It gradually assimilated the principles of natural law, not as an abstract theory, but as vital practical rules of conduct. The leaven worked slowly, but steadily.
>
> After the Norman Conquest, holy and learned clerics like Lanfranc, St. Thomas a Becket, John of Salisbury, and many others continued to infuse natural law principles into the common law. It may be said that canon law was the nurse and tutor of the common law. The very name "common law" was derived from the *ius commune* of the canonists. It was not till the twelfth century that the name began to be generally used by the lawyers, to denote not so much the general custom of the realm as the custom and judicial tradition of the king's court. Thus,

25. John C. H. Wu, *Fountain of Justice* (London, 1959), 65.

> the predominantly judicial origin of the common law was clear from its beginning.[26]

Professor Wu quoted Pollock and Maitland for a description of the court of King Henry II (AD 1154–1189) and King Richard (AD 1189–1199):

> English law was administrated by the ablest, the best educated men in the realm; not only that, it was administered by the selfsame men who were "the judges ordinary" of the church's courts, men who were bound to be, at least in some measure, learned in the canon law. At one moment Henry had three bishops for archjusticiars. The climax is reached in Richard's reign. We can then see the king's court as it sits day by day. Often enough it was composed of the archbishop of Canterbury, two other bishops, two or three archdeacons, two or three ordained clerks who were going to be bishops, and but two or three laymen. The majority of its members might at any time be called upon to hear ecclesiastical causes and learn the lessons in law that were addressed to them in paper prescripts.[27]

St. Ethelbert (AD 556–616) gave England its first system of written laws known as the "Ninety Dooms [judgments or commands] of Ethelbert." These Dooms followed many of the Old Testament criminal provisions, normally prescribing restitution as the penalty and also provided special protection for the Church. Later, King Alfred the Great (AD 871–899) developed a legal code specifically incorporating the Ten Commandments. John Canning states,

> In the annals of the English nation no man merits a higher place than Alfred the Great: stainless in character, brilliant as a writer, statesman, lawgiver, scholar, and champion of Christianity.[28] . . . Alfred now set to work to codify the laws of England, which had been a chaos of local rules and customs. He sought to revise and combine these with regulations borrowed from Mosaic laws and Christian principles. His Book of Dooms (law) forms the basis for administration of justice in the Courts of

26. Wu, 65–66.

27. Wu, 65–66.

28. John Canning, *100 Great Kings, Queens and Rulers of the World,* ed. John Canning (New York: Taplinger, 1968), 211.

> the Shires and Hundreds, and with additions and modifications became the ancestor of our Common Law of today.[29]

The late Harvard Law Professor Harold J. Berman noted the influence of the Ten Commandments upon King Alfred the Great and his law code known as the Book of Dooms:

> The Laws of Alfred (about AD 890) start with a recitation of the Ten Commandments and excerpts from the Mosaic Law; and in restating and revising the native Anglo-Saxon laws. Alfred includes such great principles as "doom (i.e. judge) very evenly; doom not one doom to the rich, another to the poor, nor doom one to your friend, another to your foe."[30] [cf. Exodus 23:1–3; Deuteronomy 1:16–18]

It is important to note the relationship between the common law and the canon law of the Church. According to Ralph Houlbrooke in *Church Courts and the People During the English Reformation 1520–1570* (Oxford: Oxford University Press, 1979), "The law of the church courts was the common law of Christendom, much of it supplemented by local custom or reinforced by local legislation."[31] Houlbrooke emphasizes efforts by Church authorities and by the Crown to inculcate the Ten Commandments to facilitate a common understanding of canon law.[32]

Canon Law was based largely upon Biblical Law. As E. Garth Moore and Timothy Briden note, in the Second Edition to *Moore's Introduction to English Canon Law* (London: Mowbray, 1–2):

> In the study of moral theology we are concerned with the whole of God's law in so far as it is immediately relevant to man. In the study of the canon law we are concerned with so much of the moral law as is enforced, directly or indirectly, by human sanctions. The basis of the canon law is theological.... If the lawyer

29. Canning, 214.

30. Harold J. Berman, *The Interaction of Law and Religion* (Parthenon Press, 1974), 55; See also, Frederick Austin Ogg, *A Sourcebook of Mediaeval History* (New York: American Book Company, 1908), 104f; William Seagle, *The History of Law* (New York: Tudor Publishing Co., 1946), 124.

31. Ralph Houlbrooke, *Church Courts and the People During the English Reformation 1520–1570* (Oxford: Oxford University Press, 1979), 8.

32. Houlbrooke, 169–72, 200–01; see also, Sir William Holdsworth, *A History of English Law* (London: Methuen & Co., 1903, 1971), 581–619.

> objects, as some do, that the divine law cannot be ascertained, the reply is again a theological one, for the Christian claims that there is a God, that God has a will, that in many instances that will has been revealed, and that, for the Christian, God's revealed will is law....
>
> ... throughout the Old Testament God's law is revealed, often implicitly, sometimes explicitly, as in the giving of the Ten Commandments to Moses; and in the New Testament our Lord in His summary gives the twofold substance of that law, both implicit and explicit, as love towards God and love towards one's neighbor, upon which hang all the law and the prophets.[33]

Hebrew Law influenced European law in another way. Throughout much of the Middle Ages, the Church prohibited money lending, based upon its interpretation of various passages of Scripture. But the Jews interpreted these passages differently, and as a result the Jewish community was a primary source of moneylending. Outstanding Jewish scholars such as the Rabbi Moses Ben Maimon (Maimonides, AD 1135–1204) developed much of the commercial code for medieval Europe, basing it in large part upon the Mosaic Law.[34] Around AD 1200 King John issued the Charter for Jewish Civil Justice which authorized Jewish residents of England to use their own tribunals to resolve civil disputes between themselves:

> John by the Grace of God, etc. Know that we have granted and by our present charter confirmed to our Jews in England that the breaches of right that shall occur among them, except such as pertain to our Crown and Justice, as touching homicide [etc.]... be examined and amended among themselves according to their Law, so that they may administer their own justice among themselves.[35]

During the thirteenth century, the English Crown commissioned Henricus Bracton to systematize the English common law. Bracton found that the common law had many gaps and inconsistent traditions in the various shire courts. He filled in the gaps and smoothed out the inconsistencies

---

33. E. Garth Moore and Timothy Briden, *Moore's Introduction to English Canon Law 2 ed.* (London: Mowbray), 1–2.

34. R.J. Rushdoony, *The Institutes of Biblical Law* (Nutley, NJ: Craig Press, 1973, 1978), 788–89.

35. King John, Charter for Jewish Civil Justice circa. AD 1200; quoted by John Henry Wigmore, *A Panorama of the World's Legal Systems* (West Publishing Co., 1928), I: 124.

with the Christianized Justinian Code of the Romans, as well as with the canon law of the Church, Gratian's Decretum, and the Decretals of Pope Gregory IX.

Since the Mosaic Law formed much of the basis for English common law, it is not surprising that those who studied to become lawyers in early England studied, among other things, Biblical Law including the Ten Commandments. For hundreds of years, legal education in England took place largely in four academic centers known as Inns of Court. These were known as Lincoln's Inn, the Inner Temple, the Middle Temple, and Gray's Inn. Barrister Robert R. Pearce, in his book *A History of the Inns of Court and Chancery: with Notices of Their Ancient Discipline, Rules, Orders, and Customs, Readings, Moots, Masques, Revels, and Entertainments; Including an Account of the Eminent Men of the Four Learned and Honourable Societies,—Lincoln's Inn, the Inner Temple, the Middle Temple, and Gray's Inn, Etc.* (Littleton, CO: Fred B. Rothman & Co., 1987), described the course of study in these Inns of Court:

> It deserves notice that, at periods long anterior to the Reformation, the Holy Scriptures were studied in the Inns of Court, a fact which has been overlooked by those who suppose that, prior to that era, the sacred volume was altogether a "sealed book" to the laity. The author of the "Miroir Aux Justices" having recounted the perversions of the law, which induced him to compile that compendium, says, "Taking the same into my serious consideration, and the foundation and original of the usages of England, given by the law, together with the rewards of good judges, and the punishments of others, I thought it needful (wherein my companions gave me their assistance), to study the Old and New Testament for the saving of souls from perpetual damnation, notwithstanding that the same were disused by false judges. And we found that the Holy Scripture remained in the Old and New Testament." Fortescue, who lived in the reign of Henry VI, in his account of the *Studies in the Inns of Court and Chancery,* expressly tells us: "On the working days, most of them [the students] apply themselves to the study of the law; and, on the holy days, to the study of the Sacred Scriptures; and out of the time of divine service, to the reading of Chronicles; for there, indeed, are virtues studied, and vices exiled." Quotations from the inspired volume occur frequently in Fortescue's work, *De Laudibus,* etc., which shew that he was

> intimately acquainted with both the Old and New Testaments. When we remember that, at this period, according to Fortescue's computation, there were, at the least, one hundred students in each of the lesser inns, and two hundred in each of the Four Inns of Court, it seems to follow, that a large portion of the educated classes among the laity in this country, had opportunities of becoming familiar with the contents of the Bible. In the *Doctor and Student,* another of our ancient books, the author of which lived AD 1460, there are also many references to Law, Prophets, and Evangelists [common title for the authors of the four Gospels]: "For a law," it is remarked, "is not properly called the law of God because it was showed by the revelation of God, but also because it directed a man by the nearest way to the felicity eternal, as being the laws of the Old Testament, that being called morals, and the laws of the Evangelists, the which were shewed in a much more excellent manner than the law of the Old Testament was; for that was shewed by the mediation of an angel, but the law of the Evangelists was shewed by the mediation of our Lord Jesus Christ, God and man. And the law of God is always righteous and just, for it was made and given after the will of God; and, therefore, all acts and deeds of man be called righteous and just, when they be done according to the law of God." [36]

Barrister Pearce offers a detailed description of the physical facilities of the Inns of Court. Of the Middle Temple he wrote,

> The arms of the Middle Temple are a holy lamb, bearing a banner, surmounted by a red cross, on a shield Argent charged with a cross Gules. In ancient times, this lamb, symbolizing our sacred Redeemer, was embroidered on a cloth, and, after episcopal benediction, was worn by the faithful, with the words of the Evangelist St. John, *agnus Dei qui tollis peccata mundi* [John 1:29: *"Lamb of God, who taketh away the sin of the world."*] (p. 271).... The hall is also lighted by a handsome louvre, on

36. Barrister Robert R. Pearce, *A History of the Inns of Court and Chancery: with Notices of Their Ancient Discipline, Rules, Orders, and Customs, Readings, Moots, Masques, Revels, and Entertainments; Including an Account of the Eminent Men of the Four Learned and Honourable Societies,—Lincoln's Inn, the Inner Temple, the Middle Temple, and Gray's Inn, Etc.* (Littleton, CO: Fred B. Rothman & Co., 1987), 75–76.

which was formerly a dial with the motto, *lux Dei, lex Dei* [light of God, law of God].[37]

America

On January 10, 1884, Oscar S. Straus (1850–1926, later U.S. Secretary of Commerce and Labor) delivered a lecture in New York City titled "The Origin of the Republican Form of Government in the United States and the Hebrew Commonwealth." As the *New York Times* described his speech, "In the conception of the American Union Mr. Straus showed how deeply Americans were imbued with religious principles. The Bible was studied as no people excepting only the Jews had studied it."[38] They, of course, studied both the Old and New Testaments, but when speaking about law and government, they relied primarily on the Old Testament, the Hebrew Scriptures. They drew parallels between the thirteen colonies and the twelve tribes of Israel, their crossing of the Atlantic and their struggles for independence were like the Hebrews' crossing the Red Sea and their struggle for freedom from slavery in Egypt, and they compared King George III to the Pharaoh of Egypt.

While colonial Americans drew parallels between themselves and Israel, many, including James Adair, Edward Winslow, and Elias Boudinot, believed the native Americans may be descended from the ten lost tribes of Israel.[39] The Rev. Cotton Mather so identified with the Jews that he began wearing a skullcap and calling himself a rabbi.[40] Hebrew was taught at Harvard, Yale, Dartmouth, and other early American colleges.[41]

Even though Thomas Paine later in life appeared to be hostile to Christianity, nevertheless in his widely-circulated pamphlet "Common Sense," he relied primarily upon the Hebrew Scriptures to build a case for independence and against hereditary monarchy:

37. Pearce, 322.

38. "The Hebrew Commonwealth: Liberty in Old Testament Lands and in the United States," *New York Times*, January 11, 1884. Straus later expanded his lecture into a book, *The Origin of Republican Form of Government in the United States of America* (Putnam, 1901).

39. Shalom Goldman, ed. *Hebrew and the Bible in America* (Brandeis University Press, 1993), 61–90, 110. Boudinot served as the first President of the Continental Congress.

40. Goldman, 105.

41. Goldman, 199–245.

> Government by kings was first introduced into the world by the heathens, from whom the children of Israel copied the custom. It was the most prosperous invention the Devil ever set on foot for the promotion of idolatry.... Monarchy is ranked in Scripture as one of the sins of the Jews, for which a curse in reserve is denounced against them.... All anti-monarchical parts of Scripture, have been very smoothly glossed over in monarchical governments, but they undoubtedly merit the attention of countries which have their governments yet to form.... But where, say some, is the king of America? I'll tell you, friend: he reigns above, and does not make havoc of mankind like the royal brute of Britain.... The Jews, elated with success [in Gideon's victory over the Midianites], and attributing it to the generalship of Gideon, proposed making him king, saying: *"Rule thou over us, thou and thy son and thy son's son."* Here was the temptation in its fullest extent; but Gideon, in the piety of his soul, replied: *"I will not rule over you, neither shall my son rule over you; the Lord shall rule over you."* Gideon doth not decline the honor, but denieth the right to give it.... These portions of Scripture are direct and positive; they admit of no equivocal construction. That the Almighty hath here entered his protest against monarchical government is true, or the Scriptures are false.[42]

The thirteen colonies established by the English on the North American Atlantic seacoast largely followed English common law. For the most part, the common law was already based upon Mosaic principles. But in many instances, particularly in New England, the colonists modified the common law to more specifically embody the legal precepts of the Bible. As Gabriel Sivan says, "Insofar as it was observed at all, English Common Law was checked for its agreement with 'the word of God.' Cases were often decided by reference to Scripture and, as the early records show, agreements of counsel and even deliberation of the General Court (or Legislature) took more heed of Mosaic injunction or Prophetic wisdom than of the Lord High Chancellor's decisions."[43] In the year

---

42. Thomas Paine, "Common Sense," quoted by Straus, 136–38. Whatever Paine's actual religious beliefs may have been at that time or later, a reading of "Common Sense" clearly bears out Straus's claim that Paine used the Bible to build his case. Even if, as is commonly believed, Paine was a religious skeptic, the fact that he felt compelled to use the Scriptures to make his argument, is itself a convincing testimony to the hold the Bible had upon colonial Americans. Paine's religious skepticism may have developed later in his life.

43. Gabriel Sivan, *The Bible and Civilization* (Keter Publishing House Jerusalem, 1973; New

1636, the general court (legislature) of colonial Massachusetts established a council to draft a body of laws "agreeable to the word of God." Until such laws were drafted and adopted at the next session of the general court, magistrates were to follow such laws as were already adopted, and where no statute governed, to decide cases "as near to the law of God as they can."[44] In 1641 the Massachusetts general court adopted the Massachusetts Body of Liberties, which had been drafted by Nathaniel Ward, a minister who had some legal training. The Body of Liberties enacted into statute many provisions of the Old Testament law and stated that no man's life was to be taken unless by some express law established by the general court or by the Word of God. It further provided that

> In all criminal offenses where the law hath prescribed no certain penalty, the judges have power to inflict penalties according to the rule of God's Word.[45]

The Massachusetts Body of Liberties, adopted by the General Court of Massachusetts (actually a legislative body) in 1636, contained the following provision:

Article 94

1. If any man after legall conviction shall have or worship any other god, but the lord god, he shall be put to death.
2. If any men or woemen be a witch, (that is hath or consulteth with a familiar spirit), They shall be put to death.
3. If any man shall Blaspheme the name of god, the father, Sonne or Holie ghost, with direct, expresse, presumptous or high handed blasphemie, or shall curse god in the like manner, he shall be put to death.

Massachusetts court documents also record a colonial magistrate named Symonds who declared in a judgment that "the fundamental law which God and nature has given to the people cannot be infringed. The

---

York Times Book Co., 1973), 135.

44. *Massachusetts Colonial Records,* I: 174; quoted by Paul Samuel Reinsch, Ph.D., L.L.B., *English Common Law in the Early American Colonies* (Madison, Wisconsin: Da Capo Press, 1898), 11.

45. *Massachusetts Body of Liberties,* 1; quoted by Reinsch, 13.

right of property is such a fundamental right."[46] The colonists of Massachusetts believed that the common law for the most part was consistent with the higher laws of nature and of nature's God, and to whatever extent they were inconsistent with that higher law, they were not law but error.[47]

The Connecticut code of 1642 was largely copied from that of Massachusetts.[48] Criminals were to be punished "according to the mind of God revealed in his word"[49]:

> In the fundamental agreement all freemen assent that the Scriptures hold forth a perfect rule for the direction and government of all men in all duties. The Scriptural laws of inheritance, dividing allotments, and all things of like nature are adopted, thus very clearly founding the entire system of civil and criminal law on the word of God.
>
> This principle is re-enacted in similar language in 1644.[50]

The influence of the Mosaic Law upon the Framers of the American republic was both direct and indirect—direct through their reading the Scriptures and listening to preaching based upon the Scriptures, and indirect through reading or listening to others who in turn derived their ideas from the Scriptures.

The direct influence is seen through the study of two political science professors, Dr. Donald S. Lutz and Charles Hyneman, who researched some 15,000 writings (speeches, diary entries, letters, articles, monographs, etc.) with explicitly political content by leading Americans from 1760 to 1805, for the purpose of identifying quotations. They found that the source more frequently quoted than any other was the Bible, accounting for 34% of all quotations. They found that the book of the Bible quoted more frequently than any other was Deuteronomy, the restatement of the Mosaic Law first recorded in Exodus. As indirect evidence, they found, further, that if one excludes the Bible and considers only non-Biblical writers, the writers quoted most frequently were Baron Montesquieu of

46. Reinsch, 16.

47. Reinsch, 20.

48. Reinsch, 25.

49. Reinsch, 26.

50. Reinsch, 26.

France (a devout Roman Catholic), 8.3%, and Sir William Blackstone of England (a devout Anglican), 7.9%.[51]

President Woodrow Wilson, who also served as President of Princeton University, wrote that "the laws of Moses as well as the laws of Rome contributed suggestions and impulse to the men and institutions which were to prepare the modern world; and if we could have but eyes to see... we should readily discover how very much besides religion we owe to the Jew."[52]

In his *Life and Literature of the Ancient Hebrews,* Lyman Abbott wrote:

> It would be impossible to mention any people of even a much later age... whose law and constitution embodied an ideal so noble as that embodied in the Hebrew civil laws, or any people whose history shows the existence of political institutions so essentially just, free, and humane.... We gentiles owe our life to Israel. It is Israel who, in bringing us the divine law, has laid the foundation of liberty. It is Israel who had the first free institutions the world ever saw.... When sometimes our own unchristian prejudices flame out against the Jewish people, let us remember that all that we have and all that we are we owe, under God, to what Judaism has given us.[53]

It is not surprising, then, that on October 4, 1982, Congress passed Public Law 97–280, declaring 1983 the "Year of the Bible." The President signed the bill into law. The opening sentences of the bill read:

> Whereas Biblical teachings inspired concepts of civil government that are contained in our Declaration of Independence and the Constitution of the United States;
>
> Whereas this Nation now faces great challenges that will test this Nation as it has never been tested before; and
>
> Whereas that renewing our knowledge of and faith in God through Holy Scripture can strengthen us as a nation and a people....

51. Donald S. Lutz, "The Relative Influence of European Writers on Later Eighteenth Century American Political Thought," *American Political Science Review* [1984], 189–97; see also Charles Hyneman and Donald Lutz, *American Political Writing during the Founding Era 1760–1805* Vols. I & II (Indianapolis: Liberty Press, 1983).

52. Woodrow Wilson, *The State* (1890), quoted by Sivan, 143.

53. Lyman Abbott, *Life and Literature of the Ancient Hebrews* (1901), quoted by Sivan, 108.

Congress, speaking for the nation at this late date, recognized the formative role of Biblical Law upon the founding of America.

Russell Kirk was less likely than Wines to look to Bible chapter and verse for specific provisions of American law. But he clearly understood that the Law of Moses inculcated in Americans a conviction that a sovereign God watches over human affairs, that man is sinful and utopian schemes are therefore doomed to failure, and that law has an ethical dimension. He wrote,

> ...American political theory and institutions, and the American moral order, cannot be well understood, or maintained, or renewed, without repairing to the Law and the Prophets. "In God we trust," the motto of the United States, is a reaffirmation of the Covenants made with Noah and Abraham and Moses and the Children of Israel, down to the last days of prophecy. The earthly Jerusalem never was an immense city: far more Jews live in New York City today than were inhabitants of all Palestine at the height of Solomon's glory. But the eternal Jerusalem, the city of spirit, still has more to do with American order than has even Boston which the Puritans founded, or New York which the Dutch founded, or Washington which arose out of a political compromise between Jeffersonians and Hamiltonians. Faith and hope may endure when earthly cities are reduced to rubble: that, indeed, is a principal lesson from the experience of Israel under God.[54]

How strange it is, then, that so many modern secular legal historians utterly ignore the Hebrew foundations of Western law. This blind spot toward the Bible and all things spiritual is endemic in the academic world.

But recognized or not, Moses stands as a colossus of history, the consummate statesman and lawgiver whose precepts have echoed through the corridors of time for thousands of years.

In the Great Hall of the U.S. Department of Justice Building in Washington D.C. are a series of large murals. One depicts Moses. The depiction of Moses is of special interest because it shows him pointing above to rays of light coming from heaven. He holds a scroll, and at his feet two figures (possibly Aaron and Joshua) are copying from the scroll onto a stone tablet. This mural is centrally located between the two other ancient

54. Russell Kirk, *The Roots of American Order* (Regnery Gateway, 1991), 48–49.

lawgivers, Menes and Hammurabi, and is slightly larger than either of them. Both Menes and Hammurabi face toward Moses, while Moses looks upward to the Divine.

In the entrance to the Rayburn House Office Building in Washington, D.C., are relief portraits of Moses and other figures on the walls of the building's subway terminal that connects with the Capitol. The portraits are as follows:

1. **Moses** is the central portrait. Of the 23 portraits, eleven face Moses from his right, and eleven face Moses from his left. Moses alone is a direct facial portrait; all of the others are side views.
2. **Hammurabi** (circa 2000 BC).
3. **Lycurgus**, whose life is variously placed from the 9th to 6th centuries BC, developed the legal code of Sparta. Herodotus wrote that Lycurgus received edicts from the oracle at Delphi, and these either were the laws that Lycurgus gave to Sparta, or were the divine sanction for the laws that he developed.
4. **Solon** (circa 638–588 BC), whose name has become almost synonymous with legislator, was an archon or ruler of Athens. Solon argued that Zeus was a just god and that he worked out his justice on earth.
5. **Gaius** (AD 110–180), whose *Institutiones* were completed around AD 161 as a manual of legal study for students, has given us our best information about the Roman Law of the Twelve Tables. It should be noted that no complete copy of the Twelve Tables is known to exist today, but authorities can piece together much of its content from the writings of Gaius and others.
6. **Papinian** (circa AD 210) served as a prime minister of Rome and was a leading jurist who reassembled the Roman legal code at a time when Roman jurisprudence was in a state of disarray. In keeping with the spirit of the times, he justified absolute monarchy, but he did so on the ground that the people had delegated absolute powers to the emperor. According to Durant, "Papinian's *Quaestiones* and *Responsa* were so distinguished by clarity, humanity, and justice that Justinian's collections leaned heavily on these works. When Caracalla killed Geta, he bade Papinian write a legal defense of the act; Papinian refused, saying that it was

'easier to commit fratricide than to justify it.'" Caracalla ordered him beheaded, and a soldier performed the deed with an ax in the presence of the emperor (III: 634). After Papinian's death, Ulpian continued his work, and nearly a third of their judgments survive in Justinian's *Digest.*

7. **Justinian** (AD 482–565) was the most famous of the Eastern Roman emperors. He undertook major revisions of the Roman legal code, culminating in the Justinian *Codex,* the *Digest,* and the *Institutes,* which three works are known collectively as the *Corpus Jurus Civilis.* The changes in Roman law wrought by Justinian brought the law more in keeping with the canon law of the Church and the principles of Christianity. In keeping with the Eastern tradition, Justinian saw himself as the vicar of Christ and, in a sense, almost the embodiment of Christ. His *Corpus* deals with matters of doctrine and heresy as well as civil and criminal matters. When later jurists like Bracton sought to introduce concepts of Roman law into English common law, the Roman law they used was the Justinian Code.
8. **Tribonian** (AD 500–547) was the jurist appointed by Justinian to head the commission that collected and codified the Roman laws into the Justinian Code.
9. **Maimonides** (AD 1135–1204).
10. **Pope Gregory IX** (circa AD 1147–1241) was known for standing against absolute monarchical power by asserting and using the papal power to excommunicate kings and place their kingdoms under interdiction. In particular he employed these weapons against Emperor Frederick II of Germany for Frederick's failure to fulfill his vow to lead a crusade to Palestine.
11. **Pope Innocent III** (AD 1161–1216) had studied jurisprudence at Bologna and theology at Paris. Besides his diplomacy and statesmanship in mediating and resolving numerous disputes among the kings and kingdoms of Europe and his leadership in the earlier Crusades, he was best known for his decretal, *Corpus Juris Canonici.* The decretal provides that the German princes have the authority to elect their emperor because that authority was given to them by the Pope when he transferred authority over the Holy

Roman Emperor from the powers of Byzantium to Charlemagne, but that if the Pope finds that the princes have elected an unworthy emperor, he can require them to elect a new one. The essence of the decretal was that civil authority derives its legitimacy from God through the intermediary of the Church.

12. **Simon de Montfort** (AD 1200–1265) is probably Simon the younger; his father Simon de Montfort was a noted leader in the Crusades. The younger de Montfort was Bishop of Lincoln and a lifelong champion of ecclesiastical and governmental reform in England. De Montfort's main contribution to English legal history was his effort to transform the old Anglo-Saxon witenagemot or Great Council into the modern Parliament, consisting of two knights from each shire and two burgesses from each borough. Much of English history over the following four centuries would consist of the struggle for supremacy between the king and the Parliament.

13. **St. Louis IX** (AD 1214–1270) was King of France and leader of one of the most successful of the Crusades, which he undertook against the counsel of his advisors in fulfillment of a vow to God. Under his reign the *curia regis* (court of the king) was established and a law book titled *Etablissements de Saint Louis,* a collection of juridical customs, was completed toward the end of his reign. French legends picture him holding court and delivering judgments under the oak tree of Vincennes.

14. **Alphonso X** (AD 1221–1284) was king of Castille, a northern kingdom in Spain. Known as Alphonso the Wise, he developed a legal code for Castille based on the Justinian Code; long after his death this legal code became the code of all Spain. He also commissioned a Spanish Bible, the Old Testament of which was translated directly from Hebrew into Spanish without the intermediary of Greek or Latin.

15. **Edward I** (AD 1239–1307), the arch-villain of the movie *Braveheart,* was the English king who tried to conquer Scotland. But he also strengthened the authority of Parliament, calling 45 parliaments during his reign, and he began the development of statutory law to supplement the common law, commissioning Henricus Bracton to systematize the common law. He also began the prac-

tice of publishing yearbooks recording the cases and precedents established each year, thus aiding the principle of *stare decisis*. His reign also began the practice of bar exams.

16. **Sulieman the Magnificent** (AD 1494–1566), Sultan of the Ottoman Empire, was a Muslim who considered the Koran to be the divine source of law.

17. **Jean Baptiste Colbert** (AD 1619–1683) was Comptroller General of the Finances for France, reformed the financial system to facilitate merchantilism and industry, infuriated many by persuading King Louis XIV to establish a Chamber of Justice to inquire into all kinds of financial malfeasance, and encouraged exploration and the establishment of colonies.

18. **Robert Joseph Pothier** (AD 1699–1772) was a French jurist and law professor known for his scholarship on French and Roman law.

19. **Blackstone** (AD 1723–1780).

20. **George Mason** (AD 1726–1792) was a Virginia delegate to the Constitutional Convention. He objected to certain provisions in the Constitution and therefore opposed its ratification. As a member of the Virginia Constitutional Convention of 1776, he played a major role in writing the Virginia Declaration of Rights. Thomas Jefferson relied in part upon this Declaration when he drafted the Declaration of Independence, and the Declaration of Rights also formed the basis for the Bill of Rights to the U.S. Constitution. A member of the Episcopal Church, Mason was one of the earliest Virginians to publicly urge freeing the slaves.

21. **Thomas Jefferson** (AD 1743–1826) is best known as the primary author of the Declaration of Independence. In his later years he probably was not an orthodox Christian, but he recognized that "The God who gave us life, gave us liberty," and asked, "Can the liberties of the people be secure when we have removed their only firm basis, a conviction in the minds of the people that these liberties are... the gift of God? That they are not to be violated but with His wrath?"

22. **Napoleon** (AD 1769–1821) was the emperor who restored order to France after the chaos of the French Revolution. He developed

> the Napoleonic Code that influenced law in parts of the United States.[55]

In *Art in the United States Capitol,* prepared by the Architect of the Capitol under the direction of the Joint Committee of the Library (Washington, D.C. U.S. Government Printing Office, 1976), the author states that the portraits in the Rayburn Office Building are plaster models, and the marble portraits are displayed in the House of Representatives Chamber. As in the Rayburn Building, the full face of Moses is central, and eleven profiles face left and eleven face right, although the order is reversed.[56]

Similarly, on the east outside wall of the U.S. Supreme Court Building is a pediment consisting of nine human figures. The central and largest of these human figures is Moses, who is seated and holding a tablet in each hand. The fact that these tablets are recognized as symbolizing the Ten Commandments, even though they contain no writing, demonstrates how thoroughly ingrained the Ten Commandments have been into American law and culture. On Moses' right hand is the Chinese lawgiver Confucius, a smaller figure than Moses even though Confucius is standing while Moses is seated. Other figures on Moses' right, in descending order and size, are a man holding a child, a man with a shield, and a woman with a book. On Moses' left, in descending order and size, are the Greek lawgiver Solon, a woman carrying a child and a sheaf of grain, a man with a shield, and a man with a cornucopia. On both sides, most of these figures face Moses; Confucius is a notable exception.[57] Clearly, those who designed our nation's capitol and other public buildings recognized the centrality of Moses and Biblical Law to the laws and institutions of America and the West.

Wines wrote that if Moses could somehow address a gathering of American lawmakers today (circa 1850), he would say something like this:

> Gentlemen, at length my word is fulfilled. What you boast of doing now, I accomplished, as far as in me lay, in a distant age. I broke the doors of the house of bondage, and proclaimed the principle of universal equality among men. I substituted for castes and privileged classes, a nation of freemen, and for arbitrary and capricious impositions, the reign of law, equal and universal. I preferred peace to war, general competence and

55. Personal observation of the author in Washington, D.C., 29 May–1 June, 2002.

56. *Art in the United States Capitol* (U.S. Govt. Printing Office, 1976), 282–93.

57. Personal observation of the author in Washington, D.C., 29 May–1 June, 2002.

happiness to the false glory of arms, substantial blessings to airy nothings. My highest efforts were constantly directed to procure for all the citizens the greatest equality practicable, both of the labors and enjoyments of life; for the whole commonwealth of Israel, lands well cultivated, good habitations, rich herds, and a population healthy, numerous, enlightened, pious, and contented. It is false, what ignorance and irreligion have charged against me, that I held in abhorrence, after the example of Egypt, foreign nations. No other legislator in the world has ever shown to the stranger an equal justice, and equal tenderness, with myself. Nor is this all: I earnestly labored to secure a universal intellectual equality. Far from being jealous of the superiority, which God and the discipline of my faculties had given me, I nourished the animating hope, that all the lights, which I possessed, would one day become the common property of all, even the humblest of my fellow-creatures. LAWS,—not men,—were the rulers of my republic; CONSENT,—not force,—the basis of my government. Conquests, and servitude; magnificent palaces, and servitude; a certain amount of science, and still servitude;—behold a brief but true picture of the governments, by which I was surrounded. It is a libel upon my name and memory to charge me with having framed my institutions upon the model of those stupendous systems of fraud and tyranny. By the wisdoms of my counsels and the energy of my policy, I overthrew, at a blow, the whole degrading apparatus of political jugglery and priestly despotism. I reduced the speculative ideas of my own and the preceding ages to a single sublime principle of simplicity. I recognized the happiness and well-being of the people, as the one supreme law of political philosophy. By the institutions founded upon this principle, I impressed a new character upon my age and species; I gave a new impulse to man, both in his individual and social energies; I fixed upon my labors the indestructible seal of a divine wisdom and beneficience. Forward, then, gentlemen, without fear or faltering, in the doctrine of Jehovah,—in those great principles of free and equal government, which, taught by the Divine Spirit, I first promulgated to the world; and to which, after so many ages of tyranny and misgovernment, you have at length returned. Cling to these principles, legislators of a world that had no being when I founded my republic. Give them a broader development, a higher activity; and the civilization,

> the prosperity, the happiness flowing from them, shall outstrip your fondest hopes, and more than realize the brightest vision of bard or prophet.[58]

Columnist Don Feder tells the story of a rabbi who was travelling in the country, when the driver of his coach realized he had forgotten to bring feed for the horses. The driver stopped the coach to take some grain from a farmer's field, asking the rabbi to keep watch in case someone saw him. As he began stealing grain, the rabbi called out, "One sees!" The driver returned to the coach, and, seeing nothing, protested that the rabbi was playing tricks on him. The rabbi pointed toward Heaven and repeated, "One sees!" Feder concluded,

> This, ladies and gentlemen, is the essence of the Jewish mission: to persuade humanity that someone indeed is watching us, one to whom we all are ultimately accountable. On the success or failure of this mission the fate of the world hinges.[59]

Questions for Reflection, Discussion, and More Reflection

1. What makes Hebrew Law and government distinctive from all others in the ancient world?
2. Explain Wines's contention that the Hebrew laws, while perfectly wise for their time and place, might not be wise as applied to other societies at other times. Do you agree with him?
3. How did the Jewish scholar Maimonides influence the commercial law of Europe?
4. What were the Inns of Court, and how were they influenced by Biblical Law?
5. In his treatise "The Age of Reason" Thomas Paine seemed hostile to Christianity. Why would he rely so heavily upon Scripture in his pamphlet "Common Sense"?

Questions continued on next page....

58. Wines, 637–39.

59. Don Feder, *A Jewish Conservative Looks at Pagan America* (Huntington House, 1993), 122–23; reprinting speech by Feder to 13th anniversary dinner of Yeshiva Migdal Torah, Chicago, IL, 21 May 1992.

Questions *continued*

6. Why was the influence of the Hebrew laws greater on legal systems in the West than in the East?
7. Define canon law and common law. How does Biblical Law influence each of these?
8. Why did New England, more than most of the other colonies, draft its laws using Old Testament Israel as the model? Was it because of the theology of the founders of the New England colonies?
9. Would you agree that Moses was the world's greatest lawgiver? What other historical figures might come close?
10. Identify some symbolic references to the Mosaic Law in Washington, D.C. today.

CHAPTER 17

HEBREW LAW IN THE AMERICAN COURTS:[1] *Citing the Moral Foundations of Law*

I. INTRODUCTION

From the beginning of our republic through the present, American courts have commonly quoted or cited the Ten Commandments and other portions of Biblical Law in their official published decisions. But how frequently are they cited, in what form, and for what purpose?

Seeking an answer to these questions, in March 2002, this writer conducted a Lexis[2] computer search to discover how often courts have cited the Decalogue. The research is far from complete, but when the words "Ten Commandments" were input, Lexis reported 515 cases in which that term has been used. This includes only published decisions of courts of record: The U.S. Supreme Court, U.S. Courts of Appeals, Federal District Courts, State Supreme Courts, and occasionally state courts of appeals.

A further search using the term "Decalogue" revealed 331 cases in which that term is quoted or cited. Searches for individual commandments, conducted in October 2002, revealed many more: "First Commandment": twenty-six cases; "Second Commandment": twenty-four cases; "Third Commandment": nine cases; "Fourth Commandment": forty-four cases; "Fifth Commandment": forty-five cases; "Sixth Commandment": twenty-seven cases; "Seventh Commandment": twenty-nine cases; "Eighth Commandment": thirty-four cases; Ninth Commandment": nine cases; and "Tenth Commandment": thirteen cases.

1. The author originally wrote this chapter as an article for the Plymouth Rock Foundation's *Letter from Plymouth Rock.* It was later reprinted in revised form under the title "The Use of the Ten Commandments in American Courts" in the *Oak Brook College Journal of Law & Public Policy,* V: 99–141 (2006) and later reprinted by the *Liberty University Law Review* (III:1 Spring 2009, 15–46).

2. Lexis and Westlaw are two companies that enable their subscribers (usually judges, lawyers, law professors, and law students) to research cases, statutes, and other legal documents online.

Added together, these citations total 1,106 cases. However, this figure needs to be qualified in several ways:

(1) One case may cite the Decalogue many times, yet this will be reported as one citation. However, if different terms are in the same case, this may result in multiple citations. For example, if a case refers to the "Decalogue" and then refers also to the "Second Commandment" and "Fourth Commandment," this will be reported as three citations. However, if the case referred to the "Second and Fourth Commandments," the Lexis search might not report this at all since the exact term "Second Commandment" or "Fourth Commandment" was not entered.

(2) Other references to the Decalogue in different terms would not be uncovered by this search. For example, if a court referred to "the stone tablets delivered on Mt. Sinai" or the "admonitions of Moses," these would escape detection. Similarly a reference to "Thou shalt not kill" without the Commandment being cited by number would not come up in this search. Likewise, if a court simply referred to Exodus 20:4, the search would not have found this citation.

(3) Frequently, when he looked up the case, the author found that the court cited other cases that the computer search did not reveal. This, plus the other factors mentioned above, lead the author to believe he has only scratched the surface of the myriad cases that employ the Decalogue. He hopes to expand this search as time permits.

(4) The Lexis search obviously does not include the innumerable cases in which local trial judges and sometimes appellate judges have quoted or cited the Ten Commandments in unpublished opinions. Nor does it include citations by administrative courts.

The different systems by which different theological traditions number the Ten Commandments can be confusing in court citations. Jews generally regard *"I am the LORD thy God"* as the First Commandment while Catholics and Protestants generally regard that declaration as the introduction or preamble. Catholics combine *"Thou shalt have no other gods before me"* and *"Thou shalt not worship a graven image"* into the First Commandment, while Jews combine them as the Second

Commandment, and most Protestants divide those commands into the First and Second. Jews and most Protestants regard *"Thou shalt not covet"* as the Tenth Commandment, while Catholics divide this prohibition into *"Thou shalt not covet thy neighbor's wife"* as the Ninth and *"Thou shalt not covet anything that is thy neighbor's"* as the Tenth. (Most Lutherans follow the Catholic enumeration of the Commandments.) Perhaps unmindful of these distinctions, some courts have referred to *"Thou shalt not kill"* as the Fifth Commandment while others have called it the Sixth. The prohibition against adultery is sometimes called the Sixth and sometimes the Seventh, while the prohibition against stealing is sometimes called the Seventh and sometimes the Eighth. The resultant confusion does not present a major problem, but it shows the wisdom of Alabama Chief Justice Roy Moore in keeping the commandments unnumbered. Later in this chapter, as we discuss the courts' treatment of the Commandments individually, we will categorize them by description (*"Thou shalt not kill,"* etc.) rather than by number.

The study reveals that the courts use the Ten Commandments in several ways:

(1) Often courts cite or quote a portion of the Decalogue to underscore the importance of a statute and enhance its moral authority.

(2) Courts likewise cite the Decalogue to establish that a certain act is in fact a common law crime.

(3) Also, at times, the courts cite the Ten Commandments to distinguish the common law from actual statutory offenses.

(4) Judges often use the Decalogue to interpret the meaning of statutes. For example, sabbatarian laws have their origin in the Commandment to *"remember the Sabbath and keep it holy."* To determine whether the Sabbath refers to Saturday or Sunday, courts have looked to the Decalogue and also to the extra-Biblical Jewish law, the practice of the New Testament church, and practices of Jews and Christians thereafter. The laws of many jurisdictions exempted "works of charity and necessity" from Sunday closing laws, and courts have often looked to the Mosaic Law, the New Testament, and Jewish and Christian history to determine the meaning and scope of these exceptions.

(5) Sometimes the courts cite the Ten Commandments to establish that a certain act is *mala in se* or of moral turpitude.[3] For example, a Louisiana school district terminated the employment of a school bus driver because she had been convicted of theft. State law provided that she could be terminated for conviction of a crime only if the crime involved moral turpitude. To establish that theft was an act of moral turpitude, the court noted that theft was a violation not only of state law but also of the Decalogue.[4]

(6) Courts have also used the Decalogue to establish moral responsibility or mental capacity. For example, in a case involving a thirteen-year-old boy charged with murder, the court admitted evidence that the boy had been taught the Ten Commandments and therefore knew that murder was wrong.[5]

(7) A few of these cases involve court challenges to public Ten Commandments displays. These citations do not establish our contention that the Ten Commandments are the moral foundation of law.

(8) A few involve those who raise Free Exercise Clause defenses, such as those who object to military service because of the Commandment *"Thou shalt not kill,"* refuse to rise for the judge in court because *"Thou shalt have no other gods before me,"* or refuse to salute the flag because *"Thou shalt not worship a graven image."* Again, these are a negligible part of the total number of cases.

(9) At times judges have employed the language of the Decalogue as a literary tool. *Bray v. United States Net & Twine Co.* involved a patent for a device that was designed to prevent fishing lines from snaggling, thereby causing the fisherman "to indulge in expressions not altogether in harmony with the precepts of the decalogue."[6] A 6th Circuit Court of Appeals Judge used his literary

3. Crimes classified as *mala in se,* such as murder and theft, are wrong in and of themselves regardless of a statute, while crimes classed *malum prohibitum* are wrong only because the law prohibits them. Many would classify traffic offenses as *malum prohibitum,* although one could argue that driving with willful disregard for the safety of others is wrong in and of itself. One might say that crimes that violate the Law of Nature are *mala in se.*

4. *Rochon v. Iberia Parish School Board,* 601 So.2d 808 (1992).

5. *People v. Thompson,* 211 P.2d 1, 4–5 (1949).

6. *Bray v. United States Net & Twine Co.*, 70 F. 1006, 1007 (1895); cf. *Wright v. United States,* 108 F. 805, 812 (1901).

> skills to refer to the "commandments" of the Bill of Rights as "thou shalt not violate anyone's right to be secure in his person against unreasonable seizure" and "thou shalt not deprive any person of life, liberty or property without due process of law."[7] *New York v. Vecchio* referred to the statute which sets forth the various factors to consider in dismissing an indictment as "the decalogue of possible determinants."[8] *Ballengee v. Florida* referenced an article by Federal District Court Chief Judge Edwin J. Devitt titled "Ten Commandments for the New Judge."[9] In *State ex rel. Lashly v. Becker,* 235 S.W. 1017, 1037–38 (1921), dissenting Judge Higbee argued by analogy that "the simple truth is that section 57 no more repeals section 1 or the proviso of section 7 of article 4 than the Sermon on the Mount abrogates the Ten Commandments. Indeed, the Master gave a new interpretation to the Commandments. Envy of another's goods is larceny; lust is adultery; hatred is murder. Still, the Law, written by God's finger on the Tables of Stone, remains the Gibraltar of civilization."

These usages demonstrate how thoroughly ingrained into our culture the Ten Commandments have become, to the point that the usage of this terminology lends instant recognition and moral authority to the injunctions they describe. Admittedly, however, increasing Biblical illiteracy may have dimmed Americans' recognition of the Ten Commandments in recent years.

The question is asked, "Are the Ten Commandments law or legislation?" This author's answer is that they are law in the sense that the Constitution is law, the supreme law of the land. But they are not, strictly speaking, legislation. The Ten Commandments are a summary of the basic values of our society, just as the Constitution is a statement of the fundamental principles upon which our nation is founded. But they need to be implemented by legislation or common law tradition, in ancient Israel as well as in modern societies. Much of the rest of the Mosaic Law is implementing legislation for the Ten Commandments.

But while each of the Ten Commandments has significance for civil society, not all of them were to be implemented by legislation or punished

7. *McDowell v. Rogers et al.*, 863 F.2d 1302, 1306 (1988).

8. *New York v. Vecchio*, 139 Misc.2d 165, 169 (1987); quoting *People v. Rickert*, 446 NE2d 419, 421 (1983).

9. *Ballengee v. Florida,* 144 S.2d 68, 73 n.1 (1962) (citing 46 A.B.A.J. (1961)).

as criminal violations. *"Thou shalt not covet"* is the last commandment, but nowhere in Scripture was anyone punished by civil government for simply coveting. Coveting led to wrongful actions like theft and adultery for which the Mosaic Law provided punishment, but people were not punished for coveting alone. Partly for this reason, American legislation and jurisprudence have dealt more with some commandments than with others.

First we will examine the courts' treatment of the Decalogue as a whole; then we will examine the courts' use of each Commandment individually. Let us note that these case citations cover a time span from the early 1800s to the present time, demonstrating an unbroken tradition of looking to the Ten Commandments as the moral foundation of law.

II. THE DECALOGUE AS A WHOLE

In the 1899 case of *Moore v. Strickling,* a fired public official argued that his termination for having solicited a prostitute was illegal because it did not involve moral turpitude. Noting the adultery Commandment, the West Virginia Supreme Court said of the Decalogue:

> These commandments, which, like a collection of diamonds, bear testimony to their own intrinsic worth, in themselves appeal to us as coming from a superhuman or divine source, and no conscientious or reasonable man has yet been able to find a flaw in them. Absolutely flawless, negative in terms, but positive in meaning, they easily stand at the head of our whole moral system, and no nation or people can long continue a happy existence in open violation of them.[10]

And in *Kithcart v. Metropolitan Life Insurance Co.*, Federal District Court Judge Otis expressed both the centrality of the Ten Commandments and his shock at the plaintiff's argument by beginning his opinion with the statement, "Plaintiff's plea to the jurisdiction is almost as startling as would be a motion to dismiss the decalogue."[11]

In the 1939 case of *Rogers v. State,* the Court of Appeals of Georgia upheld a Sunday closing law, ruling that,

> This is a Christian nation. The observance of Sunday is one of our established customs. It has come down to us from the

10. *Moore v. Strickling,* 33 S.E. 274, 277 (1899).

11. *Kithcart v. Metropolitan Life Insurance Co.,* 55 F. Supp. 200, 200 (W.D.Mo. 1944).

> same Decalogue that prohibited murder, adultery, perjury, and theft. It is more ancient than our common law or our form of government. It is recognized by constitutions and legislative enactments, both State and Federal.[12]

In an 1872 case involving water rights, *Yunker v. Nichols*, the Colorado Territory Supreme Court stated,

> The principles of the law are undoubtedly of universal application, but some latitude of construction must be allowed to meet the various conditions of life in different countries. The principles of the Decalogue may be applied to the conduct of men in every country and claim, but rules respecting the tenure of property must yield to the physical laws of nature, whenever such laws exert a controlling influence.[13]

In *Colorado ex. rel. Duke W. Dunbar, Attorney General v. Sam Weinstein*, the Colorado Supreme Court suspended Weinstein from the practice of law for two years for having committed perjury. Justice Holland dissented, calling for a 90-day suspension instead. He noted that "there is joy in the presence of the angels of God over one sinner that repenteth,"[14] that the defendant had sworn falsely not for personal gain but to protect his father, and that "[t]here is no reason to crucify one transgressor as a lesson for the overwhelming majority of the members of the bar who do not need the lesson."[15] He added,

> [W]e must not overlook the filial devotion and respect to his parents and elders, seemingly a part of the traditions of his [Jewish] race. It is not idle nor out of place to observe the laudable fact that statistics will show that there is a smaller percentage of Jewish people brought before the bars of justice for violations of our civil and moral laws than any other race....
>
> Regardless of all this, respondent admittedly violated his oath as a witness and also the decalogue formulated by his ancestral fathers, far removed, in bearing false witness. Fortunately

12. *Rogers v. State*, 4 S.E.2d 918, 919 (1939) (quoting Marchetti's *Law of Stage, Screen, and Radio*, 347, § 163).

13. *Yunker v. Nichols*, 1 Colo. 551, 553 (1872).

14. *Colorado ex. rel. Duke W. Dunbar, Attorney General v. Sam Weinstein*, 135 Colo. 541, 545 (1957) (quoting *Luke* 15:10).

15. *Colorado ex. rel. Duke* at 547.

> for respondent, as well as many of us, there are only ten commandments instead of forty....[16]

Hild v. Hild upheld the Maryland presumption against awarding custody of a child to a spouse found guilty of adultery, noting that adultery was prohibited by ancient law "[c]ommonly known as the Decalogue or Ten Commandments. See Exod. 20:1–17; Deut. 5:6–21."[17]

In *Murrow Indian Orphans Home v. Childers*, Oklahoma Supreme Court Justice Riley wrote in dissent concerning the Puritans, that

> The Ten Commandments, as a whole, constituted the warp and the woof of the social fabric to be administered alike by the clergy and magistrates. The Puritans believed that if the first four Commandments were violated (purely offenses against God, and not punished by the State), religion would be disturbed and civil society would cease to exist. The Constitution is the State's moral law.[18]

In *Hill v. Wilker*, the Georgia Supreme Court refused to enforce a contract that had been made in Kansas on a Sunday. Georgia law prohibited the making of contracts on Sunday, and Georgia public policy prohibited the enforcement of a contract made on Sunday in another state, unless the law of that state permitted contracts on Sunday. In the absence of proof of Kansas contract law, the Supreme Court of Georgia presumed that Georgia's contract law applied. The Court noted that Sunday contracts were "in violation of the decalogue,"[19] and the Court refused to presume that "the people of Kansas... have annulled the decalogue."[20]

In 1976, the District of Columbia Court of Appeals upheld the constitutionality of anti-sodomy laws, noting that such "offenses were also proscribed in the Decalogue."[21]

No discussion of the role of the Decalogue in American courts would be complete without *Vidal v. Girard's Executors Sergeant*.[22] In his will,

---

16. *Colorado ex. rel. Duke.* at 545–46.

17. *Hild v. Hild,* 157 A.2d 442, 448 n.5 (1960).

18. *Murrow Indian Orphans Home v. Childers,* 171 P.2d 600, 609 (1946).

19. *Hill v. Wilker,* 41 Ga. 449, 449 (1871).

20. *Hill* at 453.

21. *Stewart v. United States,* 364 A.2d 1205, 1209 (1976).

22. *Vidal v. Girard,* 43 U.S. 127 (1844). The Lexis version says "Oldee Jewish Records," while

Girard had provided for the establishment of a school at which no minister could be hired as a teacher or staff person. The will was challenged on the ground that it was an affront to Christianity, which was the law of the land. Binney, and the counsel for Girard's Estate, noted that charity itself has Biblical origins:

> Where did the favor with which charities are regarded, and the motive by which they are established, spring from? The doctrine is traced up to the civil law. But where did Justinian get these ideas? They came from Constantine, the first Christian emperor, and they can be traced up to a higher source than that—the Bible. The Anglo-Saxons received all their principles from the same authority. Orphan-houses were exempted from taxation. Originally the injunction of the Bible was to *"honour thy father and thy mother";* but the domestic affections are selfish, and it was reserved for Christianity to enjoin the duty of *"loving thy neighbor as thyself."* [Binney seems not to have recalled that Jesus quoted these words from Leviticus 19:18.] The Jewish lawyer asked who his neighbor was, and it was hard to convince him that a Samaritan could be so. There was the same difficulty as now respecting the uncertainty of the beneficiary. The lesson of charity is taught too in the case of the woman who, in her humility, claimed only the crumbs that fell from the table, and in the beautiful parable of visiting the sick and the prisoner: *"Inasmuch as ye have done it to the least of these, ye have done it unto me."* Even in the older Jewish records, we find the same lesson of philanthropy taught where the sheaf is left for the unknown and unacknowledged stranger. It is the uncertainty of the person upon whom the benefit may fall that gives merit to the action. A legacy to a friend is no charity. The first trustee for a charity was St. Paul....
>
> In 1138, the civil law came into England, and the canon law soon afterwards, and is part of the law of that country to this day. But how did it get into the civil law? It is said from Constantine. But wherever Christianity went, charity went too. Gibbon says "the apostate Julian complained that Christians not only relieved their own poor, but those of the heathen also." The revealed law is part of the law of England. Blackstone says so. When did Christianity come into England? It reached Rome

the WestLaw version says "Old Jewish Records."

> in the time of the Apostles, where Paul and Peter both suffered. But when England? Some say at the same time that it was carried to Rome, and was there trodden down for a time. The latest period is 597, the arrival of Augustine. An archbishop of Canterbury was then appointed, and there has been one ever since. If Christianity carried the law of charity to Rome, it must have done so to England too. It was a part of the common law after the sixth century. Where is there a spot upon earth, where Christianity is found, that the law of charity does not exist also? Alfred sent an embassy to the Christian churches in Syria, in the ninth century, and had the ten commandments translated into Saxon.[23]

Webster, counsel for the appellants, argued that the prohibition against hiring clergymen as teachers was an affront to Christianity:

> The plan of education is derogatory to the Christian religion, tending to weaken men's respect for it and their conviction of its importance. It subverts the only foundation of public morals, and therefore it is mischievous and not desirable....
>
> Ministers are the usual and appointed agents of Christ.... What country was ever Christianized by lay teaching? By what sect was religious instruction ever struck out of education? None. Both in the Old and New Testaments its importance is recognized. In the Old it is said *"Thou shalt diligently teach them to thy children,"* and in the New, *"Suffer little children to come unto me and forbid them not."*[24]

Noting that "This cause has been argued with great learning and ability,"[25] the renowned Justice Joseph Story wrote for the U.S. Supreme Court,

> *It is also said, and truly, that the Christian religion is a part of the common law of Pennsylvania. But this proposition is to be received with its appropriate qualifications, and in connection with the bill of rights of that state,* as found in its constitution of government. The constitution of 1790, (and the like provision will, in substance, be found in the constitution of 1776, and in the existing constitution of 1838) expressly declares, "That all

23. *Vidal* at 149–50, 167.

24. *Vidal* at 173, 175.

25. *Vidal* at 183.

> men have a natural and indefeasible right to worship Almighty God according to the dictates of their own consciences; no man can of right be compelled to attend, erect, or support any place of worship, or to maintain any ministry against his consent; no human authority can, in any case whatever, control or interfere with the rights of conscience; and no preference shall ever be given by law to any religious establishment or modes of worship." Language more comprehensive for the complete protection of every variety of religious opinion could scarcely be used; and it must have been intended to extend equally to all sects, whether they believed in Christianity or not, and whether they were Jews or infidels. So that we are compelled to admit that *although Christianity be a part of the common law of the state, yet it is so in this qualified sense, that its divine origin and truth are admitted, and therefore it is not to be maliciously and openly reviled and blasphemed against, to the annoyance of believers or the injury of the public.* Such was the doctrine of the Supreme Court of Pennsylvania in *Updegraff v. The Commonwealth*, 11 Serg. & R. (Pa.), 394.[26]

Justice Story concluded that the provision of Girard's will which prohibited clergymen at the school was not contrary to Christianity, because the will only prohibited clergymen, not Christians or Christianity. Story asked,

> Why may not laymen instruct in the general principles of Christianity as well as ecclesiastics[?] There is no restriction as to the religious opinions of the instructors and officers.... Why may not the Bible, and especially the New Testament, without note or comment, be read and taught as a divine revelation in the college—its general precepts expounded, its evidences explained, and its glorious principles of morality inculcated? What is there to prevent a work, not sectarian, upon the general evidences of Christianity, from being read and taught in the college by lay-teachers? Certainly there is nothing in the will, that proscribes such studies.[27]

These cases, and countless more, make clear that public acknowledgement of the Ten Commandments as the moral foundation of law is entirely consistent with the legal tradition of our nation.

26. *Vidal* at 198 (emphasis added).

27. *Vidal* at 200.

III. COURTS' USE OF EACH COMMANDMENT INDIVIDUALLY

A. I Am The Lord Thy God. Thou Shalt Have No Other Gods Before Me.

The October 2002 Lexis search for the term "First Commandment" produced twenty-six case citations. The civil application of this Commandment is as a limitation on the power of government. The pagan nations that surrounded Israel practiced state-worship and emperor-worship. The people of Israel were to respect government and honor their judges and rulers, but they were to worship God alone.

While the Commandment has secular or civic applications, the Commandment normally is not implemented by governmental legislation. Consequently, few cases have been decided in which the Commandment has been applied as the moral foundation of law.

In *In the Matter of Frederick J. Chase*, the defendant was on trial for obstructing the Selective Service, and he was cited for contempt for refusing to rise when the judge entered the courtroom. He refused, he said, because "The First Commandment states, *'I am the Lord, thy God. Thou shall not have false gods before me.'*"[28] The Court of Appeals for the Seventh Circuit upheld the contempt citation, but Judge Stevens dissented in part:

> I agree that it could not be excused by a religious or other conscientious motivation. Conversely, although I share the trial judge's appraisal of the reasons for "the rising requirement," he plainly exceeded his powers by insisting not merely that defendant must rise but also that he must do so with a particular state of mind. Valid rules of conduct must be obeyed. But a citizen's respect is his to give or to withhold according to the dictates of his own conscience. Since the defendant was not present in court by choice, I do not believe he could legitimately be forced to profess a respect he did not feel.[29]

28. *In the Matter of Frederick J. Chase,* 468 F.2d 128, 129 (1972).

29. *Chase* at 140 (Stevens, J., dissenting).

Judge Stevens cited Justice Frankfurter's dissent in *West Virginia State Board of Education v. Barnette*: "Law is concerned with external behavior and not with the inner life of man."[30]

Lulay v. Lulay involved a dispute within a family-held corporation. The Oregon Supreme Court noted that around 1947 Vincent Lulay had become distressed that the company "did not operate in accordance with Christian ethics that Vincent devotedly believed in," and that he believed his brothers were in "violation of the First Commandment, apparently because he thought the other directors were worshipping mammon [money]."[31] The Court seemed to sympathize, but barred his suit on the doctrine of laches.

B. Thou Shalt Not Worship A Graven Image.

The full Commandment states,

> *Thou shalt not make unto thee any graven image, or any likeness of any thing that is in heaven above, or that is in the earth beneath, or that is in the water under the earth: Thou shalt not bow down thyself to them, nor serve them: for I the LORD thy God am a jealous God, visiting the iniquity of the fathers upon the children unto the third and fourth generation of them that hate me; And shewing mercy unto thousands of them that love me, and keep my commandments.*[32]

The Lexis search revealed twenty-four citations of the Second Commandment. Like the previous Commandment, this Commandment limits the authority of the State to require obeisance and worship through symbols. Our attention is drawn to Daniel chapter three, where the Babylonian King Nebuchadnezzar caused to be built a large golden image of a man and compelled all his subjects to fall down and worship this image. Daniel's three friends, Shadrach, Meshach, and Abednego, refused to worship the image and were cast into a fiery furnace for execution but were delivered by God. The image represented the Babylonian State, and Nebuchadnezzar as head of state and embodiment of state.

30. *West Virginia State Board of Education v. Barnette*, 319 U.S. 624, 655 (1943).

31. *Lulay v. Lulay*, 429 P.2d 802, 803 (1967).

32. *Exodus* 20:4–6.

Like the previous Commandment, this Commandment is usually not the subject of legislation, and consequently there are few cases which cite it. Most of those which do, cite it with other Commandments in Decalogue displays or with religious objections to saluting the flag or placing photographs on drivers' licenses.

In *Rensselaer v. County of Onondaga,*[33] the Supreme Court of Judicature of New York held that the Insolvent Act had to be construed with other provisions of the law to determine the right of redemption of property. The Court illustrated its point by citing this Commandment and noting that the prohibition against "making" a graven image must be construed with the rest of the Commandment concerning bowing down to the image:

> Being penal, the statute ought not to be extended by construction beyond the fair import of the words.... We might as well stop at the first section in construing the 2[n]d commandment. *"Thou shalt not make unto thee any graven image,"*... which would prohibit the labours of the statuary. It is the second section of that commandment, *"thou shalt not bow down to them, nor serve them,"* which determines the construction, and makes it, really, a commandment to *abstain from idolatry.*[34]

C. Thou Shalt Not Take The Name of The Lord Thy God in Vain.

This Commandment is commonly understood to prohibit blasphemy or profanity, but it also prohibits perjury, as stated in *The Catechism of the Catholic Church,*[35] *Luther's Small Catechism,*[36] *The Heidelberg Catechism,*[37] and other catechisms and commentaries. A principal function of government is the dispensing of justice, and the judicial system cannot properly dispense justice unless it has a means of determining the truth. The sacredness of the oath, in which one swears to tell the truth before the Omniscient God Who knows truth from falsehood even when

33. *Rensselaer v. County of Onondaga*, 1 Cow. 443 (1823).

34. *Rensselaer* at 452 (quoting *Exodus* 20:4, 5).

35. *The Catechism of the Catholic Church* (Doubleday, 1995), 577.

36. *Concordia: The Lutheran Confessions* (Concordia, 2005), 344.

37. *Heidelberg Catechism,* 1563, Article 36, Question 99, www.reformed.org/documents/index.html?mainframe=http://www.reformed.org/documents/heidelberg.html (accessed 13 May, 2016).

police, courts, and prosecutors do not, is essential to justice. However, most court citations relate perjury to the Commandment against bearing false witness, and the cases relating to the Commandment against taking the Name of the Lord in vain refer to blasphemy and profanity.

In *Cason v. Baskin*, the Florida Supreme Court decided a right to privacy claim involving a woman who claimed a biographer had written that she engaged in profanity, although the words the biographer attributed to her were, according to the woman, not really profanity. The Court noted the Biblical origin of the prohibition against profanity:

> This court has never defined the legal meaning of the word "profanity," so far as this writer has been able to discover, but a number of other courts of last resort have done so, and practically all of them, following pretty closely the dictionary meaning, define it as the use of words importing "an imprecation of Divine vengeance," of "implying Divine condemnation," or words denoting "irreverence of God and holy things,"—blasphemous. These decisions doubtless hark back to the third Commandment of the decalogue: *"Thou shalt not take the name of the LORD thy God in vain."*[38]

Other courts have wrestled with the definition of profanity or blasphemy. The Court of Common Pleas of Franklin County, Pennsylvania, considered the question in *Commonwealth v. Brown*.[39] They examined blasphemy statutes of 1794, 1860, and 1939 and quoted Blackstone as to the difference between blasphemy and profanity:

> The fourth species of offences, therefore, more immediately against God and religion, is that of blasphemy against the Almighty by denying His being or providence; or by contumelious reproaches of our Saviour Christ. Whither also may be referred all profane scoffing at the holy scripture, or exposing it to contempt and ridicule....
>
> Somewhat allied to this, though in an inferior degree, is the offence of profane and common swearing and cursing.[40]

38. *Cason v. Baskin,* 20 So.2d 243, 247 (1944). This language is quoted with approval in *Canney v. Florida,* 298 So.2d 495 (1973).

39. *Commonwealth v. Brown,* 67 Pa. D. & C. 151 (1948).

40. *Brown,* 157 (quoting William Blackstone, 4 Commentaries *59).

The court concluded that the defendant's words, while "wholly reprehensible and a clear violation of the Third Commandment, Exodus 20:7,"[41] were not blasphemy under the Pennsylvania statute and therefore could not be prosecuted.

D. Remember The Sabbath Day, To Keep It Holy.

The Lexis search revealed forty-four cases which cited the "Fourth Commandment." Because of the different numbering systems, some of these were references to the Sabbath Commandment, others to honoring one's father and mother. A few references to the "Third Commandment" actually referred to the Sabbath Commandment.

The Supreme Court of New York, Oneida County, noted that

> Our laws for the observance of the Sabbath are founded upon the command of God at Sinai that we should *"Remember the Sabbath Day to keep it holy,"* and that "the experience of mankind demonstrates that the setting apart of one day in seven is not only conducive to the spiritual welfare of the people, but it is essential to the rest and recuperation which every one needs at stated intervals from the cares, burdens, and anxieties of life. The Sabbath, therefore, is the result of the highest dictates of public policy as well as of religious duty. The Sabbath existed before Constitutions or statutes, and was sanctioned by the common law."[42]

In *Rosenbaum v. State*, the Supreme Court of Arkansas cited several leading jurists and philosophers concerning the value of the Sabbath:

> Blackstone says: "For, besides the notorious indecency and scandal of permitting any secular business to be publicly transacted on that day, in a country professing Christianity, and the corruption of morals which usually follows its profanation, the keeping one day in the seven holy, as a time of relaxation and refreshment, as well as for public worship, is of admirable service to a state considered merely as a civil institution. It humanizes, by the help of conversation and society, the manners of the lower classes, which would otherwise degenerate into a sordid

41. *Brown*, 160.

42. *Hamlin v. Bender*, 155 N.Y.S. 963, 968 (1915) (quoting *In Matter of Rupp*, 53 N.Y.S. 927, 929 (1898)).

> ferocity and savage selfishness of spirit; it enables the industrious workman to pursue his occupation in the ensuing week with health and cheerfulness; it imprints on the minds of the people their sense of their duty to God, so necessary to make them good citizens; but which yet would be worn out and defaced by an unremitted continuance of labor, without any stated times of recalling them to the worship of their Maker."
>
> Daniel Webster says: "The longer I live the more highly do I estimate the Christian Sabbath, and the more grateful do I feel to those who impress its importance on the community."
>
> Emerson says: "The Sunday is the core of our civilization, dedicated to thought and reverence. It invites to the noblest solitude and the noblest society."
>
> McCaulay says: "If the Sunday had not been observed as a day of rest during the last three centuries, I have not the slightest doubt that we should have been at this moment a poorer people and less civilized."
>
> Henry Ward Beecher says: "Sunday is the common people's great liberty day, and they are bound to see to it that work does not come into it."[43]

In keeping with Church doctrine and Jewish tradition, many jurisdictions that have Sabbath laws exempt works of necessity and charity. In defining these terms, many courts have looked to the wording of the Commandment, and to various Jewish and Christian teachings concerning its interpretation. Deciding in *Walsh et. al. v. Delaware* that football is not a "necessity," the Superior Court noted that Leviticus 23:7 prohibits only "servile" work on the Sabbath, that Church Fathers such as Ambrose of Milan and Thomas Aquinas wrote that hunting and other games were permitted on the Sabbath.[44] The court concluded, however, that "the meaning of the statute in question clearly is not controlled by the construction placed on the Fourth Commandment by the ancient Christian Church, or by any particular religious organization or sect thereof."[45]

Oklahoma v. Chesney noted that Oklahoma law prohibited "Servile labor, except works of necessity or charity"[46] on Sunday, but held that in

43. *Rosenbaum v. State,* 199 S.W. 388, 391 (1917) (quoting WILLIAM BLACKSTONE, 4 COMMENTARIES *63, *64).

44. *Walsh et. al. v. Delaware,* 136 A. 160, 161–62 (1927).

45. *Walsh* at 162.

46. *Oklahoma v. Chesney,* 233 P. 236, 237 (1925).

recognition of the rights of those who hold to another Sabbath than Sunday, the term "servile labor" would be construed as "synonymous with the term 'secular labor.'"[47]

Swann v. Swann noted that at least as far as contracts were concerned, unlike Roman law and canon law, "The common law made no distinction between the Lord's day and any other day."[48]

The Superior Court of Pennsylvania, in *Commonwealth v. Hoover*, heard evidence and argument that the English common law did observe the Sabbath, citing the laws of Edward the Elder, and the decrees of Aethelstane, Edgar, Ethelred, and Canute, as well as the laws of Charlemagne and the Council of Rhiems on the continent.[49] The Supreme Court of New York, Kings County, in *New York v. Poole*, considered athletic games on Sunday and concluded that Scripture would be a factor in their

---

47. *Oklahama v. Chesney* at 237.

48. *Swann v. Swann*, 21 F. 299, 301, 308–309 (1884). The court commented that:

> Writers on ecclesiastical law are not quite agreed as to what extent the obligations of the commandment and the Levitical law were abrogated by the advent of our Savior; but conceding that the fourth commandment delivered to the Jews is of universal obligation, the fact remains that that commandment has never been observed by the Christians so far as relates to the day of the week. The commandment declares explicitly that "the seventh day is the Sabbath of the LORD, thy God." While many of the commandments are very short, that relating to the observance of the Sabbath is worked out at considerable length, and great stress is laid on the day of the week to be observed, and the reason for observing that day. (301)
>
> ... The celebration of the Sabbath probably existed before the time of Moses. However this may be, it has antiquity and an explicit command of the Old Testament to support its claims. The Lord's day has been the practice of the apostles and Christian church since the resurrection of our Lord. The week of seven days is not found elsewhere, except among the Egyptians, and there no day of rest was observed. At one period in their history the Jews observed the Sabbath with great strictness, not even defending themselves in time of war on that day, and punishing Sabbath-breaking capitally. Exodus, xxxi. 14; Numbers, xv. 32–36. The method of observing the day entered largely into their ceremonial code. They were much incensed at our Lord and His disciples for their desecration of the day, according to the Jewish law; and it was when challenged by the Pharisees for profaning the Sabbath that our Lord, after defending his disciples, boldly announced that *"the Sabbath was made for man and not man for the Sabbath; therefore, the son of man is LORD also of the Sabbath."* St. Mark, ii. 27, 28. By the Jews, who regarded the Sabbath as the everlasting covenant between God and Israel, (Exodus, xxxi. 15, 16), the reply of our Lord to their accusation was looked upon as sacrilege. The liberal notions of our Lord with regard to the Sabbath deepened and widened the gulf between him and the Jews, and ultimately resulted in the complete repudiation of the Jewish Sabbath by the Christians, who substituted for it the day of the week on which our Lord rose from the dead. (308–9)

49. *Commonwealth v. Hoover*, 25 Pa. Super. 133, 134 (1904).

interpretation of the statute: "It is not to be understood that the Legislature meant to be stricter than the divine law of the Hebrew scriptures, or than the rules of the Christian church, excepting the extent to which it has expressly gone."[50]

Using similar reasoning, the Supreme Court of Georgia invoked the Mosaic Law in ruling that selling gas on Sunday was a work of necessity and therefore within the exemption to the Sunday closing law:

> [W]e are of the opinion that, under the application of even ancient rules, the sale of gasoline to a traveler on the Sabbath day, who intends to continue his journey and for whom it is impossible to proceed without gasoline, must be a work of necessity. Even under the strictness of the Mosaic law, travel on Sunday was not prohibited, though a limit was prescribed for a Sabbath day's journey, and a "Sabbath day's journey" was not restricted in its purposes to worship or charity. A Sabbath day's visit might be paid as a mere matter of innocent pleasure.[51]

E. Honor Thy Father and Thy Mother.

The Lexis search revealed forty-five citations of the Fifth Commandment, most of which were applied to the Commandment to honor one's parents, though a few used the numbering by which *"Thou shalt not kill"* is the Fifth Commandment. Sometimes the command to honor one's parents is cited as the Fourth Commandment, following the Catholic numbering. The various catechisms declare that the Commandment enjoins honor and obedience toward not only parents but church and civil authorities as well.

Ryckman v. Acheson involved a native of Canada who, with her husband, became a naturalized U.S. citizen. After her husband died, she returned to Canada to care for her elderly and infirm mother. As a result, pursuant to the Nationality Act, her citizenship papers were taken for expatriation. The court ruled,

> The sole and only reason for plaintiff's going to Canada was, as before stated, the condition of her mother, and the fact that her mother (who had no other children) had no one else to look

50. *New York v. Poole,* 89 N.Y.S. 773, 775 (1904).

51. *Williams v. Georgia,* 144 S.E. 745, 746 (1928).

> after her and she did not have sufficient funds to secure the attention she needed even if such attention could have been procured by the payment of wages to someone to look after her. It was of such compelling necessity for plaintiff to take care of her mother as to amount to, and was, duress of such a nature that she did not, and should not have resisted. To have failed her mother at this time would have been in violation of all the instincts of loyalty of a child for its parent and contrary to the Fifth Commandment to *"Honor thy father and thy mother that thy days may be long upon the land which the LORD, thy God, giveth thee."* Exodus 20:12....
>
> The plaintiff... performed her God-commanded duty to her mother, with the result that certain United States agents are now attempting to forfeit her citizenship in this country....
>
> Should such a dutiful daughter be deprived of the priceless possession of her American citizenship for doing nothing other than her filial duty? I think not, and in view of all the facts and circumstances in this case, I hold that plaintiff's stay in Canada was, in legal effect, involuntary and, as such, it could not be a ground for forfeiture of her nationality and citizenship in the United States of America.[52]

Another public policy issue involving this Commandment occurred in *Equity Investments v. Paris*. Ms. Paris moved her elderly parents into the spare bedroom of her apartment, apparently in violation of her lease. The Civil Court of Queens County called the case

> [A]n interesting dilemma of a conflict between two "laws" one written in stone approximately 3,500 years ago and the other written by mere mortals in 1962. The former is the fifth of the ten commandments given to Moses on Mount Sinai and the latter is Section 52(a) of the New York City Rent Control Regulations....

---

52. *Ryckman v. Acheson,* 106 F. Supp. 739, 740–42 (1952). Similarly, *Petition for Naturalization of Yee Wing Toon,* 148 F.Supp. 657, 659–60 (1957), held that petitioner's act of sending money to China to support his mother, even though illegal, is not moral turpitude:

> In the conflict between following the Fifth Commandment (or the Chinese counterpart thereof) and the regulations respecting foreign fund controls, he chose to follow the Divine commandment rather than the technical regulations relating to foreign exchange. The Court is not convinced this is evidence that he is not disposed to the good order and happiness of the United States.

> "If we had the eyes to see the subtle elements of thought which constitute the gross substance of our present habit, both as regards the sphere of private life and as regards the action of the State, we would easily discover how very much we owe to the Jews for the... ten commandments... and other contributions to western law."...
>
> The public policy of this state (as expressed by statute and decisional law) is not in conflict with the fifth of the ten commandments. It is all too rare (in these troublesome times of self-indulgence) to find people willing to sacrifice their own comfort and serenity for the sake of their parents. Therefore, far be it for the courts to punish such devotion....[53]

In an opposite situation involving the same principle, a landlord sought to evict a tenant from an apartment so his elderly father could move in. The court said in *Beaty v. McGoldrick* that

> Consequently, the sole issue to be reviewed is the finding that the landlord failed to establish the existence of an immediate and compelling necessity. Such necessity seems to have been amply demonstrated. To give comfort and to heal the man, in his last years, who, though he may be undeserving, is the father, husband and grandfather of the family unit, conforms not only to the very essence of the Decalogue but is an immediate and compelling necessity in every sense of that term.[54]

Granting visitation rights to the father of an illegitimate child, the Family Court of New York, Ulster County wrote,

> The willingness of the Court to afford this father an opportunity to permit Joanna to come once again to know, love and respect him as her father should not be regarded as novel. In fact, it but reflects the ancient wisdom of God's law as given to Moses on Mount Sinai wherein as the Fifth Commandment of the Decalogue it is written: *"Honour thy father and thy mother: that thy days may be long upon the land which the* Lord *thy God giveth thee."*[55]

53. *Equity Investments v. Paris,* 437 N.Y.S.2d 1000, 1001, 1005 (1981) (quoting President Wilson).

54. *Beaty v. McGoldrick,* 121 N.Y.S.2d 431, 432 (1953).

55. *Pierce v. Yerkovich,* 363 N.Y.S.2d 403, 414 (1974) (quoting Exodus 20:12). (*contd. next pg.*)

In *California v. Copus*, California sued in the Texas courts to require an adult son to pay for the care of his mentally ill mother. The Supreme Court of Texas ruled that Copus could be required to make back payments up to the time of his removal to Texas. Justice Greenhill dissented, arguing that Copus should be required to pay support even after moving to Texas. Justice Greenhill noted that

> The Fifth Commandment is *"Honor thy father and thy mother . . . "* Exodus 20:12. Like others in this code of laws, it is directed to the adult citizen who is burdened with the care of an aged parent, and is a warning against the heathen habit of abandoning the aged when they can no longer support themselves.[56]
>
> . . . Texas should not become a haven for deserting providers who would ignore or repudiate their duty to support.[57]

However, the Supreme Court of Mississippi decided a very interesting case in 1889, *Westbrook v. The Mobile & Ohio Railroad Co.*[58] Westbrook, a small child, had been injured by a railroad train. He brought suit, claiming the engineer had failed to sound the warning whistle. The Railroad's defense was that Westbrook's parents were contributorily negligent, but the Court held that their contributory negligence did not bar the child from recovery:

> To charge the child with the negligence of the parent or custodian, in such case, would be, as said by the supreme court, of New York in *Lannen v. Gas-Light Co.*, 46 Barb. 264, to visit "'the sins of the fathers upon the children to an extent not contemplated in the Decalogue, or in the more imperfect digests of human law."[59]

In *Krabel v. Krabel*, 429 N.E. 2d 1105, 1106 (Ill. App. 1981), Joseph Krabel sought to change custody of his minor children because of Linda Krabel's cohabitation with her paramour. The court was highly critical of Joseph for telling the children about their mother's sexual liason:

> Joseph appears to be extremely selective in his choice of the elements in the Decalogue. It may well be asked whether one is moral by being very sanctimonious about the carnal aspects of that great pillar of ethical conduct, while at the same time teaching his children to dishonor their mother.

56. *California v. Copus*, 309 S.W.2d 227, 234 n.1 (1958) (quoting 1 Interpreter's Bible 985 [1952]).

57. *Id.*, at 234.

58. *Westbrook v. The Mobile & Ohio Railroad Co.*, 6 So. 321 (1889).

59. *Westbrook* at 322 (The "sins of the fathers" quotation is from Exodus 20:5).

The Commandment has been invoked in cases involving children striking their parents. *Sipp v. Coleman* held that beating one's mother is an act of moral turpitude, because "The obligations of the Fifth Commandment are recognized by the secular as well as the ecclesiastical law":[60]

> The family relation is the basis upon which our entire social superstructure is erected. The dishonoring of the parent by the child injuriously affects the whole social fabric. Very low, indeed, in the scale of civilization, would a community be that recognized no distinction in morals between an assault and battery by one stranger upon another and one by a son upon his mother.[61]

Landry v. Himel involved an altercation between a father and his adult daughter. The Court of Appeals of Louisiana, First Circuit, held that

> [T]he conclusion is inescapable that she frequently irritated and abused him, and failed to show the honor and respect due a parent by a child, whatever his age, required by both the civil and the moral law. Article 215 of the Civil Code provides that a child, whatever be his age, owes honor and respect to his father and mother. This rule of the Civil Law is founded on the Mosaic law, expressed in the Fifth Commandment, to honor thy father and mother. It is true this command implies that the father and the mother will conduct themselves toward their children in such a way as to merit honor and respect from them. But the first duty is on the child.[62]

In *Axe Estate* the Common Pleas Court of Philadelphia County, Pennsylvania, refused a daughter's petition to appoint a guardian for her father because "she exhibited complete indifference to the fifth commandment of the Decalogue, *'Honor thy father and thy mother...'* : Exodus 20:12."[63]

60. *Sipp v. Coleman,* 179 F. 997, 999 (1910).

61. *Sipp* at 999–1000.

62. *Landry v. Himel,* 176 So. 627, 628 (1937). Similarly, in *Beyer v. Beyer*, the court noted that "Such parents, while exacting from their children a rigid compliance with the commandment, *'Honor thy father and mother,'* forget and ignore that equally sacred and supplementary injunction, *'Provoke not thy children to wrath.'*" 21 Ohio Dec. 757, 758 (1909) (quoting Exodus 20:12 and Ephesians 6:4).

63. *Axe Estate,* 34 Pa. D. & C.2d 625, 635 (1964).

And in *Feller v. Universal Funeral Chapel,* the Supreme Court of New York County refused a daughter's request for the ashes of her father because

> She did not exhibit that respect for her father that we expect from one of her background, social as well as cultural. She was unmindful of the Fifth Commandment and sought to determine for herself, a privilege reserved only to those claiming omniscience, the standard which would justify her recognition of her father. This is not the thinking of a dutiful daughter.[64]

In *Stramler v. Coe* the Supreme Court of Texas held that "*'Honor thy father and mother'* is a command not only of the decalogue, but of nature; and suits in which rights can be claimed only through the alleged turpitude of a parent, are not to be encouraged."[65]

Finally, in *Raymond v. The Superior Court of Sacramento County,* the Court of Appeals reasoned that search and seizure law concerning police officers forcing a boy to enter his father's bedroom should be strictly construed in the family home, because "the Fourth Amendment conceivably incorporates some elements of the Biblical Fifth Commandment."[66]

F. Thou Shalt Not Kill.

The Lexis search uncovered twenty-seven cases which cite the Sixth Commandment, though some of these speak of adultery and some cite the Commandment *"Thou shalt not kill,"* sometimes translated *"Thou shalt not murder,"* as the Fifth Commandment. The Commandment is the basis of the right to life and of the various statutes prohibiting homicide.

Sometimes the Decalogue is cited to clarify the meaning and scope of a murder statute. *Gilbert v. Florida* involved a man who killed his wife and claimed it was a mercy killing. The Florida Court of Appeals ruled

64. *Feller v. Universal Funeral Chapel,* 124 N.Y.S.2d 546, 551 (1953).

65. *Stramler v. Coe,* 15 Tex. 211, 214–15 (1855). Similarly, in *Yarnall Estate,* 103 A.2d 753, 759 (1954) (quoting *Jenkins v. Fowler,* 24 Pa. 308, 310 [1855]), the Supreme Court of Pennsylvania held that children who question the veracity of their mother violate the Fifth Commandment, but "'Malicious motives make a bad act worse; but they cannot make that wrong which, in its own essence, is lawful.'" And in *Mileski v. Locker,* 178 N.Y.S.2d 911, 916–17 (1958), the court noted in a case of litigation between a mother and her children, that it had "in mind the spiritual and moral precepts of the Decalogue, and is prone to regretfully observe that the tenets of this Divine ordinance have apparently been unheeded. The Court finds that it is significant that this aged mother found it necessary to institute this action against two of her five children."

66. *Raymond v. The Superior Court of Sacramento County,* 96 Cal. Rptr 678, 680 (1971).

that euthanasia was not a defense to first-degree murder in Florida. Judge Glickstein, in a concurring opinion, noted that

> The Decalogue states categorically, *"Thou shalt not murder."* It draws no distinction between murder by members of the middle class and murder by members of an underclass. It draws no distinction between murder by a family member and murder by a stranger. It draws no distinction between murder out of a misguided notion of compassion and murder for hire.[67]

In the Matter of John Storar involved a profoundly retarded and terminally ill adult whose mother wanted to decline further treatment on his behalf. The Supreme Court of New York, Appellate Division, upheld their right to decline treatment, but Judge Cardamone, dissenting, wrote,

> The circumstances here transcend mere statutory and constitutional views and lead inexorably back to the Author of the natural law from whose foundation all law is derived. The imperative of the Fifth Commandment—Thou shalt not kill—is reflected in the beginnings of the common law. As Blackstone observed: "The law of England wisely and religiously considers, that no man hath a power to destroy life but by Commission from God, the author of it." Our founding fathers enshrined the doctrine that life is an unalienable right in the Declaration of Independence....
>
> ... There is but a short step from a mentally defective patient's "right to die" to his duty to die.[68]

The Decalogue has also been cited to establish a defendant's responsibility for his actions. *New York v. MacDowell* involved a woman who called herself "Jezreel, Lord God Woman."[69] Affirming her murder conviction and rejecting an insanity defense, the court observed that "the defendant testified at the trial that she knew that she was killing the defendant when she stabbed him, she knew that what she did was against society's laws, and she

---

67. *Gilbert v. Florida,* 487 So.2d 1185, 1192–93 (1986) (Glickstein, J., concurring).

68. *In the Matter of John Storar,* 434 N.Y.S.2d 46, 47–48 (1980) (Cardamone, J., dissenting) (citation omitted) (quoting WILLIAM BLACKSTONE, 4 COMMENTARIES *189).

69. *New York v. MacDowell,* 508 N.Y.S.2d 870, 872 (1986).

was aware of the constraints of the Fifth Commandment, but that she went by her own rules."[70]

Illinois v. McEwen suggested concerning "*Witherspoon* excludables" (prospective jurors who can be challenged for cause because they cannot under any circumstances impose the death penalty), "Since many people in our democratic society base an anti-death penalty belief on the Mosaic Fifth Commandment, it would probably be more literally correct to call such prospective jurors, 'Fifth Commandment excludables.'"[71]

People on the relation of Le Roy et. al. v. Hurlbut et. al. involved the power of the water board commissioners. Michigan Supreme Court Justice Thomas Cooley, whose *Constitutional Limitations* is considered by many the leading work on the U.S. Constitution from the second half of the 1800s, surveyed the powers given to government officials in colonial New England. He wrote,

> In Massachusetts, it was even insisted by the people's deputies that, to surrender local government was contrary to the sixth commandment, for, said they, "men may not destroy their political any more than their natural lives." So it is recorded they clung to "the civil liberties of New England" as "part of the inheritance of their fathers."[72]

G. *Thou Shalt Not Commit Adultery.*

The Lexis search found twenty-nine cases which cited the Seventh Commandment. Sometimes the Seventh Commandment was used in reference to theft, but usually it referred to adultery. Sometimes adultery was referred to as the Sixth Commandment.

Oliverson v. West Valley City, involved administrative sanctions against a police officer for acts of adultery. The court concluded that adultery was an act of moral turpitude:

---

70. *Macdowell* at 872.

71. *Illinois v. McEwen,* 510 N.E.2d 74, 76 (1987); cf. *Witherspoon v. Illinois,* 391 U.S. 510 (1968). *Farina v. Florida,* 937 So. 2d 612 (2006), and numerous other cases have addressed the propriety of judges, jurors, prosecutors, and defense attorneys using this Commandment and other Scriptural passages to support or oppose imposition of the death penalty.

72. *People on the relation of Le Roy et. al. v. Hurlbut et. al.*, 24 Mich. 44, 101–02 (1871) (citing 3 Palfrey's New England 381–83; 2 Bancroft's U.S. 125–27; 21 Mass. Hist. 74–81). Note that this case refers to the adultery commandment as the Sixth Commandment while *Storar*, *MacDowell*, and *LeRoy* refer to it as the Fifth.

> The offense of adultery was not a common law crime, under English law, but it was punished by the ecclesiastical courts which had adjunct authority to the common law courts. It was a crime in the British colonies, where ecclesiastical courts had no jurisdiction, and in the United States.... As Honoré notes, "In many societies adultery is one of the most serious crimes, and often carries the death penalty." In Hebraic law the Seventh Commandment forbade adultery. Subsequent Hebraic codes also penalized adultery. Leviticus 20:10 stated: *"And the man that committeth adultery with another man's wife, even he that committeth adultery with his neighbor's wife, the adulterer and the adulteress shall surely be put to death."*[73]
>
> *The codes are often referred to for their religious importance, however, in fact, in Hebraic history they were in part legal codes governing the social conduct of the societies to which they applied. The Biblical books are ancient legal codes and histories. It would be wrong to assume the Hebraic references are merely religious commands.*[74]

Some courts have used a Jewish interpretation of the Commandment to interpret modern adultery statutes. In *The State v. Robert Lash*, the New Jersey Supreme Court observed that the Hebrew Law considered adultery to involve sexual relations between a man (married or unmarried) and a married woman; relations with an unmarried woman were fornication rather than adultery, regardless of the man's marital status. (Some would dispute this interpretation.) Common law, the court said, followed the Hebrew Law, while Roman law and canon law considered sexual relations adultery if either party were married. Chief Justice Hornblower concluded,

> I will barely add that adultery at the common law, is limited to criminal intercourse with a *married* woman, both by *Swift* and *Reeve* who are among our most eminent American Commentators, and that I am acquainted with no treatise on the common law, English or American, to the contrary. Whether its regulation on this point, was borrowed at some early age, from the Levitical law, which the early dispersion of the Jews carried into various

73. *Oliverson v. West Valley City*, 875 F. Supp. 1465, 1473 (1995) (citations omitted) (quoting TONY HONORÉ, SEX LAW IN ENGLAND 28 [Archon Books 1978]).

74. *Oliverson* at 1473 n.5 (emphasis added).

> parts of Europe, I am not able to say; but certain it is, that this wide distinction between criminal intercourse with a *married* woman, and a *single* woman, is emphatically settled in the Levitical law; the former being punished with death, while the latter was only a fine. On the whole, I am clearly of opinion that the offence described in the indictment is not adultery; it amounts only to fornication, for which, the defendant should have been indicted; and on this ground the indictment must be quashed.[75]

A note by the reporter adds that Pennsylvania had at the time a similar law which was given a different construction; in Pennsylvania an act of intercourse was adultery only for the married party; the single party (apparently of either sex) was guilty only of fornication.[76]

Other courts have held that their states' adultery statutes apply only to open adultery or cohabitation or living as husband and wife, and that they were not simply enforcing the Seventh Commandment but rather its open violation.[77]

In *Western Union Telegraph Company v. McLaurin*, McLaurin sued the telegraph company for disclosure of a telegram concerning an adulterous act. The court ruled that McLaurin could not sue because he did not have clean hands; he has suffered because "his sins had thus found him out,"[78] and "His claim for actual damages is grounded upon and has no foundation save for the fact that he has been violating the Seventh Commandment."[79]

H. Thou Shalt Not Steal.

The Lexis search revealed thirty-four cases that have cited the Eighth Commandment, usually in reference to theft but occasionally to bearing false witness. A few cases refer to *"Thou shalt not steal"* as the Seventh Commandment, following the Catholic numbering. The Commandment is the basis for property rights and for the many laws concerning property, including laws prohibiting theft.

---

75. *The State v. Robert Lash*, 16 N.J.L. 380, 389–90 (1838) (citation omitted).

76. See *Lash* at 390.

77. See *Illinois v. Potter*, 49 N.E.2d 307 (1943); *Richey v. Indiana*, 87 N.E. 1032 (1909); *State v. Helm & Thornhill*, 6 Mo. 263 (1840).

78. *Western Union Telegraph Co. v. McLaurin*, 66 So. 739, 740 (1914) (quoting *Numbers* 32:23).

79. *Western Union Telegraph* at 741.

In one case, *Rochon v. Iberia Parish School Board,* the court cited the Commandment to establish the moral turpitude of theft. Rochon's employment as a bus driver had been terminated because of an act of theft. To constitute grounds for termination, the employee must have committed an immoral act. The court noted,

> Moses, in his sermon on the mount [sic], established ten commandments that has served the Judeo-Christian community for thousands of years. One of the commandments is *"Thou shalt not steal."* Stealing and theft are synonymous and are criminal acts. For example, Moses castigates in these same ten commandments that *"Thou shalt not commit adultery,"* which is an immoral act, yet to thus sin one does not commit a criminal act. Au contrare, to run a stop sign in a vehicle one commits a criminal act, but it is not immoral to do so. So, this Court holds that theft (especially of these funds) is an immoral act.[80]

Several cases have held that the simple wording of this Commandment provides for a broad definition of theft. In 1926 the Supreme Court of Florida stated that the meaning of the word steal "has been pretty thoroughly understood since the eighth commandment was brought down from Sinai, or at least since it was translated into English."[81] In 1928 the Florida Supreme Court again said,

> The word "steal" may not be technically synonymous in meaning with the words "to commit larceny," but it is nevertheless a very strong and significant word, and the commonly accepted meaning of that word is very well defined in the Standard Dictionary as follows: "To steal is to commit larceny." The eighth commandment of the decalogue merely reads, *"Thou shalt not steal,"* yet was it ever doubted that it prohibited larceny of all kinds?[82]

80. *Rochon v. Iberia Parish School Board,* 601 So.2d 808, 809–10 (1992) (citation omitted). Possibly the court has confused Moses's reception of the Ten Commandments (Exodus 20; Deuteronomy 5) with Jesus' Sermon on the Mount (Matthew 5–7). Also, one might argue that running a stop sign is an immoral act as it endangers other people.

81. *Fountain v. Florida,* 109 So. 463, 464 (1926).

82. *Addison v. Florida,* 116 So. 629, 629 (1928).

In *Oregon v. Jim,*[83] the defendants demurred to an indictment because it failed to charge with specificity their crime. Denying the motion, the court quoted with approval *Cameron v. Hauck*:

> "In the present case we hold that under Texas law, the crimes described by 1410 and 1413 are the same and that a charge under 1410 (theft) notifies a defendant of all elements of a 1413 (false pretenses) offense. Theft is a synoptic concept: the Eighth Commandment condemns theft without explaining every possible nuance and contrivance in its accomplishment."[84]

Sometimes courts cite the Decalogue to add moral authority to their findings, as when the Supreme Court of Missouri affirmed a conviction, declaring, "[T]his case exhibits as bold and flagrant a violation of the criminal law and of the eighth commandment as courts are ordinarily called on to pass upon. Judgment affirmed. All concur."[85] *The Isle of Mull* held that to give title to the owner "would require a frustration, not only of the charter party, but of the eighth commandment as well."[86] *Highway Truck Drivers and Helpers Local 107 v. Cohen* held that requiring the union to pay the attorney fees of officials charged with defrauding the union, would violate "basic and fundamental requirements of justice and fair play called for by §501(a) of the Act—requirements which are indeed developed but one step beyond the Seventh Commandment itself. . . ."[87]

Grand Upright Music Limited v. Warner Brothers Records noted that copyright infringement "violates not only the Seventh Commandment, but also the copyright laws of this country."[88] *Margolis v. National Bellas Hess Co.* commented that "Even in the present state of the law the piracy of styles is not entirely without the pale of the Eighth Commandment."[89]

In a case involving ballot fraud, *Doll v. Bender*, the Supreme Court of Appeals of West Virginia ruled that the Republican candidate had been elected by 2,131 votes to 2,128 votes. Judge Dent concurred, writing that,

83. *Oregon v. Jim,* 508 P.2d 462 (1973).

84. *Oregon v. Jim* at 465 (quoting *Cameron v. Hauck*, 383 F.2d 966, 971 (5th Cir. 1967), *cert. den.* 389 U.S. 1039 [1968]).

85. *State v. Good,* 33 S.W. 790, 795 (1896).

86. *The Isle of Mull,* 257 F. 798, 810 (1919).

87. *Highway Truck Drivers and Helpers Local 107 v. Cohen,* 182 F. Supp. 608, 612 (1960).

88. *Grand Upright Music Ltd. v. Warner Bros. Records,* 780 F. Supp. 182, 183 (1991).

89. *Margolis v. National Bellas Hess Co.,* 249 N.Y.S. 175, 180 (1931).

> I am aware that there are some people who at least profess to believe that elections, being human institutions, are governed solely by human inclinations, and are not subject to the supervision or control of that moral code of ethics promulgated by God through the greatest of all human law-givers from Sinai's hoary summit. This, however, is a great and grievous error, for the eighth commandment, *"Thou shalt not steal,"* forbids not only larceny as defined in the Criminal Code, but also the unjust deprivation of every person's civil, religious, political, and personal rights of life, liberty, reputation, and property—even though done under the sanction of legal procedure.[90]

Finally, in *Smyth, Executor v. United States,* the majority held that certain bondholders had lost their right to interest when the maturity of the bonds was accelerated by valid notice. Justice McReynolds, joined by Justices Sutherland and Butler, dissented, saying, "The answer ought not to be difficult where men anxiously uphold the doctrine that a contractual obligation 'remains binding upon the conscience of the sovereign' and reverently fix their gaze on the Eighth Commandment."[91]

I. Thou Shalt Not Bear False Witness Against Thy Neighbor.

The author's Lexis search revealed nine cases that cite the Ninth Commandment, again recognizing variants in the numbering. Many courts have cited this Commandment to condemn perjury, although as previously noted, perjury is also condemned by the Commandment, *"Thou shalt not take the name of the Lord thy God in vain."*

In *United States v. Ianniello,* the court stated,

> When our judicial system was established and the requirement of an oath or affirmation on the part of a witness was borrowed from the British common law, the swearing of an oath meant something—namely, that the court could be fairly sure that a witness would tell the truth. In the time of our Founding Fathers, witnesses believed that they would be subject to severe and perhaps immediate Divine retribution if they lied under oath on the witness stand, based on the Ninth Commandment's

90. *Doll v. Bender,* 47 S.E. 293, 300 (1904) (Dent, J., concurring).

91. *Smyth, Executor v. United States,* 302 U.S. 329, 368 (1937) (McReynolds, J., dissenting).

> proscription, handed down by God to Moses that *"Thou shalt not bear false witness against thy neighbor."*[92]

In *Commonwealth v. Brown,* the Supreme Court of Pennsylvania observed that a dying declaration is accepted as evidence because

> [W]hen a person is faced with death which he knows is impending and he is about to see his Maker face to face, is he not more likely to tell the truth than is a witness in Court who knows that if he lies he will have a *locus penitentiae,* an opportunity to repent, confess and be absolved of his sin?[93]

But the dissent by Justice Musmanno countered that "An expiring murderer could have as much motive to falsify as he had to kill. If the Sixth Commandment did not deter him from slaughtering his fellow-man, the Ninth Commandment would present no barrier to his bearing false witness."[94] The reason, he said, is that "there are persons who defy goodness and honor and who accept the cut rates of Mr. Satan at his sulphuric supermarket rather than pay the just price which decency and justice demand, that evil still walks the earth."[95]

Rejecting an appeal from a judgment of fraud, the Court of Appeals of California, Third Appellate District, wrote, "Counsel for the appellants cite several verses of the Bible, all of which, perhaps, are fitting when the circumstances correspond, but in this case we think the ninth commandment given effect by the judgment of the trial court, is conclusive."[96]

And in *Davis v. Queen City Furniture* the Louisiana Supreme Court concluded that "Whether in all these contradictions it is the plaintiff's witnesses who have violated the ninth commandment or if it be the defendant's witnesses, only the Supreme Judge can decide with absolute certainty."[97]

92. *United States v. Ianniello,* 740 F. Supp. 171, 192 (1990) (quoting *Exodus* 20:16).

93. *Commonwealth v. Brown,* 131 A.2d 367, 370 (1957).

94. *Brown* at 372 (Musmanno, J., dissenting).

95. *Brown* at 373 (Musmanno, J., dissenting).

96. *Aycock v. Carr,* 288 P. 448, 450 (1930).

97. *Davis v. Queen City Furniture,* 41 So. 318, 320 (1906).

J. Thou Shalt Not Covet.

This writer's Lexis search revealed thirteen cases in which the Tenth Commandment was cited. Please note that Roman Catholics and many Lutherans consider *"Thou shalt not covet thy neighbor's wife"* as the Ninth Commandment and *"Thou shalt not covet anything that is thy neighbor's"* as the Tenth Commandment, while Jews and most Protestants treat all coveting as Tenth Commandment violations.

Coveting is not simply wanting things. Rather, the various catechisms explain that coveting is (1) wanting something even though it is not God's will that one should have it; (2) wanting something obsessively; (3) wanting something so badly that one is willing to obtain it by illegal or unethical means; or (4) wanting something so badly that one resents the fact that someone else has it.

Judge Dent, whose concurring opinion in the voting fraud case of *Doll v. Bende*r, was previously quoted in its reference to the Commandment *"Thou shalt not steal"* as including theft of votes or civil liberties, spoke further of the Tenth Commandment:

> the tenth commandment, *"Thou shalt not covet,"* rebukes even the desire to do such things. The selfish disregard of these plain inhibitions of both revealed and natural law, supported by the dictates of a pure conscience, brings on political corruption, poisons the very fountain head of civil authority—the ballot box—and ends in disrespect to all law, followed by lawlessness, fraud, rapine, murder, and lynching by rope, fire, and torture. A broken moral law, by whoever done, however done, and wherever done, is certain to bring its retribution, which may fall on the head of the innocent and pure, but for which the aggressor must some day, somewhere and somehow, make full restitution. This is a lesson which men are slow to learn and unwilling to receive, although the history of the past is but a record of one half of its profound truth, while the other half awaits the revelations of eternity. With my unshaken and fixed belief in the moral law, the supreme rule of Almighty God, the final triumph of perfect righteousness, and the sure punishment of all iniquity, I could not do otherwise than concur in sustaining the expressed will of the people, bound as I am by the oath of office under which I hold my commission. A cross and a crown

> of thorns are far more to be preferred than success achieved through the broken laws of God.[98]

In *Cooley, Cooley, and the 7C Company v. United States*, the United States Court of Claims noted that regulatory takings can run afoul of the Takings Clause of the Fifth Amendment if they go too far. The court noted,

> "[F]or what is the land but the profits thereof[?]" In fact, the Tenth Commandment embodies this same principle (*"Neither shalt thou desire thy neighbour's wife, neither shalt thou covet thy neighbour's house, his field, or his manservant, or his maid-servant, his ox, or his ass, or any thing that is thy neighbour's."*)[99]

Chisman v. Moylan involved the duty of a broker to his clients. The court opined,

> What has here been said as it concerns the duty incumbent upon a broker to his principal is nothing new, but constitutes an axiomatic truth which adverts farther back than contemporary law. It flows from the highest and most everlasting authority, the Holy Writ. There the law of fairness and the ethics of man's conduct with man is given in incomparable clarity and purity through the admonition of the Tenth Commandment. *"Thou shalt not covet"* and the Golden Rule, *"Therefore all things whatsoever ye would that men should do to you, do ye even so to them: for this is the law and the prophets."*[100]

Haskins v. Royster applied the Fourth Commandment and the Tenth Commandment to the enticing away of servants or laborers:

> This is so by the common law. The relation of master and servant has existed from the earliest stages of society. It is recognized both in the 4th and 10th commandments of the decalogue, and is said by Blackstone to be founded in convenience, whereby a

98. *Doll v. Bender*, 47 S.E. 293, 300–01 (1904).

99. *Cooley, Cooley, and the 7C Co. v. United States*, 46 Fed. Cl. 538, 546 n.8 (2000) (citation omitted) (quoting 1 Edward Coke, Institutes, ch. 1, § 1 (1st Am. ed. 1812)). The "Takings Clause" of the Fifth Amendment provides that "nor shall private property be taken for public use without just compensation."

100. *Chisman v. Moylan*, 105 So.2d 186, 189 (1958) (quoting Matthew 7:12).

> person calls in the assistance of others when his skill and labor will not be sufficient to answer the cares incumbent on him.[101]

Unlike stealing, coveting is seldom the subject of legislation. But the commandment is nevertheless highly relevant to law and government, because it is a "hedge" of protection against illegal activity. A person who covets his neighbor's property is more likely to steal it. A person who covets his neighbor's spouse is more likely to commit adultery. Persons who have been trained not to covet are more likely to be honest, law-abiding citizens than those who have not been so taught.

Gaines v. Florida involved an attempt to gain Winslett's confidence and rob him. The court said "the excessive manifestations of hospitality as exhibited by Gaines, Patrick, and McRae toward Winslett immediately after the latter displayed his large roll of money were not due to his fascinating personality, but rather to a spirit of cupidity against which the Tenth Commandment had not effectively admonished them."[102]

III. CONCLUSION

These myriad cases, emanating from courts of record all across the nation and from the beginning of American constitutional history to the present, demonstrate an unbroken tradition of looking to the Ten Commandments as the moral foundation of law. In 1895 Judge Dent of the Supreme Court of Appeals of West Virginia declared that

> the common law is not agnostical, atheistical, nor even deistical, but is unswervingly theistical. As its crowning glory and chief excellence, with faith immovable it believes in the God of Moses, *"who, watching over Israel, slumbers not, nor sleeps."* ... The faithful servant of God, whose equal, save One, has never appeared in human form, in transmitting from the infinite to the finite that perfect code of laws known as the "Ten Commandments," which challenges the admiration and obedience of all mankind as the sure foundation of peace, prosperity, and happiness, also at the same time, as from the same divine source, delivered, with a tongue that forbade the utterance of

---

101. *Haskins v. Royster,* 70 N.C. 601, 602 (1874) (citing William Blackstone, 1 Commentaries *421).

102. *Gaines v. Florida,* 122 So. 525, 526 (1929).

> any untruth, the following, among other, judgments for the governance of his people....[103]

And in 2005 the Indiana Supreme Court rejected the dissenting argument that "government should not take sides by enacting legislation regarding matters involving individual conscience and religious belief." Concurring in the result, Justice Dickson wrote,

> such a proposition could be used to attack the constitutionality of much of our criminal code, particularly laws prohibiting murder, theft, and perjury because these enactments reflect values taught in the Ten Commandments.[104]

If a judge may cite the Ten Commandments in an official opinion that has the force of law, may a judge not also draw public attention to the Ten Commandments by means of a monument?

Questions for Reflection, Discussion, and More Reflection

1. What is the difference between crimes classified as *malum prohibitum* and crimes classified as *mala in se?* Can they really be sharply distinguished? Is there any crime that does not involve at least some moral considerations? Would it be accurate to say that *mala in se* crimes are violations of the Law of Nature while *malum prohibitum* crimes are not? How have courts used the Ten Commandments to establish certain crimes as *mala in se*?
2. Describe some of the ways the courts use the Ten Commandments in their decisions. Are these legitimate usages?
3. In *Rogers v. State,* what did the Georgia Court of Appeals mean when it said "This is a Christian nation"? Did the court mean that Christianity is the nation's official religion, that Christians have preferred status in America, or that others are at best second-class citizens? Or did the court mean that the basic values of

103. *Mayer v. Frobe,* 22 S.E. 58, 61 (1895).

104. *Clinic for Women, Inc. v. Brizzi,* 837 N.E. 2d 973, 994 (2005).

this nation are informed by Christianity? How is the Decalogue relevant to this question? How are the commands *"Thou shalt have no other gods before me"* and *"Thou shalt not worship a graven image"* relevant to civil government?

4. What does the command *"Thou shalt not take the name of the Lord thy God in vain"* cover besides blasphemy? Is blasphemy a legitimate subject for the government's concern? If blasphemy brings down the wrath of God upon society, does the government have a right or duty to protect society from the consequences incurred by those who blaspheme?
5. What was the original reason for the Sabbath? Why did the American colonies enforce sabbath observance by law? Why did Blackstone, Webster, Emerson, McCaulay, and Beecher endorse sabbath observance? Is there a legitimate reason for sabbath observance today? Does the State have a right or duty to enforce it?
6. How does the commandment to *"honor thy father and thy mother"* constitute a basis for civil government and other forms of authority? Why do some courts call this commandment the Fifth Commandment while others call it the Fourth? Does this reflect the judge's own theological background (or that of his law clerk) combined with ignorance of others? How can a court cite the commandments without showing a preference for one religious tradition over others?
7. Is the command *"Thou shalt not kill"* better translated *"Thou shalt not murder"*? Does the command apply to killing in war? To execution of criminals? To manslaughter? To euthanasia? To abortion?
8. How do the commands *"Thou shalt not commit adultery," "Thou shalt not steal,"* and *"Thou shalt not covet"* interact and support each other? What does coveting mean? Is capitalism, with its profit motive, based upon coveting? Or is Marxism, with its emphasis on the class struggle, based upon coveting?

Questions continued on next page....

Questions *continued*

9. Under what circumstances can *"Thou shalt not bear false witness against thy neighbor"* be a crime or a basis for a civil lawsuit? In what ways is civilization based upon the assumption that people normally tell the truth? If we can't assume that people normally tell the truth, is meaningful communication possible?
10. If it is permissible for a judge to cite the Ten Commandments in an official opinion that has legal force, why have some courts held that a judge may not display the Ten Commandments in the public arena?

The eastern façade of the Supreme Court building features Moses (center) holding the Ten Commandments. Jeff Kubina, 2009.

CHAPTER 18

INTERLUDE: *The Magi, The Monarch, and The Messiah: A Christmas Contemplation*[1]

Now when Jesus was born in Bethlehem of Judaea in the days of Herod the king, behold, there came wise men from the east to Jerusalem, Saying, Where is he that is born King of the Jews? for we have seen his star in the east, and are come to worship him. (Matthew 2:1–2)

For 2,000 years, the wise men of the East have intrigued us. Who were they? From where did they come? Whom were they seeking? And why? Could their quest have had anything to do, even in part, with the principles of law and government that western civilization has held so dear?

This writer believes it did. It should not surprise us that these kings or magi would be concerned about law and government. Christ is our personal Savior, but He is Lord of the nations as well (Isaiah 9:6–7; Revelation 12:5, 19:15). Matthew emphasizes Christ's role as Lord of the nations by presenting the account of the Magi who came to worship Him. Luke emphasizes Christ's role as personal Savior by presenting the account of the shepherds, common men who came to worship Him. Both are necessary for a complete understanding of His earthly mission.

They sought what man has sought from the beginning: the Savior who would release man from the curse of Adam's Fall and restore him to his original paradise. Genesis 3 records that God expelled our original parents from Eden and cursed the ground for their sake after they

1. This essay by the author was originally written for the Plymouth Rock Foundation's *Letter from Plymouth Rock*. In December 2008 it appeared in the Firm Foundation blog of the Foundation for Moral Law, www.morallaw.org (accessed 14 June 2016). It is incorporated as a chapter in this book as a bridge between the ancient laws of Persia and other empires, the inspired Laws of the ancient Hebrews as practiced in the Hebrew republic and the Hebrew monarchy, and the tyranny and corruption of the despotic empires of Greece and Rome.

sinned against Him. But God also promised them a Savior, the *"Seed of the Woman"* (3:15) who will bruise the head of the serpent. Throughout the generations the faithful have looked for the coming of God's promised Messiah.

The Rise of the Messianic State

But others have looked to false saviors, and counterfeit messiahs have arisen in every age. God had promised in His Word that the Savior would come first as a suffering servant (Isaiah 53:1–12) and only later as a victorious king (Revelation 19:11–21). But many, even among God's own people, looked only for the latter. The Christ on the Cross was rejected or ignored as man looked to civil government for salvation and the restoration of the Golden Age.

Not that civil government is ungodly. Quite the opposite. God ordained civil government (Romans 13:1–6; I Peter 2:13–17) to restrain the exercise of sin, enforce order, protect human rights, and foster social organization. Those who are called to civic office have a high godly responsibility to perform.

The problem arises when men look to civil government to perform the functions God has delegated to the Church, or when men look to the Church to perform the functions God has delegated to civil government—when civil rulers seek to become saviors, and when false messiahs become kings.

Most emphatically, this does not mean government must be divorced from God or that law must be divorced from Biblical morality. Government functions best when it is based upon the solid foundation of the Ten Commandments. Luther and Calvin both spoke of the Decalogue as the embodiment of natural law, and Dean Wigmore of Northwestern University School of Law called the Ten Commandments "the greatest short moral code ever formulated."[2]

But government's role is limited to enforcing legal principles of right and wrong and defending the liberty and safety of the people. God never intended that civil government should change basic human nature, eradicate all sinful impulses, and usher in the Golden Age. Government must be godly, but government must not try to become God.

---

2. John H. Wigmore, *A Panorama of the World's Legal Systems* (West Publishing Company, 1928), I: 105.

But almost from the beginning, people looked to civil rulers to usher in the Golden Age. As Ethelbert Stauffer says in his classic work *Christ and the Caesars,*

> One of the earliest longings of mankind is the longing for God to appear on earth. Egyptians and Persians, Greeks and Romans, relate mysterious myths of gods who once walked the earth in human form. In annual festivals they celebrated the cult renewal of that mythical theophany—the epiphany of Apollo, the advent of the sun-god, the birth of the heavenly child of the Age, who was to lead in a new era of salvation. With ecstatic cries and hymns they called on the god to appear: "Come and do not delay!" For where the deity moves as a man among men, the dream of the ages is fulfilled, the pain of the world is scattered, and there is heaven on earth.[3]

Such longings represent a corruption of God's promise to send the Messiah and the tendency to look to the State for that which only God can deliver. And when people expect the State to do that which only God can do, they begin to worship the State as God.

Deification of Emperors

In the pagan world, state-worship and emperor-worship were the rule rather than the exception. The Jewish historian Flavius Josephus, in his *Antiquities of the Jews,* tells us that Nimrod took a leading role in the building of the Tower of Babel to avenge himself on God for having destroyed the world by the Flood, and that Nimrod changed the government into a tyranny.[4] Alexander Hislop, in his classic work *The Two Babylons*[5] (Neptune, NJ: Loiseaux, 1916, 1959), says the Sumerians made Nimrod their king, and after his death they deified him and worshiped him as chief of their pantheon of gods.

Worshiping a ruler as though he were a god seems strange to many westerners. Through centuries of Bible teaching we have come to

3. Ethelbert Stauffer, *Christ and the Caesars: Historical Sketches* (Westminster Press, 1952, 1955), 36.

4. Flavius Josephus, *The Antiquities of the Jews,* AD 70; translated and reprinted as *Complete Works of Flavius Josephus* (William P. Nimmo, Edinburgh, Scotland, 1857; reprinted by Kregel Publications, 1960), 30.

5. Alexander Hislop, *The Two Babylons* (1853; expanded 1858; reprinted 1903; reprinted Cosimo, Inc., 2009), 23–38ff.

understand God as all-powerful and all-knowing, infinitely above all that man is or could ever be. In the western view no man could ever become God.

But the pagan view is different. Gods are superior to men in knowledge and power, but they are not all-knowing or all-powerful; nor are they perfectly just or righteous. The gods have character flaws much like ours, and they find themselves in the same intrigues and betrayals as men, only on a more colossal scale. The difference between gods and men is one of degree, and according to Greek mythology, somewhere between gods and men were heroes. Hercules was not a god but a hero, a man who achieved immortality by his courage and valor.

In the pagan view, then, the idea that the king could be a god, or descended from the gods, or ascended to godlike status, is not that far-fetched. And of course, pagan kings employed all the trappings and ceremonies to encourage that belief.

Israel vs. Pagan State-Worship

God's Word and God's people stood in marked contrast to this pagan view. Israel began as a confederate republic of twelve tribes governed by elders and judges, with no king in Israel but God Himself. The day would come when Israel would demand a king so they could be like the nations around them, but even then, Israel's king was to be a limited monarch. God spoke prophetically through Moses in Deuteronomy 17:14–20:

> *When thou art come unto the land which the LORD thy God giveth thee, and shalt possess it, and shalt dwell therein, and shalt say, I will set a king over me, like as all the nations that are about me;*
>
> *Thou shalt in any wise set him king over thee, whom the LORD thy God shall choose: one from among thy brethren shalt thou set king over thee: thou mayest not set a stranger over thee, which is not thy brother.*
>
> *But he shall not multiply horses to himself, nor cause the people to return to Egypt, to the end that he should multiply horses: forasmuch as the LORD hath said unto you, Ye shall henceforth return no more that way.*

> *Neither shall he multiply wives to himself, that his heart turn not away: neither shall he greatly multiply to himself silver and gold.*
>
> *And it shall be, when he sitteth upon the throne of his kingdom, that he shall write him a copy of this law in a book out of that which is before the priests the Levites:*
>
> *And it shall be with him, and he shall read therein all the days of his life: that he may learn to fear the LORD his God, to keep all the words of this law and these statutes, to do them:*
>
> *That his heart be not lifted up above his brethren, and that he turn not aside from the commandment, to the right hand, or to the left: to the end that he may prolong his days in his kingdom, he, and his children, in the midst of Israel.*

Unlike the Egyptian pharaoh who proclaimed himself to be a god and who was worshiped and obeyed as a god, Israel's king was to be one of the people. He must be a Jew, not a foreigner; being of one blood with them, his countrymen were less likely to regard him as a god. He was not to accumulate great wealth or power, and he was to write out a copy of the law of God, read from it daily, and follow it throughout his reign. The great object was that he be under the law of God, and that *"his heart be not lifted up above his brethren."* The king ruled by the law of God and according to the law of God, but he himself was not God but rather one of the people.

Daniel vs. State-Worship

This was the message of the prophet Daniel to the great Babylonian King Nebuchadnezzar—that God *"removeth kings, and setteth up kings."* (Daniel 2:21) Nebuchadnezzar erected a great golden image and commanded all to fall down and worship it (Chapter 3); the image represented the Babylonian state and Nebuchadnezzar as the head of state. Daniel's three friends were willing to show all the respect due a great Babylonian king, but they were willing to face death by fire rather than worship this image or that which it represented (3:17–18). As Daniel proclaimed in 4:32 and as King Nebuchadnezzar finally came to understand at the end of

Daniel Chapter 4, *"the most High ruleth in the kingdom of men, and giveth it to whomsoever he will."*

The Apostle Paul declared that the civil ruler is *"ordained of God"* and is the *"minister of God to thee for good."* (Romans 13:1–6) Yet Paul wrote these words from the Corinthian jail, indicating that governmental authority is not absolute. Peter also wrote of the duty to obey civil rulers (1 Peter 2:13–17), but when commanded to stop preaching the Gospel he and the other apostles declared, *"We ought to obey God rather than men"* (Acts 5:29).

Jesus: Render Unto Caesar

In the time of Jesus' earthly ministry the Jews faced testy relations with the Roman authorities. In Luke 20:19–25 we read that the chief priests and scribes asked Jesus whether it was lawful to pay taxes to Caesar. Jesus noted the image and superscription of Caesar on the coin and said, *"Render therefore unto Caesar the things which be Caesar's, and unto God the things which be God's."* Lord Acton wrote concerning this passage,

> ...when Christ said *"Render unto Caesar the things that are Caesar's and unto God the things that are God's,"* He gave to the state a legitimacy it had never before enjoyed, and set bounds to it that had never yet been acknowledged. And He not only delivered the precept but he also forged the instrument to execute it. To limit the power of the State ceased to be the hope of patient, ineffectual philosophers and became the perpetual charge of a universal Church.[6]

At the time of Christ, Rome was in transition from republic to empire. The SPQR (Senatus Populus Que Romana) that had governed Rome for half a millennium was becoming a rubber stamp for the emperors who increasingly claimed for themselves the attributes of divinity. Octavian subdued and organized the empire, and the Senate gave him the title Augustus Caesar (Divine King). He issued coins superinscribed *Caesar Divi Filius,* "Caesar Son of God." Throughout the Empire temples were built and sacrifices and prayers offered to the goddess Roma and the god Augustus, and the poet Virgil proclaimed of Augustus, "This is the man, the one who has been promised again and again," the world savior who

6. Lord Acton, quoted by Gertrude Himmelfarb (London, 1955), 45; in E. L. Hebden Taylor, *The Christian Philosophy of Law, Politics, and the State* (Craig Press, 1966), 445–46.

would usher in the age of gold.[7] The ancient world trembled with excitement that deliverance was at hand.

The Magi Seek the True King

And yet—the wise men of the east came not to worship Augustus, but to seek Him who is born King of the Jews.

Who were these wise men? Matthew calls them *magoi* or magi (2:1). They probably came from the eastern countries of Persia or Babylon. The priestly caste in those countries known as the Magi had existed for centuries and may have borne some similarity to the Celtic Druids. The Bible does not call them kings, but Tertullian writing around AD 200 says they were "well-nigh kings."[8] They were highly influential advisors to the Persian and Babylonian kings, as Daniel attests (Daniel 1:19–21; 2:2, 24; 4:7–9; 5:7), and probably played a prominent role in selecting a new king. In so doing, they looked to the will of the heavens, and they believed the will of the heavens was revealed through the stars. And as they looked to the heavens they saw the Star that led them to Bethlehem.

No scientific theory can adequately explain that Star. Men have called it a meteor, a comet, a heliacal rising, a supernova. But none of these theories can explain a Star that appeared in the east, led the Magi to the west slowly enough that they could follow, then suddenly reversed course in Jerusalem and led to the southeast to Bethlehem. The Star must have been a special creation of God, perhaps a theophanic appearance of God Himself in the Person of the Holy Spirit to lead these Magi to Jesus Christ.

But why would these Magi care that One had been born King of the Jews? Possibly they understood the Hebrew concept of law and government, for the Persians recognized that the king is subject to the law and powerless to change the law (Daniel 6:8, 12, 15). More likely, they remembered Daniel the Prophet, who had once led the magi himself.

Daniel: Master of the Magi

Daniel had been taken captive to Babylon around 605 BC. He was recognized to be ten times wiser than the magi and astrologers (Daniel 1:20) and rose to prominence in Babylon and later in Persia. He was a trusted advisor to the Babylonian and Persian kings, and in Daniel 2:24

7. Stauffer, 81–89.

8. *Catholic Encyclopedia* (New York: Gilmary Society, 1907, 1913), "Magi" IX: 528.

he used his influence to save the magi from execution. In Daniel 4:9 he is called *"master of the magicians (magoi),"* so very likely the learned Magi of Christ's time would recall Daniel and his writings.

In Daniel 9 we read the most precise of all Old Testament prophecies concerning the coming of Jesus Christ:

> *Seventy weeks are determined upon thy people and upon the holy city, to finish the transgression, and to make an end of sins, and to make reconciliation for iniquity, and to bring in everlasting righteousness, and to seal up the vision and prophecy, and to anoint the most Holy.*
>
> *Know therefore and understand, that from the going forth of the commandment to restore and to build Jerusalem unto the Messiah the Prince shall be seven weeks, and threescore and two weeks: the street shall be built again, and the wall, even in troublous times.*
>
> *And after threescore and two weeks shall Messiah be cut off, but not for himself: and the people of the prince that shall come shall destroy the city and the sanctuary; and the end thereof shall be with a flood, and unto the end of the war desolations are determined.*
>
> *And he shall confirm the covenant with many for one week: and in the midst of the week he shall cause the sacrifice and the oblation to cease, and for the overspreading of abominations he shall make it desolate, even until the consummation, and that determined shall be poured upon the desolate.* (Daniel 9:24–27)

The "weeks" (Hebrew *shavuot*; Greek *hephtah)* of Daniel 9 are commonly interpreted as seven-year periods. Sixty-nine seven-year periods equal 483 years. King Artaxerxes of Persia gave the decree to restore and build Jerusalem in 445 BC. Counting 483 years later would seem to be AD 38, but the Hebrew year was twelve 30-day months or 360 days. Factoring in the difference would bring us to AD 31, the likely date of Christ's crucifixion.

We do not know how much of this the Magi understood. But if they remembered the words of their old master, Daniel, then they would have known that the salvation of the world would come not through the legions of Caesar but through the One Who would be born King of the Jews. And without condoning astrology, God used the means most familiar to them to lead them to His Son.

But the world continued to look for a conquering prince, not a suffering savior. Augustus reigned well for the most part, and his reign brought in the *pax romana* or Roman peace. But the *pax romana* only restrained sin and evil; it did not conquer them. And after the death of Augustus his plan for government crumbled. But the ancient dream of the god-man who would bring heaven down to earth remained.

With the rise of the Roman Empire, the classical longing for a savior was given a political form. The coming savior was the emperor, and as the people's hopes were dashed with the tragic collapse of each emperor, they thirstily looked with equal hope to the next.

The Messianic State Turns Demonic

When Nero ascended the throne in AD 54 at the age of seventeen, the philosopher Seneca said of him,

> as the red of morning drives away dark night, as neither haze nor mist endure before the sun's rays, as everything becomes bright when my chariot appears, so it is when Nero ascends the throne. His golden locks, his fair countenance, shine like the sun as it breaks through the clouds. Strife, injustice, and envy collapse before him. He restores to the world the Golden Age.[9]

A lover of Greek culture, Nero proclaimed himself to be "Zeus the Liberator" and embarked upon a reign of madness, tyranny, and bloodbaths. He covered Christians with tar and set them up as living torches in the imperial parks, murdered his mother and wife, and kicked to death his lover who was expecting his child. After fourteen years the army revolted, and as Nero committed suicide his dying words were, "What an artist dies in me!"[10]

Succeeding emperors claimed to be the best of gods but acted as the worst of men. And still, men looked to Rome for salvation, seeking the City of God through the City of the Earth. As Stauffer so graphically wrote,

> The triumph of the *civitas dei* [City of God] was to be reached by the self-exaggeration and self-destruction of the *civitas terrena* [city of the world]. The self-exaggeration and self-destruction

9. Seneca, quoted by Stauffer, 139.

10. Stauffer, 141.

> of the classical advent philosophy was completed in the third century AD. This is the century of which the schoolboy knows nothing because no young mind can bear the knowledge of what happened then. It was the century of the assassination of the emperors, of the sarcophagi, of the dance of death, of the systematic persecutions of Christians, the century of twisted titles. Magnus, Maximus, Maximinus, Magnentius, Maxentius, Maximianus, Maximilianus are the names given to themselves by those who wanted to be accounted important. In this century the political eschatology on which men had been nourished for thousands of years ran amok through the Roman world. About the year 260 Gallienus struck a coin with the inscription, "The genius of the Roman people has entered the capital of the empire." This patron spirit was incarnate in himself, the Emperor Gallienus. In the same decade the imperial genius was murdered. In the year 275 Aurelian was celebrated as "god and lord from birth." In the same year the divine lord was murdered. The following year the Emperor Probus ascended the blood-girt throne and struck a series of coins with the famous inscription ADVENTUS AUGUSTI and the portrait of the emperor riding up with his hand raised in greeting and blessing, led by the goddess Victoria. In the year 282, Probus was murdered. In 287 a coin of the Emperor Carausius appeared, and on it we see Britannia greeting the emperor, as he arrived from the Continent, with the advent greeting EXPECTATE VENI, Come, Thou Longed-for One. In the Advent hymn the words are "Thou Longing of all the world." Carausius was murdered. . . .[11]

State-Worship Today?

And the story goes on, through the collapse of Rome, the Dark Ages, the Renaissance, the Enlightenment, mercantilism, colonialism, imperialism, the modern age, the postmodern, and so on down through the centuries. In an age in which many pride themselves as being too sophisticated to believe the state is divine, the German philosopher Hegel proclaimed that the State is god walking on earth,[12] although he used the

---

11. Stauffer, 39–40.

12. Georg Wilhelm Friedrich Hegel, *Philosophy of Right;* quoted by William P. Paterson, *German Culture: The Contribution of the Germans to Knowledge, Literature, Art, and Life* (T.C. & E.C. Jack, 1915), 58.

term "god" loosely in the sense of a universal consciousness or worldly spirit (*Weltgeist, or World Spirit)*). An age which rejects the transcendent God of the Bible places man, and the State as the greatest of man's institutions, on the throne in the place of God. We give to the State all authority, we expect the State to make all important decisions, we look to the State for all material blessings, and we trust the State to make our laws and define our values. Truly, for many of us the State has become our god.

And amid all this intrigue and carnage, Christ was born in a Bethlehem stable. He grew as a humble child in Nazareth, He lived and taught and served among men. He died on a Roman cross, and His enemies thought they had conquered Him. But there He paid the atoning price for the sins of the world, washing away forever the sins the emperors could only imperfectly restrain. And there He established His Kingdom, a Kingdom that is not of this world but that will endure forever.

Wise Men Still Seek Him

The Magi were wise men indeed. We don't know how much they understood, but we know they made wise choices. They passed by the Caesars and the Herods of their day and came to worship the newborn King. They were influential men in their day, and they respected and served the kings of their respective lands. But their souls' allegiance was to the King of Kings, to Him who wears the mitre of eternity. They respected the godly state and the ruler who governs according to Biblical principles. But they feared the messianic State that seeks to make itself god. They knew that government service is an honorable vocation, but they also knew that earthly government will never usher in the Golden Age. Only God through His true Son can do that.

And on Christmas Day God did become man. God became incarnate, taking upon Himself human flesh so that He could redeem mankind through His Death on the Cross, His Resurrection, His Ascension, and His Second Coming. Wise men sought Him then, and wise men seek Him now.

Venite, Adoremus Dominum!

"O Come, let us adore Him, Christ the Lord!"

Questions for Reflection, Discussion, and More Reflection

1. What is the source of this longing for a savior god who comes in human flesh on earth? Do you agree that it is universal, or nearly so?
2. Which is the greater danger as a false messiah—the false religious leader who claims messiahship, or the charismatic head of state who tries to usurp this role?
3. The "Golden Age" that men look for—is this a dim memory of Eden, and a foreshadowing of a millennium?
4. Explain why a polytheistic society is more conducive to emperor-worship than is a monotheistic society. Is state-worship possible in a democracy? How about in a republic?
5. Who were the *magoi* (wise men) of Matthew 2? If they were a Persian priestly caste, why would they have been interested in the birth of the King of the Jews? Could they have had ties with the Celtic Druids or other priestly castes? Could they have been influenced by the Jewish prophet Daniel?
6. Why would the Roman emperors mint coins with inscriptions proclaiming their divinity? Does this cast additional light on the Mark 12:13–17 account of Jesus, the Pharisees, and the tribute money?
7. What are some of the so-called scientific explanations of the Star of Bethlehem? Do any of them fully account for the appearance and movements of this Star? If God forbade astrology in the Bible (Deuteronomy 4:19, 18:10–12; 2 Chronicles 33:1–6; Isaiah 47:13–14), why would He use a Star to guide the Magi to Jesus Christ?
8. What did Hegel mean when he said the State is god walking on earth? In what sense was he using the term "god"?

9. Do people in this age worship the State or the King as God? Do we look to the State to supply all our needs and solve all our problems? Do we look to the Government, especially the judicial branch, as the final arbiter of what is true and false, of what is good and evil, of what is right and wrong?

10. Can one practice fervent patriotism without practicing state-worship? How do we delineate the difference?

The Adoration of the Magi
Designed 1888, woven 1894. Designed by Edward Burne Jones with details by William Morris and John Henry Dearle.

Master Index

A

D

E

F

H

I

J

O

P

S

T

U

V

W

X

Y

Z

Nordskog
Publishing inc.

Noble Novels

7th
Millennium

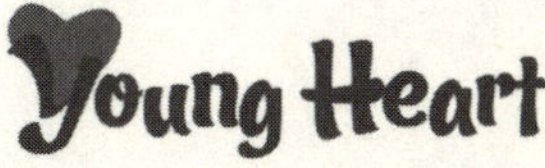
Young Heart